HISTORY OF
LATIN AMERICAN CIVILIZATION
sources and interpretations

HISTORY OF
LATIN AMERICAN
CIVILIZATION

sources and interpretations

Volume 1 / The Colonial Experience

edited by LEWIS HANKE

Little, Brown and Company • Boston

Published simultaneously in Canada
by Little, Brown & Company (Canada) Limited

PRINTED IN THE UNITED STATES OF AMERICA

Acknowledgments

Though I take full responsibility for the planning and execution of this volume, I have received much help from colleagues and students. Helen Delpar provided excellent editorial assistance throughout the preparation of the work and gave valuable advice on historical matters as well. Others who contributed with their insights and experience were: Marvin Alisky, Robert Conrad, Charles Julian Bishko, Charles C. Griffin, Joseph E. Love, Thomas F. McGann, Gunnar Mendoza, Magnus Mörner, Charles E. Nowell, Fredrick B. Pike, Frank Safford, Peter H. Smith.

E. Bradford Burns was particularly helpful in connection with the Brazilian selections, and Alfred L. Browne III and David W. Lynch fulfilled a delicate and essential function as publisher's midwives. To all of these friends I offer my grateful thanks.

Lewis Hanke

Preface

Foundations and the government have poured forth millions of dollars in recent years to develop research and graduate instruction in Latin American studies, but relatively little attention has been given to improving teaching methods and materials at any level. The present boom in undergraduate courses on Latin America could be a dubious blessing, therefore, unless we stop to consider why and how Latin American history should have an integral place in the educational structure of the United States.

Should the teacher of Latin American history consciously aim at inculcating Pan-Americanism, promoting the "Good Neighbor" concept, defending particular political actions and economic policies of the United States government, or fighting communism south of the Rio Grande? Such approaches seem to me objectionable and unhistorical. Should the Latin American past be studied because it illuminates the present or, as one historian has put it, "the cultural and institutional imperatives of the past which shape contemporary process"? Even that, although immensely important because the hand of history lies heavily on every Latin American country, is not in my view sufficient reason.

I believe that Latin American history will have a lasting place in our colleges only when it is recognized as a valuable part of world history whose study throws light upon another culture than our own, and when it is presented as the story of the long experience of many kinds of people in a New World setting. Latin America since 1492 has been, and is today, part of the Western world. But its history if properly taught also records the contact of Europe with a number of Indian civilizations and the mingling of many races to form in many areas a new mixed-race society whose future has long been of special importance to the people of the United States.

Moreover, the study of Latin American civilization, so similar to our own but also strikingly different in some respects, should aim at producing better-educated human beings, not "experts." The premise upon which this conclusion rests is that all students — especially those in the United States — need windows on the world opened to enable them to learn about other people, other cultures, and other points of view. This is no new doctrine. Bernard Moses, who gave the first course in "Spanish American History and Institutions" at the University of California in Berkeley in 1895, believed that teachers of American history should check "the tendency to narrowness and provincialism" by helping the pupil "to extend his horizon so that other countries than the United States may lie under his observation." He held that teachers "may help their students realize that the ideals of other nations are not necessarily to be rejected because they differ from our ideals, and by this enable them to acquire a broad and liberal spirit, the sign and result of the world's highest civilization. . . . A great educational achievement has been made when we have learned to appreciate this other point of view, and from it now and then to consider ourselves and our ambitions."[*]

Latin American history has certain obvious advantages which make it an unusually attractive and available "window on the world" for our students. Latin America shares with the United States the European heritage with which we are already familiar, in contrast with Chinese, Indian, and other non-Western civilizations. The long centuries of colonial rule — during which the Portuguese and Spaniards carried to America many of their ideas and attitudes as well as their languages and their religion — produced a definite way of life which still influences the value systems and institutions of Latin Americans. Their communication with Europe and the United States greatly increased during the century and a half following independence, and their fundamental world outlook is significantly similar to ours. Yet they differ sufficiently from each other and from us to offer a view of another world, in some respects a strange and exotic world whose character is not easily understood. Américo Castro's remark concerning Spain might well be applied to Latin America: "To try to fit Spanish life only to economic and down to earth criteria is truly to waste time and not to understand

---

[*] Lewis Hanke, ed., *Do the Americas Have a Common History?* (New York: Alfred A. Knopf, 1964), p. 58.

history."* Thus Latin American history offers exciting and fruitful ideas for college students to encounter as part of their general education.

To study a culture in any depth, a knowledge of its language is highly desirable. Spanish and Portuguese are far easier to learn than Arabic, Chinese, or Hindi, and Spanish is the most widely taught language in our secondary schools and colleges today. Thus Latin American history enjoys the advantage of offering no great linguistic barrier. Again, many Latin Americans live in the United States today and their presence — increasingly felt in cities far beyond Los Angeles, Miami, New York, and San Antonio — also brings our students into contact with their culture. And Latin America, except for Cuba, is open to us as a travel area. Students of history may visit some part of that large and varied region which includes urban societies with exciting modern architecture, great rural areas as well as isolated sections with ancient archaeological sites and primitive tribes, and evidences of grave social and economic and therefore political problems harassing each Latin American country today. Thus, if we can agree that American college students would benefit from exposure to another culture as part of their fundamental education, Latin American history offers an excellent opportunity to understand the confrontation of cultures resulting from conquest and colonization.

How can this history be presented most effectively? My answer is a plain one. Latin American history should not be looked upon as a "crisis" subject, but as the unfolding story of a culture, a civilization both interesting and worthy of attention in itself. Naturally the Cuban Revolution and United States intervention in the Dominican Republic have stirred our students to increased awareness of Latin American affairs. But a "current events" approach which concentrates on transitory dictators, military juntas, and economic and even social problems will not, I am convinced, provide the kind of course required by the world in which we live and by the place of the United States in that world. One need not be classified as a troglodyte if he denies that the only useful history is "contemporary" history and that anything that happened before yesterday need be studied *only* if it can be demonstrated that today's problems have their roots in the past. As one writer has expressed it: "The past is

---

* Américo Castro, *The Structure of Spanish History* (Princeton: Princeton University Press, 1954), p. 592.

not the present. On the contrary, the past is significantly different from the present — that is why we study it, that is why it can be useful to us, and that is why it has meaning and imaginative charm. General education is impoverished when we neglect this central truth in an anxiety to prepare everybody for today's world . . . difference enriches; likeness palls."*

The contents of this volume and of its companion to follow, on the period from 1810 to the present, have been drawn from the rich store of material that has appeared in widely scattered publications. The selections from the original sources illustrate the freshness and unique character of such documents. The later writers approach their subjects from varied points of view. Many are historians, but the insights and interpretations of anthropologists, geographers, librarians, and men of letters are also represented so that this collection brings together the work of many minds and disciplines.

In selecting these writings, I have made no attempt to cover the huge subject of Latin American civilization comprehensively in textbook fashion, or to present the complicated story as a series of "crises" or "problems." Yet controversy abounds in these readings, for sharp disagreement has always marked the writing of Latin American history, whether the question is on locating the bones of Columbus or the reasons for the economic underdevelopment of any Latin American country today. The readings, therefore, will help students to develop the healthy skepticism essential to the training of their minds. The "Bibliographic Suggestions" appended to each selection will show how rich this literature of controversy is, and will suggest topics for special reports and term papers.

One final point. One of the advances made in recent years has been the integration of Brazilian history into the broad stream of Latin American history. No longer is the history of Portuguese-speaking Americans considered a marginal field cultivated by a few exceptional persons; today we recognize that Latin American history cannot be adequately presented unless Brazil occupies an important place in it, and I have made a special effort to include material on its past.

One result of a volume such as this is to reveal what we do not

---

* Howard Mumford Jones, "Uses of the Past," *Harvard Educational Review* (Winter, 1966), pp. 10–11.

know. Certain important topics could not be included simply because they have not yet been sufficiently studied. But even these gaps in our knowledge can be useful: the student learns that not everything is known. I hope that some of those who use these volumes will be stimulated by their very faults and omissions to help during the coming years to fill some of these gaps, so that students in the future will have access to a more illuminating collection of sources and interpretations.

My purpose, to sum up, is to show that Latin American civilization is a significant and fascinating part of the history of mankind. Citizens of the United States, especially, need to study it.

Table of Contents

Section I

The Transit of Civilization

Why have so little effort and imagination been spent on determining what influences the Spaniards and Portuguese carried to their American colonies? More particularly, why has so little attention been given in Latin American history courses to the European scene, the background from which the conquerors and colonists came?

A partial explanation is that Iberian history is generally neglected in our universities and "contemporary history" is greatly emphasized by foundations and government agencies that, by large grants of funds, have supplied the impetus for the boom in Latin American historical studies. Another reason is the influence of politics on the writing of history. Since the sixteenth century, arguments have been loud and bitter on the role of Portugal and Spain in the New World. For some, these Iberian nations redeemed a wilderness of savages and brought them into a Christian, Western way of life; for others they were almost wholly responsible for all the ills Latin America has suffered from 1492 until today. The historical study of these important and enduring influences in the lives of Latin Americans has been hampered by the passion and dogmatism engendered all too often by political considerations.

We must remember that conquest and colonization were not a simple process, but that early modern Europe in the era of the Renaissance and Reformation carried medieval elements as well as some modern ideas into an already populated continent whose cultures had been evolving for centuries with few outside con-

1

tacts.[1] Professor Charles J. Bishko of the University of Virginia brings his sharp critical intelligence to bear on the central problems (Reading I.1), and students who want to know more about the relations between the Iberian and American worlds can do no better than read his entire article, from which the selection below is taken, and then follow up the many bibliographic leads he has brought together and carefully organized.

Mexican diplomatist and professor Luis Weckmann gives a broad-brush treatment to the subject (Reading I.2), which emphasizes medieval survivals in the New World. New World conditions stimulated many fanciful ideas (Reading I.3).

The late James Alexander Robertson, a pioneer in developing Latin American history in the United States, describes the Spaniard's fundamental contributions in bringing plants and animals (Reading I.4). Here indeed is a rich field for further study, for the early chroniclers recorded remarkably sharp and detailed observations of flora and fauna. Carl Sauer states that perhaps no other part of the world has an equal wealth of such data for that time.[2] A recently discovered Aztec map now in the Library of Congress indicates that Indian leader Don Carlos Chichimecatecotl, as early as 1536, began to develop orchards in Mexico, both by introducing Spanish apple, pear, and quince trees, and by grafting them onto native stocks.[3]

Spaniards embarked upon their conquests in America at the very moment when Antonio de Nebrija had produced the first modern grammar of any European language, the *Gramática Española* (1492), and they raced over the great stretches of the New World while the printing press was being intensively developed in Spain. The books that Spaniards brought to their colonies for pleasure or instruction, or for converting the Indians, are an impressive tribute to their love of the printed page and their conviction of the need

---

[1] See Robert S. Chamberlain's *Castilian Backgrounds of the Repartimiento-Encomienda* (Washington, D.C.: Carnegie Institute of Washington, 1939) and "The *Corregidor* in Castile in the Sixteenth Century and the Residencia as Applied to the *Corregidor*," *Hispanic American Historical Review*, XXIII (1943), pp. 222–257.

[2] *Handbook of South American Indians*, Vol. VI (Washington, D.C.: Government Printing Office, 1950), p. 487.

[3] Howard F. Cline, "The Oztoticpac Lands Map of Texcoco, 1540," *The Quarterly Journal of the Library of Congress*, XXIII, No. 2 (Washington, DC., 1966), p. 106.

to communicate through books. Their record of printing in America, as the Chilean scholar José Toríbio Medina has abundantly shown, is most impressive. The sheer quantity of research on printing and books makes it difficult to present a selection that will do justice to this aspect of the Iberian culture transfer, but Dr. Lawrence S. Thompson of the University of Kentucky Library gives an up-to-date and succinct view based upon many specialized studies (Reading I.5).

Portuguese influences in forming Brazil have been described (Reading I.6) in a lyrical way by the eminent Brazilian Gilberto Freyre, and analyzed in a systematic way by Professor Emílio Willems of Vanderbilt University (Reading I.7).

The New World's reciprocal influence upon the Old has been even less thoroughly investigated than the transit of civilization westward across the Atlantic. One obvious and important American effect was the rise in prices caused by the great influx of minerals, especially silver, from the mines in Peru and Mexico, a subject explored by Professor John Lynch of the University of London (Reading I.8). Since the fundamental contributions to economic history of Earl J. Hamilton a generation ago,[4] much attention and some criticism have been directed to this theory, and recently a Hungarian scholar, Tibor Wittman, has suggested that internal economic conditions were perhaps even more important than the influx of American treasure.[5] But a recent survey of the enormous literature on Spain's decline confirms that her economy was indeed adversely affected by riches from the New World.[6]

The Pacific Ocean as well as the Atlantic was a highway that moved ideas, plants, and products back and forth between Spanish America and the Orient. There is much documentation, mostly in rare printed chronicles and manuscripts, on trans-Pacific influences, but only a beginning has been made toward telling the full story.[7]

[4] Earl J. Hamilton, *American Treasure and the Price Revolution in Spain, 1501–1650* (Cambridge, Mass: Harvard University Press, 1934).

[5] Tibor Wittman, "Apuntes sobre los métodos de investigación de la decadencia castellana (siglos XVI–XVII)," *Nouvelles Études Historiques publiées à l'occasion du XIIᵉ Congrès International des Sciences Historiques par la Commission Nationale des Historiens Hongrois* (Budapest: Académie des Sciences de Hongrie, 1965), pp. 243–259.

[6] John H. Elliott, "The Decline of Spain," *Past and Present*, No. 26 (London, Nov., 1961), pp. 52–75.

[7] Pablo Guzmán-Rivas, "Geographic Influences of the Galleon Trade in New

Did Brazil exert a comparable influence on Portugal? No study has yet been published on this interesting subject, but Professor James Duffy of Brandeis University is at work on it and states:

> Portugal's overseas enterprise left a distinctive impression on the small nation's personality. As a result of Portugal's dramatic thrust into new and distant lands — Africa, America, India and beyond — cultural values were changed and then crystallized in the sixteenth and seventeenth centuries. On the basis of extensive study of Portuguese history, literature, and art, I will attempt to define the influence of the expansion in these two centuries and then proceed to demonstrate how subsequent cultural traditions, extending down to the present, derived from the overseas experience.
>
> I believe that the pattern of Portuguese culture, certainly more than that of any other European nation, has been shaped by the consciousness of expansion. Perhaps a large part of Portuguese historical and artistic writing has concerned itself with overseas themes. Portuguese art and architecture reflect the same preoccupation. The Portuguese Catholic Church has long seen itself as a militant missionary force. Portuguese folklore has been enriched by motifs from one part of the remote world or another. Even Portuguese science has more often centered its attention on colonial phenomena than on those of the metropolis. This constant interest in the overseas world has contributed to the formation of the unique Portuguese personality.[8]

The readings given in this section will slightly indicate the important and constant flow of ideas and materials back and forth across the Atlantic Ocean between the Iberian motherlands and their American colonies. Much more research must be undertaken but enough is known to suggest the extent of this reciprocity in the history of Latin America.

Spain," *Revista Geográfica,* XXVII, No. 53 (Rio de Janeiro, July–Dec., 1960), pp. 5–81.

[8] Statement by Professor Duffy, March 3, 1960.

A. General

1. A Major Challenge

CHARLES JULIAN BISHKO

Historians of Ibero-America, confronting a civilization that in regionally varying proportions incorporates elements of European, Indian and African origin, tend to be peculiarly conscious of "backgrounds" and of the flaming controversies that surround their analysis and evaluation; yet they have given surprisingly little attention to the scientific formulation of what might be called a backgrounds philosophy or methodology. This is especially true of the Iberian Background, despite universal recognition, by friends and foes alike, of the necessity for studying the Iberianization of much of the Western Hemisphere in the light of the historical formation of the Luso-Hispanic peoples. Does the concept embrace the whole body of Spanish and Portuguese history down to 1492 (or, alternatively, 1598, 1810, 1898 or 1956)? Or does it include only those human, institutional and cultural elements demonstrably transplanted to the New World? Can these latter legitimately be studied outside the total complex of Iberian civilization from which they may have been selected, in the colonizing of America, by historical precedent, local exigency, official decision or mere accident? And, finally, how can what is in any case a discouragingly large mass of historical materials be organized to meet the needs of the specialist in Latin American history?

The fact that in Ibero-Americanist historical circles the air does not yet ring with anguished cries for answers to these and related methodological questions can, I think, be attributed to a continuing (if largely unwarranted) faith in certain traditional practices. These

Charles Julian Bishko, "The Iberian Background of Latin American History: Recent Progress and Continuing Problems," *Hispanic American Historical Review*, XXXVI (Feb., 1956), pp. 50–55, *passim*. Reprinted by permission of the Duke University Press.

take the form of either (1) complete or virtually complete avoidance
of the Iberian Background, presumably as too large or too well
known to require the attention commonly extended the Indian Background; or (2) brief, sporadic references to Iberian origins in describing the genesis of specific Ibero-American institutions or ideas;
or (3) a Background survey genuine but conceived in terms of an
inadequate, often arbitrary and largely outworn nineteenth-century
table of contents which displays little regard for chronological or
topical relevance. Furthermore, the failure to conceive a sound
methodological approach has been compounded by confusions due
to other factors: doctrinaire stands for or against *hispanismo* and
lusitanismo; the influence of dated interpretative works like those
of Oliveira Martins, Ganivet, Blanco-Fombona and Juderías; the
relative underdevelopment of historical research in the Portuguese
and Spanish fields; the paucity of bibliographical tools and periodicals; and the poor communication between compartmentalized historians. This last lack has led the Luso-Hispanic specialist to neglect
subjects of prime interest to the Ibero-Americanist, while the latter
in turn, unaware of the advance of research in peninsular history, or
failing to make known his needs, has relied unduly upon the works
of Herculano, Altamira, Ballesteros, Merriman and others despite
their inevitable need for revision at many points in the light of subsequent investigation.

Against these ancient obstacles to proper understanding of the
Iberian Background of Latin American history, however, significant
progress has been registered in the last fifteen years on both sides
of the Atlantic. In the Western Hemisphere, the spread of ideological movements stressing Iberian roots; the stimulating effects of
residence on American soil of topdrawer peninsular scholars like
Altamira, Sánchez Albornoz, Ots Capdequí, Américo Castro and
Millares Carlo; the growing study of Ibero-American history in Latin
America as well as in the United States; have all stirred a strong
new interest in the Iberian Background and posed numerous new
problems of historical genesis. The scholarly effects of this can be
seen in the activities of the Colegio de México and the Spanish section of the Instituto de Investigaciones Históricas of the University
of Buenos Aires; the appearance of such periodicals for peninsular
studies as the outstanding *Cuadernos de Historia de España* of
Buenos Aires and the *Revista de História* of São Paulo; and the

readiness of Latin American presses like Losada or the Fondo de Cultura Económica to publish books of the caliber of Sánchez Albornoz' *La España musulmana,* Américo Castro's *España en su historia,* Marcel Bataillon's *Erasmo y España,* and Fernand Braudel's *El Mediterráneo y el mundo mediterráneo en la época de Felipe II.*

In the Iberian Peninsula itself, furthermore, historical productivity since 1940 in precisely those fields most closely related to the Iberian Background has been abundant. The Portuguese octo-tercentennial of that year provoked numerous multi-volumed historical sets, special studies, and new national and regional historical periodicals; and while this tide has since inevitably ebbed, important work continues to be produced at the Instituto de Estudos Históricos Dr. Antonio de Vasconcelos of Coimbra, by the Faculdades de Letras of Lisbon and Coimbra, and in provincial historical centers. In Spain, where enthusiasm for the Iberian Middle Ages, the Siglo de Oro and Hispanic America dominates the historiographical scene, the government-directed Consejo Superior de Investigaciones Científicas has spawned a staggering *sequela* of national and regional historical Institutos, Instituciones, Centros, Escuelas, and Congresos, organized under the Patronatos Menéndez Pelayo de Filología, Historia y Arte; José María Quadrado de Estudios e Investigaciones Locales; and others. From these as from the universities and historical societies has come a flood of books and journals in which the old dividing line between Spanish and Hispanic American history hardly exists; and this cross-fertilization of the two fields is further attested by the small but growing number of scholars who, like Virgínia Rau or Florentino Pérez Embid, contribute authoritatively to both.

To the historian of Latin America this fruitful ferment in Portuguese and Spanish historical studies inevitably poses a major challenge. It calls upon him to define more carefully than he has yet done the concept of the Iberian Background, if only as a defensive measure enabling him to extract from a growing body of historical information what is pertinent to his own needs. And it imposes upon him the necessity of becoming familiar with a wide range of new discoveries and interpretations contained in new books, periodicals and bibliographical guides. This seems then a good moment to attempt a brief and necessarily incomplete appraisal of the present state of Iberian Background studies, which, if it accomplishes nothing else, will at least serve to call attention to the problems involved, the general progress in the field, and what areas still await investigation.

It is necessary to begin with a profession of faith. In the writer's opinion, the Iberian Background is by no means identical with, but cannot possibly be understood apart from, Spanish and Portuguese history as a whole. To limit attention exclusively to the specific ethnic, institutional and cultural elements Spain and Portugal transplanted across the Atlantic from 1492 on, is to ignore the crucial historical process by which these, and not other, elements were selected for overseas survival or adaptation, and to be unaware of hitherto unenvisaged factors in problems of historical origins. Yet certain distinctions or priorities of relevance must unquestionably be established. Broadly speaking, from the chronological standpoint, the Background stretches from the first human habitation of the Peninsula right down to present-day Spanish and Portuguese influence upon Latin America. But the pre-Roman, Roman and Germanic epochs before 711 so substantially antedate the emergence of the peoples and civilization transmitted to the New World, that for the most part they fall outside the frame of reference. On the other hand, for the Ibero-American historian, the death of Philip II in 1598 marks the effective terminus of the basic epoch of the discovery, conquest and colonization of the Spanish and Portuguese Indies; thereafter metropolitan influences operate in an already firmly established American society. This leaves two periods as central to the Iberian Background of Latin American history: first, the six medieval centuries between 711 and 1300, the era of the formative evolution of the institutional and intellectual bases of Iberian civilization; and, secondly, the three transitional centuries between 1300 and 1600 of the Later Middle Ages, Renaissance and Reformation, i.e., the era of the national consolidation and explosive overseas expansion of the Luso-Hispanic peoples. Acceptance of some such scheme of chronological relevance should minimize the present tendency to discuss Celt-Iberian tribalism, prehistoric Basque origins, Roman municipalities or Visigothic kingship (all in themselves important matters, surely) in connection with Background surveys, to which such subjects as Minhotan and Beiran agriculture, Basque familial law, the late medieval Castilian *concejo* or Extremaduran population pressure would be much more pertinent.

In the second place, the Iberian Background must be marked off from the European background in general, which affects Latin America through the medium of the metropolitan countries, although of course direct contacts, as with English piracy in the Caribbean, Flemish missionaries in early Peru, German miners in Tierra Firme or French trespassers at São Sebastião, also occur. The Spanish empire in Europe or Portuguese commercial relations with the Italian trading cities and northern Europe bear more directly upon the American expansion. In the Peninsula itself Navarre and, much more, the Crown of Aragon — especially in the light of recent studies claiming for it strong administrative and institutional influence upon the Indies — possess still more immediate significance. But within this broad and necessary framework the central focus of Iberian Background studies must inevitably be the colonizing states of Portugal and Castile, not only in their own proper historical development but also, after 1400, in that projected conquest and colonization of the Afro-Atlantic area which is the direct prototype of the twin enterprises of the Indies.

To the definition of the Iberian Background thus delimited in time and space three corollaries may be added. First, that the subject should be studied not merely in terms of politico-military history and biography, but as broadly as modern historians treat Latin America itself, in its social, religious, economic, cultural and juridical aspects. Second, that the overworked mechanical formula of tracing Ibero-American ideas or institutions to their metropolitan ancestors should be expanded to include the larger problem of why, how and from what general context these and not other forms were adopted for use in the Indies. Third, that interpretations of the Background should recognize in medieval and early modern Spain and Portugal highly complex, unstable societies moving, in the midst of violent internal change and conflict, from an original dynamic diversity towards the more static ethnic, religious and constitutional uniformity and centralization of the arteriosclerotic seventeenth century, to which, not to earlier periods, so many of our glib generalizations about Spain and Portugal really apply.

B. The Spanish Background

2. The Middle Ages in the Conquest of America

LUIS WECKMANN

For the mediaevalist it is interesting to note that there exists a natural continuity between the Middle Ages in Europe — and especially the Spanish Middle Ages — and the early institutional and cultural life of the Ibero-American colonies. As I hope to prove, the Middle Ages found their last expression on this side of the Atlantic, where, after the termination of the mediaeval period in Europe, an appropriate setting for the development of mediaeval ideals existed for an extended period in the Spanish New World while, contemporarily in Europe, the Religious Reformation and the so-termed Italian Renaissance were causing the abandonment of the essentials that sustained mediaeval Christendom.

Although Renaissance thought has its importance in the shaping of early Latin American civilization, and some of the conquerors, notably Cortés, were Renaissance men in their fondness for the visible, material things — grandeur, wealth, fame — it is nonetheless true that some old mediaeval trends, perhaps nowhere stronger than in Spain, the land of the perennial crusading, greatly influenced the early course of Latin American life. That should not surprise anyone. Forced to remain long in the background of European evolution, due to her almost constant state of warfare, Spain realized, later than any other country in western Europe, the flowering of her mediaeval civilization. Thus, Spain was able to transmit to America, as a living product and not as a dead tradition, many of her mediaeval accomplishments. There was no waning of the Middle Ages in Spain as there was during the fourteenth and fifteenth centuries in

Luis Weckmann, "The Middle Ages in the Conquest of America," *Speculum*, XXVI (1951), pp. 130–139, *passim*. Reprinted by permission of the author and of the Mediaeval Academy of America.

the rest of Europe. Spain found herself in the autumn of the Middle Ages during the first two centuries of her modern history, when, against insurmountable odds, she strove to keep alive and dominant such mediaeval ideals as those embodied in the *ecclesia universalis* and in the universal empire. The conception of a universal empire, the Company of Jesus, the new mysticism of St. Theresa and of St. John of the Cross, the new scholasticism of Vitoria and Suárez, the romance of chivalry, the *Romancero* and the theater represented the late fruits which the Spanish mediaeval spirit produced well into the modern age.

Columbus, the first link between the Old World and the New, stands in a clearer light, perhaps, if we envisage him not so much as the first of the modern explorers but as the last of the great mediaeval travelers. Although there is no doubt that Columbus' mind was affected by Renaissance trends, we can still say that this man, the spiritual heir of Marco Polo, was impelled by mediaeval quests and geographical puzzles towards the exploration of new routes of navigation. Was it not on the basis of Marco Polo's report (on his first voyage Columbus took with him Marco Polo's writings), even if this was complemented by newer works, that he set out to find the fabulously rich islands, off the coast of Asia, so lavishly and imaginatively described by the Venetian? Still other mediaeval legends concerning the existence of islands to the West and current in Columbus' days were known to him and in part impelled him to the undertaking of his voyages. Antillia (whence Antilles), St. Brandan's Isle, Brasil, the Island of Seven Cities, were among those legendary isles. Columbus never outgrew these geographical conceptions. In all his travels, when navigating through the Antilles or bordering the coasts of the American mainland, he thought (as his diary shows) that he was visiting the many islands which, as he said, were depicted in mediaeval maps at the end of the Orient in the vicinity of Cathay. . . .

Perhaps most poignantly mediaeval of all was the conviction displayed by Columbus in the course of his third voyage, when he firmly asserted that he had found nothing less than the Terrestrial Paradise. To support his assertion, he quotes, in genuine mediaeval fashion, the opinions of St. Isidore, of the Venerable Bede, of the "master of scholastic history" (i.e., Petrus Comestor), of St. Ambrose and of Johannes Scotus, all of whom had placed the earthly Paradise in the East. The earth, Columbus claims, is pear-shaped

and Paradise lies in its highest summit. He reports that he was able
to locate the Terrestrial Paradise after having encountered the
mouths of the four rivers of Genesis that proceed from the Tree of
Life, when he mistook the delta of the Orinoco river for the paradisi-
acal streams. The site of Paradise was so rich, asserted the discoverer, that with its wealth he could finance an army of 100,000
infantrymen and 10,000 cavalrymen with which the old mediaeval
goal of recovering the Holy Sepulchre could be attained. Columbus
also rejoices at the thought that he has found a new land where the
Lord can be served by the divulgation of His Holy Name and Faith
among so many new peoples, a truly mediaeval attitude. In other
minor details, such as in the method of time computations, in Columbus' writings as well as in those of his pilots and staff, and in
the diaries of subsequent explorers, mediaeval usages are likewise
followed.

The mediaeval world was surrounded by a realm of fable. Beyond
the known lands there existed others, populated in mediaeval fan-
tasy (drawn, it is true, from ancient sources, and distorted) by all
kinds of mythical beings, monsters, enchantments so charmingly
depicted in mediaeval *mappaemundi*. Such were, for instance, the
giants, pygmies, gimnosophists, sciopodies, Amazons, cinocephali,
boys with white hair, people who lived only on smells, headless
beings with eyes on the stomach, bearded women, etc., so dear to
the mind of St. Isidore, together with griffons, dragons, the Sea of
Darkness, the Land of Prester John. As the discoverers of the late
fifteenth and early sixteenth centuries came to venture to the edges
of the world it was supposed that, sooner or later, they would encounter some of these mythical figures whose existence was, at least
for a great number of them, beyond dispute. Of special prominence
in the early history of Latin America is the quest for the Amazons,
which seemed to have fascinated practically every conqueror and
which has left a permanent souvenir in the names of the mightiest
river of the continent and of the northernmost of Spain's provinces
in America: California. Columbus already, in his second voyage,
refers to a certain island, Madanina, inhabited, according to Indian
versions, only by women, information that is put down soberly and
sceptically by the historian of the Indies. Cortés, in a letter to the
king in 1524, refers to what is now Lower California — presumably
an island and at that time unvisited by Spaniards — saying that it
was inhabited only by women who, at given times, received visits

of men from the mainland. Of the issue only female children were kept, the males being disposed of. The very name "California" apparently derives from an island of Amazons, ruled by Queen Calafia and mentioned in *Las Sergas de Esplandián,* a Spanish romance of chivalry and sequel of the famous *Amadís de Gaula.* . . .

Among the other recurrent legends of early American exploration, *El Dorado,* the gilded man whose kingdom was so rich that his subjects painted him every day with gold and washed him off at night, and Quivira and the Seven Cities of Cíbola, founded by seven mediaeval bishops, have conspicuous places, the second legend having led to Coronado's discovery of the American Southwest, where to this day New Mexico's folk plays represent a survival of mediaeval mystery plays. López de Gómara, author of the *Historia General de las Indias,* the first seven chapters of which are in spirit and in form still mediaeval, weighs the reasons advanced by the fathers of the church and by ancient writers for and against the existence of antipodes. After wearisome references to Lactantius, St. Augustine, St. Isidore and others, the author finally accepts the probability of their existence in the New World, after which he passes on to discuss the belief of the inhabitants of Iceland that Purgatory is to be located under their island. Among the fabulous beings which the imagination of the Spaniards places somewhere in America, room is reserved for the Devil himself. According to Gómara, the Devil is the principal god worshipped in a certain island of the Caribbean Sea where he appears many times and "even speaks" to his devotees. To balance this, we also find the Apostle St. James, the Patron Saint of Spain, fighting side by side with the Spaniards in many of their military engagements. The New World is, no doubt, a land of hidden marvels, of untrodden mysteries; the land, as Columbus said, of Alpha and Omega, where the sun rises and where the sun sets, the beginning and end of the earth.

That the Spaniard of the sixteenth century was naturally prone to believe in such marvels can be explained in part by the fact that the romances of chivalry, partially outmoded in the rest of Europe, were still very popular among Spanish readers. Ferdinand Columbus, son of the Discoverer, heads the list of prominent men in the history of the New World who were attracted by this type of reading. When the army of Cortés, after an exhausting march, finally catches its first glimpse of the city of Tenochtitlan, strange and beautiful, mirroring its colors in the lake upon which it was built,

Bernal Díaz, the soldier-chronicler of the expedition, merely comments: "We were astonished and told ourselves that this seemed
like a thing of enchantment, such as they related in the book of
Amadís," after which the conquering army entered the Aztec capital
with all the trappings of mediaeval splendor. Later on, when a re-
bellious soldier is condemned to death he finds no better way to
express his disagreement with his sentence, which he attributes to
tyranny rather than to justice, than to hope that sometime, in a
better future, the Twelve Peers will rule — a reference to the *Historia de Carlomagno y de los Doce Pares,* a romance of chivalry
first published in Spain in (the date is very revealing) 1525.

In some episodes of the civil and urban life of the early colony,
such as the dinner offered in 1538 by the first viceroy of New Spain
to commemorate the signing of a peace treaty between Charles V
and Francis I of France, all the splendor of the most magnificent of
all mediaeval courts, that of the dukes of Burgundy, was reproduced. On this occasion, the *pièces de résistance* were huge pastries
filled with live quail and rabbits. The *mises en scène,* a favorite
device of the Burgundian dukes to entertain their guests and to
display their wealth and magnificence, were also continued in New
Spain where, for example, the main square of Mexico City would
be converted into a lake and a naval battle fought around a fortress
built on an artificial island, the whole episode representing the siege
of Rhodes by the Turks. Nothing strange in this, if it is remembered
that Charles V of Spain, himself born in Ghent, was the heir of
Burgundian policies and of Burgundian grandeur through his father,
Philip the Fair.

In the legal and institutional realm of early America the mediaeval
imprint is equally patent. The Spaniards of the period retained the
ideal of a universal empire, of whose present incumbent they were
but servants. Charles V remained for them the *dominus mundi,* the
legitimate and God-ordained lord of the world. Sometimes, they
found no better reason than this to demand from Indian rulers their
submission to the king. Typical is the case of Francisco Pizarro in
Peru, and his counsellor, Fray Vicente de Valverde, both of whom
informed the last of the ruling Incas that they were the envoys of
the pope and the emperor, the lords of the world, who demanded
his submission to their authority. In the legal terminology of this and
of later ages we find many feudal reminiscences too: the Indians
are regarded as "vassals," a somewhat ideal conception badly shat-

tered by reality; in the creation of titled estates with which the conquerors were rewarded, in the terminology used in the documents of donation with their mention of woods, pools, meadows and so forth, all are mindful of feudal Europe. The oath, a basic institution of the feudal age, where it sustained the very fabric of society, plays an important role in appeasement of internal quarrels, and in setting up alliances between the conquerors. When, for instance, Almagro and Francisco Pizarro were reconciled at Cuzco, they attended mass together and, joining hands over the consecrated host, swore not to malign one another, not to send separate reports to the emperor, and to share equally all profits — a scene which recalls the famous story of the oath exacted from King Alfonso VI by the Cid and which proved, may I add, equally ineffective.

The pastimes of the conquerors are still those of a feudal class: tournaments, tourneys of canes (*juegos de cañas*), hawking, etc., all of which presupposed a mounted nobility. When Las Casas had in mind his scheme of colonization in South America, at Cumaná, he founded an order of "Knights of the Golden Spur" to finance it. Other usages, such as the cutting of boughs from trees in token of taking possession of the land and the reservation of hidden treasures to the king, the "royal fifth," are also reminiscent of feudal practices. The *derecho de lanzas* paid to the king by the early *encomenderos* corresponds in general to a feudal scutage. The *encomienda* system itself, by placing a certain number of natives under the protection and guide of a Spaniard, could be considered feudalistic because conceived in the spirit of patronage, so characteristic of the feudal world. But since land tenure was not included in this system, the *encomienda* was deprived of what could have been its most feudal characteristic. Still, a contemporary Mexican scholar, Federico Gómez de Orozco, thinks it possible to trace the *encomienda* back to mediaeval Spain, where conditions similar to those in sixteenth-century New Spain were created as the Christian kingdoms of the peninsula in their southward expansion were faced with the problem of a newly subjected class of non-Christians, and these new vassals of the crown were placed in trust (*encomienda*) with the military orders which were made responsible for their spiritual welfare. Another thought should be given to the *Capitaneas* or administrative divisions of Brazil in the colonial era that resemble very strongly the type of administration prevalent during the late Middle Ages in the Madeira and Azores islands; and the *sesmarias*, the

Portuguese mediaeval form of land grant introduced in Brazil after 1500, cannot pass unmentioned. Also, the mediaeval Spanish institution of the municipality — of ancient extraction but fortified by the role the townspeople played in the War of Reconquest — the *cabildo abierto,* already obsolete in the peninsula, was revived in America by the conquerors, eager to preserve for themselves and for their descendants a voice in the internal government of the colonies.

Perhaps nowhere else is more visible the imprint of the Middle Ages in America, and especially in Mexico, than in the realm of art. Military architecture in the beginnings of the sixteenth century, the early fortresses and castles built by the first conquerors, with their moats, drawbridges and turrets, such as the castles of Ulúa and Acapulco, are still genuinely mediaeval, and the same can be said of such walled cities as Campeche. In regard to religious edifices, conventual architecture of the first and even of the second half of the sixteenth century might be classified, according to Manuel Toussaint, Mexico's leading critic of Colonial art, as a mediaeval survival. It can be said, adds that authority, that the great fortified temples and convents of this period stand as the final expression of the Middle Ages in the world. . . .

Perhaps the most striking phenomenon in relation to mediaeval architectural survivals in America exists in the construction of Romanesque churches and other buildings of Romanesque type. The church of the Franciscan convent of Pátzcuaro is, essentially, a Spanish Romanesque church which could have been built in the twelfth century. Romanesque chapels and capitals adorn many sixteenth-century churches. This is not as surprising as it may appear: Romanesque constructions in New Spain are not, strictly speaking, afterthoughts but follow a "natural" architectural evolution. Romanesque style took a deep and lasting hold in those European countries that had long been a part of the Roman empire, such as Spain and southern France, regions in which Gothic may be regarded more or less as a foreign intrusion. Old Roman structural devices and constructions remained alive — even though suffering alterations and decay — for many centuries in the Mediterranean countries, and the fact that the Spanish *cortijo* basically follows the plan of the Roman *villa,* which likewise is copied in the plantation or *hacienda* of central and northern Mexico, is an eloquent proof of the lasting character that the Roman genius gave to its edifices. The pattern of the unwalled town with a fortified church featuring strong walls, ramparts, merlons, narrow skylights, so familiar in the Mexican central countryside, has its precedent in mediaeval mendicant practices, especially in southern France, like Spain, a Mediterranean land. . . .

The cultural atmosphere of sixteenth-century New Spain represents in many respects an unfolding of mediaeval Spain. In the colleges, and notably in the Royal and Pontifical University of Mexico founded in 1551 — whose constitutions and organization were copied from those of Salamanca, and where graduates gave each member of the cloister "six fat hens, four pounds of cold viands and a pair of gloves" after their reception — St. Thomas Aquinas and Duns Scotus reigned supreme at least until the eighteenth century. In the days of Carlos de Sigüenza y Góngora, the University of Mexico, in its government and curriculum, was still an interesting and curious survival of European mediaevalism. The early Mexican historiographers and, more notably so, the first Spanish historians of America, followed the practice of the mediaeval chroniclers, in transcribing in their writings material from older sources without bothering to acknowledge their debt. There are traces, I believe, of Spiritual Franciscanism in the teachings and writings of Friar Peter of Ghent, one of the first Franciscans to arrive in Mexico and one of the most venerable figures of the early history of the Mexican church. The councils of that period, needless to say, echoed those of contemporary Europe.

Finally, before I conclude this paper, which pretends merely to point out the existence of a potential field of study, I shall enumerate some other phenomena in the early, and even in the modern, life of Mexico which can be considered mediaeval survivals. Further research could aid in the task of understanding the vital powers that lie within many mediaeval institutions and ideas which enabled them to outlive their own epoch in a different environment, not as mere antiques but still full of energy and of potentialities.

Theology was in colonial days and even beyond, down to the Wars of Reform, the queen and pinnacle of all university studies, with the *Sententiae* of Peter Lombard the undisputed text in that field. Latin remained compulsory for university work throughout the Spanish commonwealth until the days of King Ferdinand VI, and to the study of Latin that of oriental languages and of native languages was added as the result, I believe, of the impulse given in this direction in mediaeval days by St. Raymond Lull. The power

and influence of the church in colonial Mexico, especially that of
the mendicant orders, was considerable. A distinguished contemporary Mexican historian, Pablo Martínez del Rio, has said "not
without exaggeration, of course" that the history of colonial Mexico
is the history of mediaeval Europe without the strife of the Investi-
tures. Religious festivities, the holidays *par excellence* until the nineteenth century (and, to a certain extent, even today, especially in
rural areas), combined in many instances Christian purposes and pagan ceremonies in a process of syncretism that the practical genius
of the church fostered in Europe in the era that followed the Germanic migrations. The old practice of the church in mediaeval Europe of building Christian sanctuaries on the site of heathen sacred
abodes, was repeated in Mexico, where many a church of today is
built upon a pagan pyramid. Religious theater, especially that celebrated in the *atria* of churches — in many instances today, the
atrium of the local church, is still the center of town life — is also
remindful of mediaeval practices. The dominance of religious
themes in colonial painting, architecture and sculpture (and the fact
that sculpture was in many cases ancillary to architecture) as well
as the noticeable activity of the miniaturists in the sixteenth century
and after, are very suggestive. The Inquisition was not suppressed
in Mexico until 1812. The great devotion to the Virgin, even today
the most cherished form of piety, would have been most pleasing
to St. Bernard of Clairvaux.

The mediaeval idea of law dominated the political and institutional life of the colony: natural law is considered to be paramount
and in case a royal ordinance sent from Spain contradicted it the
royal command was not carried out by the viceroys. This is, I believe, the explanation for the curious practice of the viceroys, who,
upon receiving a royal order that conflicted with natural precepts
or the customary law of the country, placed the documents upon
their heads and said: "Let us obey them but let us not carry them
out." The problems of the submission of the Indians and of the status
of their property were discussed on the basis of the doctrines of the
great theologians and canonists of the Middle Ages.

Beautiful legends such as the one that attributes to the manual
intervention of the angels the completion of the towers of the cathedral of Puebla dot here and there colonial history and traditions. The
military orders established themselves deeply on Mexican soil and
were prominent in the conquest and settlement of many areas as

well as in the setting up of the structure of colonial society. The landed nobility of early Mexico and her successor of independent days, the class of landowners (both conservative and liberal), practically dominated the economic life of the country. In this connection it should be remembered that the last great attack on *latifundia*, with wholesale expropriation of estates, where the conditions of the peasants were in many points similar to those of mediaeval serfs, was carried out only fourteen years ago.

In geographical nomenclature, there was in Latin America a great recurrence to religious names that range from the City of Our Lady of the Assumption and the Port of the Triumph of the Cross to the promontory of the Eleven Thousand Virgins. Even today typical mediaeval first names are widely used by the rural classes of Mexico, some of which possess a sixteenth-century Castilian diction: even one of our latest presidents, of humble parentage, had the charming mediaeval name of Abelard. A comparative study of mediaeval guilds and the guilds of New Spain (whose ordinances have been edited by Silvio Zavala) will, I am sure, prove fruitful. In this connection too, the importance of fairs (usually held in the *atria* of churches) as means of distribution corresponds to the economic type of organization of mediaeval Europe. The peddler, too, is still a familiar figure in some Mexican rural areas.

As I have tried to point out, the study of mediaeval survivals in America is a fascinating field of research, for the better understanding of the early history of the New World and for its later currents and developments where mediaeval ideas and practices are palpable even today, as well as for the better appreciation of the intrinsic vitality and permanence of such ideas and practices which as living forces were able to survive their own atmosphere and their own epoch and to bear magnificent fruits in a different environment beyond the seas in the New World which in many respects came to fulfill mediaeval expectancies.

❖   ❖   ❖

Scholars often have second thoughts concerning their publications. Sometimes they reach a different interpretation after further study; sometimes new material turns up which needs to be incorporated into their earlier conclusions. Dr. Weckmann, for example, was kind enough to call to my attention the fact that he had continued to investigate the subject of his *Speculum* article given above, and had collected over a thousand additional references. At my invitation, he consented to prepare a brief additional statement, which adds to his previous research and which illustrates the fact that a historian's work is never done. [*Ed. note.*]

Recent investigations confirm the fact that medieval traces can be found in Mexico in a multiplicity of aspects. In the colonial University, for example, there were offshoots of Goliardic literature and wandering monks, heirs of the clerics of Talavera. At the beginning of the "Century of Enlightenment" mathematics and astronomy were still taught according to the texts of Euclid as translated by Adelard of Bath.

Some rural classes still use diction that corresponds rather to the fifteenth century, and Américo Castro has correctly stated that our Continent is a storehouse of atrophied archaisms. At the start of the sixteenth century time was still measured according to canonic hours, and the year began on the feast of the Annunciation.

Religious life and theological problems set much of the tone of New Spain's spiritual life. There were numerous accounts, all written with medieval naivete, of miracles, revelations, visions, trances, enchantments, and the phenomena of radiance and levitation. The stigmata of St. Francis reappeared on the body of Fray Diego de Guadalcanal; Fray Francisco de Soto spoke of the "sister sea" in the manner of the humble Friar of Assisi; and Fray Juan de San Francisco destroyed idols with the same spirit that had inspired Saint Boniface in the eighth century.

Just as in the Middle Ages, mysticism brought with it a sequel of heterodoxy. Franciscan spiritualism is evident in the work of Peter of Ghent. This is not strange, for Flemish influence was powerful during the first decades of the sixteenth century, and the school of *devotio moderna* found representatives like Bishop Zumárraga. Rodrigo de Albornoz alluded to the Beguines of Flanders upon asking Charles V to establish schools for Indian girls. Juan Botello, a soldier-astrologer who accompanied Cortés, was the first of a series of friars and university graduates who found themselves at odds with the Inquisition. There were cases of pantheism in the middle of the sixteenth century, not to mention illuminists like Carbajal the Younger.

Religious syncretism occurred as in medieval Europe: homage is still paid to the Virgin of Guadalupe in the same place where Tonantzin had once been venerated. As Jiménez de Rueda pointed out, the columns of the first cathedral concealed pagan hieroglyphics. And even today, how many offerings formerly made to stone idols are accepted in the name of the calendar of saints?

For a time the Church retained some pre-Tridentine customs, such as matrimony without benefit of clergy, like that which united Doña Marina with Juan Jaramillo. The "living portraits" transplanted from the Middle Ages still survive in *posadas, pastorelas,* and *matachines.* And the Cistercian influence persisted in the bell towers of arcades constructed in the sixteenth century.

Myths and fables appeared everywhere. Columbus thought himself on the verge of finding Prester John, and he claimed to have seen the sirens, who, according to Herrera, "were not so beautiful as they were depicted." Fray Marcos de Niza asserted that he had seen a flock of unicorns in Cibola.

Accounts of the early stages of the conquest are full of statements of the uniqueness of the knightly exploit under consideration: each battle was the most difficult of all. Cortés evoked the paladin Roland and was accused by his enemies of attempting to confer knighthoods, but his soldiers found a parallel for the conquest only in the *Gesta Romanorum* or in the *Romance of Alexander.* Balbuena searched for themes in the epics of the cycles of Charlemagne and of King Artus; and even in the mid-seventeenth century the masques of the viceregal court were inspired by tales of chivalry.

The Requirement was a legacy from the colonization of the Canary Islands, and the *residencia,* which was of Roman origin according to Urquijo, was outlined in the Partidas. The origins of the *mayorazgo* can also be traced to that period. The *mesta* and *aparcería,* the latter still in use, have antecedents in Peninsular customs of the Middle Ages. Even the name of the *ejido* seems to have been derived from the *exido* (from the Latin *exitus*), that is, from the name given to communal pasture lands.

The Mexican *charro* and the North American cowboy with their rodeos and part of their attire are direct descendants, as Professors Urban Holmes and Lynn T. White, Jr. have shown, of the herdsmen of the plains of New Castile in the last stages of the Middle Ages. Our *Monte de Piedad,* or pawnshop, also has ancestors in fifteenth-century Europe.

The origins of some institutions lie beneath the Middle Ages in the classical period. The Roman *damnatio memoriae* reappeared in the placing of the stone of ignominy where the house of Alonso de Avila had stood before it was demolished as part of the sentence imposed in 1566 for the conspiracy against the crown in Mexico; and it is clear that the plans of the metropolises of Latin America, including their *Plazas mayores*, were influenced by the rectilinear Peninsular cities of Roman foundation.

I have been able to awaken the interest of my students with respect to these themes. They have written theses dealing, for example, with the influence of certain legends on geographic discoveries; with the similarities between medieval fairs and those of Jalapa and Acapulco and between the guilds of New Spain (the Mexican artisan is still called "master") and those of the Middle Ages; and finally with the evolution from the fourteenth century to the twentieth that links the "Dance of Death" with the work of the artist José Guadalupe Posada.

3. America as Fantasy

Lewis Hanke

The Spaniards who actually saw America not only became tremendously excited and stimulated but they tended to look at the New World through medieval spectacles. The wealth of ideas and legends developed with such luxuriance during the Middle Ages was transferred at once to America; this medieval influence was especially marked during the early years of the discovery and conquest.   . . .

Spanish captains went forth to their conquest expecting to encounter many kinds of mythical beings and monsters depicted in medieval literature: giants, pygmies, dragons, griffins, white-haired boys, bearded ladies, human beings adorned with tails, headless creatures with eyes in their stomachs or breasts, and other fabulous folk. For a thousand years a great reservoir of curious ideas on

Lewis Hanke, *Aristotle and the American Indians* (Chicago: Henry Regnery Co., 1959), pp. 3–11, *passim.* Reprinted by permission of Henry Regnery Company and The Bodley Head, Ltd.

man and semi-men had been forming in Europe, and was now freely drawn upon in America. St. Augustine in his *City of God* had a whole chapter on "Whether the descendants of Adam or of the sons of Noah produced monstrous races of men," and by the end of the fifteenth century a rich body of fantastic ideas was ready for use in America. Trumpet-blowing apes, for example, "formed part of a loosely defined pictorial cycle combining subjects from the world of fable with the exotic beasts of the Bestiaries and the Marvels of the East." It is not surprising, therefore, to find that the early historian Gonzalo Fernández de Oviedo had heard of a Peruvian monkey that "was no less extraordinary than the griffins," for it had a long tail, with the upper half of its body covered with many-hued feathers and the lower half with smooth, reddish fur. It could sing, "when it felt like it," in the same dulcet tones as a nightingale or a lark.

Wild men also had captured popular imagination during the Middle Ages. They were depicted on the façades of churches, as decorations for manuscripts, and in tapestries, as ferocious beings of wild mien rending lions barehanded or smashing their skulls with trees or mighty clubs. Wild men served as jamb figures on the façade of the fifteenth-century San Gregorio monastery in Valladolid in which Las Casas lived during the 1550 disputation with Sepúlveda. The wildman motif was much used in Spain, crossed the Atlantic with Spanish workmen, and is seen on the façade of the Casa del Montejo in Yucatan, built in 1549. Wild men also supported the arms of Charles V in Tlaxcala. Given this medieval mélange of man, beast, and mythical creature, we are not surprised to find that a 1498 edition of John of Holywood's *Sphaera Mundi* describes the inhabitants of the New World as being "blue in colour and with square heads." One of the earliest pictures of American natives, printed as a wood engraving about 1505, showed the same fantastic spirit. The caption read as follows:

> They go naked, both men and women; they have well-shaped bodies, and in colour nearly red; they bore holes in their cheeks, lips, noses and ears, and stuff these holes with blue stones, crystals, marble and alabaster, very fine and beautiful. This custom is followed alone by the men. They have no personal property, but all things are in common. They all live together without a king and without a government, and every one is his own master. They take for wives

whom they first meet, and in all this they have no rule. They
also war with each other, and without art or rule. And
they eat one another, and those they slay are eaten, for
human flesh is a common food. In the houses salted human
flesh is hung up to dry. They live to be a hundred and fifty
years old, and are seldom sick. . . .

Fifteenth-century Europeans had assumed their knowledge of
the world to be exact, and the appearance of a vast unknown continent across the seas shook their confidence in themselves. Ingenious attempts were made to demonstrate that the early Christian
authorities foreshadowed that shattering event, the discovery of
America. If the new lands could be related somehow to the world
they knew, a bridge could be built between the known and the unknown. The natives of this marvellous new world were, of course,
at the centre of speculation. Even before the first decade had passed,
these plumed and painted peoples — so inevitably and so erroneously
called Indians — had become the principal mystery which perplexed
the Spanish nation, conquistadores, ecclesiastics, crown, and common citizens alike. Who were they? Whence came they? What
was their nature, their capacity for Christianity and European civilization? Most important of all, what relationship would be the
right one for the Spaniards to establish with them?

The popular image, in the first feverish months, of a terrestrial
paradise was soon succeeded by that of a hostile continent peopled
with armed warriors rushing out of the tropical forests or strange
cities to resist the advance of the Spanish soldiers and the missionary efforts of their companion friars. The early suppositions that
the lost Ten Tribes of Israel were the progenitors of the Indian —
held by more than one serious writer of the day — or even the later
idea that in some mysterious way the Welsh nation had sent out
these strange shoots — failed to answer satisfactorily the urgent basic
questions: Who and what are these creatures? How shall we treat
them? Can they be Christianized and brought to a civilized way of
life? How shall this be attempted, by war or by peaceful persuasion? The conquistadores tended to ask rather pointedly: When
may just war be waged to compel the Indians to serve God and
the king and us? And the ecclesiastics asked eagerly: How can the
natives be made to change from what they are to what they ought
to be?

Two circumstances were responsible for these questions, which were asked by no other European colonizing nation with such general and genuine concern. The first was the nature of the Spanish people themselves, a people legalistic, passionate, given to extremes, and fervently Catholic. Three events of the year 1492 reflect some of the most fundamental characteristics of Spaniards and their history. Granada, the last of the Moorish kingdoms, fell to the Catholic Kings Ferdinand and Isabella on January 2, the Jews were next expelled, and on August 3 Columbus set sail. The final conquest of Granada was the climax of a long national effort to establish Christian hegemony in Spain. This long travail had helped to prepare the nation for larger tasks. Isabella herself discovered this in that same year, 1492, when she bluntly asked the scholar Antonio de Nebrija, as he presented to her his Spanish *Gramática,* the first grammar of a European modern language ever written: "What is it for?", and the Bishop of Avila, speaking on behalf of the scholar, replied: "Your Majesty, language is the perfect instrument of empire."

The second circumstance was the nature of the dominion exercised by the Spanish crown in America, by which the Spaniards felt themselves responsible for the conversion of the natives. The decrees of Pope Alexander VI, the famous bulls of donation of 1493, which were used at first to justify the exertion of Spanish power in the new lands, specifically entrusted to the crown of Castile the Christianization of these lands. Without becoming embroiled, as the Spaniards themselves became, in the legal and moral implications of these papal pronouncements, we may be clear that the Spaniards had, logically, to determine Indian nature and capacity before they could legitimately pursue either conquest or Christianization.

Most Spaniards, no matter what attitude they developed towards the Indians, were usually profoundly stirred by them. Kings and the Council of the Indies instituted prolonged and formal enquiries in both Spain and America on their nature. Few significant figures of the conquest failed to deliver themselves of opinions on the Indian's capacity for Christianity, ability to work, and general aptitude for European civilization. Among the documents which remain to us are not only opinions but also numerous and curious proposals for the protection and welfare of the Indians. Early in his career Las Casas proposed the introduction of Negro slaves to the islands, in order to spare Indians the heavy labour which was destroying them, but later repented and opposed Negro slavery as well as

Indian slavery, "and for the same reasons." Spaniards never fought, however, as hard or as consistently against Negro slavery as they did on behalf of the Indians, not even Las Casas. Despite his final rejection of Negro slavery, as late as 1544 he owned several Negro slaves and no document has come to light which reveals any concerted opposition to Negro slavery during the sixteenth century. Why did the consciences of Spaniards twinge more easily for Indians than for Negroes? Perhaps Iberian peoples had become accustomed to having Moslem Negro slaves, and Indians were not only new to them but had never had an opportunity to hear the faith before. The Jesuits Alonso de Sandoval and Pedro Claver were to work on behalf of Negroes in the seventeenth century but the moral conscience of the modern world was first roused by the plight of the American Indian.

Many men and many methods were engaged in the attempt to help the American Indians. In the same month (May, 1550) that saw the beginning of the famous discussion on the nature of the Indian, a Sevillan named Cristóbal Muñoz obtained a contract from the king to introduce 100 camels into Peru. Why? To spare the Indians the bearing of heavy burdens up and down the Andes. The archives of Spain and America are full of absorbing documentation on what the conquerors thought of the conquered people in this first widespread meeting of races in modern times. The amount and quality of the information available is unparalleled in the records of any other colonizing nation, and constitutes a wealth of material not yet fully exploited by anthropologists.

As the conquerors and clerics moved forward into America in the uneasy partnership which the crown's double purpose of political dominion and religious conversion enjoined upon them, stubborn facts and theological convictions clashed resoundingly. The voices of individuals and of different factions — ecclesiastics, soldiers, colonists, and royal officials in America as well as of men of action and thought in Spain — rose continually during the sixteenth century in a loud chorus of conflicting advice to the Spanish kings and the Council of the Indies. Each man, each faction, held a profound conviction about the nature of the Indians and all generalized about them as though they were a single race. Each made his own views on the Indians the basis of a recommendation for a government policy which he urged upon the powers in Spain as the one true solution which would once and for all set the enterprise of the

Indies on a firm and unassailable foundation. The crown considered all these recommendations and ruled above all individuals and all factions, jealous of its prerogatives and determined to prevent the growth of a powerful and turbulent aristocracy such as had just been broken in Spain by the unremitting efforts of Ferdinand and Isabella. It was the Emperor Charles V and his counsellors, therefore, who had to decide eventually what doctrine should be applied to the American Indians. In the feverish days of the early conquest, when even hard-bitten conquistadores suffered strange dreams and the New World was to some men a place of wonder and enchantment populated with mysterious and bewildering people, it is not surprising that even the ancient theory of Aristotle, that some men are born to be slaves, was borrowed from antiquity and found conveniently applicable to the Indians from the coasts of Florida to far-distant Chile.

4. The Transfer of Plants and Animals

JAMES A. ROBERTSON

"Very extraordinary," says the good Jesuit father, Bernabé Cobo, writing in 1652, "is the abundance of the increase in this New World of all the animals, fruits, vegetables, and all manner of plants which the Spaniards have taken to it since they discovered and settled it." So true was this, continues the same author, that some people doubted that certain things had been transferred from Spain at all, but declared them native to the new lands. A residence of forty years in America, however, and an acquaintance with old men who remembered when certain European animals and plants were not to be found in the Indies, or who remembered, even, when some of them were first brought over, gave Cobo a right to speak with a certain authority on the matter. Induced by friends or officials, the observant Jesuit had the prescience to write down what he knew of the bringing of new forms of life to the Indies, and his chapters on this subject are valuable testimony.

James A. Robertson, "Some Notes on the Transfer by Spain of Plants and Animals to Its Colonies Overseas," *James Sprunt Historical Studies*, XIX (Chapel Hill, N.C.: University of North Carolina Press, 1927), pp. 7–21, *passim*. Reprinted by permission.

But Cobo, although he will be used largely in this paper, is not the only authority on this phase of Spain's constructive labors in the colonies. Others — and some much earlier than he — left partial record of animal and plant transfer to and from the Indies, among them Cortés, the conqueror, Oviedo, the official, Acosta, the Jesuit (whose books have run into many editions), Herrera, the chronologist, Solórzano, the jurist, and many others. . . . Even a slight study shows that Spaniards thought of other things beside gold and precious stones, and that among the early explorers, discoverers, officials, and others, were persons with a large outlook and some with a scientific type of mind — largely untrained though they may have been in the exact tenets of science. Thus we find the great pioneer Cortés writing:

> I assure your Caesarian Majesty that, could we but obtain plants and seeds from Spain, and if Your Highness would be pleased to order them sent to us . . . the ability of these natives in cultivating the soil and making plantations would very shortly produce such abundance that great profit would accrue to the Imperial Crown of your Highness. . . .

A work of this nature, to be complete, needs the testimony of botanists and other scientists and a minute sifting of all sources. It must be premised also that the early writers, being human, and living in an age when exact observation was not regarded so necessary, perhaps, as now, were not always immune from error; so that one must check up their assertions from as many sources as possible. Cognizance must also be taken of the fact that the Spaniards sometimes transferred animals or plants into their colonies which were already to be found there. A notable instance of this was the transfer of horses to the Philippine Islands, although the Chinese horse had long been known there. In a sense, these were, however, real transfers, especially in the case of plants, for in more than one instance, the European variety throve better than the indigenous, or enriched it. With these warnings, we are ready to begin our examination of the evidence, without claiming in any way to be exhaustive and without claiming, even, to present the best evidence. This paper must be regarded merely as composed of notes that may be useful in the writing of a more definitive article on the subject of animal and plant transfers.

Cobo's evidence is especially interesting and valuable. He states that he does not know in all instances by whom introductions were made into each province; yet he remarks the problem is not a very difficult one, for most products were taken first to Isla Española, whence they were transferred to other regions. It is true, however, as he says, that some products were taken to other parts without passing through Isla Española first. Since his acquaintance was more intimate with Peru than any other region, it is not surprising that he confines himself more especially to that country.

On his very first voyage, Columbus noted the lack of European fruits, vegetables, grains, and animals. Accordingly, on his second voyage, he carried animals for breeding purposes, besides seeds and slips of plants. Later expeditions did the same thing, so that, says Cobo, "there are very few plants of all the kinds grown in Europe which have not been transferred to this land." And he makes the same observation that the transfer of animals and plants has been more advantageous to the New World than the immense wealth of gold and silver sent thence to Spain. One may predict, he continues, that every Spanish plant will thrive in the New World. One potent cause for the great increase in plants and trees has been the destruction and change of site of many Spanish and Indian settlements. Abandoned by their inhabitants, gardens have run riot, while cattle reverting to a wild state, have continued to breed and have formed immense herds. Soldiers on entering a ruined city in Chile found veritable groves of various kinds of fruit trees, which bore excellent fruit. The Indians once destroyed a Spanish settlement in the valley of Neyva, situated between Peru and the Nuevo Reino de Granada. They left some of the cattle behind, which continued to breed and within a short time had formed immense wild herds.

On their part the Indians, recognizing the benefits to be derived from the new animals and plants, ere long began to pay their tributes in wheat and cattle. The immensity of excellent grazing lands was a potent aid in the breeding and dissemination of animals; while plants, in addition to human agency (both of Spaniards and natives) were often spread by birds and in other ways.

Transfer and Spread of Animals — The American Indies were astonishingly bare of domestic animals. Dogs of questionable breeds, and cats, were not rare, and there were some wild pigs. The wild buffalo or American bison roamed the plains of North America; in South America, the Indians had tamed the vicuña and llama. But

horses and domestic cattle were unknown. Columbus, himself, took
the first horses to Isla Española in 1493. Ponce de León, Narváez,
Soto, and Luna y Arrelano had horses in their expeditions to Florida.
Cortés took this friend of man to Mexico, where the awestruck natives thought it some sort of powerful god; Pizarro, to Peru; and
Coronado, into the southwest. There is no doubt that horses aided
very materially in the conquest.

In the first years of the conquest, it was common to pay from 3,000
to 4,000 pesos for a horse, but they bred so rapidly in the New
World that the price dropped very materially within a comparatively short time. Very soon also some horses escaped into the wilds
where they quickly reverted to a wild state forming as seen above
immense herds. Wild herds were no uncommon sight in Isla Española, and they rose to uncommon proportions in the colonies of
Paraguay and Tucumán. The immense herds that roamed through
our own western country are too well known to need more than
mention. These also were often the descendants of horses that escaped from the conquistadores. In Cobo's time the best horses
came from Chile, where they had been introduced from Peru.

Shortly after their permanent entrance into the Philippines (1565),
the Spaniards also took horses thither, but the sturdy Chinese horse
had been there for many years. The small ponies that are capable of
drawing such extraordinarily large loads are descended from the
Spanish horses (often Arabs or mixed with Arab) and the Chinese
horse.

The first cattle were taken to Isla Española at the beginning of the
conquest, and to Peru three or four years after Pizarro's entrance.
Like the horse, some of them escaped into the wilds and before long
they too were formed into large herds in various regions. Indeed,
wild cattle were so numerous in Isla Española and other West Indian islands, that it was found profitable to kill them for their flesh
and hides. The men who made this their business, most frequently
English, Dutch, or French, though the scourings of many other
nations gradually drifted into the seas of the Indies, were known as
boucaniers, a word derived from an old Indian term, *boucan* or
buccan, meaning the method of drying or smoking the meat; and
since the piratical crews which scurried along the Spanish main
during the sixteenth and seventeenth centuries were usually recruited from these men, the term "buccaneer," meaning pirate came
into the English language. Acosta notes that in 1587, a single fleet

carried over 64,000 hides to Spain. The pirate Esquemelin noted the large number of wild cattle in Isla Española and says that the bulls found there were of huge bulk.

The first asses in the New World were taken to Isla Española, whence they spread into other regions, being taken to Peru by Captain Diego Maldonado, who obtained them in Jamaica. But most likely because of the abundance of horses throughout the Indies, neither asses nor their hybrid offspring, the mules, were very abundant in America in Cobo's time. However, asses could be procured in Lima for prices ranging from 10 to 15 pesos; while mules, which were very dear in early days, could be had at reasonable figures in Cobo's time, working mules fetching only 30 to 40 pesos, riding mules, 60 to 100 pesos, and choice animals, 200 to 300 pesos.

The New World had various kinds of wild, but no domesticated pigs. Because of their food value, the early conquistadores were accustomed to take large droves of European swine with them on their explorations and *entradas,* as, for instance, did Pizarro to Peru in 1531 and slightly later, Soto to Florida. Only four years after Pizarro's entrance into Peru, a slaughter house was erected in Lima, the first meat to be sold therein being pork. A decree of the cabildo of Lima, dated August 14, 1536, ordered that a pig be killed daily and the meat sold for twenty reals per *arroba,* and that no other animals were to be killed. In the middle of the seventeenth century pigs could be bought for eighteen pesos in Lima and even more cheaply in other places. Lard had a steady sale and the rendering of it was a fairly profitable business.

Sheep, when transferred from Spain to the warm regions of America (and the same was true of the transfer to the Philippine Islands), did not thrive well. Later, however, it was found that those reared in the highlands of Peru and in Chile fared better, and in those localities it was not long after their introduction before the woolen goods made from their fleece were able to compete with those of Spain. The Spaniards also early took goats and rabbits to the new lands, as well as dogs, although the Indians had plenty of the latter, albeit of poor breeds. The European dogs were used in tracking the poor Indians who fled before the cruelty of their self-appointed masters, and many a victim fell before the ferocity of the great hunting mastiffs and bloodhounds. The classic example of the dog in the early days of American colonization was the animal used by Juan Ponce de León in his conquest of Porto Rico, which shared like and like with the soldiers in all booty and wages. Pizarro took dogs to Peru, and Soto to Florida. Las Casas, the Apostle to the Indians, speaks in scathing terms of the cruelty of the dogs and the curious reader will find many interesting pictures of the dog in the great works published by Theodore de Bry in the latter part of the sixteenth century. There were instances of the dog's reverting to a wild state, and Esquemelin mentions the great, wild dogs of Isla Española descended from those brought in by the Spaniards.   . . .

Introduction of Plant Life — It was quite natural for the Spaniards on coming to their new lands to look for the plant life to which they had been accustomed; and not finding it, to attempt to introduce it, both to remind them of the land of their birth and to serve as food and for other uses. It was also quite natural for them to transfer the plant life of the colonies to Spain or from one colony to another, but with this phase of transfer we have no concern in the present article. In bringing seeds, roots, and slips from the mother country, it is not surprising that many difficulties were encountered, for methods of packing were generally crude, and in the long voyages in their insecure ships, it was not uncommon for everything to be drenched with seawater, while the intense heat as they entered the tropics caused many of the seeds to rot. The story of the transfer of wheat, for instance, is a thrilling one. Various attempts to bring seed had failed, and it seemed impossible to bring the seed alive to America. At last, however, what it seemed impossible to accomplish by design, was brought about by pure accident. It is recounted that a Negro slave of Cortés, while preparing rice for the expeditionaries one day, discovered several grains of good wheat. These were planted in New Spain and grew, and the resultant grains were also planted. In due time, the harvest was sufficient for use. A similar story is told of the introduction of wheat into Peru. Doña Inez Muñoz, wife of Martín de Alcántara — one of the conquistadores who had come to Peru with Pizarro — one day in 1535 while cleaning rice to make some soup for the family meal, found a few grains of good wheat in the rice barrel. Since she was much interested in transferring Spanish products to the new possessions, she recognized the value of her discovery. Accordingly, she planted the grains in her garden. What a gala day that must have been when the first shoots appeared above the ground, for the wheat grew rapidly and yielded abundantly. For several generations the harvest was in turn planted and in 1539 the first flour mill was erected in Peru. Next year, the cabildo of Lima regulated the sale of flour, and on November 19, 1541, bread was sold at one real for two and one-half *libras* (pounds). Other grains, including barley and rice, were early planted in Peru and flourished. . . .

The first cultivated seed or slip of the vine was taken to Lima by Hernando de Montenegro, and so rapid was the development that by 1551 grapes were being gathered in abundance. In that year, being placed on sale, under the auspices of Licentiate Rodrigo Niño, they brought half a *peso oro* or 225 *maravedis* per *libra*. However, Montenegro, to whom the grapes belonged, considered this price too low and appealed to the audiencia of Lima asking that he be permitted to sell at a higher rate. So greatly were the first plants esteemed, says Cobo, that it was necessary to have them guarded by armed men, so that the shoots should not be stolen. The first vines taken from Peru to Chile sold at 3,000 pesos, and the shoots at 100 pesos each. In Cobo's time there was an annual export from Peru of more than 100 shiploads of grapes. The price of the wine made from the grapes dropped to as low as three to four pesos per *arroba*. As time passed most of the Spanish varieties of grapes were transferred to Peru and flourished; and as might be expected, found favor not only with the whites but with the Indians as well. The Jesuit Joseph de Acosta, writing much earlier than Cobo, bears similar testimony of the vine, but says that this most useful product did not thrive in Tierra Firme or in the islands. The vines bore well in New Spain, however, but the grapes were there used only for eating, no wine being made, because as Acosta conjectures, the grapes did not ripen thoroughly on account of the rains of July and August. On the other hand, he says, excellent wine was made in Peru and Chile; and so great was the increase in those regions that the tithes of the church increased five or six times within twenty years.

The olive was first brought to Peru by Antonio de Ribera, one of the principal settlers of that country. Having been sent to Spain as procurator for the new colony, on his return in 1560, he brought many olive plants from Seville, but only two or three survived the voyage. Planting these in his garden he had them carefully guarded against theft by Indians and dogs. Notwithstanding his care, however, all the plants except one were stolen one night, and taken to Chile where being planted they throve exceedingly. The one left to Ribera became the parent of all the trees in Peru, and in Cobo's time was still living although the garden in which it had been planted had been transferred to a community of nuns. . . .

Sugarcane was first brought to the West Indies by Pedro de Atienza, an inhabitant of Concepción de la Vega in Isla Española, and from this place it spread all over the tropical Indies redeeming much territory that had been considered as only waste. The product was larger than in its former home, and grew so abundantly that sugar was made in great quantities and soon became very cheap, costing only four or five pesos per *arroba*. In Peru, notwithstanding the heavy consumption of sugar, there was a considerable export to Spain.

The first sugar in the Indies is said to have been made by Gonzalo de Vibora, who brought over sugar experts to Isla Española, and who erected a horse mill for expressing the juice. "To him alone," says Oviedo, "are due thanks for the first manufacture of sugar in America." So rapid was the development of sugar growing that despite the heavy capital needed to run a mill because slave labor only was employed, many sugar mills were early established, among mill owners being Luis Colón, Cristóbal de Tapía, Miguel de Pasamonte, Lucas Vasquez de Ayllón, and many others whose names are familiar. Until sugar became an object of export, ships had to return to Spain in ballast. In 1553, so much sugar was made in Mexico that heavy exports were made from Vera Cruz and Acapulco to Spain and Peru. One shipment of sugar to Spain before 1590 amounted to 898 boxes, each presumably of 8 *arrobas'* weight, and this notwithstanding the heavy consumption in the Indies. Sugar, indeed, became the chief product of the West Indian islands, and its abundance created a great demand for confections of various kinds. . . .

Oranges and lemons spread so rapidly that it early became not uncommon to see them growing wild in Isla Española. Acosta, indeed, says that whole forests of wild oranges were found growing in many localities. The first oranges (both sweet and sour varieties) were taken to Isla Española from Spain, and throve wonderfully both inside the city of Santo Domingo and in other parts of the island, and spread very soon to the other islands. The first oranges were taken to Peru by Baltasar Gogo and planted in a garden not far from Lima. Lemons were unknown in Peru when Cobo first went there, but when he wrote they had been flourishing for a score of years.

The mulberry was introduced into the New World by Hernando

Cortés, who tried to establish the silk industry in New Spain. The first bananas in the New World, according to Oviedo, were planted in Isla Española in 1516 by Tomás Berlanga, a Dominican priest, who is said to have brought them from the Canary Islands; but Acosta says that they had been known in America before the arrival of the Spaniards. Cobo is probably in error in his assertion that the first bananas were planted in Tierra Firme, but probably correct when he says that the first ones were taken to Peru by a lady of Panama who went to that country.

With regard to the plant life of the New World, Candolle says that of 247 plants cultivated in America, 199 originated in the Old World, 45 in America, 1 in Australia, while the native habitat of 2 can not be determined. It might be well in this connection to repeat Humboldt's warning, lest we get to believing that the New World was poorer in useful plant life than was really the case. He says:

> In general, if one considers the garden plants of the Aztecs and the great number of farinaceous and sugar roots culti-vated in Mexico and in Peru, he will see that America was not nearly so poor in food plants as would appear from the un-trustworthy evidence advanced by certain savants, who know the new continent only through the works of Herrera and Solis.

And he notes further that, before the arrival of the Spaniards in America, Mexico and the Cordilleras of South America produced several fruits quite similar to those of the temperate climate of the old continent.

On the other side of the globe, the Spaniards transferred various products to the Philippine Islands, both from the American Indies and from Spain. This story may not be taken up in any detail in this paper. Suffice it to say that Miguel López de Legazpi, who made the first permanent Spanish settlement in the Philippines (that at Cebu), in writing his official report of 1565, states that the soil was so fertile that four days after the Spanish forces had taken the native town of Cebu, "the Castilian seeds had already sprouted."

Whatever mistakes the Spaniards made in their colonization of their new possessions, whether in the western or eastern hemisphere, one can indorse much of what Claudio Gay says, namely:

> Never has a nation carried the colonizing spirit to a degree as high as the Spaniards. Although many of them expatriated

themselves with the sole object of enriching themselves at any price, the majority had the firm resolution to contribute to the civilizing and evangelizing of semi-barbaric peoples. With this object they carried with them, not only the principal elements of civilization, such as domestic animals, wheat, beans, vegetables, etc., but also a force of goodwill and of perseverance truly wonderful which naught could change.

5. The Libraries of Colonial Spanish America

LAWRENCE S. THOMPSON

The *leyenda negra* has somehow perpetuated the idea that libraries were insignificant in colonial Spanish America, and this notion was a part of the folklore of Latin American history up until a quarter of a century ago. The stern legal prohibitions against the export of fiction to the Indies and other formal controls on the book trade have been interpreted literally by some students who have not examined customs records, book lists in Jesuit and other religious archives, export records of the Casa de la Contratación (and countless other sources in the seemingly inexhaustible Archivo de Indias in Seville), Inquisition records, and other pertinent archives. The labors of scholars such as Irving A. Leonard, José Torre Revello, and Father Guillermo Furlong Cardiff, using manuscript catalogues and book lists, have pointed out the productive sources for research; and their specialized studies have suggested the need for similar work in all fields of the history of the book in the old Spanish colonies. In particular we need to identify and describe more libraries that were in monasteries, episcopal palaces, universities, private homes, and, quite late in the colonial period, public institutions sponsored by societies.

Books came to the Americas at an early date. One of the first references to Bartolomé de Las Casas (A Dominican) refers to a payment of 10,000 maravedís to the master of the vessel *Trinidad* for the passage of Las Casas "con 4 criados, librería, ropa y media cámara" on April 6, 1517. Seventeen years later and a whole hemi-

Lawrence S. Thompson, "The Libraries of Colonial Spanish America," *Bibliotheca Docet: Festgabe für Carl Wehmer* (Amsterdam: Verlag der Erasmus-Buchhandlung, 1963), pp. 257–266. Reprinted by permission of the author.

sphere to the south the Franciscans entered the River Plate and brought books with them, and Pedro de Mendoza himself brought "siete libros medianos guarnecidos de cuero negro," one "librete chico dorado que dice que es Bridia guarnecido en pergamino." Soldiers and administrators brought books to America, for they often had cultural interests in proportions equal to their desire for precious metals and *encomiendas*.

The friars — Jesuit, Dominican, Franciscan, Augustinian and Mercedarian — were the most zealous in bringing books to early Spanish America, much as the churchmen of early New England and New York laid the foundations of the libraries of Harvard, Dartmouth, Yale, and Columbia. Alonso de la Vera Cruz, an Augustinian distinguished as author, collector, and executive, came back to New Spain in 1573 with a scrap of the *lignum Crucis,* and, vastly more important, a collection of books; and he founded and nurtured libraries in Mexico, Tiripitío, and Tacámbara. Some of his books are still preserved in the Museo Michoacana in Morelia. Although we have not yet excavated records of significant libraries on the islands, we know that there was a collection in the Convento de Santo Domingo in San Juan de Puerto Rico as early as 1523 and that it endured until it was destroyed by the Dutch in 1625. Lope de Vega even celebrated the private library of Bernardo de Valbuena, bishop of Puerto Rico from 1600 to 1627, in the *Laurel de Apolo,* Silva II.

The Jesuits, more than any other order, were responsible for the spread of books and printing in Spanish America. Arriving in the Americas in the latter half of the sixteenth century, they brought with them not only the traditional vows but also concern for "a peculiar care in the education of boys." By the time of the expulsion in 1767, there were Jesuit libraries in Córdoba de Tucumán, Bogotá, and elsewhere which were at least equal to any in Saxon America. The dissolution was also the cause of the dispersal of Jesuit collections and their partial reincorporation into public and national libraries. On the other hand, there were irreparable losses after the expulsion, and biblioklepts and biblioclasts had a Roman holiday in many an old cultural center such as Cuzco. Jorge Cornejo Bouroncle found that the University of Cuzco, heir to the local Jesuit collections, was not able to inventory and to clean and repair the books until 1938; and he was properly dismayed by a rumor, probably correct, that a first edition of *Quijote* had been clandestinely removed from the library and sold.

If the surviving book lists in customs and Inquisition files, records of civil litigation, will books, and other likely sources were studied throughout Spanish America even to the extent they have been studied in Argentina, Chile, and Mexico, the rôle of Loyola's followers in developing book collections would be recognized as one of their greatest achievements. Especially in Argentina the Jesuits were active in creating libraries. Don Francisco Salcedo, dean of the Cathedral of Santiago del Estero and one of the first Jesuits to land in Argentina (around 1586), and Don Diego Suárez Babiano (d. 1593), vicar general of Córdoba, were masters of select, even if small private collections, and philology as well as theology was represented in the latter. The Jesuits imported books steadily, both for library resources and for re-sale (mainly as textbooks) during the nearly two centuries from 1586 to 1767 when they were the dominant cultural element in the old viceroyalty of the Río de la Plata. Many personal libraries of individual friars found their way to the shelves of the old University of Córdoba, a trend which Father Furlong has documented. The Colegio Máximo and the Noviciado in Córdoba contained well over 5,000 volumes in 1767, and the Colegio Grande (or of San Ignacio) in Buenos Aires had upwards of 3,000 volumes. Many of the books in these two collections as well as in the provincial Jesuit libraries found their way to the modern University of Córdoba Library, to the Argentine National Library, and to other collections in Buenos Aires and (in isolated instances) in the provinces.

In Santa Fé de Bogotá the Jesuit library of the Colegio de San Bartolomé was the cornerstone of the Biblioteca Pública, founded in 1774, barely seven years after the expulsion. It was not actually opened to the public until January 9, 1777, at which time it consisted of 4,182 volumes, mainly in theology, history, and the classics. This collection was the origin of the modern Colombian National Library.

In the opposite corner of the old kingdom of New Granada we can identify a founder of libraries in the brilliant *zambo* Francisco Javier Eugenio de Santa Cruz y Espejo (1747–1795) of Quito. A typical eighteenth century intellectual (and such there were in some abundance, in the Spanish colonies, the *leyenda negra* to the contrary), he saw an opportunity to found a public library in the Ecuadorian capital from the remains of the Jesuit collections. The especially harsh treatment of the Jesuits in Ecuador probably caused the destruction of many records, including library lists, and we may never know the full extent and importance of their collections.

In Santiago de Chile the Jesuit collections of some 5,000 volumes were deposited in the University of San Felipe in Santiago where they remained almost unused. Largely theological and legal, with some classics, this collection, and that of the University proper, amounting to some 8,000 volumes in all, became the nucleus of the Chilean National Library under the sponsorship of Manuel de Salas and San Martín. The significant fact, however, is that the Jesuits owned over 15,000 books in thirty-three different locations in Chile before 1767.

The brilliance of the Jesuits as missionaries in the Orient and in the New World sometimes tends to obscure the work of the other orders. The Augustinians were pioneers in the transplantation of Hispanic culture, and Alonso de la Vera Cruz was among the first of many distinguished representatives of this order. Toward the end of the eighteenth century there were substantial libraries of at least four orders, in addition to the Jesuit collections, in Santiago de Chile. There were 5,000 volumes in the library of the Convento de Santo Domingo and 3,000 in the Convento de San Agustín. The latter was based on a collection inherited from Fray Agustín Carrillo de Ojeda, who died in Lima in 1671, and a donation of 400 books by Fray Francisco de Loyola y Vergara in 1672. A manuscript catalogue in the Biblioteca Nacional of Santiago de Chile shows over 3,000 volumes in the Convento de San Francisco in that city. Even the Mercedarians, rarely distinguished as booklovers or scholars, had 435 books in their Convento de La Merced when it was founded in 1683; and a century later there were about 1,000 volumes in the collection.

In Buenos Aires the Dominicans had a significant library at least as early as 1739 when the Dominican Neira referred to it in complimentary terms. In 1768 the bishop of Buenos Aires wrote to Count de Aranda that the Dominican monasteries, as well as those of other orders, in his province, were poorly equipped with books, but this was probably a hint to have Jesuit property turned over to them. There were Dominican, Franciscan and Mercedarian libraries in the Río de la Plata, and it is not unusual to find books in modern Argentine libraries, public and private, with such inscriptions as "Es

de la Merced de Córdoba." The detailed study of these collections
awaits the excavation of more catalogues from archival sources.

The Franciscans were second only to the Jesuits in bold and
imaginative missionary work in which books played a major rôle.
The first library in what is now the United States was the Franciscan
collection in Santa Fé, New Mexico, and it may have come into existence three decades before John Harvard's legacy reached Cambridge, Massachusetts. While the local Franciscan archives per-
ished along with those of the provincial government in the Pueblo
Revolt of 1680, Eleanor B. Adams and France V. Scholes have made
logical guesses about the scope and content of the collection, mainly
from letters written by Fray Juan de Vidania around 1640–41 at the
time of a bitter controversy between Governor Luis de Rosas and
the Franciscans. Vidania cited many authorities, mainly religious,
but also classical, and it is likely that the original sources were at
hand.

The Franciscans in the capital were reputed to have developed
the best book collection in Mexico. Fernando Peñalosa states, without citing documentation, that the friars of the Convento de San
Francisco in Mexico City "spared neither expense nor effort in
bringing together a great collection of books, and by the end of
the eighteenth century they had the best library in New Spain."

There are several known instances, and probably many other yet
unrecorded ones, of high prelates who were book collectors and
founders of libraries. Juan de Zumárraga, first bishop and archbishop
of Mexico, and an indefatigable friend of printing, education, and
cultural development in general, was a zealous collector and donated
books to various monasteries. In a report to the Council of the Indies in 1533 he emphasized the need for good libraries in New Spain.
Another early book-loving bishop of Mexico was Vasco de Quiroga,
who became the first bishop of Michoacán in 1537. His library of
over 600 volumes must have been semi-public, for a humanitarian
of his orientation would not fail to share his books as a part of his
efforts to create a utopian society among the aborigines. Most famous of the bibliophilic Mexican prelates was Juan de Palafox y
Mendoza. An enemy of the privileged regular clergy (especially
the Jesuits) and a humanitarian comparable to Las Casas, Palafox
founded a seminary in Puebla, the Colegio de San Pedro y San
Pablo, in 1646 and donated a library of 6,000 volumes. The institution thrived under Palafox' successors, and the library continues to

be housed in a late eighteenth century building known as the Biblioteca Palafoxiana.

At the other extremity of Spanish America another private episcopal library survives in the Cabildo Eclesiástico of Santiago de
Chile. It originally belonged to Francisco Ruiz de Berecedo, born
in Concepción in 1675. According to the Archivo de Escribanos, a
rich source for documents relative to books in colonial Chile, the
collection amounted to "2,058 libros grandes y pequeños, con sus
estantes con 90 cajones." Strong in classical literature, history, and
linguistics, the library passed to Berecedo's great nephew, Manuel
de Alday y Axpée, later bishop of Santiago. He in turn left it to the
Cathedral of Santiago.

In the latter part of the eighteenth century the Archbishop of
Bogotá and Viceroy of New Granada, Antonio Caballero y Góngora,
had a distinguished private collection. He provided a subsidy for
José Celestino Mutis in 1783 to establish the famous Expedición Bo-
tánica; and it is not unreasonable to assume that such a generous
patron of science would make his library freely available to the
beneficiaries of his grants.

We know less about the university libraries of colonial Spanish
America than about libraries of the religious or of private individuals. Córdoba is the single exception to this statement, although it is
not unlikely that documents will some day be found to shed more
light on colonial academic libraries. The early library history of the
Imperial and Pontifical University of Santo Domingo, founded
ninety-eight years before Harvard opened its doors, is unrecorded
in print. The second oldest university of the New World in Mexico
(1551) had existed for two and a half centuries when the Viceroy
Marquina reported to his successor that the university "no tiene
gabinete y su biblioteca está escasa de buenas obras modernas." The
University of Havana (1728) had a library from the beginning
which served both the institution and the religious establishment
with which it was affiliated. The university was under the direction
of the clergy and remained so until the secularization in 1842, at
which time an assistant professor in the Faculty of Philosophy and
Letters was placed in charge.

The seminaries could hold university rank and privilege and perform university functions (with libraries as a necessary tool). Good
examples were the Colegio de San Bartolomé (Jesuit, *supra*) in
Bogotá and the Colegio del Rosario (Dominican) in Bogotá, both

equal in privileges to the University of Salamanca by royal decree; and their libraries were, according to Giraldo Jaramillo, "famosas en la Santafé colonial." The Seminary of Santiago de Chile, founded in 1777, had five sections (*estantes*) of books, but we do not know how many volumes there were. Palafox' solicitude for the library needs of his Colegio de San Pedro y San Pablo has already been noted.

Perhaps a contrast with North American colonial libraries is not out of order. John Harvard willed his library of some 400 books in 1638 to the two-year-old-college in Cambridge, and the books passed to the exclusive control of the institution. In 1764 when Harvard Hall burned there were 5,000 volumes, but by 1790 the 404 surviving books had been increased to a total of 13,000. A group of clergymen in Brandford, Connecticut, assembled forty folio volumes for the new Collegiate School of Connecticut, and there were nearly 1,000 when they were moved to New Haven in 1716. The school acquired its present name when Elihu Yale gave 400 volumes in 1720. In 1733 Bishop Berkeley gave 100 more books. By 1765 there were 4,000 volumes under the supervision of the college's administration. Princeton University owned some 3,000 volumes in 1802 when Nassau Hall burned, and Dartmouth College held 3,000 books by 1809. The significant fact about these and other colleges (in the Anglo-American sense) is that the clergy was not the final determinative force in the institution's destinies. Administration of the book collections was no more efficient, perhaps less efficient in some instances, and the collections in Cambridge and New Haven may even have been inferior to those of Córdoba, Bogotá, Mexico City, or Santiago de Chile. But the Calvinist and Anglican clergy did not rise and fall with the political destinies of the country; and, while they dominated the teaching faculties, the institutions had powerful friends outside of the clergy. The Roman church performed fabulous exploits in bringing culture to the New World, but there was far too intimate a connection between church and state to insure stability for the other partner when one had problems. A debacle such as the Jesuit expulsion had disastrous effects on all institutions associated with this group.

There is another side of the picture towards the end of the colonial period that was manifest from Cambridge to Córdoba: the influence of the Enlightenment. The propagation of secular libraries and freedom of learning was a fundamental notion of the new movement, and in Spanish America we even find the clergy (by no means totally reactionary) participating in the movement. The same spirit that moved Benjamin Franklin and his friends to establish the Library Company of Philadelphia and what is today the University of Pennsylvania was also abroad from New Orleans to Buenos Aires. If these libraries and universities did not thrive in nineteenth-century Spanish America, penetration of the ideas of the Enlightenment to the old Spanish colonies is nevertheless beyond question.

If some of the Jesuit persecution (especially in the Americas) was tinged with jealousy and vengefulness, it was surely a more generous attitude that inspired the conversion of old Jesuit collections to the use of semi-public, university, and later national libraries. This we have already noted in Quito, Bogotá, Córdoba and Buenos Aires, where substantial portions of Jesuit collections escaped the biblioklepts and biblioclasts to find their way to semi-public collections. The clergy often encouraged the establishment of a "public" library (actually not quite public in the nineteenth century Anglo-American sense) and made substantial donations of books for the purpose. In 1788 the Cathedral of Mexico accepted and opened for public use the Biblioteca Turriana, founded by the two brothers Torres and their uncle. The municipal government of Mexico City made contributions to its support, and it is said to have accumulated 19,000 volumes.

Perhaps the most characteristic manifestation of the spirit of the Enlightenment as far as Spanish American library development is concerned is the Sociedad Económica de Amigos del País in Havana. Founded by several Havana gentlemen, to "aumentar la instrucción y de influir el gusto de la lectura," it was to be financed by funds derived from the sale of the *Papel periódico*. The serial itself commenced in 1790 and was produced by the Imprenta de la Capitanía General. Members of the Sociedad Económica contributed books, and there was an ambitious plan to exchange with other Hispanic countries. It is doubtful that this plan was ever realized, even in part, for world political conditions and the current system of communications were hardly conducive to international cooperation at this time. It is significant to note that this institution, essentially a subscription library for the intellectual élite of the Cuban capital, thrived for another century of colonial administration and more than a half century of the first Cuban republic. In the late 1950's it was still the most practical collection in Havana for researchers in things Cuban.

Manuel del Socorro Rodríguez, a Cuban émigré to New Granada, also combined journalism and librarianship. On February 9, 1791 he published the first number of the *Papel periódico de la ciudad de Santafé de Bogotá* and continued it until January 6, 1797. In the meanwhile he catalogued both the printed books and manuscripts in the "Real Biblioteca Pública" and, presumably, made them much more accessible than at any previous time. Even if the libraries in Bogotá and Buenos Aires were precursors of actual revolution, the same spirit of rational truth-seeking nevertheless inspired these as well as the founders of the library of the Sociedad Económica in Havana, where revolution was not to be successful for another century.

Another element in the growth of libraries for laymen in the late eighteenth century was the rising economic prosperity of Spanish America. In 1802 Pedro de Mantilla, resident agent in Madrid for the Consulado (merchant guild) of Mexico, presented a list of "recognized works in political economy" which seemed appropriate for a library for the Consulado in Veracruz. There is no evidence that the library ever actually came into existence, but the list, published by Irving A. Leonard and Robert S. Smith, reveals something of the growing awareness of businessmen of the need for reference books.

They *leyenda negra* can be transformed into a smog-yellow by careful study of the zeal of intellectuals, clerical and secular, in the Spanish colonies just before the revolutions. Indeed, there was never any Plutonian darkness, from the days of Las Casas on. The. witchcraft scandals of New England and the anti-intellectualism of Virginia's seventeenth century governors might have been the basis of a similar malignancy by enemies of the English colonial administration; but, instead, Saxon America has been apotheosized (mainly by North American writers) as a cradle of modern egalitarianism. In Spanish America there are records of savage action against owners of private libraries including books not fully approved by the ecclesiastical hierarchy, but there are also numerous instances of private ownership of books which would have been vigorously condemned by orthodox Philadelphia Quakers or tidewater Anglicans. The truth of the matter is, probably, that possession of questionable books was used as an excuse by authorities for action against politically suspect individuals. The records of private libraries, abundant in lay and clerical circles alike, are known in representative samples, thanks to the work of Rodríguez Marín, Torre Revello, Leonard, O'Gorman, González Obregón, Furlong, and other delvers in the archives of two hemispheres.

The story of private bibliophily in colonial Spanish America is beyond the scope of this essay, but it cannot be ignored in this connection; for private collections have always set the tone for the public collections into which they have been incorporated or to which they are often dispersed. Religious books predominated, but we have seen that the "lying histories" found their way to the Indies despite legal prohibitions. One of Pedro de Mendoza's books was by Erasmus. It might even be a bit impious to try to guess what titles were among the two hundred books brought by Antonio de Mendoza, first viceroy of New Spain, for his entertainment in his new post. He was cautious to arrange to have them exempted from customary duties — and presumably inspection as well — by special dispensation of the Crown.

There were regrettable cases of persecution. Saddest of those recorded is the fate of Melchór Pérez de Soto, who was arrested on January 10, 1655 in his Mexico City residence and died two months later in a secret prison of the Holy Office. He had "1502 cuerpos de libros . . . en latín y en romance" (and, *horribile dictu*, in High and Low Dutch, presumably Lutheran in content). He had books in bibliography (León Pinelo's *Epitome*), the sciences (Copernicus and Euclid), Mexican imprints, and French sonnets. The existing records fail to show what the Holy Office had against Pérez de Soto in addition to his being the master of a library of a typical seventeenth century cultured layman. There must have been more to the story. In remote Santa Fé de Nuevo México the Holy Office arrested Bernardo López de Mendizabal and his wife Doña Teresa in 1662; and the inventory of their books showed such subversive titles as *Quijote,* a book of *comedias* by different authors, *Orlando Furioso,* and Espinel's *Marcos de Obregón.* By the same token, Diego de Peñalosa, successor of Luis de Rosas as governor of New Mexico, ran afoul of the Church. He was arrested and his books and property inventoried in 1665. Far to the south of Mexico, Francisco de Larrinaga, bibliophilic *corregidor* in Mendoza in the late seventeenth century, was staked out in the desert by his cruel successor, Nicolás Francisco de Retana, but fortunately was rescued by passing Indians. Retana seems not to have bothered to have indicted Larrinaga for the ownership of some seventy volumes of mathematics, architecture, law and theology, some of which may well have been by Lutheran authors.

There were, in fact, an abundance of dissident and even heretical books in Spanish American libraries toward the end of the eighteenth century. Manuel Gayoso de Lemos, governor of Louisiana from 1797 until his death in 1799, could get away with ownership of any books he wanted to read, including William Robertson's notoriously anti-Spanish *History of America*. In the Río de la Plata apparently little attention was paid by the end of the eighteenth century to formal prohibitions against importation or possession of questionable books. Ricardo R. Caillet-Bois notes in various private collections the *Encyclopédie,* works of Voltaire, Bayle, Montesquieu and even the Abbé Raynal (a founding father of the *leyenda negra*).

Even in colonial Caracas, a city ranking below Bogotá in cultural importance for New Granada, the young Bolívar could read Locke, Condillac, Buffon, d'Alembert, Helvétius, Montesquieu, Lalande, Rousseau, Voltaire, Rollin, Berthel, and the principal ancient and modern belletristic authors, philosophers, historians, and poets of western Europe, including England. Many another youngster who participated actively in fomenting and executing the revolutions of the early nineteenth century must have had a similar background.

Whether all of these books which were surely suspect to officials in Spain were also available in institutional or religious libraries is not known. If they were in the latter, they were surely available only to a select few. The doubt in our minds that is left by the absence of published lists and more detailed histories of institutional libraries suggests the urgent need for more investigations of the type that Leonard and other students with similar interests have made on private libraries and the book trade. Many original archives have been lost, but many others survive and need only to be located, transcribed, and interpreted. Until they are, our imperfect knowledge of the institutional libraries of colonial Spanish America will remain one of our greatest handicaps in adequate understanding of three centuries of American history.

C.   The Portuguese Background

6. The Mobility, Miscibility, and Adaptability of the Portuguese

GILBERTO FREYRE

The singular predisposition of the Portuguese to the hybrid, slave-exploiting colonization of the tropics is to be explained in large part by the ethnic or, better, the cultural past of a people existing indeterminately between Europe and Africa and belonging uncompromisingly to neither one nor the other of the two continents; with the African influence seething beneath the European and giving a sharp relish to sexual life, to alimentation, and to religion; with Moorish or Negro blood running throughout a great light-skinned mulatto population, when it is not the predominant strain, in regions that to this day are inhabited by a dark-skinned people; and with the hot and oleous air of Africa mitigating the Germanic harshness of institutions and cultural forms, corrupting the doctrinal and moral rigidity of the medieval Church, drawing the bones from Christianity, feudalism, Gothic architecture, canonic discipline, Visigoth law, the Latin tongue, and the very character of the people. It was Europe reigning without governing: it was Africa that governed.   . . .

Within this antecedent factor of a general nature — the bi-continentalism or, better, the dualism of culture and of race — there are other, subordinate factors that call for our special attention. One of these is the presence among the elements that united to form the Portuguese nation of individuals of Semitic origin, or stock, individuals endowed with a mobility, a plasticity, and adaptability social as well as physical that are easily to be made out in the

Portuguese navigator and cosmopolitan of the fifteenth century. Hereditarily predisposed to a life in the tropics by a long tropical habitat, it was the Semitic element, mobile and adaptable as no other, that was to confer upon the Portuguese colonizer of Brazil some of the chief physical and psychic conditions for success and for resistance — including that economic realism which from an early date tended to correct the excesses of the military and religious spirit in the formation of Brazilian society.

This mobility was one of the secrets of the Portuguese victory. Without it, it is not to be explained how a country that was practically uninhabited, with a population that was numerically insignificant as a result of all the epidemics, famines, and especially wars that had afflicted the peninsula in the Middle Ages, should have succeeded in virilely besprinkling with what was left of its blood and culture populations so diverse and at so great a distance from one another: in Asia, in Africa, in America, and in the numerous islands and archipelagoes. The scarcity of man-power was made up for by the Portuguese through mobility and miscibility, by dominating enormous spaces and, wherever they might settle, in Africa or in America, taking wives and begetting offspring with a procreative fervor that was due as much to violent instincts on the part of the individual as it was to a calculated policy stimulated by the State for obvious economic and political reasons.

Individuals of worth, warriors, administrators, technicians, were shifted about by the colonial administration in Lisbon like pieces on a backgammon board: from Asia to America and from there to Africa, depending upon the exigencies of the moment or of the region. To Duarte Coelho, grown rich from his stay in India, John III intrusts the new *capitânia* of Pernambuco. His sons, trained in fighting the American Indians, are summoned to the more difficult wars in Africa. From Madeira technicians in the manufacture of sugar are sent to the plantations of northern Brazil. Ships employed in trade with the Indies are made use of for commerce with the American colony. From Africa whole nations, almost, of Negroes are transported for agricultural labor in Brazil. An astounding mobility. An imperial domain achieved by an all but ridiculous number of Europeans running from one end to another of the known world as in a formidable game of puss-in-the-corner.

As to their miscibility, no colonizing people in modern times has exceeded or so much as equaled the Portuguese in this regard. From their first contact with women of color, they mingled with them and procreated mestizo sons; and the result was that a few thousand daring males succeeded in establishing themselves firmly in possession of a vast territory and were able to compete with great and numerous peoples in the extension of their colonial domain and in the efficiency of their colonizing activity. Miscibility rather than mobility was the process by which the Portuguese made up for their deficiency in human mass or volume in the large-scale colonization of extensive areas. For this they had been prepared by the intimate terms of social and sexual intercourse on which they had lived with the colored races that had invaded their peninsula or were close neighbors to it, one of which, of the Mohammedan faith, was technically more highly skilled and possessed an intellectual and artistic culture superior to that of the blond Christians.

Long contact with the Saracens had left with the Portuguese the idealized figure of the "enchanted Moorish woman," a charming type, brown-skinned, black-eyed, enveloped in sexual mysticism, roseate in hue, and always engaged in combing out her hair or bathing in rivers or in the waters of haunted fountains; and the Brazilian colonizers were to encounter practically a counterpart of this type in the naked Indian women with their loose-flowing hair. These latter also had dark tresses and dark eyes and bodies painted red, and, like the Moorish Nereids, were extravagantly fond of a river bath to refresh their ardent nudity, and were fond, too, of combing their hair. What was more, they were fat like the Moorish women. . . .

In opposition to the legend of the "enchanted Moorish woman," although it never attained the same prestige, there evolved that of the "Moorish hag," representing, it may be, an outlet for the blonde woman's sexual jealousy toward her colored sister. Then, there were outbreaks of religious hatred, with the blond Christians from the north pitted against the dark-skinned infidels, a hatred that was later to result in the idealization throughout Europe of the blond type as identified with angelic and divine personages, to the detriment of the brunet type, which was associated with evil and fallen angels, with the wicked, and with traitors. One thing we know is that in the fifteenth century, when ambassadors were sent by the Republic of Venice to the two Spains, bearing greetings to King Philip II, the envoys noted that in Portugal certain women of the upper classes were in the habit of dyeing their hair a "blond color," while both there and in Spain a number of them "painted their faces a white and red tint" by way of "rendering their skin, which is a trifle swarthy — which is, indeed, quite swarthy — more fair and rosy, being persuaded that all swarthy-skinned women are ugly."

Meanwhile, it may be stated that the brown-skinned woman was preferred by the Portuguese for purposes of love, at least for purposes of physical love. The fashions of the blonde woman — limited, for that matter, to the upper classes — were the reflection of influences coming from abroad rather than a genuine expression of the national taste. . . . Moreover, in our national lyricism there is no tendency more clearly revealed than one toward a glorification of the mulatto woman, the *cabocla* or Indian woman, the brown-skin or brunette type, celebrated for the beauty of her eyes, the whiteness of her teeth, for her wiles and languishments and witching ways, far more than are the "pale virgins" and the "blonde damsels." These latter, it is true, appear here and there in a sonnet or popular song (*modinha*) of the eighteenth or nineteenth century, but they do not stand out as the others do.

Another circumstance or condition that favored the Portuguese as much as did miscibility and mobility in the conquest of the land and the domination of the tropical peoples was their acclimatability. With respect to physical conditions of soil and temperature, Portugal is Africa rather than Europe. The so-called "Portuguese climate" of Martonne, unique in Europe, is one that approximates the African. Thus, the Portuguese was predisposed by his own mesology to a victorious encounter with the tropics; his removal to the torrid regions of America was not to bring with it the grave disturbances associated with adaptation nor the profound difficulties of acclimatization that were experienced by colonizers coming from cold climates.

7. Portuguese Culture in Brazil

EMÍLIO WILLEMS

It has often been stated that contemporary Brazil contains a hybrid people and a hybrid culture, the foundations of which were laid by Portuguese settlers, African slaves, and native Indians. This threefold contribution to one of America's most widely diffused Creole cultures calls for extensive anthropological research which, at the present time, seems to be only in the very beginning. Attention of ethnographers and sociologists has been attracted so far by the African and Indian ingredients rather than by Portuguese strains in the cultural make-up of contemporary Brazil. Connections with Portugal seem too obvious to deserve more than general and vague references. And yet the results of recent anthropological research work, conducted in various regions of Brazil, have furthered evidence that the common denominator of Brazilian Creole culture is basically Portuguese. Exactly what these Portuguese elements are, what changes they underwent, and how they were integrated in the total configuration of the Brazilian culture still remains, however, to be investigated. . . .

The Family — The development of an extended, multifunctional family in Brazil (erroneously called clan by some authors) has sometimes been attributed to weaknesses of the colonial government and to certain ecological characteristics of colonial Brazil.

> This kinship solidarity [says Oliveira Vianna] which we find dominating in the colonial centuries — and which clearly and imperceptibly inspires all political and party activities of our territorial aristocracy of the fourth century — certainly has its origin not in any peninsular tradition, but in the enormous and frightful dangers which, during the first centuries, surrounded our pioneering and colonizing institutions.

Emílio Willems, "Portuguese Culture in Brazil," *Proceedings of the International Colloquium on Luso-Brazilian Studies* (Nashville, Tenn.: Vanderbilt University Press, 1953), pp. 66–78, *passim.* Reprinted by permission of the Vanderbilt University Press.

Isolated by the prevailing system of land allotment, the kinship group had to defend itself against Indians, bands of pirates, and fugitive Negro slaves, and against neighboring kinship groups which enjoyed so much independence that they could even maintain small private armies. The Portuguese family is believed to have lost already much of its original cohesion at the time of discovery.

The belief in an autochthonous origin of the extended Brazilian family sharply contrasts with certain facts which were found in Portugal itself. From the most extensive sociological survey ever made in Portugal, we learn that in different regions of that country the extended, multifunctional family existed until recently and that even at the present time certain elements of the traditional kinship solidarity with some of their economic and political implications have been preserved. . . .

At least in three provinces of Portugal, an extended, multifunctional kind of family existed which agglutinated large numbers of retainers and followers. Certain structural and functional patterns show striking similarities to those of the Brazilian extended family. . . .

Another aspect of family organization which needs a careful scrutiny is the status of married women within the family. It has widely been assumed that both the Portuguese and the Brazilian family developed under a patriarchal rule of which the main features have persisted until the present time. In our studies on the Brazilian family of the middle and lower rural classes in southern Brazil, some very important exceptions to the patriarchal rule have been discovered. On the northeastern highlands of São Paulo it was found that wives of landowners who do not belong to the so-called rural aristocracy enjoy a degree of economic independence which seems incompatible with patriarchal principles. Those married women raise hogs and fowl, make corn meal, and sell the produce to merchants of their own choice. The monetary results of these transactions belong to the women and are never claimed by their husbands. Considerable amounts of money are thus accumulated and invested at the initiative of the female owners. Usually the money is lent at high interest. Also, commercial transactions of a speculative character are relatively frequent.

In the family of the lower rural classes a woman may take the initiative in changing husbands without lowering her status. This of course indicated an evaluation of female virginity quite different from that which characterizes the Brazilian family of the patriarchal type. There is no doubt that the relative instability of the lower-class rural family must be attributed, at least in part, to this practice. It might be added that these facts were gathered among people who are predominantly of Portuguese extraction.

Descamps' sociological survey of Portugal refers to facts showing that in some regions of Portugal the status of married women does not fit into the stereotype of patriarchal family structure. Matrilineal tendencies in the peasant family of Minho were characterized in the following way:

> One also notices numerous cases wherein the female line prevails with regard to names and inheritance. At the present time the civil state requires the family name; yet in the current language of common people only the first name is known. One does not say Joseph, son of Peter, but Joseph, son of Mary. If he marries Louise he becomes Joseph of Louise. And she becomes Louise of Mary's Joseph.

The tendency to call a man by his mother's name was frequently observed in the unstable forms of common-law marriage of the lower rural classes of southern Brazil. Even the connecting preposition between the two names is omitted. Thus the first name of the mother really tends to become a definite part of a man's name. "There are, for example, Augusto Rita (Augusto, son of Rita), Paulo Catarina (Paulo, son of Catarina) and Theodoro Riqueta (Theodoro, son of Riqueta), etc. Sometimes these nicknames were incorporated into the true name." . . .

Considerations of space forbid the discussion of the more obvious similarities in Portuguese and Brazilian family structure such as, for instance, the separation of the sexes, the *namoro* pattern, cousin marriage as a form of preferential mating, and common-law marriage. Let us consider very briefly only so-called polygamous tendencies which in Brazil are usually attributed to the temptations of slavery. In the survey on Portugal similar tendencies were found in Alentejo.

> Certain landowners, although legally married, are accused of supporting a mistress, sometimes several. This is believed to happen more often than elsewhere; yet one understands how difficult it is to control such a statement. The maintenance of those women is hardly ruinous; what makes it less recommendable from a social standpoint is the fact that it is

practiced openly. This may be explained however by the fact
that the people of Alentejo are scarcely puritanical and do not
judge those practices in an unfavorable way. There is a general agreement that wealth would not be worthwhile if one
could not have several wives. And everyone thinks he would
do the same if he could afford it. So far as legal wives are
concerned only a certain proportion is opposed to these customs. There is a widely spread opinion that it is a survival
of the Arabic epoch. But this is only an hypothesis.

The Rural Community — Among the numerous aspects of rural
social organization which require comparative research, only co-
operative labor as a form of mutual aid will be briefly discussed
here. In all parts of Brazil neighbors in the broadest sense of the
word help each other perform various tasks. The clearing of forests,
the weeding of corn fields and pastures, harvesting, housebuild-
ing, the repairing of roads and bridges, fishing with large drag nets
are carried out as cooperative enterprises. The landowner invites his
neighbors, some of them living miles away, to assemble on a given
day on his land and to perform a previously specified task in common. Sometimes as many as 150 people gather and usually the
work is done in one day. Breakfast, lunch, and dinner are served by
the host, and at night a dancing party is held which continues until
dawn. The work itself is accompanied by songs, jokes, and *desafios*
(challenges in the form of song). Next time, the same people gather
on the farm of another neighbor and so forth until the most pressing
work is done. Thus a double reciprocity is observed in this institution; the workers are immediately rewarded by abundant meals,
plenty of rum, and various kinds of entertainment. The postponed
reward consists of the help given by the host at the request of any
one of his guests.

There are, as is well known, different words for mutual aid: *mutirão, putirão, muchirão, adjutório, batalhão, troca-dias,* etc. None
of these terms is of African origin, although the institution was well
developed in all West-African cultures whence most Negro slaves
came. Nor is there any close resemblance to the similar African institution, in contrast to Trinidad and Haiti, where such resemblances have been found. Not only the use of Indian words like
mutirão, muchirão, putirão, apatchirú, but also the comparison of
structural elements indicate that a rather large number of Indian
elements was introduced in the current organization of mutual aid.

On the other hand it seems undeniable that at least some elements of the Brazilian *mutirão* were taken over from Portugal.   . . .

Religion and Magic — The deepest and most lasting impact upon Brazilian folk cultures has probably been produced by the religious and magical traditions of the Portuguese settlers. Attempts to distinguish modern Latin-American culture as a distinct configuration of patterns and values from other varieties of occidental culture have been based, to a large extent, upon a set of religious practices the essentials of which were taken over from the Iberian Peninsula. It is not so much the fact that Roman Catholicism became the prevailing religious belief of Hispanic America and Brazil. Emphasis has been laid upon the specific features of Catholicism as practiced in Portugal and Spain.

The outstanding characteristics of Iberian Catholicism may be interpreted in terms of exteriorization, dramatization, and humanization of religious beliefs and practices. Everywhere in the world Catholics solicit aid from the saints, but Portuguese and Brazilian images of saints are clad in silk and velvet, are covered with sparkling adornments, and are greeted by thundering *vivas* and carried in solemn street processions. Most public festivals are attached to names of saints and their commemoration attracts enormous masses of people who participate in, or watch enthusiastically, endless musical and dramatic performances accompanied or followed by fireworks and lavish distribution of food. Rather than the existence of religious brotherhoods as such, the important fact is that their members are clad in brilliant red, purple, or white costumes and that they participate in all religious performances, carrying sacred paraphernalia and symbols that produce a most dramatic effect.

Link and Hoffmansegg, who traveled through Portugal at the end of the eighteenth century, made some judicious remarks on religious customs which still hold true, at least for certain parts of Brazil:

> Among the public entertainments one should not forget religious practices which have a great influence upon the Portuguese; I should say they enjoy religious ceremonies only as entertainment. One follows the processions as one goes to the opera.

The Portuguese were found to be less fanatical than the Span-

iards: "This slightness of the Portuguese who view the cult as a kind of spectacle may be regarded as one of the principal causes of tolerance which exist in this country."

To those who are familiar with Brazil there is little doubt that tolerance is one of the outstanding characteristics of the religious life of the people. Tolerance has become manifest not only in the prevailing attitudes toward beliefs different from Catholicism and a tendency to accept elements of other religious systems and to blend them, in varying degrees, with Catholic elements, but also in the attitudes which members of primary groups develop toward each other with regard to religious observances. In numerous families of all social classes, the female members practice religion while the men stay away from church; yet this peculiar division of labor is far from acting as a disturbing factor in family life. As a rule, men show little concern for religion, which sometimes is referred to as "women's business." Attempts to stir up religious fanaticism in Brazilian communities have rarely been successful.   . . .

Belief in witchcraft or destructive magic has reached a considerable degree of complexity in many folk cultures of Brazil. Aside from the African and Indian influences there are undoubtedly Portuguese elements which in some regions have been preserved in their original form. The most widely spread elements are probably the beliefs in the evil eye and the werewolf as destructive forces in human life. Both beliefs are still very much alive in contemporary Portugal. The assumption that *lobishomens* (werewolves) are "children of incestuous parents or the fruits of marriage between *compadres,* those linked by ties of godfathership" is found in Portugal and Brazil.

Some more specific beliefs show how far the similarities between the two countries go in certain cases. For example, special protection must be given to an unbaptized child. In Portugal the child is believed to run the risk of being carried off by witches, while in Brazil the werewolf and the *saci* (a malignant Indian dwarf) are supposed to do harm to such a child. In Portugal as in Brazil a lamp must always burn to protect unbaptized children from evil forces.

Although the ritual practices related to death seem to be fewer and simpler in Brazil than in Portugal, resemblances are still numerous and close. The Portuguese belief that "the dead envy and persecute the living; and that the presence of death endangers the lives of those around" is somewhat restricted in rural Brazil in so

far that only the dead "who are not from God," or, in other words, those who are possessed of the devil, are believed to endanger the living.

In Portugal "to help the soul to escape . . . it is usual to open a window of the dead man's house," while in some regions of rural Brazil the front door must stand open at the precise moment of death. For seven days one must not close the house for the soul of the deceased is believed to stay a week. If the house is closed up, the soul cannot get out and becomes enchanted.

These are a few examples from an imposing array of Portuguese cultural elements which have been preserved in Brazil, sometimes under changed forms or performing different functions.   . . .

Luso-Brazilian National Character — Some of the findings which have been compared in the present study suggest a hypothesis concerning Luso-Brazilian national character. A tentative formulation may be started with the already mentioned attitude of tolerance. Portuguese and Brazilians live in a world which is essentially human. Human frailties are to be tolerated and sympathetically accepted as unavoidable. The tolerant attitude of the Brazilians toward delinquents and criminals has often been discussed. With regard to Portugal a revealing remark was made by Link and Hoffmansegg. After discussing the frequency of murder, usually caused by vengeance or jealousy, the authors comment upon the attitude of the people: "The evildoer almost always escapes, and, moved by a strange compassion, everybody facilitates his flight. *Coitadinho!* [poor fellow!] says the Portuguese, and they do everything to save him." Although this reaction was observed at the end of the eighteenth century, it still applies to contemporary Brazil. *Coitado* or *coitadinho* is perhaps the word most frequently heard when Brazilians comment upon the situation of the poor, the helpless, the sick, and the criminal. *Coitado* means compassion, sympathy, and understanding for unfortunate human fellows. The offender is not primarily seen as a malignant evildoer liable to punishment and seclusion. He is, above all, a disgraced human being who deserves commiseration and sympathy. He is believed to be in such a state of mental distress, caused by his unfortunate deed, that no additional punishment may be necessary to establish what is felt to be "social equilibrium."

No wonder that in this basically human world of the Luso-Brazilians emphasis is put on personal, sympathetic, or primary rather than on impersonal, categorical, or secondary relationships. One feels that human understanding and sympathy can be achieved only through the more intimate forms of contact with people. Therefore, high emotional value is attributed to blood relationship, godparent-hood, and friendship. These three types of social relations are likely to encroach upon any other form of institutional relationship, whatever be its degree of remoteness or social distance.

So pronounced is the value set upon emotional appreciation that sentiment itself has been developed into a cult. "The Portuguese," we are told by Descamps, "claim the monopoly of a kind of mental malady which they call *saudade*. This word appeared in their lan-guage at the end of the fifteenth century and has remained un-translatable. Nevertheless, one finds expressions in certain languages which have a related meaning."

"The famous *saudade* of the Portuguese," explains Aubrey Bell, "is a vague and constant desire for something other than the present, a turning toward the past or toward the future; not an active dis-content or poignant sadness, but an indolent dreaming." "In a word," Gallop adds, "*saudade* is yearning for something so indefinite as to be indefinable: an unrestrained indulgence in yearning. It is a blend of German *Sehnsucht*, French *nostalgie*, and something else besides."

If there is anything to be shared by Portuguese and Brazilians it certainly is the emotional pattern of *saudade*. Through books and broadcasting the *hora da saudade* has become a national institu-tion in Brazil with thousands of breathless listeners, even in a metropolitan city such as São Paulo. *Saudade* is perhaps the most frequent theme in Brazilian folk songs of various kinds. It may be said that Brazilian folk music is permeated with *saudade*, the ele-ment that provides its always present emotional undertone.

Portuguese and Brazilians do not feel separate from the super-natural world as do some other Christian peoples. The saints are humanized to an extent that would appear blasphemous to many Europeans. Nothing seems to be more significant in this context than the concept of the *santo pândego* or *santo folião*, bearer of hu-man virtues and weaknesses, who reacts to reward and punish-ment which his human fellows inflict upon him. Yet humanization of the saint is reciprocated by sanctification of the human in the form of the parent or superior who bestows a blessing upon his offspring or subordinates.

Gilberto Freyre has written extensively on the historical roots of this "domestic, lyric, and festive Christianity," as he calls it. And despite certain changes, these characteristics have not disappeared, either in Portugal or in Brazil. In fact, they appear to be manifest and closely integrated with other attitudes in the hypothetical picture of Portuguese and Brazilian national character.

D. The New World's Influence on the Old

8. Why Prices Rose in Europe

JOHN LYNCH

Before the arrival of American treasure in the sixteenth century, European trade was fed primarily by gold from the Sudan. But Portuguese expeditions along the Atlantic coast of Africa to the Gulf of Guinea between 1460 and 1470, and the establishment of direct trade relations between Portugal and the East Indies at the beginning of the sixteenth century, diverted the route of Sudanese gold away from the Mediterranean and caused a great scarcity of gold in Europe. This was supplied in part by the German silver mines, which enjoyed a period of relative prosperity between 1470 and 1530, coinciding with the shortage of precious metals. From 1530, however, this shortage was unexpectedly eased when American treasure began to replace the old sources of supply and gave Europe an immense stock of money, the origin of grave alteration in prices, especially in Spain, the country where the treasure arrived and from which it was distributed.

John Lynch, *Spain Under the Hapsburgs, Volume I: Empire and Absolutism, 1516–1598* (Oxford: Basil Blackwell, 1964), pp. 121–129. Reprinted by permission of Basil Blackwell & Nott, Ltd.

The influx of treasure consisted almost entirely of silver. Up to 1550, it is true, imports were mixed, but American gold was never sufficient, even in the best years, to produce an appreciable effect on prices, and after 1550 gold lost its importance altogether. Silver receipts, however, expanded enormously. They began most effectively about 1530, and remained at a relatively modest, though steadily rising, level until 1550. From then the galleons began to import silver in vast quantities, which became vaster still from 1580 and caused a profound revolution in prices. Behind the flood of silver lay a technical revolution in America itself. The new method of amalgamation devised in Germany and consisting of the treatment of silver with mercury was introduced in the mines of New Spain by Bartolomé de Medina in 1557. From 1571 it was applied to the Potosí deposits in Upper Peru. This process increased the exports of treasure tenfold, and they reached their peak in the period 1580 to 1630, the great age of Spanish imperialism. "The king has reason to say," wrote one of Philip II's secretaries, "that the emperor never disposed of as much money as himself for his enterprises."

The interest of the state in precious metals derived not merely from mercantilist prejudices but from their ability to buy what it most needed — the means of power. Spain was already a protectionist country, barricaded with customs, and a government which theoretically controlled everything entering and leaving its frontiers was unlikely to allow the new-found treasure to escape its grasp. But the monopoly, and the attempts to preserve it, were not perfect: there were frequent complaints from the cortes that the continual exit of precious metals — "as if we were Indians" — was impoverishing the country, and it was commonly said that Spain was "the Indies of other countries." Yet there were many reasons why the precious metals should escape from Spain and circulate abroad. Spain was primarily an exporter of raw materials and an importer of manufactured goods; with an unfavourable trade balance, she had to settle her payments with ready cash. This accounted for much unlicensed export of specie by Spanish merchants or by foreign merchants resident in Spain, all of which made its way to the great production centres of Europe. In a sense the precious metals were the crutches which enabled the Spanish economy to move. But alongside clandestine export, the state had to authorize some foreign payments in specie, for imports of vital food supplies and naval stores had to be bought with cash. The greatest remittances of all, however, were made by the crown itself in order to pay for its overseas commitments. Instead of investing their money in productive enterprises at home, as the Fuggers did at Augsburg with the money from their mines at Schwaz, the Spanish Habsburgs lavished more and more on foreign enterprises, the price not merely of ambition but of the very existence of the Spanish empire and its defence. The routes by which the precious metals left Spain all converged on northern Europe, either directly from Bilbao or via France and Italy, for it was here that Spain's political and military interests were most exposed and her balance of payments was most adverse. The money itself was vital not only in the conflict with France and the war in the Low Countries but also in the economy of northern Europe, for from Antwerp it made its way to Germany and England, while the latter also profited from the smuggling of specie by Spanish merchants in wool ships.

In spite of its rapid departure from Spain, however, American treasure had profound effects on the Spanish economy. The "extremely close correlation between the increase in the volume of treasure imports and the advance of commodity prices throughout the sixteenth century, particularly from 1535," has been so well established that the products of the American mines must be regarded as the principal cause of the price revolution in Spain.* The Spanish government, like its neighbours in the rest of Europe, did not understand the causal connection between the influx of precious metals and the rise of prices, and was thus hampered in its economic and financial policies. On the other hand, contemporaries were certainly aware of the price revolution, for it was reflected in the cost of living, and although there was much uncertainty and

---

* Hamilton, *American Treasure and the Price Revolution in Spain,* p. 301. Hamilton's thesis and the statistical evidence with which he sustains it are unassailable, but criticism of some of his methods and interpretations has been growing; see P. Vilar, "Problems of the formation of capitalism," *Past and Present,* X (1956), pp. 15–35; Ingrid Hammarström, "The 'Price Revolution' of the Sixteenth Century. Some Swedish evidence," *The Scandinavian Economic History Review,* V (1957), pp. 118–154; and especially, J. Nadal, "La Revolución de los Precios españoles en el siglo XVI. Estado actual de la cuestión," *Hispania,* XIX (1959), pp. 503–529. The criticisms of later commentators can be summarised as follows: (1) Hamilton worked on town prices, but a complete study ought to take account of rural prices, paid in local markets and more closely tied to crop yields. (2) A third of Spain is omitted from his investigation, including Catalonia and the Basque country,

confusion about its causes, individual economists began to appreciate the rôle of American treasure. Of these the most distinguished was the French theorist, Bodin, who established a connection between treasure imports and inflation in 1568. The views of Bodin, however, had already been anticipated in Spain. Twelve years previously, in 1556, Martín de Azpilcueta Navarro, a canon lawyer, produced the first clear statement known to exist that the high cost of living was a result of treasure imports:

> We see by experience that in France, where money is scarcer than in Spain, bread, wine, cloth, and labour are worth much less. And even in Spain, in times when money was scarcer, saleable goods and labour were given for very much less than after the discovery of the Indies, which flooded the country with gold and silver. The reason for this is that money is worth more where and when it is scarce than where and when it is abundant.

Other Spaniards of the Salamanca school showed similar awareness. The Dominican, Fray Tomás de Mercado, published his *Tratos y contratos de mercaderes y tratantes* in 1569 — it was completed by the previous year and owed nothing to Bodin — and although it was full of ethical analysis in the traditional style it also contained some acute economic observation, including the quantity theory of money and the relation between American treasure and the current inflation.

An adequate understanding of the problem, however, had to await modern scholarship. The causal relation between the influx of precious metals and the rise of prices is to be distinguished by regions and by periods. Broadly speaking, the price rise was greatest in Andalucía, which through its monopoly of the Indies trade

---

both of which perhaps were more closely related to the European economy than the rest of Spain. (3) Not all of the regions can be fitted consistently into his thesis: Valencia, after being in front up to 1530, then drops behind, but takes the lead again from 1581 to 1620. Moreover, although it is true that in general prices rose more quickly in Seville than in Valencia, that does not tell us whether at any given time the cost of living was higher in Seville than in Valencia, or vice versa. (4) His figures for entry of American treasure are defective in that he does not indicate the criterion adopted for separating royal income from private income or include unregistered receipts. (5) His price figures suffer from a defect of origin: they are of uniform provenance — hospitals and charitable establishments. In spite of the criticisms, however, no one has offered to replace Hamilton's work, which remains indispensable.

always received the first impact of treasure imports; this was followed by New Castile, then by Old Castile and León on the one hand and Valencia on the other, corresponding to their distance from the receiving centre. The general price level in Spain slightly more than doubled in the first half of the century. In this period the rise occurred largely in the first, third, and fifth decades. Prices continued to rise in the second half of the century, with plateaux of relative stability in the years 1551–56, 1562–69, and 1584–95; but from 1596 prices soared, reaching their apogee in 1601 with an index number of 143.55 on a 1571–80 base. By 1600 prices had risen to a level four times as high as that of 1501. From 1601 the process was checked, and after a period of oscillations ended in a temporary decline from 1637 to 1642 when there was a drastic drop in remittances from America, but prices never fully descended from the peak attained at the close of the sixteenth century. To this factual description, however, two considerations should be added. First, although prices reached their apogee in the second half of the sixteenth century, the price rise was proportionately greater in the first half of the century. From 1501 to 1550 the advance was 107.61 per cent, while in the last half of the century it was 97.74 per cent. Moreover, the rhythm of acceleration of the price revolution slackened in the middle years of the century. Between 1549 and 1560 prices increased only 11.9 per cent, and the year 1562 marks the transition from a rapid rise (2.8 per cent half yearly increase) to one more moderate (1.3 per cent). This mid-century phenomenon can be related to the contemporary depression in the Indies trade (the channel of American treasure) and indicates that the economic depression of the seventeenth century and its relation to the influx of treasure were already foreshadowed at the beginning of Philip II's reign. Secondly, it would be wrong to ascribe the difference between the economic progress of Spain and that of northern Europe uniquely to prices. In general, it is true, the rise of prices was later and less intense in the rest of Europe than in Spain, because of the time required for American treasure to circulate there and the dilution suffered in the process; first France then England felt the impact. But this does not give us a complete picture of the cost of living in these different countries: grain, for example, was always dearer in France than in Spain during the great inflationary period.

Moreover, treasure in itself was not the only cause of the price revolution. The quantity theory of money, by which an increase in

the quantity of money in circulation brings a proportionate increase
in the level of prices, is too crude to account for all the factors involved in the history of Spanish prices. Prices are also affected by
conditions of supply and demand. Industrial and agricultural production, therefore, must also be taken into account. An increase in
the amount of money in circulation without a corresponding increase in the production of goods means that the same amount of
goods is chasing more and more money, and therefore prices rise.
The money pumped into Spain from America was not used to increase domestic productivity, and higher prices were the inevitable
result. After an increase in industrial production in the first half of
the sixteenth century, though one which did not keep pace with the
increase of money, Spanish output then fell off and money sought
products abroad. From the side of demand, there were now more
people to be fed and clothed and housed. The growth of population enhanced the demand for goods, including foodstuffs. Agricultural producers, like industrial producers, were unable to respond to
the rising demand, and new and less fertile lands were cultivated;
in this way marginal costs increased, and *per capita* yields became
smaller, while demand continued to rise. The pressure of population
on food supplies thus increased the price of agricultural produce,
and further helped to raise the cost of living.

The consequences of the price revolution are perhaps even
more difficult to elucidate than its causes. It certainly caused a
general rise in the cost of living, but what this meant for the different classes and for the economic development of the country as a
whole is by no means clear. According to the classical explanation,
the economic backwardness of Spain was related directly to the
results of inflation there. The lag of wages behind prices in Europe
aided the accumulation of capital; the diminishing price of labour
gave entrepreneurs the opportunities of exceptional benefits which
could then be further invested. Spain, on the other hand, was
claimed as an exception to this general rule, for although there was
a lag of wages behind prices it was not enough to afford extraordinary benefits and therefore give great impetus to capitalism. A
further refinement of the argument was to note the close correspondence between periods of inflation and deflation of benefits
and those of national rise and decline; in these terms the greatness
of Spain coincided with the inflation of 1520 to 1600 and its eclipse
with the deflation of 1600 to 1630. For there was a close relation

between inflation of benefits and accumulation of capital; as wages in Spain were higher than those elsewhere, so there was less opportunity to accumulate capital, and this was the principal reason for Spain's economic inferiority. But these monetary theories leave many questions unanswered. Apart from the fact that inflation of profits does not necessarily imply an industrial boom, there is no ground for arguing that all Spanish wage-earners were better off than their foreign counterparts during the price revolution. From a comparison of the wages of builders in England and France with those in Valencia, it is clear that the latter underwent at least the same progressive losses as the former throughout the sixteenth century. In any case, builder's wages, unaccompanied by those of industrial and agricultural workers, are not representative enough to justify generalisation. It is true that the Spanish inflation did not produce an accumulation of capital for investment. But this was because those who profited from it used their wealth unproductively, either in buying a title and an estate, or in extravagant building, in the purchase of luxury consumer goods, or in simple hoarding.

How, then, did the price revolution affect the various sectors of Spanish society? Conditions in sixteenth-century England support the view that the divorce between constantly rising prices and fixed rents could impoverish the land-owner. But this does not apply to Spain, where rents were not fixed and where the greater power of landowners enabled them to raise rents and replace their tenants by those better able to pay. There is also abundant evidence that in Spain the rich were getting richer and the poor poorer. A possible inference from this is that the opening of the American market and the rise of population in the peninsula itself produced an increase in demand for agricultural products, an extension of cultivation, and a rise in the value of arable land, all of which coincided with the added stimulus of inflation. If, at the same time, the concentration of property in the hands of a few extremely wealthy families is taken into account, together with power to raise rents, then it would seem that the inflationary period was not unfavourable to the great landowners in Spain and did not deter people from investing in land. But landowners were not the only ones to gain from the price revolution. Anyone with something to sell or trade could reap the benefit of inflation, as many manufacturers and merchants did in the first half of the century. When conditions then became more difficult, and constant inflation began to make Spanish enterprise less competitive in the international and colonial markets, only the more powerful merchants were able to survive foreign competition, but those who did so undoubtedly prospered. Enormous fortunes were to be made in the Indies trade, whose expansion was related directly to the rise in prices; when prices rose in Spain there was a strong presumption of an even greater rise in America, and this encouraged further investment and more profitable returns. The latter were distributed beyond the merchant houses of Seville to entrepreneurs in other parts of Spain, for the American market took the oil and wine of Andalucía, the wool of Castile, the metallurgical products and ships of the Basque country. To at least the end of the sixteenth century there was still money to be made in Spain. On the other hand, the price revolution brought impoverishment to those who lived on fixed incomes and small rents, for these did not keep pace with prices. Small landowners of the *hidalgo* class, the lower clergy, government officials and many others all found their standard of living reduced as the price of commodities rose beyond their means. The situation of the peasant is less clear, for it is difficult to reconcile agricultural prosperity and the great rural emigration to the towns, which in turn makes it difficult to explain the alleged extension of cultivation in Spain. But one thing is certain — wages lagged behind prices, and the difference between the two was worse in the first half of the century. Even if the money value of wages subsequently picked up, their purchasing power continued to fall. By 1550 real wages were roughly 20 per cent lower than the average for 1501–20, and they continued to fall steadily from 1551–60 to 1591–1600, the decrease being now about 12 per cent. Throughout most of the sixteenth century life was difficult for the Spanish poor; indeed, for the mass of Spanish wage-earners the price revolution was a grievous blow which reduced their already low standard of living still further.

The crown, on the other hand, like its ally, the aristocracy, was less crippled by these developments than the majority of its subjects. Certainly the cost of administration, and of paying, feeding, and equipping its armed forces, rose for the crown just as the cost of goods did for the private consumer; for war was an industry like any other, and one that was more costly to Spain than to other countries because of her higher level of prices. But as the aristocracy could raise its rents, so the state could increase its revenue; this enabled it to keep up with prices, while inflation alleviated the burden of the loans which formed such a substantial part of its income.

While the Spanish crown's expenditure in the sixteenth century was immense and increasing, it also had enormous and growing resources. The figures available in contemporary budgets lack precision, but are sufficient to show the general trend. The revenues of Charles V tripled during his reign. Those of Philip II doubled in the period 1556–73 alone, and more than redoubled by the end of the reign. Debts, however, were also increasing. Philip II inherited from his father a debt of at least twenty million ducats, and seems to have left to his successor a debt of five times that amount. But all the desperate financial expedients of the reign, the raising of loans secured on future revenues and the two decrees of suspension of payments in 1575 and 1596 point to the same conclusion: expenditure was soaring beyond revenue. In 1588 the expenses of the Armada preparations alone were costing 900,000 ducats a month, as Philip himself admitted to the cortes in June of that year. During the last ten years of his reign, the crown's insolvency could hardly be disguised.

Of all the items of revenue possessed by the Spanish crown that from the Indies was the one which most impressed Spaniards and foreigners alike. Compared with receipts from other sources, however, it was not spectacular. The sums derived from the Indies — consisting of the royal fifth, the alcabala, customs duties and the *cruzada* — increased rapidly during the last two decades of the reign of Philip II, and between 1590 and 1600 they reached an annual average of more than four times as much as in the early 60's. Even so, they still formed a smaller proportion of total revenue than used to be supposed. The crown's American revenue rose from about 11 per cent of total income in 1554 to about 20 per cent in 1598. At its highest this was no more than Philip II's revenue from ecclesiastical sources and much less than the amounts extorted from the unfortunate taxpayers of Castile. Yet receipts from America were invaluable windfalls by any reckoning, and their sheer size gave Spain the extra power which she possessed in the sixteenth century. Moreover, the considerable returns derived by individual Spaniards from the Indies — averaging two-and-a-half times those of the crown during Philip II's reign — played an important part in enabling the king's subjects to pay the various domestic taxes at rates which would otherwise have been impossible.

BIBLIOGRAPHIC SUGGESTIONS

A. *On the Iberian Empires in General*

The new world territories of Portugal and Spain constituted only a part of their empires, and to attain a perspective on America's place in these empires the following publications will be helpful.

1. Boxer, Charles R. *Four Centuries of Portuguese Expansion, 1415–1825: A Succinct Survey* (Johannesburg: Witwatersrand University Press, 1961).
2. Diffie, Bailey W. *Prelude to Empire: Portugal Overseas Before Henry the Navigator* (Lincoln: University of Nebraska Press, 1960).
3. Elliott, John H. *Imperial Spain 1469–1716* (New York: St. Martin's Press, 1964). This volume and item 5 below admirably complement each other, and are fundamental for the European background.
4. Livermore, Harold V. *A New History of Portugal* (Cambridge, Eng.: Cambridge University Press, 1966).
5. Lynch, John. *Spain under the Hapsburgs,* Vol. I: *Empire and Absolutism, 1516–1598* (Oxford: Basil Blackwell, 1964).
6. Silva Rego, A. da. *Portuguese Colonization in the Sixteenth Century: A Study of the Royal Ordinances (Regimentos)* (Johannesburg: Witwatersrand University Press, 1959). A comparative study of ". . . human relations between the Portuguese on the one side and Indians, Africans, and Brazilians on the other."
7. Buarque de Holanda, Sérgio. *Raízes do Brasil,* Third ed., rev. (Rio de Janeiro: José Olympio, 1956). An important interpretation, with much scattered information on Portuguese influences in Brazil.
8. Castro, Américo. *The Structure of Spanish History* (Princeton: Princeton University Press, 1954). A much-discussed, controversial evaluation, based primarily on literary sources. See particularly "Towards an Understanding of Spain" (pp. 589–671).
9. Choy, Emilio. "De Santiago Matamoros a Santiago Mata-indios: Las ideas políticas en España desde la reconquista a la conquista de América," *Revista del Museo Nacional,* XXVII (Lima, 1958), pp. 195–272. The simplistic views of a Peruvian historian who believes that the killing of Indians in America naturally resulted from the killing of Moors in medieval Spain; he suggests that the

Indians were considered rational beings only to give the missionaries an excuse to intervene and not for the good of the Indians.

10. Marques, Antonio H. de Oliveira. *Guia do estudante de historia medieval portuguesa* (Lisbon: Edições Cosmos, 1964).

11. Parry, John H. *The Spanish Sea-Borne Empire* (New York: Alfred A. Knopf, 1966).

12. Russell, Peter E. "The Nessus — Shirt of Spanish History," *Bulletin of Hispanic Studies*, XXXV (Liverpool, 1959), pp. 219–225. An amusing and subtle commentary on the ideas of two eminent Spanish scholars, Américo Castro and Claudio Sánchez-Albornoz, who disagree sharply on the true nature of Spain and Spaniards in the medieval period.

13. Sánchez-Albornoz, Claudio. "La empresa de América y España," in *España: Un enigma histórico*, Vol. II (Buenos Aires, 1962), pp. 500–514. The conclusions of an outstanding Spanish medievalist, who has long been concerned with this problem.

14. Verlinden, Charles. "Italian Influence in Iberian Colonization," *Hispanic American Historical Review*, XXXII (1953), pp. 199–211. Spanish and Portuguese economic colonization depended heavily upon Italian precedent and experience, this Belgian scholar states.

15. ———. *Précédents médiévaux de la colonie en Amérique* (Mexico: Pan American Institute of Geography and History, 1954). Concise statement on themes for research, emphasizing economic matters. A selective bibliography.

16. Vivas, Eliseo. "The Spanish Heritage," *American Sociological Review*, X (1945), pp. 184–191. A brief but suggestive discussion of the Spanish character as an influence in developing and maintaining the class system in Spanish America.

B. *On Particular Aspects*

17. Bishko, Charles Julian. "The Peninsular Background of Latin American Cattle Ranching," *Hispanic American Historical Review*, XXXII (1952), pp. 491–515. A persuasive description of the ". . . enduring influence of medieval Iberian cattle ranching upon the history of the Americas."

18. Carro, Venancio, O. P. "Las controversias de Indias y las ideas teológico-medievales que las preparan y explican," *Anuario de la Asociación Francisco de Vitoria*, VIII (Madrid, 1948), pp. 13–53. On the medieval background for the later discussions on the justice of Spain's rule in America.

19. Domínguez Ortiz, Antonio. "Los caudales de Indias y la política exterior de Felipe IV," *Anuario de Estudios Americanos*, XIII

(Sevilla, 1956), pp. 311–383. The connection between American treasure and the foreign policy of Philip IV.

20. Gonçalves, Maria de Conceição Osoria Dias. *O indio do Brasil na literatura portuguesa dos seculos XVI, XVII e XVIII* (Coimbra: Ed. Coimbra, 1961).

21. Konetzke, Richard. "Entrepreneurial Activities of Spanish and Portuguese Noblemen in Medieval Times," *Explorations in Entrepreneurial History*, VI (Dec., 1954), pp. 115–120. Iberian noblemen did not disdain business in the Old World or the New.

22. Leonard, Irving A. "Conquerors and Amazons in Mexico," *Hispanic American Historical Review*, XXIV (1944), pp. 561–579. See also his basic work, *Books of the Brave* (Cambridge, Mass.: Harvard University Press, 1949).

23. Morrisey, Richard J. "Colonial Agriculture in New Spain," *Agricultural History*, XXXI, No. 3 (July, 1957), pp. 24–29. A recent description with bibliography.

24. Patiño, Víctor Manuel. *Plantas cultivadas y animales domésticos en América equinoccial.* Vols. I, II (Cali, Colombia: Imprenta Departamental, 1963–1964). The first volumes of a monumental five-volume work in preparation.

25. ———. *Historia de la actividad agropecuaria equinoccial* (Cali, Colombia: Imprenta Departamental, 1965). A fundamental work, with excellent bibliography.

26. Pike, Ruth. "The Sevillan Nobility and Trade with the New World in the Sixteenth Century," *Business History Review*, XXXIX (Winter, 1965), pp. 439–465.

26a. ———. *Enterprise and Adventure. The Genoese in Seville and the Opening of the New World* (Ithaca: Cornell University Press, 1966).

27. Scholes, France V. and Eleanor B. Adams. "Inventories of Church Furnishings in Some of the New Mexico Missions, 1672," *Dargan Historical Essays: Historical studies presented to Marion Dargan by his colleagues and former students.* William M. Dabney and Josiah C. Russell, eds. (Albuquerque: University of New Mexico Press, 1952), pp. 27–38. An example of how Spain furnished even the mission churches on the frontier with the objects necessary for divine worship.

28. Zavala, Silvio A. "Las conquistas de Canarias y América. Estudio comparativo," año 1, *Tierra Firme*, No. 4 (Madrid, 1935); año 2 (1936) No. 1. Spain conquered the Canary Islands in the fifteenth century, which proved to be valuable training for the later conquest of America.

Section II

Was Inca Rule Tyrannical?

Spaniards were amazed by the strange peoples they found in the New World and over the years, as they strove to conquer and Christianize the Indians, they devoted much attention to the many native languages, religions, and cultures (Reading III.12). The kind of culture the Indians had attained became part of the verbal battles over their "rationality." Bartolomé de Las Casas, the sixteenth-century Protector of the Indians, attempted in a long treatise, *Apologetic History,* to prove that the Indians were eminently rational beings with such "excellent, most subtle and natural intelligence" that they satisfied all the requirements laid down by Aristotle for the good life.[1]

As the conquest moved to the high Andean regions in Peru the arguments over the kind of civilization created by the Indians there became more acute. The youthful conquistador Pedro de Cieza de León, writing down his impressions in the days of Pizarro, admired Inca achievements (Reading II.1). The oldest survivor of the conquest, one Mancio Sierra de Leguízamo, solemnly swore on his deathbed in 1589 that not only were the Incas wise rulers but that the Spanish conquest had corrupted an ideal Indian society. This Spanish warrior had participated actively in the wars against the Indians and had been famous throughout Peru for having won as booty the celebrated golden image of the sun in Cuzco, the ancient

[1] For more information on this treatise, see the editor's *Aristotle and the American Indians* (London: Hollis & Carter, 1959).

Inca capital. He became even more famous when he promptly lost it in an all-night card game. Possibly some zealous, pro-Indian ecclesiastic actually composed his moving last will and testament (Reading II.2), and had influenced the dying conquistador to sign the document to manifest his penitence. There is much evidence, however, to indicate that a number of Spaniards suffered from a sense of guilt and provided in their wills for restitution to the Indians to compensate for any wrong they had committed against them.[2]

Garcilaso de la Vega's account of Inca culture, a classic of Spanish literature, was only one of his notable contributions to Spanish prose. Born in Cuzco, the son of a Spanish captain and an Inca princess, he learned much about Inca history as a boy but spent most of his life in Spain. His early seventeenth-century *Royal Commentaries*, the most widely read and translated source on Inca culture, also defended the civilization his maternal ancestors had created and his paternal kin had destroyed (Reading II.3).

Viceroy Francisco de Toledo discovered on his arrival in Peru in 1569 so much argument over the comparative merits of Inca and Spanish dominion that he launched a frontal attack on the Inca system (Reading II.4). One of his principal methods was commissioning Pedro Sarmiento de Gamboa, one of his trusted advisors, to demonstrate that Inca rule was unjust by composing a history which would prove that the Inca system had been tyrannical, and that the Spaniards therefore had liberated the Indians from an unjust, despotic oppressor (Reading II.5).

Inca government and Inca history continued to have a political role long after Viceroy Toledo's time. During the wars for independence in Argentina in the early nineteenth century General José de San Martín and Manuel Belgrano supported the idea of an "Inca Monarchy" to supplant that of Spain, and even had propagandistic handbills in Aymara and Quechua distributed to Indian caciques to arouse sympathy for the revolutionists against Spain.[3] A century

---

[2] Guillermo Lohmann Villena presented a paper at the Semana de Estudios Lascasianos at the University of Seville in May, 1966, on "El ideario lascasiano en el Perú: El problema moral de la restitución por conquistadores y encomenderos."

[3] Harry Bernstein, *Modern and Contemporary Latin America* (Philadelphia: Lippincott, 1952), p. 199.

later in Peru, during the early years of President Augusto B. Leguía's administration in the 1920's, Fredrick Pike states: ". . . an increasing number of Peruvian intellectuals turned their attention to Inca history, folklore, and archaeology. In Lima the Society of the Golden Arrow was formed, the purpose of its members being to study the glories of the Inca past. . . . Leguía himself joined in, and liked to be referred to as Viracocha, the white-skinned, culture-bearing deity." [4] Though Leguía did not pursue these Inca interests, other Peruvians such as José Carlos Mariátegui and Víctor Raúl Haya de la Torre did: some of the roots of the APRA political party are sunk in the Inca past. In the years between the two world wars Italian fascism found Inca "communism" a useful tool, and the Bolivian Revolution of 1952 is said to have been prepared for by renewed interest in Inca studies.[5]

Scholarly attention to all aspects of Inca history has grown during the last half century, though it has not produced a consensus. Philip Ainsworth Means, a pioneer student in the United States of Inca history, agreed with the highly favorable accounts of the sixteenth-century Spaniards (Reading II.1–II.3), and concluded: "Such was the unique civilization which Spanish culture, bringing with it Christianity and money culture, was destined to overwhelm and change beyond recognition. . . . The greatest, the fundamental and the universal source of evil brought into Peru by the Spaniards was the money-complex whence arose all the endless misery which has weighed down the Andean peoples ever since the money-less empire of the Incas was shattered." [6]

Later writers such as Louis Baudin characterized Inca culture as "socialistic" (Reading II.6). A more evaluative note was struck by a Swiss anthropologist, the late Alfred Métraux, who objected to forcing the Inca state to conform ". . . to a modern formula: a socialist, a totalitarian, or a welfare state" (Reading II.7). Though "romantic attitudes and unfounded prejudices, glib exaggerations and superficial generalizations have provided the basis for either uncritical

---

[4]Fredrick Pike, *A History of Modern Peru* (London: Weidenfeld & Nicholson, 1967), Chap. VIII.

[5] Benedetto Giacalone, *Comunismo Incaico-araucania-Florida-Colombiano* (Genoa: Bozzi, 1936); Charles Arnade, "The U.S. and the Ultimate Roots of the Bolivian Revolution," *Historia*, new series, I, No. 1 (Río Piedras, 1962), pp. 35–50.

[6] P. A. Means, *Fall of the Inca Empire* (New York: Scribners, 1932), p. 12.

exaltation or contemptuous denigration of Peru's aborigines and their historical feats," as Professor Pike declares,[7] a new realism is being brought to bear upon the Inca past. The young Swedish scholar Ake Wedin has challenged previous interpretations of Inca chronology,[8] and John V. Murra has denounced the practice of classifying the Inca system using terms applied to European economic and political history.[9] He refuses to employ the labels "socialistic," "feudal," "totalitarian," or the concepts implicit in "commoner," "nobleman," or "lumpenproletariat." The most recent author to survey the interpretations of Inca rule reaches this conclusion: "The old sources of knowledge of Inca culture . . . indicate that one cannot speak of an Inca communistic order, nor of a collectivistic system, or a socialist centralization of land tenure. The property tax of 66%, the personal service or *prestación,* the compulsory change of residence, and the impossibility of overcoming social barriers because of the static order of social classes, show very clearly that the Incas and their form of the state cannot serve as a model for our times." [10]

The study of Inca culture, however, holds rich rewards, because one may learn more about a remarkable civilization the Spaniards encountered and may see how cultural history has been manipulated for varied purposes.

[7] Fredrick Pike, *A History of Modern Peru,* Chap. 1.

[8] Åke Wedin, *La cronología de la historia incaica. Estudio crítico* (Madrid: Instituto Ibero-Americano de Gotemburgo, 1963). See also his monographs *El sistema decimal en el imperio incaico. Estudio sobre estructura política,* (Madrid: Instituto Ibero-Americano de Gotemburgo, 1965); *El concepto de lo incaico y las fuentes. Estudio crítico* (Uppsala: Scandinavian University Books, 1966). Studia Historica Gothoburgensia, VII.

[9] John V. Murra, "On Inca Political Structure," *Systems of Political Control and Bureaucracy in Human Societies,* Proceedings of the 1958 Annual Spring Meeting of the American Ethnological Society, Verne F. Ray, ed. (Seattle, 1958), p. 30. See also his "Social, Structural and Economic Themes in Andean Ethnohistory," *American Anthropologist,* XXXIV, No. 2 (1961), pp. 47–59.

[10] Horst Nachtigall, "El estado estamental de los incas peruanos," *América Indígena,* XXIV, No. 2 (1964), pp. 93–110.

A. Favorable Assessments of the Sixteenth Century

1. How the Incas Achieved So Much

PEDRO DE CIEZA DE LEÓN

One of the things most to be envied these rulers is how well they knew to conquer such vast lands and, with their forethought, bring them to the flourishing state in which the Spaniards found them when they discovered this new kingdom. Proof of this is the many times I recall hearing these same Spaniards say, when we were in some indomitable region outside these kingdoms, "Take my word for it, if the Incas had been here it would have been a different story." In a word, the Incas did not make their conquests any way just for the sake of being served and collecting tribute. In this respect they were far ahead of us, for with the order they introduced the people throve and multiplied, and arid regions were made fertile and bountiful, in the ways and goodly manner that will be told.

They always tried to do things by fair means and not by foul at the beginning; afterward, certain of the Incas meted out severe punishments in many places, but they all tell that they first used great benevolence and friendliness to win these people over to their service. They set out from Cuzco with their men and weapons, and traveled in careful manner until they were close to the place they were going and planned to conquer. There they carefully sized up the situation to learn the strength of the enemy, the support they might have, and from what direction help might come, and by what road. When they had so informed themselves, they tried in every possible way to prevent them from receiving succor, either by rich

From *The Incas of Pedro de Cieza de León,* by Pedro de Cieza de León, translated by Harriet de Onis, edited and with an introduction by Victor W. von Hagen. Copyright 1959 by the University of Oklahoma Press.

gifts or by blocking the way. Aside from this, they built fortifications on hills or slopes with high, long stockades, each with its own gate, so that if one were lost, they could retire to the next, and so on to the topmost. And they sent out scouts of their confederates to spy out the land and learn the paths and find out whether they were waiting for them, and where the most food was. And when they knew the route by which the enemy was approaching and the force in which they were coming, they sent ahead messengers to say that the Inca wanted them to be his kin and allies, and, therefore, to come out to welcome him and receive him in their province with good cheer and light heart, and swear him fealty as the others had done. And so they would do this willingly, he sent gifts to the native rulers.

In this way, and with other good methods they employed, they entered many lands without war, and the soldiers who accompanied the Inca were ordered to do no damage or harm, or robbery or violence. If there was a shortage of food in the province, he ordered supplies brought in from other regions so that those newly won to his service would not find his rule and acquaintance irksome, and that knowing and hating him would be one. If in any of these provinces there were no flocks, he instantly ordered that they be given thousands of head, ordering that they tend them well so that they would multiply and supply them with wool for their clothing, and not to venture to kill or eat any of the young during the years and time he fixed. And if there were flocks, but they lacked some other thing, he did the same. If they were living in hills and wooded places, he made them understand with courteous words that they should build their villages and houses in the level parts of the sierras and hillsides; and as many of them were not skilled in the cultivation of the land, he had them taught how they should do it, urging them to build irrigation canals and water their fields from them.

They knew how to provide for everything so well that when one of the Incas entered a province in friendship, in a little while it seemed a different place and the natives obeyed him, agreeing that his representatives should dwell there, and also the *mitimaes*. In many others, where they entered by war and force of arms, they ordered that the crops and houses of the enemy be spared, the Inca saying, "These will soon be ours like those we already possess." As this was known to all, they tried to make the war as mild as possible even though fierce battles were waged in many places, because, in spite of everything, the inhabitants of them wanted to preserve their ancient liberty and not give up their customs and religion for others that were alien. But in the end the Incas always came out victorious, and when they had vanquished the others, they did not do them further harm, but released those they had taken prisoner, if there were any, and restored the booty, and put them back in possession of their property and rule, exhorting them not to be foolish and try to compete with his royal majesty nor abandon his friendship, but to be his friends as their neighbors were. And saying this, he gave them a number of beautiful women and fine pieces of wool or gold.

With these gifts and kindly words he won the good will of all to such a degree that those who had fled to the mountains returned to their homes, and all laid down their arms, and the one who most often had sight of the Inca was considered blessed and happy.

They never deprived the native chieftains of their rule. They were all ordered to worship the sun as God, but they were not prohibited from observing their own religions and customs. However, they were ordered to be ruled by the laws and customs which prevailed in Cuzco, and all were to speak the general language.

And when the Inca had appointed a governor with a garrison of soldiers, he went on, and if the provinces were large, he at once ordered a temple built to the sun and women assigned to it as in the others, and palaces built for the Inca, and the amount of tribute to be paid fixed, without ever making this burdensome or offending the people in any way, but guiding them in the ways of their polity, and teaching them to wear long clothing and live in their settlements in orderly manner. And if they lacked for anything, they were provided with it, and taught how to plant and cultivate. So well was this done that we know of many places where there had been no flocks that had them in abundance from the time the Incas subdued them, and others where there had been no corn that later had more than they could use. Those who had lived like savages, poorly clad and barefoot, after they acknowledged this ruler wore shirts and ribbons and blankets, and their women likewise, and other good things; so much so that there will always be memory of all this. In the Collao and other regions they ordered *mitimaes* to go to the highlands of the Andes to plant corn and coca and other fruits and roots, the necessary number from all the settlements. And these and their wives always lived in the place where they planted their crops, and harvested so much of what I have described that there was no lack, for these regions produced so much that there was no village, however small, that did not receive something from these *mitimaes.*

2. The Corruption of an Ideal Indian Society by Spaniards

MANCIO SIERRA DE LEGUÍZAMO

Before beginning my will, I declare that for many years I have wished for the opportunity to advise his Catholic Majesty, King Philip, our Lord — seeing how Catholic and very Christian he is and how zealous in the service of our Lord God — of what is necessary for the relief of my soul because of the large part I played in the discovery, conquest, and settlement of these Kingdoms when we took them away from those who were Lords Inca and possessed and ruled them as their own, putting them under the royal crown. His Catholic Majesty should understand that the said Incas had these kingdoms governed in such a manner that in all of them there was not a single thief, nor man of vice, nor idle man, nor any adulterous or bad woman; nor were people of loose morals permitted among them. Men had honorable and useful occupations; uncultivated lands, mines, pastures, hunting grounds, woods, and all kinds of employments were so managed and distributed that each person knew and held his own estate, and no one else took possession of it or deprived him of it; nor was there any litigation over it. Military enterprises, although they were frequent, did not obstruct commercial matters, and the latter did not impede farming nor anything else; in everything, from the most important to the most trifling, there was order and methodical arrangement. The Incas, as well as their governors and captains, were respected and feared by their subjects as persons of great capacity and leadership; and since we found that they were the ones who had the strength and authority to offer resistance, we had to deprive them of their power and goods by force of arms in order to subdue and oppress them for the service of our Lord God and in order to take away their land

"Testamento de Mancio Sierra de Leguízamo," *Revista del Archivo Histórico del Cuzco,* IV (1953), pp. 91–102, *passim.*

and put it under the royal crown. Our Lord God having permitted it, it was possible for us to subjugate this kingdom with such a multitude of people and riches, and those who had been lords we made servants, as is well known.

. . . His Majesty should understand that my motive in making this declaration is to unburden my conscience of guilt for having destroyed by our bad example people of such good conduct as were these natives, both men and women, and so little given to crime or excess. An Indian who had 100,000 pesos in gold and silver in his house would leave it open and put a broom or small stick across the doorway as a sign that the owner was not there; with this, according to their custom, no one could go inside nor take anything from within. When they saw that we had doors and keys in our houses, they thought that this was due to fear that they would kill us, but they did not believe that anyone would take or steal the property of another; and thus when they saw that among us there were thieves and men who incited their wives and daughters to sin, they regarded us with disdain. These natives have become so dissolute with their offenses against God because of the bad example we have given them in everything that their former extreme of doing no evil has been transformed, so that today they do little or no good. . . . In addition, those who were kings and lords, wealthy and obeyed, have come to such a low estate that they and their descendants are the poorest men in the kingdom. Moreover, we Spaniards even want to force them to serve as bearers, to clean and sweep our houses, to carry refuse to the dung-heaps, and to perform even lowlier tasks. And to avoid such tasks, these Inca Lords have started to learn shoe-making and similar trades, taking advantage of an ordinance of the Viceroy, D. Francisco de Toledo, that natives who served the public did not have to perform personal service, for Toledo's ordinance has greater influence than their being free men. Many things of this nature are permitted, which His Majesty would do well to realize and correct for the relief of his conscience and those of us who were discoverers and settlers and caused these ills. I can do no more than to inform his Catholic Majesty of these conditions, and with this I beg God to absolve me of my guilt, which I myself confess. I am moved to speak because I am the last survivor of all the discoverers and conquerors since, as is well known, there is no other left in this kingdom or outside of it.

3. Land Division, Tribute, and Treatment of Vassals

Garcilaso de la Vega

How They Divided the Land Amongst the Vassals — As soon as
the Ynca had conquered any kingdom or province, and established
his Government amongst the inhabitants according to his laws and
idolatrous customs, he ordered that the cultivated land capable of
yielding maize should be extended. For this purpose he caused irrigation channels to be constructed, which were most admirable, as may
be seen to this day; both those that have been destroyed, the ruins
of which are yet visible, and those still in working order. The
engineers led the irrigation channels in directions required by the
lands to be watered; for it must be known that the greater part of
this land is barren as regards corn-yielding soil, and, for this reason,
they endeavoured to increase its fertility as much as possible. As
the land is under the torrid zone it requires irrigation. The Yncas
supplied the water with great ingenuity, and no maize crop was
sown without being also supplied with water. They also constructed
channels to irrigate the pasture land, when the autumn withheld its
rains, for they took care to fertilise the pastures as well as the arable
land, as they possessed immense flocks. These channels for the
pastures were destroyed as soon as the Spaniards came into the
country, but the ruins may be seen to this day.

Having made the irrigation channels, they levelled the fields and
arranged them in squares, so that they might get the full benefit of
the water. On the sides of the mountains, where there was good
soil, they made terraces so as to get level ground, as may be seen at
this day round Cuzco and all over Peru. These terraces or *andenes*
consisted of three walls of strong masonry, one in front and two at
the sides, slightly inclining inwards, as are all their walls, so as to
sustain the weight of the earth, which was filled in until it reached
the top of the walls. Over the first *anden* they constructed another
narrower one, and above that another still smaller. Thus they
gradually covered the whole mountain, levelling the ground after

Garcilaso de la Vega, *First Part of the Royal Commentaries,* Clements R. Markham, trans. (London: The Hakluyt Society, First Series, Nos. 41, 45, 1869–
1871), No. 45, pp. 3–29, *passim.*

the manner of a flight of stairs, and getting the use of all the land
that was suitable for sowing, and that could be irrigated. . . . So
industrious were the Indians in all work tending to enlarge the
extent of the land capable of yielding maize. In many places they
led an irrigation channel for fifteen or twenty leagues, to irrigate
only a few *fanegas* of maize land, that it might not be lost.

Having thus increased the quantity of arable land, they measured
all that was contained in each province, every village by itself, and
then divided it into three parts. The first part was for the Sun, the
second for the King, and the third for the people. These divisions
were always carefully made, in order that the people might have
sufficient land for their crops; and it was a rule that they should
rather have more than was requisite than too little. When the people
of a village or province increased in number, a portion was taken
from the lands of the Sun and of the Ynca for the vassals. Thus the
King only took for himself and for the Sun such lands as would
otherwise remain desert and without an owner. Most of the *andenes*
belong to the Sun and to the Ynca, because the sovereign had
ordered them to be made. Besides the maize lands which were
irrigated, other unirrigated tracts were portioned out, in which they
sowed pulses and other crops of much importance, such as those
they call *papas, ocas,* and *añus.* These also were divided into three
parts: for the people, the Sun, and the Ynca. But as they were not
fertile, from want of irrigation, they did not take crops off them
more than once or twice, and then portioned out other lots, that the
first might lie fallow. In this way they cultivated their poor lands,
that there might always be abundance.

The maize lands were sown every year, because, as they were
irrigated and manured like a garden, they were always fertile. They
sowed a seed like rice with the maize, called *quinua,* which is also
raised on the cold lands.

**The Arrangement They Adopted for Tilling the Land, and of
the Festival They Held When They Cultivated the Land of the
Ynca and the Sun** — They also established a regular order in the
tilling and the cultivating of the land. They first tilled the fields of
the Sun; then of the widows, orphans, aged, and sick, for all these
persons were classed as poor, and, as such, the Ynca ordered that
their fields should be tilled for them. In each village, or in each
ward, if the village was large, there were men deputed to look after

the lands of persons who were classed as poor. These deputies were named *Llacta-camayu,* which means "officers of the village." They superintended the ploughing, sowing, and harvesting; and at such times they went up into towers the night before, that were built for the purpose, and after blowing through a trumpet or shell to secure attention, cried with a loud voice that on such a day such and such lands of the poor would be tilled, warning those, whose duty it might be, to repair thither. The inhabitants of each district were thus apprised on what lands they were to give assistance, which were those of their relations or nearest neighbours. Each one was expected to bring food for himself of what he had in his house, for those who were unable to work were not required to find food for those who could. It was said that their own misery sufficed for the aged, sick, widows, and orphans, without looking after that of the neighbours. If the disabled had no seed, it was provided from the stores, of which we shall speak presently. The lands of soldiers who were employed in the wars were also tilled in this way, like those of widows and orphans; and while the husbands were serving in the wars, their wives were looked upon as widows during their absence. Great care was taken of the children of those who were killed in the wars, until such time as they were married.

After the lands of the poor and distressed had been tilled, the people worked on their own lands, the neighbours assisting each other. They then tilled the fields of the Curaca, which were the last that received attention in each village or district. In the time of Huayna Ccapac, an Indian superintendent, in the province of Chachapoyas, was hanged because he caused the land of a Curaca, who was a relative of his, to be tilled before that of a widow. He was punished as a breaker of the rules established by the Ynca for the tilling of the land, and the gallows was set up on the land of the Curaca. The Yncas ordered that the lands of their vassals should take precedence of their own, because they said that from the prosperity of his subjects was derived their faithful service to the King; for if they were poor and in need, they would not be able to serve well either in peace or war.

The last fields that were cultivated were those of the King. All the people tilled the lands of the Ynca and of the Sun in common, and they went to them with great joy and satisfaction, dressed in the clothes which they wore on their grandest festivals. These garments were covered with plates of gold and silver, and the people also wore plumes of feathers on their heads. When they ploughed (which was the labour they most enjoyed) they sang many songs, composed in praise of their Yncas, and they went through their work with joy and gladness, because it was in the service of their God and of their King.

Hard by the city of Cuzco, on the slopes of the hill where the fortress stands, there was a terrace covering many *fanegas* of ground, and it will be there still, if it has not been covered with houses. It was called the Collcampata. The suburb which contains it, takes its name from the terrace, and this terrace was the special and principal jewel, so to speak, belonging to the Sun; for it was the first land that was dedicated to that deity throughout the whole empire of the Yncas. This land was cultivated by persons of the blood royal, and none but Yncas and Pallas could work on it. The work was performed with great rejoicing, especially the ploughing, when the Yncas came forth in their richest clothes. All the songs that were sung in praise of the Sun and of their Kings, were composed with reference to the meaning of the word *Haylli,* which in the general language of Peru means "triumph." Thus they were said to triumph over the earth by ploughing it, and turning it up so that it might yield fruit. In these songs they inserted graceful references to discreet lovers and to valiant soldiers, all bearing on the triumph over the land that they were tilling. The refrain of each couplet was the word *Haylli,* repeated as often as was necessary to complete the compass which the Indians made; for they ploughed the land backwards and forwards so as to break it up more thoroughly. . . .

The songs of the Indians and their tune appearing good to the master of the choir of the cathedral church of Cuzco, he composed a chaunt, in the year 1551 or 1552, for the feast of the most holy sacrament, very like the *Haylli.* Eight mestizo boys, school-fellows of mine, came forth dressed as Indians, each with a plough in his hand, to represent the song of *Haylli* in the procession, and the whole choir joined them in the refrain of the couplets, which pleased the Spaniards, and caused great joy to the Indians to see the Spaniards solemnizing the festival of our Lord God, whom they called Pachacamac, with the native songs and dances. . . .

The Tribute That They Gave to the Yncas, with an Account of the Granaries — Now that the method the Yncas had of dividing the land has been described, and how it was cultivated by the vassals, it will be well to explain the nature of the tribute they paid to their kings. Their tribute was to cultivate the lands of the Sun and of the Ynca, to gather in the harvests, and to store them in granaries which were kept in each village. One of the chief crops was the *uchu,* which the Spaniards call *axi,* and for another name pepper.

The granaries, called *pirua,* were built of clay mixed with straw. In the time of the Yncas they were constructed with great care. The blocks of clay were of a size conformable to the height of the wall where they were placed, and were cast in different sizes in a mould. They made the granaries of sizes according to the required measurement, some larger than others, to hold from fifty to two hundred *fanegas.* Each granary was measured so as to be of the required size. It had four walls, and there was a passage down the middle, leading from one granary to another, so that they could be emptied or filled at pleasure. But they did not move them from where they were once placed. In order to empty a granary, they had small windows in front, in eight squares, opening so as to give a measurement of the quantity of grain that was poured out, and thus they knew the number of *fanegas* that had been taken out and the quantity remaining, without having to measure it further. Thus they could easily tell, by the size of the granaries, the quantity of maize in each depôt, and by the windows they knew how much had been taken out and how much was left in each granary. I saw some of these granaries, which remained from the time of the Yncas, and they were among the best, for they were in the house of the virgins of the Sun, and were built for the use of those women. When I saw them, the convent had become the house of the sons of Pedro del Barco, who were my school-fellows.

The crops of the Sun and those of the Ynca were shut up in places apart, though in the same depôt. The seeds for sowing were given by the Lord of the land, who was the Sun or the King; and in the same way for the sustenance of the Indians who worked, that they might be maintained each out of his own estate, when they tilled and cultivated their lands; so that the Indians had only to give personal labour as their tribute. The vassals paid nothing to the Ynca from their own crops.   . . .

The Vassals Were Supplied with Clothes. No Begging Was Allowed — As there were regulations for the supply of clothing, in abundance, to the soldiers; so also the wool was given to the Curacas and vassals generally every two years, to enable them to make clothes for themselves and their families; and it was the duty of the Decurions to see that the people were clothed. The Indians, and even the Curacas, had few llamas; while the Sun and the Yncas possessed innumerable flocks. The Indians said that when the Spaniards first came to the country there was scarcely sufficient pasture for the flocks, and I have heard my father and his contemporaries relate the great excesses and waste committed by some Spaniards among these flocks. . . . In the warm country cotton was distributed from the royal estates for clothing for the Indians and their families. Thus they had all that was required for human life, both in clothes, shoes, and food; and no one could be called poor, or require to seek alms. For all had as much as they would have required if they had been rich, but they were as poor as possible in unnecessary things, having nothing more than they required. Father Acosta, speaking of Peru, says briefly and compendiously what we have related with so much prolixity. At the end of the fifteenth chapter of the sixth book he has these words: "The sheep were shorn at the proper season, and each person was given wool to spin and weave into cloth for his wife and children. Visits were made to see if this was done, and the idle were punished. The wool that was over was put into the storehouses; which were full of it, and of all other things necessary for human life, when the Spaniards arrived. No thoughtful man can fail to admire so noble and provident a Government. For, without being religious or Christians, the Indians attained to a high state of perfection in providing all that was necessary, and plentifully sustaining their houses of religion, as well as those of their King and Lord. . . ."

In the following chapter, speaking of the occupations of the Indians, he . . . says what follows, copied word for word: "Another thing which the Indians of Peru practised was to teach each boy all the arts which it was necessary a man should know to sustain human life. For, among these people, they had no special tradesmen, as we have, such as tailors, shoemakers, or weavers; but each man learnt all, so that he could himself make all that he required. All men knew how to weave and make clothes; so that when the Ynca gave them wool, it was as good as giving them clothes. All could till and manure the land, without hiring labourers. All knew how to build houses. And the women knew all these arts also, practising them with great diligence, and helping their husbands. Other occupations, which were not connected with ordinary wants, had their special artizans, such as silversmiths, painters, potters, boatmen, accountants, and musicians. Even in the ordinary labours of weaving, tilling, and building, there were masters for special work, who served the Lords. But among the common people, as has been said, each could do all that was necessary in his household, without having to pay another, and it is the same at the present day. . . . In truth, these people were neither covetous nor wasteful, but were contented to pass their lives in great moderation, so that surely if their mode of living had been adopted from choice, and not from habit, we must have confessed that it was a very perfect state of existence. Nor were the seeds wanting for the reception of the doctrine of the Holy Gospel, which is so hostile to pride, avarice, and waste. But the preachers do not always make their acts agree with the doctrine they preach to the Indians." A little further on he says: "It was an inviolable law that no one should change the peculiar dress of his province, even if he moved to another; and the Yncas held this rule to be very conducive to good government. The custom is still observed, although not so strictly as it was then." So far the Father Acosta. The Indians wonder much at the way the Spaniards change the fashion of their dress every year, and attribute it to pride and presumption.

The custom of never seeking alms was still observed in my day; and up to the time when I left Peru, in 1560, throughout all the parts that I travelled over, I never saw an Indian, man or woman, begging. I only knew one old woman in Cuzco, named Isabel, who begged, and her habit was more to go jesting from house to house, like a gipsy, than to seek alms from necessity. The Indians quarrelled with her, and spat on the ground, which is a sign of contempt and abhorrence; so that she never begged of the Indians, but only of the Spaniards; and as, even in my time, there was no regular money in the country, they gave her maize as alms, which was what she wanted.   . . .

The Yncas, in their administration, did not forget the travellers, but along all the royal roads they ordered houses for travellers to be built, called *corpa-huasi*, where they were given food and all things necessary for their journeys from the royal stores kept in each village. If they fell ill, they were attended with great care and kindness; so that they had everything as if they had been in their own

houses. It is true that they did not travel for their own pleasure
or amusement, nor on their own business, for no such thing was
known; but by order of the King or of the Curacas, who sent them
from one part to another, or by direction of captains or officials,
either of war or peace. These travellers were carefully looked after,
but any who travelled without just cause, were punished as vagabonds.

B. The Spanish Justification for Conquest

4. Viceroy Toledo's Attack on Inca Rule

LEWIS HANKE

The best example of the effect produced by Fray Bartolomé de
Las Casas' theoretical writings concerning the just title Spain held
to America occurred in Peru during the rule of Viceroy Francisco
de Toledo, wise law-giver, energetic administrator, and greatest
viceroy Spain ever sent to Peru, who laid the basis for Spanish rule
there during the years 1569–1582. Before his coming, Peru had had
a most turbulent and bloody history, and Toledo arrived with one
great aim — to establish without question in this territory the position of the King of Spain. One of his earliest acts was to execute
the Inca, Lord Tupac Amaru, the Indian leader who refused to accept Spanish rule. Presently, with a view to establishing Spain's
juridical title to Peru, he undertook an extensive historical investigation which attempted to demonstrate the unjust nature of the Inca
regime and thus demolish the doctrines of Las Casas.   . . .

The Viceroy was impelled to this task by what he considered the
pernicious influence of Las Casas. Even before Toledo's arrival in
Peru, in fact in the instructions given to him by the king on January

Lewis Hanke, "Viceroy Francisco de Toledo and the Just Titles of Spain to the
Inca Empire," *The Americas*, II (July, 1946), pp. 3–19, *passim*. Reprinted by
permission of the Academy of American Franciscan History.

28, 1568, he had been warned against free-speaking friars. The king
had understood that "the ecclesiastics who have resided and reside
in those parts on the pretext of protecting the Indians have wished
to busy themselves concerning the justice and the lordship of the
Indies and in other matters which lead them into much scandal,
particularly when they treat these subjects in pulpits and public
places." Therefore, he warned Toledo to take care to prevent such
occurrences by conferring with the provincials and superiors of
these ecclesiastics, for in no wise should such scandals be permitted.
So serious did Toledo consider this problem that early in his career
as viceroy he conferred with the higher ecclesiastical authorities of
Peru to determine whether the newly established Inquisition could
not be utilized, not to smoke out heretics but to impose silence "on
preachers and confessors in this realm who hold contrary opinions
on jurisdictional matters and on security of conscience." . . .

The Viceroy took three positive steps to combat these theories.
First, he inspired the composition of a treatise against Las Casas;
second, he embarked upon an investigation of the justice of Inca rule
by collecting the so-called *Informaciones;* and finally, he arranged
for the preparation of a "true history" of Peru's past by Pedro
Sarmiento de Gamboa. This section will discuss the treatise.

The treatise is in the form of an anonymous letter dated at the
Valley of Yucay on March 16, 1571, and is entitled "Defense of
the Legitimacy of the Rule of the Kings of Spain in the Indies, in
Opposition to Friar Bartolomé de Las Casas." The author, who
appears to be rendering a formal opinion to Viceroy Toledo, has
been identified by some as Polo de Ondegardo, one of Toledo's principal jurists, by others as Pedro Sarmiento de Gamboa, another one
of Toledo's principal officers, but perhaps was neither. For at one
point, after referring to himself he mentions "many other friars" as
though he were one himself and the impression that the author is a
friar is strengthened when in closing he states that he was happy to
give an opinion "on a matter so appropriate to my profession." If
the author were an ecclesiastic, he may have been the Viceroy's
chaplain, the Franciscan Pero Gutiérrez.*

At any rate this treatise was a frontal attack on the theories of

---

* Marcel Bataillon has recently concluded that the author probably was the first
Jesuit provincial in Peru, Jerónimo Ruiz del Portillo, *Études sur Bartolomé de
Las Casa*: (Paris: Centre de Recherches de l'Institut d'Études Hispaniques,
1966), pp. 273–274.

Las Casas who, the author points out, although he was never in Peru and therefore could know nothing first hand of conditions there, has stirred up all the trouble. The author states that the Indies were given to Spain as a reward for her eight centuries of warfare against the Moslems and insists that the Incas were tyrants in Peru "which fact, Your Excellency is now making abundantly clear with great authority in the investigation you are making."   . . .

Much harm will come if the just title of the king of Spain is not clarified, continues the author. Christian government and justice will be hindered, conversion will lag, and other Christian princes will use the excuse of ill treatment of the Indians to try to take over part or all of the Indies. Moreover, and this is a curious sidelight on the times, some Spaniards have married Indian women of the Inca family in order to be in line to rule by hereditary right if the Incas should return to power, as will happen, warned the author, "if this indiscreet and mistaken Bishop has his way." Finally, Lutheran, English, and French heretics will use the beclouded title of Spain as an excuse to rob Spaniards in the Indies, to harry the land, to ascend rivers and disseminate their heresies in all the empire.

The author then proceeds to state certain basic propositions, such as, that the Incas were modern tyrants, that before Topa Inga conquered the land there was no general overlord, that the Pope made the king of Spain lord over them and that, since they had no natural or legitimate lord, the king of Spain became their ruler. The author combats the idea put forward by Las Casas that the Incas had been received voluntarily as lords, and the charge that, whereas the Spaniards levy taxes and send money abroad, the Incas levied none and spent what money they had in Peru.

In a final burst, the author expresses his amazement at those who "under the guise of zealousness try to give these Indians titles and things which did not belong to them, because God didn't choose to give them nor is it appropriate . . . for they are minors who must be governed. . . . It has been a most delicate subtlety of the Devil to select as his instrument an ecclesiastic and apparently a person of zeal, but deceived and ill-speaking and of little discretion, as may be seen by the publication of his books, and by the disturbances he created in Peru when Blasco Núñez came."   . . .

The "Informaciones" of Viceroy Francisco de Toledo — The *Informaciones* consisted of a formal inquiry, by order of the Viceroy, into the ancient history of the Incas, the conquests of Tupac Yupanqui the last Inca ruler, the institution of the *Curacas,* the Inca religious beliefs and practices, and their sacrifices, nature, and customs. Information was taken down, by means of translators, from two hundred Indians at eleven different points in Peru during the period November, 1570–March, 1572, while Viceroy Toledo was making a general inspection of Peru at the beginning of his rule there, much in the same way the Inca rulers began their administration by first formally surveying their realms. The complete record of this inquiry has only recently been made available by the Argentine historian, Roberto Levillier.

Few episodes in the colonial history of Peru have been interpreted so variously by modern historians as this inquiry. Clements Markham, José de la Riva-Agüero, Horacio Urteaga, and Philip A. Means believe that Toledo organized this as a public spectacle to present the Incas as monsters of cruelty, to falsify their history and customs in order to make certain of Spain's title. They state that senile, servile "yes-men" were chosen as witnesses, and that if a witness happened to tell an unpalatable truth his answer was changed by the interpreter from "no" to "yes," or "yes" to "no," as the occasion required. In short, that it was intended to blacken the Incas. A good example of the heat engendered among historians on this topic is the following conclusion of Means:

> I feel, however, very strongly that enough evidence has now been presented to prove the utter worthlessness of the *Informaciones* of Toledo and, consequently, of the History of the Incas by Sarmiento. In both cases the basis upon which the structure of false testimony, reared by Toledo's will, rests is the evidence of broken-spirited, baptized Indians who were densely ignorant of the truth concerning Incaic history and who constantly contradicted themselves and one another. They were cowed by the martial strength of the Viceroy's government and by the new spiritual terrorism which Catholic Christianity had put in the place of the old cults; they were unable to speak to their questioners directly because of the barrier of language, and consequently they had to talk through the mediation of an unscrupulous blackguard, Gómez Jiménez, to a ruthless and prejudiced audience — Toledo and Loarte; finally, most of them were in extreme old age when senectitude must have beclouded their memories considerably, and some of them harbored grudges against their former rulers.

Levillier rejects this conclusion vehemently. He points out that not one of these writers had available all the *Informaciones,* and insists that the inquiry was an honest and important investigation which constitutes one of the most trustworthy sources available for a reconstruction of the events and of the spirit of the prodigious Inca communist republic.

These inquiries make curious and interesting reading. The records tell us, for example, that on March 13, 1571, there were examined at Cuzco these witnesses: Don Francisco Antigualpa, Governor of Los Andesuyos, aged eighty years; Don Joan Llamoca, Principal of Los Lurinsoras, aged sixty years; Don Joan Caquya, Principal of Los Lurinsoras, aged fifty-five years; Don Lucas Chico, Cacique of Urcos, aged seventy years; Don Bautista Gualpuracana, Curaca of Cachec, aged seventy-five years; and Don Lope Martín Cunti-maycta, Curaca of Yucay, aged sixty years. Among the questions put to them were these:

1. Is it true that the first Inca, he who was called Mango Capac, tyrannically subjugated the Indians living around Cuzco by force of arms and despoiled them of their lands, killing them, warring against them, and otherwise maltreating them? And did all the rest of the Incas do likewise, until the fourth, called Maita Capac, who completed the conquest?
2. Is it true that the Indians never recognized voluntarily these Incas as their lords, and only obeyed them through fear of great cruelties inflicted against them?
3. Is it true that neither you nor your ancestors ever elected the Incas as your lords, but that they supported their tyrannical position by force of arms and the inculcation of fear?

Practically all the questions were of this yes-or-no character, and there were evidently more yes- than no-men in the group interrogated, for the answers all tended to establish that the whole history of the Incas, from 565 A.D. when Manco Capac founded the dynasty until 1533 when Francisco Pizarro won Peru for Spain, was but a succession of tyrannical and brutal overlords who ruled despotically. It was thereupon an easy transition for the interrogators to elicit that the Spanish invasion was thus a deliverance and greatly to the advantage of the Indians, who were now to be Christianized by the ecclesiastics and protected by the Crown. Another set of questions put to a different set of witnesses drew information that the Incas sacrificed to their gods and idols the most beautiful children to be found, that the Incas realized the laziness of their subjects and kept them at work, even if it had no real value, and that some of the Indians were cannibals.

Although Levillier has published all these *Informaciones* in a bulky volume and attacked the "campaign" theory vigorously in an extensive and detailed analysis, it is probable that we can never be quite certain that the last word has been said on this controversy. For the purposes of this present study it is enough to know Toledo's motive in instituting the inquiry. As his secretary, Alvaro Ruiz de Nabamuel, declared, "he had seen how badly the rights of the King of Spain to the Indies were treated in Spain and in the Indies, and how unreasonable and dangerous it was to attribute to these Incas the true lordship of these kingdoms."

Viceroy Toledo summed up his own view on the meaning of the inquiry when he transmitted to the King a summary of the *Informaciones* with a letter dated March 1, 1572, in which he declared:

1. Your Majesty is the legitimate ruler of this kingdom and the Incas are tyrannical usurpers.
2. Your Majesty may assign at will the *Cacicazgos* as you see fit, and this action would be one of the most important steps you could take for the spiritual and temporal rule of the Indians.
3. Your Majesty may therefore bestow the lands of Peru upon Spaniards and ignore the scruples of those who have claimed the Incas are the legitimate rulers.
4. Moreover, all mines and minerals, as well as the property of the Incas, belong to Your Majesty.
5. As legitimate ruler, Your Majesty rightly exercises jurisdiction over the Indians, and, given their weak reason and rude understanding, Your Majesty must devise laws for their conservation and require them to obey these ordinances.

Toledo closes this letter with the earnest hope that "such a variety of opinion on matters of great importance will cease," and the King, his ministers and the inhabitants of Peru will no longer have their consciences so disturbed and confused as in the past whenever some ignorant person dares to open his mouth and cry to high heaven.

The "Historia Indica" of Pedro Sarmiento de Gamboa — The inquiry into Inca history and Indian customs was not enough. Neither did the treatise "Defense of the Legitimacy of the Rule of the King of Spain in the Indies" wholly satisfy the Viceroy or the conquistadores and their descendants. What the situation really required, they felt, was a history — a true history, which would supplant the false histories then current.   . . .

The widespread and intense dissatisfaction among the Spanish rulers of Peru with the historical accounts of Spanish deeds in the New World and with the justification of Spanish rule in Peru is well-illustrated by the expressive memorial drawn up by the Town Council of Cuzco and forwarded to the Council of the Indies on October 24, 1572. These worthies wrote in an injured tone as follows:

> Not only did the Greek and Roman historians have a high opinion of the importance of writing history, but even barbarians who have no knowledge of writing still have by a natural instinct sought means to record their past with paintings and marks, and in Peru by a system of threads and knots and registers. Certain persons were appointed whose sole duty was to teach the meaning of it all. Such care has been taken by these Indians that they have a record for the past three hundred years of their deeds, their achievements, their edifices, their wars, and the events of their history. Truly this is to be admired and it is difficult to believe unless one has seen it with his own eyes. All the greater, then, is the fault of the discoverers, the conquistadores, and the colonizers who, having performed great feats and having labored more greatly and with more determination than any other nation in the world, permit these deeds to be forgotten.
>
> Many of those who conquered this realm still live, and we understand that chroniclers who never were here are writing the story of our deeds without ascertaining the truth. These writers do this only to get money by publishing, and sometimes to the detriment of the estates and the honor of those whose deeds they describe. Thus there has resulted a world of conflicting opinions which have left the people disturbed and depressed. When we read the histories written about us, we think they must be describing another kind of people.

We believe ours the most justified cause of all that we know because the basis was the concession which Our Lord and His Vicar-General of our Church made to the Kings of Castile, giving them sovereign dominion and making them patrons in spiritual matters charged with the conversion and evangelical preaching, with general authority to concern themselves in everything discovered and to be discovered without any limitation whatsoever.

This spiritual obligation has been fulfilled. In Cuzco alone there are five monasteries of ecclesiastics and one convent of sisters and a hospital. In this district alone are more than one hundred and twenty priests laboring for the conversion and indoctrination of the natives, not counting the priests Your Excellency has ordered to be added whose expenses are so heavy that they amount to more than one hundred thousand *castellanos*. Moreover, there are only Spanish inhabitants here and they are poor.

Therefore, considering the expense which Your Majesty bears with five tribunals of judges, and mayors, and so many *corregimientos* and the many other salaries which are paid, which consume almost all the revenue gained in Peru, we do not know if there exists in the world a dominion possessed by such just and such reasonable titles, and from which such usefulness and benefit have resulted for the service of God and the increase of His Holy Roman Church.

Moreover, those who are curious to know the origin and basis of other dominions that are in France, Germany, and many other places will discover that most of them have their rights to possession written in the bones of men. And though they have no other reason or basis for their rule than this, they have lived and continue to live so quietly and peacefully that all they have to do is maintain their defenses. They do not have to reply to scruples because nobody raises them. We, the inhabitants of this land, have been less fortunate.

Then the Spaniards resident in Cuzco in 1572 proceeded to describe the tyranny of the Incas, to deplore their bad customs — in much the same vein as the *Informaciones* — and to approve heartily Viceroy Toledo's inquiry. They concluded with the statement that of the one thousand *encomenderos* appointed by the King in Peru, eight hundred have been killed in putting down rebellions and in defense of the realm and those who remained required assistance and favors. It was to satisfy the demands for an honest history, and to meet the threat to Spanish rule in America that Toledo . . . commissioned Pedro Sarmiento de Gamboa to write a history to set at rest forever the doubts concerning the justice of Spain's rule in Peru.

Sarmiento was one of that group of able officials with whom the Viceroy had surrounded himself, and upon whom he leaned heavily in the administration of his far-flung realm. As a soldier, astronomer, and later explorer of the Solomon Islands and the Straits of Magellan, Sarmiento was typical of the principal Spanish administrative officers who kept the large and complicated machinery of empire in motion. For two years he had been traversing Peru, drawing out from the oldest inhabitants their recollection of the events of the past. To a considerable extent Sarmiento depended upon the *Informaciones* brought forth by Toledo's inquiry, but he had also carried on other investigations in the Valley of the Jauja, in Guamanga, but principally in Cuzco where the Incas had made their capital and where the best informants still lived.

Sarmiento officially presented his history to the Viceroy on February 29, 1572, for examination and correction. Toledo thereupon ordered the "principal and most able descendants" of the Incas to be brought together to listen to a reading of the history. Each Indian swore by the Cross to tell the truth and to indicate, by means of an interpreter, whatever corrections he considered necessary. Day after day the history was read, chapter by chapter. Now and then some name was corrected, or other minor change made, as when Doña María Cusi Guarcai objected to the prominent place accorded to certain Incas not of her own family, but all the listeners declared that they found the history good and true and according to the tales handed down by their fathers. The four living conquistadores who had entered Peru with Pizarro almost half a century before also testified that the history coincided with what they had been told by other Indians.

The corrected version was then legally certified and despatched to the king, with a covering letter from the Viceroy, a genealogical tree, and four painted cloths illustrating certain events of Inca history. These paintings had also been examined by various competent Indians and pronounced good. The Viceroy suggested in his letter to the king that such an accurate history, which would serve as the best possible justification of Spain's title to America, should be published, "in order to refute the other false and lying books that have circulated in these parts, and to explain the truth, not only to our own people but to foreign nations as well."

The *Historia Indica* of Sarmiento described in detail the history of the Incas, their cruelty, their revolting customs, and their tyranny, in a tone and in a spirit reminiscent of that in which Las Casas had denounced the conquistadores in his *Very Brief Account of the Destruction of the Indies.* Sarmiento concluded that because of the sins of the Incas against the law of nature they should be forced to obey this law, "as had been taught by the Archbishop of Florence and confirmed by Friar Francisco de Vitoria in the discussion he made concerning the title of the Indies. Therefore, Your Majesty, by this title alone holds just as sufficient and legitimate title to the Indies as any prince in the world holds to any realm whatsoever, because in all the lands thus far discovered in the two seas to the North and to the South there has been found this general violation of the law of nature." But the king never published the history so laboriously compiled by Pedro Sarmiento de Gamboa. It was allowed to remain in obscurity and not permitted to be spread abroad through Europe in opposition to the writings of Bishop Bartolomé de Las Casas; indeed, it has never been published in Spain and only saw the light of day in 1906, because of the interest of a German scholar.

Nor was Toledo able to convince all the Spaniards in Peru. The Jesuit José de Acosta, perhaps the outstanding ecclesiastic of the time, without mentioning Sarmiento by name, rejected the theory that Indians could be deprived of dominion if they persisted in error. Acosta affirmed: "We must reject those false titles of dominion which some persons are trying to propagate, unnecessary defenders of the royal authority in my opinion, not to say deceivers, who would prove their assertions by the tyranny of the Incas . . . which we do not understand and do not admit. For it is not lawful to rob a thief, nor does the crime committed by some one else add to our own justice."

Another prominent figure of the time, Juan de Matienzo, jurist and adviser of Toledo, was just as certain that the Viceroy was absolutely right. In the *Gobierno del Perú,* not published until three hundred years after it was written, Matienzo followed the same view set forth in Sarmiento's history. He first described the cruelty and tyranny of the Incas, how they killed five thousand persons at one time in one place and jerked out their hearts, how they sacrificed boys to their idols, how they burned alive the women and children of their chief men, and how the Incas governed in their own interest, and not for the welfare of their people. Then Matienzo made a rousing justification of Spanish rule, declaring:

> The Indies were justly won. By the concession of the pope, or because those kingdoms were found deserted by the Spaniards. Or because of their abominable sins against nature. Or because of their infidelity. Although this last reason alone would be sufficient, as would each of the others, the tyranny of the Indians is enough to establish the fact that the kingdom of Peru was justly gained and that His Majesty has a very just title to it. . . . Moreover, the Indians have learned to trade and thereby win profits, and to use mechanical and agricultural instruments, which is no less a just title than the others.

Curiously enough, just as certain historians today accuse the Spaniards of hypocritically seeking to justify their rule, so Polo de Ondegardo, another important adviser to Toledo, stated that the Incas, once they had determined upon a particular conquest, "looked for some title and pretext to accomplish what they wanted to do, which is only natural."

We have found no documents to explain the royal indifference to a history which so stoutly defended the king's title to Peru. Perhaps ecclesiastical pressure was strong enough to prevent the publication of this history so opposed to the doctrines of Las Casas. Toledo never abandoned his official interest in the history of the Incas, an interest maintained by later viceroys. Spaniards continued to question the right of their king to the Indies, and Licenciado Francisco Falcón introduced a modern idea, comparable to the mandate system under the League of Nations when he maintained that if the Incas "came to such a state as to be able to rule themselves, as they will with the aid of God, their independence should be restored by the crown."

Today there still exist two well-defined attitudes toward the history compiled by Sarmiento de Gamboa at the behest of Viceroy Toledo, similar to the divergence of opinion on the *Informaciones*. Markham attempted to discredit Sarmiento's work, and Means considers it "an abominably unjust and inaccurate account of a great but fallen dynasty" and the author a pliant tool who was willing to aid in Viceroy's "nefarious literary attack." Levillier, on the other hand, stoutly defends the essential truthfulness of Sarmiento's his-

tory, lashes out at Markham for what appears to be his plain men-
dacity, and supports Viceroy Toledo at every point. Today, just as
almost four hundred years ago, the differences of opinion on the
justice of Spanish rule in Peru are deep, bitter, and apparently
irreconcilable.

5. The Tyranny of Inca Rule

PEDRO SARMIENTO DE GAMBOA

It is a thing worthy to be noted [*for the fact that besides being a
thing certain and evident the general tyranny of these cruel and
tyrannical Incas of Peru against the natives of the land, may be
easily gathered from history*], and any one who reads and considers
with attention the order and mode of their procedure will see, that
their violent Incaship was established without the will and election
of the natives who always rose with arms in their hands on each
occasion that offered for rising against their Inca tyrants who oppressed them, to get back their liberty. Each one of the Incas not
only followed the tyranny of his father, but also began afresh the
same tyranny by force, with deaths, robberies and rapine. Hence
none of them could pretend, in good faith, to give a beginning to
time of prescription, nor did any of them hold in peaceful possession,
there being always some one to dispute and take up arms against
them and their tyranny. Moreover, and this is above all to be noted,
to understand the worst aims of these tyrants and their horrid
avarice and oppression, they were not satisfied with being evil tyrants to the natives, but also to their own proper sons, brothers and
relations, in defiance of their own laws and statutes, they were the
worst and most pertinacious tyrants with an unheard-of inhumanity.
For it was enacted among themselves and by their customs and laws
that the eldest legitimate son should succeed, yet almost always
they broke the law, as appears by the Incas who are here referred to.

Before all things Manco Ccapac, the first tyrant, coming from
Tampu-tocco, was inhuman in the case of his brother Ayar Cachi,

Pedro Sarmiento de Gamboa, *History of the Incas*, Clements R. Markham, trans.
(Cambridge, Eng.: The Hakluyt Society, Series 2, No. 22, 1907), pp. 190–194.

sending him to Tampu-tocco cunningly with orders for Tampu-chacay to kill him out of envy, because he was the bravest, and might for that reason be the most esteemed. When he arrived at the valley of Cuzco he not only tyrannized over the natives, but also over Copalimayta and Columchima who, though they had been received as natives of that valley, were his relations, for they were *orejones*. Then Sinchi Rocca, the second Inca, having an older legitimate son named Manco Sapaca who, according to the law he and his father had made, was entitled to the succession, deprived him and nominated Lloqui Yupanqui, the second son, for his successor. Likewise Mayta Ccapac, the fourth Inca, named for his successor Ccapac Yupanqui, though he had an older legitimate son named Cunti Mayta, whom he disinherited. Viracocha, the eighth Inca, although he had an older legitimate son named Inca Rocca, did not name him as his successor, nor any of his legitimate sons, but a bastard named Inca Urco. This did not come about, Inca Urco did not enjoy the succession, nor did the eldest legitimate son, for there was a new tyranny. For Inca Yupanqui deprived both the one and the other, besides despoiling his father of his honours and estate. The same Inca Yupanqui, having an elder legitimate son named Amaru Tupac Inca, did not name him, but a young son, Tupac Inca Yupanqui. The same Tupac Inca, being of the same condition as his father, having Huayna Ccapac as the eldest legitimate son, named Ccapac Huari as his successor, although the relations of Huayna Ccapac would not allow it, and rose in his favour. If Ccapac Huari was legitimate, as his relations affirm, the evil deed must be fixed on Huayna Ccapac, who deprived his brother Ccapac Huari, and killed his mother and all his relations, making them infamous as traitors, that is supposing he was legitimate. Huayna Ccapac, though he named Ninan Cuyoche, he was not the eldest, and owing to this the succession remained unsettled, and caused the differences between Huascar and Atahualpa, whence proceeded the greatest and most unnatural tyrannies. Turning their arms against their own entrails, robbing, and with inhuman intestine wars they came to a final end. Thus as they commenced by their own authority, so they destroyed all by their own proper hands.

It may be that Almighty God permits that one shall be the executioner of the other for his evil deeds, that both may give place to his most holy gospel which, by the hands of the Spaniards, and by

order of the most happy, catholic, and unconquered Emperor and
King of Spain, Charles V of glorious memory, father of your Majesty,
was sent to these blind and barbarous gentiles. Yet against the
force and power of the Incas on foot and united, it appeared that
it would be impossible for human force to do what a few Spaniards
did, numbering only 180, who at first entered with the Governor
Don Francisco Pizarro.

It is well established that it is a thing false and without reason,
and which ought not to be said, that there is now, in these kingdoms, any person of the lineage of the Incas who can pretend to a
right of succession to the Incaship of this kingdom of Peru, nor to
be natural or legitimate lords. For no one is left who, in conformity
with their laws, is able to say that he is the heir, in whole or in part
of this land. Only two sons of Huayna Ccapac escaped the cruelty
of Atahualpa. They were Paullu Tupac, afterwards called Don
Cristóval Paullu, and Manco Inca. They were bastards, which is
well known among them. And these, if any honour or estate had
belonged to them or their children, your Majesty would have granted
more than they had, their brothers retaining their estate and power.
For they would merely have been their tributaries and servants.
These were the lowest of all, for their lineage was on the side of
their mothers which is what these people look at, in a question of
birth.

And Manco Inca had been a traitor to your Majesty and was a
fugitive in the Andes where he died or was killed. Your Majesty
caused his son to be brought out, in peace, from those savage wilds.
He was named Don Diego Sayri Tupac. He became a Christian,
and provision was made for him, his sons and descendants. Sayri
Tupac died as a Christian, and he who is now in the Andes in rebellion, named Titu Cusi Yupanqui, is not a legitimate son of Manco
Inca, but a bastard and apostate. They hold that another son is
legitimate who is with the same Titu, named Tupac Amaru, but
he is incapable and the Indians called him *uti.* Neither one nor the
other are heirs of the land, because their father was not legitimate.

Your Majesty honoured Don Cristóval Paullu with titles and
granted him a good *repartimiento* of Indians, on which he principally lived. Now it is possessed by his son Don Carlos. Paullu left
two legitimate sons who are now alive, named Don Carlos and
Don Felipe. Besides these he left many illegitimate sons. Thus the
known grandsons of Huayna Ccapac, who are now alive and ad-

mitted to be so, are those above mentioned. Besides these there are Don Alonso Titu Atauchi, son of Titu Atauchi, and other bastards, but neither one nor the other has any right to be called a natural lord of the land.

For the above reasons it will be right to say to those whose duty it may be to decide, that on such clear evidence is based the most just and legitimate title that your Majesty and your successors have to these parts of the Indies, proved by the actual facts that are here written, more especially as regards these kingdoms of Peru without a point to raise against the said titles by which the crown of Spain holds them. Respecting which your Viceroy of these kingdoms, Don Francisco Toledo, has been a careful and most curious enquirer, as zealous for the clearing of the conscience of your Majesty, and for the salvation of your soul, as he has shown and now shows himself in the general visitation which he is making by order of your Majesty, in his own person, not avoiding the very great labours and dangers which he is suffering in these journeys, so long as they result in so great a service to God and your Majesty.

C. Modern Interpretations

6. The Inca Empire Was Socialistic

LOUIS BAUDIN

The basis of all regional organization, the agrarian community, was invested with such importance before the time of the Incas that Cunow and his disciples regard it as the very foundation of the social system of the empire. This community appears to have been the result of a centuries-old evolution. Its origin is lost in the ages before the dawn of history, and in many parts of South and Central America we find it still today virtually unchanged. Through it the

Louis Baudin, *A Socialist Empire: The Incas of Peru,* Katherine Woods, trans. (Princeton, N.J.: D. Van Nostrand Co., 1961), pp. 56–175, *passim.* Reprinted by permission of D. Van Nostrand Company, Inc.

empire of the Incas thrust its roots deeply into the past and continues to maintain a kind of penumbral existence in the present
within the framework of modern legislation.

The primordial cell of Peruvian society was the *ayllu,* a clan
made up of all the descendants of a common ancestor, real or supposed. Every *ayllu* had its totem (*pacarisca,* the engendering being).
Garcilaso reports that the common people believed themselves to
be descended from animals — puma, condor, snake — and, indeed,
some of the Nazca pottery represents beasts so stylized that they
seem human. But the totems were not only living creatures; sometimes they comprised inanimate objects, such as mountains or rivers,
and sometimes natural phenomena like thunder and lightning.

For the Indian, men, animals, vegetables, and minerals were all
divided into *ayllus.*

Markham, Cunow, Joyce, Bandelier, and Saavedra agree in believing that the *ayllu* is of very ancient origin and that it rests upon
a religious foundation. The group had its guardian deities, the
huaca, which were distinct from those of the family properly so
called, the *conopa,* and its own ancestors, which it confounded
neither with those of the family nor with those of the tribe or group
of *ayllus.* These ancestors were themselves divinities, and their
mummies were the objects of a cult. The religious character of the
ayllu and the Indians' veneration of the deceased and of the aged
are traits still found today on the inter-Andean plateau. Thus, at
the present time ritual ceremonies precede community toil in the
province of Huarochari in the region of Casta, and Europeans are
astonished by the authority of ancestral tradition and the respect
inspired by the aged which they observe in upper Peru, "as opposed
to the situation in so many country districts."

Was it from this family community, this kinship group that the
village community sprang? Saavedra maintains that this is the case.
Even before the time of the Incas, according to him, the *ayllu* by
lineage was becoming slowly modified; it was gradually losing its
personal character and tending to assume a territorial dimension.
When an association of families settles in a given area, the soil
comes to replace the ties of consanguinity as the basis of social
organization. In the Aymara language, the term *ayllu* denotes either
a family or a territorial association; but the bond created by place
of residence did not eclipse the bond created by blood, because the
Aymara family had two classes of members — the original kin who

formed the ancient *ayllu* and the members by adoption. Thus, in ancient times, perhaps in the Tiahuanaco era, the *ayllu* was already an economic and territorial association.

It must be acknowledged, however, that the Incas were an exception. Their *ayllus* remained pure kinship groups — which is natural, since their territory comprised the entire empire and the maintenance of racial purity was one of their essential preoccupations. But this *ayllu* of the Incas grew and multiplied according to a rule that was peculiar to it. The heir detached himself from his ancestral stock as soon as he took power and founded a new *ayllu*. In other words, every Inca gave his name to an *ayllu* that included all his descendants except his heir, who in turn formed an *ayllu* in his own name. This is the reason why the goods of the deceased sovereign passed to his *ayllu* and not to his reigning successor, who was obliged to have a new palace built and to acquire, by tribute or as gifts, whatever articles he needed. . . .

The division of the people into *ayllus* undoubtedly existed in the cities as well as the rural areas. Each of these groups would establish itself in a particular block of buildings in one of those large square enclosures containing a series of courtyards and dwellings that De Rivero and Tschudi have taken for palaces. In Machu Picchu each *ayllu* occupied from six to ten houses, and every such group of houses was distinguished by some particular characteristic, chiefly in the way the stones were dressed.

The association of a large number of *ayllus* formed a tribe.

Finally, families continued to exist as such within the *ayllu*. The Inca organization, which respected the community, was in no way destructive of the family. . . . As we shall see, children assisted their parents to the exclusion of other members of the group; assessments were always made by households; and the head of a family was the unit in terms of which the statistics were compiled. The family tie was also apparent in the common law, which expressed the customary practices of the land: children orphaned at an early age would be taken in charge by the eldest brother, or, if there was no brother, by the next of kin; and a widow would be entrusted to the care of her son, or, if she had no son, to that of her brother-in-law.

The *ayllu* continued to exist after the Spanish conquest, but as a territorial unit. It was essentially an agrarian community, its characteristic feature being collective land tenure. When an *ayllu* moved

from one place to another, it took with it the name of its original
home. In Coni, for example, there is an *ayllu* called Tiahuanaco.   . . .

It is because of the existence of these agrarian communities that
a great many authors have chosen the term "socialist" to describe
the Inca empire. No doubt the community, as organized and maintained, does appear to be a collectivist association, since it involved
the common ownership of the means of production; but it was the
resultant of a long, natural evolution, the origin of which is lost in
prehistory. It was a spontaneous development, and not a reasoned
creation; a system to which man yielded, not one that he deliberately
willed.

On the other hand, the regime that we are now about to examine
does bear the characteristic stamp of socialism, for it is *an attempt
at the rationalization of society*. Its author is man himself. It is he
who conceived the plan and imposed it, and *this plan tends toward
the virtual absorption of the individual by the state*, for the well-
being of the former is assured only as it leads to the aggrandizement
of the latter.

We have adopted the term "state socialism" to describe this
phenomenon in order to denote an organization of the whole of
society to conform to a certain ideal to be realized by way of
authority. To be sure, the doctrine of state socialism has not been
formulated with much theoretical rigor. As expounded by Rod-
bertus, Lassale, or Wagner, it is loosely defined and appears primarily as a reaction against the Manchester School. But in spite of
its vagueness it is based on the idea of the "regulative action of a
central power in social relations." Never has this action made itself
felt more powerfully than in Peru, where demand was precisely
calculated to meet implacably fixed needs, where supply was determined by a meticulous regimentation of production, and where the
adjustment of supply to demand was assured by a system of statistical tables and reserve stocks.

In Europe the modern state socialists propose to respect the existing order, that is, private property and individual initiative. In Peru
this same regard for established institutions led the Incas to preserve
the agrarian communities, which represented the existing order of
their time. Thus, in the Western Hemisphere, state socialism took
on a much more pronounced form than it has in the countries of
Western Europe, with their long tradition of private property. In

Peru it rested on a foundation of collective ownership, which, to a certain extent, facilitated its establishment, because the effacement of the individual within a limited group prepared him to allow himself to be absorbed by the state. Nevertheless, the Peruvian system cannot be called socialist without some qualification, because the sovereigns not only spared the small enclaves of private property that were already in existence, but themselves contributed, by their gifts and grants, toward the formation of others. It was, rather, as C. Rist says, in speaking of state socialism, "a particular idea of the general interest," the feeling that the state has a function to perform in promoting "civilization and well-being." In fact, it was an extreme form of interventionism, a veritable despotism conceived, not in the interests of the sovereign, but in those of the entire people.

What is really extraordinary is that a rational and strictly planned empire could have been constituted at the beginning of the fifteenth century in a country whose terrain is badly broken up and whose people lived in communities that were shut in upon themselves. The establishment of an empire under such untoward circumstances serves to provide us with some measure of the achievement of its founder, the Inca Yupanqui, called Pachacutec, that is, "the reformer of the world" (from *pacha,* "world," and *cutec,* "modified" or "changed"). The image of this sovereign dominates the whole pre-Columbian history of Peru, and his name is repeated by all the chroniclers. "The Indians had such a reverence and respect for this Inca" writes Garcilaso, "that they have not been able to forget him to this day." . . .

The Inca Pachacutec intervened in the agrarian system, settling the territorial boundaries and making various officials responsible for gathering the Indians together and counting them, for having neglected fields cultivated, for seeing that irrigation canals were dug and terraces constructed, and for drawing maps of the provinces and towns. According to Betanzos, the distribution of land and the building of public granaries took five years, at the end of which time the Inca distributed gifts among those who had most distinguished themselves, and laid down the rules for compulsory labor and military service. A year later, he had the *curacas* summoned to Cuzco, ordered great festivals, and busied himself with the clothing of the Indians — the number, quality, and design of their garments — and with taxes and centers of provisions. Then he instituted the practice of obligatory marriage. The same Spanish writer

recounts how Pachacutec established the class of the *orejones*, reformed the calendar, and had Cuzco rebuilt, and how he engaged
in great military expeditions for the extension of the borders of his
empire. According to Garcilaso, it was this Inca too who commanded
the people to speak Quechua, decreed sumptuary laws, regulated
commerce, reformed the army, founded cities, and raised temples
to the gods. His prodigious activity seems to have touched every
department of life.

The way in which the reconstruction of Cuzco was carried out is
typical of this monarch's mentality. First, he had a plan in relief
made of the city as he envisioned it. Then, he evicted the inhabitants and settled them in the neighboring provinces. Once the work
was completed, he assembled the heads of families in a field near
the capital and assigned each one a dwelling as shown on the plan,
declaring that no other Indian would be permitted to take up residence in Cuzco, since it was to remain a "city of distinction."

The Inca's way of dealing with his whole empire seems not to
have differed from his conduct in setting up his capital. His procedure there too was marked by the elaboration of a rational program, its execution by authoritarian decree, and finally the laying
down of regulations designed to prevent any occasion of disturbance
and to render the organization definite and permanent. Naturally,
this system, so logical in its plan, was bound to encounter obstacles
in adapting itself to realities. We shall see how these obstacles were
surmounted by the progressive assimilation of the peoples newly
subjugated and by the arrest of the processes of natural evolution,
i.e., by an economic crystallization.

The information we have just presented provides a general picture of the superstructure of Indian society, but certain details
need to be added.

In the first place, we are assuming that the portrait of Pachacutec
given us by most of the chroniclers is a faithful likeness. It is possible
that some of their statements may be exaggerated and that several
sovereigns should receive the credit for the measures of which we
have spoken, since a number of different emperors seem to have
borne the name of Pachacutec. But this in no way changes anything
essential to our thesis. If the plan was elaborated little by little and
put into effect gradually, the facts are less spectacular, but the
picture of the organization of the empire remains the same.

In the second place, we have noted that the Incas found an environment favorable to the establishment of socialism, without which they would probably have failed. The limitation of demand, for example, was imposed by the niggardliness of Nature, which restricted the supply. The execution of a master plan was greatly facilitated, on the one hand, by the need for communal labor in barren areas without domestic animals, tools, or slaves, and, on the other, by the persistence within the *ayllu* of an actual community not all of whose members may yet have been invested with individual rights. But this in no way diminishes the originality of the Peruvian system, which consisted in co-ordinating existing elements by working them into a plan on an imperial scale, and it is certainly a distortion of the facts to view these elements, as H. Castro Pozo does, as themselves the motive forces that brought the plan into being. After all, other peoples have found themselves in a situation similar to that of the Quechuas and have adopted very different solutions. Thus, the Chibchas, under conditions quite like those of the Incas, had recourse to a system other than that of the Peruvians and were acquainted with the institution of private property.

Thirdly, it is obvious from what has been said in the two preceding paragraphs that the plan of imperial organization very probably did not spring complete and fully formed from the brain of Pachacutec like Minerva from the head of Jove. In this respect G. Muñoz Puglisevich is right, but why does he then proceed to exaggerate by writing that the Inca system was due to a combination of different factors "like a process independent of the human will"? He adds, nevertheless, his acknowledgment of the influence of eminent individuals or powerful personalities and states that he does not mean to dim the glory that belongs to Pachacutec as the organizer of the empire.

Fourthly, having defined the sense in which we understand the word "socialism," we are at a loss to comprehend the stubborn opposition of certain critics to the use of this term. "It is an obvious error," writes Emilio Romero, "to try to apply the terminology of the modern social sciences to the facts of the ancient past." This mode of reasoning is inadmissible. Should we forego the right to characterize as communistic the city of the future envisioned by Plato, on the ground that Greek society differed from our own? What, then, should we call it? Are we to be forbidden to speak of the controlled economy in Egypt in the period of the Lagides because we are dealing with a time that antedated the Christian era? Sr. Romero believes he is being relativistic, but in fact he is stultifying science by preventing the observer from drawing comparisons between one era and another. The definition of an economic system is and must be independent of historical circumstances. Whether there are machines or not, whether we are concerned with agriculture or with industry, whether men make use of horses or llamas, makes very little difference in this respect.

Finally, an even worse error is committed by a socialist who writes: "Autocracy and communism are incompatible in our era, but they were not so in primitive societies." Socialism — and especially communism, which is the most stringent expression of it — is authoritarian by definition, by reason of its internal structure. Not only are autocracy and communism compatible; they are necessarily connected. Recent German and Russian experience should be enough to enlighten us in this regard. This author states that the Peruvian regime was despotic, and he is right; this is all the more reason for affirming its socialist character.   . . .

In spite of its superficial resemblance to a beehive or an anthill, the Peruvian system did not have the rigidity of a formal, theoretical scheme. Some room was left for *personal interest*. Not only did it continue to manifest itself in the form of family interest in the cultivation of the soil and the manufacture of articles for domestic consumption, but the Inca also endeavored to give it scope by distributing gifts, by publicly bestowing praise or blame, by granting special permits authorizing the favored individuals to possess a chair or to be carried in a litter, and, lastly, in exceptional cases, by allowing ordinary Indians to assume rank among the Incas "by prerogative," to cut their hair in a particular way and have their ears pierced — privileges which Wiener picturesquely calls "decorations."

The monarch manifested no hostility toward private property as such. On the contrary. It is thanks to his gifts that such property entered history, in Peru at least, not as the fruit of spoliation or of conquest, but under the eminently moral form of a reward for merit. Nor did the Inca seek to limit the exchange of goods among the people. Although wealth circulated by way of tribute, allotments, and gifts more than by way of barter, at least the empire was not sealed off from all contact with the rest of the world, for foreigners, whether traders or pilgrims, traveled through it in all directions.

Places were assigned to them in the towns, and special officials were made responsible for looking after their security, getting doctors for them in case they fell ill, and assuring them burial if they died.

As we have already seen, the sovereigns were so far from being intolerant that they respected local custom to the greatest extent. But it should not therefore be inferred, as so many authors have mistakenly done, that they originated nothing and merely confined themselves to the general extension of the systems that had existed before them — though this in itself would be sufficient to earn them a fine title to glory. They themselves actually originated and instituted a plan of production, distribution, and consumption and organized the population into a hierarchy that concentrated all power and all responsibility in the hands of the leaders. In such a system each farmer was acquainted only with his decurion and his centurion, scarcely ever left his own valley, received no education, and had to obey his superiors blindly, under threat of severe punishment. The centurion, in his turn, was familiar with several valleys and had a modicum of learning; and the higher one was in the social scale, the greater was one's power, the broader one's knowledge, the more refined one's sense of duty. Material, intellectual, and moral forces were marvelously co-ordinated.

This social hierarchy rested upon an economic "superorganization." With the aid of the statistical tables, production and consumption seemed bound to remain in equilibrium, and the reserve stocks served to stabilize the whole mechanism.

But this harmony was not quite so perfect as it appeared. In newly conquered regions the plan was not immediately put into effect. Its outlines, left vague for a long while, would become clear and precise as time went on. Consequently, a whole gamut of conditions could be found within the empire, from regions that were completely unified to those where the power of the Inca was demonstrated only by their being constituted as a domain of the state. It is even possible that a small number of tribes, such as the Atacamas, were not actually subjects of the Peruvians, but merely paid tribute to them. It is also possible that on certain distant frontiers a few territories enjoyed actual autonomy under governing *orejones,* who must occasionally have caused the monarch some anxiety. In Ecuador, where the Incas ruled for a generation, the rational plan was applied with less rigor than in Bolivia, which had been under the domination of Cuzco for more than two centuries. The strength of the Inca's legislation lay in its flexibility. The mass of the people were not abruptly made to conform to a socialistic pattern of existence; the process of socialization was a gradual one. The elite, on the other hand, was not individualized; it was in the process of individualization. These two divergent tendencies emphasized, with increasing rigor, the fundamental dualism of Peruvian society. All the limbs had not yet been allowed to atrophy for the sake of the head.

Even in provinces that had been under the rule of the Incas for a long time, their system remained to some degree artificial. It never adapted itself completely to reality, since the consistency of the administrative divisions changed slightly as the population varied. Besides, as the distribution of goods was made without any knowledge of what the recipients already possessed, provisions and raw materials were allotted blindly, in reliance on later exchanges to bring about the necessary rectifications. The plan remained, to a certain extent, theoretical and abstract. It was, in some sort, an ideal to be approached without cessation of effort, but with no hope of its eventual attainment. But could it have been otherwise? A completely rational social system, however perfect in plan, cannot take account of all the manifestations of life, and it would be a waste of time for even the most accomplished thinker to undertake to put it into effect. Every rigid framework will break if one tries to adapt it exactly to a society, even to one that is simplified to excess, and the all-powerful lord of Cuzco himself could not have succeeded in imposing such a Procrustean system on the people of his empire.

7. Despotism or Socialism?

Alfred Métraux

The true character of the Inca Empire is poorly set forth in works dealing with its economic and social structure. Too many historians or sociologists have attempted, in their enthusiasm, to make of it a

"The Inca Empire: Despotism or Socialism?" by Alfred Métraux from *Diogenes* (a journal of the International Council for Philosophy and Humanistic Studies, Paris; published by Mario Casalini, Montreal), No. 35, Fall 1961, pp. 78–98, *passim*. Reprinted by permission.

state corresponding to a modern formula: a socialist, a totalitarian or a welfare state. From the sixteenth century on, how many arbitrary pictures have been drawn, propped up by quotations! In fact among the chronicles and reports and documents which Spain, that rummager of old papers, has handed down to us, and in the accounts of the Indians themselves, one finds enough mixed-up assertions and facts to bolster or justify the most diverse interpretations. Reality has frequently been confused with a schematic, abstract order which was the fruit of frequently gratuitous speculations.

Undoubtedly, the Indians who described their system of government to the Spaniards gave them a somewhat idealized image, exaggerating the geometrical order and rigorous discipline which it implied. The perfection attributed to this administrative machine, in its functioning as much as in its intentions, cannot but fail to arouse suspicion in our minds. The Inca Empire, as it is usually evoked, escapes history. It is a Utopian republic and not a kingdom of this world which collapsed in a few months under the aggression of a band of adventurers. The terms used to define its institutions, constantly creating false associations, only add to the disease. Even contemporary authors often speak of the Empire of the Sun as did their colleagues of the sixteenth and seventeenth centuries who attributed the customs of its inhabitants to legislators as beneficent as they were wise and ingenious.

Professor Baudin, in a celebrated work, *The Socialist Empire of the Incas,* while admitting the traditional character of the rural communities, considers all the other institutions as a form of organization bearing the true trade-mark of socialism, for, as he explains, "it is an attempt at the rationalization of society." For this eminent economist, this organization would seem to respond to a preconceived plan tending "to realize a veritable absorption of the individual into the State, the well-being of the first being assured only in order to redound to the grandeur of the second. . . ." One of the aims of this article is to confront this concept of the Inca Empire with a new interpretation of the facts.   . . .

The myth of the great socialist State of the Incas is based upon a rather summary notion of its institutions. The property system, especially, as well as the duties of the subjects toward the emperor, have been interpreted according to a terminology and spirit only vaguely corresponding to a civilization which was still archaic despite its complexity and subtlety.

Based on Garcilaso, a picture has been drawn of an Inca economic and social system, thus briefly summed up: the monarchs of
ancient Peru, seeking to establish a reign of justice and prosperity
among their people, once a province was conquered, "divided it
into three parts, the first for the Sun, the second for the king and
the third for the natives of the country."

The fields of the Sun were cultivated for the needs of the cult
and their products served to support a numerous clergy. The domain
of the Inca, exploited for the government's profit, were drawn upon
as from a safety vault, when disaster struck some province. Finally,
the third group of arable lands were annually divided into equal
lots, then redivided among the families of each community according
to their members. Each individual's private property was reduced
to possession of a hut, an enclosure, some domestic animals, and
household goods such as clothes and utensils. All the rest belonged
to the State. The inhabitants of the Empire worked for the emperor,
who, in exchange, left the free disposition of the communal lands
to them and equitably redistributed a part of the fruits of their
labor. If the economic structure of the Inca Empire was carried on
in this manner, one would more accurately entitle it State Socialism
grafted upon agrarian collectivism. Did the reality correspond to the
ideal image here evoked?

As a matter of fact, the Incas combined the most absolute kind
of despotism with the greatest tolerance toward the social and
political order of its subject peoples. The emperor's will was primary,
but this will reached the common man via the intermediary of local
chiefs whose authority and privileges were maintained and reinforced. The centralizing tendencies of power harmonized with the
practice of indirect government, a good and bad harmony — if such
an anachronism may be permitted us.

The most original aspects of Inca civilization — the tripartite
division of the land, the convents of the Virgins of the Sun, the State
granaries, the system of statistics transcribed by means of knotted
cords, the network of roads — reflect, in great detail, the conception
of the subject's obligations toward his sovereign, and a most ingenious exploitation of resources — both in manpower and products —
which a brutally imperialist political system had set up for itself
in less than a century.   . . .

The forced labor system which the Incas imposed within their
Empire derives directly from the work-payments out of which they

formerly profited when they were only chiefs of rural communities. The peasants for whom they had been, in bygone times, the *koraka* ("elders") followed them to war, cultivated their fields, and, in turn, took it upon themselves to serve them. Having become masters of a great empire the Incas organized it in such a way as to derive the same advantages from it, but on an incomparably vaster scale.   . . .

The evidence of our sources is unanimous: the Incas avoided crushing their subjects under the weight of too-heavy tributes, and, as a rule, distributed personal services equitably. Despite its implacable discipline their government appears to us paternalistic by comparison with the truly ferocious régime which the Spaniards introduced into Peru. Perhaps we are baptising with the name of wisdom and political sense that which was only respect for norms of behavior and archaic traditions to which the Incas adapted themselves like the smallest community chief. Was not the structure of the imperial *ayllu* identical with that of other Andean *ayllu*, and did not their conceptions of the chief, as well as that of community rights, fit into the general ethic held by peoples of the same stock? What was at the beginning a simple confederation of agrarian communities in a Sierra valley was transformed into a hegemony over immense territories without fundamentally altering the primordial relationships between the ruling and ruled groups. In the mountainous region the relatively fertile earth derived its main value from the manpower available for its exploitation. Masters of an empire, the Incas imposed the obligations of work with much severity and made it a moral duty. Undoubtedly, the only condemnable idleness was that which harmed the state and which constituted for this reason an undisciplined act, almost a rebellion.

To read the numerous works treating of the Incas one would gather the impression that at the time of the Spanish conquest, their civilization had reached a dead point and that their empire had become inert in its rigidity and perfection. If one objectively examines the sources, devoting oneself to the exegesis of Spanish documentation without neglecting the teaching of modern ethnography, one would perceive that the Empire's institutions were in full evolution, and that in this apparently so harmonious system, the Incas had introduced innovations which would sooner or later have modified the structure of their State.

These as yet scarcely indicated tendencies, however, are sufficient to permit us to imagine an epoch in which, after repeated gifts, the nobles and high officials would have ended by carving out vast lordships for themselves. The Inca then would have been able to satisfy the ambition of his aides only by dispossessing a growing number of communities whose members would have changed status from freedom to servitude. Among these people uprooted from their *ayllu* were the specialized artisans, servants or tenants, Virgins of the Sun and the *mitima,* farmers transferred to conquered territories. They formed a new category of men whose status was not determined by blood ties, weakening, in proportion, the traditional communities.

Civic officials to whom land had been granted would have also been able to form a new class whose mentality and mode of life would no longer conform to the ideas of old Andean society. If the Empire's evolution had not been brutally interrupted by the Spanish conquest, would it have transformed itself into a kingdom with a structure similar in many ways with that of the late Roman Empire or the decadent Carolingians? With the multiplication of large domains, would not the ruling class have constituted a powerful aristocracy and would it not have been opposed to the central power? The number of *yana,* domestic servants of the great and tenant farmers on their properties, would certainly have augmented at the expense of free peasants. These, of course, are only conjectures based on limited clues but these do reveal the possibilities of transformation which would have operated in a directly opposed sense to the idea of a "Socialist State of the Sun."

Let us consider the political and economic system described here in terms of the famous definition of Socialism by Bertrand Russell. For him, socialism essentially means common ownership of land and capital under a democratic form of government. It implies production for use and not for profit and distributed, if not equally to all, at any rate according to inequalities justified only in the public interest.

The Inca Empire hardly corresponds to these qualifications. Subjected to the despotism of a caste, its aristocratic tendencies were emphasized as a result of the consecration which the authority of the petty kings and local chiefs had received from the conquerors. Besides, in addition to the traditional privileges enjoyed by the *koraka,* were added those deriving from their status as Inca officials. An increasing distance separated them from their former subjects.

Agrarian collectivism existed only on the level of the rural communities (*ayllu*) and represented an ancient system whose equivalent may be found in the Old as well as the New World. Therefore, it is certainly a peculiar anachronism to apply a term applicable only to industrial societies to the collective property of archaic societies.

Production was only partially influenced according to the needs of the subjects, the entire surplus reverting to a ruling caste and to its administration. Certainly a part of the excess was redistributed under the form of provisions and material allocated to work crews and soldiers or as presents made to noblemen, clergy, and officials. Assistance to the aged and to the sick which one would be tempted to compare with our social security was an obligation of the village and not of the State. This responsibility simply expressed the old group solidarity still present today among primitive farmers of the Amazon and the peasants of modern Peru.

Socialism, as its theoreticians have emphasized, is not limited to State ownership but implies that the latter be put to the service of the collectivity. In the Inca Empire the tribute paid in personal services and wrought objects profited a caste whose riches and power were growing.

The classical tradition, extolled by the Spanish chroniclers, was imposed on modern historians and sociologists, who, vying with each other, compared the Inca Empire to ancient Rome, to modern States, and to Utopian Republics, but hardly ever dreamed of comparing it with States which existed or still exist among people characterized, for good or evil, as "primitive."

There exists more than one analogy between the Inca Empire and the ancient kingdom of Dahomey. The latter was founded after successive conquests made by the sovereigns of Abomey. It was endowed with an internal organization which has often been offered as an example of the administrative genius which a people in a State of archaic civilization are capable of. Like the Incas, the kings of Dahomey respected the autonomy of the agrarian communities and permitted the traditional leaders to remain in power. Just like the Indian caciques, these were integrated into a hierarchy of civic officials who, on the highest echelons, were recruited into the royal family. The ruler of Dahomey also took care to be informed concerning the resources of his State and undertook census-taking of the population, divided into age groups. Taxation and the raising of troops were managed with the greatest rigor. The State was feared and obeyed. The king's envoys, the *recadères*, exercised the same authority as the *tokoyrikoq*, the inspectors of the Inca. The women which the villagers furnished the king were enrolled in a woman's brigade instead of being enclosed in "convents" to serve the nobles and gods according to Peruvian usage. These analogies are pointed out only as examples. They serve to demonstrate that a bureaucratic type of administration might very well develop among a people without a system of writing, whether they be American or African.

The conquistadores accustomed to fight "naked and savage" Indians were dazzled by the manifestations of high civilization among peoples whom they were naturally inclined to treat as irrational barbarians. Nothing astonished them so much as the discipline ruling the Empire. Later, the old order seemed even more just and humane to the degree that the rule introduced by the Spaniards was marked by wretchedness and cruelty. By contrast with the horrors of the conquest and colonization, the Inca despotism was molded in memory into an age of gold. And so it was, to the degree that the Cuzco emperors, respecting millennary customs, managed their subjects, and under the *pax Incaica*, guaranteed their well-being and happiness.

BIBLIOGRAPHIC SUGGESTIONS

1. Baudin, Louis. *Daily Life in Peru under the Last Incas* (New York: Macmillan, 1962). A popular description by a writer who felt that the Inca empire was a unique socio-economic experience in the history of mankind.

2. Bennett, Wendell and Junius B. Bird. *Andean Culture History* (New York: American Museum of Natural History, 1949).

3. Bingham, Hiram. *Lost City of the Incas: The Story of Macchu Picchu and Its Builders* (New York: Atheneum, 1963). For a rapid survey of Inca culture, see pp. 3–33.

4. Brundage, Burr Cartwright. *Empire of the Inca* (Norman: University of Oklahoma Press, 1963).

5. Cobo, Bernabé. *Historia del Nuevo Mundo* (Seville, 1892). A seventeenth-century description of Peru, with much information on Inca civilization, unfortunately not yet available in English.

6. Gibson, Charles. *The Inca Concept of Sovereignty and the Spanish Administration in Peru* (Austin: University of Texas

Institute of Latin American Studies, 1944). Analyzes the transition from Inca to Spanish sovereignty.

7. Kosok, Paul. *Life, Land and Water in Ancient Peru* (Brooklyn: Long Island University Press, 1965). Primarily on the Chimu empire (1250–1490), but interesting for comparative purposes.

8. Lothrop, Samuel K. *Inca Treasure as Depicted by Spanish Historians* (Los Angeles: Frederick Webb Hodge Publication Fund, 1938).

9. Mason, J. Alden. *The Ancient Civilizations of Peru* (London: Penguin Books, 1950).

10. Minnaert, P. "La morale au Pérou," *Bulletin de la Société des Américanistes de Belgique,* no. 16 (1935), pp. 25–48. On the Incas as conquerors and on their morale before and after the Spaniards arrived.

11. Moore, Sally Falk. *Power and Property in Inca Peru* (New York: Columbia University Press, 1958).

12. Rowe, John H. "Inca Culture at the Time of the Spanish Conquest," *Handbook of South American Indians,* Julian Steward, ed., Vol. II (Washington, D.C.: Government Printing Office, 1946), pp. 183–330. The most comprehensive view available in brief compass; based on an extensive bibliography.

13. ———. "The Incas under Spanish Colonial Institutions," *Hispanic American Historical Review,* XXXVII (May, 1957), pp. 155–199.

13a. *Royal Commentaries of the Incas and General History of Peru,* by Garcilaso de la Vega, *El Inca.* Tr. by Harold V. Livermore. 2 vols. (Austin: University of Texas Press, 1966).

14. Strube Erdmann, León. *Vialidad imperial de los Incas* (Córdoba, Argentina: Universidad Nacional de Córdoba, 1963). An important recent study, with good bibliography and maps, on Inca roads. Interesting chapters on inns, bridges, and the postal system.

15. Valcárcel, Luis. *La historia del Perú a través de las fuentes escritas,* 3 vols. (Buenos Aires: Mejía Vaca, 1965).

16. Von Hagen, Victor Wolfgang. *Highways of the Sun* (New York: Duell, Sloan, & Pearce, 1957). Attractively written account, profusely illustrated, based on personal inspection of the Inca road system.

17. Wedin, Åke. *El concepto de lo incaico y las fuentes. Estudio crítico* (Uppsala: Scandinavian University Books, 1966). Studia Historica Gothoburgensia, VII. The most recent review of the literature — works of fiction as well as scientific studies — on the nature of Inca rule, plus a criticism of John H. Rowe's

conclusions on Inca chronology and the application of the decimal system in various fields of Inca administration.

18. Zorita, Alonso de. *Life and Labor in Ancient Mexico*, Benjamin Keen, ed. (New Brunswick: Rutgers University Press, 1963). A useful work for comparative purposes. As Professor Keen explains, this report by a royal official ". . . offers an idealized portrait of life in Mexico before the Conquest, contrasts that pagan age with the miserable state of the Mexican Indian under Spanish rule, and searches for solutions to the insoluble problems of Spanish Indian policy" (p. 18).

Section III

Relations Between Indians and Spaniards

Such a large part of the Spanish history in America involves the relations between the conquering Spaniards and the conquered Indians that this whole volume might 'be devoted to it. So much controversy has swirled around the subject from 1492 until today that selecting representative material is a difficult task.

No great champions of the Indians came to the fore in Brazil comparable to such figures as Bartolomé de Las Casas in Spanish America except the Jesuit António de Vieira, who will be presented in Section V. This fact, combined with the condition of the Indians in Brazil, who were much more primitive than the Aztecs, Mayas, and Incas, resulted in a much less dramatic cultural clash between the Portuguese and the indigenous peoples they encountered during the colonial period in Brazil. We therefore limit this section to the Spanish experience in America, although interesting parallels may be drawn by consulting such works as Dr. Mathias Kiemen's writings.[1]

The struggle for justice for the Indians began in the conquest's earliest years, although the sermons of Antonio de Montesinos marked the first sharp, public confrontation of colonists and friars on how the Indians were to be treated justly, according to Christian

---

[1] Mathias Kiemen, "The Indian Policy of Portugal in America, with Special Reference to the Old State of Maranhão, 1500-1755," *The Americas*, V (1948), pp. 131–171; *The Indian Policy of Portugal in the Amazon Region, 1614–1693* (Washington, D.C.: Catholic University of America Press, 1954).

doctrine (Reading III.1). The struggle for justice occurred because
the crown, ecclesiastics, and even some soldiers wanted the conquest
to be conducted justly, for one of the principal aims of Spain was
to Christianize the Indians. What constituted justice and how it
could be achieved were thorny questions; they were raised frequently during the discovery, colonization, and administration of the
new dominions. One immediate problem the Spanish captains faced
in the New World was how to conduct a just war against the Indians. The Requirement, drawn up in 1512 to be read before hostilities began, was the answer of Dr. Palacios Rubios (Reading III.2).
This document rests upon principles accepted for many years by
the crown, as the Mexican scholar Silvio Zavala explains (Reading
III.3).

The Spaniards were legal-minded and within twenty years after
the landfall of Columbus had worked out the Laws of Burgos for
the treatment of the Indians (Reading III.4). In 1542, they devised
the New Laws, after terrific disputes in Spain (Reading III.5), and
by 1573 they had promulgated the basic law on conquests (Reading
III.6). Each of these laws has a long and complicated history, and
a careful reading of them and some of the controversial interpretations of them reveals much of the spirit and practice peculiar to
Spanish legislation.

The system the Spaniards used for more than a century to regulate Indian labor was the encomienda, a medieval institution adapted
to New World conditions. A representative title by which a Spaniard
received the right to an encomienda indicates the formal rights and
duties of an encomendero (Reading III.7). The way in which encomenderos and other Spaniards actually treated the Indians has
been heatedly debated. In one example the activities of the royal
court (*audiencia*) in New Galicia have been described by Professor
John H. Parry of Harvard University (Reading III.8). Spaniards
have been sensitive since the sixteenth century to attacks upon their
actions in America, particularly to the allegations — often made by
their political enemies — that they mistreated the Indians, whom
they considered as their wards to be protected and Christianized.
One of the most reasoned defenses to be made in Spain was prepared by the eminent seventeenth-century administrator and juris-
consult Juan de Solórzano y Pereira (Reading III.9). The well-
meaning segregation laws, remarks Magnus Mörner of Queens
College, ". . . only served to increase the tension which, in spite of

the mixing of the races, has endured between the red and the white inhabitants" (Reading III.10).

Interpretations of Spanish action have greatly varied. Professor Charles Gibson of the University of Michigan concludes that the Indians were in fact exploited (Reading III.11), whereas "The Dawn of Conscience in America" (Reading III.12) looks at the problem from a somewhat different angle. These and the other approaches included in the Bibliographic Suggestions will be enlightening for students of history.

A. The First Cry for Justice in America

1. The Sermons of Friar Antonio de Montesinos, 1511

On the Sunday before Christmas in 1511 a Dominican friar named Antonio de Montesinos preached a revolutionary sermon in a straw-thatched church on the island of Hispaniola. Speaking on the text "I am a voice crying in the wilderness," Montesinos delivered the first important and deliberate public protest against the kind of treatment being accorded the Indians by his Spanish countrymen. This first cry on behalf of human liberty in the New World was a turning point in the history of America and, as Pedro Henríquez Ureña termed it, one of the great events in the spiritual history of mankind.

The sermon, preached before the "best people" of the first Spanish town established in the New World, was designed to shock and terrify its hearers. Montesinos thundered, according to Las Casas:

> In order to make your sins against the Indians known to you
> I have come up on this pulpit, I who am a voice of Christ cry-
> ing in the wilderness of this island, and therefore it behooves

Lewis Hanke, *The Spanish Struggle for Justice in the Conquest of America* (Boston: Little, Brown and Company (Inc.) 1965), pp. 17–18. Copyright 1949, American Historical Association; Copyright © 1965, Little, Brown and Company (Inc.). Reprinted by permission of Little, Brown and Company and the University of Pennsylvania Press.

you to listen, not with careless attention, but with all your heart and senses, so that you may hear it; for this is going to be the strangest voice that ever you heard, the harshest and hardest and most awful and most dangerous that ever you expected to hear. . . . This voice says that you are in mortal sin, that you live and die in it, for the cruelty and tyranny you use in dealing with these innocent people. Tell me, by what right or justice do you keep these Indians in such a cruel and horrible servitude? On what authority have you waged a detestable war against these people, who dwelt quietly and peacefully on their own land? . . . Why do you keep them so oppressed and weary, not giving them enough to eat nor taking care of them in their illness? For with the excessive work you demand of them they fall ill and die, or rather you kill them with your desire to extract and acquire gold every day. And what care do you take that they should be instructed in religion? . . . Are these not men? Have they not rational souls? Are you not bound to love them as you love yourselves? . . . Be certain that, in such a state as this, you can no more be saved than the Moors or Turks.

Montesinos thereupon strode out of the church with head high, leaving a muttering crowd of colonists and officials behind him, who were astounded, but not one was converted. He had come as near to convincing his hearers of their wrongdoing as would a theological student in our day who delivered a soapbox philippic in Wall Street on the biblical text "Sell that which thou hast and give to the poor, and thou shalt have treasure in heaven."

The colonists gathered at the house of the Governor, Diego Columbus, protested against the sermon as a scandalous denial of the lordship of the king in the Indies, and delegated a group which went indignantly to the monastery to exact an apology and disavowal. The vicar, Pedro de Córdoba, unimpressed by the delegation's threat to expel the offensive friar, assured them that Montesinos had spoken for the Dominican group. He promised, however, that Montesinos would preach the next Sunday on the same topic. The colonists thereupon retired, believing they had won their point.

Word of the expected retreat spread quickly, and the following Sunday most of the leading Spaniards crowded into the church. Montesinos mounted the pulpit and announced the disquieting text "Suffer me a little, and I will show thee that I have yet to speak on God's behalf." Rather than explaining away his previous sermon with dialectic subtleties, he proceeded to belabor the colonists anew, with even more passion than before, warning them that the friars would no more receive them for confession and absolution than if they were so many highway robbers. And they might write home what they pleased, to whom they pleased.

These words were soon heard in Spain, even by the King. On March 20, 1512, Ferdinand ordered Governor Diego Columbus to reason with Montesinos. If the Dominican and his brothers persisted in their error, previously condemned by the canonists, theologians, and learned men gathered to deliberate on the problem ten years before, the Governor was instructed to send them to Spain by the first ship so that their Superior might punish them "because every hour that they remain in the islands holding such wrong ideas they will do much harm."

Three days later on March 23, 1512, the Dominican Superior in Spain, Alonso de Loaysa, reproved Montesinos in an official communication to the Dominican Provincial in Hispaniola and ordered him to prevail upon the friars to stop preaching such scandalous doctrine. The Provincial was warned that no more friars would be sent if such preaching were permitted to continue.

Thus began the first great struggle for justice in the New World.

B. Just War Against the Indians

2. The Requirement, 1512

On the part of the King, don Fernando, and of doña Juana, his daughter, Queen of Castile and Leon, subduers of the barbarous nations, we their servants notify and make known to you, as best we can, that the Lord our God, Living and Eternal, created the Heaven and the Earth, and one man and one woman, of whom you

Lewis Hanke, "The Development of Regulations for Conquistadores," *Contribuciones para el estudio de la historia de América: Homenaje al Dr. Emilio Ravignani* (Buenos Aires: Editores Peuser, Ltda., 1941), pp. 73–75. Reprinted by permission.

and I, and all the men of the world, were and are descendants, and all those who come after us. But, on account of the multitude which has sprung from this man and woman in the five thousand years since the world was created, it was necessary that some men should go one way and some another, and that they should be divided into many kingdoms and provinces, for in one alone they could not be sustained.

Of all these nations God our Lord gave charge to one man, called St. Peter, that he should be Lord and Superior of all the men in the world, that all should obey him, and that he should be head of the whole human race, wherever men should live, and under whatever law, sect, or belief they should be; and he gave him the world for his kingdom and jurisdiction.

And he commanded him to place his seat in Rome, as the spot most fitting to rule the world from; but also he permitted him to have his seat in any other part of the world, and to judge and govern all Christians, Moors, Jews, Gentiles, and all other sects. This man was called Pope, as if to say, Admirable Great Father and Governor of men. The men who lived in that time obeyed that St. Peter, and took him for Lord, King, and Superior of the universe; so also have they regarded the others who after him have been elected to the Pontificate, and so it has been continued even until now, and will continue until the end of the world.

One of these Pontiffs, who succeeded that St. Peter as Lord of the world, in the dignity and seat which I have before mentioned, made donation of these isles and Terra-firme to the aforesaid King and Queen and to their successors, our lords, with all that there are in these territories, as is contained in certain writings which passed upon the subject as aforesaid, which you can see if you wish.

So their Highnesses are kings and lords of these islands and land of Terra-firme by virtue of this donation; and some islands, and indeed almost all those to whom this has been notified, have received and served their Highnesses, as lords and kings, in the way that subjects ought to do, with good will, without any resistance, immediately, without delay, when they were informed of the aforesaid facts. And also they received and obeyed the priests whom their Highnesses sent to preach to them and to teach them our Holy Faith; and all these, of their own free will, without any reward or condition, have become Christians, and are so, and their Highnesses have joyfully and benignantly received them, and also have commanded them to be treated as their subjects and vassals; and you too are held and obliged to do the same. Wherefore as best we can, we ask and require you that you consider what we have said to you, and that you take the time that shall be necessary to understand and deliberate upon it, and that you acknowledge the Church as the Ruler and Superior of the whole world and the high priest called Pope, and in his name the King and Queen doña Juana our lords, in his place, as superiors and lords and kings of these islands and this Terra-firme by virtue of the said donation, and that you consent and give place that these religious fathers should declare and preach to you the aforesaid.

If you do so, you will do well, and that which you are obliged to do to their Highnesses, and we in their name shall receive you in all love and charity, and shall leave you your wives, and your children, and your lands, free without servitude, that you may do with them and with yourselves freely that which you like and think best, and they shall not compel you to turn Christians, unless you yourselves, when informed of the truth, should wish to be converted to our Holy Catholic Faith, as almost all the inhabitants of the rest of the islands have done. And besides this, their Highnesses award you many privileges and exceptions and will grant you many benefits.

But if you do not do this, and wickedly and intentionally delay to do so, I certify to you that, with the help of God, we shall forcibly enter into your country and shall make war against you in all ways and manners that we can, and shall subject you to the yoke and obedience of the Church and of their Highnesses; we shall take you and your wives and your children, and shall make slaves of them, and as such shall sell and dispose of them as their Highnesses may command; and we shall take away your goods, and shall do all the harm and damage that we can, as to vassals who do not obey, and refuse to receive their lord, and resist and contradict him; and we protest that the deaths and losses which shall accrue from this are your fault, and not that of their Highnesses, or ours, nor of these cavaliers who come with us. And that we have said this to you and made this Requirement, we request the notary here present to give us his testimony in writing, and we ask the rest who are present that they should be witnesses of this Requirement.

3. The Doctrine of Just War

SILVIO ZAVALA

During the period when the validity of the proclamation (*requeri-miento*) drawn up by Palacios Rubios was admitted, and even after the first statement of the problem of Spanish claims to the West Indies had been revised, systematic consideration was given to the possibility that relations between the Europeans and the Indians might take the form of war. We should therefore pause to investigate the doctrine of war which then prevailed. In doing so, we shall see that the changes that have subsequently taken place in instruments and techniques of warfare have been accompanied by a corresponding change in the philosophy of war.

In pre-Christian treatises it is easy to find allusions to the valor of rulers, their glory, and their desire for power as incentives favoring belligerent procedure. But Christians are bound by a doctrine of peace in dealing with this problem. For Christians, could war ever be permissible, or would it always be contrary to Christian doctrine because it embodies force? This was one of the great problems of patristic philosophy.

In spite of Christianity, wars continued to be fought and new views were shaped to fit this fact. Christian thinkers did not condemn all war; they merely demanded that it be just and for sufficient and reasonable cause. From the time of St. Augustine these thinkers also asked that the aim of war should be the re-establishment of peace. These basic ideas continued to develop through the medieval period, and by the time we reach the *Summa Theologica* of St. Thomas Aquinas in the thirteenth century we find a mature Christian doctrine on the problem of war.

Scholastic doctrine demands, in the first place, that war be declared by a lawful authority, that is, an authority which is not subject to another sovereign power in temporal affairs; for if the dispute

Silvio Zavala, *New Viewpoints on the Spanish Colonization of America* (Philadelphia: University of Pennsylvania Press, 1943), pp. 38–48. Reprinted by permission of the University of Pennsylvania Press.

is one between subjects, they must refer it to a judge who is above them both, that he may decide the issue. War may be waged legitimately only when a quarrel affects sovereign powers who cannot have recourse to any higher authority to bring about the re-establishment of justice. In the second place, it was held that the war must be for a just cause — that is, it might be waged if the enemy were at fault and in order to right a wrong done by him if peaceful means of reparation were refused. The third and final requirement was the upright intent of the party waging the war. His purpose must be to vindicate the wrongs done him by another and not to plunder or to inflict punishment entirely disproportionate to the extent of the injury suffered.

This theory of a just war prevailed in the universities of Europe at the time of the Conquest of America. If we examine the treatises of Vitoria, for example, we find allusions to all these principles. He maintains that only a grave wrong can justify war. Suárez says that the just cause must be absolute in character according to natural law; that is, that the rights of one of the parties shall have been violated or that the issue be that of defending innocent victims. This mention of the defense of the innocent was of considerable importance in the case of America, for it was claimed that a European power had the right to intervene to save the life of any persons, including children, who were destined for human sacrifice.

Even a glance at the development of ideas on the subject of war since the sixteenth century shows that they have greatly changed. War is no longer, as in medieval theory, a process of vindication based on reasons of justice or a means by which an aggrieved party seeks compensation for an injury done it. Of course, in the Middle Ages acts of war were not always in keeping with the prevailing doctrine. But in the modern period not only has this divorce between fact and theory continued but theory has more and more abandoned ideas of morality and justice. Thus a war is now justified on the ground that the growing power of a nation constitutes a threat, or because of commercial competition between nations, or for some other imperialistic motive. It is not for us here to make a special study of these modern ideas but only to point out that the Spanish Conquest of America is situated historically at the meeting point of medieval and modern docrines, when *just* war — not merely war without qualification — was still spoken of and the facts were interpreted in the light of Scholastic theory.

As we have pointed out from the first, the international problem of the New World was considered in terms of the proper relationship between Christendom and pagan peoples. Hence, among the various types of war this is the one that merits our closest attention.

Let us briefly review the writings of some Spanish authors regarding wars waged by Christians upon infidels.

Palacios Rubios declared that when infidels did not recognize the superiority of the Church or refused to admit Christian preachers to their territories war might justly be waged against them.   . . . He then admitted other causes for war against infidels; for example, if they combatted the faith or harassed the Christians in particular ways, or blasphemed, or committed crimes of *lèse majesté*. For it is just to vanquish the infidel in order to free Christians from danger, not only when the former actually behave in any of the aforementioned ways but when there is a strong presumption that they may do so. By this latter example he referred especially to the continuous war which was fought by the Europeans against the Saracens, and which admitted of no truce. The Saracens were considered perpetual enemies, and in their case the rules of war came to be extremely rigorous. The same author thought that the heathen dwelling in Christian kingdoms may be expelled if it was feared that they might act against the Catholic faith. In this manner the expulsion of the Jews during the reign of the Catholic monarchs was justified. Finally, he admitted that infidels might be despoiled of lands that formerly belonged to Christians; the principal example of this being, of course, the Spanish reconquest against the Moors and the fall of Granada.

Gregorio López, who was a commentator on the laws of Castile and a member of the Council of the Indies, believed an injury to missionaries or merchants to be a primary cause for war. He also held that if infidels placed impediments in the way of peaceful life with their converted brothers, this constituted another legitimate reason for taking up arms. Let us suppose that some of the inhabitants of an Indian kingdom were converted, and that others began hostilities against them for this reason. According to López, there would then exist a just cause for war on the part of the Christians, who would aid the converted Indians against the oppressing infidel group. The author finally fell back upon the argument of human sacrifice which, in his opinion, made it lawful to use force to save innocent victims.

Bartolomé de Las Casas considered war between Christian and infidels justified in three cases. First, if the latter should war upon and thus disturb Christendom, as in the case of the Saracens. Secondly, if they should maliciously persecute, disturb, or hinder the faith, whether by killing its adherents and preachers without legitimate cause, or by attempting to force those who had accepted the faith to renounce it, or by offering inducements to leave the Christian faith and accept their own. All this, according to Las Casas, comes under the head of hindering and persecuting the faith. And if the defense of temporal things is licit, how much more so must be the defense of spiritual things. In the third place, he considered the case of war against heathens in unjust possession of Christian lands or other Christian property. However, the entire philosophy of Las Casas is permeated by an evident pacifism. He declared that wars are a pestilential plague and a terrible calamity to mankind.

Ginés de Sepúlveda, although he belongs not to the group of theologians but rather to the political philosophers of the Italian Renaissance, not only thought that a just cause was necessary before undertaking a war, but also that it should be undertaken by legitimate authority only and with an upright mind, and should be conducted in an honorable manner. That is, he echoed the traditional theory of the Scholastics. But among the just causes of war which he enumerated (such as legitimate defense, the recovery of things unjustly taken away, and the imposition of merited punishment upon evildoers who have not been punished in their own city) he mentioned one cause which he himself conceded was less clear and less frequent, and which in fact formed no part of traditional Scholastic thought regarding war. This was "to subdue by force of arms, if no other means be possible, those who by their natural condition ought to obey others, but who refuse to accept their domination"; in other words, a war in behalf of a hierarchy supposedly justified by rational differences among men. The fact that the European, in the opinion of Sepúlveda, was superior to American heathen in the use of reason was sufficient to justify the forced subjugation of the latter to the domination of the former.

It may be asked whether such an inquiry as this does not lead us into juridical and theological abstractions without real significance and importance for American history. It has always been my opinion that an inquiry of this kind is indispensable to an understanding of the phenomenon of the Conquest. I shall present some reasons to justify this belief.

Let us examine the conduct of a warrior of some education like Hernán Cortés, and let us see whether in his acts we may not perceive the influence of Scholastic thought regarding war which prevailed among the writers of his time and country. In this way, we shall descend from the academic atmosphere to that of the men of action who were charged with establishing dominion over the Indians.

A law of the *Partidas* had declared that war ought to be a means toward peace, in accordance with the doctrine of St. Augustine. Just causes for war, according to the Spanish code, would be to expand the people's faith and to destroy those who wished to vex it; to fight for their lord, to the end of serving, honoring, and faithfully defending him; to protect themselves, and to increase and honor their own homeland.

When Hernán Cortés explained to his soldiers the causes of the war they had undertaken, he told them that for their part they had just motives and reasons:

> One, to fight for the increase of our holy faith and against barbarian people; another, to serve your Majesty; another, to safeguard our own lives; and for another, having many friends among the natives to aid us, this was a highly sufficient reason to lend courage to our hearts.

It is easy to see the resemblance between the text of the Spanish law and the discourse of the conqueror of Mexico. This suggests that a copy of the *Partidas* may have fallen into the hands of the soldiers, who were accustomed since the time of the Cid to know law as well as warfare.

The crusading character in defense of the faith which distinguished the enterprise of Cortés is emphasized in other documents, wherein he wrote to the Emperor that he encouraged his soldiers by telling them to remember that they were vassals of the King and that Spaniards had never been dismayed and were going to win the greatest kingdoms and fiefs then existing in the world, and that, in addition to doing what they were bound to do as Christians, "in fighting against the enemies of our faith," they would thereby gain glory in the next world and win the greatest renown and honor that any generation until that time had won in this world;

that they must remember that they had God on their side and that nothing was impossible to him, as they might see from the victories they had won.

Elsewhere Cortés informed the King of an action favorable to the Spanish arms, saying: "As we carried the banner of the cross and battled for our faith and in the service of your holy Majesty in his very royal venture, God gave us so great a victory that we killed many people, without ourselves receiving any harm."

In his will this conquistador again spoke of having always received great honor and favor from the hand of God, as much in the victories he won against the enemies of the holy Catholic faith as in the pacification and settlement of the Indian kingdoms.

In some battles, the soldiers of the conquering armies claimed to have seen St. James the Apostle mounted on his white horse and fighting against the Indians, as they believed he had so often done in the wars against the Moors in Spain, because both were crusades in defense of the propagation of the faith.

In addition to the requirement of a just cause demanded by doctrine and the laws, one may observe among the conquerors of New Spain recognition of the requirement of honorable intention. In the military ordinances that Hernán Cortés drew up in Tlaxcala when he was making ready to return against Tenochtitlán, he charged his companions that

> their principal motive and intention must be to dislodge and root out idolatry from all the natives of these regions and to bring them, or at least to desire to bring them, to salvation, and that they may be brought to a knowledge of God and of his holy Catholic faith; for if the said war were fought with any other intent, it would be unjust and everything taken in it would be obnoxious, and restitution would have to be made, and his Majesty would have no reason to order those who took part in such war to be rewarded. And I charge the consciences of the said Spaniards regarding it; and I now protest in the name of his Catholic Majesty that my principal intent and motive is to make this war and others that may be waged in order to bring and reduce the said natives to the said knowledge of our faith and belief, and later to subjugate them and bring them under the yoke and imperial and royal sovereignty of your holy Majesty, to whom the overlordship of all these regions belongs.

The requirement of legitimate authority did not worry Cortés, for he intended to carry out all his acts in the name of the King of Spain; and the difficulties which he had with the Governor of Cuba, Diego Velásquez, he endeavored to settle by means of the new power he had received from the municipal council (*cabildo*) established in Vera Cruz.

It seems reasonable to conclude that the legalistic atmosphere surrounding the actions of the conqueror of New Spain is not alien to the traditional principles of the Scholastic philosophy.

The evolution of ideas regarding the Conquest is reflected in the statutes which the Crown prepared as the military occupation of the continent proceeded.

As already explained, the proclamation of Palacios Rubios — the requerimiento — and the principles upon which it was based were accepted by the Spanish Crown as official doctrine for many years, and the conquests of Mexico and of Peru were carried out in accordance with them. Subsequently, however, criticisms of a theoretical nature began to influence the laws of the Conquest. The laws of Barcelona of 1542 restricted the war waged by the Spaniards against the Indians, and peaceful counsels regarding the nature of war predominated in the instructions given by the Crown to the captains.

A more advanced stage of this evolution is illustrated by the ordinances for pacification and settlement issued by Philip II in 1573, which not only recommended that the use of force be avoided in so far as possible but also forbade the use of the word "conquest" in official documents. The word "pacification" was to be substituted for it so that no doubt might exist regarding the intentions of the Spanish state.

Las Casas commented as follows on this change:

> Even the Turks would not dare to speak of conquest and of placing people under the yoke of servitude, as was done by the Council of the Indies through the ignorance and blindness of its members, who were not aware that such words do not become any Christian king, least of all the King of Castile; they likewise ignored the differences between infidels [of the Old World], who oppose us, who are the enemies of our faith, and who have usurped our lands, and the Indians [of the New World], who live peacefully on their own lands and who owe nothing to the Christians or to the monarchs of Castile. These expressions were used for many years in the Coun-

cil of the Indies, while the aforesaid blindness lasted, until the priest Bartolomé de Las Casas, after many years showed to them their error.

Certainly Las Casas contributed to bringing about the change and he did not conceal his satisfaction over it, but other distinguished thinkers cooperated in this important reform.

When, years later, the Laws of the Indies were codified in 1680, it was possible to put an end to the evolutionary cycle by ordering, in Law 9, Title 4, Book III, "That war cannot and shall not be made on the Indians of any province to the end that they may receive the Holy Catholic faith or yield obedience to us, or for any other reason." This represented an attitude opposite to that of the proclamation which was valid during the first years of the American conquest. Violent means were no longer considered legitimate for realizing the religious or political purposes of European colonization. The code (*Recopilación*) of 1680 admitted only a few exceptions with regard to Indians such as the Caribs and the Araucanians, who had distinguished themselves by their violent opposition to the Spaniards and who created permanent war zones in the expansive empire.

The foregoing exposition warrants the conclusion that the Spanish Conquest, in which religious and political motives were intermingled, closed the medieval cycle of crusades. We have already seen that Cortés and his companions believed that they were fighting for the faith. Later, in the modern world, religion ceased to be a fundamental cause for the expansion of nations. But we have also seen that in the Spanish Conquest some political arguments were employed which open the chapter of modern imperialism. Among these were the distinction between superior and inferior beings and the justification of the dominion of civilized peoples over the natives of other lands — a relation which, it was held, might legitimately be established by force if necessary.

Many English, North American, and German authors are beginning now to study the Spanish Conquest as an early form of imperialism and a precursor of the great developments which have taken place in this field in the modern world down to our own day. But, without leaving the field of political doctrine, properly speaking, it must not be forgotten that even the most imperialistic of all the Spanish authors, Sepúlveda, justified the tutelary mission of the

Europeans with the argument that it would elevate the aborigines
to higher levels of human reason. In this way, imperialism was invested in his argument with an intimate sense of the perfectibility
of men in political as well as in religious life. Later imperialisms
have held that the civilizing mission consists rather in the communication of material benefits or have completely forgotten that they
are under an obligation to confer any benefit at all upon subject
peoples, at times even failing to preserve their lives on the ground
that control over natural resources belongs to the strongest.

Spanish authors also went so far as to propound the contempo-
raneously burning international theme of "living room" (*Leben-
sraum*). In the treatise of Sepúlveda regarding war with the Indians,
he asks:

> If a ruler, not through avarice, nor through thirst for empire,
> but through the narrowness of the boundaries of his state or its
> poverty, makes war upon his neighbors in order to take posses-
> sion of their territories as an almost necessary step, will that
> constitute a just war?

The author promptly replies: "That would not be war but robbery."

Vitoria declared in his second "Lecture on the Indians" that
"Neither is the enlargement of empire sufficient cause for making
war." This appeared to him "too clear to need any demonstration."
The same reason might be adduced by any belligerent. Neither, he
held, is personal glorification of the ruler a just cause for war, nor
any other personal advantage to him, for a ruler must order war
as well as peace for the well-being of the nation. He may not employ the public revenues for his personal convenience or glory, and
still less may he expose his subjects to danger. A good king is distinguished from a tyrant by the fact that the tyrant orders his government for the benefit of his own affairs and comfort and the true
king orders it to the common well-being.

These quotations demonstrate the lack of sober judgment in the
generally accepted affirmation that the claim of Spain to the Indies
in the sixteenth century was the right of conquest conceded by the
"ideas of the time." It is undoubtedly a matter clouded by confusion.
The motive of expansion was not a just cause for war according
to Scholastic doctrine. Spanish authors, not excepting Sepúlveda,
did not admit the right of conquest for conquest's sake. On the other
hand, when there was legitimate cause to declare war in accordance

with their ideas, and when it was actually waged, they admitted among its just effects the possible domination of the conquered if the harm which the latter had done to the conqueror was sufficient to warrant such punishment.

C. Fundamental Ordinances

4. The Laws of Burgos, 1512

Doña Juana, etc . . .

Whereas, the King, my Lord and Father, and the Queen, my Mistress and Mother (may she rest in glory!), always desired that the chiefs and Indians of the Island of Española be brought to a knowledge of our Holy Catholic Faith, and,

Whereas, they commanded that certain ordinances be drawn up, which were indeed drawn up, by their Highnesses, as well as, at their command, by the Comendador Bobadilla and the Comendador Mayor de Alcántara, former governors of the said Island, and afterward by Don Diego Columbus, our Admiral, Viceroy, and Governor of it, and by our officers who reside there, and,

Whereas, it has become evident through long experience that nothing has sufficed to bring the said chiefs and Indians to a knowledge of our Faith (necessary for their salvation), since by nature they are inclined to idleness and vice, and have no manner of virtue or doctrine (by which Our Lord is disserved), and that the principal obstacle in the way of correcting their vices and having them profit by and impressing them with the doctrine is that their dwellings are remote from the settlements of the Spaniards who go hence to reside in the said Island, because, although at the time the Indians go to serve them they are indoctrinated in and taught the things of our Faith, after serving they return to their dwellings where, be-

Lesley Byrd Simpson, ed. and trans., *The Laws of Burgos* (San Francisco: John Howell-Books, 1960), pp. 11–39, *passim*. Reprinted by permission of John Howell-Books.

cause of the distance and their own evil inclinations, they immediately forget what they have been taught and go back to their customary idleness and vice, and when they come to serve again they are as new in the doctrine as they were at the beginning, because, although the Spaniard who accompanies them to their village, as is there ordered, reminds them of it and reprehends them, they, having no fear of him, do not profit by it and tell him to leave them in idleness, since that is their reason for returning to their said village, and that their only purpose and desire is to do with themselves what they will, without regard for any virtue, and,

Whereas, this is contrary to our Faith, and,

Whereas, it is our duty to seek a remedy for it in every way possible, it was considered by the King, my Lord and Father, and by several members of my Council and by persons of good life, letters, and conscience, and they, having informed themselves from others who had much knowledge and experience of the affairs of the said Island, and of the life and customs of the said Indians, gave it as their opinion that the most beneficial thing that could be done at present would be to remove the said chiefs and Indians to the vicinity of the village and communities of the Spaniards — this for many considerations — and thus, by continual association with them, as well as by attendance at church on feast days to hear Mass and the divine offices, and by observing the conduct of the Spaniards, as well as the preparation and care that the Spaniards will display in demonstrating and teaching them, while they are together, the things of our Holy Catholic Faith, it is clear that they will the sooner learn them and, having learned them, will not forget them as they do now. And if some Indian should fall sick he will be quickly succored and treated, and thus the lives of many, with the help of Our Lord, will be saved who now die because no one knows they are sick; and all will be spared the hardship of coming and going, which will be a great relief to them, because their dwellings are now so remote from the Spanish communities, so that those who now die from sickness and hunger on the journey, and who do not receive the sacraments which as Christians they are obligated to receive, will not die [unshriven], because they will be given the sacraments in the said communities as soon as they fall sick; and infants will be baptized at birth; and all will serve with less hardship to themselves and with greater profit to the Spaniards, because they will be with them more continually; and the visitors who have

them in charge will visit them better and more frequently and will
have them provided with everything they need, and will not permit
their wives and daughters to be taken from them, as now happens
while they live at a distance; and many other evils and hardships
will cease which the Indians now suffer because they are so remote,
and which are not described here because they are notorious; and
many other advantages will accrue to them for the salvation of their
souls, as well as for the profit and utility of their persons and the
conservation of their lives; and so,

Therefore, for these reasons and for many others that could be
adduced, it was agreed that for the improvement and remedy of
all the aforesaid, the said chiefs and Indians should forthwith be
brought to dwell near the villages and communities of the Spaniards
who inhabit that Island, so that they may be treated and taught
and looked after as is right and as we have always desired; and so
I command that henceforth that which is contained below be obeyed
and observed, as follows:

I — First, since it is our determination to remove the said Indians
and have them dwell near the Spaniards, we order and command
that the persons to whom the said Indians are given, or shall be
given, in encomienda, shall at once and forthwith build, for every
fifty Indians, four lodges [*bohíos*] of thirty by fifteen feet, and have
the Indians plant 5,000 hillocks (3,000 in cassava and 2,000 in yams),
250 pepper plants, and 5 cotton plants, and so on in like manner,
increasing or decreasing the amount according to the number of
Indians they have in encomienda, and these shall be settled next the
estates of the Spaniards who have them in encomienda, well situated
and housed, and under the eyes of you, our said Admiral and judges
and officers, and of our visitor who will be in charge of it, or of the
person whom you, our said Admiral and judges and officers, shall
send for the aforesaid purpose, and he, I charge and command you,
shall be such as will be competent in this matter; and the persons
who have the said Indians in their charge [in encomienda] shall
have them sow, in season, half a *fanega* of maize, and shall also give
them a dozen hens and a cock to raise and enjoy the fruit thereof,
the chickens as well as the eggs; and as soon as the Indians are
brought to the estates they shall be given all the aforesaid as their
own property; and the person whom you send for this purpose
shall tell them it is for their own use and that it is given them in

exchange for what they are leaving behind, to enjoy as their own property. And we command that the persons to whom they are given in encomienda shall keep it for them so that they may enjoy it as their own; and we command that this property shall not be sold or taken from them by any person to whom they may be given in encomienda, or by anyone else, but that it shall belong to the said Indians to whom it is assigned and to their descendants, even though this said person sell the estate in which they are, or the said Indians be removed from him; and we declare and command that the person to whom the said Indians are given in encomienda may utilize the goods that the said Indians abandon when they are brought to the estates of the Spaniards, each according to the number of Indians he has, in order to maintain them with such goods; and after the said persons have removed the said goods I command you, our said Admiral and judges and officers, to have the lodges of the said villages burned, since the Indians will have no further use for them: this so that they will have no reason to return whence they have been brought.

II — After the aforesaid has been done, we order and command that all the chiefs and Indians dwelling on the Island of Española, now or in the future, shall be brought from their present dwelling places to the villages and communities of the Spaniards who reside, now or in the future, on the said Island; and in order that they be brought of their own volition and suffer no harm from the removal, we hereby command Don Diego Columbus, our Admiral, Viceroy, and Governor of the said Island, and our appellate judges and officers of it, to have them brought in the manner that seems best, with the least possible harm to the said chiefs and Indians, to this end encouraging them and urging them with praise; and we charge and command them most earnestly to do this with much care, fidelity, and diligence, with greater regard for the good treatment and conservation of the said Indians than for any other respect, desire, or interest, particular or general.

III — Also, we order and command that the citizen to whom the said Indians are given in encomienda shall, upon the land that is assigned to him, be obliged to erect a structure to be used for a church, on a site selected by you, the said Admiral, judges, and officers, or by the visitor appointed by you; and in this said church he shall place an image of Our Lady and a bell with which to call the Indians to prayer; and the person who has them in encomienda shall be obliged to have them called by the bell at nightfall and go with them to the said church, and have them cross themselves and bless themselves, and together recite the *Ave Maria,* the *Pater Noster,* the *Credo,* and the *Salve Regina,* in such wise that all of them shall hear the said person, and the said person hear them, so that he may know who is performing well and who ill, and correct the one who is wrong; and since the period we command to be allowed them for rest before nightfall is principally for the purpose of having them rested at the hour of evening prayer, in case any Indian should fail to come to the said church at the said time, we command that on the day following he shall not be allowed to rest during the said period; but he shall still be urged to go to prayers the next night; and we also command that each morning, before they go to work, they shall be obliged to go to the said church and pray as they do in the evening; but they shall not be obliged on that account to rise earlier than is customary, that is, at full daylight.   . . .

IX — Also, we order and command that whoever has fifty Indians or more in encomienda shall be obliged to have a boy (the one he considers most able) taught to read and write, and the things of our Faith, so that he may later teach the said Indians, because the Indians will more readily accept what he says than what the Spaniards and settlers tell them; and if the said person has a hundred Indians or more he shall have two boys taught as prescribed; and if the person who has Indians does not have them taught as ordered, we command that the visitor who in our name has charge shall have them taught at the cost of such person. And because the King, my Lord and Father, and I have been informed that several persons are employing Indians boys as pages, we order and command that the person who does so shall be obliged to teach them to read and write, and all the other things that have been prescribed above; and if he fails to do so the boys shall be taken from him and given to another, because the principal aim and desire of the said King, my Lord and Father, and mine, is that in the said parts and in each one of them our Holy Catholic Faith shall be planted and deeply rooted, so that the souls of the said Indians may be saved.

X — Also, we order and command that each and every time an Indian falls sick in a place where there is a priest, the priest shall be obliged to go to him and recite the *Credo* and other profitable things of our Holy Catholic Faith, and, if the Indian should know how to confess, he shall confess him, without charging him any fee for it; and, because there are some Indians who already understand the things of our Holy Faith, we command that the said priests shall be obliged to have them confess once a year, and also that they shall go with a Cross to the Indians who die and shall bury them, without charging any fee for it or for the confession; and if the said Indians die on the estates we command that the Christian settlers there shall bury them in the churches of the said estates; and if they die in other places where there are no churches they shall be buried where it seems best, on pain that he who has Indians in his charge and fails to bury them or have them buried, shall pay four gold pesos, which shall be applied and distributed in the following manner: one for our treasury, one for his accuser, one for the judge who sentences him, and one for the priest at the estate or village where the said Indians are buried. . . .

XIII — Also, we order and command that, after the Indians have been brought to the estates, all the founding [of gold] that henceforth is done on the said Island shall be done in the manner prescribed below: that is, the said persons who have Indians in encomienda shall extract gold with them for five months in the year, and, at the end of these five months, the said Indians shall rest forty days, and the day they cease their labor of extracting gold shall be noted on a certificate, which shall be given to the miners who go to the mines; and upon the day thus designated all the Indians shall be released in the district where the founding is to be done, so that all the Indians of each district shall go to their houses on the same day to rest during the said forty days; and in all the said forty days no one shall employ any Indians in extracting gold, unless it is a slave, on pain that for every Indian that any person brings to the mines in the said period of forty days shall pay half a gold peso, applied in the aforesaid manner; and we command that in the said forty days you, the said officers, shall be obliged to finish the founding. And we command that the Indians who thus leave the mines shall not, during the said forty days, be ordered to do anything whatever, save to plant the hillocks necessary for their subsistence

that season; and the persons who have the said Indians in encomienda shall be obliged, during these forty days of rest, to indoc-
trinate them in the things of our Faith more than on other days,
because they will have the opportunity and means to do so. . . .

XVI — Also, we order and command that, among the other
things of our Faith that shall be taught to the Indians, they shall
be made to understand that they may not have more than one
wife at a time, nor 'may they abandon her; and if the persons who
have them in encomienda see that they have sufficient discretion
and knowledge to undertake matrimony and govern their households, they shall procure their lawful marriage, as our Holy Mother
Church commands, with the wife of their choice; and we especially
command that the chiefs be made to understand that they may not
take wives related to them, and we command that the visitors shall
be responsible for their understanding this, repeating it to them very
frequently and telling them, or having them told, all the reasons for
their so doing, and how by this action they will save their
souls. . . .

XIX — Also, we order and command that all those on the said
Island who have Indians in encomienda, now or in the future, shall
be obliged to give to each of them a hammock in which to sleep
continually; and they shall not allow them to sleep on the ground,
as hitherto they have been doing; and they shall give them this
hammock within the twelve months immediately following their
receiving the said Indians in encomienda. And we command our
visitors carefully to observe whether each Indian has the said hammock, and to urge the said persons who have them in encomienda,
if they have not already supplied hammocks, to do so within the
said following twelve months [on pain that the person who fails
to obey the aforesaid shall incur the penalty of . . . pesos], and
this penalty we command you, our said Admiral and judges, to
execute on the person who incurs it. And since it is said that when
anything is given to an Indian he immediately wishes to exchange
it for something else, we command that the said Indians be admonished by the visitors that they are not to exchange the said
hammocks for other things, and if they do exchange them, we command the said visitors to punish the Indians who do so and to void
the exchanges they have made.

XX — Also, we order and command that, in order that henceforth the Indians may have wherewith the better to clothe and adorn themselves, the person who has them in encomienda shall give to each of them a gold peso every year, which he shall be obliged to give them in wearing apparel, in the sight of and with the consent of our visitor, and this gold peso shall be understood to be in addition to the said hammock that we commanded above to be given to each of them. And since it is just that the said chiefs and their wives should be better dressed and better treated than the other Indians, we command that one *real* be deducted from the gold peso to be paid to the latter, and that with this said *real* the said visitor shall have clothing purchased for the said chiefs and their wives; and we command you, our said Admiral, judges, and officers, to have special care to see that this article is observed, obeyed, and fulfilled.   ...

XXIV — Also, we order and command that no person or persons shall dare to beat any Indian with sticks, or whip him, or call him dog, or address him by any name other than his proper name alone; and if an Indian should deserve to be punished for something he has done, the said person having him in charge shall bring him to the visitor for punishment, on pain that the person who violates this article shall pay, for every time he beats or whips an Indian or Indians, five pesos gold; and if he should call an Indian dog, or address him by any name other than his own, he shall pay one gold peso, to be distributed in the manner stated.

XXIX — Also, we order and command that in each community of the said Island there shall be two visitors in charge of inspecting the whole community, together with its mines and estates, its shepherds and swineherds, and they shall ascertain how the Indians are being taught in the things of our Faith, and how their persons are being treated, and how they are being maintained, and how they or the persons who have them in charge are obeying and fulfilling these our ordinances, and all the other things that each of them is obliged to do; and we command them to have particular care in all this, and we charge their consciences with it.   ...

XXXIV — Also, we order and command that you, the said Admiral, judges, and officers, shall inquire once every two years into the way in which the said visitors are fulfilling their duties, and you shall have their *residencias* taken, in which it shall be ascertained how they have enforced these ordinances, each according to his obligation. And we command that the said visitors shall be obliged, at the time of their residencias, to give you, the said Admiral, judges, and officers, a very complete accounting of all the Indians and their number, each reporting for the place in his charge, and how many have been born and how many have died in those two years, so that the said Admiral, judges, and officers may send us an accounting of it all, which shall be signed by you and the visitors, to the end that I may be well informed of everything.

XXXV — Also, we order and command that no inhabitant or resident of the said communities of the said Island of Española, or of any other island, shall have in encomienda, by grant or otherwise, more than a hundred and fifty Indians, or fewer than forty.

Therefore, I command you, our said Admiral, judges, and officers, and each and every one of you, present and future, and all other persons whatsoever to whom the contents of these ordinances may apply, to consider the ordinances incorporated above and those others mentioned, and to observe and obey them, and to have them observed and obeyed and executed completely, each according to its contents; and you shall execute and cause to be executed the penalties upon such as incur them; also, you shall observe and obey the said ordinances yourselves, according to the manner and form prescribed therein, under the penalties stated. Moreover, in case of disobedience, you shall incur the loss of the Indians you have in encomienda, and they shall be considered vacated, so that we may assign them to whomsoever we please; and you shall not act counter to their tenor and form, nor shall you permit them to be violated at any time or in any way. And if, in order to fulfill and execute the aforesaid, you should have need of favor and aid, I hereby command all town councils, justices, regidores, knights, squires, officers, and citizens of the said Island of Española to render you such favor and aid as you shall demand of them, under whatever penalties that you in our name shall impose, which by these presents I impose and consider imposed; and I hereby give you authority to execute them upon all those who fail to obey you.

Also, so that this my letter may be brought to the attention of all, and that none may plead ignorance of it, I command that it be read in the squares and markets and other customary places of the said Island of Española by the public crier, in the presence of a notary and witnesses, none of whom shall disobey it in any way, on pain of my displeasure and 50,000 *maravedís* for my treasury, to be levied against each offender. Moreover, I command him who shows them this my letter to cite them to appear before me at my court, wherever I may be, within one hundred days of the time they are cited, under the said penalty; and, also under the same penalty, I command any notary who should be called upon to do so, to give testimony thereof signed with his rubric, so that I may know how my command is being observed.

Done in this City of Burgos, December 27, 1512.

I, the King.

I, Lope Conchillos, Secretary to the Queen our Mistress.

The Bishop of Palencia — Count [of Pernia].

5. The New Laws, 1542

Charles by the divine clemency Emperor ever august, King of Germany, Doña Joanna his mother and the same Charles by the grace of God Sovereigns of Castile, of Leon, of Aragon, of the two Sicilies, of Jerusalem, of Navarre, of Granada, of Toledo, of Valencia, of Galicia, of the Mallorcas, of Seville, of Cerdena, of Cordova, of Corsica, of Murcia, of Jaen, of the Algarves, of Algezira, of Gibraltar, of the Canary Islands, of the Indies, Islands and Terrafirme of the Ocean Sea; Counts of Barcelona, Lords of Biscay and of Molina, Dukes of Athens and of Neopatria, Counts of Ruysellon and of Cerdania, Marquises of Oristan and of Gociano, Archdukes of Austria, Dukes of Burgundy and of Brabant, Counts of Flanders and of Tyrol, etc. To the Most Illustrious Prince Don Philip our very dear and very beloved grandson and son, and to the Infantes our grandsons and sons, and to the President, and those of our Council of the Indies, and to our Viceroys, Presidents and Auditors

Henry Stevens, ed., *The New Laws of the Indies* (London: The Chiswick Press, 1893), pp. iii–xvii, *passim.*

of our Audiencias and royal Chanceries of our said Indies, Islands and Continent of the Ocean Sea; to our Governors, Alcaldes mayores and our other Authorities thereof, and to all the Councils, magistrates, regidores, knights, esquires, officers, and commoners of all the cities, towns, and villages of our said Indies, Islands, and Tierrafirme of the Ocean Sea, discovered and to be discovered; and to any other persons, captains, discoverers, settlers, and inhabitants dwelling in and being natives thereof, of whatever state, quality, condition and pre-eminence they may be, as well to those who now are as to those who shall be from hence forward, and to every one and any of you, in your places and jurisdictions, to whom this our Letter or its copy signed by a public notary shall be shown, or who may otherwise know of its contents, and to whom any thing or part of it may touch and relate, and can pertain in any manner, Health and grace; Know ye, That having for many years had will and intention as leisure to occupy ourselves with the affairs of the Indies, on account of their great importance, as well in that touching the service of God our Lord and increase of his holy Catholic faith, as in the preservation of the natives of those parts, and the good government and preservation of their persons; and although we have endeavoured to disengage ourselves to this effect, it has not been possible through the many and continual affairs that have occurred from which we were not able to excuse ourselves, and through the absences from these kingdoms which I the King have made for most necessary causes, as is known to all: and although this incessant occupation has not ceased this present year, nevertheless we commanded persons to assemble of all ranks, both prelates and knights and the clergy with some of our Council to discuss and treat of the things of most importance, of which we had information that they ought to be provided for: the which having been maturely debated and consulted upon, and in presence of me the King divers times argued and discussed: and finally having taken the opinion of all, we resolved on commanding to enact and ordain the things contained below: which besides the other Ordinances and Provisions that at different times we have commanded to be made, as by them shall appear, we command to be from henceforwards kept inviolably as laws. . . .

Whereas one of the most important things in which the Audiencias are to serve us is in taking very especial care of the good treatment of the Indians and preservation of them, We command that the said

Audiencias enquire continually into the excesses or ill treatment which are or shall be done to them by governors or private persons; and how the ordinances and instructions which have been given to them, and are made for the good treatment of the said Indians have been observed. And if there had been any excesses, on the part of the said Governors, or should any be committed hereafter, to take care that such excesses are properly corrected, chastizing the guilty parties with all rigour conformably to justice. The Audiencias must not allow that in the suits between Indians, or with them, there be ordinary proceedings at law, nor dilatory expedients, as is wont to happen through the malice of some advocates and solicitors, but that they be determined summarily, observing their usages and customs, unless they be manifestly unjust; and that the said Audiencias take care that this be so observed by the other, inferior judges.

Item, We ordain and command that from henceforward for no cause of war nor any other whatsoever, though it be under title of rebellion, nor by ransom nor in other manner can an Indian be made a slave, and we will that they be treated as our vassals of the Crown of Castile since such they are.

No person can make use of the Indians by way of Naboria or Tapia or in any other manner against their will.

As We have ordered provision to be made that from henceforward the Indians in no way be made slaves, including those who until now have been enslaved against all reason and right and contrary to the provisions and instructions thereupon, We ordain and command that the Audiencias having first summoned the parties to their presence, without any further judicial form, but in a summary way, so that the truth may be ascertained, speedily set the said Indians at liberty unless the persons who hold them for slaves show title why they should hold and possess them legitimately. And in order that in default of persons to solicit the aforesaid, the Indians may not remain in slavery unjustly, We command that the Audiencias appoint persons who may pursue this cause for the Indians and be paid out of the Exchequer fines, provided they be men of trust and diligence.

Also, We command that with regard to the lading of the said Indians the Audiencias take especial care that they be not laden, or in case that in some parts this cannot be avoided that it be in such a manner that no risk of life, health and preservation of the said Indians may ensue from an immoderate burthen; and that against their own will and without their being paid, in no case be it permitted that they be laden, punishing very severely him who shall act contrary to this. In this there is to be no remission out of respect to any person.

Because report has been made to us that owing to the pearl fisheries not having been conducted in a proper manner deaths of many Indians and Negroes have ensued, We command that no free Indian be taken to the said fishery under pain of death, and that the bishop and the judge who shall be at Veneçuela direct what shall seem to them most fit for the preservation of the slaves working in the said fishery, both Indians and Negroes, and that the deaths may cease. If, however, it should appear to them that the risk of death cannot be avoided by the said Indians and Negroes, let the fishery of the said pearls cease, since we value much more highly (as is right) the preservation of their lives than the gain which may come to us from the pearls.

Whereas in consequence of the allotments of Indians made to the Viceroys, Governors, and their lieutenants, to our officials, and prelates, monasteries, hospitals, houses of religion and mints, offices of our Hazienda and treasury thereof, and other persons favoured by reason of their offices, disorders have occurred in the treatment of the said Indians, it is our will, and we command that forthwith there be placed under our Royal Crown all the Indians whom they hold and possess by any title and cause whatever, whoever the said parties are, or may be, whether Viceroys, Governors, or their lieutenants, or any of our officers, as well of Justice as of our Hazienda, prelates, houses of religion, or of our Hazienda, hospitals, confraternities, or other similar institutions, although the Indians may not have been allotted to them by reason of the said offices; and although such functionaries or governors may say that they wish to resign the offices or governments and keep the Indians, let this not avail them nor be an excuse for them not to fulfill what we command.

Moreover, We command that from all those persons who hold Indians without proper title, having entered into possession of them by their own authority, such Indians be taken away and be placed under our Royal Crown.

And because we are informed that other persons, although possessing a sufficient title, have had an excessive number of Indians allotted to them, We order that the Audiencias, each in its jurisdiction diligently inform themselves of this, and with all speed, and reduce the allotments made to the said persons to a fair and moderate quantity, and then place the rest under our Royal Crown notwithstanding any appeal or application which may be interposed by such persons: and send us a report with all speed of what the said Audiencias have thus done, that we may know how our command is fulfilled. And in New Spain let it be especially provided as to the Indians held by Joan Infante, Diego de Ordas, the Maestro Roa, Francisco Vasquez de Coronado, Francisco Maldonado, Bernardino Vazquez de Tapia, Joan Xaramillo, Martin Vazquez, Gil Gonçales de Venavides, and many other persons who are said to hold Indians in very excessive quantity, according to the report made to us. And, whereas we are informed that there are some persons in the said New Spain who are of the original Conquistadores and have no repartimiento of Indians, We ordain that the President and Auditors of the said New Spain do inform themselves if there be any persons of this kind, and if any, to give them out of the tribute which the Indians thus taken away have to pay, what to them may seem fit for the moderate support and honourable maintenance of the said original Conquistadores who had no Indians allotted to them.

So also, The said Audiencias are to inform themselves how the Indians have been treated by the persons who have held them in encomienda, and if it be clear that in justice they ought to be deprived of the said Indians for their excesses and the ill-usage to which they have subjected them, We ordain that they take away and place such Indians under our Royal Crown. And in Peru, besides the aforesaid, let the Viceroy and Audiencia inform themselves of the excesses committed during the occurrences between Governors Pizarro and Almagro in order to report to us thereon, and from the principal persons whom they find notoriously blameable in those feuds they then take away the Indians they have, and place them under our Royal Crown.

Moreover, We ordain and command that from henceforward no Viceroy, Governor, Audiencia, discoverer, or any other person have power to allot Indians in encomienda by new provision, or by means of resignation, donation, sale, or any other form or manner, neither by vacancy nor inheritance, but that the person dying who held the said Indians, they revert to our Royal Crown. And let the Audiencias take care to inform themselves then particularly of the person who died, of his quality, his merits and services, of how he treated the said Indians whom he held, if he left wife and children or what other heirs, and send us a report thereof with the condition of the Indians and of the land, in order that we may give directions to provide what may be best for our service, and may do such favour as may seem suitable to the wife and children of the defunct. If in the meantime it should appear to the Audiencia that there is a necessity to provide some support for such wife and children, they can do it out of the tribute which the said Indians will have to pay, or allowing them a moderate pension, if the said Indians are under our Crown, as aforesaid.

Item, We ordain and command that our said Presidents and Auditors take great care that the Indians who in any of the ways above mentioned are taken away, and those who may become vacant be very well treated and instructed in the matters of our holy Catholic faith, and as our free vassals. This is to be their chief care, that on which we principally desire them to report, and in which they can best serve us. They are also to provide that they be governed with justice in the way and manner that the Indians who are under our Royal Crown are at present governed in New Spain. . . .

6. Royal Ordinances on "Pacification," 1573

. . . Discoveries are not to be called conquests. Since we wish them to be carried out peacefully and charitably, we do not want the use of the term "conquest" to offer any excuse for the employment of force or the causing of injury to the Indians. . . .

After a town has been laid out and its buildings constructed, but not before, the government and settlers are to attempt peacefully to win all the natives of the region over to the Holy Church and obedience to our rule. In this they are to show great diligence and holy zeal and to use the best means at their disposal, including the following:

They are to gather information about the various tribes, languages, and divisions of the Indians in the province and about the lords whom they obey. They are to seek friendship with them

"Ordenanzas de Su Magestad para los nuevos descubrimientos, conquistas y pacificaciones. — Julio de 1573," *Colección de documentos inéditos relativos al descubrimiento, conquista y organización de las antiguas posesiones españolas de América y Oceanía, sacados de los archivos del reino y muy especialmente del de Indias* (Madrid, 1864–1884), XVI, pp. 142–187, *passim*.

through trade and barter, showing them great love and tenderness and giving them objects to which they will take a liking. Without displaying any greed for the possessions of the Indians, they are to establish friendship and cooperation with the lords and nobles who seem most likely to be of assistance in the pacification of the land.

Once peace and amity with the Indians have been assured, the Spaniards will try to bring them together in one spot. Then the preachers, with as much solemnity as possible, will start to teach our Holy Faith to those who wish to be instructed in it, using prudence and discretion and the gentlest methods possible. Accordingly, they are not to begin by rebuking the Indians for their vices and idolatry, nor by taking away their women and idols, so that they will not be shocked and form an aversion to Christian doctrine. Instead, it should be taught to them first, and after they have been instructed in it, they should be persuaded to give up of their own free will those things that are contrary to our Holy Catholic Faith and evangelical doctrine.

The Indians should be brought to an understanding of the position and authority which God has given us and of our zeal in serving Him by bringing to His Holy Catholic Faith all the natives of the Western Indies. They should also learn of the fleets and armies that we have sent and still send for this purpose, as well as of the many provinces and nations that have rendered us obedience and of the many benefits which they have received and are receiving as a result, especially that we have sent ecclesiastics who have taught them the Christian doctrine and faith by which they could be saved. Moreover, we have established justice in such a way that no one may aggravate another. We have maintained the peace so that there are no killings, or sacrifices, as was the custom in some parts. We have made it possible for the Indians to go safely by all roads and to peacefully carry on their civil pursuits. We have taught them good habits and the custom of wearing clothes and shoes. We have freed them from burdens and servitude; we have made known to them the use of bread, wine, oil, and many other foods, woollen cloth, silk, linen, horses, cows, tools, arms, and many other things from Spain; we have instructed them in crafts by which they live excellently. All these advantages will those Indians enjoy who embrace our Holy Faith and render obedience to us.

Even if the Indians are willing to receive the faith and the preachers in peace, the latter are to approach their villages with prudence and with precautions for their own safety. In this manner if the Indians should prove unruly, they will not be inclined to show disrespect to the preachers; otherwise, the guilty persons would have to be punished, causing great damage to the work of pacification and conversion. Although the preachers should keep this in mind when they visit the Indian settlements, it should be concealed from the natives so that they will not feel any anxiety. Difficulties may be avoided if the children of the caciques and nobles are brought to the Spanish settlements and are kept there as hostages under the pretext of entertaining them and teaching them to wear clothes. By means such as these is conversion to be undertaken in all the Indian communities which wish to receive the preachers in peace.

In areas where the Indians refuse to accept Christian doctrine peacefully, the following procedure may be used. An arrangement should be made with the principal lord who is a proponent of peace so that he will invite the belligerent Indians to his territory on one pretext or another. On this occasion the preachers, together with some Spaniards and friendly Indians, should be hidden nearby. At the opportune moment they should disclose themselves and begin teaching the faith with the aid of interpreters. In order that the Indians may hear the faith with greater awe and reverence, the preachers should carry the Cross in their hands and should be wearing at least albs or stoles; the Christians are also to be told to listen to the preaching with great respect and veneration, so that by their example the non-believers will be induced to accept instruction. If it seems advisable, the preachers may attract the attention of the non-believers by using music and singers, thereby encouraging them to join in. If the Indians seem inclined to be peaceful and request the preachers to go to their territory, the latter should do so, taking the precautions previously described. They should ask for their children under the pretext of teaching them and keep them as hostages; they should also persuade them to build churches where they can teach so that they may be safer. By these and other means are the Indians to be pacified and indoctrinated, but in no way are they to be harmed, for all we seek is their welfare and their conversion.

Once the region has been pacified and the Indian lords and subjects have tendered us their fealty, the Governor, with their consent, is to distribute the land among the settlers who are to take charge of the natives in their parcels, defending and protecting them and providing them with clerics to teach them Christian doctrine and administer the sacraments. They should also teach them to live in an orderly fashion and fulfill all the obligations of encomenderos as set forth in the clauses dealing with this subject.

The Indians who offer us obedience and are distributed among Spaniards are to be persuaded to acknowledge our sovereignty over the Indies. They are to give us tributes of local produce in moderate amounts, which are to be turned over to their Spanish encomenderos so that the latter may fulfill their obligations, reserving to us the tributes of the principal villages and the seaports, as well as an amount adequate to pay the salaries of our officials. If it appears that the pacification of the natives will be accomplished more easily by temporarily exempting them from tribute payments or by granting them other privileges, this should be done; and whatever is promised should be carried out. . . .

D. The Encomienda

7. Title of the Encomienda Given to Julián Gutiérrez Altamirano in Chile, 1566

Rodrigo de Quiroga, governor and captain-general of these provinces of Chile from Nueva Extremadura to the Straits of Magellan, on behalf of His Majesty, etc. I have been informed by you, Licentiate Julián Gutiérrez Altamirano, that twenty-three years ago you came from the kingdoms of Spain to serve His Majesty in this part of the Indies; that you went to the kingdom of Tierra Firme as an officer of the viceroy Blasco Núñez de Vela in the campaign against Gonzalo Pizarro; that afterwards you went to the kingdom of Peru and served his Majesty with the licentiate Pedro Gasca against the said Pizarro until he was captured and killed; that after peace and

José Toribio Medina, ed., *Colección de documentos inéditos para la historia de Chile: Segunda serie* (Santiago: Fondo Histórico y Bibliográfico J. T. Medina, 1956–1961), I, pp. 63–64. Reprinted by permission.

tranquility had been restored to Peru, you came to this government
fifteen years ago to further serve His Majesty and that you took
part in the discovery, conquest, and settlement of all the cities that
have been colonized from Santiago to the Straits; that in many of
them you have been a lieutenant and captain and have had many
expenses while supporting yourself in the service of His Majesty
and that you have been a captain and officer of all these provinces
and have served with your arms, horses, servants, and slaves at great
expense but with great glory in many important ventures, risking
your person, as is the custom among noble gentlemen of your quality
and profession, for as such you are esteemed; and that as a result
you are very poor and deeply in debt. For these and many other
reasons, which I will not set forth here but which are just and redound to your credit, and in order to give you partial compensation
for your many services, labors, and expenditures, in the name of His
Majesty I hereby commend to you, the said licentiate Julián Gutiérrez Altamirano, the tributary group known as Millapoa with the
cacique called Reuqueando and with the other Indian nobles and
subjects of said group, together with its division and water-hole, as
well as the nobles called Quiloioya and Taroande with their nobles
and subjects, all of whom have their land and residence in the
district of the city of Concepción on both sides of the Bío-Bío River.

I grant this encomienda to you by virtue of its relinquishment by
the licentiate Hernando de Castro, resident of the city of Concepción, to whom the said Indians were commended in the name of
His Majesty by my predecessor, the governor Pedro de Villagra,
and on the same terms in which they were held by him and by
Francisco de Castañeda, also resident in Concepción, who received
them from the governor Pedro de Valdivia, so that you may make
use of them in accordance with the royal commands and ordinances
and with the condition that you treat them well, seek their preservation and increase, and instruct them in matters pertaining to our
holy Catholic faith, the natural law, and orderly conduct; if you
are in any way negligent, let the burden fall upon your conscience,
not upon mine nor that of His Majesty. I commend the said Indians
to you with the further condition that in collecting their tributes
and benefits you abide by the regulations and assessments that have
been or may be fixed, that you keep arms and a horse in order to
serve His Majesty in time of war, that you repair the bridges and
royal road within the borders of your encomienda, and that you do

everything else which may be commanded by His Majesty's magistrates in Concepción. After the magistrates have seen this document, they are to give you possession of the said caciques and Indians and see to it that you are not deprived of them without due process of law under the penalty of a payment of 2,000 gold pesos each to His Majesty.

Done at Cañete de la Frontera on the third of June, 1566. Rodrigo de Quiroga. By command of the lord governor. Diego Ruiz de Olivier.

8. The Audiencia of New Galicia and the Indians

J. H. PARRY

The general attitude of the Crown towards the whole question of labour and tribute is well illustrated in the instructions issued to the second viceroy of New Spain, Luis de Velasco, "the liberator," who succeeded Mendoza in 1550:

> The Indians must be made to work for wages in the fields or in the cities, so that they have no excuse for idleness. . . . This order must be enforced by our justices; private Spaniards must not be allowed to bring pressure upon the Indians, even within their own *encomiendas*. You are to give orders for proper daily wages to be paid to the Indians themselves, and not to their chiefs, or to any other intermediaries. They are not to be overworked; and it must be made clear that Spaniards who disregard these orders will be severely punished.

In the matter of tributes:

> Since in many Indian *pueblos* the scale of tributes is uncertain, and no one knows exactly how much they ought to pay, with the result that they are often overtaxed: you are to issue orders for definite assessments to be made and declared, so that the Indians know what they are to pay. . . .

J. H. Parry, *The Audiencia of New Galicia in the Sixteenth Century: A Study in Spanish Colonial Government* (Cambridge, Eng.: Cambridge University Press, 1948), pp. 65–79, *passim*. Reprinted by permission of the Cambridge University Press.

In general:

> You are to do justice, and to see to it that the grievances of
> the Indians are removed, and their tributes lightened; observ-
> ing and enforcing in all things the provisions made by the
> New Laws for the good government of the Indies. You are to
> study a royal decree which we have issued concerning the
> services of the Indians, and are to observe and enforce it.

Velasco himself regarded the revised labour laws and the pension-
encomienda as indispensable, if peace was to be maintained in the
colonies. He even succeeded in extending titles to *encomiendas* to
cover a third life, by way of a legal fiction. In other respects, however, he was altogether upon the side of reform, and strove continually to achieve the abolition of personal servitude and the
reasonable assessment of Indian tributes based upon the scale of
payment existing before the conquest. His chief difficulty was to find
suitable agents to carry out the work — men of known reliability,
and of sufficient standing to be above bribes and threats, for the
encomenderos might well resort to such methods to prevent decisions being given against their interests. The *oidores* of the audiencia
of Mexico were already fully occupied. The solution came in a decree
empowering Velasco to employ two of the *oidores alcaldes mayores*
[of the audiencia of New Galicia at Compostela] in *visitas* in any
part of New Spain, at his own discretion. Incessant correspondence
on the subject had evidently convinced the Council of the Indies that
four justices of appeal were not needed in Compostela, for supplementary decrees added that when reporting to Mexico City, the
oidores visitadores were to assist in the work of the vicegral audiencia, and that in New Galicia, suits involving less than the statutory
500 *pesos* might be settled by one *oidor* sitting alone; or, in the case of
a retrial, by two. In 1551, accordingly, viceregal commissions were
issued to the licentiates Contreras and Lebrón de Quiñones to set out
upon extended *visitas* in the Pacific provinces of New Spain. [The
oidores] de la Marcha and Oseguera . . . were to remain at Compostela to continue the work of the audiencia. . . .

Lebrón's commission entrusted to him a general *visita* of the
provinces of Colima and Zacatula, including Zapotlán, Tuspa, Tama-
zula "and all other villages, whether held by the Crown or in
encomienda." The *visita* completed, he was to inspect the villages on
his way to Mexico City. He was to enforce the New Laws, and all

other decrees and ordinances; to inquire whether adequate provision was made for religious instruction; to punish *encomenderos* who placed obstacles in the way of the missionaries; and to see that proper provision was made for the bodily and spiritual welfare of Indians working in the mines. Indians illegally enslaved were to be freed, and *encomiendas* held without proper title to be annulled. Tributes were to be assessed at reasonable amounts, and penalties placed upon *encomenderos* who demanded illegal service, or over-taxed their Indians, and upon native *caciques* who embezzled tribute money. Idle Indians were to be set to work — the clergy if necessary using their powers of persuasion — and proper wages paid: 12 *maravedíses* a day to labourers, 24 to native officials. The mountain Indians were to be induced to settle in villages and till the land "like reasonable people"; Spanish stock farms were to be kept away from the cultivated land of the Indians, undesirable Spaniards expelled from the villages, and roads and bridges built to accommodate pack animals, in order to remove all excuse for employing Indian carriers. Finally, Lebrón was to investigate the records of all *corregidores, alcaldes mayores, tenientes* and *alguaciles* and to take *residencia* of those retiring. With this formidable assignment he left Compostela in the spring of 1551, accompanied by his personal servant, a notary, a constable, and a native interpreter.

Lebrón spent the next four years incessantly travelling through a rough, wild country, in a climate which at some seasons was (and is) desperately unhealthy. He was seriously ill, and heavily in debt, when he reached Mexico City. The viceroy himself, in recommending him for a special grant to cover his expenses, testified to the zeal and competence which he had displayed. Lebrón's own report — a lengthy but lucid and extremely frank document — revealed a state of affairs very different from that contemplated by the royal legislation; his findings fell under four headings: a description of all the villages visited, with the names of the *encomenderos*, and the titles, where titles existed; a survey of the town of Colima, the municipal administration, judicial arrangements, administration of *Real Hacienda;* administrative orders made by the *visitador;* and law-suits arising from the *visita* — chiefly against Spaniards holding Indians without title, or ill-treating the Indians. A diatribe against the idleness or indifference shown by the *oidores* of Mexico in these matters, completed the *visitador's* findings.

The province of Colima had been populous and rich; but now, wrote Lebrón, "of valleys filled with thriving settlements, only the names are left." Of the two hundred independent *pueblos* of the district, no fewer than seventy-seven were held without lawful title by seventeen *encomenderos,* of whom seven were permanently absent from the province without the viceroy's licence and made no attempt to fulfill their obligations of defence. Some *encomenderos* were also accused of forging deeds of sale in order to conceal their seizures of Indian land. Lebrón instituted proceedings against all those accused, to have their Indians released and their grants formally annulled.   . . .

Most of the orders issued by Lebrón concerned the treatment of Indians. He liberated during his *visita* more than six hundred slaves, and an even greater number of *naborias,* "who although they had neither deed nor brand of slavery, were treated as slaves . . . orders were given for them to receive compensation for the injustice they had suffered . . . the Spaniards took this very ill." Lebrón interpreted literally the royal decrees upon the subject of slavery which threw upon the slave-owner the burden of proof that every male slave had been taken in the act of rebellion, and was held by lawful title. In the absence of such title, the slave was released. The enslavement of women, or of children under fourteen years of age, was in all cases forbidden. The *visitador* also strictly forbade the practice whereby Indians paying tribute in kind were required to carry their produce to central depôts without pay: "for many of them come ten, twenty and thirty leagues, once every month, carrying produce over high mountains and swift rivers . . ."; in future, tributes were to be paid and assessed in the village of their origin, and reckoned at local prices. In every village, Lebrón published what he considered a reasonable assessment of tribute, and distributed copies of the assessment both in Spanish and in Aztec characters.   . . .

Like most Spanish officials, Lebrón distrusted the Indian *caciques.* In many Indian *pueblos,* these headmen were — and are — shamans and custodians of sacred ritual rather than political leaders; sometimes their very identity was secret. The Spaniards — despite the official policy of supporting and employing the *caciques* — found it difficult to make use of dignitaries of this type — impractical, unadaptable, and naturally hostile to Christianity. The village councils, in whom was vested such political authority as existed, usually allowed themselves to be guided in everything by the *caciques.* Lebrón's solution of the problem was to appoint or induce the village councils to elect Indian governors, judges and constables, who should be responsible to the local Spanish governors for collection of tribute and maintenance of the peace. The Spanish officials were thus able to side-track the power of the *caciques,* while observing the letter of royal decrees, which upheld the authority of the Indian rulers. Lebrón's procedure was followed widely throughout New Spain. In some villages, European forms of government were adopted willingly, even enthusiastically; but in many places the village councils to this day elect "governors" upon the advice of the *caciques.* The officials so elected may be quite negligible persons, while the *caciques* really rule.   . . .

The opposition with which both Lebrón and Contreras had to contend received no mention in their official reports. The covering letter which accompanied Lebrón's report, however, gave an account of the threats and beatings with which some of the *encomenderos* sought to prevent their Indians from giving evidence; of the suborning of *corregidores* and *alcaldes;* of attempts to intimidate the *visitadores* themselves, and of lampoons and public insults levelled against them. Lebrón, with his simple directness of purpose, never fully understood the power of the interests which opposed him; his denunciations contained always a note of surprise, especially when they concerned the attitude of the audiencia of Mexico. The *oidores* of that audiencia, bitterly jealous of interference in their province by justices from the subordinate court, and fearful, as always, of any policy which might lead to disaffection among the colonists, had reversed Lebrón's judgements and dismissed his charges wherever possible. A single illustration will suffice:

> One Pedro de Figueroa, *vecino* of Colima, beat and half killed an Indian governor of the province of Tuxpa, a great man according to Indian notions, to whom I had entrusted a rod of justice and a commission to investigate some disputes among the natives there. The Indian was an able and trustworthy fellow, who had previously conducted similar inquiries for the viceroy. . . . The charge of assault was not denied, and I duly gave sentence of two years of exile and a hundred *pesos* damages; thinking myself very lenient, in not sentencing the culprit to lose his hand. . . . The *oidores* of

> Your Majesty's royal audiencia laughed at the severity of the
> sentence, reversed my judgement, and remitted the case for
> settlement to the *alcalde* at Colima.

Lebrón suggested (though without giving specific examples) that
the *oidores* had friendships and economic interests throughout the
provinces, which made them reluctant to administer justice im-
partially. Even the viceroy, though a loyal servant of the king and
a good friend of the Indians, was unable to enforce the laws against
oidores owning property and engaging in business.   . . .

This letter, written with the peculiar mixture of formal deference
and confiding familiarity which the paternal government of Spain
encouraged, contained personal requests as well as political suggestions. Lebrón sought royal licence to marry a woman who held an
encomienda, not in New Galicia, but in New Spain, and asked that
if his bride were compelled to give up her Indians upon marriage
to an *oidor,* she should receive some compensation, since the salary
of an *oidor* was inadequate to support a married household, and a
virtuous single life difficult for a man of Lebrón's age. He declared
himself willing to resign his judicial office at Compostela, if that
were held an insuperable obstacle to his marriage. Finally he re-
minded the king of an old promise, that the first promotion from
the subordinate audiencia should be offered to him; in support of
his application he recited the services of his father and brother,
and begged to be removed from New Galicia — 'that inferno.' He
was beginning to realise how thoroughly he was hated for his fearless prosecution of influential law-breakers in all the provinces of his
jurisdiction. For three years the *oidores* of Mexico, the treasury
officials, the *encomenderos,* and even their own colleagues at Compostela had vied with one another in abusing Lebrón and Contreras
in letters to the authorities in Spain. Soon the campaign against
them was to take effect.

The laws of the Indies provided a means by which aggrieved persons might bring charges against officials, in the *residencia,* the
inquiry to which every servant of the Crown was required to submit,
upon relinquishing any office. Often the *residencia* was purely
formal, being conducted by a successor who proposed to practise
the same abuses as the outgoing official; often, again, the only result
might be a fine, which the offender could pay out of the more or
less legitimate perquisites of his office. A special judge, however,

might be appointed to hold a *residencia,* and if the outgoing official
had been marked down by the authorities in Spain for severe treatment, or if he had offended powerful interests in his district, his
residencia might become a terrible ordeal. Some of the most famous
conquerors — Nuño de Guzmán, for instance, and the gallant Montejo in Yucatán — had been utterly broken by their *residencias.*
Lebrón and Contreras had offended powerful interests, and complaints about the whole conduct of the audiencia had been pouring
into Spain since its foundation. Accordingly in February 1556, upon
receiving a request from de la Marcha, for permission to retire from
office and return to Spain, the Council of the Indies issued a commission to the Licentiate Pedro Morones to take de la Marcha's
place as *oidor alcalde mayor* at Compostela, to conduct de la
Marcha's *residencia,* and to hold an inquiry (*pesquisa secreta*) into
the conduct of all the *oidores alcaldes mayores* since their appointment. Ninety days were allotted for the collection of evidence and
the hearing of complaints. The justices were to be suspended from
office until their cases had been considered by the council, unless
Morones saw fit to recommend any of them for reinstatement. During the period of suspension, Morones was to carry out their duties,
allowing those dissatisfied with his decisions to appeal to Mexico.

Morones represented a common type of swashbuckling, hard-
swearing colonial lawyer, an Indian-baiter and a would-be-*conquistador.* His principal object in going to New Galicia was to organise
an expedition to Chiametla and the north for, like so many of his
contemporaries, he was attracted by tales of fabulous cities to the
north of the settled regions of New Galicia. He had been *fiscal* to
the audiencia of Mexico, until promoted to the rank of *oidor* in 1555,
the year before his appointment to New Galicia. On his new commission, no doubt after consultation with his colleagues in Mexico,
he placed two interpretations for which his instructions contained no
warrant: the first, that his jurisdiction included the *visitas* conducted
in New Spain under the viceroy's mandate; the second, that his
real duty was to break Contreras and Lebrón de Quiñones. De la
Marcha and Oseguera received scant attention. Of de la Marcha,
Morones later reported that, as he had already retired, no case had
been brought against him — an extremely frank confession of neglect of his duties by a *juez de residencia.* Oseguera, suspended
from office with the others upon Morones's arrival in Compostela
towards the end of 1556, was convicted of receiving gifts from

litigants, fined, and after due recommendation, reinstated in his post.

In the case of Lebrón, investigations were delayed by a dispute over procedure. Morones appointed a *vecino* of Guadalajara, Sancho de Cañego, to conduct an inquiry in Colima, concerning Lebrón's conduct there; Lebrón protested that Cañego was a personal enemy and that if the evidence of the inhabitants of Colima were relevant to the *pesquisa*, it should be demanded from the justices there by the ordinary writ *receptoria*, issued by authority of the audiencia. Morones refused to adopt this procedure, but offered to send, instead of Cañego, one of the members of the town council of Compostela — a body which entertained no friendly feelings towards Lebrón; this offer was naturally refused, and Cañego departed for Colima, with a commission from Morones. Arrived there, however, he was arrested by the viceroy's agents, upon the charge of attempting to set up an illegal jurisdiction in New Spain. Morones, later, experienced some difficulty in securing his release; meanwhile, the prosecution was compelled to rely upon the evidence of inhabitants of New Galicia, and though many colonists testified readily enough against Lebrón and Contreras, the Indians showed great reluctance to do so. The reluctance was attributed to fear of Lebrón's vengeance; Morones himself stated that he had ordered repeated floggings as a means of extracting evidence from Indian witnesses, but even this failed to overcome their fear of Lebrón; the Indians so beaten contradicted themselves each time they spoke. Despite the loyalty shown to them by "persons of little credit," the *juez pesquisidor* succeeded in drawing up a case against the two *oidores* within the allotted ninety days and, as a result of his findings, sentenced them both to deprivation of office and payment of very heavy fines. Contreras paid his fine; Lebrón failed to do so, having (it was alleged) placed the proceeds of eight years of extortion under the protection of the monasteries. He was duly imprisoned, and a fraction of his supposed debt to the king paid off by the forced sale of his clothes and other personal effects and of his small but treasured library. Both sentences were endorsed by the audiencia of Mexico, and both victims appealed to the Council of the Indies.

The charges brought against Lebrón by Morones were as vague as they were venomous. He was "a bad Christian . . . a slanderer of honest men . . . vicious and revengeful . . . totally devoid of education and knowledge of law . . . unfitted for judicial office."

Of his moral character, Morones wrote: "The notorious looseness of his life, and his disgraceful relations with married women, made so unpleasant a story that I forbade the witnesses to make specific statements, for fear of scandal." Some definite charges were made, however. Lebrón was alleged to have seduced the wife of one Alonso López, *vecino* of Compostela; and Contreras to have ravished the same López's daughter; both were suspected of complicity in poisoning the licentiate Villagar, *alcalde ordinario* of Compostela. The evidence cited in support of these charges was so flimsy that the judges of the Council of the Indies, when the case came before them, dismissed the charges summarily. The remaining counts consisted of unsupported accusations of cruelty practised against the Indians and seduction of Indian women; assertions of favouritism in dealing with *encomiendas;* a supremely ridiculous statement that Lebrón, during his *visita*, had spent most of his time at fiestas and bullfights; and the charge of converting to their own use the fines imposed by both *oidores* in cases tried on *visita*.

It may have been true that the treasury ledgers of New Galicia contained no entries of money paid in by the *visitadores;* but as the accounts had not been audited for twelve years, and as the treasurer of the time was convicted shortly afterwards of embezzling large sums from the royal revenue, no satisfactory evidence could be produced against Lebrón and Contreras on that score. The charge resulted only in a decree forbidding any official of the audiencia to act as "depositario de penas de cámara."

The charges against Lebrón were amply refuted by the detailed clarity of his own reports and by the testimony of Velasco and of the missionaries. The Franciscans of Guadalajara supported Lebrón as far as they could, and wrote an emphatic joint letter to the king, in which they proclaimed that

> the remedy for all these troubles . . . is clear and will cost your Majesty very little: the licentiate Lebrón de Quiñones . . . has been like a lily among thorns (*como lirio entre espinas*), a thoughtful man, devout, honest, stern and zealous for justice; he punished the injuries committed against the poor and against the helpless Indians . . . and all who knew him well were inspired by his noble example; . . . for these reasons we beseech your Majesty to appoint him governor of this kingdom of Galicia, because the present audiencia is useless.

Opinions about Contreras were more conflicting. He had been severely criticized by the friars for his hasty temper and his disorderly life, and his learning and legal attainments were often questioned. The general nature of the evidence indicates, however, that he too had been arrested principally because he had offended powerful interests, though he was less uncompromising than his colleague, and succeeded eventually in making his peace.

Audiencia rule had indeed broken down. Lebrón, despairing of justice in Compostela, took the law into his own hands in the summer of 1557, broke prison, and fled to Mexico, where he was hospitably entertained in his distress by the Franciscans, and protected from molestation by the favour of the viceroy. Velasco still befriended Lebrón, and though he had no power to reverse Morones's decisions, he offered the suspended *oidor* another commission, for a *visita* in Oaxaca, to occupy the time during which his case was awaiting review; but Lebrón refused to undertake further judicial work until he had been cleared and reinstated in office. In January, 1558 he wrote a letter to the king, begging permission to return to Spain to answer in person for his conduct, and complaining of the personal animus displayed against him, the refusal of the judge to furnish him with a list of charges, and the general conduct of the trial.

> Dr. Morones has sought to prove my guilt by bribing or intimidating reluctant witnesses, by torturing my servants until they testified according to his instructions, and by allying himself with those who were my confessed enemies, because I had formerly executed your Majesty's justice upon them. . . . It is not right that a man of quality, the son of a faithful servant of your Majesty, and one who has himself sought with all his power to serve, should be treated worse than a common malefactor, and slandered and dishonoured by a partial judge.

Lebrón followed up this letter by soliciting the help and influence of the one man in all Spain who had least love for colonial officialdom — the veteran "apostle of the Indians," Fray Bartolomé de Las Casas. Fray Bartolomé had taken a prominent part in framing the New Laws, as Lebrón had in enforcing them, and his voice still carried great weight in Indian affairs. Whether by his influence or not, Lebrón obtained his licence to return to Spain, and a writ issued by the Council of the Indies of 1560 ordered the audiencia of Mexico to forward all papers relating to the case, without informing or consulting Morones.

Lebrón's presence, and possibly Fray Bartolomé's influence, secured a quicker trial than was usual in such cases. In November 1561 he was acquitted of all the charges brought against him, and reinstated in the audiencia of New Galicia as senior *oidor*. He was to receive his salary for the period of his suspension, and an advance of 300 ducats to cover the cost of his journey. The following January, he received the necessary licences — licence to take money out of Spain; licence for the weapons needed by his household; licence for his four servants (one a Negro brought from New Galicia); and licence for his nephew, aged sixteen, to accompany him. He set sail soon afterwards, but death overtook him before he reached his post — no doubt to the relief of many in New Galicia. He was thus spared the ordeal of working with Morones as his colleague; his reinstatement in the same audiencia as his late judge was altogether characteristic of the slow, well-intentioned, utterly impersonal working of Spanish justice — that justice which he had served so well.

Contreras had been living in Mexico all this time, and his case came up for review later than Lebrón's. In 1562 he too was acquitted, except upon one charge, that of accepting gifts from litigants; the treasury officials of New Galicia were ordered to refund the fines which he had paid. Four years later he was again appointed to New Galicia as senior *oidor*, with three colleagues — the licentiates Alarcón (appointed in 1560), Mendiola (in 1564) and Orozco (in 1565). Under their joint rule the audiencia reestablished its authority and reverted to a modified form of the Indian policy of Lebrón de Quiñones. Prosecutions under the Indian laws again figured in the proceedings of the court and the slow process of incorporating *encomiendas* in the Crown was resumed, softened by arrangements for the paying of a compensatory pension over a term of years to the heirs of the *encomendero*.

E. Interpretations

9. A Seventeenth-Century Defense of Spain's Indian Policies

JUAN DE SOLÓRZANO Y PEREYRA

Although heretics and other rivals of the glories of our Spanish nation have realized the validity of its titles to the New World and the great increase that the Monarchy has achieved through its conquests and conversions, they try to discredit these titles, saying in the first place that we were impelled more by greed for the gold and silver of its provinces than by zeal for the propagation of the Gospel. They also say that since all things must be judged by their intent or principal end, if this is wicked or erroneous, then it cannot produce a title or effect that can be considered constant and legitimate. . . .

Even if we concede that greed for gold and riches . . . may have prevailed among some, this blemish does not lessen the merit of the many good men who took part so sincerely and apostolically in the conversion of the New World. Nor does it lessen the merit of the zeal and concern repeatedly displayed by our Kings in their sagacious *cédulas* and instructions. . . .

The second charge of our enemies is that this greed was the cause of the slight peacefulness and benevolence which have been shown to the Indians. . . . They also say that these are the only qualities needed for the conversion of the Indians and that gentle and pacific methods can be efficacious, as the example of our Lord Jesus Christ and His Holy Apostles shows and as is proven by many passages of Scripture. They also feel that Christians, even when they take part in just wars should always be as kind and amiable as possible. . . .

Juan de Solórzano y Pereyra, *Política indiana* (Madrid, 1930), Vol. I, pp. 117–127, *passim*.

At each step they throw in our faces the fact that the Indians have been badly treated and that in many places they have completely disappeared. To prove this they have recourse to the treatise written by the Bishop of Chiapas advancing the same argument, which, to stir up greater hatred for us, has been printed in four languages. . . .

But although I do not wish to excuse completely — nor should I — the wars that must have been waged unjustifiably against the Indians in the early days of the conquest, nor the many injuries that have been and are still being done to them, . . . I still make bold to assert that these excesses cannot wipe out all the good that has been accomplished in the conversion and instruction of these non-believers by clerics who were disinterested and punctual in the fulfillment of their mission of preaching the Gospel. Even less can they wipe out the piety and ardent zeal of our Kings, nor the justice of their titles. With great solicitude and care and without taking costs or difficulties of any kind into account, our Kings have tried to provide for the conversion of the Indians in a kind, religious, and Christian manner and have sought the services of persons of all estates, laymen as well as ecclesiastics, in order to repress bad treatment and offenses against the Indians and to carry out the obligations imposed on them by the Holy See. . . .

Thus the principles and regulations governing the conquests and conversions were always laid down with all the vigilance and Christian and human prudence that their high ends demanded, though it is understood that in their execution there may have been some excesses and Indian deaths, as our rivals, heretics, and rumor-mongers charge. However, these flaws cannot prejudice the titles and rights of our Kings, nor diminish the glory and repute of what has been achieved in those remote and extensive provinces by means of their expenditures and conscientious attention in converting so many savage infidels and in reducing them to civil life. This is a fact acknowledged by all the serious and Christian authors, both foreign and Spanish, who have dealt with this matter and have endlessly praised the way in which our conquests were organized and conducted. . . .

Although Nicetas audaciously declared that there is nothing that kings and emperors cannot correct, nor that surpasses their power and authority, much truer is the aphorism of Tacitus that wherever there are human beings there are bound to be vices and sin, especially in provinces so distant from their Kings, where royal commands tend to be ignored or diluted and the residents or governors can regard as licit anything that occurs to them. The temerity of human beings easily leads them to scorn what is very remote. And just as doctors consider the cure of diseased lungs to be extremely difficult because medicaments must reach them through the stomach, following a long and narrow route, so the distance of the Supreme Power makes it unlikely that appropriate remedies can succeed in alleviating the ailments of these provinces.

This state of affairs was even less to be wondered at in the early days of the conquest of the New World, when governors and magistrates were not yet able to protect the Indians nor rigorously execute the laws enacted for this purpose. At that time everything was ruled by captains, soldiers, and sailors — people driven by ferocity and greed who did not hesitate to violate the laws of men and, as Lucan, Seneca, Sallust and many other authors point out, were not likely to refrain from transgressing divine laws as well. People of this type regard as just only what fills the depths of their greed; they do not know how to return their swords to their sheathes without shedding blood nor to restrain themselves from despoiling the vanquished.

For this reason the Marquis of Pescara, Don Fernando Davalos, used to say that nothing is more difficult in war than to respect Christ and Mars with equal discipline. We will not pause to consider this point at present. . . . nor the question of when and how the misdeeds of servants cast a reflection on their masters, a matter that various authors have discussed at great length. All agree that when kings do not order these misdeeds nor know of them nor fail to punish them when they are discovered nor are guilty of negligence in appointing their servants, they are absolved of all blame. And this is precisely the position of our glorious and Catholic Kings, as we have shown. . . .

In addition, if this question is considered dispassionately, in many places the Indians gave cause for their mistreatment or for war to be made against them, either because of their bestial and savage customs or because of the excesses and treason that they attempted or committed against our people. . . .

Moreover, it is not the Spaniards who have exterminated them, but their own vices and drunkenness or the earthquakes and repeated epidemics of smallpox and other diseases with which God in His mysterious wisdom has seen fit to reduce their numbers, as Acosta and other eye-witness writers testify.

Everywhere they seem destined to undergo these hardships, for . . . nothing is ordered or legislated for their health, usefulness, and preservation that does not turn out to cause greater harm to them, according to what the same authors affirm. All of this, therefore, should be attributed to the wrath and punishments of God rather than to the oppression and other offenses that we are said to commit against them. Perhaps God has acted in this fashion because of their grave sins and persistent and abominable idolatry, as some historians observe with respect to similar calamities that befell the cities of Rome and Jerusalem.

In any event, I would like those persons who calumniate us to state frankly whether they would not have been guilty of greater excesses if it had been their lot to make our conquests. This is a point made by one of the very authors [Theodorus de Bry] who has depicted our cruelties in print.

Indeed, we have already seen the destruction of the islands and other lands which they have unjustly occupied and sacked with great cruelty and insatiable greed. Nor have they shown that they took any pains to instruct the natives in religion but instead have tried to pervert them with their execrable errors, without establishing bishoprics or building churches, which we have erected in large numbers.

But to put an end to this chapter, I again repeat what I said at the outset: I do not wish to extoll past excesses against the Indians and even less those that may occur in the future because the principal wealth we ought to seek from them is their conversion, instruction, and preservation, since it was for this purpose that they were commended to us, and it can be accomplished more effectively with gentleness and piety than with bad treatment and atrocities. . . .

10. The Theory and Practice of Racial Segregation in Colonial Spanish America

MAGNUS MÖRNER

The Crown pursued rather tenaciously a policy aiming at the separation of its Indian subjects from the rest. The point of departure of this policy was the concept of the two republics, the *República de españoles* and the *República de indios*. In the beginning this dualism was natural but it was soon being undermined by the process of race mixture. Whereas the early missionaries arriving in the Indies had expected the Spaniards to set the Indians "a good example," later on both ecclesiastics and many administrators, taught by bitter experience, became convinced that Spaniards and Mestizos were really more of "a bad example" to the Neophytes. As the mission of the famous Dominican, Bartolomé de Las Casas in the "Land of True Peace" in Guatemala exemplifies, missionaries preferred to work without intervention by other whites. Spanish and Mestizo vagrants very early infested Indian villages. This social problem motivated the prohibition for vagrants to live among the Indians, enacted in 1536 and 1563. Abuses were also committed by the encomenderos and their overseers (*calpisques*), often Negro slaves or freedmen whom the encomenderos left in the villages of their Indians. Consequently, Negro calpisques were excluded from residing among the Indians in 1541, calpisques in general in 1550 (modified later on) and, finally, the encomenderos themselves in 1563. The systematic exclusion of all Mestizos, Mulattoes and Negroes followed in 1578, at the suggestion of an Augustinian friar from Peru. Pure Spaniards were finally added to the list in 1600. Even non-Indians who owned land within an Indian village were

This selection comes from two works by Magnus Mörner, *Race Mixture in the History of Latin America* (Boston: Little, Brown, and Company (Inc.) 1967), Chap. IV, *passim*. Copyright © 1967, Little, Brown and Company (Inc.). Reprinted by permission of Little, Brown and Company. The second is "The Guaraní Missions and the Segregation Policy of the Spanish Crown," *Archivum Historicum Societatis Jesu*, II (1961), pp. 367–386, *passim*. Reprinted by permission of the editors of *Archivum Historicum Societatis Jesu* (Institutum Historicum S.J., Rome).

prohibited to settle down there, it was explained in 1646. On the other hand, Mestizos who had been brought up by their Indian mothers in a village were excepted from the prohibition. The laws enforcing residential separation were included in the *Recopilación* of 1680.

The background of this policy, formed especially during the 1570's, was the rapid decline of the Indian population, the systematic gathering of the remaining Indians into large mission villages, *reducciones,* or *congregaciones* and the increasing disorders in the countryside attributed to vagrants and mixed-bloods. The motivations of the policy were several. In the first place, the Crown wanted to protect the Indians not only from violence and abuse but also from influences harmful to their morals and faith. Secondly, there was a desire to maintain the dualism already established in the ecclesiastical and administrative realms. "Spaniards" could not be subjected to the jurisdiction of "Indian" town councils, nor should the cure of their souls be entrusted to friars or priests whose function was that of missionaries. Consequently, "Spaniards" and "Indians" ought to live apart, in villages or towns of their own. In fact, the policy of separation may also have been aimed to promote the foundation of new "Spanish" centers. In any case, this policy was not discriminatory in the sense of South African "apartheid," or, at least, the discrimination involved was not directed against the Indians but rather against the non-Indians. Segregation imposed to lessen inter-ethnic tension and to provide autonomy only becomes discrimination if imposed by compulsion on one or several groups (as is usually the case). In Spanish America the Indians applauded the policy of separation or segregation. Thus the victims of segregation in this case were rather the Mestizos, Mulattoes, and other non-Indians.

Though less emphasized than in the rural environment, the policy of separation was also imposed in the cities, where the Indians were supposed to live in special districts, such as the famous Cercado of Lima. When set to work in mines or textile workshops (*obrajes de paño*) the Indians according to the law would have to be kept apart from other workers.

Theoretically speaking, the policy of separation implied a conflict with another aim of the Crown, the spreading of Spanish among the Indians proclaimed with emphasis in a royal decree of 1770. Nor did this policy harmonize with the liberty of Spanish-Indian intermarriage, even if there was never, as we have just noticed, any promotion of intermarriage on the part of the Crown. On the other hand, the aversion of the Crown and the authorities to Afro-Indian miscegenation was, of course, in keeping with the policy of separation. That is why a document on intermarriage from 1781 makes explicit reference to "the laws that prohibit contact and communication between Indians and Mulattoes, Negroes, and similar races."

The conflict between the different aims of the Crown that could be envisioned, especially during the eighteenth century, never really materialized because at that time the policy of separation had already experienced a complete failure. This had been true already in 1680 when the very laws of separation were codified. The Crown simply lacked the tools to impose such a radical policy, especially when not supplemented with the systematic foundation of new towns to harbor "Spaniards," Negroes and Castas. In view of the decline of the Indian population and the increase of the Mestizos, the policy proved increasingly absurd. Although theoretically in force, the laws of separation from about 1680 onwards were only applied in isolated cases, giving rise to interminable lawsuits. It was only in the missions situated in peripheral regions, such as those of the Jesuits among the Guaraníes in Rio de la Plata, that the laws continued to be applied because they suited the missionaries. . . .

❀   ❀   ❀

One of the most striking features of the famous Guaraní Missions established by the Jesuits in the upper River Plate area was, no doubt, the isolation of the Indians from the outer world. To some observers, both then and later, this isolation policy seemed to be a crime against the law of nations and a most sinister way of building up a Jesuit Empire in the wilds of South America. To others it seemed to be a prudent measure taken by the Jesuits in order to protect their Indian wards from the bad influence and the encroachments of the Whites. Both friend and foe seemed to ascribe the isolation of the Indians in the Missions entirely to the initiative and authority of the Jesuits themselves.

It is really astonishing that the obvious connection between the isolation policy of the Jesuit Missionaries and the general segregation laws enacted by the Spanish Crown was not observed by the many students of the "Jesuit State" until 1913 when Father Pablo Hernández published his fundamental work, *Organización social de las doctrinas guaraníes de la Compañia de Jesús.* Hernández found it very easy to explain all the isolation principles adopted by the Jesuits in terms of the Spanish colonial laws, i.e., the *Recopilación de Leyes de los Reinos de las Indias* and also the so-called *Ordenanzas de Alfaro.* He also pointed out that the isolation was not by far as rigid as imagined by most of the earlier writers: both State and Church dignitaries frequently visited the Mission district, the Missions were not surrounded by fosses, etc. to prevent the entrance of aliens; indeed a few Missions, the so-called "Pueblos de Abajo," were expressly allowed to receive Spanish traders. In exceptional cases even the residence of Spaniards within the Missions was allowed, i.e., when they were professionals particularly needed by the Indians and of good behaviour.   . . .

The so-called Guaraní War of the 1750's broke the isolation of the Missions, and for several years both Portuguese and Spanish troops were quartered there. It was in this connection that Father Cardiel reported that some of the Spanish officers and other functionaries who had arrived in the Missions took up the segregation issue with the Jesuits from a theoretical point of view. "Decían . . . que, si los españoles estuvieran mezclados con los indios, dispensando en la ley que lo prohibe, tendrían más luces, entrarían en alguna codicia, lo agenciarían más bien, haciéndose a guardarlo." But Cardiel argued that the Spanish segregation laws had been judicious and based on a long experience. Even the Indians of Mexico and Peru, much more civilized than the Guaranís, had suffered rather much from the intercourse with the "Spaniards." He also maliciously asked his opponents if they had ever met any Indians who, after having cohabited with "Spaniards" for twenty or thirty years, were able to save as much as 50 pesos, i.e., about the amount which a Mulatto or Negro was able to save in a year. . . .

As we know, the Jesuit regime was re-established in the whole of the Mission district after some years of war and occupation. It was to last a very short time, however. Being expelled from the dominions of the Spanish King by the notorious decree of Charles III in 1767, the Jesuits had to leave the Guaraní Missions the following year. With them, their strict rules regarding the isolation of the Missions from aliens disappeared as well.   . . .

Some general conclusions might be drawn from the account given on these pages. It is evident that the isolation policy of the Jesuits in their famous Guaraní Missions was completely in harmony with the spirit which dictated the Spanish segregation laws. The main purpose was in both cases to protect the Indian population from abuse by more forceful elements of the population. This conformity is not at all surprising. While the Jesuits administered the Missions by delegation of the Crown, the legislation of the Crown was always deeply influenced by the viewpoints of the Church and of the Orders. . . .

. . . However, the isolation policy of the Jesuits in their Guaraní Missions cannot be explained entirely in the terms of the Royal legislation. It cannot possibly be denied that, with regard to the temporary visits of aliens to the Indian Pueblos, the Jesuits were considerably more reluctant to admit such visits than the law required. At least from the 1710's or 1720's onwards they simply denied aliens the right to enter the Missions. The exemptions from this rule granted by the Jesuit leaders never referred to more than certain Missions and certain categories of visitors, i.e., merchants and messengers. On the other hand, as far as the legal prohibition for non-Indians to settle down for long periods among the Indians was concerned, the Jesuit Fathers, . . . under the impact of economic necessity, allowed an exception of a certain amount.

The aspect of Indian isolation from aliens treated here clearly shows that the history of the Guaraní Missions cannot possibly be studied without due consideration being paid to the general legal background. On the other hand, not all the administrative rules and characteristic social features of the Guaraní Community under Jesuit leadership can be explained only in terms of Royal laws and decrees. It is understandable, indeed, that if the "ambitious" Jesuit leaders of the Guaraní Missions wanted to ensure the real welfare and protection of their wards, they sometimes felt obliged to create their own rules on this or that subject.

11. Spanish Exploitation of Indians in Central Mexico

Charles Gibson

The Black Legend provides a gross but essentially accurate interpretation of relations between Spaniards and Indians. The Legend
builds upon the record of deliberate sadism. It flourishes in an atmosphere of indignation, which removes the issue from the category
of objective understanding. It is insufficient in its awareness of the
institutions of colonial history. But the substantive content of the
Black Legend asserts that Indians were exploited by Spaniards, and
in empirical fact they were.

We have not commented in detail on the conquest itself, a separate subject, already much studied. The conquest has a bearing here
not for its military events but for its consequences, and the over-all
consequence of conquest was the condition of Spanish domination
and Indian subjugation. Aztec peoples could not confront Spaniards
as a unified nation, with diplomacy and negotiation. Conquest destroyed Aztec nationalism and fixed adjustments at a local level.
Nearly everything that could be called imperial in Aztec affairs
came to an end. If Aztec society be thought of as a graduated complex of progressively more inclusive units, from the family and
calpulli at one end to the total empire at the other, it becomes evident that conquest eliminated all the more comprehensive structures
while it permitted the local and less comprehensive ones to survive.

The demarcation or cut-off point was the jurisdiction of the
tlatoani. This became the cabecera, the essential unit of the early
colonial period, on which encomienda, the missionary church, ca-
cicazgo, and tribute and labor exactions directly depended. The
cabecera won out over alternative organizing principles of greater
or lesser range. One may suppose that this followed in part from
the role of the tlatoani in Indian society, a role that was repeatedly
affirmed in the events of pre-conquest history. But it was the con-

Reprinted from *The Aztecs Under Spanish Rule: A History of the Valley of
Mexico, 1519–1810* by Charles Gibson with the permission of the publishers,
Stanford University Press. © Copyright 1964 by the Board of Trustees of the
Leland Stanford Junior University. Pp. 403–409.

sequence also of relations between Spaniards and Indians. Conceivably a differently ordered Spanish rule might have made the tribe rather than the cabecera the essential colonial unit. An opposite type of Spanish power might have settled on the calpulli. We can glimpse some such alternative forces at work in the various readjustments and modifications made upon the standard cabecera, as when repartimiento reinvoked the tribal groups or when non-tlatoani towns were granted in encomienda and allowed to become cabeceras.

The most evident changes in Indian society occurred during the first forty or fifty years. This was the time when Indian peoples, or some of them, met the Spanish influence part way and reached positive degrees of cultural accord. The mid-sixteenth century has a special interest in the history of humanistic tutelage, with the community of Santa Fe, the Gante school, and above all the Colegio of Santa Cruz in Tlatelolco. One can speak here of a cultural florescence for upper-class Indians, and we may cite again the remarkable Badianus Herbal, a systematic catalogue of plants, classified in a European tradition, painted in an Indian style, its glosses written in Nahuatl by one learned native commentator and translated into Latin by another. The herbal was composed in 1552, and it seemed to give promise, thirty years after the conquest, of a combined culture, with enduring Indian values enriched by a European admixture.

The total possible range of Indian reaction at this time was relatively extensive. Because two complicated societies were intermeshing, opportunities for new combinations continually arose. It is in the sixteenth century that we find the most diverse individual incidents and the most unsettled conditions in both societies. But the long-term tendencies were toward the solutions of the seventeenth and eighteenth centuries, and the scope of Indian response became more limited. As the Indian population was reduced in size, Spanish controls became fixed and the traditional leaders lost power. Colonial law only partially reacted to what occurred, and local customs acquired a greater force than law. After the sixteenth century few individuals stand out in either society, and the history becomes one of localized groups. The seventeenth and eighteenth centuries have a peculiarly leaderless quality, as if all alternative solutions had been discarded.

Neither society was at first unified in its response to the conditions proffered by the other. Indians were at first divided between those who cooperated and those who resisted, and between the upper class and the maceguales. Both lines of division tended to disappear. But the geographical divisions in Indian society remained. The patterns of subordination, however uniform in their abstract characteristics, were locally bounded. Cabecera jurisdictions, encomiendas, and haciendas were discrete manifestations of localism effectively preventing a consolidation of Indian interests. All native conduct was so confined. No two towns were ever capable of uniting in organized resistance. The common qualities of Indian towns were insufficient bases for concerted action.

In Spanish society friars and encomenderos were the main conflicting parties of the early period. The friars, almost alone among Spaniards, were guided by principles of Christian humanitarianism. It could be argued that even they exploited native peoples in their coercive indoctrination and their extirpation of pagan practices. Yet their effort as a whole may be distinguished from that of other Spaniards. What happened was that the spiritual component of Hispanic imperialism disappeared or concentrated its energies elsewhere. Its effect for Indians was confined to the early period. The church ceased to be active in Indian defense as ecclesiastics adopted the methods and attitudes of civilian colonists. Churchmen could oppose encomienda in part because they were prohibited from becoming encomenderos, but ecclesiastical condemnation of latifundium would have meant condemnation of an institution that was essential to ecclesiastical wealth and power. There were many other divisions, of course, within Spanish society, but none of them bore directly upon Indian life or livelihood. Thus the creoles despised the peninsulares, but the issue between them was not native welfare, and in some degree what they were disputing over was Indian spoils.

Tribute, labor, and land were the most clearly defined categories of Spanish demand. The three were differentiated in the colonial period, and the legal instruments were different in each case. Tribute and labor were state-controlled after the mid-sixteenth century, and their consequences for Indian society, however serious, were less severe than in the case of land. Tribute and labor were periodically adjusted to population changes, and the extreme Spanish requirements were confined to the earliest times. Moreover, tribute and labor were already familiar types of pre-conquest exaction, and the degree of change between the one period and the other has often been overstated by critics of the Spanish regime.

Spanish usurpation of land has received less attention, probably because it followed the conquest by some years and did not occupy a major position among the Las Casas accusations. It occurred gradually, through many individual events over a long period, and phenomena that take place in this way lack the dramatic appeal of cataclysms like conquest. So deficient is the Black Legend with regard to land that until recently historians were interpreting hacienda as a direct outgrowth of encomienda. Only in our own time has this fundamental error been corrected, most effectively through the work of Silvio Zavala.

It is often said, with an implication of significance, that the lands of America were the property of the crown of Castile. But the point is at best legalistic, and for Indian history it is immaterial. The crown played an insignificant role either in fostering or in inhibiting latifundia. Legal possession of land by the crown did not mean that land usurpation, too, was a state-controlled enterprise. It was private and frequently illegal, though the state came to tolerate it and to profit from it through the devices of denuncia and composición. That it did not occur immediately is probably less the result of legal restriction than of sheer numbers of Indian people and the universality of Indian occupation of land. A prerequisite was available land, and this was not present when the Spaniards first came. Encomienda was therefore an appropriate institution for the early years. But with Indian depopulation, land became accessible, and when it became accessible, it was usurped.

One consequence of the historical concern with selected Black Legend themes is a weakness in our knowledge of hacienda history. The sections of this book that deal with hacienda make some contribution to the subject, but they suffer from inadequate information and lack a secure conceptual frame. Hacienda, perhaps more than any other single colonial topic, still needs systematic investigation, not alone in the Valley of Mexico but in all areas. We cannot now confidently compare our documented examples of Valley of Mexico hacienda with the institution in other regions, and until we can the Valley conditions will remain imperfectly defined. . . . My own feeling is that the hacienda is a crucial institution, that for various reasons its study has been slighted, and that we would be well advised to make a concerted effort toward solving the historical problems that it raises.

With respect to land there can be no doubt that the hacienda came to be the dominant mode of control. In the tempo of its history it contrasts with tribute and labor. The extreme Spanish demands for tribute and labor occurred early, before much land was transferred to Spanish possession. This transfer, on the other hand, took place on a large scale only in the late sixteenth century and after, when private exploitation of tribute and labor had already been brought under state control. In a sense, land represented a new avenue of exploitation for Spaniards, after other avenues were blocked. But the hacienda combined its essential control of land with secondary controls over labor and tribute, and the result was the most comprehensive institution yet devised for Spanish mastery and Indian subordination. If there appeared, as we have thought, some benign features of hacienda, these are explicable in terms of the total matrix within which hacienda developed. Human character tends toward benevolence as well as toward cruelty, and the hacienda could afford certain kinds of benevolence that would have been incongruous with the harsher, more superficial, less subtle coercions of encomienda. Thus the hacendado could appear as the protector and advocate of his Indians against outside pressures. The encomendero was intended by law to play this same role, but he never did.

That land was important to Indians is obvious. Some of the most intimate and revealing documents of all Indian history are the native títulos for community land possession. The títulos were an Indian response to Spanish usurpation and Spanish legalism. Their purpose was to integrate community opposition against alienation. They speak only sparingly, or not at all, of conquest, tribute, and labor. They see the essential threat to community existence where in fact it lay, in Spanish seizures of land.

There had been seizures of land before the conquest, as in the "lands of Montezuma," but these had been accommodated within Indian practices of land disposition. The difference is one of degree. Moreover, the pre-conquest period, so far as we know, offers no comparable situation of population change. When Indian society seemed headed for extinction, in the late sixteenth and early seventeenth centuries, its practical need for land likewise diminished, and

Indian gobernadores and others became the accomplices of Spaniards in the transfer of titles. When the population began to increase
in the late seventeenth and eighteenth centuries the need for land
correspondingly increased. But by then it was too late. Land transfer was cumulative in a way that tribute and labor exactions were
not. Every increase in Indian population in the late colonial period
meant an additional number that could not be incorporated in the
traditional calpulli tenure, or could be incorporated only with a corresponding strain on other community institutions. The available
land was hacienda land, and the new population could now be incorporated within colonial society only through the mediation of
hacienda. When the hacendado authorized the towns to rent some
of his lands or gave permission to individuals to occupy huts on the
hacienda properties, both the hacendado and the Indian beneficiaries could regard the act as one of benevolence. All surrounding
conditions were accepted as normal. An aristocracy had been created
through innumerable acts over generations of time. Even if there had
been an inclination to assign blame, there was no one to accuse, for
no one was responsible. The institution and the ethos of the institution dominated all its members. A conquistador who killed or an
encomendero who overcharged could be convincingly criticized on
moral grounds, but similar criticism appeared excessive when turned
against the hacendado, who had inherited most of his lands and
played a paternalistic role in a society he had not created. . . .

The Indian community was further beset by a series of demands
not comprehended in the three classifications of tribute, labor, and
land. Most of these were designed to extract from its economy the
increment remaining beyond minimum subsistence. Ecclesiastical
fees fall in this category, as do the forced sales in corregimiento and
the usurpations of produce. The political officials' handbook of
1777 openly declared the corregimiento of Chalco to be worth thirty
times the corregidor's salary, a statement that suggests the extent of
precedented extra-legal exploitation by officials appointed to uphold
the law.

Variations occurred from area to area in the timing and intensity
of these processes. Tacuba was an early victim. Xaltocan prospered
for a time and yielded in the seventeenth century. Tepetlaoztoc
made a late recovery based not on land but on a pack-train commerce. Chalco province attracted powerful hacendados and became
an area of extreme land pressures. By contrast, Xochimilco lacked

the kind of land that attracted hacendados and by a coincidence of circumstances maintained its craft economy and chinampa agriculture throughout the colonial period. Tenochtitlan and Tlatelolco, which lacked land from the start, remained virtually immune from the struggle against the hacienda. But Tenochtitlan made a more viable economic adjustment than Tlatelolco, which suffered progressively from drought, emigration, and neglect.

What we have studied is the deterioration of a native empire and civilization. The empire collapsed first, and the civilization was fragmented in individual communities. Some creativity appeared in the early stages of change, but the process as a whole could not be called a creative one for Indians. The community proved to be the largest Indian social unit capable of survival, and it survived in spite of manifold and severe stresses. The cofradía and the fiesta were enlisted to support it. Indians in general yielded to Spanish demands, protesting only in rare instances of community resistance. The civilization became infused with Hispanic traits at many points, but it retained an essential Indian character, partly through the conviction of its members, partly because it was depressed to a social status so low that it was given no opportunities for change. One of the earliest and most persistent individual responses was drink. If our sources may be believed, few peoples in the whole of history were more prone to drunkenness than the Indians of the Spanish colony.

12. The Dawn of Conscience in America

Lewis Hanke

The image many English-speaking people have of Spanish action in America is one of almost unrelieved cruelty to the Indians, and many unfavorable judgments have been made on Spanish action in the New World in comparison with English colonization. Spaniards naturally resented these judgments and a "war of the myths"

Lewis Hanke, "The Dawn of Conscience in America: Spanish Experiments and Experiences with Indians in the New World," *Proceedings of the American Philosophical Society*, CVII, No. 2 (April, 1963), pp. 83–92, *passim*. Reprinted by permission of the American Philosophical Society.

has resulted. One myth makes the Spaniards the heroes, the English
the villains, and the Indians the victims and the opposing myth
makes the Spaniards into villains, the English into heroes, but still
casts the Indians in the role of victims. My aim is to present some
relatively little-known aspects of Spanish-Indian relations, not to
present a well-rounded comparison of European colonial practices,
and certainly not to engage in the war of the myths.

All European explorers and colonists who came to the New World
encountered native peoples. But only the Spaniards met so many
millions of natives, whom they called Indians, in the vast stretches
of their empire which eventually reached from California to Pata-
gonia. The very fact of large numbers of natives settled under the
control of the Aztec, Inca, and Maya empires required the Spaniards
to devise a different method of treating them from that worked out
by the English, French, and Portuguese for the largely nomadic and
much smaller number of natives they found sparsely scattered in
their territories.   . . .

In the effort to govern the mass of Indians in their great empire
the Spaniards adapted some institutions from their own medieval
experience of long fighting against the Moslems and created others
to meet the needs of New World conditions. The determination of
the crown and the church to Christianize the Indians, the imperious
demand of Spaniards for labor forces to exploit the new lands for
revenue for the Crown and for themselves, and the attempts of some
Spaniards to protect the Indians resulted in a very remarkable complex of relations, laws, and institutions which even today leads
historians to contradictory conclusions on the reality of Spanish
rule in America. The encomienda system, by which groups of Indians were assigned to Spaniards, a device to provide both labor and
goods to the Spaniard and protection and religious instruction for
the Indians, was both stoutly defended as necessary and bitterly
attacked as un-Christian throughout the sixteenth century by Spaniards themselves. The Spanish imperial policy of attempting to civilize the Indians by urbanizing them led to many curious experiments
and experiences, and in the end was fatal for large numbers of
natives. George Kubler has pointed out in his substantial work on
Mexican architecture:

> no building could be achieved without the prior urbanization
> of the participants. To urbanize the Indian populations was to

dislocate and destroy the patterns of indigenous culture. Such cultural extirpation brought about, in turn, the biological decrease of the Indian race. . . . Each building, and each colonial artifact, was nourished by the destruction of a culture and the decline of a race.

Spain made many efforts to mitigate the lot of the Indians by appointing official "Protectors," setting up special courts to try cases involving them, and sending out numerous investigating groups to discover what might be done to help them. She tried many stratagems in the sixteenth century particularly to ensure that Indians would be brought under Spanish rule by peaceful means alone, and be persuaded to accept Christianity by reason instead of by force. To achieve this end the Dominican Bartolomé de Las Casas and his brother Dominicans attempted to preach the faith without the backing of the sword in Chiapas, and Vasco de Quiroga established his Utopian communities in Michoacán. In many places a system of Indian segregation was worked out by friars and royal officials to protect them from other Spaniards who would exploit them, and this practice was followed throughout the colonial period, culminating in the famous Jesuit missions in eighteenth-century Paraguay. The difficult, indeed impossible, double purpose of the crown to secure revenue and also to Christianize the Indians inevitably led in fact to a series of angry disputes, evil compromises, and some glorious episodes throughout the more than three centuries of Spanish rule in America.

Today, in looking back on the total encounter of Spaniards and Indians, two developments hold special interest for us, living as we do in a world society whose multiplicity and variety of cultures become daily more evident and more significant. For the first time in history one people — the Spaniards — paid serious attention to the nature of the culture of the peoples they met; and, perhaps most striking of all, the controversies which developed in sixteenth-century Spain and America over the just method of treating the Indians led to a fundamental consideration of the nature of man himself. This "dawn of conscience in America" was only a faint daybreak; indeed, who can say that in the twentieth century we have reached high noon? The fact that we are still struggling ourselves to discover how to live justly in a world of many races and many cultures gives the Spanish struggles of the sixteenth century a poignant and familiar ring. . . .

It was the friars, looking for souls to win, rather than the conquistadores, who first began to study Indian customs, history, and
religion. The missionaries needed to know the names and attributes
of Indian gods, the sacrifices made to them, and as accurately as
possible the mentality of the Indians in order to lead them away
from their pagan rites toward Christianity. The founder of American
anthropology was Friar Ramón Pané, who accompanied Columbus
on his second voyage for the express purpose of observing the natives and reporting on their ways and who was the first European
to learn an Indian language.

The Crown encouraged ecclesiastics throughout the sixteenth
century to study the Indians, and numerous volumes on their cultures were in fact prepared. Administration officials such as Alonso
de Zurita also compiled reports, and the questionnaires sent out
regularly to all Spanish governors in the New World by the Council
of the Indies included a number of items on Indians. The result of
all this enquiry is a magnificent body of linguistic, archaeological,
and ethnographical material which is both contradictory at times
and difficult to assess because so much remains in manuscript and
even the printed editions available are often poor, lacking indexes
and proper notes.   . . .

Closely linked with these anthropological studies and with Spain's
struggle to work out a just Indian policy was the much disputed
question of the nature of the Indians. The first twinge of official
conscience was expressed by Ferdinand and Isabella in 1495 when
they learned that a shipload of Indians Columbus had sent back
from Hispaniola had been sold as slaves because they had been taken
in rebellion. The monarchs thereupon instructed Bishop Fonseca,
who managed Indian affairs, that the money from this sale should
not be accepted until their Highnesses could inform themselves from
men learned in law whether these Indians could be sold with good
conscience. No document that I know of has recorded the answer
the sovereigns requested. A dramatic public protest in America
against Indian slavery was made by a Dominican friar named Antonio de Montesinos, who in a revolutionary sermon preached in
1511 on the island of Hispaniola thundered:

> Tell me, by what right or justice do you keep these Indians
> in cruel servitude? On what authority have you waged a de-
> testable was against these people, who dwelt quietly and

peacefully on their own land? . . . Are these not men? Have
they not rational souls?

This sermon led to serious disputes and discussions in Spain, out of
which came the 1512 Laws of Burgos to govern relations between
Spaniards and Indians as well as juridical treatises on the basis for
Spanish dominion in the New World.

The legalistic and religious nature of the Spaniards led both to
their intense preoccupation with the just basis for their newly discovered overseas territory and with the nature of the Indians whom
they were attempting to draw into the Christian world. Francisco
de Vitoria, a Dominican professor at the University of Salamanca,
discussed these matters with great vision and clarity in his lectures
and many of his students later went to America with their attitudes
determined by his teachings. Vitoria remarked in one treatise, *De
Indis:* "The Indians are stupid only because they are uneducated
and, if they live like beasts, so for the same reason do many Spanish
peasants." He also asserted that discovery alone gave Spaniards
no more right to American territory than the Indians would have
acquired had they "discovered" Spain. Vitoria and other Spanish
political theorists of the time addressed themselves to the fundamental legal questions raised when Europe invaded America and,
long before Grotius, laid down an enduring basis for international
law.

Most significant of all, the Spanish inquiry into the nature of the
Indians and their capacity for entering into the Christian commonwealth led Spaniards to grapple with that ultimate problem — the
nature of man himself. Of all the ideas churned up during the early
tumultuous years of American history, none had more dramatic
implications than the attempts made to apply to the natives there
the Aristotelian doctrine of natural slavery: that one part of mankind is set aside by nature to be slaves in the service of masters born
for a life of virtue free of manual labor. Learned authorities such
as the Spanish scholar Sepúlveda not only sustained this view with
great tenacity and erudition but also concluded, without having
visited America, that the Indians were in fact such rude and brutal
beings that war against them to make possible their forcible Christianization was not only expedient but lawful. Many ecclesiastics,
especially Las Casas, opposed this idea scornfully, with appeals to
divine and natural law as well as to their own experience in America.

The controversy became so heated and the emperor's conscience so troubled over the question of how to carry on the conquest of the Indies in a Christian way that Charles V actually ordered the suspension of all expeditions to America while a junta of foremost theologians, jurists, and officials was convoked in the royal capital of Valladolid to listen to the arguments of Las Casas and Sepúlveda. All this occurred in 1550, after Cortez had conquered Mexico, Francisco Pizarro had shattered the Inca empire, and many other lesser-known captains had carried the Spanish banners to far corners of the New World.

Las Casas and Sepúlveda duly fought their great battle of ideas before the junta in Valladolid. The details of their arguments cannot be indicated here. The foundation on which Las Casas based his argument was that the Indians were truly men capable of becoming Christians. Drawing upon the information he had brought together in his massive anthropological work the *Apologetic History,* he documented his contention that the Indians had many skills and accomplishments and in fact possessed a culture worthy of respect. He cited their agricultural methods as well as their irrigation systems; illustrated their ingenuity by the way they derived twenty-two products from the maguey tree, contrived delicate ornamental collars of fish bones, and created remarkable gold jewelry. He drew special attention to their extraordinary capacity to learn the Old World crafts which the Spaniards had brought with them, giving a careful account of the way the Indians made knives and rubber balls. He also described the cleverness of their painters, their feather work, their silver making with few tools, and, after little training, their competence in fashioning musical instruments, their work as carpenters, and their hand lettering so fine that it could sometimes not be distinguished from printing. The only thing he found an Indian could not do as well as a Spaniard was to shoe a horse. He described the Indian mining methods and included an account of their ball games. Above all, however, he claimed, the Indians excelled in the dramatic arts and demonstrated this with various illustrations. He described the military organization of both the Mexican Indians and the Incas of Peru, a topic on which relatively few data are provided by other works, and gave much information on their coca chewing and tobacco smoking, together with an excellent description of the great teeming market in Mexico City.

He devoted many pages to the religion of the Indians, and the most striking aspect of this section is his attitude toward Indian sacrifices. He considered that the most religious peoples were those which offered to God the most magnificent sacrifice, and those who offered human beings had — in his opinion — a very noble concept indeed of their God. The Indian fasts, mortifications of the body, sacrifices of animals and men, were clearly superior to the sacrifices of the ancient peoples. Under the horrible and bloody aspects of these rites Las Casas discerned a commendable spirit of religious devotion which could be directed to higher ends and enlisted in the service of the only true God.

Las Casas was deeply convinced of the importance of education and therefore was particularly impressed by the meticulous attention paid by the Mexican Indians to the education of their children in the ways of chastity, honesty, fortitude, obedience, and sobriety. He cried:

> Did Plato, Socrates, Pythagoras, or even Aristotle leave us better or more natural or more necessary exhortations to the virtuous life than these barbarians delivered to their children? Does the Christian religion teach us more, save the faith and what it teaches us of invisible and supernatural matters? Therefore, no one may deny that these people are fully capable of governing themselves and of living like men of good intelligence and that they are more than others well ordered, sensible, prudent, and rational.

Las Casas believed firmly in the capacity of all people for civilization; he emphatically rejected a static and hopeless barbarism. "All the peoples of the world are men," he insisted, and declared that God would not allow any nation to exist, "no matter how barbarous, fierce, or depraved its customs" which might not be "persuaded and brought to a good order and way of life" provided the persuasion was peaceful. To practical conquistadores and administrators, men aiming at immediate wordly goals and faced with different kinds of Indians, and perhaps to the crown as well, jealous of all royal prerogatives, Las Casas' reiteration that the only justification for the presence of Spaniards in the New World was the Christianization of Indians by peaceful means alone must have seemed dangerous nonsense. One can imagine with what contempt and horror his announcement was received that Spain ought to abandon America, with all its Indians un-Christianized, rather than to bring them into the fold by forcible and — to him — profoundly un-Christian methods. The important fact to us today is that Sepúlveda's doctrine did not triumph at Valladolid in 1550 and that his treatise was not approved for publication until late in the eighteenth century.

Since the Valladolid debate the problem of how to treat peoples unlike ourselves in color, race, religion, or customs has given rise in every century to the most diverse and inflammatory opinions. In general the idea of the inferiority of natives to Europeans appeared in whatever far corners of the world Europeans reached. In the English colonies, for example, only Roger Williams had any respect for Indian culture and small attention was given the theories about Indians.

The battle waged by Las Casas and all the other Spaniards of his opinion to win recognition of the humanity of the Indians and to understand their culture is far from won. But today those who believe that "all the peoples of the world are men" have powerful allies. Anthropologists have gone on record that "the basic principles of opportunity and equality before the law are compatible with all that is known of human biology. All races possess the abilities needed to participate fully in the democratic way of life and in modern technological civilization." The United Nations Universal Declaration of Human Rights, adopted four centuries after the Valladolid controversy, announced: "All human beings are born free and equal in dignity and rights. They are endowed with reason and conscience and should act towards one another in a spirit of brotherhood." The Ecumenical Council, now in session at the Vatican, with members "from every nation under heaven" expressed the thought even more succinctly in its Message to Humanity: "We proclaim that all men are brothers, irrespective of the race or nation to which they belong."

Only a partisan in the "war of the myths" would dare to claim that the ideals announced by the Spanish crown were generally followed in the American territory under Spanish rule. Nor should anyone claim that the Spaniards fully accomplished their purpose: to incorporate the mass of New World Indians into a Christian and a European world.

For we know in the twentieth century that the Spaniards faced impossible problems: the clash of cultures complicated by the great area in which they operated, the tremendous diversity of the Indians encountered, and the small number of Spaniards available for conversion and education of the millions of Indians. One important doctrinal question remains. Why did Negroes never receive the same solicitous attention as Indians, and why did the conscience of Spaniards twinge so much more easily for Indians than for Negroes?

The Jesuit Alonso de Sandoval did indeed write a treatise in the seventeenth century on the culture of the different tribes of Negroes brought to Cartagena and may therefore be called the first Africanist in America. But neither Sandoval nor his disciple Pedro Claver ever denounced Negro slavery as an un-Christian institution, and the moral conscience of Europe was first roused in modern times by the plight of the Indian of America. The difference between the Spanish attitude toward Indians and Negroes has not yet been satisfactorily explained, and remains an important problem for investigation.

Is it not remarkable enough, however, that some sixteenth-century Spaniards studied Indian cultures and that a whole school of powerful and articulate members of this intensely nationalistic people fought stoutly for the rights of the Indians? During the early years of expansion which eventually carried European ideas and goods to almost every corner of the earth, Spain produced, it is true, an aggressive advocate of Aristotle's doctrine of natural slavery. But she also produced the powerful champion of Indians as men, whose voice along with many other Spanish voices proclaimed the dawn of conscience in America. No matter how far rockets may reach into outer space, will any more significant problems be discovered than those which agitated many Spaniards during the conquest of America? When the story is told of man's attempts in history to grapple with this most difficult problem — how to relate to other men of unfamiliar cultures — will not this become clear: that when the Spanish Crown and Council of the Indies refrained from stigmatizing the natives of the New World as natural slaves they placed an important milestone on the long road, still under construction, which winds all too slowly toward civilizations which respect the dignity of man, that is to say of all men?

BIBLIOGRAPHIC SUGGESTIONS

1. Arjona, Doris K. "The 'Twelve' Meet a Language Requirement," *Hispania,* XXXV (Aug., 1952), pp. 259–266.

2. Aznar, Luis. "Legislación sobre indios en la América hispano-colonial: Cuestiones de criterio. Períodos legislativos," *Humanidades*, XXV, part 1 (1937), pp. 233–274.
3. Caso, Alfonso, et al. *Métodos y resultados de la política indigenista de México* (Mexico: Instituto Nacional Indigenista, 1954). A thorough and complete review of Indian policy in Mexico from the conquest until today.
4. Comas, Juan. "La cristianización del indio desde 1492 a nuestros dias," *América Indígena*, XI (1951), pp. 219–234.
5. ————. "La realidad del trato dado a las indígenas de América entre los siglos XV y XX, *América Indígena*, XI (1951), pp. 323–370.
6. Chamberlain, Robert S. "Simpson's *The Encomienda in New Spain* and Recent Encomienda Studies," *Hispanic American Historical Review*, XXXIV (1954), pp. 228–250. Valuable review article.
6a. Chevalier, François. *Land and Society in Colonial Mexico* (Berkeley: University of California Press, 1965).
7. Crespo Rodas, Alberto. "La mita de Potosí," *Revista Histórica*, XXII (Lima, 1955–1956), pp. 169–182.
7a. Gibson, Charles. *Spain in America* (New York: Harper and Row, 1966). See especially Chap. 3 on the Encomienda and Chap. 7 on Spaniards and Indians.
7b. Hanke, Lewis. *The First Social Experiments in America* (Cambridge, Mass.: Harvard University Press, 1935).
8. Jiménez Moreno, Wigberto. "The Indians of America and Christianity," *The Americas*, XIV (1958), pp. 411–431.
9. Menéndez Pidal, Ramón. *El Padre Las Casas. Su doble personalidad* (Madrid: Espasa-Calpe, 1963). For an analysis of this attack on Las Casas, see the editor's "More Heat and Some Light on the Spanish Struggle for Justice in the Conquest of America," *Hispanic American Historical Review*, XXXXIV (1964), pp. 293–340.
10. Miranda, José. *El tributo indígena en la Nueva España durante el siglo XVI* (Mexico: El Colegio de México, 1952).
11. ————. "La función económica del encomendero en los orígines del régimen colonial. Nueva España (1525–1531)," *Anales del Instituto Nacional de Antropología* (México), II (1949), pp. 421–462.
12. Parry, John H. *The Spanish Theory of Empire in the Sixteenth Century* (Cambridge, Eng.: Cambridge University Press, 1940).
12a. Poole, Stafford. "The Church and the Repartimientos in the

Light of the Third Mexican Council, 1585," *The Americas,* XX (July, 1963), pp. 3–36.

12b. ————. " 'War by Fire and Blood,' " *ibid.,* XXII (October, 1965), pp. 115–137.

13. Quirk, Robert E. "Some Notes on a Controversial Controversy: Juan Ginés de Sepúlveda and Natural Servitude," *Hispanic American Historical Review,* XXXIV (1954), pp. 357–364.

For those who enjoy polemics over Indian questions, this article should be read in conjunction with these studies: Edmundo O'Gorman, "Lewis Hanke on the Spanish Struggle for Justice in the Conquest of America," *Hispanic American Historical Review,* XXIX (1949), pp. 563–571; and the article by Lewis Hanke, "Bartolomé de Las Casas, an Essay in Hagiography and Historiography," *Hispanic American Historical Review,* XXXIII (1953), pp. 136–151.

13a. Ricard, Ricard. *The Spiritual Conquest of Mexico* (Berkeley: University of California Press, 1967).

13b. Sauer, Carl Ortwin. *The Early Spanish Main* (Berkeley: University of California Press, 1966).

14. Service, Elman R. "Indian-European Relations in Colonial Latin America," *American Anthropologist,* LVII (1957), pp. 411–425. Analysis of the relationship between the complexity of Indian societies and cultures and the various policies employed by the Spanish and Portuguese settlers, missionaries, and officials.

15. ————. "The Encomienda in Paraguay," *Hispanic American Historical Review,* XXXI (May, 1951), pp. 230–252.

16. Simpson, Lesley B. *The Encomienda in New Spain: the Beginning of Spanish Mexico* (Berkeley: University of California Press, 1966). Third edition of this standard work.

17. Zavala, Silvio. *De la encomienda y propiedad territorial en algunas regiones de la América española* (Mexico: Antigua Librería Robredo de José Porrúa e Hijos, 1940).

Section IV

Population Statistics and Social History

The social history of Latin America, as distinct from the study of conquistadores, friars, viceroys, and laws, is relatively underdeveloped. Even firm statistical knowledge on the population has been lacking. But in recent years the subject has been increasingly studied, and when more fully opened up will greatly enrich our understanding of past and present Latin American civilization.

To try to determine the number of Indians in America at the time of the conquest is not merely a statistical exercise but is closely related to some fundamental aspects of life in the New World. Bailey W. Diffie of the City College of New York questions many of the past estimates (Reading IV.1); Woodrow Borah of the University of California, Berkeley (Reading IV.2) reaches different conclusions by using different methods. Peter Boyd-Bowman of Kalamazoo College, whose field is language and literature, analyzes the records of passengers to the Indies in the Archivo de Indias to determine the regions of Spain that set the earliest standards of speech in America (Reading IV.3). The problems raised in these selections are far from solved; indeed, a lively discussion of them took place at the meeting of the XXXVII Congress of Americanists in Argentina in September, 1966.[1]

---

[1] The following papers were among those presented, in mimeographed form: Woodrow Borah, "The Historical Demography of Aboriginal and Colonial Latin America: An Attempt at Perspective"; Ángel Rosenblat, "Problemas y métodos de demografía historica. Los cálculos de la población precolombina." They will be published in the Proceedings of the Congress.

Professor Borah, a pioneer in population studies, presents the challenging hypothesis that Mexico's century of depression following 1576 caused its distinctive economy to be organized on the basis of latifundia and debt peonage, which lasted until the nineteenth century ". . . and which helped provoke the Revolution of 1910–1917" (Reading IV.4). The role of the Negroes brought as slaves to the Spanish and Portuguese colonies in America, although it has not claimed as much attention as that of the Indians, was very important indeed, as Professor Wilbur Zelinsky of Pennsylvania State University explains (Reading IV.5).

Professor Dauril Alden of the University of Washington will doubtless surprise some readers by his remark that ". . . population counts in colonial America long antedated the adoption of modern census figures in Europe." His analysis of the demographic statistics for late eighteenth-century Brazil (Reading IV.6) is a preliminary but valuable study which helps to reveal ". . . answers to such questions as the size, distribution, and racial composition of Brazil's population during the last colonial decades."

The most striking characteristic of colonial society in Spanish and Portuguese America was its varied racial strains and combinations. The careful study of this mixed-race society has just begun, as Professor Mörner has made clear in his report on the present state of knowledge on this vital and complicated subject.[2]

---

[2] Magnus Mörner, *El mestizaje en la historia* (Mexico: Instituto Panamericano de Geografía e Historia, 1961). See also the volume, to be brought out by Cornell University Press in 1967, on proceedings of the international conference on *mestizaje* organized by Dr. Mörner.

A.   Estimates of Indian Population in 1492

1. The Early Spanish Accounts Were Inflated

BAILEY W. DIFFIE

The Population of the Indies — How many people were living in America at the time of the Conquest has been a matter of dispute since the first reports of discovery. The number was placed very high by some of the earliest writers. The population of pre-Conquest America was not as large, however, nor the depopulation after the Conquest as great, as is frequently believed. The wars of conquest, enslavement, harsh treatment, and disease undoubtedly contributed to a decline in population; but much of the "Black Legend" concerning Spain in the New World has arisen from inflated estimates of the numbers of pre-Conquest peoples.

Bartolomé de Las Casas estimated the population in millions. For example, he believed that the island of Cuba had at least 200,000 Indians in 1492. Another estimate placed the population of Cuba at the beginning of the Conquest in 1511 at 1,000,000, and in 1517 at only 14,000 people. Fray Luís Bertrán, however, in an estimate made between 1555–69, gave Cuba 200,000 Indians. Yet in the same period (1553) López de Gómara asserted that while "Cuba was once heavily populated with Indians, today there are only Spaniards." His explanation was that "they all turned Christian. Many died of work, of hunger, and of smallpox, and many went to New Spain after Cortés conquered it. And thus, there is none of their race left." He estimated that Española "once had a million men." Equally high and contradictory estimates were made for the mainland. Oviedo remarks: "in this region of Castilla de Oro [a relatively small area taking in parts of Panama and Colombia] there were two million Indians, or, they were innumerable." The eighteenth-century

Bailey W. Diffie, *Latin-American Civilization: Colonial Period* (Harrisburg, Pa.: Stackpole Sons, 1945), pp. 178–186. Reprinted by permission of the author.

writer, Antonio de Ulloa, estimated that "there is not in America the eighth part of the population that existed at the time of discovery," basing his statement on the assumption that America of 1492 had 120,000,000 people. Clavigero notes that Riccoli placed the total for America at 300,000,000 people. De Pauw stated that while others estimated the pre-Conquest population at 100,000,000 he thought 30,000,000 to 40,000,000 was about right.

All these early statements are so little in agreement that it is hard to accept any of them. To illustrate the difficulties of finding the true population from early estimates, Humboldt points out that the population of the island of Otaheite [Hawaii] was estimated by Captain Cook when he discovered it at 100,000, by the missionaries at 49,000, by Captain Wilson at 16,000, and by Turnbull at 5,000. In view of this uncertainty about the population of one small Pacific island in the eighteenth century, it is not strange that there is confusion in determining the population of a much greater area in the sixteenth.

A large population for Cuba and other tropical regions has been assumed on the basis of their great fertility, which could support millions of people. Yet, wherever we find large populations in tropical regions, they have developed conventionalized civilizations with at least relatively advanced agricultural and economic systems. Pre-Conquest Cubans had no such things. They farmed but little, their trade was practically nonexistent, and their villages were small and situated many miles apart. The total population in all probability was not more than a few thousand naked and half-naked people in 1492. The same thing is true of the island of Española, Puerto Rico, and many other tropical areas.

Pre-Conquest Mexican Population — The figures given for Mexican population are subject to the same doubts, and it is necessary to use other evidence for a more accurate estimate. With the exception of Sinaloa, both coast lines and most of the northern part of Mexico were thinly populated. The great bulk of the people were concentrated in Vera Cruz, the Central Valley, Puebla, Morelos, Oaxaca, and Michoacán. Torquemada dwells on the great population, large cities, and fine buildings here when the Spaniards arrived.

Of Mexico City he writes: "It is said of this city that when the Spaniards entered, it had 120,000 houses, and in each house three, four, and up to ten people (*vecinos*), so that, according to this count, its inhabitants (*vecinos*) numbered more than 300,000." He adds, "And granted that it is true (which it is) that this city of Tenochtitlán was so populous and famous, it is so much more so now that it belongs to, and was built by the Spaniards, that there is no comparison." He estimated the population at only "7,000 Spanish vecinos" and "8,000" Indians, a total of 15,000 at the time he wrote [1615] which is difficult to reconcile with other estimates and his own statements. After the rebuilding of Mexico City in 1524, Cortés wrote to the Emperor that the city already numbered 30,000 inhabitants.

There is one indication, however, that the population of Aztec Mexico City was not great. At the time of the Conquest the lakes covered a very large part of the area which is today heavily populated. The maximum area of Tenochtitlán was about three and a half square miles, as compared with the modern Federal District of 572 square miles with a population of under 2,000,000. The discrepancy is too great to permit an assumption of a large population in 1520. Modern London, for example, has only 12,000 people to the square mile. Did Tenochtitlán have more? If so, how was the population clothed and fed in a land with no wheeled vehicles and no beasts of burden? The whole of Aztec Mexico, moreover, comprised possibly not more than one-fourth or one-fifth of the area of the present Mexican nation. The Franciscans, to be sure, claim to have baptized more than 6,000,000 Indians in the region of the capital city alone between 1524 and 1540. But if the population was so extremely dense, why the fierce competition for encomiendas far beyond the number the Spaniards could give out?

The Spaniards in this early period numbered only a few hundred, and had there been so many millions, or even hundreds of thousands of Indians, to distribute there would have been no such problem. The grants made to Cortés himself indicate that the Indian population was not great. He received 22 towns with the surrounding land and 23,000 vassals, which he interpreted as 115,000 people. His grants were in Morelos, Oaxaca, Puebla, Mexico, and Vera Cruz, the choicest and most densely populated parts of Mexico at that time as well as today. The area was not less than 25,000 square miles, equal to approximately one-fifth or one-sixth of the dominions of Montezuma. Judged from this, the population of Montezuma's empire would not have reached a million people.

Humboldt thought that in 1800 New Spain contained more people than the same area had about 1500.

The Population of the Inca Empire — The Inca Empire is usually considered to have comprised 8,000,000 or 10,000,000 people. One modern authority places the population at from 16,000,000 to 32,000,-000, with the city of Cuzco itself having as many as 200,000 people.

This view receives support from the descriptions of the early chroniclers, almost all of whom agree that the early population was dense. Cieza repeats almost monotonously as he traverses the valleys and highlands of ancient Peru, "in former times (*antiguamente*) this valley was heavily populated." For example, of the valley of Santa he says, "there were in former times many thousands of people, and today you cannot find 400 natives." He states that, whereas formerly the Indians built impressive irrigation projects throughout the valley and high up on the hillsides, "now, since there are so few Indians, as I have said, most of the fields are uncultivated, having become woods and brambles with such thickets that in many places it is impossible to penetrate them." In the valley of Parmonga, he reported that there was "nothing but deserted groves and wooded fields."

But, at the same time, there are evidences that much of the population had disappeared before the Spanish invasion, and that it was never so heavy as first appearances indicate. It may be taken as axiomatic that vast populations will of necessity form a number of cities. And yet Cieza makes it clear that Cuzco was the only town in the whole of the Inca Empire that was of any size and importance.

> And in no part of this kingdom of Peru was there found any sort of a city of beauty (*con noble ornamento*), if it was not this city of Cuzco. . . . And except for this city, the other provinces of the Indies are villages. And if there are any towns they have neither plan nor order.

Nor is the evidence clear on the population trend after the Conquest. While to Cieza it seemed that there had once been many more Indians than there were fifteen years after the Conquest, judging from the remains found everywhere, he says that "even when the Spaniards discovered them and conquered them there were a great number of people," indicating that he believed some of the depopulation occurred before Spanish discovery.

An undetermined degree of depopulation is revealed in an Ordinance issued by the Cabildo of Cuzco in 1543, ten years after the conquest of the city by the Spaniards. This Ordinance was concerned with preserving the *tambos* (supply and lodging stations along the Inca roads) and highways. More tambos were abandoned than occupied, because "in these said kingdoms and provinces there has been, and is a great diminution of the Indian natives." Yet it is not at all certain that there were tremendous decreases after the Conquest. A careful reading of the first and second parts of Cieza de Leon's *Crónica* demonstrates that very frequently when he says "antiguamente" he really means *anciently* and not *formerly*. Many of the places of which he speaks as having large and sumptuous buildings and large populations "antiguamente" were pre-Inca ruins. Hence the Spaniards cannot be held responsible for the extinction of their populations. In other places once thickly settled, only uncultivated fields with trees as big around as an ox remained, indicating that they were abandoned many years before the Spaniards entered South America.

There are other reasons to doubt the large population of ancient Peru. From the time of the first conquerors, the extremely broken and mountainous nature of the country and the vast uninhabited areas received considerable attention from Cieza and other chroniclers. The coastline was a desert absolutely barren of vegetation except for the few valleys where the rivers break through to the sea. These valleys occupy only about three per cent of the entire coastline. Probably not more than one per cent of ancient Peru was habitable. The question then arises how large a population could be sustained with the available arable and pasture land.

Squier made extensive explorations in Peru in the nineteenth century and was impressed by the small area available for cultivation. He thought that previous estimates of the population were far too high and brought his estimate down to "between ten and twelve millions." Cobo was so struck by the small amount of arable land that when he wrote his work, after more than half a century in Peru, he remarks on "the very few people who formerly inhabited it, and the still fewer it has at present, relatively to its great size and expanse." The heading he gives his chapter on this subject, "On how America was lightly populated and the causes for this," reveals his conclusions. His explanation demonstrates that because of the immense deserts where it seldom or never rained, the swamps where it never ceased raining, the jungles where the vegetation was too dense for people to live, the mountain regions that were too cold, the immense areas of bad lands composed of mountains, sand or salt flats, and finally the good land that was not settled by the Indians, the population was small. He did not, however, venture a guess at the total. After reading Cobo's description of Peru's geography and travels through the country, it is difficult to believe it was ever heavily peopled.

Most estimates of population are dependent on the translation of the Spanish word *vecino*. A vecino in the sixteenth century could mean either the head of a family, or a citizen with political rights within the community (the majority of the people did not enjoy political rights), or merely *one* person. On the one hand, vecino may be taken to represent an average family of five or ten, as Means does in his calculations, or the unit vecino may be multiplied by as much as twenty-five or thirty. On the other hand, it may be taken to mean only one person and it was so used at times by Garcilaso and Torquemada. Thus, the vecino is not a reliable basis of calculation. A better method is to estimate the number of people that ancient Peru could have supported with its methods of production.

The Inca Empire had an area of some 380,000 square miles, comprising parts of modern Ecuador, Peru, Bolivia, Argentina, and Chile. The area within the boundaries of these nations today is several times that of ancient Peru. Modern Peru alone is one-third larger, and occupies a great deal of territory not included in the Inca Empire.

Peru has in cultivation today about 3,715,000 acres, and approximately 17,000,000 in pasture. The maximum arable land (except that east of the Andes where the Inca Empire did not extend) with the maximum irrigation possible, and using modern engineering science, is about 4,000,000 acres. How many people could have been supported if the Incas had cultivated every foot of arable land?

On the basis of the probable consumption of corn per person, the corn alone necessary for 1,000,000 people each year would have been approximately 8,660,000 bushels. With a production of 20 bushels to the acre (in the United States the average yield per acre is 23 bushels, and it was undoubtedly much less in Inca Peru), each million inhabitants would have needed 433,000 acres in corn a year. Other agricultural products besides corn, however, took up much arable land; at least three times as much land was cultivated as was used for corn. Altogether 1,300,000 acres of land would have been required to support a million people. Moreover, a great deal of land could not be cultivated every year. On an average, one year's cultivation in five was the rule, making scarcely more than 2,000,000 or 3,000,000 acres in cultivation at one time in ancient Peru. Thus, that part of ancient Peru included in modern Peru could not have had more than 1,500,000 people, assuming the maximum use of the land.

As for the parts of the Inca Empire that lay outside the present-day Peru, they consisted of the high plateau of Bolivia, which Garcilaso classed as having "few people" and being "scarcely inhabited," the northwestern part of Argentina, likewise lightly populated; northern Chile, which was, and is properly a desert; and Ecuador, which could hardly have contained a greater proportion of people than Peru.

Significant also was the lack of enough Indians to give out in encomiendas. Pizarro, who of course received the largest encomienda, around Atabillos northeast of Lima, claimed 100,000 Indians. Other conquistadores received only a few hundred Indians, or less, or even none. The governors were hard put to find Indians to distribute, and this was one of the main causes of the civil wars from 1538–54.

Also pertinent to the question of population was its rapid redistribution after the Conquest. While early chroniclers point out the numerous deserted valleys, they also stress the establishment of dozens of Spanish towns stretching from Ecuador into Peru, Bolivia, Argentina, and Chile. Cieza, Garcilaso, and others make it clear that many of these towns were in regions in which there had been no previous population, or but little. Lima itself is an example. Potosí, the great silver-mining center, soon had 100,000 people, and attained 160,000 at its maximum. Besides these, there was a large number of small settlements, inhabited by Indian populations; in fact, perhaps 90 per cent or more of the people in most of these centers were Indian. The depopulation in certain areas was largely attributable to the migrations of the resettlement.

Finally, there is the city of Cuzco itself, to which have been attributed as many as 200,000 people. The area of the city, less than one square mile after Spanish settlement, when admittedly both its area and population increased, could scarcely have contained so many inhabitants. The Jesuit historian, José de Acosta, takes the view that the Indians were not decreasing but increasing in 1590.

> What causes these lands to be inhabited, and some of them heavily populated, is the wealth of the mines that are found in them, because gold and silver control everything. In these lands, thanks to the mines, there are some very large towns of Spaniards and Indians, such as Potosí and Huancavelica in Peru and Zacatecas in New Spain. Throughout all the mountains (*serranías*) there is a heavy population of Indians, and today they are maintaining their numbers, and they even say that the Indians are increasing, except that the work in the mines uses up a great many; and some general epidemics, such as the Cocoliste in New Spain have killed off a great part; but in truth, judging from their dwellings, it cannot be seen that they are decreasing.

Cobo records that the driving back of savages never conquered by the Incas resulted in the occupation and peopling of much good land.

While the population of pre-Conquest America cannot be definitely determined, it is clear that the early figures were not only in such disagreement regarding specific localities in the same period as to be subject to doubt, but were far too high. If we take into account all available evidence regarding geographical features, the sources of food and agricultural methods of the Indians, and the chroniclers' descriptions of the most populous centers, it is certain that even the most densely settled regions, such as Mexico and Peru, could not have supported anything like the huge numbers of people attributed to them.

Acceptance of the early estimates has given rise to a belief that the decline in native population as a result of the Conquest was much greater than it actually was. In reality, some of the apparent depopulation came from the rapid resettlement after the Conquest, when the Indians migrated to the new mining and agricultural centers opened up by the Spaniards. The Indians, far from being exterminated, continued to form the majority of the population of post-Conquest Latin America.

2. Sixteenth-Century Statements on the Population of Central Mexico Are Substantiated by Modern Calculations

WOODROW BORAH AND S. F. COOK

In two earlier monographs we estimated the size of the Indian population of central Mexico for various years during the first century of Spanish rule; we did not then attempt an estimate of the size of that population in central Mexico for the years immediately before the Spanish landed on the shores of the Gulf of Mexico and brought substantial new factors into operation in the area. Yet, having gone thus far backward in time, we have found ourselves unable to halt our study without an inquiry into the size of the aboriginal population just before the Spanish irruption.

The question has lured scholars into controversy ever since the second half of the eighteenth century, when William Robertson, Cornelius de Pauw, and Guillaume Raynal wrote extensive accounts of the nature and history of the European establishments in America, accounts that quickly became well known in central and western Europe. Their works were remarkable feats of comparative analysis based on critical reading of the printed texts available to them: Spanish chronicles, documents of the Conquest and early colonial period, and official histories. The skepticism nourished by the Enlightenment led all three writers to question not the tales of Spanish cruelty and massacres during the Conquest — stories of similar mistreatment by Europeans of other countries were commonplace — but the splendors of the advanced civilizations of pre-Conquest Peru and Mexico, and the reported denseness of their aboriginal populations. They found flatly unbelievable statements about the size of cities and native armies and the descriptions of vast and imposing buildings. No eighteenth-century traveler, they

Woodrow Borah and S. F. Cook, *The Aboriginal Population of Central Mexico on the Eve of the Spanish Conquest* (Ibero-Americana: 45; Berkeley, Calif.: University of California Press, 1963), pp. 1–5, 88. Reprinted by permission of the University of California Press.

commented, had mentioned seeing the great ruins that should still have been in existence had the early Spanish writers been accurate. Furthermore, Indians were known to be brutish savages still using crude implements of bone and stone, incapable of the organization and marshaling of resources necessary for building cities or maintaining imperial institutions. The Spanish conquerors, commented Robertson, had been so surprised to see any buildings at all in Mexico that they had let their imaginations run riot and turned rude and barbaric structures into huge palaces and temples. He and other writers made full allowance for the "warm imagination of the Spanish writers."

In opposition to these views, Francisco Clavijero vigorously upheld the reliability of early Spanish writers and conquerors. He pointed to the agreement of testimony by writers who could hardly have been in a general and unanimous conspiracy to deceive and would have been especially careful to remain relatively close to the truth in reports to their sovereigns. Clavijero, a Mexican-born Jesuit writing in Italy after the expulsion of the Society of Jesus from the Spanish dominions, declared that there was ample archaeological evidence of the splendor of pre-Conquest Mexico.

At the turn of the century, Alexander von Humboldt, who knew Mexico from personal observation and wide reading, prudently took a middle position. "The extended ruins of towns and villages that one finds in the interior of Mexico between 18 and 20 degrees of latitude prove beyond doubt that the population of that part of the kingdom was once much larger than at present. The letters of Cortés to Emperor Charles V, the memoirs of Bernal Díaz, and a great number of other historical monuments confirm this interesting fact." On the other hand, he indicated that it was difficult to use calculations and statements of sixteenth-century writers in estimating the pre-Conquest population of Mexico. In his day, he declared, the Indians were on the increase, and the population of Mexico was greater than at the time of the Conquest if one took into account the post-Conquest settlement of the North. In effect, Humboldt was prepared to concede that there had been something beyond a rude tribal culture in central Mexico and that the population of that area was smaller at the close of the eighteenth century than at the beginning of the sixteenth; but, he hinted, the size of the population before the Conquest and its decrease afterward had both been greatly exaggerated.

The controversy of the second half of the eighteenth century is especially interesting because it contains the basic positions scholars have taken subsequently. One group insisted that tribal societies such as Europeans knew in what is today the United States and Canada could not have given rise to the far more advanced societies described for Peru and Mexico and that therefore Spanish sources must all be used with great caution. One might call this the Bandelier position. A second group accepted these sources as reasonably accurate and held that there existed in Middle America aboriginal societies as far removed from the culture of the Plains Indians and the Eskimos as the cultures of central and western Europe were from those of the Samoyeds and Lapps in the nineteenth century. A third group attempted a compromise between these two sharply opposed positions. Although far more information is available now, after more than a century of extensive ethnographic, archaeologic, and archival research, the arguments have undergone surprisingly little change.

In 1948 Sherburne F. Cook and Lesley Byrd Simpson attempted to resolve the problem through examination of the great mass of available Spanish fiscal and administrative records of the sixteenth century. Essentially these are tribute assessments and counts of numbers of tributaries and confessants (*confesantes*). They confined their study to central Mexico, which may be defined as Mexico from the Isthmus of Tehuantepec to the northern border of sedentary settlement in 1550. The southern boundary of this area excludes Chiapas but includes the old province of Coatzacoalcos on the Gulf coast as far as the Laguna de Términos. The northern boundary is a vast semicircle stretching from Pánuco and southern Tamaulipas through the present states of Querétaro, Guanajuato, Zacatecas, Jalisco, and Nayarit, to include southern and central Sinaloa on the Pacific coast. Their estimates confirmed Spanish testimony that there was a dense aboriginal population in the area in the first half of the sixteenth century.

Subsequently we have reopened the question by examining the even more extensive tribute materials that have become available since the publication of the Cook-Simpson study. We have arrived at population figures for the Spanish period that agree essentially with those of the Cook-Simpson study, although specific estimates differ. Our figures to date are as follows:

1532	. . . .	16,800,000
1548	. . . .	6,300,000
1568	. . . .	2,650,000
1580	. . . .	1,900,000
1595	. . . .	1,375,000
1605	. . . .	1,075,000

These results show an unmistakable trend from which it would be possible to estimate the pre-Conquest population by extrapolation. For example, if we plot calendar years from 1519 on the abscissa and population directly on the ordinate, it is difficult to extrapolate the curve, but a figure of at least 50,000,000 is indicated. If we plot the logarithm of the population, the graph is approximately linear and the extended line intersects the 1519 axis at roughly the 40,000,-000 level. In a similar fashion, plotting the logarithm of the logarithm of population against calendar years yields a tentative value of 32,000,000. Rigid and uncritical extrapolation by whatever method, however, is likely to give misleading estimates of the pre-Conquest Indian population. Spanish penetration was not a uniform and massive thrust that reached all regions simultaneously. Vast areas were at most barely touched in the first years, even though they were undoubtedly affected by such factors as newly introduced diseases. Accordingly, the years from 1519 to 1531 may not have witnessed a decline that would be expressed by the curve or line derived from unmodified extrapolation of estimates for later years. Such a curve or line would express relatively uniform population change throughout the area, proceeding at a relatively uniform rate from an instantaneous origin at the moment of Spanish entry. There is, furthermore, other reason to doubt the operation in the first years of such a relatively uniform rate. Laboratory experiments on the introduction of new diseases or other massively destructive factors into animal populations suggest that the more probable pattern is one in which there is for a short initial period rather little effect of the new factor or factors, and then a steadily increasing violence of effect until the population is either destroyed or there is slowing down in the rate of decrease and eventually the beginning of recovery. In other words, there is at the beginning of the process a latent or lag phase, followed by a decline that takes the form of a sigmoid curve. For these reasons, we have wished to avoid extrapolation unless use of it could be justified by adequate external evidence.

The Cook-Simpson study examined three possible methods for

estimating pre-Conquest population: statements on the size of native armies, estimates of numbers of conversions, and a system of extrapolation based upon proportions between statements of pre-Conquest populations for certain towns and the relatively firm 1565 populations estimates for those towns. In the end the study relied upon the third method. We have based our inquiry upon another approach: an attempt to use pre-Conquest fiscal material for estimates of the pre-Conquest population of central Mexico as we applied fiscal and other administrative materials (that is, Spanish tribute assessment, counts, and parish or missionary reports) for our estimates of post-Conquest population. That pre-Conquest fiscal material we look for in the tribute system of the Triple Alliance. Success has depended upon our determining (1) that there was a relatively stable, organized levy of wide enough application to furnish a basis for estimate, (2) that there exists a reliable record of the levy that can be read and worked out to the annual charge, (3) that we can arrive at a reasonable average quota per tributary family, (4) that we can estimate the probable average size of family on the eve of the Conquest, and (5) that we can determine the basis for exemptions from tribute and the probable proportion of the exempt population. . . .

The total of our regional estimates for the population of central Mexico on the eve of the Spanish Conquest is 25.2 millions, which should be understood to be an estimate with a wide margin of error. Furthermore, it is based upon an average family size of 4.5 persons. One may postulate a family size as low as 3.6 or as high as 5.0 — about the widest range that seems possible at this time. Our estimate, adjusted to express this range, would be from 20 to 28 millions. In addition, adherents of the interpretation that every eighty days means tribute payments four times a year may wish to adjust the estimate downward by six per cent, which would make the range 18.8 to 26.3 millions. Even with such adjustment, the evidence nevertheless clearly supports the conclusion that central Mexico had a very dense aboriginal population when Cortés landed on the Gulf Coast and that, in general, early Spanish statements and accounts are in accord with fiscal evidence.

B.   Early Spanish Emigration

3. Regional Origins of the Earliest Colonists

PETER BOYD-BOWMAN

Data on regional origins are fortunately available to a surprising degree. The patient efforts of the directors of the *Archivo de Indias* in Seville in publishing extant passenger lists, and the studies of Rubio, Henríquez Ureña, Aubrey Neasham, and Rodríguez Arzúa have yielded valuable results. However, none of the latter exhausted all available sources and methods for determining regional origins, and none are organized to show periodic migration trends from individual towns and provinces in Spain to specific regions in the Indies.

Elaborating the work of these scholars, particularly that of the late Pedro Henríquez Ureña, whose manuscript notes and files are in my possession, and using a wide range of sixteenth-century Spanish and colonial sources, I have been able to establish with reasonable certainty the regional origin of some 40,000 colonists (men, women, and children) who came to the Indies prior to 1600. I would venture to guess that this figure represents, of the total number who emigrated during that time, almost 20 per cent, which I am sure statisticians would consider a highly indicative sample. The completed work will not only show migration trends from any village in Spain to any part of America, but will normally give abbreviated biographical data on each man, such as full name, parentage, place of origin, occupation, destination, marital status, year of passage, and movements and activities within America. The first part, on which this present study is based, lists both geographically and alphabetically those persons of known origin who were in the Indies between the years 1493 and 1519. It is during this critical initial

Reprinted by permission of the Modern Language Association from "The Regional Origins of the Earliest Spanish Colonists in America" by Peter Boyd-Bowman, *PMLA*, LXXI (December, 1956), pp. 1152–1163, *passim*.

period, when the Spanish colonial effort was mainly centered in the islands of the Antilles, that the earliest form of American Spanish must have developed.

Though data are not nearly as abundant for the initial period as they are for the later flood of Spanish emigration to Mexico, Peru, and the other continental areas, I have identified the names and *lugar de nacimiento* or *lugar de vecindad* of 5,481 persons known to be in the Indies prior to 1520. Many others, whose presence in the Indies prior to 1520 is possible but not certain, I have assigned to my next period (1520–40), which will be labeled "The Assault upon the Mainland." For the sake of brevity I will discuss trends mainly on the regional level and in terms of percentages.

The first incontrovertible fact I wish to make clear is that though the proportions changed in the following decades, *in the initial or Antillean period by far the largest single group, in every year, and on all major expeditions, were the Andalusians, of whom over 78 per cent came from the two single provinces of Sevilla (1259 — 58 per cent) and Huelva (439 — 20 per cent).* In fact of the 49 provinces these two alone furnished over 30 per cent (30.9 per cent) of the total number of colonists for the entire period. If we add to them just three western provinces, Badajoz (440), Cáceres (295) and Salamanca (255) we have accounted for over half.   . . .

It is a most significant fact that *for the Antillean period as a whole more than one colonist in every three was an Andalusian, one in every five was from the province of Seville and one in every six claimed the city of Seville as his home town.*   . . .

Sailors. The famous *carta* of Eugenio de Salazar, written around 1573, described the jargon of those salty veterans of ocean crossings and the lasting linguistic and lexical effect that 40 days of listening to it would leave on landlubbers from the Castilian mesetas. Especially in the Antillean period, when all communications were by sea, the sailor's *koiné* must have exerted a powerful influence on the speech of the rest.   . . .

Emigration of women to the Indies (1509–19). Though women did come to the Indies in the first half of the Antillean period I have no separate data on female emigrants until 1509. But for the period 1509–19 I have made a subtotal of the women appearing in the *Catálogo de pasajeros a Indias* and have reached the following conclusions:

The women tended to come from large cities and all but a handful went to Santo Domingo, which was at that time the safest and most civilized Spanish colony. Except for the few cases of a wife's going out alone to join her husband, most of the women traveled in parties, generally in the company of their husbands, family, parents, or relatives. A few single women, mostly from Seville, went out as *"criadas,"* a term which may have been a cover for something else.

Of the 308 women counted in this decade the town of Seville alone furnished over half. If we include the rest of the province the percentage rises to 57.5 and with the rest of Andalusia to two-thirds. The province of Badajoz contributed another 11.5 per cent, Toledo 5 per cent, Huelva and Salamanca 3 per cent each, all others together 10.5 per cent.

By regions, the breakdown is as follows: In the period 1509–19 Andalusia contributed 37 per cent of all colonists but a staggering 67 per cent of the women, Extremadura 16 per cent of all colonists but only 12.5 per cent of the women, Old Castile 19 per cent but only 8 per cent of the women, New Castile 9 per cent of all colonists and 7 per cent of the women, León 8 per cent of all colonists but only 3 per cent of the women. Except for a woman from Guipúzcoa in 1512 and one Portuguese woman in 1511 the Basques, with 4.5 per cent of the colonists, and all other regions combined with another 7 per cent, yielded no women at all.

Continually surrounded as they were by the Indian servants of their households, and no doubt lording it socially over the native wives and concubines that the majority of Spanish settlers had taken, these Spanish women of the initial colonial period must have exerted a linguistic influence far in excess of their numbers. Women have traditionally tended to play a conservative and stabilizing role in the history of a language. Conversation was no doubt even more of a woman's pastime in those days than it is today, and those Spanish women, of whom over half were *sevillanas,* must have played an important part in the development of the first Antillean dialect, envied and imitated as they were, both in speech and in conduct, by the more numerous Indian women of the island settlements.

Seville. No other town in Spain approached Seville in prestige or importance in the eyes of the colonists. A busy inland port, seat of the *Casa de Contratación* and natural center for recruiting and procurement, Seville was the base which furnished a steady stream of men, ships, and supplies for settling the Caribbean islands and exploring the coasts of the American continent. It was the adopted home of numerous merchants, moneylenders, shipbuilders, cosmologists, explorers, sailors and artisans born in other parts of Spain and even abroad, who would eventually pass over to the Indies as *vecinos de Sevilla*. At a time when other Spanish towns were still noted for their quiet dignity and conservative outlook, Seville was a fast-living, flamboyant, cosmopolitan city bursting with color and excitement, a wide open door to news and stimuli from abroad. On its streets mingled Portuguese, Venetians, and Florentines, Genoese bankers and merchants, Sicilian and Greek sailors, Basque sea captains, Gypsies, Negroes, Mulattoes, Indian slaves, and soldiers and adventurers from every part of Spain. Each ship returning with its cargo of gold, pearls, spices, and other exotic merchandise brought news of distant loved ones to families and relations residing in Seville while awaiting their return. A study of the surnames of the city's *vecinos* reveals at this time a steady drift towards Seville of families from the outlying districts of Andalusia. As fast as *sevillanos* left for the Indies, other Andalusians moved in to settle in the city. This dynamic and colorful metropolis made such a lasting impression on prospective emigrants temporarily residing there that by the time they sailed on some expedition or secured passage in the service of some employer, many of them had adopted Seville as their home and had even married Sevillan girls.

There are in all this important linguistic implications. In the sixteenth century the model for those who aspired to elegance of speech was unquestionably the speech of the aristocracy of Toledo; moreover, when the vice-regal courts of Mexico and Peru were established it is certain that these became two more cultural and linguistic foci propagating the language and letters of the Spanish court.

But what is true for the sixteenth century as a whole is *not* true for the primitive Antillean period in America (1493–1519). Different circumstances call for different speech standards. Just as the speech of the *salon* has no place in mining camps or army outposts (and vice versa), so in times of danger and violence it is not the refined manners of the court but the vivid speech and bold gestures of the veteran that excite the admiration of new recruits anxious to win acceptance. In the early days of the conquest, Seville, as no other city, embodied the spirit of colonial enterprise and impressed its speech norms upon the would-be colonist. These speech standards continued to prevail on the long, dangerous transatlantic voyage and finally in the islands, where life to the new arrival must have appeared wonderfully strange and exotic. Acclimatization involved acquiring as rapidly as possible the speech, outlook, and *savoir faire* of the colonists who had preceded him. Since in the initial Antillean period every second or third colonist was an Andalusian, and since in addition almost all the sea captains, pilots, and sailors to whom the colonists looked for supplies and news from home were either born or domiciled in Andalusia, we can appreciate the enormous prestige enjoyed by Seville at this time.

It is not my intention to discuss here just how the Castilian dialect of Andalusia may have differed in 1500 from that of Old or New Castile. The difference may have been negligible. My aim is rather to establish the fact that as far as emigration to America was concerned, it was the speech of Seville, not that of Toledo or Madrid, which set the original standards. . . .

To sum up, we are justified in saying that no matter how the trend may differ in later periods, the first or Antillean period is clearly dominated in number, unity and prestige of colonists by the Andalusian provinces of Sevilla and Huelva, and it is the insular Spanish *koiné* developed at this time, with its store of Antilleanisms, that was carried by island settlers to the mainland. The degree to which this pattern was altered by subsequent waves of emigration will be the subject of further study.

C.   The Colonial Population

4. New Spain's Century of Depression

WOODROW BORAH

In this paper I shall interpret the movement of Mexican colonial economy in terms of demographic findings. I shall indicate that

Woodrow Borah, *New Spain's Century of Depression* (Ibero-Americana: 35; Berkeley, Calif.: University of California Press, 1951), pp. 1–5, 44. Reprinted by permission of the University of California Press.

from 1576 until well over a century later New Spain had a con-
tracting economy. Further, this long period of depression was a
major factor in molding the Mexican land and labor systems which
became dominant in the seventeenth century and remained so down
to the Revolution of 1910. My interpretation is obviously a hypothesis which needs much additional investigation.

Historians have tended to assume that New Spain had a continuously expanding economy. That interpretation can be briefly summarized. During the sixteenth century the European conquerors
grafted a new economy upon the Indian base which they found
in the central areas of present-day Mexico, and eventually European and Indian techniques were fused in a mestizo culture
which was and remains distinctively Mexican. During the seventeenth century New Spain slowly reached higher quantitative levels
of production within the areas of early conquest while colonial authority was extended northward over the present northern Mexican
states and our State of New Mexico. In the eighteenth century the
colonial economy continued to expand at an accelerating rate at
the same time that Spanish rule was established over more than
half the present area of the United States.

The effect which this interpretation has had upon the treatment
of data is strikingly illustrated in the calculations of Mexican mining
output by the noted nineteenth-century scholar, Adolf Soetbeer.
For the period 1521–1587 Soetbeer had a list of shipments of treasure to Spain; for the period 1690 to the end of the colonial period,
he had the surviving Mexico City mint figures as reported by Alexander von Humboldt. For the one-hundred-and-two-year period
1588-1689 inclusive, he had no data whatever. On first treatment of
the data available, Soetbeer found with concern that his calculations
gave him a production figure for 1587 that was higher than calculated specie output for New Spain in 1690. Rather than accept a
figure which ran directly counter to the prevailing idea of the movement of New Spanish economy, he at once concluded that his
method was wrong and arbitrarily adjusted all his calculations for
the sixteenth century sharply downward. He then arranged estimates for the one-hundred-and-two-year gap to show a slow, steady
rise in output throughout the sixteenth and seventeenth centuries
until the relatively reliable calculations based upon the mint statistics beginning with 1690. Agreement with the same idea of steady
if gradual expansion in the colonial Mexican economy was so gen-

eral that Soetbeer's contemporary, W. Lexis, who subjected these calculations to severe and even hostile examination, accepted Soetbeer's formulation of general trend in mining output without discussion. Soetbeer's calculations, incidentally, are still reproduced without question in the official Mexican *Anuario Estadístico*. Nevertheless, as the present paper will indicate, Soetbeer's calculations were nearer the mark before he adjusted them to conform to the prevailing conception of the trend of the colonial economy.

The interpretation that the colonial Mexican economy had a continuous if gradual growth has been based, I suspect, upon studies of territorial expansion. For Mexico, the colonial period did indeed show almost continual acquisition of territory, although at a fluctuating rate. Demographic research, however, indicates that a steady upward trend, if postulated for the movement of Mexican colonial economy, would have run directly counter to population movement during most of the colonial period.

In recent years investigations have given us a much clearer idea of the movement of Mexican population during the colonial period. Investigators by and large agree that at the time of the Conquest there was a relatively dense aboriginal population in central Mexico; that thereafter this population declined by reason of exposure to new diseases, disruption of native economy, and poor living conditions under the post-Conquest regime. Miguel O. de Mendizábal, after examining sixteenth-century summaries of the answers to royal tax and census inquiries, postulated an average Indian natural family of 3.2 for the middle decades of the sixteenth century. Since the birth rate probably remained fairly constant in a population lacking widespread knowledge of contraceptive measures, an average family of this size presupposes so high a continuing death rate, infant, child, and adult, that the population could not have been maintained at equilibrium. Even without the factor of epidemic disease, therefore, the Indians were gradually but steadily declining in numbers. The great epidemics, such as those of 1545–1546 and 1576–1579 brought catastrophic drops in this general downward trend.

A monograph by Cook and Simpson (1948) based upon examination of tribute rolls and population counts for the sixteenth century and upon the viceregal census of 1790–1793 arrived at the population estimates for central Mexico listed in the table. Their figures

for 1540–1607 are for Indians alone and hence ignore the presence
of small numbers of persons of other races and mixed-bloods; estimates for 1650–1793 are for total population. These figures point
to: (1) a sharp initial decrease in Indian population under the shock
of the Conquest; (2) a period of relative stability between the two
great epidemics of the 1540's and the 1570's during which the
downward movement slackened so that it would be shown on a
graph as a gentle slope; and (3) thereafter, a sharp decrease through
the rest of the sixteenth century and the early half of the seventeenth
century. The low point would appear to have occurred in the middle
of the seventeenth century at the bottom of a long shallow trough
on the population graph. Cook and Simpson assign a value of 1,500,-
000 to the total central Mexican population at this low point.
By then mixed-bloods, Negroes, and whites were elements of demographic importance, numbering together perhaps 300,000. The Indian population *ca.* 1650 was thus approximately 1,200,000.

Population of Central Mexico, According
to Cook and Simpson

	Year	Total Population
	1519........................	app. 11,000,000
	1540........................	6,427,466
	1565........................	4,409,180
	1597........................	app. 2,500,000
	1607........................	2,014,000
ca.	1650........................	1,500,000
	1700........................	app. 2,000,000
	1793........................	3,700,000

Demographic recovery began toward the end of the seventeenth
century. It meant at first a slow and then a relatively rapid rise in
numbers. By 1793 the total population of central Mexico was perhaps 3,700,000, approximately two-and-one-half times the value for
ca. 1650 but only four-fifths of the Indian population in 1565.

Recovery involved a substantial change in the racial composition
of the population. Whereas the decline occurred among the Indian
majority, the recovery was due, more largely, to increase in the
number of non-Indians and mixed-bloods. During the latter part of
the seventeenth century and the early part of the eighteenth, demographic recovery was due, probably entirely, to increase among
the last two groups, whereas the Indian population remained rela-

tively stable or may even have decreased slightly. Only by the middle decades of the eighteenth century did Indians clearly begin to
increase although always at a lower rate than the mixed-bloods
and non-Indians. As a result, the ratio of the Indians to whole population continued to shrink, so that today Mexico is a mestizo rather
than an Indian country.

The large mixed-blood element, which developed in the later
colonial period and speeded up demographic recovery, would
show a relatively steady upward trend if its growth were charted
separately on a population graph. The Indians would show precipitate and prolonged decline from 1519 with recovery beginning only
in the eighteenth century. The demographic trend for total population was a decline from 1519 to perhaps the last quarter of the
seventeenth century and then partial recovery at a gradually accelerating rate.

The figures in the table indicate beyond question that contraction must have taken place at least in the Indian economy of central
Mexico as distinct from the economy associated with the European
conquerors. Until we possess detailed studies of the effects of this
population decline upon the Indian economy, any comments are
mere surmises, but we may guess that the economic contraction
was nearly, though not quite equal, to the decline in Indian numbers. The new techniques and crops introduced by the Spaniards
would have increased Indian production wherever the natives
adopted wheeled vehicles, the plow, winter cereals permitting
growing two crops a year, and domestic animals for clothing, food,
and traction, and the resulting greater efficiency in production
would have tended to counteract in the effects of the decrease in
numbers of workers. It is doubtful, however, that the adoption of
European techniques, animals, and crops could have increased efficiency of production to make up more than a small fraction of the
loss because of depopulation. Moreover, during the colonial period
a large proportion of the natives probably continued to use pre-
Conquest crops and methods. Some improvement in crop yields
also would have resulted from the contraction of the cultivated
area, since the Indian villages would tend to retire marginal land
from production and concentrate crop-raising upon their better and
more easily worked soils. Again, the differential gain from this retirement of poorer areas from cultivation was probably small as

against the decrease in production because of loss of workers. Any tendency for a proportionate increase in the working capacity of the population because the sturdier adults would have a lower death rate than children, aged, and the weak was probably balanced by enfeeblement among the survivors of disease. It seems likely, therefore, that during the sixteenth and seventeenth centuries the Indian villages progressively lost productive power proportionately to and probably nearly equal to the decrease in the number of their inhabitants.

We may safely postulate further that the contraction of the Indian economy was accompanied by a decrease in the demands upon production from within the Indian villages. Reduction in Indian numbers meant automatic reduction in the number of mouths which had to be fed. On the other hand, the heavy demands upon the villages for the support of their local officials, community activities, and the large class of Indian nobles probably failed to decrease at a rate equal to the decline in the general Indian population. Village governments and religious cults had to be maintained regardless of the number of inhabitants. Similarly the Indian nobility, being better fed and housed, would show a somewhat lower death rate in the epidemics than the mass of Indian commoners. The burden upon the general Indian population which support of nobles and community activities represented therefore probably became proportionately heavier as the villages shrank in size. In consequence, the ability of the Indian villages to contribute to the support of the new European segment of the population introduced by the Conquest was reduced not only by the sharp curtailment in their production but by greater pressure from within Indian society itself upon the remaining output of food and services.   . . .

The sharp and long-continued decrease of Mexico's Indians from the Conquest until the beginning of the eighteenth century must be accounted one of the most important factors in Mexican history. Had the aboriginal populations of central Mexico borne the impact of Conquest with little demographic loss, there would have been scant room for their conquerors except as administrators and receivers of tribute. Mexico today would be an Indian area from which, in the process of achieving independence from Spain, a white upper stratum holding itself apart, like the British in India, could easily have been expelled. In Haiti, expulsion and massacre at the time of the great slave uprisings disposed rather easily of a similar group of owners and administrators.

The hypothesis of a century-long depression developed in this paper can only be established by further research in Mexican economic and social history. If this hypothesis is sound, the precipitate and sustained decrease in the Indian hewers of wood and drawers of water after the demographic plateau of 1546–1576, the years when the white upper stratum became firmly established in the colony, confronted the new dominant group with one of the most severe and difficult problems of the colonial period. The problem was made more difficult by the fact that the Spanish actually increased steadily as the Indians diminished. The efforts of the Spanish to solve the problem, to continue to draw products and services in accustomed volume from the Indian understrata, speeded up and perhaps led directly to a radical reorganization of land holding and labor forms which greatly extended and strengthened the emerging hybrid Mexican culture. At the end of the seventeenth century, the distinctively Mexican economy was already organized on the basis of latifundia and debt peonage, the twin aspects of Mexican life which continued nearly to our day and which helped provoke the Revolution of 1910–1917.

5. The Geographical Distribution of the Negro

WILBUR ZELINSKY

The fact that slavery had had a continuous existence among the Iberian peoples from a prehistoric era through the period of colonization and that, hence, the Portuguese and the Spanish were by social heritage especially well-equipped to cope with the problems consequent upon slavery in the New World, was a matter of profound significance in the social history of Latin America. In Spain and Portugal the Negro slave existed alongside the Moorish and

Wilbur Zelinsky, "The Historical Geography of the Negro Population of Latin America," *Journal of Negro History*, XXXIV (1949), pp. 153–221, *passim*. Reprinted by permission of the *Journal of Negro History*.

Berber slave, and servitude was a matter of military misfortune or social class rather than of race. Because of this historical background and possibly because of the initial importance of Indian slavery in the New World, the Negro people were never quite regarded as equivalent to a slave race.

The major factor operating to bring the Negro to America in large numbers was the labor situation. Over much of the area of the Americas the level of culture among the aborigines was such that they did not possess the requisite aptitudes for becoming useful workmen for the conquerors, or in some cases, such as among the Boriqueños of Puerto Rico or the Chibchas of Colombia, the people lacked the physical or social resilience to withstand the first onslaughts of the Europeans. It was only in parts of Mexico and the highlands of Central America, Ecuador, Peru, and Bolivia that the native population was available and adaptable for work under European management, and even here the process of reconciling the people to such servitude was not always simple or rapid. In Latin America, then, there was a whole world of resources to be exploited and fewer and fewer hands for the work. The experiments with free white labor in early times quickly failed as might be expected under the conditions of a rapidly expanding frontier where every settler expected to become wealthy and independent within a few years and could not be confined to manual labor for more than a minimal period. The attempts to use indentured white labor in the 17th and 18th centuries were likewise destined to miscarry. The only alternative was the importation of a group of laborers who could be kept under permanent subjection. Any of the non-Christian peoples of the Old World having the necesaary cultural aptitudes would have satisfied the requirements of the masters of the New World. In fact, the Spanish did attempt shipping Filipinos, Malays, and various peoples from the lands around the Indian Ocean to Mexico, but only a very few such non-Negroid slaves ever arrived in America. Africa was the most obvious source of labor: the trip to America was relatively short, the numbers of Negroes were apparently inexhaustible, and the Negro slave had already demonstrated his proficiency in Portugal and Spain. . . .

How many Negroes were sent to Latin America and when? The record is so incomplete that only weak generalizations can be made. The best over-all estimate, although admittedly a rather conservative one, is probably that given by Kuczynski.

Number of Negro Slaves Imported
into the Americas

16th Century	nearly 900,000
17th Century	2,750,000
18th Century	7,000,000
19th Century	over 4,000,000
	Total, perhaps 15,000,000

Although several significant studies of the slave trade have been
made, for no area except Cuba and some of the Lesser Antilles do
we yet have a coherent statistical account of the influx of Negro
slaves. The reasons for the incompleteness of our knowledge are
the generally poor status of all statistics on international migration
in the era involved, the loss or inaccessibility of some of the records,
the illicit character of much of the trade, and the lack of demographic interest in most studies of the slave trade in which attention has usually been focussed on diplomatic and legalistic matters.
Even so, it has been maintained that we know more about the
movement of Negroes to Latin America than about that of white
settlers.

It appears likely that significant numbers of Africans were
shipped to Latin America very soon after the original settlement
and exploitation had begun and that this flow of black manpower
increased rather steadily until the beginning of the 19th century
with certain minor fluctuations incident upon military and diplomatic events and with important shifts in areal emphasis as the
economic complexion of Latin America altered with the passage of
time. Any attempt at present to tabulate the number of arrivals by
year and by country of destination is bound to fail.   . . .

The mechanics of the movement were relatively simple. Slavery
was a long-established practice throughout Africa although its cultural context and the mode in which it was pursued differed vastly
from the nakedly exploitative methods followed under the European
system. War captives, political and criminal prisoners, debtors, a
variety of other unfortunates and, increasingly, individuals kid-
napped for the trade — all forming a group by no means necessarily
inferior physically, socially, or culturally — were traded by the
leaders of the Negro community to dealers, almost always Negro,
on the basis of a quite sophisticated system of exchange. The middlemen would, in turn, lead their charges to harbors along the
coast which were equipped with barracks and warehouses where

ships from Europe and America would call at irregular intervals to acquire boatloads of slaves in return for currency and goods. When the holds had been filled, the vessels would set sail westward. No one has ever really ascertained the casualty rates for these voyages, but that they were frightful is beyond any doubt.

The termini of these trips were the major ports of Brazil, the harbors of the La Plata, and the more important ports of the Antilles and the Caribbean mainland. There were actually only a few really important receiving ports for the legally introduced slave. After he had been purchased at the marts by the ultimate consumer or by contractors or middlemen, the Negro would then be transported to his destination along the established land and sea routes. The large contraband trade in slaves, induced by Spain's attempt to retain the trade as a royal monopoly, confuses the pattern. The practices of using the West Indies for the storage and "breaking-in" of freshly arrived slaves and the often complex shuffling of slave merchandise around the Caribbean was a further complication.

Generally, there is a very loose latitudinal correlation in the places of origin and destination, the routes tending to be roughly east-west. Thus in Southern Brazil and Uruguay the Congo and Angola Negroes were relatively conspicuous. In Northeastern Brazil those of Guinea and Sudanese origin were preponderant; they may possibly have been even more so around the American Mediterranean.

Except in Northeastern Brazil, deliberate efforts were made to break up tribal units in the process of transplanting Negro population in order to discourage the organized resistance which a feeling of unity, social or cultural, might have promoted. The result was a Latin American Negro population composed of rather ill-assorted lumps of various peoples and cultures in a state of deculturation and demoralization. Nevertheless, enough of the old cultural distinctions may have carried over to make it necessary for us to reckon with the precise provenience of the Negroes of various parts of Latin America in order to understand thoroughly the cultural geography of these areas. The tracing out of these significant differences will be a project of great interest when our informational base has been sufficiently broadened.

The ethics of the slave trade need not directly concern us here; but aside from the incalculable misery produced by this commerce, for which the responsible individuals can gain no absolution by claiming that the Negro was thereby exposed to a superior culture and the option of spiritual salvation or by stating — without truth — that the trade did no more than take advantage of the normal social situation of Negro Africa, aside from the moral implications of the phenomenon, it can be said that the transportation of Negro labor to America created more problems than it solved. It has been argued that the early settlers had no alternative to using slave labor if they were to develop the land and that they frequently regretted the choice. Yet, rather than any genuine development of the region, the prodigal use of slave labor seems to be tied in with an utterly destructive exploitation of the land, which is well known in the Southeastern United States and the Lesser Antilles, and is an apparently irreversible process of economic disaster. The use of slaves was an easy device, not a wise one. The loss to the New World in material and human values has been incalculably great, and against this the compensation in the form of increased cultural diversity is trifling in significance. A rational exploitation of the New World was perhaps a program beyond the cultural capacity of the settler of the colonial period, or the pathology of the situation may have originated with Western European civilization itself. At any rate, the actual outcome is one of the great tragedies of human history. . . .

The question of what cultural cargo was carried along with the Negro to Latin America reduces itself to the matter of the nature of the pertinent African cultures and the degree to which these cultures were able to resist the deliberate as well as casual processes of deculturation. Much nonsense has been written about the weight and value of the Negro contribution to American life. Most of it has been by the apologists for slavery and its heritage who would deny or minimize African survivals among the American Negroes and the impact of the Negro on American ways; there have also been those who would credit too much of American culture to Africa. The truth is rather hard to get at but it seems sound to assume that the Negro did not come ashore in the New World as a culturally naked savage. The degree of retention of the original culture has varied enormously from area to area. In places, the initial amount of deculturation was huge, and in subsequent generations almost all recognizable traces of an African cultural origin have vanished; in other localities the casual observer might suppose himself to be in Africa from the cultural evidence. The Negro in Latin

America has certainly received much more in the way of culture, for better or worse, than he has contributed or preserved, but, nonetheless, the importance of this contribution is greater than most persons have realized. . . .

The transculturation of the Negro in Latin America has been a tremendously complex process of vast import for the Negro migrant and, to a degree varying with time, place, and the nature of the non-Negro cultures, of significance to the cultural geography of the region. It has involved contact between a rather wide range of African cultures on the one hand as against cultures of all western European peoples from the Portuguese to the Danes and a very wide variety of aboriginal American cultures on the other. Often there has been an intricate interplay of influences among these three cultural camps — European, African, and aboriginal — that has contributed strongly to whatever differences mark off the basically European cultures of modern Latin America from those of the homelands.

Of equal or greater prominence than cultural interchange has been the process whereby vast numbers of Negroes in Latin America have become physically assimilated into the European and aboriginal populations or have formed various hybrid strains in the process of amalgamation. The outcome has been a Latin America of great heterogeneity in racial composition from region to region and with patterns of physical types unique in the world. Miscegenation began even before the transport of the slaves to America since a considerable amount of mixture had always been going on among the various African strains with the result that, like the sub-races of Europe, these groups had succeeded in maintaining only an approximate physical identity. Wherever the white personnel of the slaving industry had access to the slaves in African factories and compounds or on the slave ships, miscegenation occurred. In America not only was the previous mixing of the African strains accelerated but an abundant mulatto progeny was produced by female slaves who were often regarded by the masters as being quite as much their legitimate sexual property as an economic utility. In addition, there was a large amount of intermarriage among Negro, white, and Indian persons who had been reduced to the same social and economic strata. . . .

The study of the social status of the Negro in Latin America reveals some interesting regional variations. Among the Ibero-Ameri-

can whites a relatively liberal attitude toward race differences based
on the racial history of Iberia, a sexual predilection for colored
women, the Catholic ideology and the Church's policy toward slavery, and the institutional history of slavery among these people has
frequently enabled the Negroes to avoid the stigma of caste (*i.e.,*
a group with a hereditary social status) and has resulted in at least a
moderate vertical social mobility for Negroes. As a whole, they are
a lower class group regarded in much the same light as lower class
whites.

6. The Population of Brazil

Dauril Alden

Population counts in colonial America long antedated the adoption of modern census procedures in Europe. As early as 1511 King
Ferdinand ordered Governor Diego Columbus to report on the size
of the Spanish population in the Indies, and a few years later the
Council of the Indies began to call upon secular and ecclesiastical
authorities in the New World to furnish numerical descriptions of
the Spanish and Indian population in the new conquests. Throughout the next two and a half centuries a stream of such reports poured
into the Peninsula, comprising a demographic record unmatched
during this period in quantity or in abundance of detail by Portuguese Brazil or by any European nation with the possible exception
of England. But such data always flowed across the Atlantic irreg-
ularly, and despite repeated reforms, designed to improve the reg-
ularity and quality of the reportage, the Council was seldom able
to obtain an accurate determination of the population of the entire
Spanish empire at any one time. With the exception of the French
province of Quebec, where periodic enumerations of a much
smaller and less dispersed population began in 1665 and continued
until the eve of the fall of New France, no successful attempts were
made in the New World to collect population data on a recurring
basis prior to the second half of the eighteenth century.

Dauril Alden, "The Population of Brazil in the Late Eighteenth Century: A
Preliminary Survey," *Hispanic American Historical Review*, XLIII (May, 1963),
pp. 173–201, *passim*. Reprinted by permission of the Duke University Press.

During the third quarter of the eighteenth century three major imperial powers in America introduced measures designed to provide the home governments with more accurate and more frequent demographic information concerning their colonies than had previously been available. The fact that each was engaged in an increasingly bitter rivalry for hegemony in the New World and required better information about the numbers of its colonists for purposes of increased taxation and military recruitment in part explains the reasons for the reforms. But they were also a reflection of enlightened governments' and individuals' preoccupation in the eighteenth century with measurements of all kinds, whether they involved the accurate determination of the longitude and latitude of key colonial cities, the maximum and minimum temperatures recorded in various parts of the empire, the elevations of mountains, or the heat of volcanos and bodies of water. It should be recalled too that during this period both Iberian powers tried (without notable success) to introduce double-entry bookkeeping systems in their colonial exchequers to improve the collection and dispersement of royal income. Both governments also established a series of so-called commercial balances in which the annual volume of trade between intra-colonial and Peninsular ports was itemized in great detail. Colonial administrators were also required to submit endless tables showing the numbers and kinds of troops garrisoned in various parts of the empire. In short, both for military and nonmilitary reasons the colonial powers were becoming increasingly statistics conscious.

The first to introduce standard census methods in its colonies was England. In 1761 the Board of Trade directed each of His Majesty's governors in America to "from time to time give Us frequent & very full Information on the State and Condition of the Province under Your government." The governors were to provide answers to a list of "queries" concerning the number of whites, blacks, and Indians, and the reasons for their increase or decrease during the previous biennium. Pursuant to this order, the governors of six of the thirteen mainland colonies submitted at least one general return between 1765 and 1776.

In 1776 Spain and Portugal acted almost simultaneously to secure even more detailed information concerning the inhabitants in their colonies. The Spanish cedula of November, 1776, which seems to have been sent to all parts of the Indies, called upon secular

authorities to submit to the Minister of the Indies annual *padrones*
"with proper distinction of classes, [marital] status, and castes of
all persons of both sexes, without omitting the infants" residing
within their jurisdiction. While it proved beyond the capacity of
the colonial bureaucracy to supply such data yearly, at least one
comprehensive general census along the lines specified by the cedula was taken in New Spain, Guatemala, Nueva Granada, Peru,
Chile, and the Río de la Plata in the course of the next two decades.

The Portuguese circular of May, 1776, extended to all parts of
Brazil demographic procedures previously tried in Pará, Goiás, and
São Paulo during the early 'seventies. They, in turn, may have been
influenced by the techniques adopted for the Castilian census of
1768, for the Portuguese employed a similar system of age grouping. This classification, which was followed by some (though regret-
tably not by all) compilers of Brazilian censuses for the next quarter
of a century, divided the population into the following classes:

Class	Description
I	male children (*crianças*) under age seven
II	boys (*rapazes*) between seven and fifteen
III	adult males (*homens*) between fifteen and sixty
IV	men over sixty (*homens velhos*)
V	female children (*crianças*) under seven
VI	girls (*raparigas*) between seven and fourteen
VII	adult women (*mulheres*) between fourteen and forty
VIII	women over forty (*adultas e as velhas*)
IX	number of births during the year
X	number of deaths during the year

Several features of this classification merit comment. First, unlike the coeval Spanish directive, the Portuguese circular did not
require data on racial or caste status, though, as will be seen later,
several governors included such information in their reports. Second,
it is apparent that those who devised the classification not only
recognized the fact that girls mature earlier than boys, but also
(unchivalrous as it may seem!) the tendency of women to age more
rapidly than men in Colonial America because of the rigors of child
bearing and domestic labor. Third, the inclusion of Class IX (annual births) caused confusion in the minds of some enumerators,
since it duplicated data already recorded in Classes I and V (children under seven). As a result some compilers mistakenly added
the figures for Class IX to those for Classes I-VIII, and thereby in-
advertently inflated their totals. On the other hand, at least one
functionary failed to count children who had not reached their first

birthday. Fourth, the inclusion of children under seven in the censuses required the tabulation of information not contained in the parish registers which did not list children below the confessional age. Presumably the purpose of Classes I and V was for projections of the colonial population in future decades, but one is at a loss to know why the king's ministers insisted upon the names of all persons in each parish who had passed the ninetieth year, unless the Portuguese were simply following the practice of the Swedes, though both may have been inspired by the example of Roman enumerators during the late Republic who, according to Pliny, recorded the number of persons over one hundred years in parts of Italy.

Three groups were excluded from the Portuguese censuses: regular troops (*tropas pagas*), ecclesiastics, and untamed Indians. The omission of the first two did not seriously affect the results, since their numbers were not appreciable. Though far more numerous, it was obviously impossible to enumerate unreduced Indians living in areas not effectively under Portuguese control, such as southern Espíritu Santo, western Goiás, much of Mato Grosso and Rio Negro.

As a matter of fact royal officials found it difficult enough to tabulate the Christian population of Brazil. Many of their problems were the same that confronted enumerators in the Spanish and English colonies, such as the dispersion of a relatively small population over a large area, the hardships of travel particularly in remote districts, and the lack of special compensation for those charged with preparing the reports. If Portuguese governors did not have to cajole unfriendly colonial assemblies to co-operate in the preparation of the censuses, as did their English contemporaries, they did encounter passive resistance among colonials who regarded head counts as portents of future financial exactions and increased conscriptions of their sons for the unpopular militia. Such intransigence prompted the captain-general of Bahia de Todos os Santos to warn Salvadoreans in 1776 that their refusal to divulge the names, numbers, and ages of their children and slaves would render them liable to heavy fines and thirty days' labor on the royal fortifications. Even so, he was obliged to post his warning a second time two years later.

But even if Brazilians had been more co-operative than traditionally has been the case where censuses have been newly introduced, it is probable that the compilation of accurate returns would have exceeded the technical competence of the Portuguese bureaucracy, just as it did that of officials in the Spanish and English colonies and also those charged with the preparation of the early Federal censuses in the United States. In Brazil many — perhaps too many — hands were involved in the organization of the reports. As soon as the captains-general and the bishops received instructions to proceed with the stocktaking, they issued appropriate directions to their respective underlings. These included the governors of subordinate captaincies, circuit judges (*ouvidores* or *juizes de fora*) and commanders of the local militia (*mestres do campo*) in the secular branch, and various members of the episcopal hierarchy down to the level of the parish priest. Primary responsibility for the construction of the tables or *mapas* in the prescribed form fell upon the shoulders of the mestres do campo and the parish priests. Their data were compiled mainly from the *lista de desobrigas,* the register of persons who received communion at Easter. However, that list did not include children under seven, so that the local officials were obliged to determine their numbers by actual count or estimates.

Since the secular and ecclesiastical government shared responsibility for the compilation of the census reports, the lack of symmetry between units of the two branches frequently complicated effective co-operation. In interior Minas Gerais, for example, the limits of the bishopric of Mariana were considerably smaller than those of the secular administration. As a result the parishes of Sapucaí, Jacuí, and Cabo Verde pertained to the bishopric of São Paulo; those of São Romão and Paracutú were suffragan to the bishopric of Pernambuco; while the four parishes of the Minas Novas district belonged to the archbishopric of Bahia. Because of the involved correspondence that such arrangements necessitated, it is not surprising that the returns from such parishes often arrived late, if at all.

As the parish lists (*mapas particulares*) were completed, they were condensed and forwarded to the circuit judge of the appropriate *comarca* or county, who sent the subtotals for his district to the governor of the subcaptaincy for transmission to the captain-general. In the secretariat of the captain-general the sums for the various subdivisions of that government were entered in the appropriate columns of the master sheets which were supposedly scrutinized by the captain-general, the bishop, and other dignitaries. When the tables were found to be defective, particularly where local officials had departed from the prescribed system of classification, the mapas were sometimes returned to the parish for correction. More often, however, the master sheets were forwarded to Lisbon with an admission of their defects and assurances from the captain-general that the next reports would be free of such inadequacies. Sometimes a second mapa geral was forwarded the following year, but . . . more often than not several years passed before the next census results were dispatched to the court.

What the crown actually did with these laboriously compiled reports is unknown. It is unlikely that they were subjected to any sophisticated analysis, for Portugal, like Spain, lacked trained staffs of statisticians comparable to those in Sweden's Tabular Commission. It seems probable that Peninsular officials were content to derive the obvious totals, and then filed the reports away to gather dust.

It must be conceded that the chaotic nature of many of the reports — their lack of uniformity, the frequency of gross errors in the recorded totals, obvious transpositions, and certain baffling lacunae — tends to discourage further examination. And yet, despite these shortcomings, a study of these materials sheds considerable light upon various features of Brazil's population in the late colonial years. . . .

The methods employed in the construction of Table I require explanation. Where the totals in the sources are confirmed by the various subtotals, they have been entered as given, but where they are inconsistent with the values represented by the subtotals and the latter appear accurate, the corrected sum has been placed in parenthesis. In three cases — those of the captaincies of Rio de Janeiro, Rio Grande de São Pedro, and Mato Grosso — it is evident that the sources do not include complete enumerations of all age groups. Children under seven were omitted in the Rio Grande and Mato Grosso censuses of 1780, while the Rio de Janeiro count for the same year fails to list minors, i.e., males below the fifteenth year and females under fourteen. It is possible, however, to extrapolate the missing data by determining from other sources what percentage of the population fell within these age limits in other parts of Brazil at this time. In the seven areas for which such information is available, the censuses show that about 11.75 per cent of the population was seven years of age or less, and that 20.7 per cent was between zero and fourteen (females) or fifteen (males) years. Even though these

Table I   Distribution of the Population of Brazil, 1772–1782

Place	Original total	Per cent	Adjusted total	Per cent
Rio Negro	(10,386)	.6	(10,386)	.6
Pará	(55,315)	3.7	(55,315)	3.5
Maranhão	47,410	3.1	47,410	3.0
Piauí	26,410	1.7	26,410	1.7
Pernambuco	239,713	15.9	239,713	15.4
Paraíba	52,468	3.5	52,468	3.4
Rio Grande do Norte	23,812	1.6	23,812	1.5
Ceará	61,408	4.0	61,408	3.9
Bahia	(288,848)	19.2	(288,848)	18.5
Rio de Janeiro	(171,033)	11.3	[215,678]	13.8
Santa Catarina	[10,000]	.6	[10,000]	.6
Rio Grande de São Pedro	17,923	1.1	[20,309]	1.3
São Paulo	116,975	7.7	116,975	7.5
Minas Gerais	319,769	21.2	319,769	20.5
Goiás	55,514	3.6	55,514	3.5
Mato Grosso	18,503	1.2	[20,966]	1.3
Totals	1,505,706	100.0	1,555,200	100.0

percentages appear considerably lower than might be expected for these age groups, they are surprisingly uniform for the seven captaincies, and I am inclined to believe that the extrapolated figures more accurately resemble the correct sums than do the original totals. Accordingly, the population of Rio Grande de São Pedro and Mato Grosso have been adjusted upward by 11.75 per cent and that of Rio de Janeiro by 20.7 per cent. It is apparent that these adjustments do not change the ranking order of any captaincy. . . .

It is apparent that most of the colony's enumerated inhabitants continued to concentrate in the river valleys and harbors of the littoral, thus ignoring the lament of the seventeenth-century chronicler Frei Vicente do Salvador, who scorned the proclivity of the Portuguese for "living like crabs along the coast" of Brazil. Moreover, in spite of repeated land "rushes" during the eighteenth century, first to the mining zones of Minas Gerais, Goiás, and Mato Grosso, and later to the southern pastoral lands of Santa Catarina and Rio Grande de São Pedro, the old sugar and dyewood captaincies of the Northeast, first settled during the second quarter of the sixteenth century, continued to retain a large proportion of Brazil's inhabitants. The censuses of the 1770's and early 'eighties reveal that 38.8 per cent of the population lived in the captaincies-general of Bahia and Pernambuco, compared with 20.5 per cent residing in Minas Gerais. On the other hand, about 14 per cent lived within the confines of the captaincy of Rio de Janeiro, and less than 16 per cent dwelt in the captaincy-general of which it was the principal part. São Paulo, today Brazil's most populous state, ranked only fifth in the 1770's. . . .

As previously noted, the royal circular of 1776 did not inquire into the caste or racial composition of Brazil's population. Nevertheless, some of the governors, notably those who had reason to be concerned about the large numbers of unfree Negroes confined to their jurisdictions, directed their subordinates to include such information in their reports. In such cases the population was segregated into three or four primary racial strains: *brancos,* meaning whites or at least persons socially accepted as Caucasians; pardos or mulattoes; pretos or Negroes; and (Christian) Indians. Interestingly enough, no special category was reserved for *mestiços* who presumably were grouped under brancos or pardos depending upon their physical appearance.

Table II indicates the racial composition of slightly over half of Brazil's enumerated inhabitants during the 1770's. Two of the largest slaveholding areas, the captaincies-general of Bahia de Todos os Santos and Pernambuco, are unreported. But included are two

Table II   Racial Composition or Civil Status of the Population of Eight Captaincies, 1772–1780

Place	Brancos	Per cent	Pardos	Per cent	Pretos	Per cent	Free-men	Per cent	Slaves	Per cent	Indios	Per cent
Rio Negro	—	—	—	—	—	—	927	9.0	191	2.0	9,268	89.0
Pará	—	—	—	—	—	—	24,779	44.8	11,413	20.6	19,123	34.6
Maranhão	[15,366]	32.4	[11,757]	24.8	[20,291]	42.8	—	—	—	—	—	—
Rio de Janeiro	—	—	—	—	—	—	86,751	50.7	84,282	49.3	—	—
Rio Grande de São Pedro	—	—	—	—	—	—	12,821	71.5	5,102	28.5	—	—
São Paulo	[65,974]	56.4	[22,459]	19.2	[28,542]	24.4	—	—	—	—	—	—
Minas Gerais	76,664?	24.0	76,110?	23.8	166,995	52.2	—	—	—	—	—	—
Mato Grosso	[3,313]	15.8	[5,703]	27.2	[11,154]	53.2	—	—	—	—	[797]	3.8

northern captaincies-general, Pará and Maranhão, both leaders in the agricultural revival of Brazil during the second half of the eighteenth century and heavy importers of African slaves; three central governments, Rio de Janeiro, São Paulo, and Minas Gerais; one southern captaincy, Rio Grande de São Pedro; and the western captaincy-general of Mato Grosso. Because of transpositions in the published source, the numbers of brancos and pardos listed for Minas Gerais can be only approximated. The bracketed totals for Maranhão, São Paulo, and Mato Grosso represent extrapolations from censuses taken between 1797 and 1800. Some error is doubtless inherent in our assumption that the racial proportions in the 1770's were the same as they were at the end of the century, but the possible distortion would appear to be minor.

The same table shows the civil status of the inhabitants of four captaincies for which direct information on racial composition is lacking. Since Indian slavery was abolished in the 1750's, it may be assumed that all persons listed as slaves were pardos or pretos. It is also likely that the majority of those counted as freemen were considered whites. Surprisingly few Indians are tabulated in the censuses, and most of those enumerated lived in the Amazon where Jesuits, Franciscans, and others had proselyted since the early seventeenth century. The high proportion of slaves to freemen in Rio de Janeiro is noticeable; undoubtedly the majority of the population of Minas Gerais, Bahia de Todos os Santos, and Pernambuco were captives at this time, though specific evidence on this point is unavailable. The presence of a higher proportion of slaves in pastoral Rio Grande de São Pedro than in agricultural Pará comes as something of a surprise, though the ratio between freemen and *captivos* in the southern captaincy appears to have remained about the same for at least the next four decades.

As in Spanish America, some Negroes and mulattoes were members of the free population of eighteenth-century Brazil. Toward the end of the century one contemporary declared that out of 3,250,000 persons living in Brazil, 406,000 or 12.4 per cent were *"Negros libertos,"* as compared with 1,582,000 or 49.4 per cent of the population who were slaves. The censuses of 1798 and 1802 for Rio Grande de São Pedro — the only eighteenth-century reports which supply this kind of information — indicate that while over half of the pardos were freemen, only about 5 per cent of the pretos enjoyed that status. On the other hand, the census of 1815 reveals that in Mato Grosso where, in contrast with Rio Grande, the majority of the population was wholly or partly Negro, nearly four-fifths of the pardos and almost one-third of the pretos were libertos. Though specific evidence is lacking, it is likely that manumission was more prevalent in the great plantation captaincies-general of Pernambuco and Bahia de Todos os Santos than in Brazil's Far South where slavery had been introduced more recently and involved far fewer numbers. The extent to which manumission was practiced in different parts of Brazil at this time and its effects upon the social structure of the colony deserve to be studied. . . .

A satisfactory social history of colonial Brazil cannot be written until we have a clearer understanding of the demographic characteristics of the peoples who lived there. We have too long ignored the value of the colonial censuses, particularly those of late-colonial Brazil. Despite their shortcomings, they furnished a good deal of useful information which cannot be gleaned from any other type of source. As such distinguished historians as Francisco A. Encina and Rodolfo Barón Castro have written with respect to the coeval Spanish colonial censuses, they provide us with more complete and more reliable statistics on the population of late-colonial Latin America than do the writings of chroniclers, foreign travelers, and other contemporaries whose more or less informed guesses have too often commanded more respect from scholars than they deserve. And as this essay has tried to show, the censuses reveal tentative answers to such questions as the size, distribution, and racial composition of Brazil's population during the last colonial decades.

Undoubtedly the discovery of much corroborative evidence — additional census records, parish registers, episcopal surveys, registers of arrivals of slaves and freemen in Brazil, militia and tax rolls — would make possible a more thorough study of Brazil's population during these years than has been possible here.

BIBLIOGRAPHIC SUGGESTIONS

1. Borah, Woodrow. "Race and Class in Mexico," *Pacific Historical Review*, XXIII (1954), pp. 331–342.
2. Boyd-Bowman, Peter. *Índice geobiográfico de cuarenta mil pobladores españoles de América en el siglo XVI (1493–1519)* (Bogotá: Instituto Caro y Cuervo, 1964).
3. Cook, Sherburne F. "The Population of Mexico in 1793," *Human Biology*, XIV (1942), pp. 499–515.
4. Dusenberry, William H. "Discriminatory Aspects of Legislation in Colonial Mexico," *The Journal of Negro History*, III (1948), pp. 284–302.
5. Endrek, Emiliano. *El mestizaje in Córdoba* (Córdoba, Argentina: Universidad Nacional de Córdoba, 1966).
6. Friede, Juan. "The *Catálogo de pasajeros* and Spanish Emigration to America in 1550," *Hispanic American Historical Review*,

XXX (1951), pp. 333–348. Analyzes this basic source on emigrations, and points out its deficiencies.

7. Gerhard, Peter. *México en 1742* (Mexico: Porrúa, 1962). Political and demographic analysis of Mexico in the mid-eighteenth century, principally from the *Teatro americano* of José Antonio de Villaseñor y Sánchez. Maps of the jurisdictions and tables of their populations. A basic systematization of available data.

8. Guarda, Gabriel. "Santo Tomás de Aquino y las fuentes del urbanismo indiano," *Boletín de la Academia Chilena de la Historia,* No. 72 (1965).

9. Guthrie, Chester L. "Trade, Industry, and Labor in Seventeenth Century Mexico City," *Revista de Historia de América,* No. 7 (1939), pp. 103–134.

10. King, James F. "The Negro in Continental Spanish America: a select bibliography," *Hispanic American Historical Review,* XXIV (1944), pp. 547–559.

11. Konetzke, Richard. "Las fuentes para la historia demográfica de Hispano-américa durante la época colonial," *Anuario de Estudios Americanos,* V (Seville, 1948), pp. 267–324.

12. Kubler, George. "Cities and Cultures in the Colonial Period of Latin America," *Diogenes,* 47 (Fall, 1964), pp. 53–62.

13. Leonard, Irving A. *Baroque Times in Old Mexico* (Ann Arbor: University of Michigan Press, 1959). A vivid re-creation of seventeenth-century Mexico.

14. Lipschutz, Alejandro. "La despoblación de las Indias después de la conquista," *America Indígena,* XXVI (1966), pp. 229–247. Up-to-date summary, with charts, based on a variety of sources.

15. López Sarrelangue, Delfina E. "Población indígena de la Nueva España en el siglo XVIII," *Historia Mexicana,* XII (1963), pp. 516–530.

16. Miranda, José. "La poblacion indígena de México en el siglo XVII," *Historia Mexicana,* XII (1962), pp. 182–189.

17. Mörner, Magnus. *El mestizaje en la historia de Ibero-América* (Mexico: Instituto Panamericano de Geografía e Historia, 1961).

18. ———. *Race Mixture in Latin America: A History* (Boston: Little, Brown and Company, 1967).

19. Neasham, V. Aubrey. "Spain's Emigrants to the New World, 1492–1592," *Hispanic American Historical Review,* XIX (1939), pp. 147–160.

20. Woodbridge, Hensley C. "Glossary of Names Used in Colonial Latin America for Crosses Among Indians, Negroes, and Whites," *Journal of the Washington Academy of Sciences,* XXXVIII, no. 15 (Washington, D.C., 1948), pp. 353–362.

Section V

Vieira and the Crises of Seventeenth-Century Brazil

Considerable material is available on the Dutch in Brazil in the seventeenth century, and on the end of Spanish domination of Brazil in 1640, but there is little to read in English on António Vieira, the Jesuit preacher whom Professor Charles Boxer of the University of London acclaims as a great historical and literary figure who ". . . was certainly the most remarkable man in the seventeenth-century" Luso-Brazilian world. The best and indeed the only treatment of Vieira in English is by Professor Boxer, who has done so much to advance our knowledge of Luso-Brazilian history (Reading V.1).

One of the reasons why Vieira is neglected in our courses is that his sermons, letters, and state papers, which Professor Boxer considers ". . . the best collective source for the understanding of the 'climate of opinion' in seventeenth-century Portugal, Brazil, and the Maranhão," have never been translated into English. A one-volume selection is badly needed. Samples of Vieira's fire and eloquence are his "Sermon Condemning Indian Slavery, 1653" (Reading V.3) and his account of "The Conversion of the Nheengaíbas, 1659" (Reading V.4). Students with a knowledge of Portuguese will find a treasure trove in the collections of his works listed in the Bibliographic Suggestions.

Because Vieira's efforts to abolish Indian slavery were most important to his role in Brazilian history, Dr. Mathias C. Kiemen's exposition of the Indian policy of Portugal is given (Reading V.2) as a general background. Dr. Kiemen is on the staff of the Academy of American Franciscan History of Washington, D.C.

1. A Great Luso-Brazilian Figure

C. R. Boxer

`"Não quero ensinar o Padre Nosso ao Vigário," and I do not pretend that this paper contains anything new for Portuguese and Brazilians, although so many-sided a man as Vieira can never make exactly the same impact on any two people. Vieira was recognized as the greatest master of Portuguese prose in his own day and generation, and Fernando Pessoa in ours has called him "O Imperador da lingua Portuguesa." His work as missionary, orator, prophet, diplomat, and statesman, has been frequently discussed (and variously assessed) by some of the most competent writers in the Portuguese-speaking world. But although Vieira is incontestably one of the greatest figures in the history of Portugal and Brazil, as he is certainly one of the most interesting, his name is practically unknown in this country. It was of Vieira that Robert Southey was primarily thinking when he wrote that Portuguese "is a language which is inferior to no modern speech, and which contains some of the most original and admirable works that I have ever perused." Unfortunately, Southey's plea that more of his compatriots should interest themselves in the language of Camões and Vieira still awaits a satisfactory response. I cannot hope to succeed where Southey failed, but [shall here] briefly recall the career of one of the most remarkable Portuguese who ever lived.

Vieira's life-span roughly coincided with the seventeenth century, when the course of events brought about the definitive separation of Portugal from Spain, and ensured that Brazil would not fall, in whole or in part, under Protestant Dutch control, as at one time seemed likely. Vieira took an active and often a leading role in these stirring and momentous events, and on one occasion at least his in-

C. R. Boxer, *A Great Luso-Brazilian Figure: Padre António Vieira, S.J., 1608–1697* (London: The Hispanic and Luso-Brazilian Councils, 1957). Reprinted by permission of the author and The Hispanic and Luso-Brazilian Councils (Canning House, London).

tervention was probably decisive. Moreover, his sermons, letters, and state-papers form the best collective source for the understanding of the "climate of opinion" in seventeenth-century Portugal, Brazil and the Maranhão. In an age when the pulpit occupied the place which is filled nowadays by the newspapers, the wireless, and television as moulders of public opinion, Vieira's sermons were among the most famous and influential, nor was their fame confined to Portugal and Brazil. Letter-writers have never been too plentiful in these otherwise admirable countries, and Vieira was not merely a prolific letter-writer, but a highly intelligent and keenly critical observer who frequently wrote at white heat and without reserve. His state-papers on such varied subjects as diplomatic negotiations with the Dutch, Portugal's economic ills and their remedies, toleration for the crypto-Jews or "New-Christians," and freedom for the Amerindians of Brazil, are also models of clear and incisive reasoning, and they invariably exercised great weight in the councils of the Crown. All in all, Vieira ranks as a great historical as well as a great literary figure, and he was certainly the most remarkable man in the seventeenth-century Luso-Brazilian world.

António Vieira was born at Lisbon on February 6, 1608, in a working class family of Alemtejan origin. One of his grand-parents was a Mulatto serving-woman, the others being respectively an armourer, a baker-wife, and a manservant of the Counts of Unhão. When six years old he accompanied his parents to Bahia, where his father had been given a small post in the recently established colonial High Court. He remained in Brazil for the next twenty-seven years, and thus grew up in the colony which had already become Portugal's most prized and profitable overseas possession. He went to school at the Jesuit College in Bahia, where he was first impelled towards a religious vocation by hearing a lurid description of the tortures of Hell in a sermon preached in March, 1623. He became a novice in the Society a few weeks later, and it was in this capacity that he witnessed the Dutch attack on and occupation of Bahia in the following year. Within a week of the recapture of the colonial capital in May, 1625, Vieira took the three ordinary vows of poverty, chastity, and obedience, and an additional voluntary one pledging himself to missionary work among the Amerindians and the Negro slaves, for which purpose he learnt Tupí-Guaraní and Kimbundu. In the next year he wrote the Jesuit Annual Letter from Brazil which contains a graphic account of the Dutch campaign. This is the earliest of Vieira's surviving writings, and it already displays all the qualities of style, clarity, and crispness which subsequently made him a celebrated writer. Like so much of his work, it is not merely a piece of edifying religious literature, but a first-class historical source for the events which it describes.

Vieira asked his superiors to release him from the long and arduous course of study prescribed for Jesuit priests, so that he could devote his life to missionary work among the coloured races, but they declined to do this since they realised his exceptional abilities. He taught rhetoric and the humanities for a year in the Jesuit College at Olinda, but was back at Bahia when the Dutch launched their invasion of Northeastern Brazil in 1630. While continuing his theological and philosophical studies, he contrived to do some work in the *aldeias* or mission-villages of the Amerindians near Bahia, and his second recorded sermon was one preached to the Negro slaves of an *engenho* or sugar-mill in the *Reconcavo* in 1633. He was ordained a priest and celebrated his first mass in December of the following year, and he speedily became the most popular preacher in the colony. As such, he took a prominent part in the defense of Bahia against Count Johan Maurits of Nassau in 1638, and was chosen to preach the victory sermon after the Dutch withdrawal. Vieira's sermons during this period are largely and inevitably concerned with the Dutch peril, since about half of Brazil was then in heretic hands, but they are not merely patriotic rhapsodies or empty exhortations to fight the good fight. On the contrary, Vieira trenchantly denounced the corrupt and rapacious colonial officials, and laid bare the causes of the mismanagement of the war. He voiced the complaints of the underfed and underpaid soldiery, observing on one occasion that the King should give the shirt off his back rather than let his infantry in Brazil be so ill-supplied as they were.

Nor were Vieira's criticisms confined to temporal monarchies and to "os poderosos da terra," the great ones of the earth. Perhaps the most famous sermon of the many he preached in the course of sixty years was that delivered at Bahia after the defeat of a combined Spanish-Portuguese Armada by an inferior Dutch fleet off Pernambuco in January, 1640. This sermon "contra as armas de Holanda" was preached to the text of Psalm XLIV, 23: "Awake, why sleepest thou, O Lord? arise, cast us not off forever," and it has been rightly described by the Abbé Raynal as "the most vehement and extra-

ordinary ever heard in a Christian pulpit." Vieira, addressing God
as much in anger as in sorrow, bitterly denounces the Deity for
favouring the heretic Dutch at the expense of the Catholic Portuguese, and he urges him to change his mind before it is too late.

If You were resolved to give these same lands to the pirates
of Holland, why did You not do so when they were still wild
and uncultivated instead of now? Has this perverse and apostate people rendered You such services that You first sent us
here as their harbingers, so that we might cultivate the lands
and build the cities for them; and after we had cultivated and
enriched the same, hand these over to them? Must heretics
and enemies of the Faith thus enjoy the fruits of the work of
the Portuguese and of the sweat of Catholic brows? *En queis
conservimus agros?* Behold for whom we have worked for so
many years!

But since You, O Lord, wish and ordain it thus, do whatever seems good to You. Give Brazil to the Dutch, give them
the Indies, give them the Spains (for the result of the loss of
Brazil will be no less perilous), give them whatever we still
have and possess (as You have already given them so much),
and place the world in their hands. As for us, we Portuguese
and Spaniards, abandon us, repudiate us, destroy us, finish us.
But I cannot forbear to tell and remind Your Majesty, O Lord,
that it may chance one day that You will need these same
whom You now spurn and cast from You, and You will then
no longer have them.   . . .

Burn, destroy, consume us all, but it may chance one day
that You will need Spaniards and Portuguese, and that You
will not be able to find them. Holland will give you apostolic
conquerors who will carry through the world the standards of
the cross; Holland will give You Gospel preachers who will
sow the Catholic doctrine in savage lands and water it with
their own blood; Holland will defend the truth of Your Sacraments and the authority of the Roman Catholic Church; Holland will build temples; Holland will raise altars; Holland will
consecrate priests and will offer the sacrifice of Your most
Holy Body; Holland, in short, will serve You and will venerate
You as religiously as they do daily in Amsterdam, Middelburg
and Flushing, and in all the other colonies of that cold and
watery hell!

The darkest hour proverbially comes just before the dawn, and this sermon which expressed the feeling of many people that "Deus não quer a restauração do Brasil," was preached only a few months before the Lisbon revolution of December 1, 1640. This event ended the so-called "Sixty Years' Captivity" of Portugal to Spain, enthroned the Duke of Braganza as Dom João IV, and led, after some tortuous negotiations, to the conclusion of a ten-year truce with the Dutch. It is a clear indication of the position which Vieira had already achieved at Bahia that he was selected as a member of the delegation which was sent by the viceroy of Brazil, Marquis of Montalvão, to announce the colony's enthusiastic adherence to the new monarch. Two of Montalvão's sons had fled from Lisbon to Seville shortly after the revolution, and this led to the delegation's (which was headed by a third son) being nearly lynched by an angry mob when they landed at Peniche at the end of April, 1641. Having been rescued with considerable difficulty, Vieira and his companions were sent to Lisbon, where they were presented to the King.

Dom João IV at once fell under the spell of Vieira's self-assured and magnetic personality and within a very short time he came to regard the tall, lean, and dynamic Jesuit as "o primeiro homem do mundo." Vieira repaid him with a passionate devotion which never wavered as long as the monarch lived, and after his death this became a hallucination that Dom João would rise from the dead to inaugurate the fifth Biblical universal monarchy under Portuguese leadership. From the day of their first meeting until the King's death sixteen years later, the relationship between the two men was not so much that of monarch and vassal as that of two friends who had no secret from each other. The King never failed to consult Vieira about the most important matters of state so long as the Jesuit remained in Portugal; and when Vieira wrote to him from abroad he wrote in terms which only someone who was much more than an *éminence grise* would use. It was particularly on Brazilian problems that the king deferred to the Jesuit's advice, for so impressed was Dom João by Vieira's knowledge of the colony that he assumed he was born there. The King's opinion was, incidentally, shared by many others; and Vieira found it necessary to insert a notice in the eighth volume of his *Sermoens* (published in 1694) stating that he was born at Lisbon and not at Bahia as most people seemed to think.

Vieira's influence was not limited to the monarch alone. The Spanish-born Queen, Dona Luisa de Gusmão, was another fervent admirer, and the Infante Dom Theodosio followed his parents' example. Vieira's fiery eloquency and patriotic fervour, the topical nature of his sermons, and the freedom with which he lashed abuses and criticized offenders, soon made him the most popular preacher in Lisbon. "Lançar tapete de madrugada em São Roque" quickly became the seventeenth-century Lisbon equivalent of queuing for seats at dawn for the Russian Ballet in the London of 1956. His intimacy with the king and the royal family, and the fact that he was virtually acting as a minister of the Crown, naturally made him many enemies; but he could also count on the admiring friendship of the Duke of Cadaval and others among the premier nobility. His sermons were often the sounding board for government propaganda, and they still afford us an admirable mirror for the times and the society which they reflect. Vieira used all his arts of eloquence and persuasion to induce the *fidalguia* and clergy to contribute more liberally to the cost of the war against Castile, and to persuade the working-classes to bear uncomplainingly the increasingly heavy burdens which were laid on them.

Although not officially appointed Court-preacher until 1644, Vieira had to all intents and purposes secured this post with the sermon which he delivered before the king and court in the royal chapel on New Year's Day, 1642. In this, he strove to discredit the widespread belief that King Sebastian, apparently killed crusading against the Moors in 1578, would return from some mysterious Atlantic island where he lay enchanted like King Arthur, to resume the crown, lead Portugal against the Ottoman Turks for the recapture of Constantinople and Jerusalem, and thus inaugurate a universal Christian empire which would render obedience to the Pope. Vieira insisted that the prophecies, whether Biblical or otherwise, on which these expectations were based, applied not to King Sebastian but to King John IV. He based his arguments not only on the Book of Daniel and the more recondite parts of the Old Testament, but on the lucubrations of a rather dim Spanish Dominican saint called Fray Gil. Both Vieira and the died-in-the-wool Sebastianists whom he was trying to confute also relied heavily on the prophetic doggerel verses of the sixteenth-century cobbler of Trancoso, Gonçalo Anes Bandarra. These jingling rhymes had been banned by the Inquisition in 1541, but they attained a wide circulation in manuscript during the "Sixty Years' Captivity." They were so cryptically worded that with a little ingenuity they could be applied to almost anything. Vieira differed from the Sebastianists in his explanation of Bandarra's verses, but he agreed with them that the cobbler was a true prophet, fully entitled to as much credit as those of the Old Testament.

Like many people in seventeenth-century Europe, whether Protestant or Catholic, Vieira believed that the prophetical books of the Old Testament could be largely interpreted in terms of the present and the immediate future. He had no inclination towards abstract thought, but a veritable passion for messianic lore and Biblical commentary. He boasted that he had acted as librarian in all the Jesuit establishments in which he had served, and when abroad he made a special point of visiting the most famous European libraries, eagerly studying all the best books on the subjects which interested him. As the English envoy at Lisbon noted in 1668, Vieira "besides his natural eloquence has the art of making the scriptures say what he pleases," and like many of his contemporaries he concentrated on the Old Testament rather than on the New. His God was in many respects the God of battles, as was perhaps inevitable with so pugnacious a personality in an age of such violent theological and confessional conflict. For instance, he concludes his New Year sermon of 1642 with the hope that the fratricidal struggle with Catholic Castile will soon cease, thus enabling the victorious Portuguese to bathe their swords in "the blood of heretics in Europe, and the blood of Muslims in Africa, the blood of heathen in Asia and in America, conquering and subjugating all the regions of the earth under one sole empire, so that they may all, under the aegis of one crown, be placed gloriously beneath the feet of the successor of Saint Peter." We may smile at such extravagances today, but Vieira was by no means the only Christian preacher to be blissfully unconscious of the incongruities in which his addiction to the Old Testament landed him. Did not the Calvinist ministers of the Scots army at Dunbar a few years later select as their battle-cry "Jesus and No Quarter!"? And did not Major-General Thomas Harrison and the Fifth Monarchy men believe that Cromwellian England was destined to play the part which Vieira assigned to Portugal?

If in his sermons Vieira appealed more frequently to the patriotism, the emotion and the imagination of his hearers than to their intelligence, the same criticism cannot be levelled at his state-papers. The depth and conviction of his messianic beliefs certainly did not affect the clarity and cogency of his reasoning on many severely practical matters. Apart from the war of independence against Castile, King John IV's principal preoccupation was the Dutch threat to the Portuguese colonies, and particularly to what he called his Brazilian "milch-cow." This was a subject on which Vieira had very definite if highly unpopular views. Both he and the King were convinced that Portugal could not possibly fight Spain and the United Provinces at the same time, and that peace with the Dutch must be made at any price. The upshot showed that they were wrong, but they had plenty of good reasons for their attitude, since the economic and demographic resources of the Northern Netherlands were vastly superior to those of Portugal.

Vieira may have exaggerated somewhat when he wrote that the Dutch had over 14,000 vessels which could be used as warships and a quarter of a million sailors wherewith to man them, whereas Portugal had only thirteen warships and 4,000 mariners all told, but there can be no doubt that Dutch naval superiority was crushing. Moreover, Amsterdam was the commercial capital of Europe, and the Dutch could draw freely on Germany and Scandinavia for additional manpower; whereas Portugal was a poor country which had no means of increasing the military potential of its population of about a million souls. Brazil was not the colossus which we know today, but a narrow coastal strip extending from the Amazon delta to São Vicente. This was nowhere colonised for a greater depth than thirty miles inland, save in the remote highland plateau of São Paulo in the extreme south. The country was about evenly divided between the Portuguese and the Dutch, with the latter holding the northern and the richer half. The Dutch held unchallenged command of the sea, and how, Vieira argued, could Portugal hope to reconquer Pernambuco, when she had need of every man and ship to fight Spain, and when the combined efforts of Spain and Portugal had failed miserably in the last ten years?

Vieira's advice was that the King should try to induce the Dutch to sell their half of Brazil to the Portuguese Crown in exchange for a huge indemnity in money and sugar; but that if the Dutch insisted on retaining Pernambuco, then the King should, as a last resort, recognize their claim in return for the conclusion of a firm and lasting peace. By way of atoning for Portugal's economic and maritime weakness in the face of Dutch commercial and naval superiority, Vieira further urged the creation of two great chartered India Companies, one for the East and one for the West, after the Dutch models. As neither the Portuguese Crown nor the merchants possessed sufficient capital to found these corporations, he advised the king to attract the necessary capital by granting a fair degree of toleration to the New-Christian who formed the wealthier portion of the merchant-class, many of whom had emigrated to avoid the rigours of the Holy Office of the Inquisition.

Although the king, the queen, and a few of the nobility — particularly the Portuguese envoys at Paris and the Hague — agreed with Vieira's views, the great bulk of the nation was resolutely opposed to them. When the *moradores* of Pernambuco rose against their Dutch overlords in June, 1645, and were joined by Portuguese troops sent by the Governor of Bahia, Vieira argued strenuously that no support should be sent from Portugal to the insurgents, and that, on the contrary, the Dutch demands for the restitution of Pernambuco should be complied with. Public opinion was violently opposed to this appeasement policy, and equally so to any toleration of the hated New-Christians; but the king, who believed with Vieira that "war with Holland is obviously impossible and peace absolutely necessary" sent the Jesuit abroad on two confidential diplomatic missions with the object of speeding up the negotiations.

From February to July, 1646, Vieira was employed (disguised as a layman in scarlet broadcloth and with a sword at his side, pointed mustachios and no tonsure) as adviser to Francisco de Sousa Coutinho, the Portuguese envoy at the Hague, in an abortive attempt to reach an agreement with the Dutch over the purchase of Pernambuco. Despite the failure of this effort, he was employed on another similar mission from August, 1647 to October, 1648, which this time envisaged the outright cession of Pernambuco to the Dutch. He was also ordered to ascertain the possibility of arranging a suitable French marriage for the Infante Dom Theodosio. With the renewal of the struggle with the Dutch in 1645, King John IV found Portugal's prospects so hopeless that he was prepared to resign his throne in favour of a French son-in-law, retiring to rule an Atlantic dominion of his own in the Azores and the Maranhão. Both these projects failed, since Cardinal Mazarin flatly rejected King John's defeatist suggestion, and the cross-purposes of Dutch internal politics thwarted the desire of the powerful city of Amsterdam to reach an agreement over Pernambuco.

On his way to Holland, Vieira was captured by pirates in the English Channel and landed at Dover in September, 1647. He visited London to get some money to continue his voyage, but naturally his main idea was to get out of the country as quickly as possible, and in any case England was not an attractive place for an abstemious Portuguese. Dr. António de Sousa de Macedo, King John IV's Resident in London, had written to his colleague at Paris in 1646: "For five years I have not seen the sun as God made it. In the winter I am shivering with cold, and in the summer I am terrified of the plague, nor have I ever met a man who was not at least half-drunk." Vieira was more charitable to us than the irascible diplomat, and he cordially approved of some aspects of the Puritan Sabbath. In a sermon preached nine years later on Palm Sunday in the Maranhão, he recalled approvingly how two of his companions had been stopped from gambling in an inn at Dover. The landlord told them that it was as much as his life was worth to let them play draughts on the Lord's Day. "And this," added Vieira impressively, "in a maritime town or port, where all, without a single exception, are heretics. What a shame on us who so pride ourselves on the name of Catholics! If in a land of heretics it is sacrilege to play draughts on an ordinary Sunday, what will it be to play these or other games of chance in Holy Week, in a land where the Cross and images of Christ are worshipped, and where the mysteries of his death are celebrated."

The failure of Vieira's diplomatic missions to France and Holland coincided with the crisis of the war against the Dutch in Brazil. This had gone well for the Luso-Brazilians on land, since they had driven their opponents into the shelter of Recife, Paraíba, and a few other fortified places on the Northeast coast; and they had even captured Angola, which was on the point of being entirely lost in August, 1648. But it was a very different story by sea, for between January 1, 1647 and December 31, 1648, some 220 Portuguese ships bound to or from Brazil had been taken by Dutch privateers in the South Atlantic. No merchant-marine in the world could survive such staggering losses, and it was clear that if they continued much longer all the victories of the insurgent patriots on land would be of no ultimate avail. Brazil had no arms industry of her own, and the Luso-Brazilians could not rely indefinitely on captured weapons. If they could neither send their sugar for sale in Portugal, nor receive essential military supplies from the mother-country, then they would either have to abandon the struggle, or retire into the bush (*sertão*) and lead a half-savage life. At the end of 1648, King John IV had either to do something drastic, or else abandon Pernambuco to the stranglehold of superior Dutch sea-power.

Screwing up his courage to the sticking-point, the king decided to take Vieira's advice and to organize a great chartered company for the Brazil trade with the aid of Jewish capital. This company, formally incorporated on March 8, 1649, was to provide convoys for all shipping engaged in the Brazil trade in return for a monopoly of the chief colonial imports from the mother-country — codfish, wine, flour, and olive-oil. On Vieira's insistence, all capital invested in the Brazil Company was specifically exempted from confiscation by the Inquisition, even if the investor was found guilty of heresy, Judaism, or apostasy. This bold move was bitterly resented by many people besides the Inquisitors. In fact, only Jesuit theologians could be found to support the lawfulness of this ruling, all other civil and canon-lawyers who were consulted voting against it. The Brazil Company was equally unpopular in Brazil, owing to the monopoly prices which it charged for its imports, and the irregularity with which its convoys functioned. But this was not Vieira's fault, and he was triumphantly successful in his principal aim. Shipping was to a great extent safeguarded against the depredations of the Dutch privateers; and thanks to the co-operation of the Brazil Company's Armada, the patriots of Pernambuco were finally able to eject the Dutch from Northeast Brazil in January, 1654. Well might Vieira claim forty years later that it was *his* Company which "brought always from Brazil the sinews wherewith to sustain the war against Castile, to maintain the kingdom, to recover Pernambuco, and still today helps with prompt and lavish means in times of greatest need."

If Vieira's outspoken advocacy of the hated New-Christians made him unpopular with all sorts and conditions of men, he also aroused considerable opposition in his own Society by warmly supporting King John IV's scheme to split the Jesuit Province of Portugal into two. So embarrassed was the Society's headquarters at Rome by Vieira's multifarious activities, that the General resolved to dismiss him, and ordered him to seek admission to another Order. At this point King John IV intervened, and offered to present to Vieira a bishopric. When Vieira declined this honour on the ground that he would rather be a scullion in the service of the Society of Jesus than a mitred prelate outside it, the King refused to allow the General's order to be implemented. Vieira, who had taken his fourth and final vow in January, 1646, thus remained in the Order to which he was so devotedly attached, as the General dropped his demand in view of the King's intransigence.

From January to July, 1650, Vieira was employed on a secret diplomatic mission to Rome, partly with the object of putting out feelers for a Spanish marriage with Dom Theodosio, and partly to try to add fuel to the flames of the popular revolt at Naples against the suzerainty of Spain. In neither respect was he able to achieve anything, and he was forced to leave Rome precipitately, in order to escape being assassinated by hirelings of the Spanish ambassador. This evidently blunted the edge of his keenness for diplomacy, since two years later he rejected the invitation of the Count of Penaguião to accompany him as his chaplain on his embassy to Cromwellian England.

Vieira had for some time been interested in the neglected Maranhão mission-field, and in 1652 he allotted his emoluments as court-preacher to the missions of the Maranhão and Grão-Pará. His first attempt to leave for that field was thwarted by the King in 1651, but a year later the monarch changed his mind, perhaps at the instigation of some other members of the Society. Although this time Vieira was not particularly keen to go, he was sent thither by his superiors at the end of 1652, with orders to refound the Jesuit mission which had lapsed with the death of the last three missionaries in 1649. On their way, Vieira's party stopped at the Cape Verde Islands for Christmas week, where he was greatly impressed by some of the indigenous clergy. "There are here," he wrote, "clergy and canons as black as jet, but so well-bred, so authoritative, so learned, such great musicians, so discreet, and so accomplished that they may well be envied by those in our own cathedrals at home." The admiration was mutual, and the islanders begged Vieira and his companions to stay there instead of going on to the Maranhão. They were seriously tempted to do so, but finally decided to leave for their proper destination, which they reached on January 16, 1653.

Vieira remained in the mission-fields of the Maranhão-Pará for the next nine years, with the exception of a brief but eventful visit to Portugal (June, 1654–April, 1655). During all these years he displayed as much energy, zeal, and ardour in missionary work among the savages of the American rivers and jungles, as he had previously exhibited in his political activities in the European capitals and courts. He later claimed to have travelled nearly six thousand miles either by canoe along the rivers, or on foot through jungle and bush, making converts wherever he went and confirming others in the faith. He composed catechisms in six of the many local (and exceedingly complex) Amerindian languages, and he imported many church furnishings and instruments at his own expense from Europe — not forgetting masks and rattles "to show the heathen, much addicted to their dances, that the Christian religion is not sad."

Vieira's missionary efforts were both strenuous and continuous, but an even greater proportion of his remarkable energy was devoted to combating the colonists who strove to enslave the Amerindians for work in their fields and households. The colony was still very sparsely populated by white settlers. There was virtually no money in circulation, and the primitive economy was based on the interchange of local products, principally cotton, but also sugar, tobacco, and cacao. For reasons which I need not go into here, white men in the tropics have (until very recent times) always sought for coloured people to do the donkey-work for them, and the Portuguese colonists in the Maranhão were no exceptions to this rule. They were too poor to afford the cost of importing Negro slaves from West Africa, as their wealthier compatriots in Pernambuco, Bahia, and Rio de Janeiro did. They therefore fell back on the use of Amerindian slave or forced labour, unsatisfactory in many ways as this proved to be.

The Jesuits alone among the Religious Orders in Brazil had a long tradition of upholding the freedom of the Amerindians against all the efforts of the colonists to enslave and exploit them, and Vieira soon became famous (or infamous, so far as the colonists were concerned) as their most outspoken champion. His sermons on this theme were inspired by the words of the Prophet Isaiah: "Cry aloud, spare not; lift up thy voice like a trumpet, and show my people their sins." Never a man to mince his words, his denunciation of the colonists at times verged on the abusive. "*M* stands for Maranhão, in the ABC of vices," he told them on one occasion: "*M* Maranhão, *M* murmurar, *M* motejar, *M* maldizer, *M* mexericar, e sobretudo, *M* mentir: mentir com as palavras, mentir com as obras, mentir com os pensamentos, que de todos e por todos os modos aqui se mente." Not content with castigating the colonists in his sermons, Vieira kept the King informed of their real and alleged misdeeds in his confidential correspondence with the Crown. He did not scruple to assert that Portuguese mistreatment of the Amerindians in Amazonia had resulted in the death of over two millions of them in forty years, and his exaggerations in this respect recall those of Las Casas. He was equally scathing in his condemnation of the rapacity and venality of some of the regional governors. When King John IV asked him whether the unwieldy colony should be governed by two Captain-Majors or by one Governor, Vieira replied that a single governor was preferable since one thief was a lesser evil than two.

Vieira's attitude naturally made him extremely unpopular with most of the colonists and the Crown officials, to say nothing of the friars of the Mendicant Orders, with whom, as he said, he waged "continual and cruel war" over their disregard of the Amerindians' interests. His enemies reacted vigorously in kind, denouncing him to Lisbon as a mischievous trouble-maker, and alleging that the Jesuits merely wished to deprive the colonists of their Amerindian labourers in order to exploit them for their own purposes. King John IV sympathized with Vieira, but he could not afford to ignore entirely the protests of the colonists and the friars. The laws which were framed at Lisbon to protect the Amerindians were thus inevitably of a compromise character which satisfied neither party to the dispute. Vieira reluctantly accepted them as better than nothing, although he declared later that it would be a lesser evil for the whole colony to collapse rather than exist on Amerindian slave-labour. On an earlier occasion he advanced the scarcely less heretical view that the colonists should perform the necessary manual labour themselves rather than rely on their Amerindian "hands and feet" as they called them. "For it is better to live by the sweat of one's own brow," he wrote, "than by another's blood."

Some admirers of Vieira have also claimed him as a pioneer abolitionist of Negro slavery, but this claim cannot be substantiated. Unlike the great Las Casas, who, after first condoning Negro slavery later unreservedly condemned it, Vieira limited himself to denouncing the sadistic ill-treatment of Negro slaves by many of their owners. In one of his earliest sermons he compared the sufferings of the Negroes in the sugar-mills at harvest-time to those of Christ upon the Cross; but he adjured the slaves if not exactly to "grin and bear it" at any rate to pray and bear it, assuring them that this Christian resignation would be suitably recompensed in Paradise. Admittedly, his condemnation of their treatment became stronger in later life, as can be seen by comparing the sermon preached to the masters and slaves of an *engenho* in the Reconcavo in 1633, with that delivered in similar circumstances some fifty years later. But even this last sermon, which lashes the cruelty and callousness of the *senhores de engenho,* does not imply that the enslavement of Negroes, was necessarily wrong in itself. Not that Vieira believed in any theory of master-race, or in the innate superiority of the white man over the coloured. "Can there be," he asked in his celebrated Epiphany sermon of 1662, "a greater want of understanding, or a greater error of judgment between men as men, than for me to think that I must be your master because I was born further away from the sun, and that you must be my slave because you were born nearer to it?" And again: "An Ethiope if he be cleansed in the waters of the Zaire [Congo] is clean, but he is not white; but if in the water of baptism, he is both." This did not prevent Vieira from arguing to the end of his days that the freedom of the Amerindians could best be secured by increasing the importation of Negro slaves from West Africa. In this respect, Vieira's views were far less advanced than those of his Spanish precursors and contemporaries, the Dominicans Las Casas and Mercado, and the Jesuit Alonso de Sandoval, whose vitriolic denunciations of the slave-trade and its attendant evils were more far-reaching.

Vieira's preoccupation with the freedom of the Amerindians during his nine years in the Maranhão and Grão-Pará did not prevent him from developing his ideas about Portugal's future as the fifth world-monarchy, which became a fixed obsession with him after the death of King John IV in 1656. This belief was closely connected with his intense conviction that Portugal "has for its particular and special end the propagation and extension of the Catholic faith in heathen lands, for which purpose God raised and founded it. And the more that Portugal acts in keeping with this end, the more sure and certain is its preservation; and the more it diverges therefrom, the more doubtful and dangerous is its future."

His belief in Portugal as the fifth universal monarchy was greatly strengthened by his own experience in the wilds of South America. He remarked on the exiguous number of missionaries who, even in the most favorable circumstances, would be available for evangelising the teeming millions of three continents; and he stressed the virtual impossibility of catechising hostile cannibals armed with poisoned arrows, who would let no one approach them in the depths of the Amazonian jungle. From these premises he argued that the conversion of the world to Christianity could not possibly be expected from the labours of a few thousand European missionaries, however devoted. It must await the direct intervention of God, working through his chosen kingdom of Portugal, the fifth great universal monarchy, as prophesied in the Old Testament and in the *Trovas* of Bandarra.

Vieira's most spectacular success as a missionary was his conversion of the savage Nheengaíbas on the island of Marajó in the Amazon estuary. This feat was all the more remarkable as these islanders had always been exceedingly hostile to the Portuguese and on friendly terms with the Dutch. The triumph was particularly Vieira's own, as the savages refused to communicate in the first place with anyone save himself — the *Payagassú*, or "Padre Grande" as they called him, both on account of his tall stature and the confidence which his character inspired. Their conversion was all the more welcome as otherwise the Dutch, who had declared war on Portugal two years previously, could easily have established themselves there and overrun both Pará and the Maranhão in short order.

Although the colonists realised that possession of Marajó gave them the strategic key to Amazonia, they could not forgive Vieira his championship of the Amerindians; and Vieira, after his resounding success at Marajó, was less than ever inclined to compromise with the colonists. King John IV had died in November, 1656, and although the Queen-Regent was likewise his ardent supporter, she did not, as a woman and a widow, inspire the same respect in the rough frontiersmen of the Maranhão. Encouraged by the weakness or duplicity of the regional governor, Dom Pedro de Mello, and allegedly egged on by some of the friars, the *moradores* of the Maranhão tumultuously arrested the local Jesuits, and their example was soon followed by the settlers of Pará. Vieira and his companions were in some danger of being manhandled if not lynched, but eventually they were deported to Portugal in September, 1661.

On his enforced return to Lisbon, Vieira was at first received with sympathy and favour at Court; but the palace-revolution of June, 1662, which relegated the Queen-Regent to a convent and brought the Count of Castel-Melhor to power, likewise resulted in the downfall of the Jesuit. He had long been an object of dislike and suspicion to the Holy Office, partly on account of his messianic beliefs, but mainly because of his outspoken advocacy of toleration for the New-Christians. He was arraigned by this tribunal at Coimbra for a lengthy disquisition entitled *Esperanças de Portugal, quinto imperio do mundo, primeira e segunda vida de El-rei D. João o quarto* which he had composed in Amazonia, and in which he affirmed his conviction that Bandarra was a true prophet and that King John IV would rise from the dead to inaugurate the conquest of the world by Portugal. Though suffering from very poor health at this period, he defended himself with great skill and pertinacity for two years, but was finally sentenced to be deprived of his faculties for preaching and to be imprisoned in a Jesuit House. With the object of inflicting additional humiliation on him and on the Society of Jesus, the lengthy judgment and sentence were read out in the crowded hall of the Jesuit College at Coimbra on Christmas Eve, 1667. When Vieira stood up to hear this rigmarole, all the assembled Jesuits likewise rose to their feet and remained standing throughout the proceedings which lasted for more than two hours. They thus demonstrated their sympathy with him and by implication their opposition to the Holy Office.

Many people thought that Vieira was lucky to have escaped the stake, and the relative lightness of his sentence was evidently due to the fact that the final stages of his trial coincided with another palace-revolution which overthrew the dictatorship of Castel-Melhor and brought his friends to power. Vieira was speedily released from his confinement, but although reappointed court-preacher, he did not find the same grace and favour in the eyes of the Prince-Regent, Dom Pedro, as he had in those of his father. Disappointed that his old influence at Court was gone, he left for Rome in August, 1669, partly to plead his own cause there, and partly to help that of the New-Christians by securing some mitigation of the savage rigour with which they were treated by the Portuguese branch of the Holy Office. He obtained from the Pope a Brief which explicitly exempted him from the jurisdiction of the Portuguese Inquisition, but his efforts to secure a drastic reform of the barbarous procedure of this institution were unsuccessful in the long run. Nevertheless, they led to the Pope's imposing a seven-year suspension of all inquisitorial trials and *autos-da-fé* in Portugal while the matter was being debated, and thus no victims were burned at the stake between 1674 and 1681.

Vieira enjoyed as much renown as an orator at Rome, where he preached in both Portuguese and Italian, as he did at Lisbon. He became the favorite preacher of that formidable blue-stocking, Queen Christina of Sweden, and of the Jesuit General, Oliva, who was himself a famous orator. Finally disillusioned with the prospect of obtaining toleration for the New-Christians, and full of *saudades* for his native land, that "cantinho da Europa, mas cantinho de terra pura e mimosa de Deus" as he called it in one of his Roman sermons, he resolved at length to return to Lisbon. He went by way of France, sailing from La Rochelle in the English frigate *Portsmouth*, in company with the Duke of Cadaval's thirteen-year-old French bride in August, 1675. Once back in Lisbon, Dom Pedro gave him every encouragement to publish the collected edition of his *Sermoens*, the first volume of which appeared in 1679; but the Prince-Regent still declined to treat Vieira as a confidential adviser, to the latter's unconcealed annoyance. Asked to return to Rome as confessor to Queen Christina, Vieira declined on the plea of ill-health, asking instead to be sent once more as a missionary to the Maranhão. When this was turned down on account of his advanced age, he decided to go back to Bahia, which he had left forty years previously, and to end his days amid the beautiful Brazilian scenery he loved so well.

He sailed for Bahia January, 1681, and there he remained until his death sixteen years later. His natural pugnacity was little abated in his old age, and he was involved in several bitter quarrels with some of his colleagues, and on one occasion with the Governor-General. He served as Visitor-General of the Brazil and Maranhão missions in 1688–91, and he continued to forward the cause of the Amerindians with all his old zest and conviction, if at times with a trifle more tact. His whole-hearted sympathy for the Amerindians was not always matched by a corresponding cordiality towards the Brazilian Creoles or *Mazombos*. Although he called Brazil his "segunda patria," and jokingly referred to himself as a *Mazombo*, and although he advocated the establishment of a seminary in the Maranhão for training the sons of the colonists as missionaries, in his old age he wrote a scathing denunciation of the Brazilian members of the Society, arguing that they were not the equals of the European-born Portuguese. On the other hand, he loaded his own countrymen with scornful abuse on several occasions, and more than once criticized the short-sighted selfishness with which the home government sometimes treated Brazil. Despite these perio-

dic outbursts of not always righteous indignation, Vieira's correspondence ranging over seventy years shows time and again how
sincerely he loved his country on both sides of the Atlantic, "all
earthly things above."

Vieira's physical health declined rapidly in his last three years,
but his intelligence remained unimpaired. Though nearly ninety
years of age, almost totally blind, and partly paralyzed, he continued to correspond with his friends at Lisbon, who included the
Dowager Queen Catherine of Great Britain. He also continued to
work on his *Clavis Prophetarum,* an enormous codex of Biblical
exegesis, with the aid of various amanuenses. The ship which carried the news of his death to Lisbon, also brought letters dictated
by him a week before he died in his cell at the Jesuit College of
Bahia, at one o'clock in the morning of July 18, 1697.

João Lucio d'Azevedo, Vieira's best biographer, entitled his final
chapter on Vieira's last sixteen years at Bahia, *O Vencido,* "The Vanquished." This seems to me to be a misnomer. Vieira died at the
height of his literary fame, with his sermons still being regularly
published and eagerly read. His renown reached as far as Mexico,
where he was officially honoured by the University, and politely
criticized by the celebrated Sor Juana Inés de la Cruz. He was the
acknowledged master of Portuguese prose in his lifetime, and, unlike the case with most great authors, his fame did not undergo even
a temporary eclipse after his death. Indeed, English is the only major European language which lacks a representative translation of
Vieira's works. As regards the Luso-Brazilian world, Dom Francisco
Alexandre Lobo merely expressed the feeling of successive generations when he wrote in 1823: "Se o uso da nossa língua se perder, e
com ele por acaso acabarem todos os nossos escritos, que não são
'Os Lusiadas' e as obras de Vieira: o português, quer no estilo da
prosa, quer no poético, ainda viverá na sua perfeita índole natíva, na
sua riquíssima cópia e louçania."

If Vieira's battle for the New-Christians had ended in defeat, his
struggle for the freedom of the Amerindians had not, even if the
final victory had to wait until the dictatorship of Pombal, who
blackened Vieira's memory while carrying out (in many respects)
his policies. If some of his cherished plans, such as the foundation
of an East-Indian Company, met with a cool reception at Court, his
advice was still heard with respect on other matters. It was largely
due to his representations that various Indian spices were trans-

planted to Bahia before the end of the century, and that a colonial mint was established there in 1694.

Vieira was nothing if not a bonny fighter, but he had the defects of his pugnacious temperament. He did not suffer fools — or friars — gladly, although he remarked resignedly on more than one occasion that even Our Lord with all his miracles had never cured anyone of folly. We may smile — or yawn — today at some of Vieira's oratorical flights, and wonder at his credulous — some would say cretinous — belief in Portugal as the fifth universal monarchy. But these chimeras served to encourage many people in the dark days of the war with Spain and Holland, and in any case (as noted above) they never interfered with his grasp of practical matters and the commonsense advice which he gave on numerous occasions. Above all, in an age when anti-Semitism raged with a virulence only surpassed in our own day and generation, Vieira's fearless championship of the New-Christians marks him out as a truly admirable man. António Vieira may not have been what King John IV called him, "the greatest man in the world," but he is entitled to an honoured place not only in the history of Portugal and Brazil but in the story of Western civilisation.

2. The Indian Policy of Portugal in America

MATHIAS C. KIEMEN

The story of Indian labor legislation in Portuguese America from 1500 to 1755 is a story of the conflict between the European or Europeanized colonists, who wished to enslave the Indian for economic reasons, and the missionaries, who were determined to prevent such a practice. For this purpose the missionaries of the various religious Orders established missions where the Indians under their control were protected from the colonists, civilized according to European standards, and taught the Catholic faith. The two protagonists in our story, which has never been adequately told, en-

Mathias C. Kiemen, "The Indian Policy of Portugal in America, with Special Reference to the Old State of Maranhão, 1500–1755," *The Americas*, V (1948), pp. 131–171, *passim*. Reprinted by permission of the author and the Academy of American Franciscan History.

deavored at various times to influence the course of royal legislation to achieve their respective aims. . . .

Consideration of Indian legislation in the first century of Brazilian colonization has shown the development of an ever-increasing interest in slave labor among the colonists. This interest was probably due in part to the essentially *rural* or *plantation* character of Portuguese colonization in America. Gold and silver were not found until the eighteenth century; by force of necessity the early colonists turned for a livelihood first to brazilwood, and then to sugar. For both of these occupations much labor was needed. Where were the laborers to be found? Not in Portugal: the Far East was already draining far too much of that tiny country's manpower; not in the other countries of Europe: they were occupied with religious or economic troubles of their own. In the mind of the Portuguese in Brazil, the answer to the labor problem was twofold: use of the African Negro and use of the native Indian.

The Negro was utilized quite early in Brazil, his hardy physique and greater knowledge of agriculture making him preferable to the weaker native Indian, unused to regular labor. By 1600 there were about 20,000 Africans in the colony. But the supply was uncertain, and the prices were exorbitant. The price of one Negro slave ranged from 50 to 300 *milreis,* a sum equivalent in modern money to from 20 to 100 pounds sterling or about $100 to $500. This alone would limit the importation of a sufficient number to provide adequate labor.

The utilization of the native Indian was the other alternative. And it was to this labor supply, near at hand, that the colonists generally turned. They relied upon the Indian to supply them with food by hunting and fishing, to transport building materials, to row boats up the jungle rivers, to guide them through the forests, to perform domestic work, to labor on sugar plantations and in sugar mills, — in a word, to do almost all the manual labor necessary in a primitive tropical colony.

The nomadic Indian of Brazil was unused to such constant labor and his physical constitution could not long endure it; hence he proved unwilling to work freely for the white colonists. Therefore in mind of the settlers, the only solution was forced labor and slavery of the natives. Against this slavery and its abuses was directed [this] legislation. In these few laws we can see the first moves of the royal government to curb this cruel enslavement-policy of the colonists. Later legislation, to be presently considered, regulated still more exactly the relations between Indian and colonist. The home government experimented during the seventeenth century with different methods of control, until, finally, at the end of the century, the Crown gave control of the Indian definitively to the missionaries of the religious Orders, who in turn, contracted with the colonists for the labor of their mission Indians. . . .

In the struggle for the emancipation of the Indian of Maranhão, the name of Fr. Antônio Vieira of the Society of Jesus looms large. By his influence at the court of Lisbon he introduced many far-reaching reforms in the treatment of the Indians. Fr. Vieira arrived in Maranhão in 1653, armed with a royal letter giving him a free hand to organize the missions and Indian labor. But conditions were very bad in the State of Maranhão when he arrived. In 1652 Baltasar de Sousa Pereira had been sent as *Capitão-Mór* (Military Chief) of Maranhão. In one of the chapters of his *Regimento* he was ordered to free all Indians that had been enslaved up to that time. Unfortunately, this royal order was promulgated a few days after Fr. Vieira arrived in Maranhão. As a result a grave tumult arose, directed against the government, but mainly against the Jesuits, and this provision of the *Regimento* had to be suspended for the time being.

It was in the midst of such tumultuous events that Fr. Vieira arrived with the royal letter of October 21, 1652, giving him full authority to erect churches, establish missions, bring Indians from the backlands, settle them in *aldeias*, etc., as he saw fit. The letter also empowered him to requisition any Indian help, canoes, etc., he might need in his work from the governor or other authorities, who were required to comply on the pain of incurring royal displeasure.

The colonists of Maranhão felt very bitter over the course of events, and they complained to Lisbon in 1653.

> . . . It was deplorable [they said] to compare the situation of this captaincy (Maranhão) with that of the State of Brazil, where every month large numbers of Negro slaves enter. Here the only help is the Indian; and the new settlements, placed on islands and on the shores of rivers, at great distances, cannot dispense with the services of this people [the Indians] for rowers on voyages.

In the face of the complaints, the King passed a new law on October 17, 1653, which in effect was a compromise intended to placate the angry colonists. Under it the captivity of the Indians was to be permitted in the following cases:

1. During a just war. Warfare against the Indians was just when they impeded the preaching of the Gospel and refused to defend the lives and property of the King's vassals.

2. When Indians allied themselves with enemies of Portugal and gave aid against the vassals of the King.

3. When Indians robbed by sea or land, or infested the roads, impeding commerce, etc.

4. When the Indians subject to the King failed in their obligations agreed upon at the beginning of the conquest, by refusing to pay the tributes and not obeying when called upon to work in the King's service or to fight the enemies of the King.

5. When subject Indians ate human flesh.

For any of these reasons, the Indians might justly be captured. *Entradas* or expeditions into the wilderness were authorized for the purpose of ransoming "Indians of the cord," or of securing the possession of Indians who were the legitimate slaves of Indian chiefs, provided that religious accompanied these expeditions to convert the natives. The law of 1653 was obviously a step in a backward direction. There was no time limit on the captivity of the Indians taken. In effect it permitted slavery, although the word is never mentioned.

Vieira, who had been absent in the interior when the latest law was promulgated, left for Portugal in 1654, to endeavor to change the King's mind on the matter of Indian slavery, for Vieira realized that all missionary work would be in vain unless the law were changed. He succeeded partially in his effort. A *Junta* of the principal theologians and lawyers of the kingdom was called at which the question of Indian servitude was discussed. The Archbishop of Braga presided, and the prelates of the religious Orders working in Maranhão were also present, together with Vieira, who represented the Jesuits, the procurators of Maranhão and Grão Pará who had been sent by the colonists to Portugal, and André Vidal de Negreiros, who was to be the new governor of the State of Maranhão. After the deliberations were over, the King passed the compromise law of April 9, 1655. In substance, it decreed that

1. A *Junta das Missões e Propagação da Fé* (Committee on Missions and Propagation of the Faith) be established, as a kind of consultive tribunal, with its authority restricted to matters dealing with missionary problems and Indian slavery.

2. The *aldeias* and the Indians of the whole state be governed and be under the discipline of the Jesuits alone. Antônio Vieira, as superior of all the missions, was authorized to determine the sites of the missions, to grant or refuse permission for *entradas* to the backlands, and to dispose of the converted Indians as he should judge it most convenient.

3. The governors must give all help and favor to the missionaries, so that they may be enabled to convert the Indians and avoid the tyranny of the past.

4. The missionaries were to have a vote in the destination of the captured slaves, in order to prevent violence to the Indians of the *Sertão*. The person selected to head the *entradas* was to be approved by the same missionaries, and the location of the new missions was to be at the choice of the Father Superior of the missions.

5. The Christian Indians and inhabitants of the *aldeias* were not to be forced to serve more than six months of each year for the colonists. Such Indians were to be paid two *varas* or yards of cloth for each month of labor.

The law was a disappointment in that it did nothing regarding the principle of enslavement, nor did it define what constituted a just war. Perpetual captivity was still allowed in four cases, i.e., when the Indians were taken in a just war; when they impeded the preaching of the Gospel; when they were "Indians of the cord" and were ransomed by the Portuguese; and finally, when they were sold to the Portuguese by other Indians, who had taken them in a war of their own. The great innovation in the law of 1655 consisted in the turning over of all power over the Indians to the Jesuit Fathers, or rather, to Fr. Vieira. As regards the economic life of the State of Maranhão, this made the colonists more or less subject to the Society of Jesus, since slaves were necessary for the development of the country.

To safeguard the Jesuit control over the Indians, the King on April 14, 1655, issued a *Regimento* to the new governor of the State of Maranhão, André Vidal de Negreiros, ordering him to place his authority solidly behind the Jesuits. The *Regimento* provided that the division of the captured Indians was to be made by two judges, one from the *Câmara* or city council, and the other from among the missionaries. It further provided that a record be kept of the Indians farmed out to work, and for whom, so that the colonists, rich and poor, might best be served. The Father Superior of the missions was ordered to determine the time of the *entradas;* the governor, to furnish an armed guard where this was necessary. The number of Indian villages was to be reduced, but the population of each was to be increased. Wherever possible, each village was to contain at least 150 houses, so that the Indians might be better taught the Catholic religion. Again, the governor was urged to make vassals out of as many Indian tribes as were willing to submit; no harm, however, would be done to those who refused.

When this latest piece of legislation was made known in the State of Maranhão, it provoked general discontent, both among the settlers and the other religious. The people saw themselves stopped in their efforts to obtain as many slaves as they desired; the other religious looked with displeasure on the monopoly of Vieira and the Jesuits. Both people and religious felt that Vieira had gone too far in his demands. So strong, in fact, was the opposition that only the firm hand of Governor Negreiros kept the people from revolting against the law. Fr. Vieira was aware of the opposition. On December 8, 1655, he wrote to King John IV:

> We have against us the people, the religious Orders, the donataries of the major captaincies, and also all those who in that Kingdom and State are interested in the blood and sweat of the Indians, whose minority we alone defend.

Despite the temper of the colonists and the repeated protests that were made at the Court of Lisbon, the law was sullenly complied with at the insistence of Vieira. During the next five years (1655–1660) the reduction of Indians in *aldeias* was carried out unmolestedly. By the end of the year 1655, the Jesuits controlled 54 such *aldeias* in the State of Maranhão. Vieira, meanwhile, realizing their needs, tried to placate the colonists by organizing large *entradas* into the interior. Of the Indians brought back on these raids, the larger number went to the Jesuit missions, but many were enslaved, according to the precepts of the law.

Such raids, however, were apparently nothing more than palliatives. On January 15, 1661, the *Senado,* or town council, of São Luiz sent a strong representation to Fr. Vieira, setting forth the misery of the people who, as the *Senado* alleged, because of the lack of Indian labor could not make enough money to pay their taxes or support the army. In his reply, couched in moderate terms, Vieira observed that the suffering of the Portuguese also proceeded from causes other than the one alleged, and promised more slaves for the use of the people, as the result of the *entradas* then in progress or planned. Vieira's answer did not satisfy the members of the *Senado*, who sent a more sharply-worded letter to the priest on February 15. The second letter accused the Jesuits, among other things, of entirely overstepping legal bounds in taking complete temporal control of the converted Indians; to which Fr. Vieira replied that he could do nothing more than he had already promised.

The storm that arose between the settlers and the Jesuits broke in 1661. The colonists rose up against the Jesuits in Belém, and the revolt spread south. Before long the Jesuits were imprisoned in their colleges, and finally were put on board ships and sent to Lisbon. A few Jesuits in the backlands managed to escape the fury for a few months, but by the beginning of 1662 all members of the Company were either detained or on their way to Portugal.

Father Vieira was among the Jesuits expelled from Maranhão by the enraged colonists. As soon as he arrived in Portugal he went to the Queen Regent, Luiza de Gusmão, and told her what had occurred. So cogent, apparently, were his arguments that within a year the Jesuits had royal permission to go back to their missions in Maranhão, with the same extensive powers which they had formerly enjoyed. Vieira's triumph, however, was short-lived. In 1662 a palace-revolution deprived Queen Luiza of power, and the crown prince became king as Afonso VI. The new king was definitely not as friendly to Father Vieira as the Queen Mother was. He banished the Jesuit from Court, and gave a ready ear to Vieira's enemies. Out of this about-face in court circles came the law of September 12, 1663.

This law, in effect, was a return to the legislation of 1653. . . . The Jesuits, therefore, were allowed to continue in their missions, although their power over mission activity generally was curtailed. An exception, however, was made in the case of Father Vieira, whose services were not reputed advantageous to the King.

Father Vieira, in fact, was in grave difficulty in Portugal. He was haled before the Inquisition for alleged errors of faith contained in his preachings and in an unpublished book called *History of the Future*. Accused of Judaism and other errors, Vieira, according to Leite, was condemned to the privation of the right of preaching and of his active and passive voice forever, and to confinement for an indefinite period in a house of the Society. But his defeat was not permanent. When Dom Pedro II came into power on November 23, 1667, he freed Vieira and restored all the prestige formerly his under King John IV.

Despite the rebuff of the Jesuits and the passage of the law of 1663, which, from the point of view of the settlers, was in many ways an improvement over previous legislation, the colonists were not satisfied, and received the new law very coldly. They were displeased with the provisions limiting the forays into the interior to official *entradas*. So violent was the reaction that in São Luiz it was impossible to execute the law. In Belém an attempt was made by the *câmara* to carry out the prescripts of the law, but without much success. The temper of the people was such that governmental interference was not immediately possible. Only in 1673 was the law observed in all its rigor in the captaincy of Maranhão; in Pará it was never observed at all.

It was not until 1680 that the administrative anarchy in the State of Maranhão over the Indian question was ended. One of the factors in the return to normality was the law of April 1, 1680, inspired by Father Vieira. The Jesuit missionary, now bowed with age, had returned to royal favor in 1667 when Pedro II ascended the throne. Until his death in 1697 he was to keep within the good graces of the king.

The law of April 1, 1680, is one of the best known pieces of Portuguese legislation on Indian labor, and the most often quoted in any discussion of Portugal's Indian policy. After a long preamble, in which the laws of 1570, 1587, 1595, 1653, and 1655 were acknowledged as failures, the law decrees:

1. That, renewing the disposition of the law of 1609, *no Indian shall henceforth be enslaved in any capacity,* not even in cases permitted in the earlier laws.

2. That if any person of whatever quality or condition, captures or orders the capture of Indians, under any title or pretext, he shall be arrested by the *ouvidor geral* of the State and sent on the first ship to Portugal.

3. That the *ouvidor* shall immediately place at liberty the Indians already captured and send them to *aldeias* if they are Catholic Indians.

4. That the governor, the bishop [Dom Gregorio dos Anjos, Bishop of Maranhão], and the prelates of religious Orders in the State shall take care to inform the king of any infractions of the law, so that the proper measures may be taken.

5. That Indians taken in an authorized defensive or offensive war shall be treated not as slaves but as prisoners of war, as the term was understood in Europe.

6. That the governor alone shall have the power to apportion the Indians among the *aldeias* of free Indians, where they may be converted to the Faith, be treated properly, and serve the State, while yet retaining their liberty.

7. That those who inflict any harm on the Indians shall be severely chastized, and those who do so during the time the Indians are working for them shall be even more severely punished.

On the day that the law was put into effect, a series of royal orders was promulgated for the purpose of clarifying certain details. These royal orders, among other things, ordained the following:

1. That every year five or six hundred Negroes shall be offered for sale in the State of Maranhão at moderate prices to take the place of Indian slaves.

2. That the Indians capable of working shall be divided into three groups: one third shall remain at the *aldeias* for the purpose of working for themselves and families; one third shall serve the colonists; and one third shall be used to accompany the missionaries to the interior missions. The division of these Indians shall be made by the bishop together with the Superior of the Franciscan Province of Santo Antônio, in Maranhão, and with one other person elected by the *câmara,* on the basis of lists furnished them by the pastors of the *aldeias.*

3. That missions to the interior shall be made only by the religious of the Society of Jesus.

4. That the *aldeias* of Christianized Indians shall be controlled by their pastors and their own chiefs, and not by captains or administrators of any kind.

5. That the Jesuits shall control all *aldeias* of Christianized In-

dians, except those which other religious may have had before the
coming of the bishop to the state of Maranhão.

6. That all the other *aldeias* along the Gurupá and Amazon Rivers
and those without pastors of their own shall be turned over to the
Jesuits.

7. That the Jesuits shall be pastors of all Indians brought from
the interior and of the *aldeias* and churches that may be newly established.

8. That no Indian shall be allowed to serve the colonists until
his wages shall have first been deposited by them.

9. That the Jesuits shall be in charge of missions set up in the
interior for the more remote Indians who cannot or will not live
among the Portuguese.

The most significant point in the legislation of 1680 is the proposal to use Negro in place of Indian slaves. If it is true, as all authors say, that Father Vieira is the sponsor of the legislation of 1680,
he must be held responsible for the clause on the introduction of
Negroes. This is further proof of the fact that at least some ecclesiastics of the time did not condemn slavery as such, but rather the
horrors of enslavement as it was then practiced. One other point is
significant; the Jesuits were endeavoring once more to obtain a
monopoly over the Indian missions at the expense of the other religious Orders, notably the Franciscans. Furthermore, the clause
permitting the Jesuits to establish missions far in the interior, from
which the Indians could bring their products to the coast settlements for trade, carried the seeds of future discord. In the eighteenth century the enemies of the Jesuits were to charge them with
using their Indian wards for commercial gain.   . . .

In February, 1684, a few malcontents, led by Manuel Beckman
or Bequimão, a rich proprietor, seized the governor and the missionaries. Beckman won the support of his followers by promising them
slaves. The revolt, however, was purely local; it never spread beyond
the borders of the captaincy of Maranhão. Pará, for example, because of its dislike of Maranhão, never took part in the uprising.

As a result of the uprising, the Jesuits were expelled once more
from Maranhão. But this time the home government did not side
with their enemies. Insofar as the Crown was concerned, the question was not merely one of Indian slavery; the very principle of authority had been impugned. General Gomes Freire de Andrade was

therefore given extraordinary powers to put down the revolt, which he did in 1685, and by September 23 of that year, the Jesuits were back.

The events of 1684–1685 mark a turning point in the Jesuit attitude towards the missions of Maranhão. A dilemma was now posed to the Fathers of the Society. Should they forsake the mission field and retire to other work, or should they adapt themselves to local conditions and give up their idea of monopolizing the control of the Indians? Both possibilities were discussed by the Order in Maranhão. The Jesuits finally compromised. They would no longer oppose the admittance of other religious Orders to the government of the Indians, and they would be more generous in answering the demands of the colonists for Indian laborers. With this compromise the Jesuits were able to remain comparatively unmolested in Maranhão until 1755.

3. Sermon Condemning Indian Slavery, 1653

ANTÓNIO VIEIRA

At what a different price the devil today buys souls compared to what he offered for them previously! There is no market in the world where the devil can get them more cheaply than right here in our own land. In the Gospel, he offered all the kingdoms of the world for one soul; in Maranhão the devil does not need to offer one-tenth as much for all the souls. It is not necessary to offer worlds, nor kingdoms; it is not necessary to offer cities, nor towns, nor villages. All he has to do is offer a couple of Tapuya Indians and at once he is adored on both knees. What a cheap market! An Indian for a soul! That Indian will be your slave for the few days that he lives; and your soul will be a slave for eternity, as long as God is God. This is the contract that the devil makes with you. Not only do you accept it but you pay him money on top of it. . . .

Christians, nobles, and people of Maranhão, do you know what God wants of you during this Lent? That you break the chains of

From A Documentary History of Brazil, pp. 82–89, E. Bradford Burns, ed. © Copyright 1966 by E. Bradford Burns. Reprinted by permission of Alfred A. Knopf, Inc.

injustice and let free those whom you have captive and oppressed. These are the sins of Maranhão; these are what God commanded me to denounce to you. Christians, God commanded me to clarify these matters to you and so I do it. All of you are in mortal sin; all of you live in a state of condemnation; and all of you are going directly to Hell. Indeed, many are there now and you will soon join them if you do not change your life.

Is it possible that an entire people live in sin, that an entire people will go to hell? Who questions thus does not understand the evil of unjust captivity. The sons of Israel went down into Egypt, and after the death of Joseph, the Pharaoh seized them and made slaves of them. God wanted to liberate those miserable people, and He sent Moses there with no other escort than a rod. God knew that in order to free the captives a rod was sufficient, even though He was dealing with a ruler as tyrannical as Pharaoh and with a people as cruel as the Egyptians. When Pharaoh refused to free the captives, the plagues rained down upon him. The land was covered with frogs and the air clouded with mosquitos; the rivers flowed with blood; the clouds poured forth thunder and lightning. All Egypt was dumbfounded and threatened with death. Do you know what brought those plagues to the earth? Unjust captivity. Who brought to Maranhão the plague of the Dutch? Who brought the smallpox? Who brought hunger and drought? These captives. Moses insisted and pressed the Pharaoh to free the people, and what did Pharaoh respond? He said one thing and he did another. What he said was, I do not know God and I do not have to free the captives. However, it appears to me proper and I do declare them free. Do you know why you do not give freedom to your illicitly gotten slaves? Because you do not know God. Lack of Faith is the cause of everything. If you possessed true faith, if you believed that there was an eternal Hell, then you would not take so lightly the captivity of a single Tapuya. With what confidence can the devil today say to you: *Si cadens adoraveris me?* With all the confidence of having offered you the world. The devil made this speech: I offer to this man everything; if he is greedy and covetous, he must accept. If he accepts, then, he worships me because greed and covetousness are a form of idolatry. It is an idea expressed by St. Paul. Such was the greed of Pharaoh in wanting to keep and not to free the captive sons of Israel, confessing at the same time that he did not know God. This is what he said.

What he did was to take out after the fleeing Israelites with all the power of his kingdom in order to recapture them. And what happened? The Red Sea opened so that the captives could pass on dry land (because God knows how to make miracles in order to free captives). It did not matter that the Hebrews did not merit this. They were worse than the Tapuyas. A few days later they worshiped a golden calf and of all the six hundred thousand men only two entered into the promised land, but God is so favorable to the cause of liberty that he grants it even to those who do not deserve it. When the Hebrews had reached the other side, Pharaoh entered between the walls of water which were still open, and as he crossed, the waters fell over his army and drowned them all. What impresses me is the way Moses tells this: that the waters enveloped them and the sea drowned them and the earth swallowed them up. Now, if the sea drowned them how could the earth swallow them? Those men, like his, had both a body and a soul. The waters drowned the bodies because they were at the bottom of the sea; the earth swallowed the souls because they descended to Hell. All went to Hell, without a single exception, because where all pursue and all capture, all are condemned. This is an excellent example. Now, let us look at the reasoning.

Any man who deprives others of their freedom and being able to restore that freedom does not do so is condemned. All or nearly all are therefore condemned. You will say to me that even if this were true they did not think about it or know it and that their good faith will save them. I deny that. They did think about it and know it just as you think of it and know it. If they did not think of it nor know it, they ought to have thought of it and to have known it. Some are condemned by their knowledge, others by their doubt, and still others by their ignorance. . . . If only the graves would open and some who died in that unhappy state could appear before you, and in the fire of their misery you could clearly read this truth. Do you know why God does not permit them to appear before you? It is exactly as Abraham said to the rich miser when he asked him to send Lazarus to this world: *Habent Moysen et Prophetas* (Luc. 16.29). It is not necessary for one to appear on earth from Hell to tell you the truth because you already have Moses and the Law, you have the prophets and learned men. My brothers, if there are any among you who doubt this, here are the laws, here are the learned men, question them. There are in this State, three religious orders which have members of great virtue and learning. Ask them. Study the matter and inform yourselves. But it is not necessary to question the religious: go to Turkey, go to Hell, because there is no Turk so Turkish in Turkey nor no devil so devilish in Hell who will tell you that a free man can be a slave. Is there one among you with natural intelligence who can deny it? What do you doubt?

I know what you are going to tell me . . . our people, our country, our government cannot be sustained without Indians. Who will fetch a pail of water for us or carry a load of wood? Who will grind our manioc? Will our wives have to do it? Will our sons? In the first place, this is not the state into which I am placing you as you soon will see. But when necessity and conscience require such a thing, I answer yes and repeat again yes. You, your wives, your sons, all of us are able to sustain ourselves with our own labor. It is better to live from your own sweat than from the blood of others! . . .

You will tell me that your slaves are your very feet and hands. Also, you will say how much you love them because you raised them like children and took care of them as you would your very own. It may be so, but Christ said to this land: *Si oculus tuus scandalizat te, erue eum et si manus, vel pes tuus scandalizat te, amputa eum* (Math. 5.29; Marc. 9.42.44). Christ did not mean to say that we should pull out our eyes nor that we ought to cut off our hands and feet. What he meant was that if that which we loved as our eyes harmed us, or that which was as necessary as our hands and feet harmed us, we should cast away from us that source of harm even if it hurts us as if we had cut it off from us. Who amongst you does not love his arm or his hand but should it become gangrenous would not permit its amputation in order to save his life. . . . If, in order to quiet your conscience or save your soul, it is necessary to lose everything and remain as miserable as Job, lose everything.

But take heart, my friends, it is not necessary to arrive at such a state, far from it. I have studied the matter carefully and in accordance with the most lenient and favorable opinions and have come to a conclusion by which, with only minor worldly losses, all the inhabitants of this state can ease their consciences and build for a better future. Give me your attention.

All the Indians of this State are either those who serve as slaves or those who live as free inhabitants in the King's villages, or those who live in the hinterlands in their natural or free condition. These latter are the ones you go upriver to buy or "to rescue" (as they say), giving the pious verb "to rescue" to a sale so involuntary and violent that at times it is made at pistol point. These are held, owned, and bequeathed in bad faith: therefore they will be doing no small task if they forgive you for their past treatment. However, if after you have set them free, they, particularly those domestics whom you raised in your house and treated as your children, spontaneously and voluntarily wish to continue to serve you and remain in your home, no one will or can separate them from your service. And what will happen to those who do not wish to remain in your service? These will be obliged to live in the King's villages where they also will serve you in the manner which I shall mention. Each year you will be able to make your expeditions into the interior during which time you can really rescue those who are prisoners ready to be eaten. Those justly saved from death will remain your slaves. Also, all those captured in just wars will be made slaves. Upon this matter the proper judges will be the Governor of the State, the Chief Justice of the State, the Vicars of Maranhão or of Pará, and the Prelates of the four orders: Carmelite, Franciscan, Mercedarian, and the Company of Jesus. All of these who after judgment are qualified to be true captives, will be returned to the inhabitants. And what will happen to those captured in a war not classified as just? All of them will be placed in new villages or divided among the villages which exist today. There, along with the other village Indians they will be hired out to the inhabitants of this State to work for them for six months of every year alternating two months of hired work with two months devoted to their own labors and families. Thus, in this manner, all the Indians of this State will serve the Portuguese either as legitimate slaves, that is those rescued from death or captured in a just war, or those former slaves who freely and voluntarily wish to serve their old masters, or those from the King's villages who will work half the year for the good and growth of the State. It only remains to set the wages of those village Indians for their labor and service. It is a subject which would make any other nation of the world laugh and only in this land is not appreciated. The money of this land is cloth and cotton, and the ordinary price for which the Indians work and will work each month is seven feet of this cloth which has a market value of about twenty cents. An Indian will work for less than a penny a day. It is an insignificant amount and it is unworthy of a man of reason and of Christian faith not to pay such a slight price to save his soul and to avoid Hell.

Could there be anything more moderate? Could there be anything more reasonable than this? Whoever is dissatisfied or discontent with this proposal either is not a Christian or has no understanding. To conclude this point, let us look at the advantages and disadvantages of this proposal.

The single disadvantage is that some of you will lose a few Indians. I promise you they will be very few. But to you who question this, I ask: Do not some of your Indians die or flee? Many do. Will death do what reason will not? Will chance do what a good conscience will not? If smallpox strikes and carries off your Indians, what will you do? You will have to show patience. Well, is it not better to lose the Indians to the service of God than to lose them by a punishment of God? The answer is obvious.

Let us look at the advantages of which there are four principal ones. The first is that you will have a clear conscience. You will no longer live in a state of mortal sin. You will live like Christians, you will be confessed as Christians, you will die like Christians, you will bequeath your goods as Christians. In short, you will go to Heaven and not to Hell, which would certainly be a tragic ending.

The second advantage is that you will remove this curse from your homes. There is no greater curse on a home or a family than to be unjustly supported by the sweat and blood of others. . . .

The third advantage is that in this way more Indians will be rescued from cannibal practices. . . . It is important to invade the forest to save Indians from being killed and eaten.

The fourth and last advantage is that henceforth your proposals on the labor problem will be worthy of submission to His Majesty, and worthy of His Majesty's approval and confirmation. Whoever asks for the illegal and unjust deserves to have the legal and just denied him, and whoever petitions with justice, reason, and good conscience deserves the fulfillment of his request. You know the proposal which you made? It was a proposal which vassals could not make in good conscience, nor could ministers consult it in good conscience. And even if the King might have permitted it, what good would it have done you? If the King permits me to swear falsely, will it mean that the false oath is no sin? If the King permits me to steal, will the theft be any less a sin? The same thing applies to the Indians. The King can command the slaves to be free, but his jurisdiction does not extend to the power to order the free to become slaves. If such a request went to Lisbon, the stones of the street would have to rise up against the men of Maranhão. On the other hand, if you submit a just, legal, and Christian request, those very same stones would take your part. . . .

4. Report on the Conversion of the Nheengaíbas, Letter to Alfonso VI, November 28, 1659

ANTÓNIO VIEIRA

. . . The great mouth of the Amazon River is obstructed by an island which is larger than the entire kingdom of Portugal and which is inhabited by many tribes of Indians, who are generally called Nheengaíbas because of the many different and incomprehensible languages they speak. At first these tribes received our conquerors with friendship, but after long experience had shown them that the false words of peace with which the conquerors arrived turned into declarations of captivity, they took up arms in defense of their liberty and began to make war on the Portuguese everywhere. . . .

Past governors, and most recently André Vidal de Negreiros, often tried to rid the State of this very troublesome problem, employing all their forces, both Indian and Portuguese, and their most experienced captains in their campaigns. But the only effect of these wars was to strengthen the conviction that the Nheengaíbas were unconquerable because of their audacity, astuteness, and constancy but most of all because of the impregnable position with which nature itself defended them. . . .

Finally, last year, 1658, Governor D. Pedro de Melo arrived with news of the war declared against the Dutch, with whom some of the Nheengaíba nations had long traded because of the nearness of their ports to those of the Northern Cape, where each year they loaded twenty Dutch ships with manatees. The government of Pará realized that if the Nheengaíbas allied themselves with the Dutch, they would become masters of these captaincies, for the State lacked

J. Lúcio D'Azevedo, ed., *Cartas do Padre António Vieira* (Coimbra: Imprensa da Universidade, 1925), Vol. I, pp. 549–571, *passim*.

the power to resist them. Accordingly, a private citizen was sent to the Governor to ask for help and for permission to invade the territory of the Nheengaíbas with as large a force as possible before their alliance with the Dutch could render this precaution ineffective and cause the loss of the entire State.

After the justification and necessity for the war had been settled by the vote of all the secular and ecclesiastical dignitaries whose consultation Your Majesty requires, Father António Vieira expressed the opinion that, since the war was being prepared in secret and in order to give it additional justification, peace should first be offered to the Nheengaíbas, but without the soldiers and clash of arms that aroused their suspicions, as had occurred in the time of André Vidal. And since this proposal of peace seemed as hazardous as war because of the ferocity which was ascribed to these people, the same Father volunteered to act as an intermediary. Everyone believed, however, that not only would the Nheengaíbas refuse to consider the peace overtures but that they would reply with arrows to those who bore such a proposal, just as they had done for the twenty years since the outbreak of the war.

On Christmas Day of the same year, 1658, Father Vieira sent two Indian nobles with a letter to all the Nheengaíba tribes in which he assured them that by virtue of Your Majesty's new law, which he had gone to Portugal to seek, unjust captures and all the other injuries done to them by the Portuguese had ended forever. He also said that he would await a message from them so that he might go to their territory and that they were to believe whatever the bearers of the letter said in his name.

The ambassadors, who were themselves of the Nheengaíba nation, set out like persons going to their sacrifice (so great was the horror of the fierceness of these tribes even among those of their own blood). Thus they took their leave, stating that if they had not returned by the end of the next moon, we should conclude that they had been killed or captured. . . .

On Ash Wednesday, when they were no longer expected, the two ambassadors returned, alive and very happy, bringing with them seven Nheengaíba nobles and many other Indians of the same tribes, who were received with the acclamation and demonstrations of joy that were due to such guests. They made a lengthy defense of their conduct, in which they blamed the past war entirely on the Portuguese, as was true, and concluded as follows: "But we gave full credence to the letter of the 'Great Father,' of whom we had already heard and who for love of us and of other people of our skin had risked the waves of the sea and had obtained from the King good things for us. Therefore, having forgotten all the injuries of the Portuguese, we have come here to put ourselves in your hands and in the mouths of your firearms. We are certain, however, that with the protection of the priests, of whom we will henceforth call ourselves sons, no one will do us harm." . . .

The Father wished to leave with them for their territory at once, but they replied with surprising courtesy that they had hitherto lived like animals under the trees and asked for permission to move one of the Indian settlements down to the edge of the river. They said that after they had built a house and a church in which to receive the Father, they would return in large numbers so that he would be suitably escorted, stating that this would be at the time of St. John, the expression they use to distinguish between winter and summer. Although the Nheengaíbas were still hardly believed, they fulfilled exactly what they promised. Five days before the feast of St. John they arrived at the settlements of Pará with seventeen canoes, which, with thirteen of the Combocas tribe, who also inhabit the same island, brought the number to thirty. In the canoes there were as many nobles, accompanied by so many people that the fortress and city secretly armed itself.

The Father was unable to leave at this time because he was gravely ill. But it was God's will that on August 16 he was able to leave . . . in twelve large canoes, accompanied by nobles from all the Christian tribes and by only six Portuguese, including the master-sergeant of the garrison, in order to indicate our trust. On the fifth day of the journey they entered the river of the Mapuaezes, the Nheengaíba tribe that had promised to build a settlement outside the bush in which to receive the priests. Two leagues from the harbor the nobles came out to meet us in a large and well-equipped canoe which was decorated with plumes of various colors. They were playing horns and shouting *pocêmas*, which are cries of happiness and praise that they utter in unison at intervals and are considered the greatest demonstration of joy among them. All of us responded in the same manner. . . .

After they had finally reached the settlement, the priests disembarked, together with the Portuguese and the Christian nobles, and the Nheengaíbas took them to the church, which they had made of palms, according to the custom of the country, and was very clean and well built. It was then dedicated with the name of the Church of the Holy Christ, and a *Te Deum laudamus* was said in thanksgiving. . . .

Messages were then sent to the various tribes. But since the tribes that lived closest to the settlement did not appear in five days, the devil was not idle, introducing into the minds of the Christian Indians and also of the Portuguese such distrust, suspicion, and fear that they almost abandoned the enterprise, which would have been lost forever. Father António Vieira settled the matter by saying to them that he thought their reasons well founded and that they should all leave; he would stay behind with his colleague, for it was they whom the Nheengaíbas were expecting and with whom they would deal.

But on the following day the Mamaianázes, of whom there was the greatest distrust because of their fierceness, began to arrive in their canoes. And so great were their demonstrations of festivity, trust, and true peace that the suspicions and fears of our people gradually disappeared, and soon their faces and minds and even their speech took on a different aspect.

After a large number of nobles had arrived and the new state of affairs had been explained to them at length both by the priests and by the Indian converts, an order was given for the oath of obedience and fidelity to be taken; and so that it might be done with due solemnity and outward ceremony (which is very important for these people, who are ruled by their senses), it was arranged in the following manner. On the right side of the church were the nobles of the Christian tribes, wearing their best clothes but without any weapons other than their swords. On the other side were the pagan nobles, naked and adorned with feathers in the manner of savages, with bows and arrows in their hands. The Portuguese were scattered among them. Father António Vieira then said the mass of the Adoration of the Kings before a richly decorated altar. The Indians heard the mass on bended knee, and it was a great source of consolation to those present to see them beat their breasts and adore the host and chalice with such strong devotion to that very precious blood, which, having been shed for all men, had a more powerful influence on them than on their grandfathers.

After the mass, the Father, still dressed in his sacerdotal vestments, preached a sermon in which he told them through interpreters of the dignity of the place in which they were standing and of their obligation to answer truthfully to all the questions that they would be asked and to faithfully carry out what they promised. Then each of the nobles was asked if he wished to receive the faith of the true God and to be a vassal of the king of Portugal, as were the Portuguese and the Indians of the Christian tribes whose nobles were present. They were also told that vassals were obliged to obey the orders of Your Majesty in everything and to keep perpetual and inviolable peace with all his vassals, being friends to his friends and enemies to his enemies. If they did this, they would enjoy with freedom and security all the possessions and privileges that had been granted to the Indians of this State by Your Majesty in the law of 1655.

They all responded in the affirmative. Only one noble, who was called Piyé and was the most intelligent of all, said that he did not want to make these promises. And since the onlookers were struck by this unexpected reply, he went on to say that "the questions and sermons of the Father should be addressed to the Portuguese and not to the Indians, for they had always been faithful to the King and had always recognized him as their lord from the beginning of the conquest. They had always been friends and servitors of the Portuguese, and if this friendship had been broken, it was the fault of the Portuguese. Therefore, it was the Portuguese who now had to make promises since they had violated them many times, while the Indians had always kept their word."

The reasoning of this savage was greeted with delight, as were the terms with which he qualified his fealty. Then the leading noble came to the altar where the Father was standing and, throwing his bow and arrows to the ground, fell to his knees. With his hands in those of the Father, he swore as follows: "I promise to God and the King of Portugal in my name and in that of all my subjects to have faith in our Lord Jesus Christ and to be the vassal of His Majesty. I also promise to keep perpetual peace with the Portuguese, to be a friend to their friends and an enemy to their enemies, and to fulfill these obligations forever." After this had been said, he kissed the hands of the Father, who gave him his blessing. Then the other nobles did the same in turn.

After the oath-taking had ended, all of them came to embrace the Father, then the Portuguese, and finally the nobles of the Christian tribes, with whom they had also been at war. And it was an occasion for great thanksgiving to God to see the happiness and true friendship with which these embraces were given and received and to hear the things that were said among them in their fashion.

Finally, they all got to their knees and the priests said a *Te Deum laudamus.* After they had left the church, the Christian nobles picked up their bows and arrows, which had been left outside. In order to make a public demonstration of what had been done in the church, the Portuguese removed the balls from their harquebuses, threw them into the river, and fired without them. Then all the nobles broke their arrows and also threw them into the river, thereby fulfilling the statement: *Arcum conteret et confringet arma.* All this was done to the accompaniment of trumpets, horns, drums, and other instruments and of the continuous shouting with which the crowd declared its happiness. . . .

The triumph of the faith was sealed with the erection on the same spot of a very handsome cross, which the fathers did not allow to be touched by any Indian of low rank. Accordingly, fifty-three nobles carried it on their shoulders to the great joy of the Christians and of the tribes, all of whom adored it. The tribes of different languages who came here were the Mamaianás, the Aruans and the Anajás, among whom are included Mapuás, Paucacás, Guajarás, Pixipixis, and others. The number of souls cannot be counted with certainty; some say that it is 40,000. Among those who came was a noble of the Tucujús, which is a province on the mainland of the Amazon, opposite the island of the Nheengaíbas, and it is reported that they greatly exceed the latter in number, both groups totalling more than 100,000 souls. . . .

BIBLIOGRAPHIC SUGGESTIONS

A. *Vieira's Writings*

1. *Cartas,* 3 vols., João Lúcio d'Azevedo, ed. (Coimbra: Biblioteca de Escritores Portugueses, 1925–1938).
2. *Obras escolhidas,* 2 vols. Notes by António Sérgio and Hernâni Cidade (Lisbon: Coleccão de Classicos Sá da Costa, 1951).
3. *Sermões,* 4 vols. Hernâni Cidade, ed. (Lisbon, 1940).

B. *Writings About Vieira*

4. Azevedo, João Lúcio de. *História de António Vieira,* second ed., 2 vols. (Lisbon, 1931).

5. Azevedo, Thales de. "Aculturação dirigida: notas sobre a catequese indígena no período colonial brasileiro," *Trabalhos de Antropologia e Etnologia*, XVII (Porto: Sociedade Portuguese de Antropologia e Etnologia na Faculdade de Ciências do Porto, 1959), pp. 491–512.
6. Boxer, Charles R. "Padre António Vieira, S.J., and the Institution of the Brazil Company in 1649," *Hispanic American Historical Review*, XXIX (1949), pp. 474–497.
7. Gotaas, Mary C. *Bossuet and Vieira; a study in national, epochal, and individual style* (Washington, D.C.: Catholic University of America Press, 1953).
8. Leite, Serafim, S.J. *Historia da Companhia de Jesus no Brasil*, 10 vols. (Rio de Janeiro-Lisbon, 1938–1950). See especially Vol. IX, pp. 192–363.
9. Ricard, Robert. "Prophecy and Messianism in the Works of António Vieira," *The Americas*, XVII (1961), pp. 357–368.
10. Rodrigues, José Honório. "António Vieira, doutrinador do imperialismo português," *Kriterion*, Nos. 61–62 (Belo Horizonte, 1962), pp. 628–651.
11. ———. [On Vieira as a Historian], in *Historiografía del Brasil, siglo XVII* (Mexico: Pan American Institute of Geography and History, 1963), pp. 191–210.
12. Saraiva, A. J. "Le Père António Vieira, S.J., et la Liberté des Indiens," *Travaux de L'Institut D'Études Latino-Américaines de L'Université de Strasbourg*, Vol. III (Strasbourg, 1963), pp. 85–118.

C. *Other Writings*

13. Boxer, Charles R. *The Dutch in Brazil, 1624–1654* (Oxford: Clarendon Press, 1957).
14. ———. *Salvador de Sá and the Struggle for Brazil and Angola, 1602–1686* (London: Athlone Press, 1952).
15. Mauro, Frédéric. *Le Brésil au XVIIᵉ Siècle. Documents inédits relatifs à l'Atlantique portugais*, in *Brasília*, XI (Coimbra, 1961), pp. 1–310.

Section VI

Urban Life

Spaniards have long been known for their devotion to town and city life, and in America they paid great attention to establishing and properly administering the centers of population they created. The royal ordinances of 1573 for laying out new towns reflected this concern (Reading VI.1), and were incorporated into the Laws of the Indies. But a Renaissance spirit was also present, as Professor Robert C. Smith of the University of Pennsylvania points out (Reading VI.2). Spanish towns in America, therefore, sometimes radically departed from the system that prevailed in the mother country, whereas in Brazil the Portuguese established more medieval and traditional towns which repeated the specific town plans of Portugal.

The emphasis on town life, at least in Spanish America, was disastrous for the Indians. As Professor George Kubler of Yale writes: "This urbanization was responsible, at least in part, for high Indian mortality. The heavy burden of labor, and the unhygienic conditions of work in new and improperly equipped settlements gave epidemic disease a rich harvest. . . . To urbanize the Indian populations was to destroy the patterns of indigenous culture. Such cultural extirpation brought about, in turn, the biological decrease of the Indian race."[1]

Through more than three centuries the cast of colonial life was so definitely urban that important events usually occurred in the

[1] George Kubler, *Mexican Architecture of the Sixteenth Century*, Vol. I (New Haven: Yale University Press, 1948), pp. 66–67.

towns. The readings have been selected to illustrate the variety of the urban scene: a description of academic life in the newly established University of Mexico, written in 1554 by Francisco Cervantes de Salazar, one of its professors and an outstanding scholar (Reading VI.3); the impressive funeral services of a viceroy in Mexico City (Reading VI.4); and the riots that made life in seventeenth-century Mexico City so exciting and dangerous, analyzed by Dr. Chester Lyle Guthrie of the National Archives (Reading VI.5). Professor John J. TePaske, of Ohio State University, gives a glimpse of what the daily round was like in the many small towns where fiestas and funerals occasionally broke the monotony (Reading VI.7); and the selection on the booming mining camp at Potosí (Reading VI.6) exemplifies, in gaudy colors, the passion for wealth that drew many Spaniards to the New World.

Brazilian cities were much less the focus of life than were Spanish American cities. The Brazilian scholar José Arthur Rios says that their character throughout the colonial period was "marginal," but his general description of urban growth shows that important centers of population grew up, although political and economic power was usually concentrated in the hands of the great landholding *senhores* (Reading VI.8). One town, Bahia, the "Bay of All Saints," remained important until 1808 when the Portuguese Prince Regent Dom João VI, settled down in Rio de Janeiro. Professor Charles Boxer of the University of London gives a lively picture of this ancient city in northeast Brazil noted both for its sanctity and its sinfulness (Reading VI.9).

A. Patterns of Settlement

1. Spanish Royal Ordinances for the Laying Out of New Towns, 1573

Royal Ordinances for the laying out of new cities, towns or villages. . . . San Lorenzo, July 3, 1573.

(Archivo Nacional, Madrid, MS 3017 Bulas y Cedulas para el Gobierno de las Indias)

I the King

Ordinances for discoveries, new settlements and pacifications.

110. . . . After having made the discovery and selected the province, district and land to be peopled and the sites where new settlements are to be founded those who intend to settle are to proceed in the following manner:

On arriving at the locality where the new settlement is to be founded (which according to our will and ordinance must be one which is vacant and can be occupied without doing harm to the Indians and natives or with their free consent) the plan of the place, with its squares, streets and building lots is to be outlined by means of measuring by cord and ruler, beginning with the main square from which streets are to run to the gates and principal roads and leaving sufficient open space so that even if the town grows it can always spread in a symmetrical manner. Having thus laid out the chosen site the settlement is to be founded in the following form.

111. The chosen site shall be on an elevation; healthful; with means of fortification; fertile and with plenty of land for farming and pasturage; fuel and timber; fresh water, a native population, commodiousness; resources and of convenient access and egress. It

"Royal Ordinances Concerning the Laying Out of New Towns," Zelia Nuttall, trans., *Hispanic American Historical Review,* V (May, 1922), pp. 249–254. Reprinted by permission of the Duke University Press.

shall be open to the north wind. If on the coast care is to be taken that the sea does not lie to the south or west of the harbor. If possible the port is not to be near lagoons or marshes in which poisonous animals and corruption of air and water breed.

112. In the case of a sea-coast town the main plaza which is to be the starting point for the building of the town, is to be situated near the landing place of the port. In inland towns the main plaza should be in the centre of the town and of an oblong shape, its length being equal to at least one and a half times its width, as this proportion is the best for festivals in which horses are used and any other celebrations which have to be held.

113. The size of the plaza shall be in proportion to the number of residents, heed being given to the fact that towns of Indians, being new are bound to grow and it is intended that they shall do so. Therefore the plaza is to be planned with reference to the possible growth of the town. It shall not be smaller than two hundred feet wide and three hundred feet long nor larger than eight hundred feet long and three hundred feet wide.

114. From the plaza the four principal streets are to diverge, one from the middle of each of its sides and two streets are to meet at each of its corners. The four corners of the plaza are to face the four points of the compass, because thus the streets diverging from the plaza will not be directly exposed to the four principal winds, which would cause much inconvenience.

115. The whole plaza and the four main streets diverging from it shall have arcades, for these are a great convenience for those who resort thither for trade. The eight streets which run into the plaza and its four corners are to do so freely without being obstructed by the arcades of the plaza. These arcades are to end at the corners in such a way that the sidewalks of the streets can evenly join those of the plaza.*

116. In cold climates the streets shall be wide; in hot climates narrow, however, for purposes of defense and where horses are kept the streets had better be wide.

117. The other streets laid out consecutively around the plaza are to be so planned that even if the town should increase considerably in size it would meet with no obstruction which might disfigure

* An interesting example of the carrying out of these instructions can be seen at the southwestern corner of the principal square of the City of Mexico.

what had already been built or be a detriment to the defense or convenience of the town.

118. At certain distances in the town smaller, well proportioned plazas are to be laid out on which the main church, the parish church or monastery shall be built so that the teaching of religious doctrine may be evenly distributed.

119. If the town lies on the coast its main church shall be so situated that it may be visible from the landing place and so built that its structure may serve as means of defense for the port itself.

120. After the plaza and streets have been laid out building lots are to be designated, in the first place, for the erection of the main church, the parish church or monastery and these are to occupy respectively an entire block so that no other structure can be built next to them excepting such as contribute to their commodiousness or beauty.

121. Immediately afterwards the place and site are to be assigned for the Royal and Town Council House, the Custom-House and Arsenal which is to be close to the church and port so that in case of necessity one can protect the other. The hospital for the poor and sick of non-contagious diseases shall be built next to the church forming its cloister.

122. The lots and sites for slaughter houses, fisheries, tanneries and such like productive of garbage shall be so situated that the latter can be easily disposed of.

123. It would be of great advantage if inland towns, at a distance from ports, were built on the banks of a navigable river, in which case an endeavor should be made to build on the northern river bank, all occupations producing garbage being relegated to the river bank or sea situated below the town.

124. In inland towns the church is not to be on the plaza but at a distance from it in a situation where it can stand by itself, separate from other buildings so that it can be seen from all sides. It can thus be made more beautiful and it will inspire more respect. It would be built on high ground so that in order to reach its entrance people will have to ascend a flight of steps. Near-by and between it and the main plaza the Royal Council and Town House and the Custom-House are to be erected in order to increase its impressiveness but without obstructing it in any way. The hospital of the poor who are ill with non-contagious diseases shall be built facing the north and so planned that it will enjoy a southern exposure.

125. The same plan shall be carried out in any inland settlements where there are no rivers, much care being taken that they enjoy other conveniences requisite and necessary.

126. No building lots surrounding the main plaza are to be given to private individuals for these are to be reserved for the church, Royal and Town house, also shops and dwellings for the merchants, which are to be the first erected. For the erection of the public buildings the settlers shall contribute and for this purpose a moderate tax shall be imposed on all merchandise.

127. The remaining building lots shall be distributed by lottery to those of the settlers who are entitled to build around the main plaza. Those left over are to be held for us to grant to settlers who may come later or to dispose of at our pleasure. In order that entries of these assignments be better made a plan of the town is always to be made in advance.

128. After the plan of the town and the distribution of the lots have been made each settler is to set up his tent on his lot if he has one, for which purpose the captains shall persuade them to carry tents with them. Those who own none are to build huts of such materials as are available, wherever they can be collected. All settlers, with greatest possible haste, are to erect jointly some kind of palisade or dig a ditch around the main plaza so that the Indians cannot do them harm.

129. A common shall be assigned to each town, of adequate size so that even though it should grow greatly there would always be sufficient space for its inhabitants to find recreation and for cattle to pasture without encroaching upon private property.

130. Adjoining the common there shall be assigned pastures for team oxen, for horses, for cattle destined for slaughter and for the regular number of cattle which according to law, the settlers are obliged to have, so that they can be employed for public purposes by the council. The remainder of land is to be sub-divided into as many plots for cultivation as there are town lots and the settlers are to draw lots for these. Should there be any land which can be irrigated it is to be distributed to the first settlers in the same proportion and drawn for by lottery. What remains over is to be reserved for us so that we can make grants to those who may settle later.

131. As soon as the plots for cultivation have been distributed the settlers shall immediately plant all the seeds that they have brought or are obtainable, for which reason it is advisable that all

go well provided. All cattle transported thither by the settlers or collected, are to be taken to the pasture lands so that they can begin at once to breed and multiply.

132. Having sown their seeds and provided accommodation for their cattle in such quantities and with such diligence that they can reasonably hope for an abundance of food, the settlers, with great care and activity are to erect their houses, with solid foundations and walls for which purpose they shall go provided with moulds or planks for making adobes and all other tools for building quickly and at little cost.

133. The building lots and the structures erected thereon are to be so situated that in the living rooms one can enjoy air from the south and from the north, which are the best. All town homes are to be so planned that they can serve as a defense or fortress against those who might attempt to create disturbances or occupy the town. Each house is to be so constructed that horses and household animals can be kept therein, the courtyards and stockyards being as large as possible to insure health and cleanliness.

134. Settlers are to endeavor, as far as possible, to make all structures uniform, for the sake of the beauty of the town.

135. The faithful executors and architects and persons who may be deputed by the governor for the purpose shall be most scrupulous in carrying out the above instructions and in hurrying both field labor and house building so that the town may be completed in a short time.

136. If the natives should wish to oppose the establishment of a settlement they are to be given to understand that the settlers desire to build a town there not in order to deprive them of their property but for the purpose of being on friendly terms with them; of teaching them to live in a civilized way; of teaching them to know God and His Law by means of which they shall be saved. This shall be explained to them by the friars and clergy and persons deputied by the governor, by means of good interpreters. Attempts are to be made by all fair means to establish the settlement peaceably and with the consent of the natives. If, after many different attempts have been made to gain their consent, the natives still withhold it then the settlers are to proceed to establish their town but are not to take any of the personal belongings of the Indians or to do them more hurt than what may be necessary in order to protect the settlers and enable them to build without interference.

137. While the new town is being built the settlers, as far as possible, shall try to avoid communication and intercourse with the Indians and are not to go to their villages or amuse themselves or disperse themselves over the country. Nor are the Indians to enter the circuit of the settlement until the latter is complete and in condition for defense and the houses built, so that when the Indians see them they will be filled with wonder and will realize that the Spaniards are settling there permanently and not temporarily. They will consequently fear the Spaniards so much that they will not dare to offend them and will respect them and desire their friendship. When the settlers begin to construct the town the governor is to appoint someone to take charge of the sowing and cultivating of wheat and vegetables so that the settlers can immediately employ these for their maintenance. The cattle are to graze and be tended in a safe place where they can do no injury to the cultivated lands or anything else belonging to the Indians. The aforesaid cattle and their offspring are to be at the service of the settlers and for their use and subsistence.   . . .

2. Colonial Towns of Spanish and Portuguese America

ROBERT C. SMITH

In the two centuries between 1500 and 1700 six European nations established towns and colonies in the Americas. Of these only Spain laid out towns according to a regular and unvarying plan. This plan represented an orderly practical concept without precedent in the immediate background of Europe. It involved not only the careful consideration of the site from the standpoint of terrain and climate but also the introduction of a gridiron plan of broad straight streets intersecting one another at right angles to form rectangular blocks and open squares. The plan was the result of a number of royal orders first codified in 1523 at the time of the conquest of Mexico and incorporated in what are known as the Laws of the Indies, which were followed in all subsequent Spanish colonization until the end of the colonial period.

Robert C. Smith, "Colonial Towns of Spanish and Portuguese America," *Journal of the Society of Architectural Historians*, XIV (December, 1955), pp. 3–12, *passim*. Reprinted by permission.

The gridiron plan, used in Mesopotamia and in ancient Egyptian cities, had been the standard scheme for plotting Graeco-Roman cities. It was almost entirely abandoned, however, in medieval times in favor of an irregular system of crooked streets and uneven spaces that obeyed a very different kind of planning. The revival of the gridiron in Spanish America was, therefore, a revival of a commonplace of antiquity and as such is characteristic of the Renaissance. It was also one of the outstanding American contributions to the history of urbanism because the revival of the gridiron plan took place in the new world before it became accepted in Europe.

Before the conquest of Mexico one important urban site had been laid out in Spanish America. This was the town of Santo Domingo on Columbus' island of Hispaniola, the modern Ciudad Trujillo, capital of the Dominican Republic, which was founded in 1496. King Ferdinand, writing to his military governor Nicolás de Ovando, said that "from here it is not possible to give precise instructions" and left to the governor himself the responsibility of determining the plan to be followed. The one that was adopted on the spot is, however, related to the whole subsequent development because it includes a number of regular arteries running parallel from a principal square containing the cathedral and city hall and a number of less regular open spaces with their respective churches. The result was sufficiently impressive to lead the Italian bishop Geraldini upon his arrival at Santo Domingo in 1520 to commend the streets as broader and straighter than those of his native Florence. In contriving this plan it is probable that the soldier Ovando and his associates were less concerned with the theory of an ideal city than with the recollection of a hastily contrived but efficiently laid-out military camp which some of them had known. This was the temporary castrum of Santa Fé, which Ferdinand and Isabella had created in two and one-half months in 1491 in order to launch the successful siege of Granada which drove the last Moors from Spain. Santa Fé was drawn up as a fortified rectangle intersected by the crossing of two perpendicular axes and approached by four cardinal gates. Santo Domingo was provided with walls for defense from marauders approaching by sea and was thus the forerunner of all the subsequent heavily fortified Spanish strongholds of the Antilles and the Gulf of Mexico.

In 1520 Hernando Cortés took the Aztec capital of Tenochtitlán and completed the conquest of Mexico, which now became New

Spain. Almost at once it was decided to rebuild the city, devastated by the terrible campaign, upon the same site; thus was laid the groundwork for the modern City of Mexico. The Spanish surveyor Alonso García Bravo was employed in 1524 to draw up the plan. This was the first example of the gridiron scheme, the use of which was by now specifically required by law, having been already suggested in the royal instructions to Pedrarias Dávila on the occasion of his first expedition to the mainland in 1513. Fourteen streets intersecting each other at right angles were laid out around a central Plaza Mayor, which was to contain the cathedral and the residence of the governor. This was in reality the center of the old Aztec city, as is shown by a woodcut map published with a letter from Cortés at Nuremberg in 1524. It was there that the principal temples and palaces had been located, approached by broad thoroughfares in four directions like those in other Indian towns described by the Spanish friar Motolinía, who called attention to "the large square court in the best part of the town" and "the very straight highways" that led to it. In this respect the new Spanish urbanism followed an Aztec tradition but there is no proof that the Indians knew or used the full gridiron arrangement.

In devising their plan the Spaniards were obeying the trend established by Italian humanists of the 15th century, who revived in theory, if not in fact, the orderly layout of classical cities, for none of their designs were actually carried out. Men like Alberti and Filarete based their plans for ideal cities upon the monumental concept they obtained from reading the text of Vitruvius, the chief original written source for information on Graeco-Roman architecture. From him they developed their taste for broad squares, stately colonnades and straight thoroughfares, but they used these features on a radial rather than a gridiron basis, apparently because Vitruvius was not sufficiently specific in describing the street pattern of his city and because the radial system was common in the middle ages. Thus none of the town plans of the Italian humanists which came to be known in Spain by the early years of the 16th century can be considered precise models for the master plan of the Laws of the Indies. Some other explanation of the origin of the Spanish gridiron must, therefore, be sought. It may have come from a new interpretation of Vitruvius on ancient urbanism; it may have been derived (but this is improbable) from the Roman towns of Spain; or again it may have evolved from the camp at Santa Fé, which in turn may

have been influenced by the only real gridiron plans of the middle
ages, which occur at Montpazier, Mirande and other 13th-century
bastides of southern France. Whatever its origin, the plan in Spanish America was effectively combined with the monumental classical
concept of the city advanced by the humanists of Italy. The dia-
logue of Cervantes de Salazar, published in 1554 after the rebuilding of Mexico City, proves beyond question that the fine streets
with regular façades joining handsome symmetrical squares, which
were so highly praised by foreign visitors of the period, were
accepted in New Spain as an essential part of the Italian understanding of urbanism based on Vitruvius. At the same time, however,
this concept bore no practical fruit in Old Spain, where even in
Philip II's new capital of Madrid the whole 16th century passed
without an end being put to the irregularities and crowding of
medieval construction. It was not, in fact, until 1617 that the building of the Plaza Mayor gave Madrid a large symmetrical square
handsomely adorned in the fashion of the broad open spaces of
Mexico and the other urban centers of Spanish America.   . . .

Neither Mexico City, Cholula nor any of the inland towns except Lima in Peru was fortified with walls and towers of defense
as were those on the seacoast. It was customary, however, in the
16th century for large houses to have some form of protection from
enemies within the city. Likewise, the members of the religious
orders who founded their rural convents all over Mexico in the 16th
century took the precaution of fortifying their churches with towers
of defense, buttresses and battlements. The resulting buildings
resemble the fortified churches which continued to be erected after
the Albigensian heresy in unwalled towns of southern France. A
1580 map of Huejutla in the state of Hidalgo shows the regular
streets intersecting at right angles that were provided for the Indian
villages constructed by Spaniards adjacent to the convents and their
churches. These village plans in imitation of the gridirons of the
cities gave impressive vistas to modest settings, not only in Mexico
but all over Spanish America.

The same laws of town planning were applied in every part of
the Indies during the 16th century, the crucial period for the laying
out of towns in the Spanish domains of the New World. From Bogotá, founded in 1538, to Santiago de Chile, a town created in 1541,
and La Paz in Bolivia of 1548, the regular scheme of the gridiron
was repeated all over Spanish South America, following the prece-

dents already created in Mexico. In the Laws of the Indies the founders were cautioned against selecting sites that were either too high or too low for the good health of the inhabitants or of such irregular terrain as to interfere with the proper use of the gridiron plan. At Lima in 1535 Pizarro and his companions chose a site that was practically ideal since the ground was almost completely level. The level site is characteristic of Popayán in Colombia, Puebla in Mexico, Antigua in Guatemala and indeed of almost all the early centers of the Spanish colonies. Exceptions like Quito in Ecuador do exist, where the whole city is spread out on a hillside, but that is because of the decision made in 1534, at the time the old Inca settlement was captured, to establish the new town on the old site.

After the site was chosen, the Laws directed that the pre-existent plan be laid out *a cordel y regla*, with rigorous exactitude. The first concern was the location of the principal square, "symmetrical, harmonious and monumental," as George Kubler has called it, so that "the four corners of the plaza face to the four principal winds, because in this way the streets leaving the plaza are not exposed to the principal winds, which would be of great inconvenience." In this respect (and there are others) the Laws of the Indies follow instructions laid down long before by Vitruvius. For the plaza mayor the Laws recommended an ideal size of six hundred by four hundred feet so that it would be big enough for the *fiestas de caballos*, the traditional equestrian sports of Spain. In inland towns the principal square was to be in the center of the city and in port settlements at the water's edge. This, for example, is still the disposition of Buenos Aires, where the city is focused upon the Plaza de Mayo, which was laid out on the waterfront at the time of the refounding of the old town in 1580.

The principal square is almost invariably dominated by the metropolitan church, generally in large centers a cathedral, "raised up somewhat," according to the Laws of the Indies, so that it can be seen advantageously, as Vitruvius had recommended for the chief temples of Roman cities. In regard to the location of these buildings there is what seems to be a discrepancy between the codified instructions and the actual practice because the Laws specifically direct that the cathedral was to be erected not in the principal square but in "some separate and prominent place." Perhaps the explanation of this confusing expression is that the Laws were forbidding the construction of the cathedral *inside the periphery of the square,* as was often the custom in the Middle Ages, a custom which it is important to note was still followed at Santo Domingo where the cathedral occupies a position within the principal plaza. In contra-distinction, the "separate place" of the Laws probably meant the side of the square, where churches, following the laying-out of Mexico City, were invariably placed.   . . .

Colonial Paraguay comprised an immense territory including modern Paraguay, almost all of Argentina, as well as part of Brazil, Bolivia and Chile. It was here that Jesuit missionaries, arriving from Peru in 1587, set up the famous República, which endured until the expulsion of their order from all the territories of Spain in 1767. To convert the Indians they established towns or *reducciones,* as the missionary friars in Mexico had already done, but because of the absence in this distant colony of regular civil organizations, these towns of the Jesuit missionaries were the only settlements in the area. Constructed and maintained by communal labor and containing sometimes as many as 7000 inhabitants, the *reducciones* all reflected in miniature the gridiron plan. Now, unfortunately, the Jesuit missions of Paraguay have almost entirely disappeared. They can, however, be partly reconstructed through the engraving representing that of Candelaria, considered a model for others, which was published by Father José Manuel Peramás in 1793. In the center was the single great square, each side of which measured some four hundred feet. Around it were grouped long rectangular houses called *galpones* occupying blocks some ninety feet in length, which were divided by broad streets. All these houses had covered porches or porticoes which produced a continuous peristyle around the entire block.

Facing the square, which contained a statue of the Virgin upon a column, was the mission church. At its right were located the cemetery and a large building for widows and orphaned girls. On the other side was the residence of the two Jesuit priests who directed the mission, constructed in characteristic fashion around a patio, and beside it, occupying identical space, another court with warehouses and workshops, like the Atarazanas that stood beside metropolitan churches in the civil towns.

There is reason to believe that the Portuguese Jesuits, who first reached Brazil in 1549 and there became a great colonizing force, founding as they did four hundred years ago the present city of S. Paulo, used a not dissimilar plan for their *aldeias* or Indian estates.

These were all, however, much smaller than the missions in Paraguay and almost nothing is known about the details of their arrangement. A drawing of 1793 in the colonial archive of Lisbon representing the nucleus of the mission at Espírito Santo in the state of Bahia, shows the church and Jesuit residence at the head of the same broad square found in the Paraguayan missions. But the way in which the houses are located unevenly around this square and the diagonal streets leading off from its angles represent a departure from the gridiron plan.

That plan in fact was not a characteristic of the colonial settlements of Brazil. At no time did the Portuguese, who discovered the country in 1500 and held it until 1822, provide a code of rules for urban development. Their cities grew without being planned in a kind of picturesque confusion that is as typical of Luso-Brazilian cities as order and clarity are typical of the urbanism of Spanish America. Lisbon itself served as a model which was followed in various degrees of exactitude in different sites all over the Portuguese empire. That city, one of the most beautiful in Europe, is constructed upon a series of steep hills overlooking the broad expanse of the estuary of the Tagus River. The tops of these hills have been from an early time occupied by churches and convents, isolated in height and extremely difficult of access. Around them wind narrow, twisting streets and lanes, so sharply inclined that they have always presented a serious barrier to vehicular traffic. Nowhere in Europe, as a result, were litters and sedan chairs more frequently utilized than at Lisbon and Oporto, another city built in a quite similar fashion. Far below, at the port level, is the business center, constituting a lower city quite separate from the upper town. In this lower area of Lisbon the old streets were almost as narrow and irregular as those of the zone above until in 1755 an earthquake of major proportions opened the way to a great rebuilding. Then the architects of the prime minister Marquis of Pombal imposed the gridiron plan with two great squares connected by parallel streets regularly intersecting. . . .

The pattern of a city at two or more levels sprawling in disordered strip formation was repeated in the Portuguese colonies almost wherever the terrain permitted. . . .

In following this uncomfortable system of planning the Portuguese settlers seem at least in part to have been obeying the medieval concept of defence through height. Another location which recommended itself for purposes of protection was the island city and this was utilized at Goa and Diu in India and at Moçambique and Luanda in Africa. Both situations are found in colonial Brazil, where almost all the early settlements were made directly on the seacoast, in contrast to those of the Spanish, who in their territories preferred inland locations for their capital establishments.

Salvador in the captaincy of Bahia, which remained from its foundation in 1549 until 1763 the colonial capital of Brazil, is the closest approximation in the new world to the site and plan of Lisbon. At Salvador the administrative buildings as well as most of the major churches and great houses were built in the upper city, superbly overlooking the vast expanse of the Bay of All Saints and enjoying at intervals a cooling breeze from the sea. Commerce and shipping, on the other hand, took up the lower level. Here was a network of lofty tenements on narrow streets, broken by dark passageways and stuffy courts, that probably represented the most faithful reproduction in colonial America of the complexities of medieval conglomerate housing in Europe. The extraordinary watercolor at the Museu do Estado da Bahia showing the now demolished Morgado de Sta. Bárbara, expresses better than any verbal description the confusion of the port zone as it was described at the end of the 18th century by the Portuguese schoolmaster, Luiz dos Santos Vilhena. "Not only are these people jealous of the land they occupy," he wrote, "but also of the very air, because not satisfied with building houses like cages in four or five stories, they set them so close that from the upper floors the street can scarcely be seen . . . and the streets are extremely dark and disagreeable for those who walk upon them."   . . .

The founders of S. Paulo likewise chose a difficult location for the same motives of defense, while at Rio de Janeiro, established in 1567, the almost fantastic land formations impeded the development of the city, which at the beginning was pretty well confined, like some medieval hill town of Italy, to the summit of the Morro do Castelo. Thus Frei Agostinho de Sta. Maria wrote in 1714: "The first foundations of this City were on a hill, where still can be seen the Cathedral, the Jesuit College, the fort of St. Sebastian and some old houses of the first colonists; but with the development of commerce the site became too small for new constructions and the new inhabitants began to build their houses . . . along the shore." But then he added "the City is still thrust between two mountain peaks that occupy the ends of the shoreline."

Here in the lower city which rapidly became the real city of Rio de Janeiro, there grew up the same irregular network of streets and passageways as at Salvador and Recife, some of which, like the Rua Gonçalves Dias, were so narrow that they have now been closed to vehicular traffic. Between the cone-like hills still occupied in true Portuguese fashion by the Franciscans and Benedictines ran the principal artery which like the main thoroughfare of Salvador was "so narrow and formless, with so many salient and re-entrant angles, that a carriage could scarcely move along it." This was surprisingly named the Rua Direita or Straight Street, following a custom long used in Portugal which is comparable to the English tradition of calling the principal thoroughfare of a town the High Street. In fairness to this Portuguese custom, however, it should be noted that in old maps and documents the words "Rua Direita" are generally followed by some such expression as "que vai da Cadêa para a Ponte" (Running from the Prison to the Bridge) indicating that the term was used to mean that the street ran not in a straight line but continuously between two given landmarks. Thus, neither at Rio de Janeiro nor elsewhere was there a system of broad thoroughfares running straight and parallel like the ones that distinguish almost every colonial urban center of Spanish America. . . .

In conclusion, we can summarize the history of colonial town planning in Latin America as follows: The Spanish employed throughout the period the rigid formula of the gridiron plan for all their settlements after 1523. These were generally made on level inland sites carefully chosen according to a code of rules incorporated in the Laws of the Indies. As a result the old cities of Spanish America were almost all alike except for a certain variation in the placing of the minor squares and an element of contrast provided occasionally by changes of terrain. There was a sameness about the streets of these cities with which we are well acquainted in this country because in the 19th century most of our cities were built in the same fashion. (This sameness in Spanish America has been intensified in recent times by a tendency to adopt the North American custom of numbered streets.) Broad and level thoroughfares provided easy communication throughout the town and until recently were entirely adequate to the volume of traffic. The colonnades and squares were an encouragement to commerce and to outdoor living. The gridiron system may have lacked originality but it did have these advantages. It also allowed practically unlimited expansion upon the same plan and provided a stamp of imperial uniformity to a whole colonial development. In Portuguese America, on the contrary, an opposite system almost exclusively prevailed. Settlements were made in rugged coastal areas. They developed without formal plans in strip formation at several levels, with narrow steep streets that rendered any communication difficult. The resulting plans are all different, disordered but picturesque.

It would then be difficult indeed to imagine two forms of urbanism more distinct than those that were employed in Portuguese and Spanish America. The one was a survival of medieval procedure which involved the repetition in America of the specific town plans of Portugal. The other, on the contrary, was a product of the Renaissance, which represented a most radical departure from the system that prevailed in the mother country. It was an early experiment in America that was to become almost universally accepted in the future.

B. The Texture of Urban Life: Spanish America

3. An Academic Dialogue in Sixteenth-Century Mexico City

Francisco Cervantes de Salazar

MESA, GUTIÉRREZ (INTERLOCUTORS)

MESA. I am indeed happy that you have arrived in this country; and, since I understand that you are familiar with many Spanish

Francisco Cervantes de Salazar, *Life in the Imperial and Loyal City of Mexico in New Spain, and the Royal and Pontifical University of Mexico*, Minnie Lee Barrett Shepard, trans., and Carlos Eduardo Castañeda, ed. (Austin: University of Texas Press, 1953), pp. 25–35. Reprinted by permission of the University of Texas Press.

colleges and are eager to get new ideas, as your very visit manifests, I shall learn what I wish to know while showing you the sights that you have not seen before.

GUT. Nothing is so natural, as Aristotle, too, testifies, as for man to be seized of his own will and carried away into the discovery of wisdom, which, having acquainted with many important ideas, delights us with its variety. Nature, too, delights in variety, and in a brief space she produces a wide diversity, for which she is always beloved of mortals. As the eyes are captivated by the varied aspect of objects, so the mind always turns toward things new and never seen before, and grows wearied with endless repetition everywhere. All these remarks have this in view, that you may clearly understand that it was not for gain that I sailed across so great and perilous an ocean, as many do, but to see unknown things.

ME. "Everyone is drawn by his own pleasure." As you are led by this desire, so others are by other desires; but this of yours is more pleasing to me.

GUT. So it goes. But tell me, please, what I haven't wished to ask of another: What is this building with one side full of many large windows, facing the plaza, and with its front, the public street? Entering it, sometimes by twos, sometimes by threes, and again in crowds, as though in dutiful attendance upon a master, are young men clad in long cloaks, with square caps pulled down to their ears.

ME. It is the university, the molding place of the youth; those entering are students, lovers of Minerva and the Muses.

GUT. Has wisdom any place where avarice holds sway?

ME. That conquers which is stronger and the more greatly desired.

GUT. It does among those who, in passing judgment on things evaluate everything as it is, and do not take the base for the beautiful, or the beautiful for the base.

ME. In the very beginning such people were conquered by wisdom and made subject to her sway. Otherwise, they would make a perverted judgment about all matters.

GUT. You are right. Now, please, let us go in together. The entrance is indeed large, and the corridors on the ground floor quite spacious.

ME. The same is true of those above.

GUT. The courtyard is ample enough for the crowded throng

of students. On the left, there is more than enough space for the erection of a fourth wing as large as that on the right. But what sort of instructors does it have, a matter of greater importance and one that truly ennobles a university?

ME. The very best.

GUT. I am not asking about their integrity, but about their scholarship and their skill in teaching.

ME. They are diligent and well versed in every science. If I may say so, they are by no means ordinary men, and Spain has few like them.

GUT. Who was the founder of so great an institution?

ME. The emperor, under whose auspices and leadership many glorious achievements have been performed all over the world.

GUT. What are their immunities and privileges?

ME. Very great and many, and in all respects not unlike those of the University of Salamanca.

GUT. Those who teach so far from their native land, as well as the students who live with their parents in the midst of great wealth and pleasures, are worthy of many more and, if it were possible, of greater ones.

ME. What you should have said, instead, is that both should be honored for the reason that by the brilliance of their wisdom they are the first to free the New World from the cloud of ignorance with which it was obscured, and to confirm the Indians in the faith and worship of God, so that an ever stronger integrity is transmitted to posterity.

GUT. Your judgment is entirely correct, none more so. But now explain to me what I earnestly desire to know: Who are these zealous molders of youth, what salary do they receive, and for how long a time?

ME. The same stipend is not paid to all. Some are employed for two hundred gold coins a year, others for three hundred, according to the importance of the instruction and the scholarship of the professors. On the whole, however, when one considers their zeal in teaching and the high prices in this province, their salaries are quite low. You will never believe this unless you try it: the things that you buy in Spain for a copper coin, three pence or four pence, you will not find on sale here even for two silver coins, I should say, three.

GUT. I well believe you, since I have unwillingly made the experiment. Even the cheapest article that I bought, on sale everywhere, cost me a silver coin. There is no money here of small value as there is in Spain, and a silver coin there is worth as much as a gold coin here.

ME. Therefore teachers ought to get a sufficient salary to be able to engage in the one thing that they are doing, without being distracted by other things, and be able thereby to support themselves and their families moderately. It would then happen, as it must in every good school, that there would be a great increase of learned men, and that the young men who will eventually become teachers would study with greater progress.

GUT. The Emperor Charles will increase their remuneration when he is informed about the situation, and will inspire great resolution in all studious men to continue unwearied, if, as I hear, he should conclude that ecclesiastical offices and other posts should come only to those who are manifestly more worthy, as shown by a prior test of their scholarship.

ME. There is great hope that it will be thus. But now, that you may know the other things that you ask about, you should know that on every day that is not a holiday continuous lectures and interpretations of authors are given, in the morning from seven until eleven, and in the afternoon from two until six. Some of the instructors lecture twice a day, some only once.

GUT. The same is true at the University of Salamanca.

ME. In the sciences of language and logic, which furnish an introduction to the other sciences, there are three distinguished professors.

GUT. Tell me who they are and at what hours they teach.

ME. The man whom you see walking up and down through that large lecture hall on the lower floor, in the midst of so great a throng of students, is Professor Bustamante. From eight until nine in the morning and from two until three in the afternoon, with earnestness as well as diligence, he teaches grammar, of which he is the chief professor. He interprets the authors carefully, solves the difficulties, and subtly notes the more important points. He is well versed in dialectics and philosophy, of which he is also professor; and because he has taught the Mexican youth for twenty-six years, there is scarcely anyone lecturing or teaching who has not been his student.

GUT. How many grandsons he will have if he who molds the mind is a father no less than he who begets the body.

ME. Very many indeed! All those whom he has taught to their great profit and has fruitfully instructed toward virtuous living in so far as their natures allowed. Now let us go upstairs, for the rest of the classrooms are on the upper floor. The one on the right is the lecture hall dedicated to the interpretation of sacred theology; here from two until three, Professor Cervantes teaches rhetoric, and he is heard by many students of the other sciences as well as those interested in oratory, because rhetoric is an equipment for these studies.

GUT. Unless I am mistaken, he is the man who was also professor of the art of speech at the University of Osuna.

ME. The very same. In that corner behind that magnificent classroom in which canon and civil law are interpreted, are two very large rooms, in the first of which Juan García, priest and also Master of Arts, teaches dialectics with great zeal and no less success. He does this twice daily. He is a man to be commended both for his learning and his integrity.

GUT. Great heavens! With what shouting and waving of hands is that fat scholar arguing with the thin one! See how he presses him and incites him!

ME. He also is doing the same thing and is very vigorously defending himself. Both, however, as I see it, are contending about a mere trifle, although they appear to be arguing about an important matter.

GUT. The many Augustinian monks now entering the theology lecture hall along with other priests, whom are they going to hear?

ME. Fray Alonso de la Veracruz, the most learned professor of arts and theology that our province has, the foremost interpreter of this most sacred and divine science, a man of varied and manifold erudition, in whom the highest virtue vies with rare and admirable learning.

GUT. You are describing to me a most extraordinary man, and above all else, as I hear, a man of so great modesty that he admires all men, despises none, and is always unassuming himself.

ME. Dr. Morones, to whom jurisprudence owes much, a man who plays a most important part in the interpretation of canon law, is about to lecture on the sacred canons and is ascending to his chair.

He is pleasing to his listeners, of whom he has many, because of his clarity.

GUT. Many do follow him.

ME. And deservedly so. From ten until eleven in the same place Dr. Arévalo Sedeño interprets and elucidates the papal decrees with such accuracy and finish that the most skilled jurists can find nothing to censure, but much to admire, as if his pronouncements came from some oracle. He is prolific in abstract argument, concise in the concrete, prompt in citing his sources, keen in his inferences, and when he turns his attention to the subtleties, he solves them. There is nothing important or obscure in law that he is not aware of, and to say it once for all, he is the only one who can make jurisconsults of his students.

GUT. I heard him at the University of Salamanca, and daily he increased more and more the great expectation that he had always given of himself.

ME. In the afternoon from three until four, Juan Negrete, Master of Arts and Theology, who last year was rector of the university, lectures on theology. He is also admirably versed in philosophy and mathematics, and that he might fail in nothing to comprise an encyclopedia of learning, he is not ignorant of medicine.

GUT. He is indeed a man indispensable to so great a university.

ME. In the afternoon also, from four until five, Dr. Frías, likewise a Master of Arts, and most learned in Greek and Latin, very ably expounds the Institutes of Justinian, a fact the more surprising because he is only thirty-four years of age.

GUT. You are setting before me men of great distinction in this newly born university, each of whom in a well-established and fully developed university could have performed his duties with many rich returns in his own right. Is there no other grammarian in Mexico? I doubt that one can be enough, even though he is very proficient.

ME. Up to now, there have been Puebla, Vázquez, Tarragona, and Martín Fernández, a man unusually skilled in dialectics and metaphysics, and a certain Cervantes, who in the testimony of many is exceptionally well versed in Greek and Latin literature. There are many others who have taught not unsuccessfully, but they have ceased to teach at the call of other plans. However, there recently came from Spain a certain Diego Díez, who in a private school explains with great accuracy both his sources and the basic principles of language. He is going to be ever more useful to the youth, for I hear that he is zealously devoting himself to the study of literature.

GUT. Indeed you are right. But who is that tall man in a robe down to his ankles, carrying a silver mace on his shoulders?

ME. He is the mace-bearer of the university, whom in Spain we call the beadle. He is a man not unlearned, a fact that accords well with his duties.

GUT. What is he announcing, with head uncovered, to the professor of theology?

ME. That on tomorrow, which is a holiday in accordance with university regulations, he must refrain from the labor of lecturing.

GUT. Is Thursday an established and constituted holiday, if another festal day does not fall within the week?

ME. Such is the custom of the university.

GUT. What does that paper contain that is fastened to the door?

ME. Theses posing certain questions in metaphysics and theology, some affirmative, some negative, as is written there at the bottom, which are to be defended and attacked in the theological auditorium on Tuesday, or as scholars say, *feria tertia* [the third day of the week].

GUT. Are those sharply attacked who enter the arena of debate to defend their principles?

ME. Very sharply; and the contest is begun between the defender and the attacker, who join in hand to hand combat in such fashion that both appear to be fighting with swords for nothing less than their altars and firesides. In a high seat, with robe and mantle, the doctoral insignia of his order and rank, sits the president of the contest, as Vives calls him, who acts as judge of the debate in settling disputes and deciding questions. He is one of the professors to whose lot the task has fallen according to the regulations of the university.

GUT. Do those who descend into the arena fight and contend with equal valor and zeal?

ME. Not at all. Some rush at the throat and force their opponents to a retraction; others attempt the same thing without success. Some attack with a leaden sword which is soon blunted, either because they are beginners who have never entered combat, or because they are not yet keen enough in ability.

GUT. Does a defender ever surrender?

ME. Almost never, because he is aided by the president or some one of the veterans who have often been in combat. It sometimes happens that between the doctors and the licentiates who hold opposite opinions a much more violent controversy arises than between the original defender and attacker.

GUT. By whom is it broken off and settled?

ME. By the night, for no other Palaemon is present; because in many cases the presiding officer of the contest, or the supporter of the defender is attacked more severely than the pupil or the client to whom he gives protection, or whom he undertakes to defend while he is receiving weapons and hurling them back.

GUT. Is there already a list of candidates for degrees?

ME. Not yet, because the students in dialectics have not obtained the first degree of the baccalaureate; but there will be a list soon, which up to now the shortness of time has not permitted. However, Bernardo López, a priest second from the vice-general in the administration of the bishopric of Oaxaca, a man of no mean learning, and Dr. Frías and Professor Cervantes have received the first degree in canon law, for which they studied at the University of Salamanca.

GUT. From whom?

ME. From Dr. Quesada, judge in the Royal Court, a man worthy to be compared with the ancients in both kinds of law, as men will testify at the University of Salamanca and of Alcalá.

GUT. With what ceremony is the doctoral cap bestowed, and at what expense?

ME. With the utmost ceremony and at so great an expenditure of money that it costs much less at the University of Salamanca.

GUT. How large is the number of doctors and professors?

ME. There are so many of those who have obtained the highest degree in Mexico and of those upon whom it has been conferred elsewhere, who are now alumni of the university enrolled according to their rank, that there are scarcely more at the University of Salamanca. To this good fortune of so great a university is added the fact that Alonso de Montúfar, Archbishop of Mexico, distinguished Professor in Sacred Theology, would be placed first in any listing and classification of doctors. He is so devoted to literature and men of letters that he cares for nothing so earnestly as the manner in which ever greater progress in literature may be made.

GUT. How correctly that famous man said: "Give me Maecenases, O Flaccus, and Virgils will not be lacking!" At what risk do those who are candidates for degrees either in theology, metaphysics, or law come to the private examination?

ME. Cearly at the greatest risk to their honor, which by most of them is considered more important than life; for no one has such confidence in himself that he does not greatly fear that in this contest the black *cita* will be placed before his name, since in himself no one is ever perfect in every respect.

GUT. Are the same letters, *A* and *R*, used here for approval and rejection as at the University of Salamanca?

ME. The very same. However, the ancients used three letters for casting their votes: *C*, which condemned, from which that famous man [Cicero] said, "prefix the black *cita*"; *A*, which approved; *L* and *N*, which signified *non liquet* [it is not clear].

GUT. Doesn't the university have a library?

ME. There will be a large one when the university becomes established. Meanwhile, the libraries in the monasteries are not small, and will greatly aid those willing to visit them.

4. Burial of an Archbishop-Viceroy in Mexico City, 1612

HUBERT HOWE BANCROFT

The embalmed body, arrayed in pontifical robes of purple taffeta garnished with gold and silver, rested in the chapel on a catafalque, covered with black gold-bordered velvet, and surrounded with candles. The interior of the chapel was draped in black. The head of the corpse reclined on a black velvet cushion, ornamented with gold and silver, and bore on the brow a mitre. Close to it rose the guidon of the captain-general, a rank held by the deceased in virtue of his office as viceroy. At the left shoulder rested the pastoral staff, and in the right hand the archiepiscopal cross; at the feet were two royal maces of gilt silver, and between them the prelate's hat.

For three days a constant stream of visitors appeared at the

Hubert Howe Bancroft, *The Works of Hubert Howe Bancroft: The Conquest of Mexico* (New York: The Bancroft Co., 1883–1888), Vol. III, pp. 21–23.

chapel to give a last look at the beloved face, while friars and clergy held vigils, masses, and chants here as well as at other temples. The bells tolled solemnly all the while, and nearly every person exhibited some token of mourning, especially officials and men of means.

On the 25th a vast concourse gathered at the palace to escort the body to the cathedral tomb. First marched the school children with white lighted tapers; then came thirty-eight brotherhoods, according to age, with standards, crosses, and other paraphernalia; the different monastic orders, closing with the Dominicans, to whom belonged the deceased, followed by over four hundred members of the clergy, the prebendaries of the Chapter being last. Then came the coffin, having at the feet the prelate's hat, and a cap with white tassel, the insignia of a master of theology. Behind were borne the cross and guidon, draped in black, between two kings-at-arms. On either side of the coffin strode the viceregal guard, while halberdiers assisted in keeping back the crowd. Following the guard came the deacons; the commercial court; the university representation, with sixty-four of its graduated doctors bearing the insignia of the faculty; the municipality, preceded by their mace-bearers; the audiencia, with three nephews of the deceased; the royal officers, bearing a black standard with royal arms in gold; three companies of infantry in lines of seven, with arms reversed, marching to the sound of four muffled drums and two fifes; the maestre de sala of the viceroy, bearing aloft on a half-pike the arms of the deceased, gilded on a black surface; the master of horse and chamberlain, leading a steed in deep mourning with a long train; another gentleman of the court, on horseback, bore the guidon of captain-general, with royal arms on crimson velvet. The procession closed with the servants of the palace, led by the major-domo.

Between the palace and the cathedral five catafalques had been erected, to serve as resting-places for the coffin as it was transferred to different bearers. The oidores bore it from the chapel to the first station; then the cathedral chapter, the municipality, the university corporation, and the commercial representatives carried it successively, the oidores taking it from the last station into the cathedral, where it was placed in a lofty position, amid a blaze of lights. As the alféreces approached they lowered the standards, and placed them at the foot of the coffin. On the left rested Guerra's coat of arms; on the right were the cross and the guidon. After service the coffin was buried at a late hour by the high altar, on the evangel side. It was a grand and glorious casting-forth.

During the novenary each religious order came to chant masses, assisted by ecclesiastic and civil bodies. On March 7th the members of the procession marched in the same order as before to the cathedral, where the vigil was chanted, and funeral oration delivered in Latin. The following day the funeral sermon was preached by the dominican provincial.

5. Riots in Seventeenth-Century Mexico City

CHESTER LYLE GUTHRIE

When the Pilgrim Fathers were making their first settlement in America, indeed when Jamestown was still a struggling community, New Spain already possessed a world-famous metropolis, Mexico City. Time and two empires had established it as perhaps the greatest in the New World. Well-nigh a century under Spanish control, Mexico City spoke of Hernán Cortés as a figure of the dim past, and had seen the children of the conquistadors grow white-haired.

In the aftermath of conquest, social and economic problems had arisen which were both grave and troublesome. The soldiers of fortune became less and less important, while the merchant, the artisan, the farmer, and other more stable if less romantic elements gained in influence. A man without a profession or trade, or without financial resources, was finding it harder and harder to make a living. Many were forced to accept public or private charity, or else had to depend on begging and the soup of the monasteries. Furthermore, the large, conquered Indian population was still in the city and had to be absorbed into the body politic. The time had passed when the Indian problem could be thrust aside by military repression, for the conquered natives had by now attained to a certain legal status. Also, free Negroes and a multitude of racial mix-

Chester Lyle Guthrie, "Riots in Seventeenth-Century Mexico City: A Study of Social and Economic Conditions," *Greater America: Essays in Honor of Herbert Eugene Bolton* (Berkeley: University of California Press, 1945), pp. 243–258, *passim*. Reprinted by permission of the University of California Press.

tures, each requiring a place in society, had arisen. Mestizos, mulattoes, *castizos, lobos, chinos, zambos,* to mention only a few of the blood combinations, had to be fitted into the social scale. Riots and unrest followed almost as a natural consequence from such numerous and varied social and economic stresses. The following brief discussion of the events surrounding the two major riots of the century may assist the reader to an understanding and evaluation of the underlying causes of the discontent.

The first outbreak occurred on January 15, 1624. On that day the people emerged from early morning Mass in the great cathedral of Mexico with one of the most dreaded edicts ever issued in New Spain ringing in their ears. The pronouncement had been to the effect that all churches would be closed under an order of *cessatio a divinis.* Furthermore, the viceroy, at that time the haughty and unpopular Diego Carrillo de Mendoza y Pimentel, Marqués de Gelves, had been called a heretic and excommunicated. Soon the populace were giving voice to their disapproval of the administration, which they held responsible for the course of events. Scattered at first, then from all sides, came shouts of "Long live the Church!" "Long live the Faith!" "Death to bad government!" "Death to this excommunicated heretic!"

At this unfortunate moment the viceroy's secretary, Cristóbal Osorio, drove into the square in an open carriage. He was recognized, and some urchins selling vegetables in the market raised the shout of "Heretic!" "Heretic!" Osorio ordered a halt and called to his retainers to discipline the youthful hecklers. It was a mistake. In self-defense the boys pelted the servants with stones and even directed some at the secretary himself. Soon other boys joined in hurling missiles, and before long they were assisted by their elders. Indians, mulattoes, mestizoes, and Negroes made up the mass of the first attackers. Even some poor whites joined the mob. Under such a barrage, Osorio had to make the best escape possible; there was not time then to uphold dignity and rank. Consequently, he shouted to the driver to whip the horses to a run, and the carriage thundered into the courtyard of the viceregal palace just ahead of a cloud of flying stones and debris. In haste the guards forced shut the ponderous doors in the face of the raging people.

From that moment the fury of the mob was turned against the palace. With each hour the position of the defenders grew more and more precarious, for the unrelenting pressure of thousands of milling, shouting rioters was more than the civil and military power of Mexico City could withstand. In vain did the viceroy make promise after promise to the people; in vain revoked, even, the edict which had brought about his excommunication. Vainly also did the Inquisition, the great councils, and even the influential citizens strive to calm the rioters. Not until hope of saving the palace was gone did the supporters of the viceroy, especially the audiencia, the greatest of the governing councils, withdraw its aid. By five o'clock in the evening the rioters had burned and sacked the palace. Viceroy Gelves escaped with his life only by the device of putting on servant's clothing and mingling with the crowd, shouting with the rest, "Death to this heretic viceroy!"

A series of events had contributed to this serious outbreak in Mexico City. In the first place, a critical food shortage had caused a virtual famine. Maize, which supplied the principal sustenance of most of the population, had more than quadrupled in price. The resulting misery was very great. And prices of other foodstuffs rose, thus adding to the discontent.

Perhaps second to hunger as a cause of unrest was the viceroy's unfortunate inability to make himself acceptable. By means of impolitic moves he had alienated almost every group in the society of the capital. To the official class he was an unjust and insulting taskmaster, whose arbitrary and retroactive punishments seemed quite out of proportion to the crimes for which they were inflicted. To the rich he was a dangerous reformer; to the poor, an implacable tax collector, law enforcer, and general meddler. Even in executing his reforms he allowed himself to be outmaneuvered and placed in the false position of favoring monopoly and oppression, while other men and institutions, particularly the Church, were credited with any betterments achieved.

Especially violent, however, were the viceroy's quarrels with the Church. After many disagreements, Gelves and the strong-minded archbishop, then a certain Juan Pérez de la Serna, clashed over the use of churches as asylums for fugitives from justice. Neither the archbishop nor the viceroy would give way in the matter. In the end, both parties resorted to their most potent weapons. The viceroy obtained a decree exiling the archbishop, and the archbishop in turn placed the city under an interdict and excommunicated the viceroy. Each made every effort to see his sentence imposed, with the result that the restless population improved its opportunity to riot against the government.

Thus the first riot of the century passed in violence and bloodshed, and for many years there were no great hostile outbreaks to disturb the administrative calm of the city, though other rumblings of discontent were heard from time to time. The danger of mob violence soon gave little concern to the minds of the representatives of the sovereigns of Spain. The old fundamental complaints against the colonial order remained, however, and in less than two generations the greatest riot of the century occurred in Mexico City.

Nature as well as society seemed to conspire to bring misery upon the people of the capital of New Spain. The summer of 1691 was an unusually wet season. Lake Texcoco, from which Mexico City was separated only by a dike and with which it was connected by canals, was changed from a dry, dusty plain into a large body of water. Roads became impassable; supplies ran low; pastures were flooded; and many of the adobe walls of the poorer houses melted, leaving the inhabitants wet, shivering, and hungry. To add to the general distress, the following winter was unusually severe, with snow blanketing the surrounding hills and making it impossible to bring supplies into the city. As a result of the inclement weather, the summer crops in the vicinity of Mexico City were so weakened and rotted that they fell victim to a blight, called by the Indians *chahuistle*. The winter and spring crops were failures, also. Prices began rising, as in 1624.

Under such conditions, the public granary, or *alhóndiga*, was called upon in greater and greater measure to allay the distress. At first it was an agency for stabilizing prices, but soon it became one of the most important sources of food supply. From dispensing a normal amount of six to eight hundred *fanegas* of grain a day (a *fanega* being about one and six-tenths bushels), the *alhóndiga* was soon called upon to dole out as much as six thousand *fanegas* a day. Under pressure, the government strove frantically to keep enough grain on hand, both by public means and through private initiative, but to little avail.

As famine increased, the lower class became more and more restless and intractable. Not only was food scarce, but more and more the wheat-eating, Spanish-descended part of the population was forced to turn to maize as the principal stay of its diet. This, as it

happened, provided a new employment for the Indians since maize
was most generally eaten by them in the form of tortillas, and they
were the ones who best knew how to make that substitute for
wheaten bread; and, impressed by their new importance, they became difficult to control. At the *alhóndiga* there was bedlam. Each
Indian woman strove to obtain as much maize as possible before the
supply should run short, in order to be the first to get her wares to
market. Much of the newly found opulence, so far as the men were
concerned, went for pulque, which happened to be plentiful that
season. Soon in the smoke-filled, dimly lighted *pulquerías,* as the
native liquor shops were called, Indians were giving vent both to
their old irritations and to their new feeling of superiority. Did not
the laws of the land state, said they, that the natives should be
served first at the *alhóndiga?* Certainly the Spaniards had grown
afraid of the noble Aztecs. Encouraging these beliefs were the mestizos, the mulattoes, and the other malcontents. As a result, to the
increasing restlessness in the city, growing out of the misery and discontent of all the lower class, was further added a combative spirit
on the part of what was usually the most humble of the social elements in Mexico City, the once-conquered Indian.

As the year 1692 progressed, the scarcity of food became greater
and greater. The government of the viceroy looked on all sides for
supplies, in a desperate effort to curb the growing discontent. Only
by keeping the city quiet until the new harvest should be reaped
could the crisis be passed peacefully. The attempt was a failure.
An adequate food supply was nowhere to be found.

Early in the afternoon of June 6, word was given out that the
maize had been exhausted, and in the ensuing disorder an Indian
child was suffocated. This, of course, aroused the anger of the native population. Next day, the crowd at the grain market was sullen
and quarrelsome, with the result that the viceroy appointed two of
his high-ranking officials to watch over the transactions and keep
order. All went well until the maize was once more exhausted and
the officials had finally left the market. Then the crowd again became unmanageable; and in the uproar which followed, word flew
from mouth to mouth that an Indian woman had been whipped to
death by one of the *alhóndiga's* attendants. The *alhóndiga* was
promptly deserted as the angry Indians and their supporters
marched to the palace, there to seek redress. They were turned
away by the palace guards, and consequently went to the palace of

the archbishop, where again they were refused a hearing. From there they swarmed back to the government palace, where rioting began in earnest. The Indians were soon joined by Negroes, mulattoes, mestizos, and poor whites, called *saramullos.*

Even more terrible, perhaps, than the riot of 1624 was this new uprising of the lower class. With few weapons other than sticks, stones, fire, and their bare hands, the rioters laid siege to the palace. The outbreak found the administration of the viceroy unable to protect itself. The military forces of the city had become greatly reduced in man power and efficiency during the two generations of peace following 1624, and, as chance would have it, this lack of preparedness was made even more disastrous to the administration by the fact that the crisis came on a church holiday, when many of the officers and men, including even the viceroy, were absent from the palace.

"Long live the Virgen del Rosario!" "Long live the king!" "Long live pulque!" cried the mob as they strove harder and harder to break into the palace. At the same time, and with even more zest, they howled "Death to the viceroy!" "Death to his wife!" "Death to the *corregidor!*" "Death to the Spaniards!" "Down with bad government!" To these cries they added curses of such ingenuity and expressiveness that even the Spaniards were astonished. Shouts of "Death to the Gachupines who eat up all our maize!" did not reassure the onlookers, who, afraid to oppose the mob, had gathered in the streets leading into the square. It soon seemed impossible that the palace could hold out much longer. Especially was the mob successful in setting fires. Most of the palace was blazing, and some of the other government structures, such as the buildings of the *cabildo,* or town council, in which was the *alhóndiga,* were fired. Before the rioters were halted, they had even tried to burn the palace of Pedro Cortés, Marqués del Valle, heir to the title of the famous conquistador.

The mob was diverted only by the action of the clergy and — perhaps more effectively — by the opportunity offered to the rioters for looting the rich market in the Plaza Mayor. While the Indians were trying to take the palace, many of the *saramullos,* and others of the lower class, broke into the *cajones,* as the shops in the plaza were called. First, the stores containing axes, bars, swords, and knives were ransacked for arms and tools. Then the shops with weak doors or roofs were forced open. When the Indians and those be-

sieging the palace saw what was going on, they promptly left what
they were doing and joined the plundering of the market. . . .

Among the clergy, the tardily aroused archbishop was the one
who took the initiative. He had at first paid little heed to threats of
mob action, but once violence occurred he realized the seriousness
of the situation. His first move was to call all the churchmen together
to plan a course of action, but it was not until nine o'clock in the evening that the forces he organized were ready to act. Two processions, one of Jesuits and the other of friars of Our Lady of Mercy,
bravely entered the square singing, praying, and carrying saintly
images. . . .

Although a few stopped to listen to the Jesuits and the friars, it
was one of the secular clergy who was most successful in diverting
the rioters from their purpose. The treasurer of the cathedral, Manuel de Escalante y Mendoza, accompanied by two priests and a
friar, took the Holy Sacrament and went into the plaza. The viceregal palace seemed to be beyond help so he forced his way to the
palace of the Marqués del Valle, where the Indians had started a fire
against the portals. The flames were mounting fast, but the padre
was able to persuade the rioters to desist and to put out the blaze.
Then the mob turned to the house of one of the important officials,
with the intention of burning it, and once more the treasurer prevented them. In fact, he succeeded in keeping them from starting
more fires anywhere. Other priests came to his assistance, and soon
one was preaching in the native tongue, persuading the Indians to
go home, and was heeded.

The destruction caused by this second riot was very great both in
lives and property. Undoubtedly, scores were killed and many more
were injured, though casualties were never counted since every attempt was made to keep the identity of the rioters secret from the
avenging officials. As for the material losses, they were staggering.
The great viceregal palace was so badly burned that it had to be
rebuilt. The shops in the square had been thoroughly ransacked,
and the buildings of the *cabildo* in large part demolished. In all, it
was estimated that damage amounting to some three millions of
pesos had been done.

For an understanding of the causes underlying the riots, one
must delve into the social history of the period. There were at least
three reasons for unrest in Mexico City in the seventeenth century.
First, there was great social inequality, produced by sharply marked

class distinctions which were mainly racial. Second, there was the precarious economic status of the largest part of the population, the part which in the main suffered most from the irritations and restrictions of differences in caste. Finally, administrative weaknesses offered an opportunity for major demonstrations to break out; for, as events showed, the viceregal government was unable to defend itself quickly and effectively against a determined domestic disturbance.

Three fundamental class divisions, based upon likenesses of interest and occupation, were discernible in colonial Mexico City. The first of these, the upper or ruling class, was composed of the rich and the nobility of Spanish extraction. Associated with them were the great merchants and others of the wealthy middle class, between whom and the nobility there was very little social differentiation. Even for a gentleman of noble birth, trading on a large scale was considered a satisfactory occupation. If any cleavage existed, it was between those born in Spain and those born in the New World.

Fallen from high estate, and now perhaps more properly to be considered as of the middle class, was a small, clannish group, the impoverished descendants of the conquistadors. Turbulent and haughty, they usually engaged in some trade or minor occupation. Sometimes, out of deference to the services rendered by their ancestors, the most needy of these were appointed to minor positions in the government.

Aping the nobility, but for the most part economically nearer to the masses, was the lower middle class, including the artisans and poorer shopkeepers. This group, however, was few in numbers and of little influence in the direction of the city's affairs. Instead of absorbing many of the masses, it kept its ranks closed by means of exclusive guild regulations, with the result that a large and restive lower class remained unaccommodated in the community. Consequently, the city's class struggle was essentially between the two extremes, and was emphasized by the great size of the lower class.

By far the most numerous and restless social group was this lower one. In an estimated population of a quarter million, its members represented from three to five times the total of those above them. Most of the viceroys had already been aware that their poverty, their vices, and the hopelessness of their position in the social scale might ripen them for crime and violence.

Among the more difficult to control were those outcast whites,

together with some Indians and mixed-bloods, who were called vagabonds. Petty thievery and chicanery were their stock in trade,
and any untoward disturbance would at once enlist them as rioters.

Of the non-Spanish elements which helped to form the lower
class, the one which ranked the highest in the social scale was that
composed of the mestizos, those who had a mixture of Indian and
Spanish blood. Their number was quite large. It was admitted that
they were presumptuous and almost as troublesome as the other
groups among the masses, but the officials pointed out that they
showed more promise of development than others of the racial
mixtures.

Many and diverse were the strains which included Negro blood.
The Negroes, both of mixed and of pure descent, formed a sizable
part of the population of seventeenth-century Mexico City. As a rule
they were considered untrustworthy by the rest of the citizens.

Outnumbering the mestizo and Negro elements were the Indians.
They were the ones upon whom fell the chief burden of manual
labor in colonial society. If an aqueduct had to be repaired, Indians
were promptly assigned to the job. If a load was to be moved, or
any other task of similar nature was to be performed, Indians were
always called upon. Consequently, their very low position in the
scheme of colonial life, as well as the fact that their interests,
by the same token, were so widely separated from those of the
ruling class, made them especially inclined to join subversive
movements.   . . .

For the most part, members of the lower class depended upon
wages for their livelihood. Trade and industry employed a large
number in the lesser capacities, while personal service and government projects accounted for another sizable group. Ordinarily, the
wages paid were just enough to meet the needs of the laborer.

In industry, the lower class suffered many restrictions. Although
a large proportion was employed in the trades, the rules of the
guilds were so formulated that persons of non-Spanish origin, of
which the lower class was mostly composed, could never hope to
rise higher than the unskilled, low-paid levels. Even the very poor
whites could hope for little from the guilds, for the expense of going
through the period of apprenticeship, and of paying the fees and fulfilling the requirements attendant upon examination for entrance
into one of the trades, made such a course a practical impossibility.
In fact, restrictions were so stringent that Viceroy Linares com-

plained that there was a marked lack of opportunity even for Spanish youths to enter a trade.

For those who were not absorbed into industry, domestic service, or governmental activities, there was little left to do but to peddle fruit, vegetables, flowers, grass, and similar goods in the public markets. Should this fail, only begging or crime was left.

Unemployment and partial unemployment added greatly to the problems of the wage earners. Many of the Indians, especially, worked at seasonal occupations in the country. Out of season, they spent almost their entire time in idleness; or so said Viceroy Juan de Mendoza y Luna, Marqués de Montesclaros. Furthermore, the presence of so many vagabonds of all races and mixtures in the city indicated that there was a great deal of unemployment. To Giovanni Gemelli Careri, a noted Italian observer, it seemed as if almost all the Indians were idle and therefore reduced to cheating in order to make a living. Viceroy Linares complained of the great number of idlers who lived by doing occasional odd jobs and, the rest of the time, by dishonesty. . . .

Under such circumstances a fluctuation in the price of any basic commodity, such as maize, was a matter of great importance. There were a number of times when the price of maize became very high, notably in 1624 and in 1692, the years of the two riots, when it rose to four and five times its normal figure, or about ten *reales*. In several other periods of scarcity, high prices caused unrest and demonstrations among the poor — without violence, however.

To counteract the fluctuating cost of living, the government felt obliged to give some aid to the poor. This help, together with direct charity, was one of the characteristics of colonial Mexico City. It was believed that without governmental regulation the price of the fundamental necessities would rise so high that none but the well-to-do and the rich could live comfortably, or perhaps even exist at all. Besides, charity was not only a civic duty; it was an important part of the religious life of the time. The poor, the widows, and the orphans found a place in the financial budgets of the government, institutions, and private individuals. Nevertheless, in spite of these mitigating influences, the fundamental problem of a low standard of living, barely at the subsistence level, helped to keep society unstable.

Many means of price fixing were tried. Perhaps most noteworthy was the supervision and operation of the public grain market, the

alhóndiga. For the institution the government established numerous
and complicated rules, which somewhat alleviated the general situation. The difficulty was that during the years of plenty most of the
rules and regulations would fall into disuse and the market would
be practically abandoned as a major activity of the government.
When a time of scarcity arrived, this shortsighted policy left the
alhóndiga too badly crippled to act as efficiently as it should have
done. Besides grain, almost all other commodities, such as meat,
fruit, vegetables, and bread, were carefully regulated in price, in an
attempt at fairness both to the consuming public and to business.

As the social and economic conditions of the era were basic factors in the development of movements of unrest, so in turn was the
failure of the government to provide itself with adequate forces to
suppress those outbreaks which led to rioting. When uprisings
threatened the capital, three forces of protection were available
to the viceroy: the regularly constituted police authority, the
guard of soldiers kept in Mexico City, and the citizen militia, which
was supposedly ready to answer a call to arms in case of an emer-
gency. Twice in the seventeenth century all three of these agencies
failed. . . .

There remains the question why the great tumults of the century
occurred only in the years 1624 and in 1692. Two reasons present
themselves. First, there was the difference in the degree to which
scarcity in foodstuffs was felt. In 1624 and in 1692 the suffering was
much greater, and continued over longer periods of time, than during other crises which developed in the seventeenth century. Hence
the people were driven to extremes of desperation. Second, there
was the difference in the administrative ability of the persons in authority. Several times the poor were so far aroused that many of
them went in a body to the palace, and each time obtained satisfaction quickly and with a minimum of irritation because the viceroys proved equal to the occasion. This was not true in 1624 and in
1692, when the potentially dangerous conditions in Mexico City
ended in uprisings.

The tumults achieved few permanent results, by reason of their
nature. In the first place, although the riots were exceedingly
violent, they lasted only for very short periods, thus quickly relieving
the government from pressure for reform. Second, they were spontaneous outbreaks without plan, program, or leadership, and flared
up from immediate resentment. Consequently, the riots prompted

administrative reform in the city but brought about no permanent social or economic improvement. Once quiet was restored, and there was no longer any reason for the government to be alarmed, most of the new regulations were relaxed until another period of crisis arrived. The importance of the riots, then, lies in the light which they throw upon social and economic conditions under the viceroys, and not upon the reforms which followed close upon them.

6. The Imperial City of Potosí, Boom Town Supreme

LEWIS HANKE

No city in all of the vast territory of America won for the King of Spain — save perhaps Mexico City — has had a more interesting or more important history than Potosí, located in the Viceroyalty of Peru. The colorful story of this great mountain of silver began when the Inca Emperor Huayna Capac started digging almost a century before the Spaniards arrived. He was halted — so legend has it — by a terrible noise and a mysterious voice which commanded, in the Quechua Indian language: "Take no silver from this hill. It is destined for other owners." The *conquistadores* heard no such prohibitory voice in 1545 when they were told of the rich silver ore by Indians who had accidentally discovered it, and indeed, if they had, would doubtless have considered themselves the rightful owners. They immediately began to develop Potosí, which was to become one of the most famous mines in the history of the world.

Treasure seekers flocked from Spain and many other parts of the world to this bleak and uninviting spot high up in the Andes, to exploit the silver in the *Cerro*, or sugar-loaf mountain, which rises majestically over the plateau to a height of almost 16,000 feet above sea level. The first census, taken by Viceroy Francisco de Toledo about twenty-five years after the news of the lode first burst upon the world, showed the unbelievable total of 120,000 inhabitants. By 1650 the population had risen — we are told — to 160,000, and Potosí was incomparably the largest city in South America. At a time

Lewis Hanke, *The Imperial City of Potosí: An Unwritten Chapter in the History of Spanish America* (The Hague: Martinus Nijhoff, 1956), pp. 1–42, *passim*. Reprinted by permission of the publisher.

when Virginia and the Massachusetts Bay Colony were puling infant colonies, unsure of their next harvest, Potosí had produced such quantities of silver that its very name had become so common a symbol for untold wealth that Don Quijote quoted it to Sancho Panza. *Vale un Potosí,* the Spaniards expressed it. The phrase "as rich as Potosí" became current in English literature as well, for within a generation of its discovery the astronomical quantities of silver mined there had become known to Spain's enemies and to others in far corners of the world. Potosí was soon marked on maps by the Portuguese, always the vigilant rivals of Spain, and even on the Chinese world map of Father Ricci, where it was placed in its correct position and called Mount *Pei-tu-hsi.*

The flush times of Potosí lasted for almost two centuries, and during this period the Imperial City (as it was officially designated by the Emperor Charles V) developed a wealthy and disorderly society. The vice, the piety, the crimes, the *fiestas* of these Potosinos, all were on a vast scale. In 1556, for example, eleven years after the founding of the city, the inhabitants celebrated the accession of Philip II to the throne of Spain with a party which lasted twenty-four days and cost eight million pesos. In 1577 three million pesos were spent on water works, an improvement which ushered in a period of even greater prosperity. By the end of the sixteenth century, miners in search of recreation could choose among the fourteen dance halls, the thirty-six gambling houses, and the one theater, the price of admission to which ranged from forty to fifty pesos. Later, one of the governors organized a "grandiosa fiesta," to celebrate an ecclesiastical event, which included the establishment in one plaza of a circus "with as many different kinds of animals as in Noah's Ark, as well as fountains simultaneously spouting wine, water, and the native drink *chicha.*" The seventeenth-century ecclesiastical chronicler Antonio de la Calancha declared: "In Potosí the signs of Libra and Venus predominate, and thus most of those who live there incline to be covetous, friends of music and festivities, zealous in the pursuit of riches, and somewhat given to venery." The scanty literature now available emphasizes about equally the carnal pleasures obtainable in the silver-rich mining camp, and the curious, awe-inspiring, and stupendous events of its uproarious history. Our knowledge of Potosí may be said to be still in the folklore stage.

For many years Potosí was boom town supreme and full of turbulence. Treachery, assassination, and civil war flourished as the

natural result of the gambling, the intrigues, the antagonism between Peninsular Spaniards and American born Creoles, and the
rivalries for the favor of women. Fighting became a pastime, a
recognized social activity. Even the members of the town council
came to their meetings armed with swords and pistols, and wearing
coats of mail. The Dominican friar Rodrigo de Loaysa described
the "accurséd hill of Potosí" as a sink of iniquity, but the Viceroy
García Hurtado de Mendoza declared that the mine was the *nervio
principal en aquel reino,* "the principal support of that realm."

At one time, in the early part of the seventeenth century, there
were some 700 or 800 professional gamblers in the city and 120
prostitutes, among them the redoubtable courtesan Doña Clara,
whose wealth and beauty, the chroniclers assure us, were unrivalled.
The most extravagant woman in Potosí, she was able to fill her home
with the luxuries of Europe and the Orient, for her salon was frequented by the richest miners, who competed enthusiastically for
her favors. Vagabonds abounded, and royal officials indignantly
reported that these ne'er-do-wells did nothing but dress extravagantly
and eat and drink to excess. So high were the stakes that one Juan
Fernández dared to start a revolution in 1583, by which he hoped to
make himself king of Potosí. He and his brothers planned to seize
the city and, "despite the fact that he was a married man, Fernández had selected a widow, María Alvarez, to share the throne of his
kingdom-to-be." The government learned of this plot and captured
Fernández before his revolution could erupt, but this was not the
last time that the wealth of Potosí engendered a fever of boundless
hope and all-consuming desire among the bold spirits attracted to
that cold and windy city. A thick volume could be compiled on the
plots that were hatched. One was the conspiracy led by Gonzalo
Luis de Cabrera and the *relator* of the Audiencia de La Plata named
Juan Díaz Ortiz. They caused royal officials much trouble in 1599
because they tried to smuggle in hundreds of Englishmen through
the port of Buenos Aires to help them with their plans to take over
Potosí.

When other mines were discovered, particularly after 1640, production began to slacken at Potosí. It continued to decline steadily
throughout the eighteenth century, despite frantic efforts to improve
the methods by which the silver was exploited, and at last the glory
departed. The War for Independence was a decisive influence in
the final decline of Potosí under Spanish rule. During this agitated

period the Indians practically stopped working in the mine, and it was difficult to obtain materials needed for its operation. Up to 1816 Potosí was lost and won by the opposing forces three times. After 1816 Upper Peru was wholly occupied by royalist forces despatched by the Viceroy in Lima, and continuous guerrilla warfare was the rule. . . .

The citizens of Potosí early felt the growing pains of greatness and from the earliest years demanded royal recognition of their city's value to the crown. The Emperor Charles V bestowed upon Potosí the title Imperial City, and placed upon its first coat of arms the words: "I am rich Potosí, the treasure of the world, and the envy of kings." His prudent son Philip II devised the scarcely less modest legend on the shield he sent them, which is used to the present day: "For the powerful Emperor, for the wise King, this lofty mountain of silver could conquer the whole world." Here was a slightly veiled royal hint that it took money to make the wheels of empire turn around. Besides the royal cut of one-fifth of all silver mined there was also the possibility of "gifts" or "loans" by individual Potosinos to a succession of ever necessitous kings whose coffers held too little for their needs. A number of documents in the archives attest to the fact that Potosinos did assist the crown in this way.

The Potosinos naturally expected some return for their assistance. As the old Spanish proverb has it: "You trim my whiskers and I'll do your topknot." Therefore the Villa Imperial regularly sent representatives to the court thousands of miles away to make known their desires. Potosí early became irked at the fact that the City of La Plata, some 150 miles away, held jurisdiction over it. The miners at Potosí struggled to throw off this yoke and by 1561 had gained their independence.

The *cabildos* or municipal councils in America were relatively weak creatures in the Spanish colonies, but not so the group that ran the affairs of rich Potosí. Their representatives enjoyed real bargaining power, and they presented their demands in well-executed and detailed documents. Antonio de León Pinelo, one of the most outstanding administrators, lawyers, and bibliographers of the seventeenth century, drew up briefs and petitions on behalf of Potosí. Sebastián de Sandoval y Guzmán was particularly active, and his *Pretensiones de la Villa Imperial de Potosí*, printed in excellent fashion in Madrid in 1634, was typical of a whole literature which might be labeled "Pretensiones de Potosí."

What did the miners want? A steady supply of Indians for the *mita,* mercury at a low price, and freedom from bureaucratic interference by royal officials were some of the demands; and loud and insistent complaints of the miners on these and other problems fill many volumes in the archives. They resisted the drawing off of miners to fight as soldiers in Chile or other threatened parts of the empire. They felt that the regulation of Viceroy Toledo, establishing that miners should never be imprisoned for debt or their property sold to satisfy debts, was a wise law which should never be revoked, because it assured a steady production upon which depended the economic health of Potosí and consequently a steady revenue to the crown. The Real Banco de San Carlos was designed to help the miners, too, and the history of this bank will doubtless provide a valuable chapter in the fiscal history of Potosí.

The Potosinos agitated for an exemption from the *alcabala,* or sales tax, and also urged the crown to see to it that merchants in Panama and Peru sent sufficient merchandise to the ever-thirsty markets of Potosí. Above all, the Potosinos wanted the royal share of silver mined cut down from one fifth to one tenth of production.

All these and other privileges and exemptions were clamored for by a city conscious of its power and aware of the king's constant need for funds. Sometimes these requests were granted in part and for limited periods, but the Potosinos were never completely satisfied. As late as 1783 we find the king decorating the Villa Imperial with the title of "Fidelísima" or "Most Faithful," in another royal attempt to assuage some of their feelings with fine words. The struggle between a succession of hard-pressed monarchs and Potosí was in fact a continuous seesaw, ending only with the successful revolution against Spain. . . .

The wealth of Potosí drew to this Andean mining center Indians from many parts of Peru, a forced migration movement of great proportions that had never before been seen in the land, for under Inca rule only Indians on royal business had moved along the Inca highways. Negroes were also brought to Potosí, despite the doubts concerning their usefulness in the cold, rarefied atmosphere of Potosí. Spaniards from most parts of the peninsula and from all walks of life participated in the rush to explore the mine, and it does not seem strange to learn that one of the miners was a descendant of Columbus.

Foreigners were so numerous that the crown became alarmed

at the dangers of their presence. A document dated 1581 lists the foreigners then in the city, and many other censuses of foreigners and reports on what they were doing, and whether their presence was "inconvenient" or not, were prepared by the hard-working representatives of the crown. The Inquisition documents provide information on suspected heretics and also on various Portuguese, who seem to have prospered in Potosí.

Another concern of the crown was the large number of vagabonds and ne'er-do-wells that flourished in the city. Not only did these lazy fellows not produce silver, but they might even be potentially dangerous, as a rebel group. Orders were despatched regularly for the "vagabonds that infest the city" to be punished and summarily ejected. These measures failing, the crown suggested that they be discreetly encouraged to engage in new discoveries and colonization attempts. If not killed in the frontier battles, at least they would be drawn away from Potosí and established far away, perhaps never to return!

The whole round of social life in this ebullient community has a sort of wild-west atmosphere. It was a vast melting pot, even more so than some other parts of the empire, for few white women could stand the climate; childbirth was particularly difficult because of the altitude. By 1586 enough *mestizos* or mixed bloods were present to provoke a riot, and the history of Potosí is well laced with disturbances which probably derived, in part at least, from the tremendous mixing of peoples that went on steadily. One little-known rebellion was attempted in 1599 with the help of the English.

This mixing of racial strains produced some interesting results. From time to time legal documents are found in the archives concerning the action of an individual who wished to be recognized legally as a *mestizo*, because otherwise he would be forced to work in the mines as an Indian. And at least one legal process relates to a person who stated that he was an Indian and did not want to be considered a *mestizo*.

Tailors went berserk in 1604 over an election of their guild officers and even Augustinian friars once had to be reproved by the government for resisting the law with swords. Some ecclesiastics engaged in commerce or led loose lives, the crown interested itself in sending married men back to their wives in Spain or in other parts of the empire, excess ostentation in funerals had to be reproved, bull fights held in holy years were frowned upon, Indians who had fancy merchandise forced upon them against their will protested, priests quarrelled about preferential places in processions, and the descendants of Diego Huallpa, the discoverer of the mountain of silver, claimed special rights and privileges they considered due them. The detail on the social life of Potosí is rich, copious, and unexploited. . . .

Even if all the thousands of pages of manuscripts on Potosí were to be organized and made available for study, and even if monographs were prepared on all the topics listed above, problems of interpretation would still remain.

One great pitfall to be avoided is that of exaggerating everything connected with the mine. Historians writing on Potosí have not infrequently fallen victims of the boom spirit so typical of the city itself. . . . Américo Castro reaffirms the belief in the overriding importance of American treasure in the history of Spain in Europe, and Víctor Andrés Belaunde has remarked that the entire colonial epoch in Peru might be designated as a "vast religious and political organization for the exploitation of the mines." The Cerro was the most noted of these mines and just as the Portuguese classic seventeenth-century historian Francisco Manoel de Melo referred to that "inestimable Potosí," other writers old and new, Spanish and foreigner, beat the drum on behalf of Potosí. The belief in the opulence of Peru generally began when Atahualpa in 1532 paid over to Francisco Pizarro a roomful of gold and two more of silver. And even after New Spain began in the seventeenth century to produce more silver than Peru, the Viceroy of Peru still received a higher salary than the Viceroy of New Spain, whose position was considered an inferior one. Was this due, in part at least, to the influence of Potosí and the general belief in its supposedly inexhaustible wealth? Myths about Potosí still influence the historians who study its past.

We know that Charles V and Philip II were usually hard pressed for cash, but did Potosí really provide funds for running the empire, in the splendid way it is supposed to have done? Or were the undramatic and mundane factories in the Low Countries the solid economic base for Spain, as R. H. Tawney stated years ago? If so, was not the revenue from Potosí still a fairly steady flow which permitted the Spanish crown to act more independently than if it had to rely on Spanish revenue alone?

Did Potosí also affect the economy of the other parts of Europe?

Did its cheaply produced silver cause the collapse of such mining centers as those directed by the Fuggers in Tyrol? We know, from the classic study of Earl J. Hamilton, of the influence of American treasure on prices in Spain. G. N. Clark is even more emphatic and has this to say, in commenting on the discovery of Potosí and the fact that in a few years silver was flowing to Europe in quantities that had never been imagined before: "This might in other conditions have affected silversmiths and ladies more than anyone else; but coming at this time it played a part, and perhaps a very great part, in changing the hunger for the precious metals as money into a surfeit of them. All over Europe metallic money became easier to get; in other words there was a great rise in prices, which is called 'the price revolution.' . . . Some men became suddenly rich. All those who were entitled to fixed sums, whether as rents or as taxes or dues, could buy less with these sums than before; all those who were free to demand what prices they could exact had new and rising opportunities. So, broadly speaking, the old world of landlords and peasants found it harder to carry on; the traders and bankers found it easier, and capitalism advanced."

What was the influence of Potosí in America itself? Did mining play a progressive role, as Bailey W. Diffie believes, through which "an urban civilization came into existence, a middle class was created, the buying power of the people increased . . . and in general America was able to grow"? Or did Potosí help to fasten upon the Viceroyalty of Peru a pernicious economic and social system which exacted quick profits from the mines, and kept agriculture in such a secondary place that its growth was dangerously retarded and a feudal society prolonged for centuries? If the answer is "yes" to this last question, can one escape the conclusion that some of the present desperate problems of Bolivia constitute, in part at least, a heritage from Potosí? Or, perhaps, did the mountain of silver rather help to develop a Bolivian nationality by establishing an economic, governmental, and social nucleus around which a nation could be organized, as that energetic historian of La Paz, Humberto Vásquez Machicado, has suggested? Or is it possible that each proposition contains some measure of truth? . . .

One final observation must be made which affects all the problems of interpretation raised above. Potosí was a part, albeit a particularly important and flamboyant part, of a vast empire and functioned within the structure which Spain established in America. Its history, therefore, must be written with one eye on the rest of the empire. Potosí was necessarily influenced by the legislation, policies, and foreign entanglements of Spain just as the mountain of silver exerted an influence on other parts of America and the mother country as well. The history of Potosí is a broad and complicated story, and therefore a tale which cannot be told adequately from the vantage point of the Cerro alone. If its historians are to avoid myopia, they must always remember that Potosí, although physically isolated from most of the other New World possessions of Spain, was in fact an integral part of lands governed by the crown of Spain from its capital thousands of miles away. Potosí was unusual, of course, in some ways. The rapidity of its growth, for example, sets Potosí apart from Mexico City, whose population grew rather slowly until recent years, and from Lima, which never suffered the spectacular decline that came upon Potosí in the eighteenth century.

The truly unique aspects of Potosí, however, were its size and dramatic history. Other mining centers existed in the empire and developed somewhat similar societies and sets of institutions. But Potosí came to exhibit those common characteristics of all mining societies in such a theatrical way that it became symbolic of the process that was going on everywhere. Perhaps herein lies the real justification for assigning to Potosí a long and significant chapter in the history of Spain in America. Just as the vociferous and learned Dominican Bartolomé de Las Casas, although not the only defender of the Indians, most persistently captured the imagination of his contemporaries and later generations as The Defender, so Potosí exemplified, in the gaudiest and most memorable colors, the passion for wealth that drew many Spaniards to the New World. Bernal Díaz del Castillo, the famous and articulate foot-soldier of Cortez, exhibited the remarkable combination of *Gott und Gewinn* which characterized the Spanish conquest of America when he exclaimed: "We came here to serve God, and also to get rich." As the mountain of Potosí towers above the surrounding peaks, so will this mine, once its story is adequately told, stand as the towering symbol for the spirit of all Spaniards who came to the New World to get rich.

7. St. Augustine, Outpost of Empire

JOHN J. TEPASKE

The drab social life of early eighteenth-century St. Augustine contrasted sharply with the glitter and pomp of life in the viceregal
centers of New Spain and Peru. Amusements, which gave pleasure
to the people of Mexico City and Lima, were unknown in this fringe
outpost of the Spanish Empire in America. The soldiers of the Castillo de San Marcos and their wives and children had little opportunity to enjoy plays, operas, tournaments of poetasters, bull fights,
cock fights, horse racing, parades, mock jousts, or the joyous *recibi-
miento*. Even the dubious pleasures to be obtained from the inquisitorial *auto de fe* were denied them. Floridians had to be content
with the common amusements and pleasures. St. Augustine was a
harsh, out-of-the way frontier area, where life was seldom lightened by the amenities or diversions common in the more populous
centers of the empire.

Social activities for the Floridians of the early eighteenth century
had a crude simplicity. Soldiers tippled wine, drank smuggled English rum, played cards, or cavorted with the local trollops. Wives
found their outlet in the church, in gossip, and an infrequent public
festival or dance, all of which helped to relieve the monotony of an
existence characterized by grinding poverty. Florida was not like
other areas of the Spanish Empire where social life found its focus
in the local parish or convent church. In St. Augustine, both the
secular and regular clergy were impoverished. Unable to provide
adequately even for the religious welfare of the colony, the priests
and friars found it difficult to sponsor the religious fiestas which had
become the emotional catharsis for so many of Spain's imperial subjects, from the remotest hamlet in the high Andes to the wilds of
northern Mexico. The principal holidays in the Roman Catholic
calendar, so scrupulously and riotously observed elsewhere, passed
virtually unnoticed or received only token recognition. Even Saint

John J. TePaske, "Funerals and Fiestas in Early Eighteenth-Century St. Augustine," *Florida Historical Quarterly*, XLIV, Nos. 1 and 2 (1965), pp. 97–104.
Reprinted by permission of the Florida Historical Society.

Augustine's Day, August 28, which should have been a time for feasting and gaiety, passed by year after year without a suitable celebration on the part of the people of the Florida capital.

The moribund social and cultural life in Florida had its roots in two factors — poverty and the military nature of the colony. Without productive enterprises or a self-sustaining economy, the province depended almost entirely upon outside aid for its existence. The *situado,* a yearly subsidy of specie and supplies, shipped into the colony from Mexico by way of Havana, maintained the residents. The total amount of the *situado* was approximately 100,000 pesos in 1736. The colonists might have been able to live comfortably or at least provide for their needs with such support, but they encountered many difficulties. Sometimes the subsidy was delayed by the viceroy in New Spain, who did not wish to release the goods and money for Florida; by the bishop of Puebla de Los Angeles, who provided the subsidy from his sales taxes (*alcabalas*); or by the governor of Cuba, who often took for his own the goods and specie intended for St. Augustine. Occasionally *situado* ships were seized by English or Dutch pirates, who found it easy to prey on Spanish vessels as they sailed through the narrow, dangerous Bahama Channel. Frequently, delays in Vera Cruz or Havana caused shipments of flour and corn to mold or rot and meat to spoil, putting new strains upon the colonial economy. Forced to lead virtually a hand-to-mouth existence, soldiers and their families had few extra pesos to spend on frivolous amusements. The poor soldier needed what little money he obtained to feed his family and to provide himself with a little rum to forget his hard lot and his bad luck in getting an assignment in Florida.

A second reason for the drab character of social life was the nature of this wilderness colony. Florida was purely a military outpost, untempered either by the civilian populace or by the regular or secular clergy. St. Augustine was governed by trained soldiers; residents were soldiers or the wives and children of military personnel; and shopkeepers, clergy, and civil officials catered mainly to the needs of the soldiers. Life had a military texture, and it is not surprising that Floridians did not taste the more pleasurable amenities enjoyed by those in the viceregal capitals, whose backgrounds and environment better fitted them for a variety of amusements.

In the eighteenth century there were at least a few occasions on which the colonial populace could let go, on which it could break its routine. These were celebrations of significant events in the lives of the royal house in Spain. The accession of a new king, birth of an heir, death of one of the royal family, pregnancy of the queen, a great military victory, or the marriage of one of the royal children were all occasions that demanded a suitable expression of joy or grief on the part of the king's colonial subjects. The monarch hoped, too, that his subjects in the New World would reinforce their expressions of loyalty with offerings of money as a tangible symbol of their love and respect.

In St. Augustine two events especially stirred the Floridians to a show of pomp and panoply. These were memorial funeral rites for a deceased monarch and the celebrations on the accession of a new king. The governor bore the responsibility for commemorating these occasions in the proper fashion, and it was he who insured that his colonists made the appropriate demonstrations of loyalty to the monarch. He was always careful to give official recognition in his correspondence to other significant events in the life of the royal family, such as the marriage of a prince or princess or the pregnancy of the queen, but formal celebrations occurred only upon the death or accession of the monarch.

Despite their somber character, funerals brought a change of pace to the Florida colony. Although hardly in the tradition of an Irish wake, burial rites forced a variation in the tempo of life in St. Augustine and helped to break the terrible monotony. For funerals the governor set aside two days to celebrate the obsequies for a monarch and one day for the death of one of the royal family. The governor also prescribed the conduct of the residents of the town for the mourning period. Houses and public buildings in St. Augustine were draped with black crepe and everyone wore appropriate mourning dress. Women donned black gowns and head dresses. Soldiers and civil officials wore dress uniforms or their best clothes, suitably adorned with black symbols of mourning. Flags flew at half mast. On each day of the formal ceremonies the sacristan tolled the bells of the parish church continuously from five in the morning until ten in the evening. Both the curate of the parish church and the guardian of the convent recited a funeral Mass for the deceased, burning votive candles at their respective altars. The governor and the important civil and military leaders marched together to the parish church for the service, where they gave funeral orations, eulogizing the king or the deceased person of the royal family.

During the first half of the eighteenth century the most lavish memorial services in Florida were celebrated for the death of three monarchs. The best known are the rites on March 28, 1702, commemorating the death of Charles II in 1700; on February 9 and 10, 1747, for the death of Philip V which occurred the year before; and, on March 27, 1760, for the passing of Ferdinand VI in 1759. Generally the death of a royal personage received little notice in St. Augustine. The governor and his soldiers were too preoccupied with other more immediate tasks, and there was little time, energy, or money to devote to a eulogy of a Spanish prince or princess three thousand miles away. While the people may have sympathized with the king's grief, most of St. Augustine's residents in the early eighteenth century were Creoles with little attachment either to the mother country or to the royal house, outside the king himself. Their world was narrow, their outlook limited, and their pocketbooks empty. While the death caused little consternation, the funeral services were highly significant.

Like obsequies in the Middle Ages, funeral rites in Florida for a dead monarch assumed the character of a spectacle. There was a tendency both to exaggerate expressions of sorrow and to formalize the emotions. This might be explained in two ways: the funeral was both an honest expression of grief and an emotional outlet. Johan Huizinga has pointed out in his study of the Middle Ages that, "The manifestations of sorrow at the death of a prince, if at times purposely exaggerated, undoubtedly often enfolded a deep and unfeigned grief. The general instability of the soul, the extreme horror of death, the fervour of family attachment and loyalty, all contributed to make the decease of a king or a prince an afflicting event." He also points out that "the nobler the deceased the more heroic will be the mourning." The Floridians demonstrated much of the medieval tendency toward exaggeration, but this was only part of it. The obsequies, eulogies, mournful processions, tolling of bells, crepe-bedecked buildings, and black-clad spectators all helped to relieve the colonist's humdrum existence and to furnish them with an emotional outlet.

In sharp contrast to the somber atmosphere pervading royal funeral rites, public festivals were joyous events in St. Augustine. Although no more frequent than funeral obsequies, the fiestas occurring upon the accession of a new monarch or on the occasion of a royal wedding were eagerly anticipated by the residents of St.

Augustine. These celebrations were times of approved license in which they could feast freely on the food provided by the governor and drink deeply of his liquor. If they were fortunate enough to have some enterprising impresario to put together a drama, they enjoyed a play — extremely amateurish, to be sure — but a theatrical, nonetheless. They enjoyed the music of the trumpeters, drummers, and pipers of the presidio, who gladly turned their talents away from martial music and joined guitarists of the town to play for dancing and singing. Candles lighted St. Augustine's narrow streets, doorways, and the windows of her houses and put the town in a festive mood. Church and convent bells were rung joyously in contrast to the sonorous tolling on funeral days. Soldiers in dress uniforms, civil officials in their best clothes, and women in their most elegant finery promenaded along the gaily decorated streets and attended Mass at the parish or convent church.

To honor a new monarch's assumption of the throne, formal ceremonies usually preceded informal celebrations in the colonies. The governor opened the formal rites with an official proclamation, stating that the new king had come to the throne, and followed this with a short eulogy. The residents then gave their own voluble demonstration of love and loyalty. On January 7, 1702, for example, His Majesty's Florida subjects assembled in St. Augustine's public square to hear Governor Joseph de Zúñiga y Cerda honor the newly crowned Philip V. After his speech extolling the virtues of the new Bourbon monarch, soldiers and residents shouted their tribute to Philip, and cries of *"Castilla Florida, Castilla Florida, por el rey católico, Don Felipe Quinto"* rang out from those standing along one side of the square. Those on the other side joyously replied, *"Viva, viva, viva."* Three times the enthusiastic crowd repeated these cries. At the close of the formal ceremony, the governor announced that he was freeing prisoners from the St. Augustine jail in honor of the happy occasion.

The informal celebration then followed. There were chocolates and sweetmeats to delight the children, and barrels of rum and wine to please the adults, and then there was dancing. Festivities continued throughout the afternoon, and often it was early morning before the revelers, exhausted from feasting and carousing, returned to their homes and beds. One of the *fiesta's* unsavory features was a request for donations for a royal gift, and while rum and wine generally loosened the pursestrings and made for more cheerful givers, unfortunately for the king, the soldiers of Florida had little to offer.

Perhaps the most festive occasion in Florida during the first half of the eighteenth century occurred in the spring of 1747 during the tenure of Governor Manuel de Montiano, when a gala festival was held honoring the accession of Ferdinand VI to the throne of Spain the year before. Having held the obsequies for Philip V in February, the governor declared April 30 and May 1 as the time to honor the newly crowned king. The first morning soldiers of the Castillo de San Marcos raised the banner of the new monarch high atop the fort and the town. In the plaza on a stage constructed especially for the festival, the officials of St. Augustine including Treasurer Juan Esteban de Peña, proclaimed their great love and devotion for Ferdinand VI and solicited donations from the crowd. Afterwards, the citizens dispersed to spend the rest of the day in their own private merry making.

The following morning, the entire town attended a high Mass at the Church of San Francisco and heard another panegyric for the king delivered by the parish priest. After Mass, Governor Montiano announced in accordance with custom that he was pardoning several criminals held in the St. Augustine jail. After the formal ceremonies, the populace turned to the public festivities. For the informal celebrations there was some class distinction. Montiano entertained the principal military, civil, and religious officials, and a "few notable residents" at a resplendent banquet in his residence. The rank-and-file, not important or fortunate enough to enjoy the governor's well-laden table or fine wines and brandy, feasted on a liberal supply of free food and imbibed a prodigious amount of free liquor in the public square and in the surrounding streets of the town. As they celebrated, the residents shouted continually, "Long live our king, Ferdinand VI." Plays, masquerades, and dancing on the newly constructed stage entertained the residents throughout the afternoon and gave local people a chance to display their talents. Improvised horse races satisfied those with gambling blood.

Montiano also arranged a bull fight for the afternoon of May 1. Using all his ingenuity, the governor ordered six bulls from an English cattle raiser in Georgia. (One can only speculate on Montiano's fervent hope that the *toros* be of the same quality as the brave bulls of Jerez in southern Spain.) As it turned out the Englishman could only furnish five animals and while they were being put into fighting trim, three wandered off and could not be found anywhere on the appointed day of the spectacle. Left with only two bulls whose fighting prowess was suspect, Montiano called off the *corrida,* which disappointed an eager crowd and several erstwhile matadors.

The liquor continued to flow far into the night, and some of the soldiers, emboldened by the heady draughts, left the public square to intrude on the governor's private, more sedate gathering. Entering the courtyard of the governor's residence, the soldiers began shouting loudly to get Montiano's attention. When he appeared, they pointed out boisterously that no festival in Havana had ever compared with the one now taking place in St. Augustine. Admitting their discontent with conditions in Florida and their own penchant for complaint about the poverty and isolation of the colony, they now saw the advantages of service in this rough, frontier province. Montiano listened politely, and then urged them to leave, personally accompanying them to the door of the courtyard where they finally made a noisy exit. Later, the governor wrote that he was proud of the loyalty of his men, despite the fact that an excess of drink may have clouded their judgment.

Fiestas and celebrations enlivened the colony, adding zest and color to its otherwise drab existence. Festivities were the high point of social life in early eighteenth-century St. Augustine and were eagerly anticipated by the residents. But these events occurred all too seldom. The accession of Philip V, Ferdinand VI, and Charles III were times for rejoicing, but they took place only three times in sixty years, an average of once every twenty years. It is no wonder that they took on the aspects of a bacchanalian revelry. The fact that they occurred so infrequently, however, is testimony to the nature of the colony. It was a struggling, military outpost on the fringe of empire with few of the amenities of civilization.

C. The Texture of Urban Life: Brazil

8. The Cities of Colonial Brazil

JOSÉ ARTHUR RIOS

A struggle between city and country has characterized the history of cities, whether in medieval Europe or Brazil. In Brazil, the superficiality of the process, its relatively recent character, and the aspects under which it occurs show that the struggle has not reached a decisive phase. An analysis of this process will better explain present tendencies.

In the period of discovery, Portugal was going through a phase of urban development that was a serious threat to its economy. Though scanty and unreliable, the statistics that we possess seem to indicate an urban concentration that was entirely disproportionate to the size of the kingdom and to the agrarian interests that dominated its economy. Scholars are unanimous in accepting as a cause of this phenomenon the vicious regime of rural property, hampered by servitudes and privileges, persecuted by the royal treasury, and monopolized by a land-hungry nobility. This helped to create in the soul of the countryman a hatred for the soil — which we shall find repeated in overseas possessions — aggravated now by the vision of easy wealth in the newly discovered lands. Maps show us the completely medieval outline of this fifteenth-century Lisbon, with its acropolis crowned by the fortress, its church, its Jewish or Moorish quarters, the walls over which the city had already spilled, the narrow and poorly aligned streets. This typical picture of the medieval city, which was infiltrated with Moorish elements and had been transformed into one of the great emporiums of European

José Arthur Rios, "The Cities of Brazil," *Brazil: Portrait of Half a Continent,* T. Lynn Smith and Alexander Marchant, eds. (New York: The Dryden Press, 1951), pp. 188–203, *passim.* Reprinted by permission of T. Lynn Smith and John Saunders.

commerce and into one of the first really cosmopolitan centers in the history of the West, was repeated in many American copies. It was this picture that the colonists took to Brazil and reproduced here, adapting it to the new environment.

Until almost the middle of the sixteenth century, then, Brazil had no human groupings that would in any way deserve the name of towns. Factories flourished, however, as provisional counting-houses for barter with the Indians and for the cutting of the dyewood that gave the country its name. They consisted of rude buildings surrounded by stockades, with a shed for the shelter of the goods, and at times also a little cleared land for the food of the factor. In the more active factories it is possible that houses of wattle and daub were built in order to shelter the few dwellers.   . . .

The factories were a transitory form of colonization. In the measure that the "mirage of India" faded, the crown began to turn more toward the colonization of Brazil, where the French also had begun to build factories. The new policy of the crown was characterized by the voyage of Martim Afonso de Souza in 1530, which looked toward the expulsion of the pirates and the initiation of colonization.   . . .

The voyage of Martim Afonso represented a transition. He was still on Brazilian soil when he received news of the division of the territory into hereditary captaincies. The new regime sought to intensify the peopling of the land by handing it over to private persons who would have feudal privileges and, at the same time, would achieve a sort of capitalism, a typical combination of an epoch of economic transition. The regime of the *donatários* dotted the Brazilian coast with settlements similar to those that we have already described.   . . .

Many of these settlements founded by the *donatários* never blossomed into cities. Of all the captaincies, only Pernambuco and São Vicente withstood Indian attack. The Crown then resolved to intervene directly in colonization by itself taking the initiative. From this the first Brazilian city arose.

The *regimento* of Tomé de Souza, the first governor general, is singularly clear and precise on this point. The king ordered him expressly "to make a fortress and strong settlement in a place fit to give favor and aid to the other settlements and to administer justice and to provide the things required by my service and the affairs of my treasury and the good of the region." For the first time, the interference of the crown went to the point of designating the site of the city — Bahia de Todos os Santos. It even went into details concerning the need for good air, abundant water, and a port of good depth, assigning to it a *termo* of six leagues.   . . .

The *regimento* of Tomé de Souza, which Varnhagen considered a monument of administration, is also a singularly explicit document concerning the features of Portuguese colonization in Brazil. These were: defense, exploration of the land, conversion of the heathen. Defense was expressed by the fort. The vital importance of taxation to the crown was expressed by the custom house. And the conversion of the heathen — "because the principal thing that moved me to command the settlement of the said lands of Brazil was in order that its people would be converted to our holy Catholic faith" — was attended to by the sending of the first Jesuits and the building of the mud-walled churches.   . . .

The "city" of Salvador da Bahia was no more than a modest village. Founded in May, 1549, it had about a hundred houses in August. Two years later, the *provedor,* compelled to use a certain realism in language by the very necessity of assessing the king's taxes in hard cash, complained to him that the city continued to be "very empty of houses as of people, granted that some are being made every day . . . the people wish to God that more will come. . . ." It seems that, acceding to the pleas of the *provedor,* God wished more people to come. The very change in the economy, from brazilwood to sugar cane, requiring mills, slaves, and cattle, increased this growth. Fifty years later, Bahia possessed three fortresses, the Cathedral, and four monasteries of different orders. And Frei Vicente do Salvador exclaimed that, if enemies invaded Portugal, the king would not find a better land than this in which to shelter. This proved to be prophetic.

In 1553, Nóbrega and the other Jesuits journeyed to São Vicente and, climbing onto the plateau, founded the college of Piratininga in the vicinity of Santo André da Borda do Campo. The two settlements, regarding each other with distrust, offered the first example of competing nuclei, one of which succeeded in predominating. This was a conflict between old cities and new cities repeated many times in Brazilian history. The Jesuits lived in Piratininga with the Indians whom they catechized and taught religious offices. In Santo André lived *mamelucos* and adventurers who wished to enslave the Indians.

Around the humble *colégio* of logs and mud, covered with straw, where were the rude quarters, school, infirmary, dormitory, refectory, and storehouses, the Indian huts were grouped. On January 25, 1555, Nóbrega said mass in the house that was to take the name of São Paulo and which came to be one of the greatest industrial centers of South America. São Paulo absorbed Santo André. Impelled by motives of safety, perhaps because they sought the religious help and medical science of the Jesuits, the *mamelucos* abandoned their settlement and went to the native village, in the shadow of the college. In 1560 the municipal life of São Paulo as a *município* began and lasted until 1711, when Dom João V granted it the rights of a city. . . .

Meanwhile, in Guanabara Bay a decisive battle was raging between Portuguese and French for possession of the new land. In 1555, French Huguenots, commanded by Villegaignon, had established themselves there on a little island where they built a stone fortress. After successive combats, the Portuguese, aided by allied Indians, succeeded in expelling them from their redoubt and, to consolidate the occupation of the land, transformed the military camp built at the foot of the Sugar Loaf into a city. Thus the village of São Sebastião do Rio de Janeiro was founded on March 1, 1565. Full of Indian allies, the village was completely *mameluco*, with Indian huts and adobe houses roofed with tile, an architectural mixture reflecting the mixture of bloods. In 1567, for strategic reasons, it was decided to move the city to a nearby hill, which came to be called Morro do Castello (Castle Hill). In the expectation of new attacks the city was surrounded by walls and forts. But at once it was ennobled by a church, the council house, the jail, warehouses and custom house — buildings already of two stories, expressing the importance of their functions in colonial society. Still more; they were built of stone and mortar. "Of stone and mortar" is still an expression in our language to express the guarantee of a promise. The houses went on multiplying and the two-storied ones increased, until the hill became too small and the houses went running downhill, looking for flat land or, on the other side, seeking the sea that brought goods, new ideas, wealth. The attraction of the beach below was the only thing that would make the inhabitants leave the hill, because the flat land, down below, was cut across by lagoons and swamps. Rio de Janeiro was built on filled land in an incessant battle against the swamp and its derivatives, miasmas and fevers. Already in the sixteenth century, however, there were important buildings of stone and mortar on the flat country by the sea.

These, then, were the principal nuclei of settlement at the end of the sixteenth century: Olinda, Bahia, Rio de Janeiro, and São Paulo. The others were insignificant settlements crowded around a fort or a church. These nuclei, through the centralizing rôle that they played in their respective regions, by the functions that accumulated around them, and because they served as bases for the later expansion of settlement, had greater importance. It should not be thought, however, that population was concentrated in these towns. However great their importance might be, the population was scanty and without prestige in the social scale, if we except the few functionaries of the Crown or the Church. The rôle of the city was marginal, dependent on the rural environment. Social control was in the hands of the powerful families, owning vast *sesmarias,* lands and slaves, and possessing prestige. The city was only an entrepôt where they went to get what they needed, the little that their *engenhos* did not produce. Or it played the rôle of outlet through which agricultural products went forth. It did not have a nucleus of consumers, an extensive use of money, or a bourgeoisie in the colonial period. Only tardily did these factors arise, and even then their action did not extend itself uniformly to the whole national territory.   . . .

The latifundia crushed the city. The latifundia were antiurban. They not only looked at the city with superiority but sought to restrict it by all means, including hunger, as, for example, by preventing the planting of food crops. In Pernambuco one of the principal complaints of the *senhores de engenho* against the Dutch was that they were forced to plant *mandioca.* The principal *câmaras* were controlled by the rural clans and reflected their interests. Only occasionally did they represent the voice of the oppressed urban classes. One of the best examples of this conflict between rural lords and the inhabitants of towns was in Campos, in the then Captaincy of Rio de Janeiro, where the landowners, in a century-long armed struggle, attempted to prevent the settlers from setting up the *pelourinho* in the settlement. And today, in the Brazilian West, Nelson Werneck Sodré discovers the same phenomenon: large estates suffocating the urban nucleus.

In the seventeenth century, however, Brazil undertook a short-lived experiment of artificial urban growth fostered by invasion and conquest. Though of brief duration, it is no less interesting in the eyes of the sociologist. It was the experiment of Dutch Recife. Writing in 1587, the chronicler Gabriel Soares described the population as follows: "In this place live some fishermen and officials of Ribeira, and there are some storehouses in which the merchants protect sugar and other wares." These words clearly indicate a modest shipping place for the sugar produced in Olinda and the surrounding mills. This is also the impression gained from examination of a contemporary map. Olinda bulks large with its six churches, the bell towers of which emerge from the crowded houses. In the place where Recife was being built, a few houses can barely be distinguished, and perhaps a chapel. The activity of the port, however, concentrated the inhabitants and increased the number of houses, warehouses, shops, and inns. Forts were built to protect the loading of ships against sudden attacks by pirates. Thus, at least, Frei Vicente do Salvador describes it in 1627, for he considers it "the most renowned and frequented by ships of all the other ports of Brazil."

Nothing of this, however, allows us to foresee the development that Recife was to have under the Dutch domination. The Dutch seem not to have liked Olinda. Its strategic advantages did not interest them. In 1631, they hastened to burn it and concentrated themselves in Recife. Josué de Castro explains this fact by the familiarity of the Recife landscape in the eyes of the Dutch because it presented urban problems identical with those that they had already solved in their native land: the same flat land, with arms of the sea, cut by canals, turned into lakes by the floods of the river. Recife had to shelter not only the invaders but also the population from the two thousand houses of Olinda. The process of filling land commenced immediately. The city extended itself in the direction of the island of Antônio Vaz. This did not suffice, and the houses had to take on height, with the first two-storied structures appearing. The counselor Johan Ghiselin, who had already been in Brazil, could not restrain his admiration, on returning with Nassau in 1637: "I find here in Recife, since my departure, an extraordinary change in the houses of the merchants, in the businesses and construction that are begun daily in great numbers, and as fine as in the fatherland, so that it is difficult to find room to lodge us and much less to build on, the best points already being taken; some Portuguese already live here." . . .

In all this, however, we must not omit a most important cultural factor: the clear-cut type of urban colonization of the Dutch. Indeed, Holland never sent agriculturists to Brazil. After the soldiers conquered the land, only bureaucrats and merchants came. The soldiers themselves were transformed into employees, merchants, innkeepers. In a short time, a concentration of 7,000 persons on a very straitened isthmus created typically urban problems of lodging, hygiene, supply, and safety. Dutch, Germans, Norwegians, and Scots mingled in its streets with the native population of Portuguese, *mestiços*, Negro slaves, and Indians. The Jews, in a considerable number, built a synagogue. The Protestants accommodated themselves in the former Catholic churches. Entire families, with women and children, gave great stability to the colonization. There was an evident preoccupation with public works. The market was built, a fire service was organized, the accumulation of trash was prohibited in the sand-covered streets. The city had its own administration. The showing of comedies and satires to amuse this population was not forgotten. An ecological diversification, foreign to the other Brazilian cities of the period, appeared in Dutch Recife. What we know of city taxes leads us to believe that there were fine streets and squares. The price of houses, as well as of rents, went up considerably. There arose, for the first time in Brazil, a bourgeoisie composed of merchants, capitalists, houseowners, slaveowners, artisans, and functionaries of the West Indies Company. . . .

In the urban evolution of Dutch Recife, the arrival of Maurice of Nassau in 1637 marked an epoch. Nassau had the city of Mauricia planned and built on the island of Antônio Vaz to serve him as a residence and also to shelter the overflow of the population of Recife. This plan included streets laid out regularly, bridges and dikes, sanitation measures, and even tree-filled parks. Thus it was the transplantation of a baroque city to the tropics. In the project for Mauritzstaadt, Dutch urbanistic genius did not betray its European traditions. Nassau built two palaces; one called Freiburg, where the influence of the Italian Renaissance may be noted, and the other called Boa Vista, in which Portuguese and Dutch architecture were blended. For the park he brought collections of animals, planted it with coco palms, lemon trees, oranges, and mangoes. He transformed it into a zoological garden, a botanical nursery, and, at the same time, into a recreational center to which families came to lunch *sur l'herbe*. . . .

Because of all this, the failure of the Dutch urban experiment is even more interesting. It had no immediate successors in Brazil. The discontinuity of the process shows its artificiality. What happened with the Dutch colony was the predominance of commercial interests and urban occupations. This urbanization was unbalanced. Recife was a temporary urban graft on a stem of latifundia and monoculture. Hence the hunger crisis that it suffered for want of food crops. Nassau saw the problem and attempted to settle it but without success. Dutch Recife had no base in the land and never succeeded in allying itself with the classes of rural proprietors. This was the principal reason for its fall. There are some who consider the Portuguese restoration as a cane-field revolution, a class struggle, with the *senhores de engenhos* expelling their bourgeois creditors. Recife was too early and it did not find ground on which to grow. The deviation into urbanism was corrected and Brazilian civilization reintegrated itself in its rural destiny.

In the meantime, the same calm life of the first century was prolonged in other types of towns that followed the oscillations of economic cycles, with these in their turn dictated by international commerce. Thus, we had cities of sugar, cotton, tobacco, and, later, coffee. When the international market shifted, the cultures died and the cities also died. Brazil is full of these dead cities — houses in ruins, silent bell towers, streets overgrown with grass. They declined with the same rapidity with which they had grown.

We also had aborted types of cities — types that went in new directions counter to the rhythm of the latifundiary and patriarchal economy, but that did not live long enough to extend it to a broader reach of territory. The Negro city of Palmares is an example. In that redoubt of slaves that had fled from the *fazendas* an organization developed on a socialistic base in which the product of collective labor was gathered into a common storehouse. The Negro Troy was, however, razed by an army commanded by *bandeirantes* from São Paulo. These were the same men who annihilated another form of urban agglomeration that had developed in the south of the country: the Jesuit reductions. It is true that other religious orders had set up throughout Brazil the same type of Indian villages. Franciscans, Dominicans, and Salesians even today in Mato Grosso and Amazônia are performing the same work of catechism by means of these reductions. All followed a single type: before the church a large rectangular square was laid out and, on each side of this, the huts of the Indians were built. Thus the Indians could be watched with ease and rapidly brought together. Many of the Brazilian cities of today originated from these former reductions.

On the other hand, the need for defense continued to strew forts along the coast and on the banks of rivers. They spread to the Amazon, afterward to the West and South, in the region threatened by the incursions of the Spanish. Belém and Manaus were, in the beginning, fortresses. Numerous cities of the South were born from military encampments produced by the long struggle with Spain.

The discovery of the mines, at the end of the seventeenth century, caused a great dislocation of the population. Until then, the penetration had occurred slowly, following the lines of least resistance, along rivers, and in the trails of wandering cattle. Now, it gave a great leap that carried settlement into the heart of the country. In their search for slaves and precious metals, the *bandeiras* from São Paulo left stopping places that became villages, towns, and cities. According to the old orientation given by the Crown, which Martim Afonso and Tomé de Souza had obeyed, instructions in 1765 ordered towns set up in the Indian villages in order that "all the vagabonds, those who lived apart, and those who live on nomadic farms be congregated in civil settlements." In these *bandeirante* cities, where the first buildings were the council house, jail, chapel, and the corral, the human torrent poured out in search of the new things, stopped and desisted, or recoiled, defeated by the jungle or the Indians. The first finds of gold in the alluvium of the rivers of Minas Gerais needed only the simple pan. In this phase of individual and nomadic mining, the adventurers founded villages that did not take root in the soil. The discovery of veins of ore, however, required greater stability and created an urban civilization.

Those fabulous mining cities then arose that today surprise us as if they had forgotten the passage of time — cities that achieved the definitive acclimation of the baroque to the Brazilian countryside. Delicately worked churches, fountains, and statues of saints and prophets flourished. The abundance of wealth created luxury and the arts, fashion, and even etiquette. A literary school arose and with it the first movements toward autonomy. The turbulent miners made a considerable police force necessary. The weight of authority on intelligent men and sensitive minds caused such men as Felipe dos Santos and the participants in the Conspiracy of Minas to resist.

To all this pomp was opposed the misery of the countryside. The forests were devastated to serve as fuel; nothing was planted, nor were cattle raised. At first, the lack of foresight of the miners, who paid no attention to the support of the towns, created crises of hunger. Little by little, supply became normal with cattle brought from other captaincies. Trains of burros and mules brought salt, food, flour, and took away loads of precious metals, coffee, rum and sugar. The stops on the roads, simple huts covered with thatch, were nuclei of cities, as were the famous *registros,* inevitable in the descriptions of travelers in the eighteenth and nineteenth centuries, where the trains were examined to see if they carried precious metals and stones. The number of shops and inns increased by the side of the roads, true purgatories for the travelers who spent the night in them. Even contraband, creating clandestine roads, created new nuclei. These cities proved less ephemeral than those resulting from mining, only because of the continuity of the traffic that created them. With the exhaustion of the mines, the population took up agriculture and stock raising. The cities of gold and diamonds were in their death struggle, becoming dead cities or museum cities in the midst of a devastated countryside.

The marginal character of cities continued during the colonial period. Power remained in the hands of those who possessed the slaves and the land, which were the productive forces of the country. Against them, however, during the eighteenth century, a very marked reaction began, which started with groups interested in the weakening of the *senhores de engenho,* the *fazendeiros,* the landowners. The Portuguese State was one of these groups, and the others were the new social classes that gathered in the cities — a mere outline of a bourgeoisie, made up of artisans, merchants, moneylenders, shopkeepers. This silent conflict at times broke out in armed struggle. The War of the Mascates, for example, as interpreted by Gilberto Freyre, was a collision between the townsmen of Recife and the rural lords of Olinda, a lack of understanding between the big house and the shop. Even before banks were created the city began to extend its dominion over the country in the form of loans. Through a process well known in European history, the aristocracy of the *engenhos* and the bourgeoisie of the *sobrados* became identified with one another, originating new social types, such as the bachelor of laws. The relations between country and city underwent a slow modification. The new-rich built their *sobrados* in the city and bought a country place, where they spent feast days. It appears that the Crown, encouraging the foundation of towns, perceived the allies that these represented in the struggle against the feudal tendencies of the landholding *senhores.*

This transformation, which was, at the same time, a class struggle and a modification of the social structure, was to find its decisive agent in Dom João VI. It is true that, on reaching Brazil, the road to centralization had already been smoothed by the despotic viceroys who had subjugated the caprices, more aristocratic than nativist, of the *senhores* of Pernambuco, Minas, and São Paulo. Nevertheless, the coming of the Prince Regent was a revolution in our history. Rio de Janeiro was the first city to feel the consequences of this movement. His choosing it — instead of Bahia, as had seemed indicated — for the residence of the Court, started Brazilian civilization off in a new direction. What this change represented in purely material things is easily seen by observing what Rio had been before Dom João. Oliveira Lima describes it as "a sort of Lisbon, irregular and still rather banal, with fewer artistic documents and more very leafy vegetation," inhabited by functionaries, merchants, religious, slaves, gypsies, and beggars, these last in great numbers. The changes brought by Dom João caused a profound differentiation between this city and the others.   . . .

More than anything else, the installing of the Portuguese court in Rio created a clear-cut separation between "the capital," or "the court," and the "the interior," "the province," "the country." Summoning to himself the most outstanding representatives of this unsubordinated rural nobility, the Prince Regent accentuated the prestige of the city, which began to dictate fashions, attitudes, and opinions to the vast rural zone of the country. The social and economic consequences of this shift soon began to make themselves felt. The city expanded. The number of buildings increased. Dredging, the filling in of land, and the opening of new streets continued. The Botanical Garden, the Public Library, the Academy of Fine Arts, the Royal São João Theater, the Marine Accounting Office, the Royal Police Guard were founded. The principal streets of the center, which by name seemed to indicate a more or less special grouping of professions (Street of the Tinsmiths, of the Goldsmiths, of the Fishermen, etc.) began to be paved with paving blocks in place of the old stone slabs. At the same time, a differentiation began to appear between the center and the periphery. The Catete was transformed into a residential suburb. Laranjeiras became an area of

sítios and *chácaras,* ornamented with stone bridges and esteemed by
the English. Botafogo, which during the Empire was to be the aristocratic suburb par excellence, began to be sought out by rich
merchants and persons of importance.

In the beginning, Rio de Janeiro was a commercial center that
supplied the rural nuclei in the vicinity. It sufficed to cross the bay
to Niterói or to visit Tijuca to find oneself in a purely rural surrounding of *engenhos* and *fazendas.* Later, the city began to play
the rôle of a port through which the products of the mines flowed
out and through which they were supplied. The opening of the
ports to international commerce meant a greater influx of ships, an
invitation to immigrants, especially merchants, who established
themselves in great numbers in Rio. At the end of the eighteenth century, the Carioca population counted about 40,000 inhabitants. In 1821, when Dom João returned to Portugal, it had risen to
more than 110,000 souls. At the beginning of the century, Bahia was,
in the unanimous opinion of travelers, the first city of Brazil. A few
years later, Rio surpassed it. In eight years Eschwege noted profound modifications in the surroundings of Rio, above all, in the
appearance of true suburbs. The first palace-like houses were built of
stone and tile. With the library, schools, and museum, the city
went on gaining strength as a cultural center. And the creation of
the Bank of Brazil, lending money to the agriculturists at 8 per cent,
emphasized the financial predominance of the city.

9. The Bay of All Saints

C. R. Boxer

The famous Brazilian sociologist, Gilberto Freyre, is the author of
a small work on Bahia which is humorously entitled, "Bay of All
Saints and of nearly all the sins," and in truth the city's reputation
for both sanctity and sinfulness was not undeserved. As is the way
with mankind the world over, sinners rather than saints predominated in the capital of colonial Brazil; but colorful manifestations of

C. R. Boxer, *The Golden Age of Brazil, 1695–1750* (Berkeley: University of
California Press, 1962), pp. 126–161, *passim.* Reprinted by permission of the
University of California Press.

both the sacred and the profane in the daily life of the city are
recorded by many observant travelers. On the one hand were the
numerous and richly decorated churches — popularly if erroneously
supposed to number three hundred and sixty-five, one for every day
in the year — crowded with worshippers, whose real or apparent
devotion impressed even prejudiced Protestant visitors. On the other
hand were the daily — or rather, nightly — deaths by murder most
foul, and the sexual license typified by the richly dressed mulata
prostitutes. The multitude of Negro slaves, on whom the life of the
city and the cultivation of the neighboring sugar and tobacco plantations depended, formed a perpetual reminder that Brazil had an
African soul.

   The City of the Savior (*Cidade do Salvador*) was the capital of
Brazil from 1549, when it was founded on the southeastern shore of
the Bay of All Saints (*Bahia de Todos os Santos*), until 1763, when
the seat of the colonial government was moved to Rio de Janeiro.
Though Salvador was the name of the city, the looser designation of
Bahia was usually employed instead, even in official correspondence.
The term Bahia was also applied to the vast captaincy of that name,
which confined roughly with the river São Francisco on the north
and west, and with the captaincies of Ilheus and Minas Gerais on
the south. Since bay, city, and captaincy alike were indiscriminately
termed "Bahia" for centuries, it will, I hope, be apparent from the
context to which one I am referring hereafter.

   . . . Bahia had long since outstripped "Golden Goa" to become
the second city in the Portuguese empire, being surpassed only by
Lisbon in population and in importance. An Italian visitor in 1699
estimated the population of the city and its environs at 700,000
souls. This is certainly a great exaggeration, and about 100,000 would
seem a more reasonable figure, although we have insufficient data for
anything more than very rough estimates. It was the seat of the governors-general and viceroys, and, from 1675 onward, of the only
archbishopric in Portuguese America. It was a thriving entrepôt of
trade with Portugal and West Africa, the chief whaling station in the
South Atlantic, and boasted a shipbuilding yard of some importance.
It was also the seat of a *Relação* or High Court; and if it did not
possess a university, as did several cities in Spanish America, this
was because the citizens' petition that the local Jesuit College should
be raised to that status was rejected by the Crown on the advice of
the University of Coimbra.

The city was built, like Lisbon and Porto in the mother country, or like Luanda in Angola, Macao in China, and Rio de Janeiro and Olinda in Brazil, on very uneven and hilly ground, running steeply into the sea. The commanding heights were occupied by churches, convents, public buildings, and the town houses of the gentry. The long narrow waterfront contained the commercial quarter with warehouses, stores, shops, and the like. There was thus an upper and a lower city, connected by narrow, tortuous, and steep streets and alleys, which made wheeled traffic virtually impossible. Slaves and (to a lesser degree) pack horses or mules were used for the transport of goods, and litters were employed by the gentry and merchants instead of coaches or carriages. In other words, it was a typical Portuguese city, medieval in its lack of planning and in its haphazard growth, forming a strong contrast to the methodically laid out Spanish-American towns.

One of the best descriptions of Bahia at the end of the seventeenth century, is that by William Dampier, who stayed there in April and May, 1699. His description is worth reproducing in full, although he does not mention the great windlass which was used for hauling heavy goods between the upper and lower towns, and which was the forerunner of the electric elevator that is such a prominent feature of the city today. His description of the streets is evidently rather flattering; but the general accuracy of his observations is attested by comparison with those of Ramponi and others who were there about the same time.

> The town itself consists of about 2,000 houses; the major part of which cannot be seen from the harbour; but so many as appear in sight, with a great mixture of trees between them, and all placed on a rising hill, make a very pleasant prospect. . . . Here lives an Archbishop, who has a fine palace in the town; and the governor's palace is a fair stone building, and looks handsome to the sea, though but indifferently furnished within. Both Spaniards and Portuguese in their plantations abroad, as I have generally observed, affecting to have large houses; but are little curious about furniture, except pictures some of them. The houses of the town are two or three stories high, the walls thick and strong, being built with stone, with a covering of pantile; and many of them have balconies. The principal streets are large, and all of them paved or pitched with small stones. There are also parades on the

most eminent places of the town, and many gardens, as well
within the town as in the outparts of it, wherein are fruit
trees, herbs, salladings and flowers in great variety, but
ordered with no great care nor art.

Nearly all visitors to eighteenth-century Bahia were deeply
impressed by the number and magnificence of its convents and
churches. Even Mrs. Nathaniel Edward Kindersley, who felt that
"no Protestant ever saw a monastery, without reflecting as I do
now, on the indolence and inutility of a monastic life, and the folly
of its mortifications," felt constrained to admit that the convents at
Bahia were "handsome buildings." She was still more complimentary about the churches. "Some of them are large and superb," she
wrote, "and by being unencumbered with pews, the double rows of
pillars have a very fine effect, and give the whole choir an open airy
appearance which our churches can never have: they are kept in the
greatest order, and adorned, particularly the altars, with carving,
paintings, and gilding; with candlesticks and ornaments of gold and
silver to a vast expence." . . .
The frequent complaints of the misdemeanors of many of the
colonial clergy did not alter the fact that as a body they were most
powerful and influential, being held in awesome regard by the
majority of the laity. The Portuguese had a deep-rooted tradition
of respect (amounting to veneration) for the Cloth, though some
contemporaries claimed that it was less noticeable in Brazil than
in the mother country and in Portuguese Asia. Be this as it may, it
was a common theme in classical Portuguese literature that the
worst priest was superior to the best layman. Nuno Marques
Pereira, who is not sparing in his criticisms of the Luso-Brazilian
clergy, explains that nevertheless the Roman Catholic priesthood is
superior to all other human callings and even to that of the angels.
"With five words they can bring God Himself down into their
hands; and with another five they can open the gates of heaven to a
sinner and close those of hell: the first five words being those of consecration, and the second five those of absolution." . . .
However much Protestant observers might deplore the all-pervad-
ing prevalence of "Popery" at Bahia, they could not deny the
devotional fervor displayed by all classes of the population. No
respectable man was to be seen in the streets without a sword at his
side and a rosary in his hand, and with another, as often as not,

round his neck. At the sound of the Angelus bell, passersby knelt down in the streets and said their prayers. The churches were thronged with worshipers of all classes, and even the censorious Mrs. Kindersley felt bound to commend "the warm and steady devotion of the common people here." She was particularly impressed by the piety of the converted Negro slaves. "They are all made Christians as soon as bought, and it is amazing to see the effect the pageantry of the Roman Catholic religion has upon their uninformed minds; they are as devout as the common people in our cities are profane; constant at their worship, obedient to their preceptors without scruple, and inspired with all the enthusiasm of devotion; the gilded pomp, the solemnity of processions, the mysterious rites, the fear as well as the admiration of their ghostly fathers, all conspire to render them so."

The religious processions which took place on many of the feast days of the Church were indeed a striking feature of life at Bahia, blending the sacred and the profane together in the most intriguing way. Portuguese Catholicism has always tended to concentrate on the external manifestations of the Christian cult, and the large African element at Bahia undoubtedly strengthened this tendency. Popular amusements were few, and the gaily dressed and richly decorated religious processions, with their masqueraders, musicians, and dancers, served social needs which are nowadays supplied by the dance-hall, the theater, and the cinema. They afforded the sole opportunity for the mingling of all classes on terms approaching equality, even if they sometimes ended in rioting and disorder. A French voyager in 1718 was astonished to see the elderly and dignified viceroy dancing before the high altar in honor of São Gonçalo d'Amarante, just as if he had been a choirboy in Seville Cathedral on the Feast of Corpus Christi. Le Gentil de la Barbinais added that a Brazilian Portuguese was quite capable of spending his whole year's income on celebrating his patron saint's feast day. "Si on ôtoit aux Portuguais leurs Saints et leurs Maitresses," he concluded, "ils deviendront trop riches."

These colorful religious processions were organized by the lay brotherhoods or confraternities (*Irmandades*), which were voluntary associations of the faithful for charitable and pious ends. Much of the social work that would be done nowadays (if at all) by the government or by the Church, was then performed by the brotherhoods. The principal Religious Orders each had their own affiliations of such laymen, and there was often considerable rivalry between them. Their social status varied from those restricted to pure whites of good family to others whose members were composed solely of Negro slaves. As a rule their composition was on racial lines, whites, mulattoes, and Negroes each having their own *Irmandade;* but a few made no distinctions of class or color, or between bond and free. Some brotherhoods were devoted to purely pious ends; others had a guild character, their membership being limited to a particular trade or calling; and others combined social and religious activities in about equal proportions.

The first half of the eighteenth century saw the full flowering of these brotherhoods in Brazil, where some of them amassed very considerable wealth. Childless members, who had made their money in mining, mercantile, or other pursuits, often bequeathed their entire fortune to their brotherhood. The palatial hospice for respectable women attached to the Misericordia at Bahia was built with a legacy of 80,000 *cruzados* left by João de Mattos. Even those with family responsibilities often bequeathed a considerable sum, and smaller legacies were an almost daily occurrence.   . . .

Membership of these brotherhoods was naturally confined to men, but women were at least allowed to watch their processions, which was one of the very few diversions permitted them in colonial days. Even the Spaniards made fun of the jealous seclusion in which the Portuguese of all classes kept — or strove to keep — their wives and daughters. The Portuguese themselves were not ashamed of this, save for a few eccentrics like Thomé Pinheiro da Veiga, whose *Fastigimia,* written in the early seventeenth century, is full of mordant criticism of his compatriots' habit of secluding their women. The more general attitude was exemplified by the proverb that a really virtuous woman left her house only thrice during her lifetime: for her christening, for her marriage, and for her funeral. The harem-like seclusion in which nearly all upper-class women were kept, inevitably gave their menfolk an unenviable reputation as husbands abroad. A Portuguese envoy in London, Dr. António de Sousa de Macedo, observed in 1642: "The English women are so convinced of the subjection in which Portuguese women are kept, that it would be very difficult for a Portuguese man to find anyone willing to marry him here," although he slyly added, "there are women who would like them as lovers." All travelers in the Portuguese empire were equally uncomplimentary about the rigorous seclusion

of Portuguese women, from Huighen van Linschoten in sixteenth-
century Goa to Maria Graham in nineteenth-century Bahia.

The misogynistic attitude is attributed by some authorities to
the influence of the long Moorish occupation during the Middle
Ages, and by others to the Roman Catholic Church. Admittedly
this latter body was certainly no advocate of the equality of the
sexes, but Luso-Brazilian custom went too far even for those prelates who took a Pauline view of women. We find the Archbishop of
Bahia complaining in 1751 that the local girls could not be induced
to attend the lessons given in the Ursuline Convent, owing to the
opposition of their parents. These latter, "despite the continual complaints of prelates, missionaries, confessors, and preachers, kept their
daughters in such strict seclusion that they rarely let them go out to
hear Mass, much less for any other reason." The Archbishop added
that this practice was not confined to white women, but was imitated by colored girls, "and by any others who can make confession
at home." This attitude did not help to enliven family life in colonial
Brazil, which the great Brazilian historian, Capistrano de Abreu,
characterized as "taciturn father, obedient wife, cowed children."

However tedious the lives of the Bahian ladies may have been,
their lot was in most ways more enviable than that of their slaves.
. . . A royal dispatch of March 1, 1700, denouncing the barbarity
with which many slaveowners of both sexes treated their slaves,
stated that these atrocities originated on plantations in the interior,
but had lately spread to the cities and towns. The Crown condemned as particularly shameful the practice of lady owners living
on the immoral earnings of their female slaves, who were not merely
encouraged but forced into a life of prostitution. This practice was
a reprehensible extension of the more common habit whereby
women slaves were allowed to work on their own account as cooks,
seamstresses, or street hawkers, provided they paid their owners a
fixed sum out of their daily or weekly earnings. Similarly, male
slaves who were skilled laborers were often allowed to work as jour-
neymen, on condition that they paid their masters an agreed proportion of their wages. . . .

One of the matters which had been left to the decision of the
Brazilian viceroys or governors-general by a decree of 1693 was
the creation of new townships in the interior, provided that the expense of erecting a council house, jail, and municipal buildings was
borne by the local inhabitants. The more capable and energetic

administrators, such as Dom João de Lencastre, the Marquis of Angeja, and the Count of Sabugosa made full use of their powers. They were rightly convinced that the erection of such townships was the best means of civilizing and developing the rough settlements of the *sertão*. When the Overseas Councillors claimed prior consultation on this matter, the Marquis of Angeja tartly observed that if the viceroy of Bahia was not competent to make such decisions on his own responsibility then the king should not have chosen him to govern Brazil. This reproach seems to have had the desired effect, at any rate for a time.

The Count of Sabugosa was particularly active in founding townships in the *Reconcavo*. On erecting that of Maragogipe in 1724, he pointed with pride to the precedent of Jacobina. No fewer than 532 persons had been murdered with firearms in that unruly mining camp between 1710 and 1721, when he promoted it to a municipality, complete with a town council, magistrate, and militia. In the three years which had elapsed since that date, only three murders had been recorded, and these were unpremeditated affairs with knives and swords. Similarly, Maragogipe, which was described as a "den of thieves" (*covil de ladrões*) in 1716, became a model municipality in 1724, when the grateful townsmen offered the viceroy an annual contribution of 2,000 *alqueires* of manioc flour for the Bahia garrison's basic ration. . . .

Brazilian historians differ on whether the municipal councils were genuine representatives of the people, or merely of a self-perpetuating and selfish oligarchy. They also argue over whether the councils were largely autonomous or were merely rubber stamps for governors and viceroys. The answer, I think, depends largely on the time and the place. The distant *Camara* of São Paulo (which has been the most publicized, since its history is the best documented in print) was in a much stronger position regarding the central authority at Bahia before 1720, than was the Senate of Salvador in the shadow of the viceroy's palace. A senior Crown official in Minas Gerais in the late 1730's, accused the town councillors of that captaincy of acting as if they were "seditious parliamentarians" in England, adding that they were openly hostile to any extension of the authority of the Crown. Such a truculent attitude was not possible at Bahia. But even the Bahia council had a will of its own during the period with which we are dealing, and its members not infrequently differed from so powerful a personality as the Count of Sabugosa.

The sugar planters of the *Reconcavo* had their representatives on the council but they did not necessarily dominate it. On the other hand, planters, council and viceroy sometimes made common cause against the Crown. A royal edict of 1687 forbade the council to fix the prices of sugar and ordered that this commodity should be sold freely. Ten years later this policy was reversed, and the Crown ordained that the annual sugar prices should be fixed by agreement between two representatives of the planters and two of the local merchants, under the supervision of the municipal council of Salvador. All sugar chests were to be inspected, graded, and weighed in accordance with certain specifications before they were shipped to Portugal. Planters who adulterated their sugars were to be fined and exiled from Bahia for two years. Another edict of 1698 fixed the maximum weight of a loaded sugar chest at forty *arrobas*, "including the wood." Experience had shown that the Lisbon stevedores could not cope with heavier chests, "with the result that many of them left their jobs and absented themselves for fear of imperiling their life and health with a weight which was more than they could bear." With the connivance of the *Camara* and of successive governors, the Bahia planters systematically evaded compliance with these edicts for more than thirty years, and the Crown was only able to call them to order in 1732.

Since sugar was for so long the mainstay of the Brazilian economy, the *senhores de engenho* (as the planters were termed) came to be recognized as the rural aristocracy and were awarded corresponding privileges and immunities. Gubernatorial and royal decrees exempted their sugar mills, technical equipment, and slaves from being seized or distrained for outstanding debts. Their creditors were only allowed to take a portion of the cane ground at harvest time. These privileges were later extended to the *lavradores* or copyholders who cultivated smaller fields and had their cane ground by the planters. The production of sugar in the *Reconcavo* varied greatly in the first half of the eighteenth century owing to the fluctuating demand in Europe and to periods of unseasonable weather in Brazil. A good harvest, such as that of 1725–1726, produced between 12,000 and 13,000 chests for export to Portugal, which may be compared with the corresponding figure of 14,000 chests in Antonil's day. . . .

As is apparent from this chapter, it was gold, sugar, and tobacco that occupied the minds of educated laymen at Bahia rather than literature, art, or music. Nevertheless these latter manifestations of the spirit were not neglected, even if they did not normally reach very high standards. The chief focus of culture was inevitably the local Jesuit College, where instruction was not confined to actual or potential members of the Society, and whose library contained in 1694 some 3,000 volumes "by every kind of writer who could be desired." The Jesuits had many lay brothers and priests who were professional painters, sculptors, woodcarvers, and metalworkers. Though much of their work has disappeared, enough survives to show that in woodwork particularly they often attained more than a merely mechanical skill. There were also numerous goldsmiths and silversmiths in Bahia, but such of their works as survive do not indicate that they possessed more than mediocre abilities. The local school of military engineering (*aula de fortificação*) produced some competent practitioners; but the intellectual caliber of the officers of the Bahia garrison does not seem to have attained the standard reached by their colleagues at Rio de Janeiro under the patronage of Gomes Freire de Andrada.

Poets and poetasters abounded at Bahia, as everywhere and always in the Portuguese-speaking world; but the only one of outstanding merit, the satirist Gregorio de Mattos, died in 1696 just when our concern with Bahia begins. His verses were too pungently critical to be printed in his lifetime and for long afterwards, but they circulated in manuscript during this period.   . . .

Historical studies received an impulse when the Count of Sabugosa was commanded by the king to collect information that might be useful for the Royal Academy of History. This body had been founded at Lisbon in 1720, and was entrusted with the task of compiling a history of the Portuguese empire in all its aspects. The royal order stimulated the viceroy to found an academy at Bahia, whose members decided, with what was obviously mock modesty, to call themselves "The Forgotten" at their inaugural session in March, 1724. The "Academia dos Esquecidos" only flourished for a short time, during which period the forty-four members limited themselves to exchanging poetical effusions, laudatory speeches, and dissertations on trivial themes, in the manner of similar literary academies which waxed and waned in Portugal. Sabugosa's intitiative was not entirely wasted, however. The corresponding members of the Academy included Pedro Leonel Mariz, who spent most of his life in the turbulent mining camps of the Bahia *sertão,* and this indicates that some of the graces of life may have penetrated there. The only production of a Bahian academician that achieved the dignity of print during its author's lifetime was Sebastião da Rocha Pitta's *Historia da America Portuguesa,* published at Lisbon in 1730. Though scornfully dismissed by Robert Southey as being "a meagre and inaccurate work which has been accounted valuable, merely because there is no other," the *Historia* does not deserve this censure. For all its Gongoric turgidity, it contains some valuable and authentic information, being on some points more fair-minded and accurate than Southey's better written but more prejudiced work.

The indefatigable Count of Sabugosa was also responsible for the establishment of the first secular theater in Bahia, with the object of "acting comedies on occasions celebrating royal festivities." This theater was built at his own expense as an adjunct of the municipal hall, but it was pulled down in 1733 by order of his pet aversion, the Royal Judge, Dr. Joseph dos Santos Varjão, which led to an acrimonious correspondence between those concerned. During the few years it lasted, this comedy theater may have provided a welcome change from the Jesuit tragicomedies or religious operas which they staged on occasional high days and holy days. Early eighteenth-century Bahia also witnessed the flowering of the *modinha,* which was later transplanted to Portugal and described by William Beckford in glowing terms: "Those who have never heard this original sort of music, must and will remain ignorant of the most bewitching melodies that ever existed since the days of the Sybarites." But despite the popularity of the *modinha,* the introduction of African musical influences through the slaves, and the initiative of the Count of Sabugosa, the culture of the educated élite at Bahia remained preponderantly a clerical one.   . . .

BIBLIOGRAPHIC SUGGESTIONS

A. *General*

1. Morse, Richard M. "Some Characteristics of Latin American Urban History," *American Historical Review,* XVII (1962), pp. 317–338. "A search for hypotheses toward a theory that will have a special explanatory value for Latin America."

B. *Brazil*

2. Boxer, Charles R. *Portuguese Society in the Tropics: The Munici-*

pal Councils of Goa, Macao, Bahia and Luanda, 1510–1800 (Madison: University of Wisconsin Press, 1965).

2a. Cardozo, Manuel da Silveira Soares. "The Lay Brotherhoods of Colonial Bahia," *The Catholic Historical Review*, XXXIII, No. 1 (1947), pp. 12–30.

3. Costa, Luis Edmundo da. *Rio in the Time of the Viceroys*, Dorothea H. Momsen, trans. (Rio de Janeiro: J. R. de Oliveira, 1936). Social history with a light touch.

4. Morse, Richard M. *From Community to Metropolis: A Biography of São Paulo* (Gainesville: University of Florida Press, 1958). The earlier chapters treat the colonial period.

C. *Spanish America*

5. Carrera Stampa, Manuel. "Planos de la ciudad de Mexico," *Boletín de la Sociedad Mexicana de Geografía y Estadística*, LXVII, Nos. 2–3 (1949), pp. 265–427. Here is reproduced a series of maps and pictures of Mexico City from 1521 to the present time, vividly portraying the evolution of this magnificent capital. The provisioning of the city with water, firewood, milk, meat, cereals, and firewater forms a separate and very interesting chapter. The author makes one relive the glorious days in Mexico City and at the same time makes an original and worthwhile contribution to urban geography.

6. Dusenberry, William H. "The Regulation of Meat Supply in Sixteenth-Century Mexico City," *Hispanic American Historical Review*, XXVIII (1948), pp. 38–52.

7a. Moore, John Preston. *The Cabildo in Peru under the Hapsburgs. A Study in the Origins and Powers of the Town Council in the Viceroyalty of Peru, 1530–1700* (Durham, N.C.: Duke University Press, 1954).

8. Muñoz Pérez, José. "Una descripción comparativa de las ciudades americanos en el siglo XVIII," *Estudios Geográficos*, XV (Madrid: Feb., 1954), pp. 89–129. Calls attention to the document *Consideraciones americanas* (1789) in the Biblioteca de Palacio in Madrid, written by Raimundo Diosdado Caballero. The document contains a comparative description and evaluation of sample English, French, and Spanish cities in the New World.

9. Parry, J. H. *The Sale of Public Office in the Spanish Indies under the Hapsburgs* (Berkeley: University of California Press, 1953).

Section VII

The Inquisition

The Inquisition charged with locating and exterminating heresy in the New World had one special problem: how to treat the Indians. Were they subject to the jurisdiction of the Holy Office? Dr. Richard E. Greenleaf, Vice-President of the University of the Americas in Mexico City, explains the intricacies of this question (Reading VII.1). Professor France V. Scholes, of the University of New Mexico, and the late Ralph L. Roys, long on the staff of the Carnegie Institution of Washington, describe one of the most famous cases in which Indians were brought before inquisitors (Reading VII.2).

English merchants and seamen who had gone to Mexico for trade or piracy in the time of Queen Elizabeth were also hauled before the Inquisition. Two were burned at the stake there, but most of those who were tried ". . . were sentenced to abjure their heresies in public, each man wearing the penitential garment of San Benito, walking barefoot with a candle in his hand, to undergo the lash, and to serve periods of six to ten years in the galleys in Spain."[1] One of the luckiest was Robert Tomson, whose description of his adventures in Mexico was first printed by Hakluyt. He had only to wear the San Benito for two years and then spend a year in the Inquisition prison in Seville. Having duly served this sentence and regained his freedom, he married the daughter of a Spaniard who had grown rich in the mines of Mexico and his fortune was made.[2]

[1] Frank Aydelotte, "Elizabethan Seamen in Mexico," *American Historical Review*, XLVIII (1942), p. 9.
[2] *Ibid.*, p. 3.

His generally favorable account (Reading VII.3) of life in Mexico helps to explain how some of the Englishmen captured by the Inquisition formed friendships in Mexico and fell sufficiently in love with the country to remain there for the rest of their lives.

Portuguese America never saw the Inquisition formally established, illustrating the truth of the oft-mentioned claim that "Brazil is different from Spanish America." But the long arm of the Holy Office occasionally stretched to Brazil (Reading VII.4). Many Portuguese went to Spanish America, especially to Peru, and Henry Charles Lea, the Philadelphia publisher who wrote so many substantial volumes on Inquisition history, described how they were handled by the Inquisition there (Reading VII.5).

That the Holy Office was a political instrument has long been accepted, but the extent to which its power lasted into the eighteenth century is still in dispute. Dr. Greenleaf, basing his conclusions on prolonged investigations in Mexican archives, argues that the Inquisition remained powerful to the end of the eighteenth century primarily because of its increased political activities in the latter part of the century (Reading VII.6).

A. The Inquisitors and the Indians

1. Jurisdictional Confusion

RICHARD E. GREENLEAF

The question of the jurisdiction of the Holy Office of the Inquisition over the native populations in New Spain and the rest of the empire has been one of controversy and confusion since the earliest days of the conquest. The perplexing problem of enforcing orthodoxy among the recently converted Indians was linked with the debate over whether or not the Indian was a rational human being

Richard E. Greenleaf, "The Inquisition and the Indians: A Study in Jurisdictional Confusion," *The Americas*, XXII (October, 1965), pp. 138–166, *passim*. Reprinted by permission of the Academy of American Franciscan History.

who had the capacity to comprehend the Roman Catholic faith and
enjoy the full sacramental system of the Church. As in the case of
the rationality controversy, the position of the Indian vis-à-vis the
Holy Office of the Inquisition was not resolved articulately, and
after the first decades of the spiritual conquest the question took on
added importance as the Mexican clergy discovered recurrent idolatry and religious syncretism among their flocks.

The Episcopal Inquisition 1522–1571 — Formal ecclesiastical
administration established in medieval times conferred upon the
bishop the duty to enforce morality and orthodoxy within his diocese. When the thirteenth-century Inquisition was founded, the
jurisdiction over heresy became invested in that tribunal. After the
mainland conquests in America, and before formal Inquisition tribunals were established in the 1570's, bishops re-assumed the inquisitorial function in their dioceses under the portfolio of Ecclesiastical
Judge Ordinary. Because the spiritual conquest was carried on by
regular clergy and these latter normally did not enjoy full privileges
in administering the sacramental rites of the Church, the Papacy
found it necessary to grant the mendicant orders extraordinary powers. On April 10, 1521, Pope Leo X granted to the Franciscan Order
the right to perform as secular clergy in areas where there were no
priests or bishops. Pope Adrian VI, by the bull *Exponi nobis*
(known in New Spain as the *Omnímoda*) of May 10, 1522, extended
to prelates of all mendicant orders in America the right to exercise
almost all episcopal powers except ordination in areas where there
was no resident bishop or where he was two days distant.

In New Spain from 1522 to 1571 an episcopal Inquisition operated
and bishops tried cases as ordinaries, or monastic prelates acted as
ordinaries under the *Omnímoda*. Bishop Juan de Zumárraga (1528–
1548) and Visitor General Francisco Tello de Sandoval (1544–
1547) received commissions as Apostolic Inquisitors but this title
did not differentiate their activities from the ordinary function.

It is significant for this study that the first trial before the Mexican
Inquisition was that of an Indian, Marcos of Acolhuacán, for the
crime of concubinage in 1522. Since the *proceso* has disappeared
from the Mexican archive, details of the trial are lacking. Procesos
of Indians before the Holy Office are missing for the decade of the
1520's, but there is some evidence that the Franciscan Martín de
Valencia did mete out capital punishment to native idolaters. Bishop

Juan de Zumárraga, O.F.M., really launched the Indian Inquisition between 1536 and 1543 when at least nineteen different trials involving some seventy-five Indians were initiated and brought to conclusion. Zumárraga realized the frailty of the Indian in the new religion because of inadequate instruction, but he also felt the necessity to deal harshly with those native leaders who by word and deed tried to undermine the spiritual conquest. When Zumárraga relaxed the Cacique Don Carlos of Texcoco to the secular arm for burning in 1539 for attacking the teachings of the friars and urging the Indian to return to pagan practices, he was reprimanded from Spain for his harsh sentence, and he was eventually removed as Apostolic Inquisitor.

Prior to his dismissal as Apostolic Inquisitor, Zumárraga himself had some doubts about the efficacy of inquisitorial jurisdiction over the native populations and he urged the crown in 1537 to place the Indian under the less stringent episcopal supervision. Among Tello de Sandoval's inquisitorial activities during the 1544–1547 interval were the investigation and trial of groups of Indian caciques in Oaxaca for idolatry and human sacrifice. Masses of documentation exist in the Mexican archive on Yanhuitlán, Tilantongo, Coatlán and environs. For some strange reason the procesos were never completed and the inference is that perhaps the Tello Inquisition left the matter up to the bishop of Oaxaca or his delegate Pedro Maraver. After Tello de Sandoval left Mexico in 1547, and until the erection of the Tribunal of the Holy Office in 1571, the jurisdiction over Indian orthodoxy was exercised by the bishop as ordinary or by the prelate of the friars in the absence of the bishop. Indian trials in Tecoaloya, Zumpango, Santiago de Guatemala, Teiticpac (Oaxaca), Zacatecas, and Yucatán clearly indicate that this was the procedure.

The Yucatán idolatry trials of the 1560's carried on by Fray Diego de Landa, O.F.M., and the alcalde mayor of Yucatán, Diego de Quijada, are well documented from materials in the Justicia and Escribanía de Cámara sections of the Archivo General de Indias in Sevilla. In connection with the Yucatán trials a great ecclesiastical debate was waged in Spain over the question of whether Landa as Franciscan prelate of Yucatán had the powers of an inquisitor. The *pareceres* of church lawyers concluded that the Omnímoda was still in effect and that, as prelate of Yucatán, Landa justly acted in an inquisitorial capacity.

The Yucatán trials, preceded by the burning of Carlos of Texcoco three decades earlier, gave impetus to the movement for permanent exclusion of the Indians from the jurisdiction of the Holy Office. When the Mexican Tribunal of the Holy Office of the Inquisition was established in 1571, it was refused the right to hear Indian cases. Indians were to remain under the ordinary jurisdiction in the bishopric. Because of an unclear understanding on the part of the new inquisitors and the clergy alike, the functions, titles, and procedures of the Holy Office and the ordinary jurisdiction in Indian matters were confused for several decades. Perhaps this situation resulted from the similar approach of these two branches of the Church in their dealings with the native populations.

The Tribunal of the Holy Office and the Provisorato of the Bishopric — The extirpation of idolatry and pagan superstitions in New Spain continued under an institutional framework quite similar to the Inquisition. After 1571 the Tribunal of the Holy Office acted as a fact-finding agency in the uncovering and disciplining of Indian transgressions against orthodoxy. Actual control over Indian orthodoxy reverted to the bishop's or archbishop's office and was placed under the care of the *Provisor,* or Vicar General, of the diocese or archdiocese. The provisoratos contrived an entire bureaucracy of officials to cope with the new function and they appointed delegates and commissaries in provincial areas. Following the tradition established during the period of the episcopal Inquisition, the Provisor and his commissaries often called themselves inquisitors ordinary and established tribunals and *juzgados* for Indians of the bishopric.

For several decades the provisorato set-up functioned without much competition or invasion of power by the Inquisition Tribunal, but in the actual operation of enforcement of orthodoxy there was still fusion and confusion of authority and responsibility of the inquisitorial and the ordinary functions. Quarrels over the competence of the Provisorato and the Tribunal in cases involving Indians in the seventeenth and eighteenth centuries occupy many pages of testimony in the actual procesos and comprise several *legajos* of administrative documents sent to Spain for resolution. Often, because many of the colonial Mexican clergy occupied several portfolios or exercised a multiple function, the personnel of the Provisorato and the Holy Office were mixed in the conduct of trials, thus adding to the confusion over jurisdiction, especially in the remote provincial areas.

Investigatory activities of the Inquisition into Indian affairs continued throughout the colonial period in New Spain. Of particular concern were studies of recurrent paganism and idolatry and violation of the degrees of carnal and spiritual relationship permitted by the Church in the sacrament of marriage. The Inquisition usually kept meticulous records of these investigations, but because of the burden of work for ministers of the spiritual flock, the Provisor or his agent kept sparse records or none at all. Therefore we must conclude that only the more serious deviations from orthodoxy came to light in the archives. Oftentimes materials on heresy and crimes against the faith are mixed with data on the spiritual activities of the regular and secular clergy. Especially between 1620 and 1700 was concern focused on the evaluation of missionizing techniques seen against the background of continued pagan practices and the process of religious syncretism taking place in many of the Mexican provinces. Friars of several of the orders were charged to write full reports, and these *relaciones* document the fears of the Inquisitors and ordinaries as to the extent of paganism in the supposedly Christianized viceregal area.   . . .

Investigatory Functions of the Holy Office — As stated previously, there was a confusion among the clergy in jurisdiction over Indian orthodoxy and there was divergence of opinion as to how long the Indian should remain outside of the competence of the Holy Office. In addition to investigating idolatries, the provincial commissaries of the Inquisition also tried cases of Indian heterodoxy in the seventeenth century. In 1625 in Chiautla of the Villa Alta area of Oaxaca, Fray Fernando de Porras, an Augustinian who acted as Inquisition Commissary, tried and convicted a Zapotec for eating the hallucinatory mushroom (el ololuque). The Commissary made the Indian strip to the waist and wear the coroza (conical mitre) during Mass and, after the religious service, ordered fifty lashes given him in the patio of the church. The Mexico City tribunal took steps to repudiate the action but the document does not inform whether or not Porras was punished or admonished for exceeding his authority. Furthermore, the Tribunal continued to initiate cases of Indian bigamy and concubinage and intervene in cases of a mixed Indian and Spanish nature when it came to the polygamous relations of the two groups. By 1650 most of these cases were referred to the Provisor. . . . The Tribunal of the Holy Office and the ordinary jurisdiction often clashed. Semantical problems over the use of the term "Inquisición" and "Inquisición Ordinaria" led to grave administrative problems in the Viceroyalty of New Spain. . . .

The Question of Limpieza de Sangre: Pure Indians Versus Mestizos — The frontier nature of many of the provinces of New Spain and the factor of administrative distance often combined to make it necessary to employ stopgap measures to cope with enforcement of orthodoxy. These circumstances, combined with a confusion over jurisdiction of the ordinary and inquisitorial authorities vis-à-vis the Indian and mestizo inhabitants of the viceroyalty, led to unusual proceedings in the Tribunal of the Holy Office. A particularly difficult problem to resolve was how to define "indio puro" (pure Indian) as opposed to mestizo, a problem all the more critical and delicate since it meant a change of jurisdiction for the person accused of idolatry, sorcery, bigamy, or any other unorthodox conduct. As Father Cuevas reasoned correctly, quite soon after the 1570's many bigamists, blasphemers, and sorcerers *claimed* to be Indians in order to escape the Holy Office's jurisdiction and remain subject to the ordinaries.

Genealogical proof of an Indian's or mestizo's *limpieza de sangre* or his *casta* (caste or breed) was difficult to obtain and many hours of testimony before Inquisition officials were needed prior to remanding the case to the ordinary. Other exigencies demanding swift punishment of pagan practices as an example to the populace led to an overhasty conviction of Indians and mixed-bloods by Inquisition commissaries. It must be noted, though, that when the evidence pointed to the fact that the accused was a pure Indian, the Inquisitors lost no time in remanding the case to the ordinary authorities. More nebulous cases of *mestizaje* induced the Holy Office to be less pliable, and the judges demanded proof of lineage before relinquishing their authority in the matter, referring to the accused as a mestizo until the contrary was proved.

Problems of limpieza on the northern frontier were especially troublesome to the Tribunal. In March, 1631, the Commissary of Zacatecas, Lic. Diego de Herrera y Arteaga, wrote Mexico City about two cases of heresy. One concerned Sebastián Fabián, an Indian sorcerer who had entered into a pact with the devil, and the other was a man of dubious casta named Agustín Morisco o Mulato who was convicted of idolatry. The Superior Tribunal ordered a complete investigation of the limpieza of the "Moorish-mulatto" and then had the autos sent to the Commissary of the Holy Office. The documents concerning the Indian, Sebastián Fabián, were remanded to the Ordinary. . . .

The "Provisorato de la Inquisición Ordinaria de Indios y Chinos," 1766–1785 — During the first half of the eighteenth century the Holy Office continued to make investigations of Indian idolatry and pagan practices and occasionally to initiate trials. At the same time the Provisor of Indians developed a well-defined pattern of staging autos de fe in Mexico City and the provinces when Indians were convicted of unorthodox conduct. The most spectacular Indian auto in the early eighteenth century is recounted by Joseph Antonio de Villaseñor in his famous chronicle, when he reviews the 1718 visit of the Nayarit cacique, Tonatiuh, to the viceregal capital, and the subsequent 1723 auto de fe staged by the Provisor in the Convent of San Francisco and the Plaza of San Diego when the skeletal remains of Tonatiuh's great-grandfather were burned, along with idols and other sacrificial paraphernalia uncovered in a Nayarit cave by the Spaniards. The account tells us that the skeleton was found seated on a throne in the cave surrounded by idols, and the throne was actually a kind of altar where it was suspected that human sacrifices took place.

Other autos de fe of Indians are well documented by the *Gaceta de México* as extracted by Joaquín García Icazbalceta in the nineteenth century. There is evidence that on many occasions procesos were passed back and forth between the Provisor and the Tribunal and that the Provisorato actually alerted the Inquisitors to cases of heresy when they were related with Indian affairs.

The foregoing data indicate clearly that by the middle of the eighteenth century Inquisitorial procedures vis-à-vis the Indians had become more formalized and that recognizable institutions had emerged by the 1760's. Furthermore, the Crown had issued other regulations that somewhat revamped the jurisdiction. Of special note were a set of royal cédulas and deliberations of the Council of the Indies that removed the Indian bigamist and polygamist from the power of the ordinary jurisdiction and placed him again under the discipline of the Holy Office of the Inquisition. This action was

taken in 1766 by Charles III as the culmination of a series of de-
bates in the Council of the Indies and a set of petitions from the
Inquisitors that this be done.

Of special significance was the continued close identification of
the two functions of Ordinary and Inquisitor after 1750. By the time
of a celebrated confrontation in 1766, the ordinary jurisdiction of
the archiepiscopal see was calling itself *Provisorato del Santo Oficio
de la Inquisición Ordinaria de los Indios y Chinos de este Arzobis-
pado,* a term which was furiously resented by the Inquisitors.   . . .

Epilogue to Confusion — The jurisdiction over Indian orthodoxy
of the Ecclesiastical Judge Ordinary, as it was organized under the
Provisorato and that of the Holy Office of the Inquisition, remained
clear in theory but confused in practice because the two functions
had not only the same subjects but also similar procedures, ceremonies, and titles. The question of title was particularly crucial in
colonial Mexico because the level of sophistication of Indian and
Spanish populations alike was relatively low. Clergy as well as in-
digenes did not understand the nature of the two jurisdictions of
Inquisition and Provisorato. The Ordinaries and the Inquisitors
did little to clear up the general misconceptions; indeed, they
seemed more interested in confusion of competencies and invasions
of the functions of the others, when such action could be taken
without fear of unpleasant confrontation or royal and ecclesiastical
censures.

Documents of an inquisitorial nature, whether originating from
the Holy Office or the Provisor, are scattered over the various
branches of the Mexican national and provincial archives because
of the sensitive nature of competencies. Interestingly enough, there
are no extant investigations or trials in the Ramo de Obispos y
Arzobispos, even though from a logical standpoint the late eighteenth century data should be filed there. Correspondence of bishops and archbishops gave little attention to the problems of Indian
orthodoxy. No doubt a multitude of cases were initiated, but like
most trials of faith and morals, they were handled quietly, and
perhaps no records were kept of the affair or of the penances prescribed. Perhaps the Indians understood that the Bishops were less
stringent than the Inquisition and acted accordingly when they
became involved in pagan accusations.

It is justifiable to conclude that the struggle over control of Indian idolatry and superstition was more of a problem of jurisdic-

tional semantics than a question of the humanity or rationality of the native. It is also more than conjecture to suggest that in the later years the Crown encouraged this fusion and confusion of authority and responsibility for enforcing native orthodoxy because of a Bourbon policy of conciliation after 1750 — a policy of balancing forces against one another in colonial society and a desire to hasten the decline of the power of the Holy Office of the Inquisition in the eighteenth century.

2. Fray Diego de Landa and the Problem of Idolatry in Yucatan

FRANCE V. SCHOLES AND RALPH L. ROYS

Toward the beginning of May 1562, two Indian boys of Mani discovered some idols and skeletons in a near-by cave. They immediately informed Fray Pedro de Cuidad Rodrigo, *guardián* of the monastery of Mani, who gave orders to have the idols and skeletons brought to the patio of the monastery. Fray Pedro apparently transmitted news of the discovery to Fray Diego de Landa [Franciscan provincial of Yucatan], who commissioned him to make an inquiry. At this time several other friars were residing in Mani, having been sent there to learn Maya, and with their aid Fray Pedro made a preliminary investigation. During the succeeding three or four weeks hundreds of Indians were arrested and questioned. Torture was used in order to obtain confessions. Many Indians confessed that they possessed idols and had performed various idolatrous rites, and as punishment for their offenses the friars had them whipped, imposed small fines, and forced them to take part in *autos de fe* that were held in the cemetery and patio of the monastery on three or four succeeding Sundays.

Convinced that the practice of idolatry was widespread, the friars sent letters to Merida urging Landa to come to Mani and take personal charge of the proceedings. Landa conferred with Dr. Diego

France V. Scholes and Ralph L. Roys, "Fray Diego de Landa and the Problem of Idolatry in Yucatan," *Cooperation in Research* (Washington, D.C.: Carnegie Institution of Washington, Pub. No. 501, 1938), pp. 585–620, *passim.* Reprinted by permission of the Carnegie Institution of Washington.

Quijada, *alcalde mayor* of the province, who agreed to appoint
an *alguacil,* or bailiff, with instructions to aid the provincial, arrest
Indians accused of idolatry, and execute such sentences as he might
impose. Soon after Landa arrived in Mani early in June, a definite
plan of action was adopted for the continuation of the inquiry. It
was decided that the provincial, together with Fray Pedro de Cuidad Rodrigo, Fray Miguel de la Puebla, and Fray Juan Pizarro,
should remain in Mani to serve as judges of the Inquisition for the
trial of the idolators, and that the other friars should go to the surrounding pueblos to inquire into the prevalence of idolatry, punish
minor offenders, and send to Mani for formal trial and sentence
those Indians who were guilty of serious offenses. In order to avoid
delay and the duplication of legal costs, it was also agreed that full
legal procedure should be omitted in the cases of minor offenders,
especially the common people (*maceguales*), by combining them
into one general process. The prosecution of major offenders, however, was to be in accordance with the customary forms of procedure.

By what right did Landa assume authority to act as judge of
Inquisition? Prior to 1571, when a tribunal of the Holy Office was
established in Mexico City with jurisdiction over New Spain and
Guatemala, the duty of trying cases of heresy and other offenses
against the Church devolved on the bishops in their respective dioceses. But at this time there was no bishop in Yucatan, although
Fray Francisco de Toral, a veteran of the Mexican missions, had already been appointed and consecrated bishop of the province and
was then on his way from Spain. By virtue of papal bulls, however, the prelates of monastic orders in America in areas where
there was no resident bishop had authority to exercise all episcopal
functions except those that could be performed only by a consecrated bishop. Thus, from 1545 to 1562, the Franciscan prelates of
Yucatan had possessed supreme ecclesiastical authority in Yucatan
and had served as ecclesiastical judges ordinary in cases pertaining
to the Church and the canon law. By a decree of February 28, 1558,
the Audiencia of Guatemala had officially recognized and confirmed
their authority.

During the month of June and the first half of July the investigation moved forward rapidly. Hundreds of Indians were questioned.
Many voluntarily confessed their guilt, others only after being subjected to torture. Landa and his associates soon became convinced

that the caciques, *principales,* schoolmasters, and other prominent Indians were the chief offenders, and were responsible for the backsliding of the common people. Orders were given for the arrest of some forty Indians of the upper class, including ten governors and caciques of the Mani area, among whom was Francisco de Montejo Xiu.

The proceedings soon aroused increasing hostility on the part of the Indians, and Landa began to fear that they might resort to violence. He also desired the presence of the *alcalde mayor* at the time when he would pronounce sentences in all pending cases. Consequently, toward the end of June he sent word to Quijada asking him to come to Mani and to bring an escort of Spaniards, especially those who held *encomiendas* in the Mani area. Quijada arrived early in the following month, and soon began actively to participate in the inquiry. With Landa's permission he questioned several Indians, even subjecting them to torture in order to force them to confess the full extent of their guilt.

On July 11 the provincial pronounced sentence in most cases. The Indians guilty of minor offenses, especially the common people, were condemned to pay small fines, to participate in a general *auto de fe,* and, in certain cases, to be whipped. Certain major offenders, including several *principales* and schoolmasters, were condemned to receive one to two hundred lashes of the whip, to have their hair shorn (a grievous thing for an Indian), to pay heavier fines, to be deprived of local office, or to serve terms of forced labor for one to ten years. Inasmuch as the documents contain very little direct testimony given by the Indians at Mani, there is not much information available concerning the nature of the offenses for which these penalties were imposed. Most of the common people, however, were probably guilty of little more than mere possession of idols. Persons regarded as guilty of more serious offenses had apparently burned copal before the idols or had performed sacrificial rites, such as the offering of birds and deer or acts of self-mortification. Although we have very little evidence of human sacrifice in the Mani area, this is doubtless due to the marked lack of Indian testimony from Mani in the available documents. There is no reason to suppose that human sacrifices were performed less frequently in the Mani district than in other parts of the province. . . .

The cases of twenty-five caciques, *principales,* and other major offenders were continued for further investigation. In view of their prominence as leaders of the native population, it was decided that they should be removed to Merida and held in confinement pending final action on the charges that had been filed against them. Included in this group were Francisco de Montejo Xiu, cacique of the pueblo of Mani, and seven other governors and caciques of the Mani area.

The friars now transferred their activities to the former *cacicazgos* of Sotuta and Hocaba-Homun. In these areas they followed the same procedure as at Mani, arresting large numbers of Indians, using torture in order to obtain confessions, and dispensing with full legal procedure except in the most important cases. . . .

On August 14, 1562, Fray Francisco de Toral, first resident bishop of Yucatan, arrived in Merida. Landa's authority to serve as ecclesiastical judge came to an end and the bishop took charge. This event marked a sharp change in the character of the inquiry, for the bishop immediately made it known that he disapproved the use of torture and severely censured the friars for the manner in which the investigation had been conducted.

The activities of Landa and his associates had aroused considerable unrest among the Indians. Indeed, according to Bishop Toral, the province "was on the point of being lost." The chief cause of unrest was the severe torture to which many of the natives had been subjected. The method most frequently employed was to suspend the Indians in mid-air by means of ropes tied to their wrists. If this proved ineffective, heavy stones were then tied to their feet. They were also whipped while in this position, and in many cases hot wax was dropped on their naked bodies. In certain cases the ancient form of torment by water was employed, as well as the *burro*, the latter being a wooden frame to which the Indians were tied and then subjected to other forms of punishment. So severe were these measures in some cases that they resulted in permanent injury or death. There is also evidence that a few Indians committed suicide — of whom the most prominent was Lorenzo Cocom, who had succeeded his brother Juan Cocom as cacique of Sotuta in 1561 — in order to escape from the torment, or because of fear of the penalties that the inquisitors would impose as sentence for their idolatries.

The Indians also protested that much of the testimony concerning the practice of human sacrifice that had been given during the inquiry was false, that they had deliberately committed perjury in order to escape further tortures. They protested that in certain instances they had agreed in advance to make false statements, or that when one of their number had given perjured testimony he told the others what he had said and the latter then repeated his story. Likewise, they asserted that many of the idols that they had handed over to the friars had been newly made for that purpose, that others were objects of worship long abandoned, and that in some cases they had gone to abandoned sites, in one case as far away as Coba, to gather up idols in order to meet the insistent demands of the friars. . . .

The bishop's refusal to sanction the continued use of torture, his general attitude of moderation, even partiality, in dealing with the cases of the caciques and chieftains imprisoned in Merida, and his decision not to extend the judicial hearings to other parts of the province, as the Franciscans proposed, decreased the tension and unrest among the native population. He found it possible, therefore, to proceed slowly with the cases of the caciques and *principales*, in accordance with customary legal formulae, and it was not until January 2, 1563, that he announced the final sentences. Unfortunately, a copy of the sentences has not been preserved in the documentary materials relating to the inquiry, but from other sources we gather that mild forms of physical punishment were imposed, as well as certain ecclesiastical censures. In reports to the king, the bishop stated that he believed the sentences to be just, "taking into account the long imprisonment [the Indians] had endured, as well as the banishment from their pueblos and provinces [and] loss of property, and that more severe punishment therefore was not advisable."

The failure to acquit the Indians of the charges of idolatry and the justification cited for the light penalties that were imposed sustain the view . . . that Bishop Toral was aware of the existence of idolatry. His decisions in these cases were based on expediency and a genuine desire to see justice done. The imposition of rigorous punishment on one hundred and twenty-three caciques, *principales*, and other native leaders, several of whom were former rulers of some prominence, would have caused tremendous unrest, if not violence, on the part of the Maya. But it was also Toral's sincere view that it was contrary to the spirit of Christian charity and justice to subject the Indians, so recently converted, to penalties of a dras-

tic kind. The same considerations prompted his decision, made a
month later, to revoke the sentences of all the Indians whom Landa
had condemned to terms of forced labor.

By this time Landa and Toral had become hopelessly alienated,
and each now turned his attention to the preparation of reports to
be sent to Spain. At the bishop's request witnesses were summoned
to testify concerning certain alleged usurpations of authority by
Landa and other Franciscan prelates in earlier years, the careless, if
not improper, manner in which the Franciscans, in Toral's opinion,
had conducted the missions, and the proceedings of the provincial
and his associates during the idolatry inquiry. This report and an
incomplete and somewhat circumstantial résumé of the whole investigation were sent to Spain in March 1563. They were accompanied by two covering letters in which the bishop denounced
Landa and the friars in scathing terms.   . . .

The bishop's reports and letters were received in Spain early in
1564 and they made a profound impression. Consequently, when
Landa arrived later in the year, having been delayed by illness and
other circumstances, he found the members of the Council of the
Indies in a hostile frame of mind. But with the aid of friends, he
was permitted to present his version of the case and to file with the
Council numerous papers, including copies of part of the Indian
testimony concerning human sacrifices, in justification of his actions.
One of the major questions involved was whether Landa had legal
authority in 1562 to serve as inquisitor and ecclesiastical judge. Because of this aspect of the case and the wider implications that
would follow if the Council imposed discipline on a prominent
ecclesiastic, as well as the fact that many of the accusations that
Toral had made related to the internal affairs of the Franciscan
Order, it was decided to remit the entire matter to the provincial
of the Franciscan province of Castile for review and decision, with
authority to impose upon Landa whatever punishment he might
deem necessary.

During the spring of 1565 Landa presented an elaborate defense
before the person appointed by the provincial of Castile to review
the case. Inasmuch as the crucial question was whether Landa, as
provincial of the Franciscan Order in 1562 prior to the arrival of
Bishop Toral, had the right to serve as ecclesiastical judge, legal
opinions on this point were sought from a number of civil and
canon law jurists, of whom one was Lic. Tomas López, who had

governed Yucatan for a year (1552–1553) by virtue of a commission from the Audiencia of Guatemala. These legal specialists all agreed that various papal bulls and colonial administrative decrees warranted Landa's exercise of jurisdiction and that the penalties he had imposed had not been excessive.

The filing of these opinions assured Landa's acquittal, although owing to the death of the provincial of Castile, a decision was not rendered until four years later. On January 29, 1569, the provincial's successor made a formal pronouncement to the effect (1) that Landa had not exceeded his authority, and (2) that it had been his duty to act as inquisitor and punish the Indians guilty of idolatry, invoking the aid of the secular arm. It was his decision, therefore, that Landa was without guilt and was free of all the charges on which he had been accused. Landa's vindication was complete when, three years later, Philip II nominated him as bishop of Yucatan to succeed Fray Francisco de Toral. . . .

It has often been stated that the inquiry of 1562 was the occasion of a wholesale destruction of Maya antiquities, especially priceless codices written in hieroglyphs. Consequently Landa's name has been anathema to many students of ancient American life. What are the facts as revealed by the documents?

Thousands of idols were destroyed. Most of these were small pottery objects and a few were of wood. So few references to stone idols are found in the record of the inquiry that we may doubt whether many important sculptured stone objects were lost at this time. The question of the codices is, of course, the important one. It has been reported, on the basis of early nineteenth century documents, that twenty-seven codices were burned during the investigation. In view of the fact that the papers of 1562–1563 contain so many references to idols and that the friars cited the great numbers that were collected and destroyed as evidence of the guilt of the Indians, we should also expect to find numerous statements concerning books if many of the latter had been found. It is significant, therefore, that the record of the inquiry contains only one reference to "books." This is in the declaration of an Indian who gave evidence at Homun in September 1562. The document briefly states without comment that the witnesses admitted

. . . that he has had idols and books and masks, and that he brought and displayed four masks and some books.

In his "Relación de las cosas de Yucatán," Landa states:

> These people used certain characters or letters, with which
> they wrote in their books about the antiquities and their
> sciences; . . . We found a great number of books in these
> letters, and since they contained nothing but superstitions
> and falsehoods of the devil we burned them, all of which they
> took most grievously, and which gave them great pain.

We cannot be sure whether Landa refers here to the inquiry of
1562, or to a general practice adopted as part of the missionary program. It seems reasonable to believe, however, that if a large number of codices were destroyed in 1562, the contemporary record of
the inquiry would contain explicit statements to that effect.

The idolatry proceedings of 1562 also had a direct relation to
Landa's treatise on Maya antiquities. Landa had undoubtedly
started collecting data for the "Relación" during the decade from
1550 to 1560, but apparently it was not until after he went to Spain
to defend himself before the king and the Council of the Indies
that he actually whipped the materials into shape. At least, we may
infer this from the fact that the only manuscript version of the
"Relación" that has been preserved bears the date 1566, and from
internal evidence in the work itself. It is also reasonable to suppose
that one of his motives for writing it at that time was the fact that
it would serve to illustrate those religious rites and idolatrous practices which he had so actively sought to extirpate.

In the same year that Landa was acquitted by the decision of
the provincial of Castile, Philip II gave orders for the establishment
of tribunals of the Holy Office of the Inquisition in Mexico City and
Lima. Jurisdiction in all cases of heresy, blasphemy, bigamy, propositions contrary to Catholic doctrine, evil-sounding words, and other
offenses against the Church was transferred from the bishops and
other local prelates in America to these special courts. There had
been numerous complaints against the activities of the bishops and
prelates as inquisitors, but it may be doubted whether any of these
had caused such a deep impression as the Landa case. Indeed, it
seems reasonable to assume that the latter had a direct and immediate influence on the king's decision to establish separate tribunals
for the trial of offenses against the Faith. Moreover, the laws defining the authority of these tribunals specifically exempted the Indians
from their jurisdiction, because of their incapacity and lack of un-

derstanding concerning Christian doctrine and because many were not well instructed in the teachings of the Church. This statement of policy vindicates the point of view held by Bishop Toral in 1562, and we may venture to suggest that the Landa episode was a contributing factor in the formulation of such a policy.

In retrospect the inquiry of 1562 is seen as an incident, albeit a spectacular one, of that conflict of cultures in Hispano-Indian America deriving from the Conquest, an illustration of the stresses and strains in native life produced by the introduction of European civilization. Not only in Yucatan, but also in other areas the forced acceptance of Christianity had an important influence on the course of colonial history. The Pueblo Revolt of 1680 in New Mexico was a movement to throw off Christianity and return to aboriginal customs and modes of life. The rebellion of the Tzendal Indians of Chiapas, inspired by the belief that an Indian girl had received messages from the Virgin and organized by another Indian who proclaimed "that St. Peter had taken him up to heaven and appointed him as his vicar on earth, with power to elect bishops and priests," illustrates another phase of the problem. Other examples of the interaction of Christian and native religions could be cited for other parts of Spanish America. For students of Central American antiquities, however, the investigation of 1562 has special interest because of the rôle played by Fray Diego de Landa, the founder of Maya research.

B. An Englishman and the Inquisition

3. Robert Tomson in Mexico, 1555

By friendship of one Thomas Blake a Scottishman borne, who had dwelt and had bene married in the said Citie [Mexico] above twentie yeeres before I came to the saide Citie, I was preferred to the service of a gentleman a Spaniard dwelling there, a man of great wealth, and one of the first conquerours of the said Citie, whose name was Gonzalo Cerezo, with whom I dwelt twelve moneths and a halfe. At the ende of which I was maliciously accused by the Holy house for matters of Religion, and so apprehended and caried to prison, where I lay close prisoner seven moneths, without speaking to any creature, but to the Jailer that kept the said prison, when he brought me my meat and drinke. In the meane time was brought into the saide prison one Augustin Boacio an Italian of Genoua also for matters of Religion, who was taken at Sacatecas 80. leagues to the Northwest of the Citie of Mexico: At the ende of the said seven moneths, we were both caried to the high Church of Mexico, to doe open penance upon an high scaffold, made before the high Altar, upon a Sunday, in the presence of a very great number of people, who were at the least five or sixe thousand. For there were that came one hundreth mile off, to see the saide Auto (as they call it) for that there were never none before, that had done the like in the said Countrey, nor could not tell what Lutheranes were, nor what it meant: for they never heard of any such thing before. We were brought into the Church, every one with a S. Benito upon his backe, which is halfe a yard of yellow cloth, with a hole to put in a mans head in the middest, and cast over a mans head: both flaps hang one before, and another behinde, and in the middest of every flap, a S. Andrewes crosse, made of red

G. R. G. Conway, ed., *An Englishman and the Mexican Inquisition* (Mexico City: By the editor, 1927), pp. 11–17.

cloth, sowed on upon the same, and that is called S. Benito. The common people before they sawe the penitents come into the Church, were given to understand that wee were heretiques, infidels, and people that did despise God, and his workes, and that wee had bene more like devils then men, and thought wee had had the favour of some monsters, or heathen people. And when they saw us come into the Church in our players coates, the women and children beganne to cry out, and made such a noise, that it was strange to see and heare, saying, that they never sawe goodlier men in all their lives, and that it was not possible that there could be in us so much evill as was reported of us, and that we were more like Angels among men, then such persons of such evill Religion as by the Priestes and friers wee were reported to be, and that it was great pitie that wee should bee so used for so small an offence. So that being brought into the saide high Church, and set upon the scaffold which was made before the high Altar, in the presence of all the people, untill high Masse was done, and the sermon made by a frier, concerning our matter, they did put us in all the disgrace they could, to cause the people not to take so much compassion upon us, for that wee were heretiques, & people that were seduced of the devill, & had forsaken the faith of the Catholique Church of Rome, with divers other reprochfull wordes, which were too long to recite in this place. High Masse and Sermon being done, our offences, as they called them, were recited, every man what he had said and done, and presently was the sentence pronounced against us. That was, that the said Augustine Boacio was condemned to weare his S. Benito all the dayes of his life, and put into perpetuall prison, where hee should fulfill the same, and all his goods confiscated and lost. And I the saide Tomson to weare the S. Benito for three yeeres, and then to be set at libertie. And for the accomplishing of this sentence or condemnation, we must be presently sent downe from Mexico, to Vera Cruz, and from thence to S. John de Ullua, and there to be shipped for Spaine, which was 65. leagues by land, with strait commandement, that upon paine of 1000. duckets, the Masters every one should looke straitly unto us, and carry us to Spaine, and deliver us unto the Inquisitors of the Holy house of Sivill, that they should put us in the places, where we should fulfill our penances that the Archbishop of Mexico had enjoyned unto us, by his sentence there given. For performance of the which, we were sent downe from Mexico, to the Sea side, which was 65. leagues,

with fetters upon our feete, and there delivered to the Masters of
the ships, to be caried for Spaine, as before is said. And it was so,
that the Italian, fearing that if he had presented himselfe in Spaine
before the Inquisitors, that they would have burned him, to prevent that danger, when wee were comming homeward, and were arrived at the yland of Tercera, one of the ysles of the Azores, the
first night that we came into the said port to an ancker, about mid-
night he found the meanes to get him naked out of the ship into the
sea, & swam naked a shoare, and so presently got him to the further
side of the yland, where hee found a little Carvel ready to depart
for Portugal, in the which he came to Lisbone, and passed into
France, and so into England, where hee ended his life in the Citie
of London. And I for my part kept still aboord the ship, and came
into Spaine, and was delivered to the Inquisitors of the Holy house
of Sivill, where they kept me in close prison, till I had fulfilled the
three yeeres of my penance. Which time being expired, I was freely
put out of prison, and set at libertie: and being in the Citie of Sivil
a casher of one Hugh Typton, an English marchant of great doing,
by the space of one yeere, it fortuned that there came out of the Citie
of Mexico, a Spaniard, called John de la Barrera, that had bene long
time in the Indies, and had got great summes of golde and silver,
and with one onely daughter shipped himselfe for to come for
Spaine, and by the way chanced to die, and gave all that hee had
unto his onely daughter, whose name was Marie de la Barrera,
and being arrived at the Citie of Sivil, it was my chance to marry
with her. The marriage was worth to mee 2500. pounds in barres of
golde and silver, besides jewels of great price. This I thought good
to speake of, to shew the goodnes of God to all them that put their
trust in him, that I being brought out of the Indies, in such great
misery and infamy to the world, should be provided at Gods hand
in one moment, of more then in all my life before I could attaine
unto by my owne labour.

After we departed from Mexico, our S. Benitoes were set up in
the high Church of the said Citie, with our names written in the
same, according to their use and custome, which is and will be a
monument and a remembrance of us, as long as the Romish Church
doth raigne in that country. The same have bene seene since by one
John Chilton, and divers others of our nation, which were left in
that countrey long since, by Sir John Hawkins. And because it shalbe
knowen wherefore it was that I was so punished by the Clergies

hande, as before is mentioned, I will in briefe words declare the same.

It is so, that being in Mexico at the table, among many principall people at dinner, they began to inquire of me being an Englishman, whether it were true, that in England they had overthrowen all their Churches and houses of Religion, and that all the images of the Saints of heaven that were in them were throwen downe, broken, and burned, and in some places high wayes stoned with them, and whether the English nation denied their obedience to the Pope of Rome, as they had bene certified out of Spaine by their friends. To whom I made answere, that it was so, that in deed they had in England put downe all the Religious houses of friers and monks that were in England, and the images that were in their Churches and other places were taken away, and used there no more: for that (as they say) the making of them, and putting of them where they were adored, was cleane contrary to the expresse commandement of Almighty God, Thou shalt not make to thy selfe any graven image, &c. and that for that cause they thought it not lawfull that they should stand in the Church, which is the house of adoration. One that was at the declaring of these words, who was my master Gonsalo Cereso, answered and said, if it were against the commandement of God, to have images in the Churches, that then he had spent a great deale of money in vaine, for that two yeres past he had made in the monastery of Santo Domingo, in the said citie of Mexico, an image of our Lady of pure silver & golde, with pearles and precious stones, which cost him 7000. and odde pesos, and every peso is 4.s. 8.d. of our money: which indeed was true, for that I have seene it many times my selfe where it stands. At the table was another gentleman, who presuming to defend the cause more then any other that was there, saide, that they knew well ynough that they were made but of stockes and stones, and that to them was no worship given, but that there was a certaine veneration due unto them after they were set up in the Church, and that they were set there to a good intent: the one, for that they were books for the simple people, to make them understand the glory of the saints that were in heaven, & a shape of them to put us in remembrance to cal upon them, to be our intercessors unto God for us, for that we are such miserable sinners, that we are not worthy to appeare before God, & that using devotion to saints in heaven, they may obtaine at Gods hands the sooner, the thing that we demand of him. As for example, said he, imagin that a subject hath offended his king upon the earth in any kind of respect, is it for the party to go boldly to the king in person, & to demand pardon for his offences? No, saith he, the presumption were too great, & possibly he might be repulsed, and have a great rebuke for his labour. Better it is for such a person to seek some private man neere the king in his Court, and make him acquainted with his matter, & let him be a mediator to his Majesty for him, & for the matter he hath to do with him, and so might he the better come to his purpose, and obteine the thing which he doeth demand: even so saith he, it is with God and his saints in heaven: for we are wretched sinners: and not worthy to appeare nor present our selves before the Majesty of God, to demand of him the thing that we have need of: therefore thou hast need to be devout, and have devotion to the mother of God, and the saints of heaven, to be intercessors to God for thee, and so mayest thou the better obteine of God the thing that thou dost demand. To this I answered, & said, sir, as touching the comparison you made of the intercessors to the king, how necessary they were, I would but aske you this question. Set the case that this king you speak of, if he be so merciful, as, when he knoweth that one, or any of his subjects hath offended him, he send for him to his owne towne, or to his owne house, or palace, & say unto him, come hither, I know that thou hast offended many lawes, if thou doest know thereof, and doest repent thee of the same, with ful intent to offend no more, I wil forgive thy trespasse, and remember it no more: said I, if this be done by the kings owne person, what then hath this man need to go seeke friendship at any of the kings privat servants hands, but go to the principal, seeing that he is readier to forgive thee, then thou art to demand forgivenes at his hands? Even so is it with our gracious God, who calleth and crieth out unto us throughout all the world, by the mouth of his Prophets, Apostles, and by his owne mouth, saying, Come unto me al ye that labour and are over laden, and I will refresh you: besides 1000. other offers and proffers which hee doth make unto us in his holy Scriptures. What then have we need of the saints helpe that are in heaven, whereas the Lord himself doth so freely offer himselfe unto us? At which sayings, many of the hearers were astonied, and said, that by that reason, I would give to understand, that the invocation of Saints was to be disanulled, and by the Lawes of God not commanded. I answered, that they were not my words but the words of God himselfe: looke into the Scriptures your selfe, and you shall so finde it. The talke was perceived to be prejudiciall to the Romish doctrine, and therefore it was commanded to be no more entreated of, and all remained unthought upon, had it not bene for a villanous Portugal that was in the company, who said, Basta ser Ingles para saber todo esto y mas: who the next day, without imparting any thing to any body, went to the Bishop of Mexico, and his Provisor, and said, that in a place where he had bene the day before, was an Englishman, who had said, that there was no need of Saints in the Church, nor of any invocation of Saints, upon whose denomination I was apprehended for the same words here rehearsed, and none other thing, and thereupon was used, as before is written.

C. Brazil

4. The Holy Office Visits Brazil, 1591–1595

ARNOLD WIZNITZER

The Inquisition was never formally introduced in Brazil, but about 1580 the bishop of Bahia was given inquisitioral powers by the Holy Office in Lisbon. Jesuits were empowered to assist the bishop in preparing proceedings against heretics, and in extraditing offenders to the tribunals of the Inquisition in Lisbon.

After the unification of Portugal and Spain in 1580, the activities of the Inquisition everywhere were intensified in severity and enlarged in scope. On March 26, 1591, Albert, archduke of Austria, a cardinal and Inquisitor General for Portugal and the Colonies, appointed the *licenciado* Heitor Furtado de Mendoça as *visitador* for São Thomé, Cabo Verde, Brazil, and the administration of São Vicente or Rio de Janeiro.

The *visitador* Mendoça arrived in Bahia on June 9, 1591. On July 28, 1591, after having appointed the inquisitorial commission, he published an Edict of Faith, a Monitory Letter, and a Term of

Arnold Wiznitzer, *Jews in Colonial Brazil* (New York: Columbia University Press, 1960), pp. 12–32, *passim*. Reprinted by permission.

Grace for the city of Bahia and an area of one league surrounding
Bahia. The population could, within thirty days, make confessions
and denounce other persons in order to obtain merciful treatment
from the Inquisition. The objectives of the visitation included the
discovery of unnatural sexual practices, sorcery, and insults to the
Catholic Church, also exposure of Lutherans, and Judaizers among
the New Christians. All offenses against the established order were
to be harshly punished. The Judaizers, or "persons of the Nation,"
who professed Catholicism but secretly observed Jewish rites
and customs, were the most important game hunted by the Inquisition. . . .

It is easy to imagine the panic which the *visitador's* publications
produced among the few thousand white people who lived in Bahia in 1591. Those who knew the methods of the Inquisition were
alarmed. Others were aroused to carnality and a thirst for vengeance.
Dozens of people appeared before the inquisitorial commissions to
make confessions, and hundreds came with denunciations against
strangers, friends, relatives, and even deceased persons. Many of
these people probably told the truth in asserting that, prior to reading the Monitory Letter, they were completely ignorant of the fact
that some of the rites practiced by themselves or others constituted
Judaizing activities. . . .

Most of the confessions and denunciations affected the inhabitants of the town of Matoim in the captaincy of Bahia, where there
was a great deal of intermarriage between New and Old Christians.
The Judaizers of Bahia had secret synagogues, rabbis, and perhaps
a Sefer Torah brought by Heitor Antunes from Portugal in 1557.
Whenever it was not too dangerous, they circumcized their sons,
observed Jewish holidays, fast days, and ritual food laws, as well as
various Jewish ceremonies and customs. Some of their practices
were based on superstition; others, such as the flogging of crucifixes,
were induced by the years of festering hatred which persecution by
the Inquisition had aroused.

Most of these New Christians lived as secret Jews without much
interference by the Church, and they do not appear to have taken
any great precautions to hide the fact. At first, the visit of an inquisitorial inspector caused a panic among them, and many considered emigration. However, the *visitador* lacked sufficient evidence
to start proceedings against many of the Judaizers in Bahia, and

only a few were turned over to the tribunal of the Inquisition in Lisbon.

On September 21, 1593, Heitor Furtado de Mendoça arrived in Recife. On October 24, 1593, he established an inquisitorial commission in the town of Olinda near Recife by promulgating an Edict of Faith, a Monitory Letter, and a Term of Grace for certain parishes. He also visited Itamaracá and Parahiba.

At that time, the captaincy of Pernambuco was populated by some eight thousand whites, two thousand peaceful Indians, and ten thousand African Negro slaves. As the sixteenth century ended, Pernambuco was the most advanced and prosperous captaincy in Brazil, Jorge de Albuquerque then serving as its governor. The economy of the area was based on sugar, cotton, and dyewood, on exports and imports, and Pernambuco had many wealthy families whose standard of living included a measure of luxury.

The denunciations and confessions occasioned by the visitation in Pernambuco deserve special attention for the light they shed on the nature of alleged transgressions. Particularly interesting are thirteen denunciations against the deceased Diogo Fernandes and his wife, Branca Dias, brought before the inquisitorial commission in Olinda. . . . According to rumors, Branca Dias had come to Brazil after having been persecuted by the Inquisition, and her husband had followed her after her escape from Portugal, sometime between 1535 and 1542.

On their arrival in Olinda, Diogo Fernandes and Branca Dias established a boarding school for young girls, in which they gave instruction in cooking and sewing. Later, they moved to Camaragibe, where Diogo Fernandes became the administrator of the sugar mill and farm of Bento Dias Santiago, a rich New Christian and a relative of Branca Dias. Santiago was the tax-farmer for the captaincies of Bahia, Pernambuco, and Itamaracá from 1575. . . .

Former pupils of Branca Dias's boarding school reported that with the help of Negro slave girls they had cleaned and washed the house every Friday, and that no one in that house worked on Saturdays. Branca Dias and her daughters, it was alleged, had worn their best clothes on the Jewish Sabbath; on that day Branca shared her meals with her daughters. A special yellow-colored dish was prepared for the Fernandes family on the Sabbath. According to Branca's younger daughters, it consisted of ground grains, meat, oil, onions, and spices. Others reported that, on Sundays in church, when the words "alevantavão ao Senhor na ostia consagrada" were recited, Branca Dias used to murmur "there are chained dogs." It was further asserted that Diogo Fernandes did not permit his slaves to work in the sugar mill on Saturday, and he worked outside Camaragibe during the week but always came home on Friday and stayed until Monday morning. It was also reported that the candlesticks were cleaned and equipped with new twisted thread and fresh oil on Friday. It was charged that there was a synagogue in Camaragibe, in which Jews gathered, arriving in carriages adorned with tree branches, to celebrate the fast day of "Gujpurr" (Yom Kippur) and other holidays. Diogo, his brother Duarte, and his son-in-law Diogo, all of them administrators of the farm and sugar mill in Camaragibe, were said to have lived in conformity with the Jewish law, rites, and customs. It was further stated that, at a later date, the new administrators of this sugar mill, members of the Vas family, continued these Judaizing activities. The schoolteacher Bento Teixeira was accused of frequent visits to Violante Fernandes, to whom he would explain the Latin Bible.

The denunciations continued. A likeness of the head of an ox, made of wood and about a span and a half (13½ inches) long, had been seen in the house of Diogo and Branca; Branca Dias and Jorge Dias de Caja had possessed a "toura," which they worshipped; Dona Brites de Albuquerque, widow of Duarte Coelho, the first governor and *donatário* of Pernambuco, had visited Diogo Fernandes before he died and had reportedly advised him to invoke the name of Jesus, but Diogo had refused to follow her advice.

Diogo Dias Fernandes and his wife are the first Brazilian Marranos to be identified by name. There is no doubt that Diogo Fernandes and Branca Dias and their family were Marranos, and that the synagogue of Camaragibe on the farm of Bento Dias Santiago was the center of Judaizers in Pernambuco. The name of Branca Dias became legendary in Brazil, and it has found its way into the literature of later generations. Not only Diogo Fernandes and Branca Dias, but also their daughters Ines, Violante, Guiomar, and Felippa were dead by the time the *visitador* came to Pernambuco in 1593. This functionary did not hesitate, however, to imprison on August 28, 1595, the unmarried daughter of Diogo and Branca, the crippled Beatriz Fernandes. The initial sentence pronounced against Beatriz Fernandes at an auto-da-fé of January 31, 1599, condemned her to go to the public auto-da-fé and to abjure her heresies. She was there sentenced to life imprisonment and to the wearing of the *habito* (prison garb) for life. Thus did the Holy Inquisition wreak its vengeance on the family of Diogo Fernandes and Branca Dias, the first known Judaizers in Brazil. . . .

The records presented throughout these pages indicate that a considerable part of the white population of the captaincy of Pernambuco were Judaizers. They began to come to Pernambuco very early in the sixteenth century. They were farmers, owners, and administrators of sugar plantations and sugar mills, merchants, manufacturers of confections, teachers, and owners of boarding houses. The richest among them were Bento Dias Santiago and João Nunes. Their spiritual center was Camaragibe, which had a synagogue and a "toura" (probably not a Sefer Torah but only a *mezuzah*). This center was evidently organized by Diogo Fernandes and his wife, Branca Dias, the first known couple of New Christians who settled in Brazil. For Yom Kippur, the Judaizers of Pernambuco came to Camaragibe. In Olinda they had a Shammash to call them to the divine services held in Camaragibe. It is almost certain that the author of the *Dialogos das Grandezas do Brasil,* one of the greatest books ever written about that country, was the Judaizer Ambrosio Fernandes Brandão of Pernambuco. The first Brazilian poet, author of the famous *Prosopopea,* was Bento Teixeira, another Judaizer, who spent about twenty-five years in Brazil. The records reveal other important facts: Many of the officials of the Catholic Church in Brazil were New Christians; others were bribed by Marranos to tolerate Judaizing activities. The curate Cortiçado, for example, was charged with having accepted bribes from Judaizers in return for tolerating the practice of their customs. Even the ecclesiastical auditor of Pernambuco, the vicar Diogo de Couto, who was still in office in 1593, was reported to be a New Christian on his father's side, and to have been bribed by Judaizers.

D. The Inquisition in Seventeenth-Century Peru

5. Portuguese Judaizers in Peru

HENRY CHARLES LEA

The most serious business of the tribunal, in the line of its proper functions, was with the apostasy of the Jewish New Christians. From the very foundation of the colonies . . . restrictions were laid on the emigration of Conversos and a law of 1543, preserved in the Recopilacion, orders that search be made for all descendants of Jews who were to be rigorously expelled. In spite, however, of the jealous care observed to preserve the colonies from all danger of Jewish infection, the commercial attractions were so powerful that the New Christians eluded all precautions. At first, however, they occupied but a small portion of the energies of the tribunal. . . . The first appearance of Jews is in the auto of October 29, 1581, when Manuel López, a Portuguese, was reconciled with confiscation and perpetual prison, and Diego de la Rosa, described as a native of Quito, was required to abjure *de levi* and was exiled — showing that the evidence against him was very dubious. . . .

The conquest of Portugal, in 1580, had led to a large emigration to Castile, where Portuguese soon became synonymous with Judaizer, and this was beginning to make itself manifest in the colonies. The auto of December 17, 1595, gave impressive evidence of this. Five Portuguese — Juan Méndez, Antonio Núñez, Juan López, Francisco Báez and Manuel Rodríguez — were reconciled. Another, Herman Jorje, had died during trial and his memory was not prosecuted. There were also four martyrs. Jorje Núñez denied until he was tied upon the rack; he then confessed and refused to be converted, but after his sentence of relaxation was read he weakened and was strangled before burning. Francisco Rodríguez endured torture without confessing; when threatened with repetition he endeavored unsuccessfully to commit suicide; he was voted to relaxation with torture *in caput alienum,* and under it he accused several persons but revoked at ratification. He was pertinacious to the last and was burnt alive. Juan Fernández was relaxed, although insane; the Suprema expressed doubts whether he had intelligence enough to render him responsible. Pedro de Contreras had been tortured for confession and again *in caput alienum;* he denied Judaism throughout and was relaxed as a *negativo;* at the auto he manifested great devotion to a crucifix and presumably was strangled; in all probability he was really a Christian. . . .

In 1626 there commenced a trial which illustrates forcibly the inexorable discipline of the Church, rendering it the supreme duty of the Christian to persecute and destroy all heresy. Francisco Maldonado de Silva was a surgeon of high repute in Concepcion de Chile. He was of Portuguese descent. His father had suffered in the Inquisition, had been reconciled and brought up his children, two girls and a boy, as Christians. Francisco was a good Catholic until at the age of 18, he chanced to read the *Scrutinium Scripturarum* of Pablo de Santa María, Bishop of Búrgos — a controversial work written for the conversion of Jews. So far from confirming him in the faith it raised doubts leading him to consult his father, who told him to study the Bible and instructed him in the Law of Moses. He became an ardent convert to Judaism, but kept his secret from his mother and two sisters and from his wife, for he was married and had a child, and his wife was pregnant when he was arrested. During her absence, a year or two before, he had circumcised himself. At the age of 35, considering that his sister Isabel who was about 33, was mature enough for religious independence, he revealed his secret to her and endeavored to convert her, but in vain, and he was impervious to her entreaties to abandon his faith. They seem to have been tenderly attached to each other; he was her sole support as well as that of her mother and sister, but she could not escape the necessity of communicating the facts in confession to her confessor. The prescriptions of the Church were absolute; no family ties relieved one from the obligation of denouncing heresy, and she could not hope for sacramental absolution without discharging the duty. We can picture to ourselves the torment of that agonized soul as she nerved herself to the awful duty which could cost her a lifetime of remorse and misery when she obeyed her confessor's commands and denounced her brother to the Inquisition.

The warrant for his arrest was issued December 12, 1626, and executed at Concepcion April 29, 1627. His friend, the Dominican Fray Diego de Ureña, visited him in his place of confinement, May 2, and sought to convert him, but he was resolved to die in the faith in which his father had died. So when transferred to Santiago, the Augustinian Fray Alonso de Almeida made similar efforts with like ill-success; he knew that he should die for the faith, he had never spoken to any one but his sister and she had betrayed him. He was received in Lima July 23d and was admitted to an audience the same day. When required to swear on the cross he refused, saying that he was a Jew and would live and die as such; if he had to swear it would be by the living God, the God of Israel. His trial went on through all the customary formalities, protracted by the repeated conferences held with theologians who endeavored to convince him of his errors. Eleven of these were held without weakening his pertinacity until, on January 26, 1633, the consulta de fe unanimously condemned him to relaxation.

A long sickness followed, caused by a fast of eighty days which had reduced him almost to a skeleton covered with sores. On convalescing, he asked for another conference, to solve the doubts which he had drawn up in writing. It was held June 26, 1634, and left him as pertinacious as ever. Meanwhile the prison was filling with Judaizers, of whom a number had been discovered in Lima. He asked for maize husks in place of his ration of bread, and with them made a rope by which he escaped through a window and visited two neighboring cells, urging the prisoners to be steadfast in their law; they denounced him and he made no secret of it, confessing freely what he had done. It was a mercy of God, we are told, that his prolonged fast had rendered him deaf, or he would have learned much from them of what had been going on.

The tribunal was so preoccupied, with the numerous trials on foot at the time, that Maldonado was left undisturbed, awaiting the general auto that was to follow. We hear nothing more until, after an interval of four years, a thirteenth conference was held at his request, November 12, 1638. It was as fruitless as its predecessors and, at its conclusion, he produced two books (each of them of more than a hundred leaves), made with marvellous ingenuity out of scraps of paper and written with ink made of charcoal and pens cut out of egg-shells with a knife fashioned from a nail, which he said he delivered up for the discharge of his conscience. Then on December 9th and 10th were held two more conferences in which his pertinacity remained unshaken. The long tragedy was now drawing to an end after an imprisonment which had lasted for nearly thirteen years. He was brought out in the great auto of January 23, 1639, where, when the sentences of relaxation were read, a sudden whirlwind tore away the awning and, looking up, he exclaimed "The God of Israel does this to look upon me face to face!" He was unshrinking to the last and was burnt alive a true martyr to his faith. His two paper books were hung around his neck to burn with him and assist in burning him.

This auto of 1639, the greatest that had as yet been held in the New World, was the culmination of the "complicidad grande" — the name given by the inquisitors to a number of Judaizers whom they had discovered. As they described the situation, in a report of 1636, large numbers of Portuguese had entered the kingdom by way of Buenos Ayres, Brazil, Mexico, Granada and Puerto Bello, thus increasing the already numerous bands of their compatriots. They became masters of the commerce of the kingdom; from brocade to sack-cloth, from diamonds to cumin-seed, everything passed through their hands; the Castilian who had not a Portuguese partner could look for no success in trade. They would buy the cargoes of whole fleets with the fictitious credits which they exchanged, thus rendering capital unnecessary, and would distribute the merchandise throughout the land by their agents, who were likewise Portuguese, and their capacity developed until, in 1634, they negotiated for the farming of the royal customs.

In August, 1634, Joan de Salazar, a merchant, denounced to the Inquisition Antonio Cordero, clerk of a trader from Seville, because he refused to make a sale on a Saturday. On another occasion, going to his store on a Friday morning, he found Cordero breakfasting on a piece of bread and an apple and, on asking him whether he had not better take a rasher of bacon, Cordero replied "Must I eat what my father and grandfather never ate?" The evidence was weak and no immediate action was taken, but, in October, the commissioners were instructed secretly to ascertain and report the number of Portuguese in their several districts. The matter rested and, as nothing new was developed, in March, 1635, the evidence against Cordero was laid before a consulta de fe and it was resolved to arrest him secretly, without sequestration, so that the hand of the Inquisition might not be apparent. Bartolomé de Larrea, a familiar, called on him, April 2d, under pretence of settling an account, and locked him in a room; a sedan-chair was brought, and he was conveyed to the secret prison. His disappearance excited much talk and he was supposed to have fled, for the supposition of arrest by the Inquisition was scouted, seeing that there had not been sequestration.

Cordero confessed at once that he was a Jew and, under torture, implicated his employer and two others. These were arrested on May 11th and the free employment of torture obtained the names of numerous accomplices. The prisons were full and to empty them an auto in the chapel was hurriedly arranged and preparations were made for the hasty construction of additional cells. On August 11th, between 12:30 and 2 o'clock, seventeen arrests were made, so quietly and simultaneously that it was all effected before the people were conscious of it. These were among the most prominent citizens and greatest merchants of Lima, and we are told that the impression produced on the community was like the Day of Judgement. Torture and inquisitorial methods elicited further information resulting in additional arrests; the affrighted Portuguese began to scatter and, at the request of the tribunal, the Viceroy Chinchon prohibited for a year any one to leave Peru without its license. . . .

One matter which vexed the souls of the inquisitors was the effort made by the threatened Portuguese to hide their property from sequestration. A proclamation was issued, ordering all who knew of such matters to reveal them within nine days under pain of excommunication and other penalties. This was successful to some extent, but the difficulties in the way were illustrated in the case of Enrique de Paz, for whom Melchor de los Reies secreted much silver, jewels and merchandise. Among other things he deposited with his friend Don Dionisio Manrique, Knight of Santiago, senior alcalde de corte and a consultor of the tribunal, a quantity of silver and some fifty or sixty pieces of rich silks. Manrique did not deny receiving them, but said that the same night Melchor ordered them taken away by a young man who was a stranger to him. The inquisitors evidently disbelieved the story; they reported that they had unsuccessfully tried friendly methods with Manrique and asked the Suprema for instructions.

The sequestration of so much property brought all trade to a stand-still and produced indescribable confusion, aggravated, in 1635, by the consequent failure of the bank. The men arrested had nearly all the trade of the colony in their hands; they were involved in an infinity of complicated transactions and suits sprang up on all sides. Creditors and suitors pressed their claims desperately, fearing that with delay witnesses might disappear, in the widening circle of arrests. There were many suits pending already in the Audiencia which were claimed by the tribunal and surrendered to it. It was puzzled by the new business thus thrown upon it; to a suit there had to be two parties, but the prisoners could not plead, so it appointed Manuel de Monte Alegre as their "defensor" to appear for them, and it went on hearing and deciding complicated civil suits while conducting the prosecutions for heresy. Mondays and Thursdays were assigned for civil business, and every afternoon, from 3 P.M. until dark, was devoted to examination of the documents. The inquisitors claimed that they pushed forward strenuously in settling accounts and paying debts, for otherwise all commerce would be destroyed to the irreparable damage of the Republic, which was already exhausted in so many ways. This did not suit the Suprema, which, by letters of October 22d and November 9, 1635, forbade the surrender of any sequestrated or confiscated property, no matter what evidence was produced of ownership or claims, without first consulting it. This exacting payment of all debts and postponing payment of claims threatened general bankruptcy when the rich merchants were arrested, for their aggregate liabilities amounted to eight hundred thousand pesos, which was estimated as equal to the whole capital of Lima. To avert this, some payments were made but only on the strength of competent security being furnished. . . .

Meanwhile the trials of the accused were pushed forward as rapidly as the perplexities of the situation admitted. Torture was not spared. Murcia de Luna, a woman of 27, died under it. Antonio de Acuña was subjected to it for three hours and when he was carried out, Alcaide Pradeda described his arms as being torn to pieces. Progress was impeded, however, by the devices of the prisoners, who were in hopes that influences at work in Spain would secure a general pardon like that of 1604. With this object they revoked their confessions and their accusations of each other, giving rise to endless complications. Some of the latter revocations, however, were genuine and were adhered to, even through the torture which was freely

used in these cases. Besides this, to cast doubt on the whole affair,
they accused the innocent and even Old Christians. . . . The
inquisitors add that they abstained in many cases from making arrests, when the testimony was insufficient and the parties were not
Portuguese.

The tribunal was manned with four inquisitors, who struggled
resolutely through this complicated mass of business, and at length
were ready to make public the results of their labors in the auto of
January 23, 1639. This was celebrated with unexampled pomp and
ostentation, for now money was abundant and the opportunity of
making an impression on the popular mind was not to be lost.
During the previous night, when their sentences were made known
to those who were to be relaxed, two of them, Enrique de Paz and
Manuel de Espinosa, professed conversion; the inquisitors came and
examined them, a consulta was assembled and they were admitted
to reconciliation. There was great rivalry among men of position for
the honor of accompanying the penitents and Don Salvadoro Veláz-
quez, one of the principal Indians, *sargento mayor* of the Indian
militia, begged to be allowed to carry one of the effigies, which
he did in resplendent uniform. Conspicuous in a place of honor in the
procession were the seven who had been acquitted, richly dressed,
mounted on white horses and carrying palms of victory.

Besides the Judaizers there was a bigamist and five women pen-
anced for sorcery. There was also the alcaide's assistant Valcázar,
who was deprived of his familiarship and was exiled for four years.
Juan de Canelas Albarran, the occupant of a house adjoining the
prison, who had permitted an opening through the walls for communications, received a hundred lashes and five years of exile, and
Ana María González, who was concerned in the matter, had also a
hundred lashes and four years of exile.

Of the Judaizers there were seven who escaped with abjuration
de vehementi, various penalties and fines aggregating eight hundred
pesos. There were forty-four reconciled with punishments varied according to their deserts. Those who had confessed readily as to
themselves and others were let off with confiscation and deportation
to Spain. Those who prevaricated or gave trouble had, in addition,
lashes or galleys or both. Of these there were twenty-one, the aggregate lashes amounting to four thousand and the years of galleys
to a hundred and six, besides two condemnations for life. In addition to these were the mother of the Murcia de Luna who died under

torture, Doña Mayor de Luna, a woman of high social position, and her daughter Doña Isabel de Luna, a girl of 18, who, for endeavoring to communicate with each other in prison, were sentenced to a hundred lashes through the streets, naked from the waist up. There was also one reconciliation in effigy of a culprit who had died in prison.

There were eleven relaxations in person and the effigy of one who had committed suicide during trial. Of the eleven, seven are said to have died pertinacious and impenitent and therefore presumably were burnt alive, true martyrs to their belief. Of these there were two especially notable — Maldonado whose case has been mentioned above, and Manuel Bautista Pérez. The latter was the leader and chief among the Portuguese, who styled him the *capitan grande*. He was the greatest merchant in Lima and his fortune was popularly estimated at half a million pesos. It was in his house that were held the secret meetings in which he joined in the learned theological discussions, but outwardly he was a zealous Christian and had priests to educate his children; he was greatly esteemed by the clergy who dedicated to him their literary effusions in terms of the warmest adulation. He owned rich silver mines in Huarochirí and two extensive plantations; his confiscated house has since been known as the *casa de Pilatos*, and his ostentatious mode of life may be judged by the fact that when his carriage was sold by the tribunal it fetched thirty-four hundred pesos. He had endeavored to commit suicide by stabbing himself, but he never faltered at the end. He listened proudly to his sentence and died impenitent, telling the executioner to do his duty. There was one other prisoner who did not appear. Enrique Jorje Tavares, a youth of 18, was among those arrested in August, 1635. He denied under torture and after various alternations became permanently insane, for which reason his case was suspended in 1639.

The next day the mob of Lima enjoyed the further sensation of the scourging through the streets. These exhibitions always attracted a large crowd, in which there were many horsemen who thus had a better view, while boys commonly pelted the bigamists and sorceresses who were the usual patients. On this occasion the tribunal issued a proclamation forbidding horses or carriages in the streets through which the procession passed, and any pelting of the penitents under pain, for Spaniards, of banishment to Chile, and for Indians and Negroes, of a hundred lashes. There were twenty-nine sufferers in all; they were marched in squads of ten, guarded by soldiers and familiars, while the executioners plied the scourges, and the brutalizing spectacle passed off without disturbance, and with the pious wish of the tribunal that it would please God to make it serve as a warning.

E. The Inquisition in Eighteenth-Century Mexico

6. The Mexican Inquisition and the Enlightenment

RICHARD E. GREENLEAF

Many scholars have called attention to the fact that the Holy Office of the Inquisition was a political instrument. What has not been examined in detail is the relationship that existed between heresy and treason during the three centuries of Spanish and Spanish colonial Inquisition history. The belief that heretics were traitors and traitors were heretics led to the conviction that dissenters of any kind were social revolutionaries trying to subvert the political and religious stability of the community. These tenets were not later developments in the history of the Spanish Inquisition; they were inherent in the rationale of the institution from the fifteenth century onward, and were apparent in the Holy Office's dealing with the Jews, Protestants, and other heretics during the sixteenth century. The use of the Inquisition by the later eighteenth-century Bourbon kings in Spain as an instrument of regalism was not a departure from tradition. Particularly in the Viceroyalty of New Spain during the late eighteenth century do the Inquisition trials show how the Crown sought to promote political and religious orthodoxy.

The Age of Science and the Age of Reason in seventeenth- and eighteenth-century Europe had powerful reverberations in the new

Richard E. Greenleaf, "The Mexican Inquisition and the Enlightenment, 1763–1805," *New Mexico Historical Review*, XLI (July, 1966), pp. 181–191. Copyright 1966 by the University of New Mexico Press. Reprinted by permission of the author and the University of New Mexico Press.

world colonies of Spain. The attack on Scholasticism and the campaign against divine right kingship represented a joint political-religious venture all the more significant because the papacy was also a divine right institution. Regalist prelates came to dominate the Church in Spain and Spanish America, and they were just as combative in their efforts to quell the new exponents of natural laws of politics and economics as were the Spanish monarchs. The environmentalism of Montesquieu and Rousseau was as much a challenge to Spanish rule in America as were the doctrines of empiricism and methodical doubt to the supremacy of the Roman Catholic faith and dogmas. During the period 1760 to 1805, the vicissitudes of Spanish-French politics and the shifting diplomatic and military alliances of the Spanish rulers in Europe complicated the problem of stemming the tide of rationalism in Mexico. The opening decade of the century had heralded the arrival of the French Bourbons on the Spanish throne, and the Spanish royal house and the French monarchy coordinated their diplomacies by the Family Compact of 1761. This made it difficult to prevent the circulation of Francophile ideas in the empire.

The Frenchmen in New Spain openly espoused Enlightenment ideas. Before 1763 they had infiltrated the periphery of the Viceroyalty of New Spain — merchants, sailors, and even clergy who came from Louisiana or the French-held islands of the Caribbean. In addition to French Protestantism, they began to disseminate the pre-revolutionary ideas of the *philosophes* and French literary figures. Technicians at the military-naval department of San Blas on the Pacific, physicians all over the empire, royal cooks and hairdressers in the viceregal capital, regiments of soldiers — all of these added to the Francophile *ambiente* in eighteenth-century Mexico. In the two decades, 1763 to 1783, and even afterwards, the residuum of French influence in Louisiana caused New Orleans to be a center of sedition.

Before philosophe thought culminated in the bloody French uprisings of 1789–1793, the Holy Office of the Inquisition found itself hamstrung in enforcing orthodoxy because of the *afrancesado* leanings of Charles III (1759–1788) in his administrative techniques and his economic theories. For all of these reasons French literature was read in Mexico, not only for its freshness and its vitality, but as a guide for the "promotion of useful knowledge." An inherently dangerous ingredient of this milieu was the Holy Office's necessary relaxation of censorship, with the subsequent proliferation of French ideas on many levels of Mexican society. As the French Revolution gained momentum, the fear of its export to Mexico gave impetus to a resurgence of inquisitorial activity, demands for expulsion of Frenchmen and other suspicious foreigners from Mexico, and confiscation of their properties. This cycle of Francophobia gradually ended as the political alliances of Spain vis-à-vis France and England again shifted, and as the reactionary Directorate consolidated its power in revolutionary France. After 1800, it soon became apparent that Napoleon Bonaparte was unwittingly spreading libertine doctrines over Europe, and the Holy Office once again had the task of defining and enforcing Mexican orthodoxy in a confused ideological and diplomatic environment. The investigatory activities of the Mexican Inquisition and the trials of the era must be examined against this background.

Enlightenment men in France — and in New Spain — were talking of popular sovereignty and the inalienable rights of man. The men who questioned the divine right of kings and severed the royal head of Louis XVI from his divine body were also prone to question papal authority, the practice of indulgences, the Triune God, the Immaculate Conception of Mary, and the doctrine of original sin. Both Voltaire and Rousseau had unorthodox religious ideas as well as iconoclastic social and political ones. Those who analyzed orthodox Christianity and established Mexican societal patterns from the philosophe point of view, often found them wanting. Fear lest the French Revolution spread to the Mexican viceroyalty was so great that after 1789 the Holy Office forbade citizens to read about the deplorable event. Late in 1794 plans were made to expel all Frenchmen and French sympathizers in the manner of the Jesuit expulsion three decades earlier.

The Inquisition's control over printed matter, including books, pamphlets, manuscripts — and even printed designs, some of which, for example, showed the Tree of Reason — extended well beyond mere censorship of questionable material. In theory, all books which entered New Spain were inspected by the Inquisition; much of the data in the Inquisition archive of Mexico consists of lengthy lists from the *aduana,* together with inventories of books being detained in the port of Veracruz. With the aid of these lists one can trace the evolving definition of orthodoxy by noting what works, once banned, were later passed. The books ordered by individual Mexicans throw light on colonial mentality through a knowledge of what men were reading.

Monelisa Lina Pérez-Marchand made an extensive study of the books prohibited in Mexico by the Inquisition, and her research determined that in the latter part of the eighteenth century, works of political philosophy predominated. It is important to note that the majority of books proscribed by Holy Office edicts during 1763–1805 did not simply question specific policies but rather challenged the theoretical existence or *raison d'être* of the State. This indirect attack made it possible for the colonist to read and apply general theories to particular circumstances — Spanish mercantilism, monopolization of office by peninsular Spaniards, monolithic religion, etc. Because the colonists saw the French Revolution as an attempt to put these ideas into practice, accounts of it had to be zealously prohibited. Such works always carried heretical religious propositions. The banned *Lettres d'une Péruvienne* (1797) are a case in point. The Holy Office charged that they were filled with sedition and heresy and "injurious to monarchs and Catholic rulers of Spain . . . and to religion itself." The same decree also prohibited *Les Ruines ou Meditation sur les revolutions des Empires* by M. Volney and others. A separate ban of the Volney tract alleged that:

> its author affirmed that there neither is nor could be revealed religion, that all (people) are daughters of curiosity, ignorance, interest, and imposture, and that the mystery of the birth of Jesus Christ, and the rest of the Christian religion are mystical allegories.

The Holy Office of the Inquisition did not limit its censorship to French books; English Enlightenment works were also a matter of concern. The works of Alexander Pope were most frequently mentioned in edicts of the Inquisition, particularly his *Cartas de Abelardo y Heloisa*, a translation of *Eloise to Abelard,* telling the tale of a nun's love for Peter Abelard. Proscriptions of Pope occurred in 1792 and 1799, and by 1815 all of his works were banned. Other English books on the lists were *Gulliver's Travels* (1803), *Tom Jones* (1803), and *Pamela* (1803). The most important edict of the period was the one issued on August 25, 1805, for it presents a comprehensive and alphabetical listing of all books prohibited since 1789.

Several hundred works appear on the list. The edict not only reflects concern with the French Revolution, but also with the ascendancy of Napoleon.

In many cases the Inquisition not only found it necessary to prohibit political philosophy, but to deny its content and validity. An example of this was the edict of November 13, 1794 with regard to a volume published in Philadelphia by Santiago Felipe Puglia entitled *Desengaño del Hombre:*

> The author of this book, writing in their own language, blows his raucous trumpet to excite the faithful people of the Spanish nation to rebellion of the most infamous sort. . . . The pedantic writer has made of himself a bankrupt merchant in such sublime goods as politics and the universal right, and [is] equally detestable for his impiety and insolence that, for his ignorance of sacred and profane literature and for the vile and ignominious style with which he speaks of Kings divined by God, imputes the odious name of despotism and tyranny to the monarchial regime and royal authority that arises from God himself and from His divine will . . . and the universal consent of all the people who from most remote antiquity have been governed by Kings. . . . [He attempts] to introduce the rebellious oligarchy of France with the presumption to propose [it] as a model of liberty and happiness of republics, while [it is] in reality the best example of desolation brought on by pestilences and anti-evangelical principles.

Of course many of the polemics of the rationalists were against the Inquisition itself, and to maintain its station in colonial life the Holy Office could not tolerate them. In the ban of *Borroquía o la Víctima de la Inquisición* the judge condemned the book as full of "ridiculous falsehoods that the enemies of religion have vomited against the Holy Office." He claimed that the purpose of the tract was to weaken and eventually destroy the Inquisition and to introduce heresy.

Such "book reviews" as these must have greatly whetted the colonists' appetite for prohibited foreign books. For those unable to read there were the French prints, and there were watches, snuffboxes, and coins bearing the figure of the goddess Liberty. But many could read, and large quantities of revolutionary literature were being assimilated into colonial thinking. Among the most avid readers were the clergy, who naturally made up a large part of the literate classes. In his letter of October 4, 1794, the Mexican Archbishop lauded the Inquisition for its zeal, and took pride in the fact that until that time he had had no knowledge of any priests being involved in foreign intrigues. His Reverence was being naive if he thought that the exciting new publications from abroad were not being read by members of the clergy. In the same month the Holy Office commenced the trial of Juan Pastor Morales, a professor at the Royal and Pontifical Seminary of Mexico who had read the prohibited French books extensively and who openly espoused seditious ideas. It was alleged that he approved of the republican system, defended the execution of Louis XVI, and claimed that the King of Spain was an oppressive "puritan rogue" who ought to be dealt with in the same way as his French counterpart. He was also accused of speaking against the Pope and the Inquisition.

Juan Ramírez, a member of the Franciscan Order, was also tried in late 1794 for appearing to be an "assemblyist" who applauded the execution of the French monarch, possessed prints of scenes from the revolution, and called Voltaire the "holy father of the century." Anastasio Pérez de Alamillo, the priest and ecclesiastical judge of Otumba, was tried in the same year on counts of religious and political heresy. He maintained a little shop where he sold works by Voltaire and small images of the French philosopher Ferney. Copies of many revolutionary manuscripts and books were found in his possession. Perhaps French philosophy inspired Pérez de Alamillo to express disbelief in the apparition of the Virgin of Guadalupe and the miracles purported to have accompanied the event. The padre was defended in this famous trial by the later-renowned Carlos María Bustamante. Inquisition processes against the Franciscan Ramírez and the hierarchy clergyman Pérez de Alamillo are forerunners of the great trials of Hidalgo and Morelos after 1810. In each of the four cases it appeared as though the clergy had tried to remain theologically orthodox while embracing philosophical eclecticism. For the most part, however, the Mexican clergy rejected the new thought of the Age of Science and the Age of Reason and cooperated in ferreting out heretics. Priests were under orders promptly to report any evidence of French influence they might encounter in casual conversation, or in the confessional. "The people were to be taught the 'ancient and true' principles of obedience and fidelity 'to the king and to all their superiors.'" In the main, however, the Church, like the State, looked to the Holy Office of the Inquisition to deal with the men, books, and ideas which threatened both.

The best evidence of the union of heresy and treason appears in the trials of men haled before the tribunal of the Holy Office during the 1790's. Unorthodox clergymen received special treatment and their trials and punishments were private matters. On the other hand, great pains were taken to make a public example of foreigners who were active disseminators of the dreaded libertine ideas. On Sunday, August 9, 1795, the residents of Mexico City witnessed their first major auto de fe in six years. The procession included five heretics convicted of Enlightenment ideas — three of them in person, and two in effigy. The latter were Don Juan María Murgier and Don Esteban Morel, both of whom had committed suicide in the Inquisition jail. The effigy of Murgier was burned with his bones, but since Morel had given signs of repentance in the last moments of his life, he was reconciled posthumously. The cases of Murgier and Morel had caused a scandal and great embarrassment to the Inquisitors.

The most interesting case of this auto de fe, obscured by the attention given to the sensational suicides of Murgier and Morel, was the trial of Don Juan Longouran of Bordeaux, who had lived in Cuba and Honduras as well as New Orleans before he emigrated to Mexico. In addition to having a lucrative career as a merchant, Longouran was an army doctor. His rationalistic medical view of the universe and the nature of man led him to question religious phenomena. Rash statement of his views in public led him into the halls of the Tribunal of the Holy Office. Shortly after his arrival in the viceregal capital in 1790, Longouran was invited to a dinner where he blatantly expounded heretical ideas. His host made him leave the house, and the next morning denounced Longouran to the Inquisition. He reported that Don Juan had said that fornication was not a sin, and that in taking the women they desired, men simply followed natural law, which was, after all, the guiding motivation of the world. He had claimed that Hell was nothing more than the labors and sufferings men undergo in their mortal lives. He opined that a God of Mercy would not save Christians alone, for there were only three and one half million of them in a world of thirty-three million souls. Such a situation would make for a "small Heaven and very great Hell." He also questioned the doctrine of the Incarnation, the adoration of images, and various other mysteries of the faith, saying he would not kiss the hands of bishops and popes or call for a priest at the hour of his death. He had spoken at length in favor of the French Revolution, and claimed it was legal and just to deny obedience to the Papacy.

The Holy Office of the Inquisition made a secret investigation of the Longouran affair, quietly gathering testimony and keeping the accused under surveillance as a "Protestant" and "secret spy." Perhaps he escaped immediate arrest while the Holy Office gathered more data on his background from Cuba, Honduras, and Louisiana. As the Reign of Terror in France intensified, and as the Spanish prepared to expel Frenchmen from the viceroyalty, the Holy Office arrested Longouran on July 17, 1793, and confiscated his property. After long judicial proceedings, Juan Longouran was convicted of heresy and sedition. He was reconciled in the auto de fe of August 9, 1795, did lengthy penance in the monastery of the Holy Cross at Querétaro, and was finally deported from Veracruz in October 1797, to serve eight years of exile in a Spanish prison. Juan Longouran was the typical example of the learned man who had separated religion and science in his thinking, and whose eclecticism undermined his orthodoxy.

The Inquisition's concern with French Enlightenment thought continued after the crowning of Napoleon Bonaparte, and as the Napoleonic soldiers spread philosophe doctrines in the areas they occupied. Don Antonio Castro y Salagado, another native of Bordeaux, was tried for francophile sentiments in 1802. Castro, who had been in France at the time of the Revolution, was a devotee of Rousseau and, as one witness put it, "infected" with revolutionary ideas. Lic. Manuel Faboada testified that Castro could recite entire passages of *Émile* from memory, and that he spoke of Rousseau as "the greatest man of the universe," while he denounced St. Augustine as "a horse" and St. Thomas as "beast" and spoke of theology as a "useless science." Other testimony proved that he was an agnostic, if not an atheist, and detailed his formal lack of respect for established religious principles. Castro heard his sentence in a private auto conducted in the chambers of the tribunal with only the Inquisitors and his family present. Apparently this procedure was necessary because he was a man of great influence in the viceregal capital. After an abjuration ceremony *de levi*, Antonio Castro y Salagado spent a year in the monastery of Santo Domingo doing penance for his sins. He was then banished from the realms of New

Spain for ten years. He was to spend six years in the service of Spain in the Philippine Islands, where his conduct would be supervised by the Inquisition Commissary in Manila.

At the same time that the Holy Office of the Inquisition was pre-occupied with the impact of philosophe thought, Freemasonry made its first inroads in the Viceroyalty of New Spain. Foreshadow-ing the nineteenth-century Mexican Masonic movement, the think-ing of the late eighteenth-century group tended to be more political than religious. First formal notice of Masonry in the Indies was taken by the Supreme Council of the Spanish Inquisition in 1751, when that body sent a letter of warning to the New World bishops requesting them to send lists of soldiers and foreigners who might have Masonic affiliations. Unfortunately, the Holy Office never made a clearly defined distinction among Masonry, Enlightenment phi-losophy, and Protestantism, and the term *Francomason* took on a very broad meaning.

To conclude, as some writers have, that the Holy Office of the Inquisition in Mexico declined in power and became decadent in the late eighteenth century because it developed into a political instrument is clearly fallacious. It is obvious that it had always been a political instrument from the time of its founding in New Spain. Only when the Enlightenment publicists, and the French Revolu-tionary activists, tried to split religion and politics did the distinc-tion between political heresy and religious heresy become manifest in New Spain. For the most part, the Spanish monarchy and the Mexican Inquisition rejected the idea that politics and religion could be separated. The Holy Office tried heretics as traitors, and traitors as heretics. For the Mexican inquisitors, Enlightenment social and political philosophy *was* heresy.

The seeming decadence of the Mexican Tribunal of the Inquisi-tion after 1763 resulted from a whole complex of political and diplo-matic circumstances which, in the end, led to a weakening of the institution. The shift of diplomatic and military alliances between Spain and France, and Spain and England, made it difficult for the Holy Office to punish foreign heretics within the Viceroyalty of New Spain. It was equally difficult, if not impossible, to contain foreign political ideas. From the standpoint of domestic politics and Empire policy, the activities of the Holy Office were severely hampered and began to atrophy because of the tendency of royal and ecclesiastical officialdom to embrace philosophical eclecticism.

Certainly in the case of the clergy this became a dangerous trend, since, in the final analysis, the new philosophical and political ideas tended to undermine orthodoxy. Social and economic tensions in the Mexican colony, pragmatically evident, were reinforced by consideration of the new natural laws of politics and economics being expounded from abroad. On the threshold of this societal discontent, the Holy Office was often forced to make an ideological retreat, adopting an attitude of tolerance or inaction instead of its former firmness — in reality a new kind of "flexible orthodoxy."

The total documentation in the Mexican Inquisition archive for 1763 to 1805 reveals that the Holy Office cannot be indicted as loath to prosecute unorthodoxy of any kind. It only confirms the fact that the overriding political considerations of the State made the Inquisitors responsible for enforcing a rapidly changing "party-line" kind of orthodoxy, an almost hopeless task. It was impossible to police the far frontiers from California to Florida, from Colorado to Guatemala, from Havana to Manila, a problem as serious to the Inquisitors as the problem of "flexible orthodoxy." Perhaps it was a sense of frustration in coping with the larger problems that led the Holy Office to concentrate on smaller ones. The tendency to engage in hairsplitting and tedious controversies over jurisdiction and judicial competencies was one result of this frustration. Another was the preoccupation with protecting the position and dignity of the Tribunal of the Inquisition.

The interpretation that the clergy (and the Inquisition) mirrored the times and the society to which they ministered is no doubt true of the Mexican experience during the second half of the eighteenth century. Would the Inquisition and the Crown have reacted any differently had the revolutionary political themes then in vogue been circulating fifty or one hundred years earlier? Probably not. At all events, the policies of Charles III (1759–1788) and Charles IV (1788–1808) did little to strengthen the Mexican Inquisition's mission to preserve political and religious orthodoxy. Indeed the Spanish kings weakened the institution by failing to define the place of the Holy Office of the Inquisition in defining the Imperial self-interest.

BIBLIOGRAPHIC SUGGESTIONS

1. Aydelotte, Frank. "Elizabethan Seamen in Mexico and Ports of the Spanish Main," *The American Historical Review,* XLVIII (1942), pp. 1–19. Based on Inquisition records in Mexico City.
2. Báez-Camargo, Gonzalo. *Protestantes enjuiciados por la inquisición en Iberoamérica* (Mexico: Casa Unida de Publicaciones, 1960).
3. Castanien, Donald G. "The Mexican Inquisition Censors a Private Library," *Hispanic American Historical Review,* XXXIV (1954), pp. 373–392.
3a. García de Proodian, Lucía. *Los judíos en América. Sus actividades en los virreinatos de Nueva Castilla y Nueva Granada siglo XVII* (Madrid: Consejo Superior de Investigaciones Históricas, 1966).
4. Greenleaf, Richard E. *Zumárraga and the Mexican Inquisition, 1536–1543* (Washington, D.C.: Academy of American Franciscan History, 1961). A basic monograph built on extensive archival research.
5. ———. "Francisco Millán Before the Mexican Inquisition," *The Americas,* XXI (1964), pp. 184–195. A splendidly detailed account of the trial of Millán, which provides a vivid first-hand picture of Mexican Judaism in the 1530's. Based on the original trial record.
6. ———. "North American Protestants and the Mexican Inquisition, 1765–1820," *The Journal of Church and State,* VIII (Spring, 1966), pp. 186–199.
7. ———. "Mexican Inquisition Materials in Spanish Archives," *The Americas,* XX (1964), pp. 416–420.
7a. Hanke, Lewis. "The Portuguese in Spanish America, with Special Reference to the Villa Imperial de Potosi," *Revista de Historia de América,* No. 51 (June, 1961), pp. 1–48.
8. Junco, Alfonso. *Inquisición sobre la inquisición* (Mexico: Jus, 1949). This book defends the Inquisition and the following item attacks it.
9. Lewin, Boleslao. *La inquisición en Hispanoamérica. Judíos, protestantes y patriotas* (Buenos Aires: Projección, 1962).
10. Liebman, Seymour B. *A Guide to Jewish References in the Mexican Colonial Era, 1521–1821* (Philadelphia: University of Pennsylvania Press, 1964). Detailed list of Jews brought before the Inquisition, with guides to pertinent manuscript material in the Mexican archives.

11. Neuman, Abraham A. "Medina, Historian of the Inquisition," *José Toribio Medina, Humanist of the Americas: An Appraisal,* Maury A. Bromsen, ed. (Washington, D.C.: Pan American Union, 1960). A summary and evaluation of the contributions to Inquisition history made by this remarkable Chilean scholar.
12. *Primeira visitação do Santo Ofício ás partes do Brasil, pelo licenciado Heitor Furtado de Mendoça. Confissões da Bahia, 1591–1592.* Introduction by J. Capistrano de Abreu (Rio de Janeiro, 1935).
13. Ricard, Robert. "Algunas enseñanzas de los documentos inquisitoriales del Brasil, 1591–1595," *Anuario de Estudios Americanos,* V (1948), pp. 705–715.
14. Tambs, Lewis A. "The Inquisition in Eighteenth-Century Mexico," *The Americas,* XXII (1965), pp. 167–181. Professor Tambs considers the Inquisition ". . . on the defensive and in decline at the close of the eighteenth century," a judgment to be compared with Professor Greenleaf's interpretation (Reading VII.6).

Section VIII

Science and Medicine

Many Europeans in the colonial period held the curious belief that the sons of European parents in the Spanish Colonies declined prematurely in their mental facilities. A balanced judgment could scarcely be expected, they felt, coming from those distant lands. American-born scholars resented the tolerant condescension and even outright contempt that their supercilious cousins across the Atlantic evidenced, and they reacted strongly. Carlos Sigüenza y Góngora, an outstanding scientist of seventeenth-century Mexico, once exclaimed: "In some parts of Europe . . . they think that not only the original Indian inhabitants of these countries but also those of us who were, by chance, born in them of Spanish parents either walk on two legs by divine dispensation or that, even by making use of English microscopes, they are hardly able to discover anything rational in us."[1] European condescension continued into the eighteenth century, and beyond. Perhaps some readers will be surprised to find in this volume a section on "Science and Medicine," since most accounts in English on the Iberian colonies pay little attention to these subjects. The readings given here were selected from the large bibliography, mostly in Spanish, which when fully known should alter the world's view of scientific developments in Spanish and Portuguese America.

Spaniards were alert to the medical possibilities of America; as

[1] Irving A. Leonard, "A Great Savant of Colonial Peru: Don Pedro de Peralta," *Philological Quarterly*, XII (1933), p. 59.

early as 1528 a druggist named Antonio de Villasante signed a contract with the crown which permitted him to produce and sell medicines, especially balsam, which he had discovered in the island of Hispaniola.[2] Philip II dispatched Francisco Hernández to Mexico in 1570 to investigate the medicinal virtues of plants there (Reading VIII.1), and a few years later sent the Valencian cosmographer and mathematician Jaime Juan to make astronomical observations in New Spain and the Philippines. As the continuing conquest revealed more vast regions and variegated peoples of the New World, scientific problems attracted Spaniards such as the sixteenth-century Jesuit José de Acosta, who not only described carefully what he saw in his extensive travels but also speculated about the puzzles presented by the phenomena he observed (Reading VIII.2).

One of the outstanding scientists in seventeenth-century Peru was Don Pedro de Peralta, whose remarkable life is well told by Professor Emeritus Irving A. Leonard of the University of Michigan (Reading VIII.3). Professor Leonard has been one of the important pioneers in the United States in clarifying the intellectual history of colonial Spanish America.

The Portuguese showed less concern than the Spaniards for scientific matters, but historians of science may discover in Brazilian and Portuguese archives activities which will change the picture. Meanwhile, what is known has been brought together by Dr. Fernando de Azevedo (Reading VIII.4), the scholar who has produced the best general view of Brazilian culture.

It was the explorer-naturalists of the eighteenth century who opened up America scientifically to the world:

> They dispelled legends, they uncovered facts. They rediscovered rubber, studied quinine, and coca leaf. They measured the earth's surface, entered the jungle and collected plants, studied the animals, measured the tides and developed the science of meteorology. The natural phenomena of America were investigated, codified, and embodied in literature — a literature that freed the continent from the fantasies which had persisted for some three hundred years.[3]

[2] Ernst Schafer, "Antonio de Villasante, descubridor droguista en la isla Española," *Investigación y Progreso*, Vol. 9 (Madrid, 1936), pp. 13–15.

[3] Philip Louis Astuto, "Scientific Expeditions and Colonial Hispanic America," *Thought Patterns*, VI (Brooklyn, N.Y.: St. John's University Press, 1959), p. 1.

Professor Arthur Robert Steele of the University of Toledo has recently explained why Spain spent so much money on botany (Reading VIII.5) that the great German scientist Alexander von Humboldt asserted: "No European government has laid out greater sums to advance the knowledge of plants than the Spanish government."

Francisco Xavier Balmis led the most dramatic expedition to carry the newly discovered vaccination against smallpox to the Spanish dominion overseas. During the years 1804–1806 Balmis' expedition vaccinated some hundred thousand persons in the West Indies, Mexico, Central America, much of South America, the Philippine Islands, the East Indies, and China. Professor Sherburne F. Cook of the University of California, Berkeley, states: "Through this one act on the part of the corrupt and decadent government of Spain more lives probably were saved than were lost in all the battles of Napoleon" (Reading VIII.6). Once we have seen the interest so long displayed by the Spanish government in science and medicine, we may understand why Professor John Tate Lanning of Duke University, another pioneer in intellectual history, has written that the Spanish colonies were not intellectually isolated and the policy of the mother country not obscurantist.

A. Scientific Investigation of the New World in the Sixteenth Century

1. Francisco Hernández in New Spain

GERMÁN SOMOLINOS D'ARDOIS

In the countryside Hernández travelled on a litter drawn by two mules. . . . His companions went on foot or on horseback. No exact account of the members of the expedition has come down

Francisco Hernández, *Obras Completas*, Vol. I (Mexico: Universidad Nacional de México, 1960): Germán Somolinos D'Ardois, *Vida y obra de Francisco Hernández*, pp. 195–224, *passim*. Reprinted by permission.

to us, but from Hernández' own letters and descriptions we can assume that it was a fairly sizable group. It was made up of two or three painters, an equal number of scribes, the interpreter, and the herbalists, or gatherers of plants, of whom Hernández said in his letters that he needed at least three; in addition, native doctors must have gone along on several trips, as well as the inevitable muleteers in charge of transporting the equipment of the expedition. The immediate head of the entire company was Hernández' son, without whose help, his father said, he "could not have completed so great an undertaking in so short a time."

The method of investigation was the standard one used in that period: old Indians were sought out and interrogated, and everything that they said was taken down. The figure of the inquisitive Spaniard, who was indispensable for the acquisition of knowledge about the new country, came to be so popular among the natives that, when they depicted the Spanish authorities on one occasion, they included among them the "inquirer" (*el preguntador*). In each locality Hernández questioned the native doctors especially closely, trying to obtain from them information about the uses of the plants that he had gathered. His work is full of references to his medical lore; at times he expresses wonder at the doctors' skill, elsewhere he calls them ignorant and uncouth. However, it was not easy to obtain the information. He often complains that the Indians, "either to look out for themselves or out of hatred for us, make a mystery of what they have studied and learned." Sometimes, as when he speaks of *Chuprei,* he exclaims: "The natives hold this plant in great esteem and conceal its properties with a great deal of secrecy, but with diligence and care we managed to get the truth out of them." It should not be believed that this problem occurred only in Spain; it existed throughout the New World. In a letter to Monardes, Pedro de Osma includes a paragraph that might have been written by Hernández. Referring to some plants, he says: "We do not know how many more herbs and plants with qualities similar to these there may be in our Indies because the Indians, since they are bad people and enemies of ours, will not reveal the secret nor the powers of an herb even if they see us dying, or if we torture them." This is obviously an exaggeration, but it is certain that the investigation of the curative powers of plants was an arduous task for Hernández and his staff. . . .

During the entire trip Hernández reacted strongly to unfamiliar plants, to small ethnographic discoveries, to the beauties of nature, and in general to everything new with a youthful enthusiasm that reveals his highly inquisitive and restless spirit. His attention was drawn by such novelties as the wood that "serves to produce fire, like a flint, when one twig is rubbed against another"; at the same time "cords stronger than those made of hemp" are woven out of its bark, and painters use it "to achieve the color scarlet." And he was struck by the gourds that, besides serving as water jars, when joined together unbroken "in rows of seven, make excellent rafts for the transportation of men, horses, or anything else."

On other occasions a plant furnishes him with the opportunity of giving a long and documented description of native customs. . . . Of this type are his chapters on corn, tobacco, chilli, the coconut tree, the nopal (in which he describes the use of cochineal for ink), the brazil tree, and the various species of maguey.

He was especially interested in the industrial uses to which the elements of nature might be put and was always careful to note the plants that were useful in the production of rope, ink, perfumes, etc. The manufacture of paper by pre-Columbian native methods attracted his notice, and he described it carefully. Whenever he found something that might be used industrially, he made experiments to test his observations; in his description of the *zaquanquá-huitl,* for example, he says that the fruit is similar to "a small melon, and is full of a white and shiny fibrous down, very much like loose and wavy silk threads, which can easily be woven, as we proved in an experiment, and converted into a silk-like fabric with much less expense and labor." He was surprised that the Indians, who had flax, were unfamiliar with its use. On the other hand, he was amazed at the Indians' skill in weaving rabbit hairs into cloth and garments and exclaims: "How diligent and industrious these people are in making use of the most insignificant things!"

The journey, with its changes of lodgings and food, must have yielded agreeable moments to Hernández. Throughout the entire work we discover that Hernández, like many men of the Renaissance, delighted in the pleasures of the table. He frequently praises a sauce, a stew, or some other dish that was served to him. For example, in speaking of the *tomatl,* he informs us that "ground and mixed with chilli [they make] a very pleasant sauce that improves the flavor of nearly all foods and stimulates the appetite." He has lavish praise for corn and its nutritive value; he considers cacao and the beverages derived from it "very pleasing." He also extols the *quauhixílotl,* which he identifies with the plantain, especially when it is eaten roasted and with wine. . . . In the chapters dedicated to the description of animals — quadrupeds and birds, as well as reptiles, including the iguana — he nearly always inserts a paragraph on the nutritional value and flavor of each animal. He sampled almost all of them; some, like the rabbit, seemed "less tasty and tougher than ours." On the other hand, he found the turkeys delicious. . . .

Finally, during his travels he discovered the barbecue, which he described enthusiastically with full historical and culinary detail. After telling us that he had cooked and eaten of one, he adds that "nothing pertaining to the delights and glories of the palate remains hidden to us."

In his accounts of plants, there also appear the small daily tragedies of the expedition. While speaking of the *anónima,* for example, he says: "I gathered among the Mechoacanos an herb that I was careful to paint and describe at once with all its properties, and although the description has been lost, perhaps through the negligence of the servants, I was able to save the drawing, which I wish to give to posterity." In speaking of the *comadreja,* he informs us of a similar mishap, for he relates that "we lost the drawing through the carelessness of the painters or perhaps through its theft by some dishonest person." On occasion he also made errors, which he admits freely, so that there are duplications of drawings and descriptions; for example, while speaking of the *eloxóchitl,* he says: "It is a form of wild lupin described here by mistake and painted twice in two other phases of its development."

Hernández was probably referring to these minor misadventures when, back in Spain, . . . he complained of his "stupid flock of servants." Nevertheless, we should take into account the difficulties of packing and unpacking the materials that accompanied Hernández on muleback along all the roads of New Spain. And if the servants lost a paper or mislaid a drawing from time to time, we cannot fail to acknowledge their great zeal and carefulness, to which we owe in large part the success of the expedition. Today, after so much time has elapsed, when the comforts and services available to man have improved in an almost inconceivable fashion, it is difficult to form an exact idea of Hernández' epochal journey, to which the natural history of Mexico owes so much and which took

place, like the feats of the conquerors, amid dangers, hostile encounters, and hardships of all kinds, defeated by a humanistic
spirit and an unwavering faith in victory.

2. The Scientific Ideas of José de Acosta

THEODORE HORNBERGER

By the rights of discovery and of conquest, the New World belonged in the sixteenth century to the Spaniards. They were the
first to report upon the geography of the new-found western lands;
their voyagers were the first to describe the strange inhabitants,
animals, and plants of the Americas, and to point out in glowing
terms the economic possibilities across the Atlantic. So swiftly did
the Spaniards take advantage of their opportunities, intellectual as
well as economic, that only thirty-four years after the first voyage
of Columbus there appeared a systematic treatise on the natural
history of the new world: *De la Natural Hystoria de las Indias*
(Toledo, 1526), by Gonzalo Fernández de Oviedo y Valdés. By the
end of the century Spanish knowledge of America had been bril-
liantly summarized by José de Acosta, sometimes known as the
American Pliny. Although Acosta's *Historia Natural y Moral de las
Indias* (Seville, 1590) has been recognized as the most useful and
the most learned of the early commentaries, one cannot say that its
truly central place in American cultural history has been widely
appreciated. The purpose of the present article is to suggest its
unique value as a point of reference, not only for students of Latin-
American science but also for those concerned with the history of
ideas in English-speaking North America. Quite possibly, Acosta's
book reveals, more clearly than any other single work, two important facts: (1) that the intellectual conquest of the New World
owed more to the ancients than is generally suspected, and (2)
that new hypotheses developed along lines determined by certain

Theodore Hornberger, "Acosta's *Historia Natural y Moral de las Indias*: A
Guide to the Source and Growth of the American Scientific Tradition," *Studies
in English* (Austin: University of Texas Press, Pub. No. 3826, 1938), pp. 139–
162, *passim.* Reprinted by permission of the author and the University of
Texas Press.

puzzling questions which grew out of men's actual experience in America.

Most of the meagre outline of Acosta's life is derived from his own books. He was born in 1540 at Medina del Campo, between Valladolid and Salamanca in northwestern Spain. At the age of thirteen he joined the Society of Jesus, and was presumably educated in one of the colleges of that order. His work leaves no question of his profound learning, much of it doubtless acquired before 1570, when he left Spain to go to the Jesuit college at Juli, near the western shore of Lake Titicaca, in what is now southern Peru. . . .

Acosta was in Peru for about fifteen years, first in Juli and then in Lima. Besides taking an active part in the Jesuit work and in the third Council of Lima, he found time to write a number of books, which he took with him in manuscript when he returned to Spain in 1587. In the course of that homeward journey he stopped for a good part of 1586 in Mexico, where he continued to amass information on the natural history and civilization of the new colonies, the activity which had shared his attention with theology in Peru. Back in Spain, he quickly published the result of his labors, those of a scientific nature appearing at Salamanca in 1588, as *De Natura Novi Orbis Libri Duo*. Two years later, at Seville, there was published a translation of the two books of the *De Natura*, together with five additional books, under the title of *Historia Natural y Moral de las Indias*. Before his death in 1600 at Salamanca, where he was head of the Jesuit college, he had published, in addition, six theological treatises.

The *Historia Natural y Moral de las Indias* is divided into seven sections, the first four of which deal with natural history. Of these, as has been said, the two first appeared originally in Latin. In its complete form, Acosta's book became enormously popular. There were later Spanish editions in 1591, 1608, 1610, and 1792; an Italian translation appeared in 1596; a French translation of 1597 was reprinted in 1600, 1606, and 1616; a Dutch translation came out in 1598 and 1624; a German translation appeared in 1601; a Latin translation was printed at Frankfort in 1602 and 1603; Edward Grimston's English translation was issued in 1604. Portions of the work also appeared in compilations and collections of voyages, in Latin, German, Dutch, and English, the most important of these being *Purchas His Pilgrimes* (London, 1625), which reprints practically all of Acosta's third and fourth books. Purchas explains, anent the first and second books, that he had already "handled the same" in *Purchas His Pilgrimage* (London, 1613), Bk. VIII, chaps. 1 and 2. . . .

In his advertisement to the reader, Acosta states exactly what, in the way of scientific information, he has in his mind to convey. Other writers, he says, have written of the new and strange things in the New World at the West Indies, but "hitherto I have not seene any other Author which treats of the causes and reasons of these novelties and wonders of nature, or that hath made any search thereof." In fact, he continues, such search is difficult,

> being the works of Nature, contrarie to the antient and re-
> ceived Philosophy, as to shew that the region which they call
> the burning Zone is very moist, and in many places very tem-
> perate, and that it raines there, whenas the Sunne is neerest,
> with such like things. For such as have written of the West
> Indies have not made profession of so deepe Philosophie; yea,
> the greatest part of those Writers have had no knowledge
> thereof.

His intent, in other words, is to correct those parts of natural philosophy (that is, science in general) which the New World, by its very existence, had demonstrated to be most obviously in error.

From Acosta's citations it is possible to know with fair accuracy what he meant by "the ancient and received Philosophy," what writers he had read, and which of them he most respected. This evidence has the added interest of suggesting what kind of library the Jesuits may have taken with them to such a remote corner of the sixteenth-century world as Peru. For it was in Peru that Acosta wrote the first two sections of his book, which deal in the main, despite some reference to astronomical theories, with what is now called physical geography, that is, with the external features and changes of the earth. To read these sections is to review the geographical literature of antiquity. Acosta knew that most persistent of geographical fables — Plato's description in the *Timaeus* of the great lost continent of Atlantis — a powerful factor in determining European preconceptions of the New World. He knew the works of Aristotle, in particular the *De Caelo* and the *Meteorologica* (of whose authenticity scholars have considerable doubt), books which for centuries were fundamental to the cosmography of the educated man. He mentions the writings of Agartharchides of Cnidus and

Eudoxus of Cyzicus, from the Alexandrian period, although he does not appear to have known Erathosthenes' work in mathematical geography. He was thoroughly acquainted with the *Historia Naturalis* of the elder Pliny, and he had at least heard of Strabo, Pomponius Mela, and Macrobius, the most famous of the Roman geographers. Ptolemy, curiously, is mentioned only once, as the "most excellent Astrologer and Cosmographer." In addition, Acosta refers to geographical or otherwise pertinent notions in the writings of Parmenides, Theophrastus, Dioscorides, Lucretius, Plutarch, Lucan, Virgil, Ovid, Seneca the Younger, and Boethius. Finally, as became a Jesuit, he was well read in the church fathers, especially those of the second, third, and fourth centuries, a period which well deserved, geographically speaking, its recent description as "The Dark Age of Early Christian Teaching." Of the many theologians whom he names, the most important to him were Lactantius, St. Jerome, and St. Augustine; a fuller list would give the names of Eusebius, Gregory Nazianzen, St. Basil, St. Chrysostom, St. Ambrose, Theodoret, Theophilus, Paulus Orosius, Procopius of Gaza, and, as Acosta's sole contemporary to have the honor of citation, Arias Montano, a Spanish Biblical commentator. The opinions of these writers tended, by and large, to narrow the bounds of the known world, to deny the sphericity of the earth, and to ignore the evidence of Ptolemy's time that the equatorial zones were inhabited. . . .

In Book I Acosta deals with five questions of physical geography which had already, by 1590, led to marked disagreement among the learned: (1) What is the shape of the heavens and the earth? (2) Do the antipodes actually exist? (3) Are the torrid zones inhabitable? (4) Did the ancients have any knowledge of the New World? (5) How was the New World populated with men and beasts? No better illustration can be found of the way in which actualities forced men in Acosta's age to devise better working hypotheses than their traditional learning supplied.

With Aristotle, Acosta holds that both the heaven and the earth are round. Against this opinion, and in support of the alternative that the earth is flat and the heaven like a roof over it, were Chrysostom, Theodoret, Theophilus, Lactantius, Procopius, Jerome, and even Augustine. Acosta does not wish to belittle the church fathers, who may perhaps have "well imployed their studies in causes of greater waight," but he concludes that

there is no doubt but the opinion which Aristotle and the other
Peripateticks held with the Stoicks (that the figure of Heaven
was round, and did moove circularly in his course), is so perfectly true, as we which doe now live in Peru see it visibly.
Wherin experience should be of more force then all Philo-
sophicall demonstrations, being sufficient to proove that the
Heaven is round, and comprehends and contaynes the earth
within it of al parts.

Nevertheless, Acosta marshals his arguments carefully: Heaven is
round because it is the most perfect body, demanding the most
perfect figure; in Peru, moreover, dark spots in the Milky Way
can be seen circling continually about the earth, always relatively
in the same position to certain fixed stars, "alwaies of one forme
and bignes, as we haue noted by infallible observation." That the
earth is round is proved by Magellan's circumnavigation of it, by
the evidence of the shadow made in an eclipse of the moon, "which
could not chance if the earth were not in the midst of the world,
compassed in and invironed by the whole Heaven," and by the testimony of Scripture itself (as Gregory Nazianzen, Jerome, Basil, and
Ambrose are forced to admit). We must conclude, says Acosta, "that
in the holy scriptures we ought not to follow the letter which killes,
but the spirit which quickeneth, as saith S. Paul." Yet Acosta, as
Andrew Dickson White long ago pointed out, was still among the
conservatives, since he left the earth in the midst of a round and
finite universe, failing even to mention the Copernican astronomy.

Acosta is likewise on the side of experience as against authority
in his remarks upon the distribution of land and sea; one could
not well live in Peru and deny that in the antipodes, although the
greater part be sea, "there is likewise land, so as in all parts of the
world, the earth and water imbrace one another, which truely is a
thing to make vs admire and glorifie the Arte of the soveraigne Creator." Yet the belief that the known world was surrounded by an
encircling ocean had been held by Aristotle and most other ancient
philosophers, the great exceptions being Crates of Mallos and
Ptolemy, whom Acosta does not mention. . . . But "although he
were a great Philosopher," Aristotle was deceived on this matter,
as were Pliny, Virgil, and Ovid. Their reasons, Acosta admits, were
good, and would seem so still "if visible experience did not vnfold
this doubt."

In his discussion of the fourth question, Acosta's patriotism comes

to the fore; he is disturbed that "some at this day, seeking to obscure the felicitie of this age and the Glory of our Nation, strive to
proove that the new-found world was knowne to the Ancients." He
is at pains, therefore, to discount the stories of extraordinary voyages
in Pliny, the allusions in Seneca's *Medea*, the "great Atlanticke
Iland" of Plato, and the suggestions of Arias Montano and Jo-
sephus that the Biblical Ophir and Tharsis (or Tarshish) are references to Peru. Nor can he accept the twentieth verse of Obadiah
as a prophecy "that this new worlde should be converted to Iesus
Christ by the Spanish nation." He is, in fact, constrained to doubt

> that the Ancients had knowledge in the Art of Navigation,
> whereby men at this day passe the Ocean, . . . I find not
> that in ancient bookes there is any mention made of the vse
> of the Iman or Loadstone, nor of the Compasse to saile by;
> yea, I beleeve they had no knowledge thereof.

How, then, did men and animals come to the New World? On
this problem Acosta's authorities afford no theories; he will write,
therefore, "what I have conceived, and what comes presently into
my minde, seeing that testimonies faile mee whom I might follow,
suffering myselfe to be guided by the rule of reason, although it be
very subtill." Men must have come to Peru either by sea or by land.
If they came by sea, it must have been by accident, since they lacked
the modern aids to navigation, in particular the compass needle
magnetized by the loadstone. Acosta is well-informed about the
compass, even to the extent of knowing about magnetic variation.
Yet, admitting that men may have come by accident, there remains
the puzzle of how wild beasts got to the Indies, after the Deluge
had destroyed all except those in Noah's ark. Acosta's conclusion,
after considering the possibilities of their swimming or flying hither,
is

> that the new world, which we call Indies, is not altogether
> severed and disioyned from the other world; . . . no man
> knowes how farre the land runnes beyond the Cape of Men-
> dozino in the South sea, . . . no man knowes the lands on the
> other part of the Straight of Magellan.   . . .

The prominent place of Acosta's questions in the minds of the
first Americans may be gauged by recalling briefly a few of the
relevant comments in the literature of the Anglo-American colonists.   . . .

Increase Mather, in 1709, wrote condescendingly that

> It is certain that the *American Hemisphere* was unknown to
> the Ancients a long Time after the Apostles Days: Nay, the
> Notion of the *Antipodes* was as incredible to them as the
> *Earth's Motion* is to some in these Days. I remember one of
> them derides that Opinion; he says, they are idle men who
> think there are Inhabitants in the opposite Part of the Earth,
> for then (says he) they must walk with their Feet superior to
> their Heads, and Trees would grow downwards, . . . and the
> Rain fall upwards. And *Austin* calls it a Fable, and says, it is
> *nulla ratione credendum,* that it is in no wise to be believed
> that there are Men on the other Side of the Earth, walking
> with their Feet against ours.

Even more frequently encountered are English speculations upon
the origin and descent of the aborigines. Representative opinions
are those of John Eliot, who wrote in 1647 that "his reasons are most
probable who thinke they are *Tartars* passing out of *Asia* into
America by the straits of *Anian*," and of James Adair, whose *History of the American Indians* (London, 1775) was designed to "explode that weak opinion, of the American Aborigines being lineally
descended from the Tartars, or ancient Scythians." Adair's elaborate
argument was devoted to proving the descent of the Indians from
the Lost Tribes of Israel, a theory which antedated Acosta himself.
Volumes could be written on all of these matters; the point here
is simply that Acosta draws together in his first book a number of
the most characteristic perplexities and attitudes of the entire colonial era.

Book II consists of discussion of why the equatorial zone is not
only habitable, to the confounding of Aristotle and Pliny, but also
sometimes actually more comfortable than the regions just outside
the tropics. Acosta finds this problem so fascinating that he is moved
"to search out the causes, not moved therevnto so much by the doctrine of ancient Philosophers, as by reason and certaine experience."
There are difficulties, of course, in accounting by a single rule for
all the diversities of climate under the line: what is true of Peru is
not true of Ethiopia; what is true of some parts of Peru is not true of
others. In general, however, the first thing to remember is Aristotle's
error in thinking that where the sun is nearest the earth the climate
will necessarily be most hot and dry. On the contrary, it is when the
sun is most directly overhead that Peru has most rain and humidity.

The reason, Acosta thinks, is that the sun draws from the ocean a great abundance of vapors, which dissolve into rain, usually in the afternoon. In the other zones there is, on the other hand, most moisture when the sun is farthest away, which is paradoxical until one considers that

> A thousand effects in naturall causes proceede of contrarie things by divers meanes: we drie linnen by the fire and in the aire, and yet the one heats and the other cooles; . . . in candles of tallow or waxe: if the wike bee great, it melts the tallow or the waxe, for that the heat cannot consume the moistnes which riseth; but if the flame be proporcionable, the waxe melts nor droppes not, for that the flame doth waste it by little and little as it riseth. The which seemeth to me the true reason, why vnder the Equinoctiall and burning Zone, the violence of the heat doth cause raine, the which in other Regions growes through want thereof.

Other things contribute to the comfort of living in Peru: the longer nights, the nearness of the ocean, the highness of the land, and, most important of all, the freshness of the winds which commonly come up in the afternoon. Each of these Acosta treats briefly, but he leaves the particular "discourse of windes, waters, landes, mettalls, plants, and beasts (whereof there is great aboundance at the Indies)" to Books III and IV. . . .

Acosta's scheme in Books III and IV is roughly Aristotelian or Scholastic, although he does not attempt to write of natural history in full. Book III treats of the simple bodies, or elements: air, water, earth, and fire — the subject of such Aristotelian writings as the *De Mundo*, the *De Generatione et Corruptione*, and the *Meterologica*. Book IV deals with the mixed bodies, both inanimate and animate: metals, plants, and beasts. These divisions are among the most ancient in natural philosophy, going back, in the case of the four elements, at least as far as Empedocles, who lived in the fifth century B.C. . . .

By far the largest portion of Acosta's third book deals with the air, or winds. A deep dissatisfaction with Aristotle's explanations is again apparent, as Acosta notes the great diversities in the winds, and concludes that

> it is needefull to seeke further to knowe the true and originall cause of these so strange differences which we see in the

windes. I cannot conceive any other, but that the same efficient cause which bringeth foorth and maketh the winds to
grow dooth withall give them this originall qualitie, for in
trueth the matter whereon the windes are made, which is no
other thing (according to Aristotle) but the exhalation of the
interior Elements, may well cause in effect a great parte of
this diversitie, being more grosse, more subtile, more drie, and
more moist. But yet this is no pertinent reason, seeing that we
see in one region, where the vapours and exhalations are of
one sorte and qualitie, that there rise windes and effects quite
contrary. We must therefore referre the cause to the higher
and celestiall efficient, which must be the Sunne, and to the
motion and influence of the heavens, the which by their contrary motions give and cause divers influences.

Thus Acosta takes up, with marked intelligence, the problem of the
trade winds, or Brizes (as they were called in the sixteenth and
seventeenth centuries). He recognizes their importance to navigation, since they make possible an easy voyage from east to west,
and he describes them meticulously. Unfortunately, although he
approximates the true explanation of their cause, he falls short of
stating it because of his ignorance or rejection of the Copernican
demonstration of the motion of the earth. "The earth," he insists, "is
not moved," nor is the element of water, "for that it is vnited to the
earth and makes one sphere, so as the earth keeps it from all circular motion." . . .

The relatively large amount of space devoted by Acosta to meteorology and climatology has a significance which is not wholly
obvious. From the first, colonial Americans appear to have been
keenly interested in the weather, in part, no doubt, because of economic reasons and an understandable curiosity. Some of them, John
Cotton, for instance, were as thoroughly grounded in Aristotle as
Acosta himself, and tended therefore to write of exhalations and
the drawing power of the sun. A goodly number, including Thomas
Robie, William Douglass, John Lining, and Professor Winthrop of
Harvard, followed Edmund Halley and other members of the Royal
Society of London in the collection, by the use of barometer and
thermometer, of statistical data. What is surprising, however, is that
at least three Anglo-Americans, John Mitchell, John Bartram, and
Benjamin Franklin, were carried by their weather interest into bold
and sweeping hypotheses, of considerable importance to the history

of science. Mitchell explained the fact that it was colder in North America than in Europe by ten or fifteen degrees of latitude on the basis of the greater land masses to the north in the former continent. Bartram suggested shrewdly that the ranges of mountains along the eastern seaboard might have some effect upon air currents and rainfall. Franklin, as is more widely known, after discovering by accident that what seemed northeast storms in Philadelphia actually came from the southwest, developed the earliest theory of cyclonic winds. In the light of these facts, Acosta would seem to have had a sure instinct for what his successors would find perplexing.

The greater part of Acosta's discussion of the element of water is actually descriptive geography. He indicates the position of the North and South Seas (the Atlantic and Pacific Oceans), of the Strait of Magellan, of the supposed Northwest Passage, of lakes in Peru and Mexico, of unusual springs and fountains, and of the Amazon and Plata Rivers. There are inserted chapters on tides and on Indian methods of fishing. These pages reveal a fairly good grasp of the geographical knowledge of his day, when the western world had absorbed the information derived from Magellan's voyage.   . . .

Acosta's discussion of the element of earth is largely a description of the topography of Peru and Mexico, with comments on the economic possibilities of the various regions. Like almost all Americans of the colonial era, he is keenly conscious of how much of the New World remains unexplored and anxious to estimate the extent of the continents. Relevant to the element of fire, he sees "no special matter at the Indies which is not in other regions." Volcanoes he explains as "places that have the propertie to draw vnto them hote exhalations, and to convert them into fire and smoke which, by their force and violence, cast out other thicke matter which dissolves into ashes, into pumico stone, or such like substance." This is mere acceptance of certain basic theories of the *Meteorologica*. Acosta is sure that volcanic flames are not hell fire, as Basil and others taught, because hell fire is without light.   . . .

Acosta's fourth book is divided fairly evenly among his three "mixtures and compounds": metals, plants, and animals. From the point of view of the history of technology and biology, this section is probably the most important of the work, because of its full account of Spanish-American mining processes, and its descriptions of the more unusual American plants and animals.   . . .

Besides accounts of the gold, silver, and mercury mines of Peru,

and the methods used to find and refine these metals, Acosta has
brief chapters on emeralds and pearls. Throughout these sections he
is heavily indebted to the twenty-third book of Pliny's *Historia
Naturalis*. His material on plants is divided into comment on those
"proper and peculiar to the Indies" and briefer mention of "the rest
that are common to the Indies and Europe." He speaks of the planting and the uses of maize, or Indian corn, noting in passing the
curious mistake by which it came to be called "Turkie graine," and
he displays the long-enduring kinship of botany with medicine in
his assertion that maize is not inferior to wheat "in strength nor
substance, but is more hote and grosse, and engenders more bloud,
wherevpon they that have not bin accustomed therevnto, if they
eat too much, they swell and become scabbed." The use of maize
as food leads him naturally to a full description of cassava bread
(made, so Acosta says, from the root of the yucca, as the cassava
seems to have been called by the people) and of "Papas" or potatoes. Briefer, but even more interesting, is his comparison of the
garden vegetables of Peru with those of Spain. In the latter country,
he says, there are radishes, turnips, parsnips, carrots, leeks, garlic,
and some other profitable roots, but in New Spain there are so many
that we cannot remember them all. He mentions roots of the wood
sorrel family ("Ocas," "Yanaocas," and "Cavi"), sweet potatoes
("Camotes" and "Batatas"), peanuts ("Mani" and, perhaps, "Co-
chuchu"), and the cat-tail ("Totora"), together with some others.
Fruits from Europe prosper better in the Indies than Indian plants
in Europe, perhaps because the temperature is more even in America. Peruvian onions, garlic, and parsnips are better than those of
Spain; turnips grow so abundantly that they can hardly be destroyed
to grow corn; radish roots are "as bigge as a mans arme, very ten-
der, and of a good taste." Other native American plants described
are the pineapple, the watermelon, the tomato, and the gourd. He
did not find any pepper, cloves, cinnamon, nutmeg, or ginger,

> but the naturall spice that God hath given to the West Indies,
> is that we call in Castille, Indian pepper, and in India, *Axi*, as
> a generall worde taken from the first land of the Ilands, which
> they conquered. In the language of Cusco, it is called *Vchu*,
> and in that of Mexico, *Chili*.   . . .

The general impression conveyed is that plant life flourishes abundantly in the New World, although Acosta admits that some im-

portations, such as cherries, have not done well, "the which I do not
impute to want of temperature, for that there is of all sorts, but to
carelessness, or that they have not well observed the temperature." His remarks, in short, are an invaluable source of knowledge
of Spanish-American agriculture at the end of the sixteenth century,
and have been used extensively by commentators on that subject.
Economics and natural curiosity urged Acosta's Anglo-American
successors to a similar concern with the plants of the New World,
so that botany is generally recognized as the leading science of
the entire colonial period. It had a prominent place in the literature
of exploration and promotion; it attracted a considerable number
of fieldworkers and classifiers; it was even graced by a few experi-
menters who advanced the world's knowledge of hybridization.

Last of all, Acosta describes the animals of the New World, those
"carried from Spaine," those "of the same kinde we have in Europe,
and yet not carried by the Spaniardes," and those "proper to the
Indies, whereof there are none in Spaine." The first class has increased enormously; Acosta hints that fortunes are still being made
in hides and wool, almost without exertion. The second class he
has spoken of before; that there are lions, tigers, bears, boars, foxes,
and other wild beasts in the New World is good evidence that there
is some connection by land with the Old, "being impossible to
swimme the ocean: and it were a follie to imagine that men had
imbarked them with them." Many of these wild beasts, he points
out, are slightly unlike the European varieties. The birds, he con-
ceives, might more easily have passed to America. The real problem falls under his third heading:

> It were a matter more difficult to shew and prove, what be-
> ginning many and sundry sorts of beasts had, which are found
> at the Indies, of whose kindes we have none in this continent.
> For if the Creator had made them there, wee may not then
> alleadge nor flie to Noahs Arke, neither was it then necessary
> to save all sorts of birds and beasts, if others were to be created
> anew. Moreover, wee could not affirme that the creation of the
> world was made and finished in six days, if there were yet
> other kinds to make, and specially perfit beasts, and no lesse
> excellent than those that are knowen vnto vs. If we say then
> that all these kinds of creatures were preserved in the Arke by
> Noah, it followes that those beasts, of whose kindes we finde
> not any but at the Indies, have passed thither from this conti-

nent, as we have said of other beasts that are knowne vnto vs.
This supposed, I demand how it is possible that none of their
kinde should remaine heere? and how they are found there,
being as it were travellers and strangers. Truly it is a question
that hath long held me in suspense.

As Andrew Dickson White has shown, the old theological theories
of the number of species and their geographical distribution were
soon to be overthrown by just such evidence as this. "It may be,"
Acosta suggests, "God hath made a new creation of beasts." Or it
may be that, although all came out of the ark, diverse kinds dispersed themselves into the most suitable regions. Acosta is not too
sure that the latter theory is the better one, an uncertainty that led
Samuel Purchas, in a long footnote in his reprint of the discussion,
to emphasize the more orthodox position. Purchas says unequivo-
cally that

> The same providence which brought all beasts and fowles
> from all their native diversified residences thorow all the world
> to the Arke (which no naturall instinct in such antipathies and
> at once, could doe) and kept them safe in the Arke, did also
> dispose them to their designed abodes after. For I hold it un-
> christian with Mercator to say, America was not drowned with
> the Flood. . . . In things above nature (as in both the historie
> and mysterie of the Arke) we must flee necessarily to a super-
> naturall cause.

The problem perceived by Acosta was to trouble Americans for
many generations. Cotton Mather touched upon it in *Work upon
the Ark* (Boston, 1689), where he sought to explain how Noah stored
away all the animals and their food. Elsewhere he shows awareness
of the uncertainty of the number of species. The best example of the
later importance of the matter is, however, the discussion of the
American mastodon, or mammoth, beginning in 1752, when fossil
teeth from Big Bone Lick, on the Ohio River, came to the attention
of European naturalists. The speculations which followed, participated in by such American thinkers as John Bartram and Benjamin
Franklin, may be reviewed in the *Philosophical Transactions* of the
Royal Society of London, or in summaries in Buffon's *Epoques.* So
assured was the eighteenth century of the constancy of species that
even Thomas Jefferson could write: "Such is the economy of nature, that no instance can be produced, of her having permitted any

one race of her animals to become extinct." The point, once more, is that the whole discussion illustrates Acosta's astuteness in perceiving significant problems.

Like all the early travelers, Acosta was mightily impressed with the number and strangeness of the birds and beasts of the Indies. He describes the humming bird, the condor, the turkey buzzard, the macaw, and the sea fowl whose dung, guano, so wonderfully fattens the ground. He points out the singularities of the peccary, the tapir, the armadillo, the iguana, the chinchilla, the guinea pig. Indian monkeys are given a whole chapter, including "the fooleries, tricks, traverses, and pleasant sportes they make when they are taught, which seem not to come from brute breasts, but from a man-like vnderstanding." He deals with the various varieties of the llama at some length, distinguishing the vicuna, the alpaca, and the guanaco. . . .

So much for the content of Acosta's four books on the natural history of the Indies, written, as has been said, to correct the errors of Scholastic science in the light of the new evidence from America. As has been shown, much of his work was descriptive, and in his curiosity about strange plants and animals and their possible economic uses he is representative rather than distinctive. To be sure, he was more than ordinarily familiar with the backgrounds of ancient and medieval science, a fact which made him discriminating in his selection of things to be described and systematic in his treatment of them. His unique qualities, however, derive from his having been a scientific theorist, curious about the puzzles presented by the phenomena he had observed and not unduly respectful of "the ancient and received Philosophy." He went beyond mere observation to develop and weigh scientific hypotheses, naive now, perhaps, but by no means naive at the time he wrote or in the two centuries thereafter.

One cannot but be impressed, indeed, with the way in which Acosta's speculations foreshadowed most of the main directions of colonial science. His interest in geography, his curiosity about the aborigines, his concern with meteorology and climatology, his speculations about the number and distribution of species — all these are characteristic of his successors in the English colonies to the north. Nowhere else, perhaps, can one find them altogether; the English, surely, produced no such sweeping view of the problems posed by the observed facts of the New World. It is not too much

to say, therefore, that Acosta is the best available guide to the source
and the growth of the colonial scientific tradition, a tradition thus
far imperfectly understood.   . . .

B. A Seventeenth-Century Scholar

3. A Great Savant of Colonial Peru: Don Pedro de Peralta

Irving A. Leonard

A curious belief was current in Spain and in Europe generally
that the Creole sons of European parentage in the colonies of the
New World entered upon a decline of their mental faculties at a
premature age. Since a certain precocity was noted among many
of the colonists who visited the homeland it was felt that there must
be a correspondingly early decadence of intellectual power. It was
reasoned, therefore, that little work requiring the balanced judgment and seasoned experience of many years could be expected
from these distant lands so sparsely inhabited by Europeans. For
this and for other reasons besides men of learning in Europe continued to view their colleagues on the other side of the Atlantic
with cold indifference during the whole colonial period and even
later. In fact, the prevalent attitude was frequently that of tolerant
condescension or outright contempt. So pronounced was this tendency in the latter part of the seventeenth century that it moved one
of the foremost scholars of New Spain to declare with some acerbity
that

> in some parts of Europe, especially in the north through being
> more remote, they think that not only the original Indian in-
> habitants of these countries [of the Western hemisphere] but
> also those of us who were, by chance, born in them of Spanish

Irving A. Leonard, "A Great Savant of Colonial Peru: Don Pedro de Peralta,"
Philological Quarterly, XII (January, 1933), pp. 54–72, *passim.* Reprinted by
permission of the State University of Iowa.

parents either walk on two legs by divine dispensation or that, even by making use of English microscopes, they are hardly able to discover anything rational in us.

But the cause of the Creoles found a champion in one of the keenest and most independent minds of Spain in the eighteenth century, the Benedictine friar, Feijóo, whose mission in life, apparently, was to attack every form of superstition and error. In one of his essays he devotes his attention to Spanish Americans and lists a number of them whose intellectual accomplishments, even at a comparatively advanced age, were truly exceptional. Of a certain Peruvian, Doctor Pedro de Peralta, he observes, before enumerating some of his attainments, that "[he is] a person about whom one cannot speak without wonder for in all Europe there hardly (and not even hardly) will be found any man of superior talent and learning." Perhaps it will be of value to investigate further this scholar of the New World who won such high approval from the celebrated Spanish critic and arch-foe of obscurantism. . . .

Don Pedro de Peralta was born November 26, 1663, in Lima where his whole life was spent. His father, Don Francisco de Peralta, was a native of Castile, and served his king as an accountant of the Audiencia in the far-off viceroyalty of Peru. His literary predilections, which manifested themselves publicly in occasional verse, were imitated by his more talented son and carried to greater heights of accomplishment. Of his mother, Doña Magdalena Rocha y Benavides, practically nothing more than her name is known. During his early youth Don Pedro does not appear to have betrayed an unusual precocity although he completed creditably his studies in Roman and Canonical law at the University of Lima and received a doctorate from that venerable institution. Soon he was practicing law in a brilliant fashion before the Royal Audiencia of which, like his father, he became an accountant as well as holding similar offices in other tribunals of the "City of the Kings." . . .

Don Pedro's devotion to his studies probably began very early in his career and, in the course of time, became more intense as his knowledge grew more profound. Natural and mathematical sciences had for him an especial appeal; these included investigations in botany, chemistry, and medicine as well as astronomy and engineering. Along with these purely scientific pursuits went his studies of languages and literatures, both ancient and modern, in which he rapidly perfected himself. It is but natural, of course, that he should have mastered the intricacies of Latin syntax and learned to express himself well in that classic medium; it is, however, somewhat surprising to be informed that at the age of twenty-four he wrote his first published work which was a long poem in Greek. This ambitious effort, which describes a great earthquake occurring in October, 1687, bears the Spanish title *Apolo Fúnebre*. . . .

Turning back for a moment to his more strictly scientific activities, we learn that he did particularly distinguished work in the fields of astronomy and practical engineering. His rapid progress in these studies soon opened the way to advancement in the official circles of Lima and a recognition of his abilities by the bestowing of an increasing number of titles in the service of the king. In 1709 the chair of Mathematics in the University of Lima was left vacant by the famous Flemish engineer, John Raymond Koenig. Don Pedro was then appointed to fill it, which he did efficiently until his death thirty-four years later. Since the office of Chief Cosmographer of the realm was usually associated with the position of professor of Mathematics in the Royal University, Don Pedro was soon preoccupied with the planning and management of engineering enterprises as well as with the theoretical demands of his academic work. His fitness for the more practical tasks was quickly demonstrated. In 1712 the Viceroy, Ladrón de Guevara, petitioned the king to approve the elevation of Don Pedro to the post of Chief Engineer of the realm — an appointment that he had already made, acting upon his own responsibility — together with the substantial increase in salary he had assigned to Peralta.

His rare executive ability in conjunction with his prodigious activity soon made Don Pedro the logical choice as Rector of the University and for this position he was duly chosen in 1715. During the early part of the eighteenth century this "Salamanca of America" had fallen upon degenerate days for its luster had been dimmed by corrupt practices and a general decline in morale. Some years later the Memoria of the Viceroy, the Marqués de Castel-Fuerte, in whose composition Don Pedro undoubtedly had a hand, reported that while the University had thirty-three *cátedras* the number of students had fallen to such an extent that there were then more professors than potential graduates; and the bestowal of degrees upon unworthies — for a consideration — and similar abuses had become flagrant.

The new Rector addressed himself vigorously to the duties of his office and endeavored to bring about improvements, both physical and moral, in this ancient seat of learning. His exceptional architectural talents were brought into play in the remodeling of the General Lecture Hall of the University in which his own designs and plans were adopted. Under his direction various rooms of the institution were equipped with new furniture, which they sorely needed, and the archives were more conveniently arranged. These matters, together with occupations of a literary nature such as the composition in Latin of a sort of detailed history of the University entitled *Fastos Académicos,* moved him at the conclusion of his administrative labors to report to the Viceroy that "this year, Sir, has been made up of more difficulties than hours for me, so much so that my watchfulness has hardly left me time enough for even the necessary functions of life. . . ." No doubt this unwonted industry was appreciated for he was re-elected as head of the University in 1716 and, at the request of the *claustro,* his term was extended in 1717.

Even the remoteness of Lima from Europe and the comparative infrequency of communication with the continent did not long prevent the fame of Don Pedro from extending beyond the confines of the viceroyalty of Peru. . . . Through the Franciscan scientist and student of the great Cassini, Father Louis Feuillé, and other visitors to the western shores of South America such as Frezier and La Condamine, with whom he exchanged observations, astronomical and geographical, Don Pedro probably came into epistolary communication with distinguished members of the French Academy of Science. No doubt these travelers appreciated his familiarity with the French language (learned before their arrival) as well as his worth as a scientist which they acknowledged; and it is likely that these qualities as well as his high reputation in Lima made him an invaluable ally in their scientific investigations since he could procure for them an easy entrée into the official circles of the capital. But let us consider in more detail some of his claims to distinction as a man of learning. . . .

His effort to improve the seaport of Callao was one of his chief engineering enterprises. This essential gateway of the capital and the vast hinterland of Peru was exposed to the not infrequent assaults of storms and tidal waves which wrought havoc not only upon the shipping in that unprotected harbor but upon the small population that lived upon its shores. Fruitless attempts had been made to combat this menace on previous occasions but no definite solution of the pressing problem had been found. After one of these recurrent disasters the Viceroy, the Marqués de Castel-Fuerte, went down to Callao to view what he was pleased to term "a maritime Troy." This tragic scene moved him to appoint a commission at once to study the situation and to determine upon a suitable remedy. General Luis de Guendica, a *maestre de campo,* Don Pedro de Medranda and Don Pedro de Peralta, who had already given considerable attention to this problem, composed the new consultative body. A plan for the construction of a retaining wall was submitted to them by an engineer named Don Nicolás Rodríguez and it fell to the Peruvian professor to pass judgment upon its effectiveness. Possibly using this as a basis Don Pedro worked out another scheme which he elaborated with the necessary drawings and an estimate of cost. One of the features of his plan which impressed the commission as entirely new was a sort of coffer-dam; within this a stone wall forming a breakwater was to be erected. As Peralta's suggestions seemed sound and practical they were adopted and, much to his satisfaction, carried through to a successful conclusion. This construction continued to stand during the remainder of his life but it was fortunate for his pride, perhaps, that he did not live three years longer. In 1746 this whole engineering project was swept away "like a grain of sand" by the jealous Pacific in one of its violent moods. If this product of his technical skill could not remain as a lasting monument to his ability he had, at least, been more successful in his efforts than his predecessors.   . . .

Among the manifold interests which absorbed Don Pedro perhaps none was more profound and constant than his astronomical observations. Despite handicaps in the form of inaccurate instruments and the frequently hazy condition of the atmosphere about Lima — a circumstance which moved him to call the capital "the purgatory of astronomers" — his achievements in this field were by no means negligible. Long before his elevation to the chair of Mathematics his eye was trained upon the heavens and all during his life he continued to regard them with scientific attention. This occupation was a source of great pride to him and the notes of his *Lima Fundada,* especially those of the ninth Canto, abound in references to his observations. With unmistakable satisfaction he announces that he was the first in Lima to recognize the appearance of a comet on February 26, 1702, which had been observed by distinguished European scholars elsewhere. Later the Count of Pontchartrain communicated Don Pedro's observations of an eclipse of the moon occurring in Lima in December, 1713, to the French Academy of Science in whose journal they duly appeared. Twelve years later other results of his study were similarly recorded in the publication of this famous learned body. These were the observations of another eclipse of the moon on March 26, 1717, a total obscuration of this same heavenly body on April 27, 1725, and the median height of the sun to determine the latitude of Lima. Perhaps it should be added, as indicative of the general suspicion in which the work of Creole scientists was held in Europe, that a note was attached to this report of the Peruvian scholar's findings to the effect that "as it is not known of what instruments Don Pedro de Peralta made use it is not possible to pass certain judgment upon their accuracy." Other evidence of his knowledge of astronomy is found in a little volume in Latin published in Lima in 1717 under the title *Observationes Astronomicae*.

From 1719 and possibly earlier he issued annually a sort of almanac which he called "El conocimiento de los tiempos." In this little publication he set forth the position and movements of the various planets together with astronomical prognostications, a calendar of the Saints' days and other holidays, among which were interspersed data of geographical and historical interest. He even ventured upon the hazardous task of phophesying earthquakes which were, unfortunately, common incidents of the colonial life of Peru. Apparently these predictions of the professor did not always prove as accurate as he may possibly have desired for we read that a certain Don José Bermúdez unkindly remarked on one occasion, "today the earth is to shake according to the almanac of Doctor Peralta. So, for that reason, I'm going to sleep up in the Santo Domingo tower." The latter structure was the highest one in Lima and, therefore, considered the most dangerous place in the capital when the earth was in one of its turbulent moods. Notwithstanding some of their features, however, these almanacs were of considerable interest and scientific value and Don Pedro continued to publish them until his death. In fact, the "Conocimiento de los tiempos" of 1743 was the last work of the scholar to be printed.

It is unfortunate that so many of the worthwhile products of the pen of Don Pedro (and those of other scientific investigators in the

colonies who were not few in number) were not put in the more
permanent form of books while his works of a lighter and more
transitory sort were carefully, even elaborately, printed and have
come down to us in larger numbers. His production of a purely
literary nature as distinguished from his scientific tracts is voluminous and most of it of little value or interest today. Though we may
feel inclined to condemn the author for this apparent lack of
discrimination, it should be remembered that he was, in some measure, the victim of his environment and the circumstances in which
he lived. That he preferred to bring forth his more serious studies
is altogether probable; that he secretly resented the frequent calls
made upon him for an almost uninterrupted stream of *versos al-
tisonantes* and descriptions of purely local events is also a reasonable
conjecture. Life in the colonies was not favorable to literary effort
or scientific work other than that which glorified the Church or
gratified the pride of ecclesiastical and secular authorities. Hence
it is that the literature of the period is composed chiefly of religious
tracts, the lives of saints, and an endless number of extravagant
descriptions of fiestas, *recibimientos* of Viceroys and other officials,
celebrations of royal births, marriages, and deaths and similar
events, with here and there a work of real merit. This generalization
relating to colonial literature is equally applicable to the individual
case of Don Pedro; the number of printed works credited to him is
truly impressive yet only a few are worthy of his genius.   . . .

No discussion of Don Pedro's poetical activities is complete, however, without some reference to his most ambitious undertaking —
an epic poem. This was entitled *Lima Fundada o Conquista del
Perú* and in it he sought to immortalize in a fitting fashion the valiant
exploits of Francisco Pizarro in ten cantos with a total of 1,183
octaves.   . . .

The judgments of critics on this work have not been gentle and
today his epic is scarcely read. The shortness of the time employed
in its composition (Don Pedro wrote in the prologue that he had
spent hardly a year and a half with many interruptions on the actual
writing) together with its all-too-faithful reflection of the current
evils of the literature of the day, made it fall far short of the aspirations of its creator. Yet here and there the dullness of his epopee is
relieved by an octave of lyric quality and it still preserves some
interest to the historian.

A work of Peralta with greater claim upon the attention of the

student of history is the *Historia de España Vindicada* which appeared in 1730 in the capital of Peru. This ranks among the greatest
historical works published in any of the Spanish colonies and is an
eloquent testimony of the scholarly zeal and industry of its author.
To attempt a comprehensive history of the motherland from its
legendary beginnings to contemporary times was a bold undertaking in this remote possession of Spain. Don Pedro earnestly endeavored to utilize all previous historical investigations in his effort to
make the work authentic. That the finished product fell short of
the mark is not hard to understand; yet, considering the heavy disadvantages under which Don Pedro was compelled to labor, the
result was truly remarkable. Though he had never visited Spain
itself, many of his geographical descriptions were amazingly accurate. Even one of his severest critics acknowledges his skillful
handling of classic sources and applauds his vigorous attack on the
false chronicles. If the Creole historian was too credulous in accepting certain myths, he was not unique in this. Other historians in
Europe with better opportunities for research fell into the same
error.   . . .

Today it is easy to perceive the defects of the character and work
of this remarkable Creole, and we can wish that he had been less
willing to debase his pen to the stupid and blind adulation of the
constituted authorities and the established institutions among which
he spent all his life. There is little that is picturesque or stirring in
his career nor do we note those positive and virile virtues of fear-
lessness and independence in thought and action which characterized his correspondent and admirer, Feijóo, for example. He was
essentially a conformist to whom, apparently, the existing order was
satisfactory and against which it did not occur to him to rebel. But
let us consider briefly the environment in which he was reared and
from which he never escaped. While it was the eighteenth century
in Europe Don Pedro was really living in the Middle Ages — the
Middle Ages before the freshening breath of the renaissance had
begun to make itself felt. If in Europe the clergy as well as the secular were becoming divided into two camps on the question of the
reaction against scholasticism, the colonies of Spanish America, and
especially the viceroyalty of Peru, were unaware of it. The authority
of the Church was paramount and undisturbed; the subversive doctrines of Bacon, Descartes, and Leibnitz were practically unknown.
The intellectual life of the colony was completely dominated by the

clergy so that Don Pedro breathed in the stuffy atmosphere of an environment almost hermetically sealed against new ideas. It would be
interesting to speculate upon the effect that the unimpeded current
of new thought might have had upon this Peruvian scholar if he
had been permitted to feel the full force of it. But this was not to
be and his encyclopedic mind and remarkable talents were compelled to limit their sphere of activities to those approved by a
jealous and suspicious hierarchy. It is a matter of profound regret
that the intellectual genius of Don Pedro was not permitted to bloom
in surroundings more favorable to its growth and development.

C. Brazil

4. An Overview of Science in Colonial Brazil

FERNANDO DE AZEVEDO

What immediately attracts our attention in the history of Brazilian literature is not only the continuity of the literary movement,
through three centuries, the growing variety of talents of the first
class in each one of these periods, but the vitality and strength with
which the originality of our national literature asserts itself progressively in the different phases of its evolution, and especially beginning with the romantic movement. In no other activity of the
mind has the intelligence of Brazil expanded with so much vigor,
nor manifested so great a power of invention. We may even consider literature as the most characteristic Brazilian product, the
least contestable witness of originality on the part of the national spirit. If we compare, however, the progress in this domain of
activity with that of the sciences, what strikes us in this contrast,
established even in the most summary analysis, is the disconcerting

impression of the disproportion between literary progress and scientific development which, in a rigorous sense, began to take place
only in the nineteenth century, and then with its attention turned
only to the realm of the natural sciences and with extreme slowness.
This preponderance of the literary spirit over the scientific spirit
has been so marked and so persistent in the whole history of our
culture that there have not been lacking critics who have attributed
it, after a superficial examination, to a particular form of the mind
related to ethnic and therefore biological factors, as if it were a
question of a natural and irremovable lack of aptitude for scientific
studies and research, for pure science and speculation. Certainly
the Brazilian people, like any other, presents us with a complex of
fundamental traits which characterize it and which reflect upon their
institutions and tendencies, marking them with a special stamp. But
whatever may be the traits or the salient facts which can be pointed
out as peculiar to a race, they are susceptible of being modified
with transformations of social life. The variations of mentality
which they make up are related in the first place to social variations
and given a constant relation between these two types of change,
we cannot deliver a sentence on the lack of aptitude of a people for
any branch whatever of human activity except in the face of its attitudes and reactions in a new social state created by the contacts of
different cultures. Moreover, this slowness of scientific progress
and our backward state in this field comes, it is easy to prove, from
political, economic, and cultural factors which have contributed
powerfully to create a social atmosphere that for a long time was
unfavorable to the cultivation of science and which has driven our
activity into other directions.

During the whole colonial period, from the discovery to the coming of Dom João VI to Brazil, there were in fact not recorded in the
history of our culture anything but sporadic and isolated manifestations — of strangers who, seizing advantage of the opportunity
of their stay in the colony, took the inhabitants and the natural
wealth of the country as the object of their study; and of some exceptional figures of Brazilians who had lived outside the country,
and in the home country and later in the colony devoted themselves
to scientific activity. Neither the foreign savants who collected in
American countries the material for their work nor the eminent
Brazilians who, educated in Europe, accomplished work of scientific
value abroad exercised any influence whatever upon the develop-

ment of a scientific attitude and methods in Brazil. It is in the Dutch period, or more exactly, under the government of Maurice of Nassau (1637–1644) — "a brilliant parenthesis" opened by the arrival and closed by the departure of the Flemish prince — that there was inaugurated in colonial Brazil a period of scientific activity, carried on by a group of scientific men that the Count of Nassau brought to Pernambuco. This important mission, the first which he brought to Brazil, arrived in Recife in 1637, a century after the beginning of the populating of the newly discovered lands by the Portuguese. In this mission there was, among other men, Wilhelm Piso, a physician of Amsterdam and the founder, along with J. Bontius, of colonial medicine, and Georg Marggraf, a German naturalist. These authors left us in their *Historia Naturalis Brasiliae* (first edition, 1648; second edition, 1658) a work of the first importance for its wealth of data and observation, and the most notable that was published on medicine, and the flora and fauna of the country in the colonial period. If, as a result of his observations upon the chief diseases in northern Brazil and the therapeutic action of medicinal plants, Wilhelm Piso — the first physician who treated ancylostomiasis, who indicated the transmission of snake poison by the teeth of the serpent, and who made examination of tissues in Brazil — is justly considered the creator of the Brazilian study of disease, the glory of having laid the foundations of natural history goes to G. Marggraf, who collected, drew, and described all the plants and animals which he met in his numerous scientific explorations. So enormous was the bulk of the material collected in these expeditions, even into neighboring captaincies, that according to Alfredo de Carvalho, "the study of the count, the museums of two universities, and various private collections (among them that of Sebasch, afterward so famous) were enriched with them and for more than a century science was nourished on this provision." The scientific activities of G. Marggraf were not, however, restricted to the field of natural sciences. In the observatory installed between the years of 1637 and 1644 by the Prince of Nassau — the oldest of the Southern Hemisphere — he carried on important meteorological and astronomical observations from which there have remained for us, preserved by Barleus, only the calculations relating to the solar eclipse of November 12, 1640; and he wrote a topographical and meterological treatise on Brazil, published in an appendix to the second edition (1658) of the great work in which there figures in eight books out of the twelve which make it up, the enormous scientific spoil collected by the German savant.

It is certain that Judaic-Dutch Recife became, in the period of the occupation, as Gilberto Freyre says, "the greatest center of intellectual differentiation in the colony, which the Catholic effort in the direction of integration was trying to preserve intact as against the new sciences and new languages. With Count Maurice of Nassau, there arose in the midst of the cashew trees the first astronomical observatory in America. A botanical garden and a zoological garden rose among the gitiranas and the mango trees, where formerly there had been only crab holes. There appeared Piso and Marggraf, the first scientific eyes to study the Indians, the trees, and the animals of Brazil; pastors of the religion of Calvin preaching new forms of Christianity; Franz Post painting plantation houses, the thatch-covered huts of Indians, the Negro shacks, cashew trees along the rivers, Negroes carrying dirty linen on their heads; Pieter Post, tracing the plans of a great city of high mansions and of deep canals through which one could pass in a canoe as in Holland." But these little scattered foci, the last witnesses of the great flame of the spirit of culture which Maurice of Nassau left, were not slow in being extinguished, on the one hand by the short duration of the Dutch rule, which had been maintained by force, and on the other by the growing hostilities directed against the invaders, heretics, in whom the colonists came to see the enemies of their country and of religion. The spirit of integration in the Catholic and Portuguese direction was to end by dissolving differences, attracting the population of Pernambuco once more into the orbit of Iberian influence. Marggraf died in 1644, in the very year of the retirement of the Prince of Nassau to Holland, where four years afterward W. Piso published the first edition of a notable work in which the Flemish physician and the German naturalist had collaborated. The great agitation which followed the departure of Nassau in May, 1644; the wars against the Batavians, defeated in Europe by England and in America by the Brazilians, in the two battles of Guararapes, and finally, the capitulation in 1654 of the invaders, who gave up their conquest, left the whole civilization which the Flemish prince had tried to build on the soil of Portuguese America completely unarmed and on the point of breaking up entirely. "Of the work of the administrator nothing survived," writes Capistrano de Abreu; "his palaces and gardens were consumed and devoured in the fire and blood of the following year; his artistic collections went to enrich various establishments in Europe, and the Americanists are studying them"; and the books of Barleus, Piso, and Marggraf which "because of their patronage attained a height which no Portuguese or Brazilian work can be compared with in colonial times, appear even to have been little read in Brazil in spite of being written in Latin, the universal language of the time, so insignificant are the remains which we find of them."

Down to the nineteenth century, no other missions of foreign savants came to Brazil; and if among the visitors of colonial Brazil some showed an interest in the nature of our country, like the Frenchman Dampier (Bahia, 1704), La Barbinnais (1714), and Bougainville, who was in Santa Catarina in 1763 and in Rio in 1765, their observations did not in general involve anything more than that feeling for the picturesque expressed by travelers who are amazed by tropical landscapes. A taste for traveling, the spirit of adventure, the interest in the newly discovered land in America and in Asia stimulated these isolated undertakings of foreigners who left no vestige of their passage through the colony, whence passing naturalists, however — a Ph. Commerson (1767) and Joseph Banks (1768), who spent three weeks in Guanabara — sent respectively to the Museum of Natural History of Paris and to London herbariums collected in Rio de Janeiro. The colony continued to be alien to the scientific revolution which was going on in the old world and sunk in the thick obscurity in which the home country was, in this respect, wrapped, like the whole peninsula "outside the isothermic line of this revolution." Over the whole surface of the peninsula, considers Rui Barbosa, "scientific instruction did not exist. In the middle of this century (the eighteenth) there was not in Spain a practical chemist. More than a hundred and fifty years after Harvey, they were still ignorant there of the circulation of the blood. The University of Salamanca in 1771 had refused public entry, disdainfully and in no uncertain terms, to the discoveries of Newton, Gassendi, and Descartes, because they could not be harmonized with Aristotle. In Portugal, university studies were vegetating under theological routine, just as the colleges were monopolies of the religious orders and also the rare primary schools which were nothing more, we may say, than diocesan establishments under the direction of the clergy and the inspection of the bishops." Teaching, subject to the administration of the clergy and transferred in 1555 to the hands of the Jesuits, without doubt the best humanists of the time, was characterized by the teaching of grammar, rhetoric, and scholasticism, and was reduced on the higher level to theological and juridical letters, beside the medicine of Galen, remaining almost completely closed for more than two centuries to the study of experimental science. It was a whole cultural system erected for the training of priests, men of letters, and scholars, and which, developing in its autonomous orbit, resisted the powerful attraction of the new methods and progressive tendencies which were agitating the civilized world. If to this cultural atmosphere, satisfied with the purely bookish and dogmatic forms and the controversies inspired by the old scholastic spirit, we add the policy of isolation adopted by Portugal with relation to the colony, which reached the point of depriving it of all communication and commerce with the nations of Europe; the regime oppressing liberty of thought and of criticism and the desperate tenacity with which the home country suffocated all the manifestations of living culture in the country and all the means of its propagation, we will have the sad picture of the almost invincible obstacles which rose in Brazil, preventing the penetration of the critical and scientific spirit and the spread of the study of the sciences of observation.

In this long period of obscurantism, interrupted only by the breach which was opened in it by the administration of the Flemish prince, the sterile discussions, precious to the point of the ridiculous, in which the intelligence of literary academies which followed one another in the colonies continued to split hairs, we do not meet any rigorous examination of ideas and of facts. Nature in the variety of its landscapes and aspects was rather a savage force, defying the boldness of adventurers and explorers, a spectacle with which poets and men of letters entertained themselves, or a springboard whence the mystic imagination threw itself into the infinite. Rarely did it appear to the eyes of the Brazilians as an inexhaustible field of observation awakening their scientific curiosity. For tens of literary academies which followed one another in the colony, one does not meet until 1770 even a single academy of sciences. The first of this kind, the Academia Científica, which was founded in 1771 in Rio de Janeiro, three years after the reform of the University of Coimbra by the Marquis de Pombal, had only an ephemeral duration (1771–1779), and with its activity reduced to the creation of a botanical garden on the Morro do Castelo and to some undertakings of a practical character and to interchange with foreign academies, it did not exercise any influence upon the evolution of Brazilian thought. Although it proposed to make studies of pure science and of applied science, uniting in the same society those who claimed to devote themselves to physics, as well as those who studied medicine, surgery, pharmacy, and agriculture, the Scientific Academy begun by the viceroy Marquis de Lavradio — forerunner of a National Academy of Medicine and the Brazilian Academy of Sciences — did not meet in the variety of its objects nor in the amplitude of its plan of action sufficient means to assure the continuity of its existence and its progress. While a student at Coimbra, Silva Alvarenga of Vila Rica, who had received in Portugal the impression of the current of new ideas, attacked in his satire *O desertor das letras,* the old methods of teaching while he was at the university before the reform of the Marquis de Pombal. Returning to Brazil, to which he brought his taste for science, he founded a scientific society which also had a short duration and was reborn later, in 1786, and restored by the poet with the approval of the Viceroy Luiz de Vasconcelos under the name of Literary Society of Rio de Janeiro. . . . In its broad outlines, stratified in rigid formulae, colonial culture maintained a climate entirely unfavorable to any movement showing an interest in the sciences; and it was not surprising when, even in the home country, in which the reforms of education promoted by the ministry of Dom José produced a true revolution, the natural sciences, looked upon askance as yet, "were like bastards to whom the generosity and clemency of Pombal had given a place to stay and a shelter in that arrogant, literary group of inheritors who made their home in Coimbra. They were sciences of plebeians and were almost unknown as being too recently arrived and lacking in genealogical coats of arms." But a small group of Brazilians who were studying at Coimbra at this time, between 1760 and 1788, and breathed there the new cultural atmosphere, was the first to take advantage of the teaching in the university, reorganized in 1768 by Pombal, who added to the program of the courses, studied natural history and mathematics, established an observatory, created laboratories and museums, and "recognized the dignity of the teaching of science."

If at the dawn of the eighteenth century there stands out in Portugal the extraordinary figure of a Brazilian, Father Bartolomeu Lourenço, who rose above his environment to take part in the first experiments with the aerostat and to whom justice assures in the annals of scientific progress a place among the immortal forerunners of aviation, there arose after 1775, in the twilight of that century, a consummate geographer like Lacerda e Almeida, a Conceição Veloso, and an Alexandre Rodrigues Ferreira, great naturalists, and a mineralogist of the value of José Bonifácio de Andrada e Silva, "the greatest and the most cultivated of the Brazilians of his time." The first, Francisco José de Lacerda e Almeida (São Paulo, 1750), educated at Coimbra around 1776, plunged into the interior on his return to Brazil, "sweeping the territory from west to east, from a southern branch of the Amazon and across the water system of the Paraguay and Paraná," and fixing the coordinates of hundreds of localities. He embarked in 1790 for Lisbon with his notes and maps, which he was to present to the Royal Academy of Sciences, and left in 1796 on a geographic mission to the colonies of Portuguese Africa, where death found him in October, 1798, after he had passed the upper Zambesi, searching for the central region of the African continent. In his *Diário da viagem de Moçambique para os rios de Sena*, published only in 1936, he describes for us the great wealth of data and observation, the great enterprise in which he succumbed and which was attempted by the expedition of which he made a part, almost a century before the glorious exploration (1871) of Livingstone and Stanley to the upper sources of the river Nile. But "the greatest profit for Brazil in the reform of the Marquis de Pombal, beside the Andradas, was," according to Juliano Moreira, "the fact that it produced a naturalist, Alexandre Rodrigues Ferreira" (Bahia, 1756–Lisbon, 1815), a physician of Bahia who had come to Brazil charged with making an inventory of the natural wealth of the country, having disembarked in Belem in 1783, and who, by his scientific explorations in the Amazon and by his notable work, above all in the fields of botany and zoology, merited the name of "the Brazilian Humboldt." The author of *Viagem filosófica*, illustrated by colored drawings, and of more than a hundred books and memorials not published even today, he passed through the bitterness not only by knowing they would not be published, but also of seeing his originals and designs and precious collections of natural history requisitioned by General Junot in 1808 on the request of Geoffroy de Saint-Hilaire; they were transported from the Museum of Ajuda to that of Paris, and the French naturalist used them, relying in his research on the work of the great Brazilian naturalist. The spoil which under these official orders G. de Saint-Hilaire seized in Portugal on the occasion of the invasion of the French troops was not limited to the material collected by Alexandre Rodrigues Ferreira. On August 29, 1808, in the same two-wheeled carriage in which he rode to the Royal Press of Lisbon, he took with him 554 plates belonging to the notable *Flora Fluminense* of Brother José Mariano da Conceição Veloso (Minas, 1742–1811), a victim, like the naturalist of Bahia, "of a lack of comprehension of the community in which they lived," writes Artur Neiva, "and of the unheard of usurpation which scholars of such great value practiced upon them." Of the Brazilians who studied at the University of Coimbra after its reform by the Marquis de Pombal, the greatest of all, José Bonifácio, a notable mineralogist, "the Portuguese Andrada" whom Bruhns mentions among savants of universal reputation, companions of Humboldt, carried on an intense scientific activity in European countries, published memoirs on the mines of Portugal, and occupied the chair of metallurgy at the University of Coimbra. However, on his return to Brazil, the agitated political life of the time drew him away from his sciences, to the progress of which no one could have made a greater contribution, in order to make of him one of the great builders of the nation.

It is, however, with the installation of the Portuguese court in Brazil that, properly speaking, the history of our culture begins, for, until this time, one cannot find anything but sporadic manifestations of exceptional figures, educated in Portugal and under foreign influence in the eighteenth century and sent, some of them, to Brazil as foreign functionaries to carry on studies and observations of a scientific character.

D. Late Colonial Developments

5. Flowers for the King

ARTHUR ROBERT STEELE

The lure of a rendezvous with the "Maids of Honor" and Goya's "Naked Maja" draws crowds of sightseers daily into the far-famed Prado Museum of Art. But next door, behind the high iron fence of the Jardín Botánico de Madrid, scarcely anyone comes. Even the gardeners are too often absent for want of money to pay them. The director fondles his maroon and gold guestbook, proudly pointing to the signature of Umberto, onetime king of Italy, but lamenting the lack of Spanish names among the distinguished company.

The dignified gate to the garden, fronting on the noise and gasoline fumes of the busy Paseo del Prado, is the symbol of a vanished age. Dating from 1781, the gate honors the king who gave life to the garden, Charles III, "restorer of the botanic art for the health and delight of his citizens." Through the portal one enters that age now vanished, an age when the botanic garden was new and Spain yearned to become, and spent money freely trying to become, the world leader in plant exploration, an age when botany was a matter of state and ministers were not strangers to the botanical scene.

Hispanophiles, to ward off the buffeting so often their lot in the field of world opinion, have seized upon these words of Alexander von Humboldt, the great German scholar who witnessed first hand this moment of Spanish glory:

> No European government has laid out greater sums to advance the knowledge of plants than the Spanish government. Three *botanical expeditions,* those of Peru, New Granada, and

Arthur Robert Steele, *Flowers for the King: The Expedition of Ruiz and Pavón and the Flora of Peru* (Durham, N.C.: Duke University Press, 1964), pp. vii–viii, 46–49. Reprinted by permission of the Duke University Press.

New Spain, . . . have cost the state about two million francs. Besides, botanic gardens have been established at Manila and in the Canary Islands. The commission destined to survey the Güines canal was also charged with examining the vegetable products of the island of Cuba. All this research, made during twenty years in the most fertile regions of the new continent, has not only enriched the domain of science with more than four thousand new species of plants; it has also contributed greatly to spread the taste for natural history among the inhabitants of the country.

Dr. Samuel L. Mitchill, professor of natural history at Columbia College in New York, passed on Humboldt's information to the members of the historical society of his state at their annual meeting in 1813. "I wish it was in my power," he said, "to state the particulars of the great exertions for the improvement of American botany made by the kings of Spain." Dr. Mitchill put the outlay for the expeditions at $370,000. . . .

Though its beginnings were tortuous and slow, Spanish botany entered an era of excited ferment in the last half of the eighteenth century. Observers ever since, viewing the stimulation of botany as only a part of Charles III's comprehensive plan to reform the intellectual and scientific life of the nation, have tried to explain the large share of attention allotted to the plant sciences.

It is customary to point out the good standing of botany in the spiritual realm. As long as mutability of species was not yet a question, botany did indeed seem a fairly innocuous form of scientific activity, upsetting no sacred credos. In fact, from a more positive standpoint, as Miguel Barnades commented in his text, the beauty of growing things demonstrates to us God's wisdom; their preservation, multiplication, and renewal show us His power; and their usefulness to men reveals His ineffable goodness. Numerous churchmen were attracted to botany. This argument implies that clerical opposition to most forms of new learning hindered the development of the scientific spirit in Spain. It suggests a government ready to burst into scientific prominence, all the while held back by a powerful church, and forced to turn to plant study for want of another outlet. There is a grain of truth in this grotesque distortion, but we should beware of making a stir about it.

A more positive explanation is demanded for the official interest in botany, and in part it lies in the economic value of plants. This seems almost too obvious for comment. Yet it becomes especially significant when we consider that attempts to revive Spain economically were an inconsequential part of public policy until the second half of the eighteenth century.

The Count of Campomanes, councilor of His Majesty, in 1774 wrote his celebrated *Discurso sobre el fomento de la industria popular,* drawn up by order of the king and council, to suggest means of relieving unemployment in Spain. Among the twenty-one "paragraphs" of his work, one explained the necessity for the study of natural history. The nation, he urged, should give prizes to those who could demonstrate the value of plants to manufacturing. Another proposal urged that so-called economic societies, similar to one already functioning since 1765 in Basque territory, be established in the capital of each province; and within a year (July 17, 1775) the Sociedad Económica de Madrid was licensed by the crown. This event, occurring at the seat of government and with the blessing of the Spanish king, set off a chain reaction. By 1787, during the very years that the Ruiz-Pavón expedition was carrying out its studies, more than fifty Spanish cities had requested authority to form economic societies: Zaragoza in 1776; Valencia and Seville, 1777; Palma and Tudela, 1778; Segovia, 1780; Oviedo, 1781.

All were quite similarly organized, and all drew support from influential classes of society. Of the estimated five thousand members in the years of 1808, most were "enlightened nobles, reformist ecclesiastics, and persons of the middle class imbued with the current philanthropism," as well as "a striking number of public officials." Intellectuals played a lesser part. In their efforts to stimulate by all means possible the improvement of agriculture, industry, and commerce, the societies demonstrated the passion for "useful knowledge" so characteristic of the Enlightenment. Material prosperity was their main concern; they sought to promote it by condemnation of idleness, by improved technology, and by better vocational education. The Madrid society dotted its *memorias* with statistics and cautioned its members against the "monstrous paradoxes" and "vain questions" so frequent in Spanish argument.

Botany felt the influence of this pursuit of "useful knowledge." Statutes of the societies usually spoke of the "cultivation of all plants and trees from which some utility can be derived" as a matter of grave concern. One of the first memoirs published by the Basque society in 1765 dealt with the plants that could grow most favorably on the diversified terrain of the province. The society in Madrid printed a memoir in 1777 on the use of gums and resins in the manufacture of linen. Of less immediately recognizable usefulness was the plan of the Real Sociedad Aragonesa to arrange a "cabinet" according to Linnaean principles. Stimulated by the prospect of a prize of fifty doubloons, it became in 1786 the first group to draw up an outline for a natural history of Spain.

Botany as a science for its own sake was obviously of little concern to these groups. Nor were many of them, especially in the smaller towns, able to survive the handicap of a shortage of talented members. But the societies in the major cities must have exerted some influence in keeping alive for a time in the Peninsula the urge for scientific knowledge. If this is so, botany benefited indirectly, just as did every other branch of science.

Campomanes performed another service by rescuing Bernardo Ward's *Proyecto económico* from the forgotten files. Among many other details, this plan, drafted in 1762 and based on an earlier report by José del Campillo y Cosío in 1743, called for the collection of samples, from all the realms, of trees, fruits, herbs, and grains which "they say by well-founded tradition, and confirm by experiment, have some special virtue for health, pleasure, or other use."

Certain authors have pursued the illusive, but fascinating, goal of analyzing Spain's affinity for the natural sciences in terms of a "national characteristic." Thus the French scholar, G. Desdevises du Dezert:

> These sciences of observation, whose object is always concrete, and which especially call for order, patience, and memory, seem better suited to the national temperament [of the Spanish] than the abstract speculations of mathematics or the lengthy meditations which the experimental sciences demand.

There are those who might not agree; for example, a modern Spaniard, Celso Arévalo: "The . . . hostility with which the Linnaean orientation was received in Spain is a proof of the resistance that the Spanish genius offered to the dry taxonomic orientation." In Spain, Arévalo maintains, science always had a "human character."

But such speculation aside, other reasons exist to help clarify the Spanish interest in botany. Since the earliest days of discovery in America, many writers had mentioned plants — a necessary result of their full-measured curiosity. The collector's urge, sweeping natural history into favor among the upper classes of other European lands, exerted a new kind of persuasion: witness the growth of the "cabinet" in Madrid. Enthusiasm touched off in Europe by the Linnaean revolution had begun to penetrate Spanish thought by 1776. And certainly, prodding by the master himself, aimed toward Spain, did not go unheeded. It would seem that Spain, determined to promote the sciences and having such vast unstudied domains, drifted into herborization because, together with metallurgy, it was the most obvious and readily available type of scientific activity upon which to lavish official funds.

6. Balmis and the Introduction of Vaccination to Spanish America

SHERBURNE F. COOK

On November 30, 1803 Francisco Xavier Balmis sailed from Coruña, Spain for the purpose of carrying the newly discovered vaccination to the wide dominions of the Spanish Empire. Seldom, perhaps never, in the history of medicine has there embarked an expedition so grandly conceived, so well executed, so uniformly successful as that of Balmis. Certainly no new therapeutic procedure of similar magnitude has ever been made available by a single agency to such a wide segment of the world's population. By it the discovery of Jenner was made available to the populations of the West Indies, Mexico, Central America, much of South America, the Philippine Islands, the East Indies and China. Through this one act on the part of the corrupt and decadent government of Spain more lives probably were saved than were lost in all the battles of Napoleon. Yet this magnificent experiment in social welfare and public health has gone substantially unnoticed and unrecorded by both medical and political historians. . . .

The plans involved three principal items: the administrative personnel, the mode of conservation of the vaccine, and the route to

"Francisco Xavier Balmis and the Introduction of Vaccine to Latin America" by S. F. Cook from *Bulletin of the History of Medicine* (The Johns Hopkins Press, Baltimore), Vol. XI, pp. 543–557, Vol. XII, pp. 70–89 (1941–1942), *passim*. Reprinted by permission of the Johns Hopkins Press.

be followed. With respect to personnel, Balmis was named Director. His salary was set at 2,000 pesos annually to run from his departure from Madrid to the return of the expedition. Thereafter, until he secured a position appropriate to his standing he was to receive half pay, and in addition he was granted a subsidy of 200 doubloons wherewith to purchase an outfit. As principal lieutenants his majesty appointed the following four physicians: Don Joseph Salvani, Don Ramon Fernandez Ochoa, Don Manuel Julian Grajales, and Don Antonio Gutierrez y Robredo. Each of these was to be paid just one half that assigned to Balmis.   . . .

The problem of vaccine transport was serious. The voyage was certainly to be of long duration, involving a minimum of several weeks passage from the Canary Islands to the West Indies. Several rather different methods were in vogue at the time. The first was to prepare the virus by placing active matter from a pustule of a cow between two small plates of glass or otherwise sealing it in glass out of contact with the air. Another was to impregnate cloth, or silk threads with the virus and allow it to dry. Both these procedures suffered from lack of aseptic precautions and moreover the virus was very likely to deteriorate. Since these and similar devices were notoriously unreliable, it was determined to utilize another safer although much more cumbersome and expensive method. The latter consisted of transporting the vaccine fluid in human reservoirs. At the outset of the voyage a small, non-immune boy was to be vaccinated with a potent preparation of cow pox virus. At the point when the reaction was at its peak, matter was to be transferred from this individual to the arm of another boy who would preserve the active principle until it was transferred to the next. This chain vaccination was to be continued until the New World was reached, at which time any number of new patients would be available. The royal orders specified simply a "sufficient number" of children. The boys were to be selected from various orphan asylums, with permission of relatives if known, and were to be well cared for. They were to be retained in the colonies after arrival, and of course after their usefulness had ceased. Nevertheless they were to be given every consideration and were to be educated at the expense of the state until they were able to enter some regular employment. Actually twenty-two sailed from Spain. Unfortunately since their names were not recorded they must forever remain anonymous contributors to the cause of medical progress.

The route to be followed was carefully worked out in advance. On arrival in the West Indies the expedition was to split. The main party under Balmis was to proceed to Mexico City and introduce vaccination throughout the Viceroyalty of New Spain, subsequent to which it was to sail for the Philippines. The remainder of the group was to go to the region of the present Colombian Republic, then over the Andes to Ecuador and Peru and finally, by an undetermined route to the settlements on the Rio Plata in present Argentina and Uruguay. This itinerary was carried out in all essentials although in detail it was determined by local circumstances.

The first stop was at the Canary Islands where a public demonstration was organized by the Governor and where the first vaccinations were performed. After what must have been a quick trip across the Atlantic the party reached Puerto Rico sometime in February, 1804. Here Balmis encountered for the first time a situation which baffled and irritated him more than once during the course of his journey. He found vaccine had already been introduced, in fact "established." It had been brought from the Island of St. Thomas by an undisclosed agency but as soon as he began to examine the vaccinations he found them to be spurious because "they did not protect against the smallpox."

The events of March, April and May are obscure. From Puerto Rico Balmis evidently proceeded to the northern coast of South America, in conformity with instructions. According to the standard account he made his third stop at Caracas in Venezuela. Here the party split. Balmis and several assistants went on to Havana. The remainder, under Assistant Director Don Francisco Salvani, started by ship for Peru presumably via Panama.   . . .

The expedition arrived in Havana in early June. On the 8th of that month the Royal Patriotic Society convened to consider the vaccination question. They informed themselves "in minute detail" of the matter, ordering two copies of the instructions to be placed in the library of the Society, and elected Balmis to an honorary membership. At the same time a central vaccination board was formed for the dissemination of the fluid among the inhabitants of the Island of Cuba. However, Balmis was anxious to continue his journey for he wrote the Viceroy on June 10 that he intended to depart on or about June 17 for Yucatan whence he would proceed to Vera Cruz, arriving there toward the end of July. Since the original royal instructions directed the expedition to go directly to Vera Cruz from Havana, the decision to make a detour to Yucatan seems to have been reached by Balmis while on the voyage. Whether any extraordinary motives prompted him to take this course is doubtful, but it may perhaps have been more than coincidence that when he arrived he found vaccine already introduced both on the peninsula and the region of Vera Cruz. . . .

It is quite clear that vaccine was in the Caribbean colonies prior to the arrival of the Royal Expedition, although its ultimate origin is obscure. Two introductions seem to have occurred, probably independently, one in Vera Cruz, the other in Yucatan.

Late in March, Bernardo de Casas, physician of the Royal Navy, shipped some vaccine from Havana to Vera Cruz on the frigates *Amphitrite* and *Nuestra Señora de la O*. It is not entirely apparent where Casas secured the virus although very probably he secured it from Doña Maria Bustamente, who brought it from Puerto Rico. This incident is discussed below in connection with events in Yucatan.

During the voyage and prior to arrival at Vera Cruz on April 1, 1804, the second officer of the *Nuestra Señora de la O* caused to be vaccinated two sailors, Manuel Sierra and Francisco Montero. From the sailors the vaccine was communicated to several other persons, the operation being performed by Don Miguel Perez Carillo, surgeon of the ship. He first vaccinated five children, then twelve more. The purpose was stated to be in order that the virus might not become vitiated. On April 24 further reserves were built up at the request of a practitioner, Dr. Don Francisco Hernández, by vaccinating six musicians attached to the local military units. By the following day the Ayuntamiento was able to write the Viceroy the municipal medical board's opinion that "the legitimate vaccine is established in this city." The introduction of vaccination in Vera Cruz must, therefore, be regarded as having been accomplished. . . .

Early in the spring of 1804 the governor of Yucatan, Don Benito Perez y Valdelomar saw an opportunity to secure the new vaccine for his province. As related previously Doña Maria Bustamente had arrived in Havana on February 10, accompanied by her son and two Negro servant girls, all of whom had been vaccinated in Puerto Rico. The governor of Havana had caused the virus from these children to be preserved in vials and had forwarded some to Vera Cruz on the *Nuestra Señora de la O*. Another vial he sent to Perez at Merida in Yucatan. The latter turned the material over to the army surgeon, Don Antonio Poveda, with instructions to propagate the treatment. On March 19, a small Negro boy was vaccinated and evidently some others, although there is no mention of a specific number. By early April, however, it was apparent that all hopes were doomed to disappointment. The virus had lost its potency and gave no results whatever. The governor then commissioned three prominent physicians to "resort to every means to see if the original pus could be found in cows in the province, utilizing the basic knowledge contained in those physiological descriptions that we have been able to acquire." This was a slim chance, and Perez was prone to regard their only hope as being the expected arrival of the Balmis expedition. Meanwhile, he pointed out, smallpox was still continuing its ravages. Most providential, therefore, from his point of view was the arrival at Campeche about the tenth of May of the brigantine *Salta* which had sailed from Vera Cruz on the first of the month bearing the surgeon Don Miguel José Monzón with several vaccinated boys.

The reception of the Monzón party was most cordial. The governor ordered all officials to cooperate to the fullest extent and even went so far as to promise the financial support of the Royal Treasury, a matter in which he may well have exceeded his authority. In turn Monzón lost no time. Having scarcely landed at Campeche he began his work. Using vaccine he had brought from Vera Cruz in vials he inoculated 13 persons. This material, however, was ineffective in all cases, an experience reminiscent of the useless Poveda vaccinations two months previously. Indeed, it is generally noteworthy that the *in vitro* methods of virus preservation were very unreliable. Perhaps the percentage of failures was no greater in Latin America at this epoch than elsewhere in the world, but on the other hand the heat and humidity of the tropics may have accentuated the inevitable tendency toward deterioration. The *in vivo* method was much more successful. On May 19 Monzón vaccinated 20 persons "from arm to arm," using the children he had brought with him.

The subsequent career of Monzón in Yucatan need not be set forth in detail. He evidently was a conscientious and capable physician, devoted to his mission, and quite successful as a pioneer in vaccination. Indeed, he went so far as to borrow a cow from a country curate, Don Manuel Suarez. This animal he inoculated "with the fluid from a pustule of his niece Juana Suarez." Although there is no indication of a successful outcome of this experiment the attempt marks Monzón as a man of scientific interest and initiative, qualities not always to be found among the practitioners of colonial Mexico. His primary task, that of vaccine distribution, he carried out with effectiveness and dispatch. According to his final report he performed 55 series of vaccinations, involving a total of 1,366 persons, most of which operations were attended by favorable results. Since this work was done in sixty days (May 10–July 10), and since he had no assistance of a competent nature, the record of more than 20 vaccinations daily is highly creditable. It was indeed unfortunate that this obscure but sincere practitioner through no fault of his own was forced into a humiliating controversy with Balmis himself.

It will be remembered that Balmis, having written the Viceroy of his intention to proceed to Vera Cruz set sail from Havana for the mainland in the middle of June. He also had notified Governor Perez to the same effect. The latter immediately wrote to Monzón in Campeche directing him to submit a full report of all his activities to Balmis. Monzón acknowledged the letter and promised complete cooperation. On June 30, Perez again wrote Monzón. Balmis had already arrived and the governor was about to turn over to him all the papers pertaining to vaccination in the province. Within the next three days Balmis reached Merida and conferred with the governor. As a result of this interview, the content of which Balmis evidently set forth in a written communication, the governor informed Monzón that Balmis was highly dissatisfied with the Campeche vaccinations, regarding them as prejudicial to public health. Indeed, he deemed it necessary to send his assistant, Gutierrez, to that town for the purpose of instituting a formal investigation.   . . . Monzón answered one week later in very indignant vein. He pointed out that his vaccinations had been highly successful, that the vaccine he had used was potent by all known standards, that no secondary ill effects had been observed, and that every practitioner in the city — even every barber — was by now well acquainted with the method. Moreover, he caustically observed, if his vaccine was as worthless as Balmis stated, then why did the latter send four boys with Gutierrez to be inoculated with that very same vaccine, "since it is more logical that in case doubt existed, as is pretended . . . he would have utilized the fluid brought from Europe. . . ."

The issue of the investigation was clearly a personal vindication for Monzón. Gutierrez examined the vaccine and some of Monzón's cases before the Ayuntamiento of Campeche on July 9, and not only pronounced the treatment legitimate but proceeded to vaccinate his four boys. Following this favorable outcome, the Ayuntamiento requested Monzón to continue his work and voted him a formal expression of thanks and confidence. Monzón, however, discontinued active vaccination and soon afterward returned to Vera Cruz. He either accompanied Balmis on this trip or immediately preceded him, for Balmis reached Vera Cruz on July 24.

His arrival was the signal for another rather acrimonious controversy. It being necessary to transmit the vaccine in order to ensure its propagation, he attempted to find persons in Vera Cruz who might be vaccinated. To his great chagrin he was unsuccessful. As he described the situation to the Viceroy: "Since the pustules brought with me were in perfect state for their fluid to be employed, I endeavored to obtain persons into whom to inject it so as to ensure its propagation but all the efforts and assiduity on the part of the two councilmen (*Regidores*) and other zealous professional men proved futile. Observing the impending danger of losing a treasure that I have conserved at the cost of great labor and affliction, I imparted the extremely critical situation to the governor, who, appreciating the seriousness of the matter furnished ten individuals of the Garrison Regiment, and I have just finished vaccinating them."

Subsequently — long after Balmis had departed from Vera Cruz — the Viceroy wrote the City Government demanding an explanation. He stated that he was "not able to reconcile this information with repeated assurances given by the governor that the fluid brought by the frigates 'O' and '*Amphitrite*' was being accepted and successfully propagated without ever indicating any resistance on the part of the populace."

To this demand the city replied in a very vituperative missive in which certain charges were brought against the conduct of Balmis. The City Council first claimed that it had been impossible to secure unvaccinated persons because every non-immune individual had previously been immunized by the local authorities, or had been a victim of the disease itself. Consequently an accusation of indifference on the part of the citizens was no less than a calumny and the necessity for making an explanation was humiliating in the extreme. The document then goes on to point with pride to the noble and fruitful efforts of the city itself, as a result of which no less than 3,027 persons had been vaccinated in various towns "before the arrival of the expedition. This appears to have incurred the displeasure of Don Francisco Xavier Balmis, obliging him to manifest it openly." Finally the heart of the matter was reached when the Ayuntamiento came to the treatment accorded Monzón in Campeche. A terrible insult had been given the city when Gutierrez was sent to examine Monzón's vaccine. Gutierrez had actually stolen this vaccine — through the four boys he brought with him. Balmis had been offensive to Monzón personally and had maltreated the children sent with Monzón as carriers. And so on for several pages in like tenor the diatribe continued.

This entire episode might be regarded as too trivial for serious consideration did it not possess significance as an illustration of the difficulties attending even great undertakings. But for the timely intervention of the Governor of Vera Cruz, the vaccine might have been lost and the entire scheme might have failed in its object. It is quite clear that the fault lay on both sides. When the vaccinated sailors arrived in Vera Cruz, the Ayuntamiento of that city, knowing of the royal expedition, doubtless saw an opportunity to anticipate Balmis and achieve publicity and merit in the eyes of the Viceroy. . . .   In support of this point of view may be noted the obsequious care with which they notified the Viceroy of their every action and on the other hand the carelessness with which they permitted the smallpox virus to disappear from their own town as soon as it had served its purpose. Entirely in line with such policy was the rude treatment they accorded Balmis and their utter indifference to the welfare of the king's expedition.

At the other end of the controversy the behavior of Balmis was, to say the least, undiplomatic. Instead of being in any way gratified that the great humanitarian object of his visit was being accomplished by private individuals in advance of his arrival he obviously became subject to strong irritation. Judging by his actions in Yucatan, and his letters from Vera Cruz he regarded any efforts by others toward introduction of vaccine as a personal affront and a presumption upon his own prerogatives as the king's emissary. In short, all parties concerned behaved as if the propagation of vaccine in the interest of the public welfare were wholly secondary to considerations of personal aggrandizement and royal or viceregal favor.

Tarrying only a few days in the inhospitable atmosphere of Vera Cruz, Balmis, Gutierrez and 22 boys departed on July 28 for Mexico. Passing by the old road through Jalapa and Perote, the group arrived at the suburb of Guadalupe on August 8.   . . .

The introduction of vaccine into Mexico City was the most vital single necessity confronting the Balmis expedition. The capital of New Spain exercised an enormous influence upon the entire stretch of the continent from San Francisco Bay to Panama. That capital was the physical or spiritual home of the entire ruling class, the group which moulded and determined public opinion. It was absolutely essential for the success of the new therapy to establish its desirability in the minds of the Mexican upper class. Hence Balmis made a particularly strong effort in this direction.

For some reason every attempt to perform vaccinations in Mexico City met with remarkable lack of success. Indeed, the amazing reluctance on the part of the inhabitants lends weight to the theory that certain persons in high places, perhaps the Viceroy himself, were engaged in secret sabotage. It will be remembered that in Vera Cruz, despite numerous previous vaccinations at the hands of local authorities, Balmis was unable to find a single individual upon whom to perform the operation. In Mexico City much the same situation presented itself. Some months previously Don Alexandro Garcia Arboleya had been commissioned by the Viceroy himself to propagate vaccine in the suburbs of Coyoacan and Tacuba where he had encountered little difficulty and had performed several hundred operations. The consistent support of the Viceroy in favor of pre-expedition introduction of vaccine argues a definite policy which manifested itself not only in Mexico City but in Vera Cruz, Yucatan and various other regions. It is very probable that colonial politics and ambitions were involved although there is no concrete documentary evidence bearing on the point. If so, this will not have been the first occasion on which a protagonist of some form of public health improvement met with reverses at the hands of ignorant and selfish political appointees.

Apart from the motivation, however, Balmis found that when he issued a call for volunteers to be vaccinated at a free public clinic on August 19 and 20 not a single soul responded. What occurred at that clinic is most vividly told by Balmis himself:

> Another proof of this (popular resistance) is seen in the fact that no person whatever has presented himself in order to participate in this immense benefaction, . . . the *Alcalde,* commissioned by your Excellency, having to resort to force to obtain 12 children to be vaccinated for the purpose of insuring continuance of the precious vaccine brought from Madrid.

> . . . On the 19th and 20th of this month I might have lost the
> fluid . . . had it not been for the zealous *Alcalde*. He
> dragged in as many as twenty Indian mothers, whose children
> we finally vaccinated after much persuasion on our part and
> after loud vociferation and exclaiming that they were not
> under obligation to anybody. Some admitted that it was right
> but that they could not pay, and every single one went to the
> apothecary, demanding an antidote against the venom that
> had just been introduced into the arm of her child. . . .

Since the primary purpose of the Royal Expedition was to introduce vaccination to the inhabitants of the territories visited, it was
necessary for the Director or selected assistants to make personal
contact with the officials and leading citizens of as many towns as
possible. Mere regulations and orders promulgated by the viceregal
government or even the clerical hierarchy were likely to be received
with indifference. Haphazard introduction depending upon local
intitiative or the exigency of epidemics likewise would be too uncertain and risky. To depend upon the nearly non-existent national
medical profession or the caprice of municipal politicians was manifestly out of the question since the former were too ignorant and the
latter too selfish and corrupt to ensure proper handling of the treatment. For these reasons it was desirable for competent and disinterested persons to go as emissaries or missionaries and make the
people themelves acquainted with the procedure and merits of vaccination. . . .

In the space of approximately six months the director, or his assistants, visited every important city, and many of the small towns
of Mexico. The medical profession was given such complete training in the practice of the new method that numerous persons remained after the departure of Balmis who were qualified to continue the work. At all key points an adequate supply existed both of
preserved vaccine and living carriers. The administration of small
pox prevention was vested in a series of local vaccination boards
which in turn were under the direct authority of the colonial government. A system of free public clinics was established. Finally, a
great many thousand inhabitants were actually vaccinated and, perhaps more important, caused to lose their initial fear and suspicion of the strange procedure.

Concerning the actual number of vaccinations performed from
July, 1804 to January, 1806, we have only the scattered estimates

cited previously. From these data it is evident that the numbers varied enormously from district to district. Moreover, it is probable that many vaccinations were never recorded officially. If a specific figure were demanded I should be inclined to feel that 100,000 might not be an overestimate. This would represent roughly two per cent of the entire population. If this is regarded as, after all a rather insignificant total, it should be remembered that not only were large sections of the country skipped by the expedition (such as Sinaloa, Sonora, Chihuahua, Coahuila, Tamaulipas and Nuevo Leon) but also vaccinations were confined to children. This was due to the fact that in 1804 practically every individual over twenty had already been exposed to smallpox in the sweeping epidemics of 1779 and 1797. If we make the fairly safe assumptions that the expedition reached only half the population by area and that only 20 per cent of the inhabitants were non-immune, then we may conclude that Balmis and his helpers reached twenty per cent of those who might have benefited by their ministrations. Such a record on the part of an introductory and propagandising expedition by strangers rather than on the part of a long-term public health program sponsored by the local government represents a real achievement.

BIBLIOGRAPHIC SUGGESTIONS

A. *Medicine*

1. Ashburn, P. M. *The Ranks of Death: A medical history of the conquest of America* (New York: Coward McCann, 1947). Has a good bibliography, with a rather general text.
1a. Cook, Sherburne F. "The Smallpox Epidemic of 1797 in Mexico," *Bulletin of the History of Medicine,* VIII (April, 1940), pp. 937–969.
1b. ———. "Smallpox in Spanish and Mexican California: 1770–1845," *ibid.,* VII (October, 1939), pp. 153–191.
2. Cooper, Donald B. *Epidemic Disease in Mexico City, 1761–1813* (Austin: University of Texas Press, 1965).
3. Díaz de Iraola, Gonzalo. "La vuelta al mundo de la expedición de la vacuna," *Anuario de Estudios Americanos,* IV (1948), pp. 103–266. The main expedition under Francisco Javier de Balmis left Corunna late in 1803 and reached Manila in April, 1805, after passing through the Antilles and Mexico. Meanwhile

branch expeditions proceeded overland from Cartagena to Bolivia (1804–1809) and to Buenos Aires. Balmis returned to Mexico (1809–1813) after reaching Cádiz from Manila via the Portuguese possessions in Asia. Much related information is included on the state of scientific affairs in the countries visited. Based mostly on documentation in the Archivo General de Indias, Seville, Indiferente General 1588. Illustrations.

4. Dobyns, Henry F. "An Outline of Andean Epidemic History to 1720," *Bulletin of the History of Medicine*, XXXVII (1936), pp. 493–515. A detailed account, with substantial bibliography, which shows that ". . . the Andean area was subjected to severe epidemic depopulation prior to 1720."

5. Duran-Reynals, Marie Louise de Ayala. *The Fever Bark Tree: The Pageant of Quinine* (Garden City: Doubleday, 1948). Has a chapter on "The Botanical Institute of the New Kingdom of Granada" (pp. 109–134).

6. Moll, Aristedes A. *Aesculapius in America* (Philadelphia: W. B. Saunders, 1944). A compendium of useful information, but not a satisfactory history.

7. Sigerist, Henry E. "Medical History in Central and South America," *Bulletin of the History of Medicine*, IX (1942), pp. 343–360.

B. *Science*

8. Delanglez, Jean. "An Astronomical Expedition to Lower California," *Mid-America*, XX (1939), pp. 284–291.

9. Garcia, Rodolfo. "Historia das explorações científicas," *Diccionario Histórico e Geográfico Brasileiro*, Vol. I (Rio de Janeiro, 1922), pp. 856–910. Detailed statement on expeditions to Brazil from many nations from 1500 to 1914.

10. Leonard, Irving A. "A Great Savant of Colonial Peru: Don Pedro de Peralta," *Philological Review, XII* (1933), pp. 54–72.

11. ———. "Science, Technology, and Hispanic America," *Michigan Quarterly Review* (Autumn, 1963), pp. 237–245. An attempt to explain the relatively backward state of science in Hispanic America.

12. Rickett, Harold W. *The Royal Botanical Expedition to New Spain, Chronica Botanica*, XI (1947), pp. 1–86. Principally a translation of documents from Mexican archives. The expedition established botanical gardens.

13. Ruiz, Hipólito. *Travels of Ruiz, Pavón and Dombey in Peru and Chile (1777–1788), with an Epilogue and Official Documents Added by Augustín Jesus Barreiro*, B. E. Dahlgren, trans. (Chicago: Field Museum of Natural History, 1940).

14. Schaedel, Richard P. "Martínez de Compañón, Founder of Peruvian Archaeology," *American Antiquity*, XV (1951), pp. 161–163. Calls attention to the fact that the great illustrated reports compiled between 1782 and 1791 by Baltasar Jaime Martínez de Compañón, bishop of Trujillo, contain important contributions to Peruvian archaeology as well as to the cultural history of the time. On this remarkable collection, see also Philip Ainsworth Means, "A Great Prelate and Archaeologist," *Hispanic American Essays. A Memorial to James Alexander Robertson*, ed. by A. Curtis Wilgus (Chapel Hill: University of North Carolina Press, 1942), pp. 67–77.
15. Wilson, Iris Higbie. "Scientists in New Spain: the Eighteenth-Century Expeditions," *Journal of the West*, I (1962), pp. 24–44.

Section IX

Climax and Crisis in the Eighteenth Century

The century before the Portuguese and Spanish colonies in America won their independence brought great cultural, economic, and political change. Tensions between the mother countries and the New World increased, despite many improvements in the lot of the overseas colonists.

One of the significant inequalities in eighteenth-century Mexico was the *fuero militar,* which granted such privileges and immunities to the well-born young men of the country as to create a military officer class exempt from civil responsibility. Professor Lyle N. McAlister, of the University of Florida, concludes his account of Mexican military development: ". . . it was this class which was to produce an Agustín de Iturbide and an Antonio López de Santa Anna" the nineteenth century military dictators (Reading IX.1).

The famous German scientist Alexander von Humboldt, in his overview of Mexico about 1800, lauded Mexico City: "No new city of the new continent, without even excepting those of the United States, can display such great and solid scientific achievements as the capital of Mexico." He added, however: "Mexico is the country of inequality. Nowhere does there exist such a fearful difference in the distribution of fortune, civilization, cultivation of the soil, and population" (Reading IX.2).

Eighteenth-century Peru was the locale of probably the most significant Indian rebellion in the whole colonial period. Led by José

Gabriel Tupac Amaru in the years 1780–1781, the revolt has been described as an attempt to achieve an independent Peruvian Indian state. Professor George Kubler of Yale University concludes in his succinct account, however, that ". . . the Indians wished to capture Spanish institutions, not destroy or displace them by others" (Reading IX.3).

Another problem in Peru was declining mineral production, upon which its economy had been based ever since the Potosí silver mines were discovered in 1545. Silver production depended upon mercury, which the Huancavelica mine had provided in great quantities since about 1570. Professor Emeritus Arthur P. Whitaker of the University of Pennsylvania examines the many expedients the crown used to revive Huancavelica during the eighteenth century. (Reading IX.4).

Stagnation and decay did not characterize the Spanish American empire generally in the eighteenth century, however, and the late Professor C. H. Haring of Harvard University stated in his fundamental work that ". . . at the end of the colonial era most of the American provinces enjoyed greater prosperity and well-being than ever before."[1]

Professor R. A. Humphreys of the University of London concurs with this view and presents an excellent general analysis and description of the fall of the Spanish empire in America which stretched ". . . in unbroken line from California to Cape Horn. From Stockholm to Cape Town is less distant, and within the area ruled by Spain all western Europe from Madrid to Moscow might lie and be lost" (Reading IX.5).

[1] C. H. Haring, *The Spanish Empire in America* (New York: Harcourt, Brace and World, 1963), p. 322.

A. New Spain

1. The Reorganization of the Army
LYLE N. MCALISTER

The military situation in New Spain was fairly representative of Spanish America as a whole. The armed forces of the colonies were strong enough to maintain internal security and defense against the hostile Indians or sudden raids by enemy forces. They were completely inadequate, however, to repulse a strong, well-organized expeditionary force. Their deficiencies were emphatically demonstrated by the loss of Habana and Manila to the English in 1762.

As a result of the lessons learned during the Seven Years War, a secret committee for imperial defense was organized in Madrid consisting of the principal ministers of the crown. This body met once a week to discuss measures for the defense of the Spanish Indies and early in 1764, presented the outlines of a general plan. To provide a first line of defense, the fortifications of the important American ports were to be strengthened, but the fate of Habana had illustrated the folly of too much dependence on fixed defenses. Fortifications, therefore, were to be supplemented by the creation of colonial armies. The nuclei of these armies were to be regular troops of two classes: First, *fijo* units, that is, regiments and battalions which were raised and stationed permanently in the colonies, and second, peninsular units which would rotate in overseas service. Considerations of economy, however, made it impossible to maintain enough regular units in America to bear the burden of defense alone. The mass of the armies would have to consist of colonial militia, greatly augmented in numbers and organized on a disciplined footing like the provincials of Spain.

Lyle N. McAlister, "The Reorganization of the Army of New Spain, 1763–1766," *Hispanic American Historical Review,* XXXIII (February, 1953), pp. 8–32, *passim.* Reprinted by permission of the Duke University Press.

The execution of the new military program in New Spain was entrusted to Lieutenant-General Juan de Villalba y Angulo, then captain-general of Andalusia and an officer of firmness and energy. As an indication of the importance the crown attached to his mission, Villalba was given authority and discretionary powers of an extent generally denied even to the viceroys. In matters relating to the reorganization of the army his authority was supreme and even the viceroy could not veto his plans or decisions. To provide him with the rank and title commensurate with his jurisdiction, he was named "commandante general de las armas de Nueva España" and inspector-general of all the regular and militia troops of the kingdom. On the other hand, with its customary reluctance to give a clear cut definition of authority to any of its officers, the Spanish government ordered Villalba to recognize the authority of the viceroy as captain general. This ambiguity left some doubt as to just who was the supreme military commander in New Spain. . . .

In addition to the administrative problems involved in forming a disciplined provincial militia, there were certain political considerations that had to be taken into account. The program could succeed only with public support, and military service was not popular in New Spain. The experiences of [Viceroy] Cruillas during the mobilization of 1762 had clearly illustrated this point. In spite of the danger of an English attack on Veracruz the inhabitants of the kingdom were extremely reluctant to enlist in the militia, and the most arbitrary methods had to be used to fill the companies. In addition to popular opposition and apathy, Cruillas had to contend with lack of coöperation from the *justicias* themselves. These officials, by regulation responsible for providing men, procrastinated, made excuses, and sometimes openly refused to coöperate with the viceroy and his lieutenants. In the procurement of personnel, therefore, Villalba was ordered to use the most diplomatic methods possible. His instructions contained the following admonition:

> It will be your inalterable maxim and that of the *mariscales de campo* who accompany you, to establish your labor principally in the hearts of the inhabitants of New Spain, treating them in all matters as my true and loving vassals, making them understand with more or less firmness according to your prudent observations, that the changing times require different policies than those followed up to now; that the security of their families and homes make it necessary to take steps

to repulse the enemies of their liberty and possessions; and
finally you will make use of every idea and method which
will make this service mild and agreeable to them, since the
maintenance and development of this program will depend on
a solid and favorable impression at the beginning.

The crown emphasized that the regular officers and noncommis-
sioned officers assigned to milita duty must maintain good relations
with the provincial troops and ordered that any regular who, in an
excess of soldierly zeal, treated a militiaman with unnecessary harshness, be returned to Spain immediately and there be punished with
the severity that his offense deserved.

The crown hoped to gain the support of the upper classes for the
military program by appealing to the creole love of titles and honors. Commissions as senior officers were to be offered to members
of the nobility or of the best families of the kingdom, while company grade officers were to be chosen from among the most distinguished and worthy *vecinos* of the communities in which the
companies were raised. Thus the leading citizens of New Spain
would be flattered by a recognition of their position and merit. An
additional attraction was to be provided by granting the *fuero militar* and other privileges and exemptions to the provincial officers.
By these appeals to the vanity and self-interest of upper class creoles, it was hoped to build a loyal and enthusiastic officer corps
which would have a personal interest in the success of the militia
program.

A problem which did not exist in the mother country but which
assumed serious proportions in New Spain, where racial mixture
had been in progress for over two centuries, was how to combine
whites, mestizos, mulattoes and all the other shadings of color and
caste in the formation of the militia. Here, again, Villalba was allowed to use his discretion. The crown suggested that with the exceptions of Negroes and Indians, it might be practical to recruit
indiscriminately, or at least allow one-third of each company to be
made up of castes. If, however, combining castes and whites in the
same unit was repugnant to the latter or for some other reason was
impractical, the inspector-general was authorized to raise separate
units of each group.   . . .

Unfortunately for the success of the militia program, the inspector-general disregarded both the letter and spirit of his commission.
His instructions emphasized the importance of treating the people

of New Spain with the utmost consideration. Instead, he and his officers acted in the most arbitrary and high-handed manner. . . . Villalba's lieutenants intervened in the selection of men by ignoring the classifications and exemptions established by law, dispensing with the *sorteo* [or drawing of lots to determine who would serve] and arbitrarily drafting recruits regardless of their age, marital status, physical condition or occupation. Whites and castes were mixed indiscriminately in the companies and, in the selection of officers, the suggestions of the *ayuntamientos* were ignored and the viceroy was not consulted. Villalba had his side of the case to present, however. The *ayuntamientos,* he complained, were lax in their responsibilities; they procrastinated in conducting censuses, in classifying personnel, and in conducting the *sorteos*. The members of the upper class refused to apply for commissions, and the common people tried every means to avoid military service. The inspector-general was a professional military man accustomed to issuing orders and obtaining results. He had been directed to raise an army in New Spain and proposed to do so with or without the coöperation of civil authorities.

Regardless of where the blame lay, the military program produced unrest and resentment throughout the kingdom. In Pátzcuaro, a mob forcibly liberated a body of draftees from a recruiting detail of regular troops and stoned the party out of the city. Puebla experienced riots in connection with the enlistment of the provincials, and in that city the *ayuntamiento* abruptly voted to dispose of 15,000 *pesos* in the municipal treasury so that the money could not be used for the purchase of uniforms for the militia. In the capital mobs stoned and jeered detachments of regular troops.

In order to popularize militia service, Viceroy Cruillas, on May 3, published a declaration conceding extensive privileges and exemptions to the provincials. By this instrument the officers of the provincial units were granted the complete *fuero militar,* that is, military jurisdiction in all their legal affairs, civil and criminal, except when they were claimants, accusers, or if they were prosecutors, and except for offenses specified by law or regulations. Chief among these special offenses were smuggling and frauds against the royal treasury. Enlisted personnel, when not on active service, were granted the protection of the *fuero* only in criminal cases, but when their unit was mobilized they also enjoyed the complete *fuero*. In addition to these general concessions, there were certain additions and exceptions. . . .

The publication of the privileges and exemptions to be enjoyed by the provincials carried significant implications for the future welfare of the kingdom. It had, however, no immediate effect on the popular attitude toward the new military program. Resistance to the enlistment of militia continued and, to add to the unrest, the regular troops stationed in Mexico, Veracruz, and Puebla experienced a decline in discipline and morale. Desertion became a serious problem, and other military offenses were common. Confronted by a hostile population, the regulars committed crimes and excesses against civilians, and often these offenses were not properly punished because of the protection of the *fuero militar*. The viceroy reported that the situation was so serious that a general uprising was not unlikely. If the English should invade, he predicted, they would find more partisans than enemies. . . .

The difficulties expressed and implied above were inherent in the character of the population, in the social structure, in the economic circumstances, and in the political organization of New Spain. The fact that Inspector-General Villalba was unable to overcome them does not detract from the significance of his mission. Although successive viceroys and inspectors reorganized the army on several occasions, the basic structure of the armed forces of New Spain was established in the instructions issued to the inspector-general, and basic procedures were introduced during the period when he was in charge of the military program.

Aside from its military aspects, the formation of a standing army of regular troops and a large corps of militia had far-reaching social, economic, and political results. The impact of the new military establishment was felt by all sections of society. Members of the upper classes provided the officer corps, lower-class families furnished their sons and husbands for the ranks, merchants and landowners contributed in money for military expenses. As the army increased in size during the remainder of the century, officials of the kingdom from the viceroy down to the *alcaldes* became more and more preoccupied with military affairs, while military expenses absorbed a larger and larger share of the national income. Before the Seven Years War the obligations of military service were largely theoretical except in infrequent crises. After the organization of the new militia and regular formations the common people of the kingdom faced the ever-present prospect of being forcibly enlisted in one of the regiments of the army. Perhaps the most significant feature of the military program was the *fuero militar* with its associated privileges and immunities. As the army increased in numbers and importance, this concession, with subsequent amplifications, tended to create a military class exempt from civil responsibility and liability. This situation was particularly dangerous in the case of officers. Although the declaration of Viceroy Cruillas produced no immediate rush to the colors, as time passed the advantages of the *fuero* became more obvious. This attraction and the lure of honors and prestige connected with military service moved the sons of the best families in New Spain to accept commissions in the militia or regular regiments. Thereafter, their primary interests lay outside constructive spheres. "In military service," as Lesley Byrd Simpson has so aptly put it, "with its immediate satisfactions in the form of honors and brilliant uniforms, the young men of New Spain found their true calling." It was this class which was to produce an Agustín de Iturbide and an Antonio López de Santa Anna.

2. Problems and Progress in New Spain

ALEXANDER VON HUMBOLDT

Mexico is the country of inequality. No where does there exist such a fearful difference in the distribution of fortune, civilization, cultivation of the soil, and population. The interior of the country contains four cities, which are not more than one or two days' journey distant from one another, and possess a population of 35,000, 67,000, 70,000, and 135,000. The central table-land from la Puebla to Mexico, and from thence to Salamanca and Zelaya, is covered with villages and hamlets like the most cultivated part of Lombardy. To the east and west of this narrow strip succeed tracts of uncultivated ground, on which cannot be found ten or twelve persons to

Alexander von Humboldt, *Political Essay on the Kingdom of New Spain,* trans. John Black (London: Longman, Hurst, Rees, Orme, and Brown, 1811), Vol. I, pp. 134–217, *passim.*

the square league. The capital and several other cities have scientific establishments, which will bear a comparison with those of Europe. The architecture of the public and private edifices, the elegance of the furniture, the equipages, the luxury and dress of the women, the tone of society, all announce a refinement to which the nakedness, ignorance, and vulgarity of the lower people form the most striking contrast. This immense inequality of fortune does not only exist among the cast of whites (Europeans or Creoles), it is even discoverable among the Indians.

The Mexican Indians, when we consider them *en masse,* offer a picture of extreme misery. Banished into the most barren districts, and indolent from nature, and more still from their political situation, the natives live only from hand to mouth. We should seek almost in vain among them for individuals who enjoy anything like a certain mediocrity of fortune. Instead, however, of a comfortable independency, we find a few families whose fortune appears so much the more colossal, as we least expect it among the lowest class of the people. In the intendancies of Oaxaca and Valladolid, in the valley of Toluca, and especially in the environs of the great city of la Puebla de los Angeles, we find several Indians, who under an appearance of poverty conceal considerable wealth. When I visited the small city of Cholula, an old Indian woman was buried there, who left to her children plantations of *maguey* (agave) worth more than 360,000 francs. These plantations are the vineyards and sole wealth of the country. However, there are no caciques at Cholula; and the Indians there are all tributary, and distinguished for their great sobriety, and their gentle and peaceable manners. The manners of the Cholulans exhibit a singular contrast to those of their neighbors of Tlascala, of whom a great number pretend to be the descendants of the highest titled nobility, and who increase their poverty by a litigious disposition and a restless and turbulent turn of mind. Among the most wealthy Indian families at Cholula are the Axcotlan, the Sarmientos and the Romeros; at Guaxocingo, the Sochipiltecatl; and especially the Tecuanouegues in the village de los Reyes. Each of these families possesses a capital of from 800,000 to 1,000,000 of livres. They enjoy, as we have already stated, great consideration among the tributary Indians; but they generally go barefooted, and covered with a Mexican tunic of coarse texture and a brown colour, approaching to black, in the same way as the very lowest of the Indians are usually dressed.

The Indians are exempted from every sort of indirect impost. They pay no *alcavala;* and the law allows them full liberty for the sale of their productions. The supreme council of finances of Mexico, called the *Junta superior de Real Hacienda,* endeavored from time to time, especially within these last five or six years, to subject the Indians to the alcavala. We must hope that the court of Madrid, which in all times has endeavored to protect this unfortunate race, will preserve to them their immunity so long as they shall continue subject to the direct impost of the *tributos.* This impost is a real capitation tax, paid by the male Indians between the ages of ten and fifty. The tribute is not the same in all the provinces of New Spain; and it has been diminished within the last two hundred years. In 1601, the Indian paid yearly 32 reals of plata of *tributo,* and four reals of *servicio real,* in all nearly 23 francs. It was gradually reduced in some intendancies to 15 and even to five francs. In the bishopric of Mechoacan, and in the greatest part of Mexico, the capitation amounts at present to 11 francs. Besides, the Indians pay a parochial duty (*derechos parroquiales*) of 10 francs for baptism, 20 francs for a certificate of marriage, and 20 francs for interment. We must also add to these 61 francs, which the church levies as an impost on every individual, from 25 to 30 francs for offerings which are called voluntary, and which go under the names of *cargos de cofradias, responsos* and *misas para sacar animas.*

If the legislation of Queen Isabella and the Emperor Charles V appears to favour the Indians with regard to imposts, it has deprived them, on the other hand, of the most important rights enjoyed by the other citizens. In an age when it was formally discussed if the Indians were rational beings, it was conceived granting them a benefit to treat them like minors, to put them under the perpetual tutory of the whites, and to declare null every act signed by a native of the copper-coloured race, and every obligation which he contracted beyond the value of 15 francs. These laws are maintained in full vigour; and they place insurmountable barriers between the Indians and the other casts, with whom all intercourse is almost prohibited. Thousands of inhabitants can enter into no contract which is binding (*no pueden tratar y contratar*); and condemned to a perpetual minority, they become a charge to themselves and the state in which they live. . . .

Amongst the inhabitants of pure origin the whites would occupy the second place, considering them only in the relation of number.

They are divided into whites born in Europe, and descendants of Europeans born in the Spanish colonies of America or in the Asiatic islands. The former bear the name of *Chapetones* or *Gachupines,* and the second that of *Criollos.* The natives of the Canary islands, who go under the general denomination of *Islenos* (islanders), and who are the *gerans* of the plantations, are considered as Europeans. The Spanish laws allow the same rights to all whites; but those who have the execution of the laws endeavour to destroy an equality which shocks the European pride. The government, suspicious of the Creoles, bestows the great places exclusively on the natives of Old Spain. For some years back they have disposed at Madrid even of the most trifling employments in the administration of the customs and the tobacco revenue. At an epoch when every thing tended to a uniform relaxation in the springs of the state, the system of venality made an alarming progress. For the most part it was by no means a suspicious and distrustful policy; it was pecuniary interest alone which bestowed all employments on Europeans. The result has been a jealous and perpetual hatred between the Chapetons and the Creoles. The most miserable European, without education, and without intellectual cultivation, thinks himself superior to the whites born in the new continent. He knows that, protected by his countrymen, and favored by chances common enough in a country where fortunes are as rapidly acquired as they are lost, he may one day reach places to which the access is almost interdicted to the natives, even to those of men distinguished for their talents, knowledge and moral qualities. The natives prefer the denomination of *Americans* to that of Creoles. Since the peace of Versailles, and, in particular, since the year 1789, we frequently hear proudly declared, "I am not a *Spaniard,* I am an *American!*" words which betray the workings of a long resentment. In the eye of law every white Creole is a Spaniard; but the abuse of the laws, the false measures of the colonial government, the example of the United States of America, and the influence of the opinions of the age, have relaxed the ties which formerly united more closely the Spanish Creoles to the European Spaniards. A wise administration may reestablish harmony, calm their passions and resentments, and yet preserve for a long time the union among the members of one and the same great family scattered over Europe and America, from the Patagonian coast to the north of California. . . .

The Spanish laws prohibit all entry into the American possessions to every European not born in the peninsula. The words European and Spaniard are become synonymous in Mexico and Peru. The inhabitants of the remote provinces have therefore a difficulty in conceiving that there can be Europeans who do not speak their language; and they consider this ignorance as a mark of low extraction, because, everywhere around them, all, except the very lowest class of the people, speak Spanish. Better acquainted with the history of the sixteenth century than with that of our own times, they imagine that Spain continues to possess a decided preponderance over the rest of Europe. To them the peninsula appears the very centre of European civilization. It is otherwise with the Americans of the capital. Those of them who are acquainted with the French or English literature fall easily into a contrary extreme; and have still a more unfavorable opinion of the mother country than the French had at a time when communication was less frequent between Spain and the rest of Europe. They prefer strangers from other countries to the Spaniards; and they flatter themselves with the idea that intellectual cultivation has made more rapid progress in the colonies than in the peninsula.

This progress is indeed very remarkable at the Havannah, Lima, Santa Fe, Quito, Popayan, and Caraccas. Of all these great cities the Havannah bears the greatest resemblance to those of Europe in customs, refinements of luxury, and the tone of society. At Havannah, the state of politics and their influence on commerce is best understood. However, nothwithstanding the efforts of the *patriotic society of the island of Cuba,* which encourages the sciences with the most generous zeal, they prosper very slowly in a country where cultivation and the price of colonial produce engross the whole attention of the inhabitants. The study of the mathematics, chemistry, mineralogy, and botany, is more general at Mexico, Santa Fe, and Lima. We everywhere observe a great intellectual activity, and among the youth a wonderful facility of seizing the principles of science. It is said that this facility is still more remarkable among the inhabitants of Quito and Lima than at Mexico and Santa Fe. The former appear to possess more versatility of mind and a more lively imagination; while the Mexicans and the natives of Santa Fe have the reputation of greater perseverance in the studies to which they have once addicted themselves.

No city of the new continent, without even excepting those of the United States, can display such great and solid scientific establish-

ments as the capital of Mexico. I shall content myself here with
naming the School of Mines, directed by the learned Elhuyar, to
which we shall return when we come to speak of the mines; the
Botanic Garden; and the Academy of Painting and Sculpture. This
academy bears the title of *Academia de los Nobles Artes de Mexico.*
It owes its existence to the patriotism of several Mexican individuals,
and the protection of the minister Galvez. The government assigned
it a spacious building, in which there is a much finer and more complete collection of casts than is to be found in any part of Germany.
We are astonished on seeing that the Appollo of Belvidere, the
group of Laocoon, and still more colossal statues, have been conveyed through mountainous roads at least as narrow as those of St.
Gothard; and we are surprised at finding these masterpieces of antiquity collected together under the torrid zone, in a table-land
higher than the convent of the great St. Bernard. The collection of
casts brought to Mexico cost the king 200,000 francs. The remains of
the Mexican sculpture, those colossal statues of basaltes and por-
phyry, which are covered with Aztec hieroglyphics, and bear some
relation to the Egyptian and Hindoo style, ought to be collected together in the edifice of the academy, or rather in one of the courts
which belong to it. It would be curious to see these monuments of
the first cultivation of our species, the works of a semibarbarous
people inhabiting the Mexican Andes, placed beside the beautiful
forms produced under the sky of Greece and Italy.

The revenues of the Academy of Fine Arts at Mexico amount
to 125,000 francs, of which the government gives 60,000, the body
of Mexican miners nearly 25,000, the *consulado,* or association of
merchants of the capital, more than 1,500. It is impossible not to
perceive the influence of this establishment on the taste of the nation. This influence is particularly visible in the symmetry of the
buildings, in the perfection with which the hewing of stone is conducted, and in the ornaments of the capitals and stucco relievos.
What a number of beautiful edifices are to be seen at Mexico! nay,
even in provincial towns like Guanaxuato and Queretaro! These
monuments, which frequently cost a million and a million and a
half of francs, would appear to advantage in the finest streets of
Paris, Berlin, and Petersburg. M. Tolsa, professor of sculpture at
Mexico, was even able to cast an equestrian statue of King Charles
the Fourth; a work which, with the exception of the Marcus Au-
relius at Rome, surpasses in beauty and purity of style everything

which remains in this way in Europe. Instruction is communicated *gratis* at the Academy of Fine Arts. It is not confined alone to the drawing of landscapes and figures; they have had the good sense to employ other means for exciting the national industry. The academy labours successfully to introduce among the artisans a taste for elegance and beautiful forms. Large rooms, well lighted by Argand's lamps, contain every evening some hundreds of young people, of whom some draw from relievo or living models, while others copy drawings of furniture, chandeliers, or other ornaments in bronze. In this assemblage (and this is very remarkable in the midst of a country where the prejudices of the nobility against the casts are so inveterate) rank, colour, and race is confounded: we see the Indian and the Mestizo sitting beside the white, and the son of a poor artisan in emulation with the children of the great lords of the country. It is a consolation to observe, that under every zone the cultivation of science and art establishes a certain equality among men, and obliterates for a time, at least, all those petty passions of which the effects are so prejudicial to social happiness.

Since the close of the reign of Charles the Third, and under that of Charles the Fourth, the study of the physical sciences has made great progress, not only in Mexico, but in general in all the Spanish colonies. No European government has sacrificed greater sums to advance the knowledge of the vegetable kingdom than the Spanish government. Three *botanical expeditions* in Peru, New Granada and New Spain, under the direction of MM. Ruiz and Pavon, Don Jose Celestino Mutis, and MM. Sesse and Mocino, have cost the state nearly two millions of francs. Moreover, botanical gardens have been established at Manilla and the Canary islands. The commission destined to draw plans of the canal of *los Guines*, was also appointed to examine the vegetable productions of the island of Cuba. All these researches, conducted during twenty years in the most fertile regions of the new continent, have not only enriched science with more than four thousand new species of plants, but have also contributed much to diffuse a taste for natural history among the inhabitants of the country. The city of Mexico exhibits a very interesting botanical garden within the very precincts of the viceroy's palace. Professor Cervantes gives annual courses there, which are very well attended. This *savant* possesses, besides his herbals, a rich collection of Mexican minerals. M. Mocino, whom we just now mentioned as one of the coadjutors of M. Sesse, and

who has pushed his laborious excursions from the kingdom of Gua-
timala to the north-west coast or island of Vancouver and Quadra;
and M. Echeveria, a painter of plants and animals, whose works will
bear a comparison with the most perfect productions of the kind in
Europe, are both of them natives of New Spain. They had both
attained a distinguished rank among *savans* and artists before quit-
ting their country.

The principles of the new chemistry, which is known in the Spanish colonies by the equivocal appellation of new philosophy (*nueva
filosofia*), are more diffused in Mexico than in many parts of the
peninsula. A European traveller cannot undoubtedly but be surprised to meet in the interior of the country, on the very borders of
California, with young Mexicans who reason on the decomposition
of water in the process of amalgamation with free air. The School of
Mines possesses a chemical laboratory; a geological collection, arranged according to the system of Werner; a physical cabinet, in
which we not only find the valuable instruments of Ramsden, Adams, Le Noir, and Louis Berthoud, but also models executed in
the capital, even with the greatest precision, and from the finest
wood in the country. The best mineralogical work in the Spanish
language was printed at Mexico, I mean the Manual of Oryctog-
nosy, composed by M. del Rio, according to the principles of the
school of Freyberg, in which the author was formed. The first Spanish translation of Lavater's Elements of Chemistry was also published at Mexico. I cite these isolated facts because they give us
the measure of the ardour with which the exact sciences are begun
to be studied in the capital of New Spain. This ardour is much
greater than that with which they addict themselves to the study of
languages and ancient literature.

B. Peru

3. The Great Revolt of Tupac Amaru

George Kubler

The last century of the Colonial era was punctuated by Indian rebellions, occurring at frequent intervals throughout Perú. The normal form was that of local riots, occasionally involving whole provinces, in which the animosity of the Indians was directed against their corregidores. Indian rebellion was usually conducted within a framework of loyalty to Church and Crown; these institutions were rarely questioned, and the causes of social oppression were identified by the Indians with the minor resident officials. None of the rebellions achieved pan-Peruvian proportions, not even the great revolt of the 1780's, under the brief leadership of José Gabriel Tupac Amaru and his associates.   . . .

The history of the revolt of Tupac Amaru is intricate and obscure; to clarify its course, the reader may refer to the following list of its episodes and their general calendar:

1. The Chayanta Rebellion (August 1779 to May 1781).
2. José Gabriel Tupac Amaru and the Siege of Cuzco (November 1780 to May 1781).
3. Julián Apasa and the First Siege of La Paz (March to June 1781).
4. Andrés Tupac Amaru and the Second Siege of La Paz (August to October 1781).
5. Final Episodes: Miguel Bastidas, Felipe Velasco Tupac Amaru.

George Kubler, "The Quechua in the Colonial World," *Handbook of South American Indians,* Julian H. Steward, ed. (Bureau of American Ethnology, Smithsonian Institution; Washington, D.C.: United States Government Printing Office, 1946), Vol. II. pp. 331–410, *passim.*

These various episodes, it should be emphasized, were confined to the southern Highlands of Perú. Their relation to one another is not that of an organized rebellion conducted simultaneously in various theaters under unified direction. On the contrary, as one episode waned, another matured to take its place, and the rebel groups migrated accordingly. Leadership was discrete and confused, but it is likely that fighting Indians from certain provinces, such as Pacajes or Chayanta, participated in nearly all the major episodes.

The Chayanta rebellion unfolded in the Viceroyalty of Buenos Aires, but its participants were *Quechua* and *Aymara* Indians resisting the extortions of corregidores. La Paz was briefly besieged in February 1781, until the arrival of troops from Buenos Aires.

By this time, the revolt of Tupac Amaru was well underway; Cuzco had been besieged in January 1781, and there is no doubt that the rebels of Chayanta were in communication with their colleagues to the northwest. In general, the revolt of Tupac Amaru, insofar as it was directly under his control, suffered from inadequate force and organization. At no time did he command the full resources of more than five provinces: Lampa, Asángaro, Carabaya, Chucuito, and Paucarcolla. Neighboring *Aymara* provinces, such as Larecaxa, Omasuyos, and Pacajes, never unconditionally supported his insurrection. In public declarations, Tupac Amaru phrased the aims of the rebellion in the language of administrative reform and did not formally offer his followers the promise of an independent Peruvian Indian state. Others did so in his name after his death, such as the illiterate Julián Apasa; they, however, were *Aymara*-speaking, and far less Hispanicized than the descendant of the *Inca* rulers.

Tupac Amaru's communications were poor. He was unable to make effective use both of the Chayanta Rebellion and the *Aymara* insurrection about La Paz. His rebellion was constructed only within the weak pattern of the hereditary local curacaships; it was sustained by no other Indian administrative network, for with the institution of the corregidores, the Indians themselves had long since been occluded from the higher processes of Colonial government. Although the rebellion of the 1780's takes its name from the episode staged by the idealizing and romantic Tupac Amaru, its most sustained and substantial achievement occurred in the long sieve of La Paz after his execution. Thus, in 1781, three distinct and separate insurrections were in progress, connected only by the

most tenuous relations: the Chayanta rebellion, the rebellion of Tupac Amaru, and the siege of La Paz under the command of Julián
Apasa. That none of them succeeded may be attributed in large
part to the fact that they remained separate and unrelated.

The tactical conduct of the siege of La Paz reveals remarkable
variety and inventiveness, vitiated, however, by the lack of discipline
and training among the peasant levies. Early in the campaign, the
Indians were armed only with stones, and they attacked most heavily during rainy weather, in the justifiable hope that the European
firearms would be made ineffective. At this stage, Indian morale was
good; it is reported that the attackers were most solicitous to conceal and bury their dead; the few prisoners preferred suicide to captivity. Soon the Indians managed to spread the siege by burning
surrounding communities, impounding all livestock, and by investing the roads over which reinforcements might come. Firearms were
procured and aimed by snipers sheltered within the ruins of the
burned houses at the city's edges. Captive Spaniards were made
to serve the newly acquired artillery, and the rebel effectives were
augmented by Mestizo deserters from the city. By April the attackers could circulate unseen all about the city, using the burnt-out
shells of houses. Attacks in force were delivered by files of foot soldiers moving behind the cover of horses and pack animals. Their
armament then included cannon, mortars, and muskets. The cannon were used to fire hand grenades; explosives, sling missiles,
rockets, and incendiary arrows wrought much damage. The artillery, however, did little harm, for the fire of the four mortars was
laid by Mariano Murillo, a captive and naturally uncooperative
loyalist, whose arms Julián Apasa later had struck off in punishment
for attempting to communicate with the city.

Meanwhile, the Indian host had encamped upon the plateau
above La Paz, in what has been described as "another city," with a
church, many dwellings, a prison, and other buildings, in a manner
suggesting the practice of the great *Inca* sieges. The camp had 24
cabildos, each with its gallows and whipping post. A great tent was
called the Palacio; in it lived Julián Apasa with his young chola
wife, a government of four "oidores," various ambassadors, two captive priests, and Bonifacio Chuquimamani, the cholo secretary. The
"oidores" administered the sale of coca and the estates of the deceased; they were also the treasurers and the supply officers for the
army. The ritual life of the camp was punctuated by frequent per-

formances of great wheel dances (bailes de rueda). It is striking to note that, as in the revolt of Manco Capac and in the siege of Cuzco in 1536–37, the dances were performed every 20 days. During them, military activities were suspended.

The collapse of the first siege of La Paz late in June 1781 happened less because of local conditions at the site of the siege than because of Spanish depredations among the supporting provinces. The crushing of the revolt of Tupac Amaru did not become generally known about La Paz until September, but the consequent demoralization of the rebel provinces bore results far earlier.

The second unsuccessful siege of La Paz began on August 4, under the direction of Andrés Tupac Amaru, who styled himself the son and heir of José Gabriel Tupac Amaru. Precisely who he was and where he came from have not been determined. The new leader, in order to legitimize his position, invented and circulated a strange account of the rebellion. According to Andrés, in a forged letter purporting to be from José Gabriel and dated July 1 at Tinta, he had been bequeathed all his "father's" powers. These powers, it was claimed, derived immediately and legitimately from Charles III. Andrés had little to do with the actual conduct of the second siege, but its military leaders acknowledged his authority. As in the first siege, the Indians attempted the ruse of impersonating Spanish soldiers. When this failed, an effort was made to flood the city. By October 12, the headwaters of the river had been dammed; a great head of water collected, and when the dam was suddenly removed, a torrent rolled down upon the Spaniards. The device was common in mining enterprises; at La Paz, however, it was unsuccessful. Another Indian stratagem was for venders to offer food to the starved Spaniards at the edge of the city, and to take captive those who came forth.

Over the last episodes of the great rebellion, the spirit of José Gabriel seemed constantly to hover. His relatives, real and fictitious, dominated the scene. Finally, in May 1783, the flames of the revolt flickered once again in Huarochiri Province. An individual styling himself Felipe Velasco Tupac Inca Yupanqui, invoked his "cousin," José Gabriel, in calling the Indians of the corregimiento of Parinacochas to his banner. They were assured that José Gabriel was still alive, seated upon the imperial throne in the realm of the Gran Paititi. During the month of June Spaniards were imprisoned, the roads and bridges leading into the province from Lima were cut, and a general Peruvian rebellion was planned for August 29. The conspirators, however, were apprehended and executed before its eruption.

For present purposes, the most significant aspect of the Indian rebellion is its striking lack of formal indigenous cultural content. Had the rebellion been successful, and had it resulted in the creation of an independent Peruvian Indian state, that commonwealth would have assumed and continued the institutional culture of the Colonial era. Such a prospect would have been inconceivable or repugnant to the Neo-*Inca* in Vilcabamba; conversely, the cultural autonomy of the *Quechua* in Vilcabamba in the 16th century would have been unsatisfactory to the Christianized and Hispanicized Indians of the late 18th century. At all points the late Colonial Indian philosophy of rebellion found its limits within the horizons of Spanish institutional culture. In essence, the Indians wished to capture Spanish institutions, not destroy or displace them by others.

A quantitative measure for the processes of Colonial acculturation is suggested by the similarities and differences between the rebellions of Manco Inca and José Gabriel Tupac Amaru. To both leaders a relatively stable Andean community pattern was available for manipulation. For Tupac Amaru, however, formal government and established religion were to remain Hispanic and Catholic. Hence, most changes within the basic Andean community pattern must be treated as functions of the spread of formal Hispanic culture; the constant and unchanging traits, accordingly, are those which never came into direct conflict with the Church or with Colonial government.

4. The Failure at the Huancavelica Mercury Mine

ARTHUR P. WHITAKER

Colonial Huancavelica owed its title of "Villa Rica," its uniqueness, and its vital importance in Peruvian economy to the fact that the methods of silver refining employed in the rich mines of Potosí in the Spanish period required large quantities of mercury and that in a mountain on the outskirts of Huancavelica lay the only mercury mine in Spanish America. It was, in fact, one of the three largest mercury mines in the world. . . .

Other mercury deposits were known to exist in Peru and some of these had been mined for a time; but Huancavelica was far richer and more dependable than any of the rest, and in the belief that the mercury business could be managed more efficiently and frauds on the royal treasury prevented more easily if operations were confined to a single mine, the court closed all of them but Huancavelica. Thus the virtual monopoly conferred upon it by nature was made absolute by the crown.

Towards the end of the eighteenth century, when its declining production was no longer adequate to the needs of Peru, the government tried to develop other known deposits and to discover new ones elsewhere in Peru, and in Mexico as well; but none of these efforts produced results of any importance. When supplementary supplies of mercury had to be sent to Peru from Europe, they were sold at approximately the Huancavelica price. Thus, to all intents and purposes, the monopoly was maintained from the establishment of government control of the mine in 1570 to its virtual abandonment in 1813. . . . Though production and profits fluctuated widely, on the whole the monopoly was a valuable source of revenue to the crown until the eighteenth century, and throughout the colonial period the mine was an indispensable part of the economic life of Peru.

It is important to note that until the close of the eighteenth century the Huancavelica mine was a crown property and that it formed a part of the crown's larger monopoly of the mercury business throughout the empire, which was not only a valuable source of royal revenue but also the principal safeguard against tax evasion on the part of the silver miners. That is to say, the crown derived a large revenue from taxes on the production of mercury and from its middleman's profits on the mercury which it bought from the miners and resold at a higher price to the silver miners; and it then protected itself against tax evasion on the part of the latter by computing the *quinto* or *diezmo* (a tax on silver production) not on the basis of the silver which the miners reported that they had produced, but on the basis of the amount of mercury which the records of the mercury administration showed they had bought. Consequently, the Huancavelica mine was no less important to the crown from a fiscal point of view than it was to the Peruvian silver miners from an economic point of view.

From first to last this precious jewel caused the Spanish court frequently recurring headaches; but it was not until the eighteenth century, when these increased sharply in number, violence, and duration, that the court made anything approaching a serious and sustained effort to diagnose the disease and provide a remedy for it. The effort led to a protracted struggle which reached its greatest intensity in the period from the 1730's to the 1780's. After a brief description of the old Huancavelica system, the following pages deal mainly with this half-century of conflict and the unexpectedly liberal system of free enterprise that emerged from it. The collapse which, perhaps less unexpectedly, ensued upon this liberation is then described; and the concluding chapter seeks to extract some meaning from these ores of fact.

That the story of the mine is one of ultimate failure does not diminish its claim upon the interest of historians. The problem of Huancavelica was important because, while it was unique in some respects, in others it was only an unusually acute case of a malady which was widespread in Peru. The problem is also important because the mercury mine was a vital factor in the economic life of the viceroyalty and the fiscal system of the crown, and because its ramifications extended all over Peru and beyond it to Mexico, Buenos Aires, and Spain and even to Germany. The case is all the more interesting because this period of travail in the history of Huancavelica and much of the rest of Peru coincided with the climax of the Bourbon renaissance in Spain and other parts of the Spanish empire. This renaissance found notable expression in many fields, including the political, economic, and scientific; and since talents and resources in all three fields were demanded by the Huancavelica problem, it is worth studying for the light that it throws on the quality and achievements of the Bourbon renaissance. . . .

The Huancavelica mine was not discovered until 1563 — a long generation after Pizarro's conquest of Peru and nearly a score of years after the discovery of the silver mines of Potosí. Even then several years elapsed before the amalgamation process was introduced into Peru from Mexico; and in this interval Huancavelica was freely exploited by its discoverers and its mercury was sold only in Mexico.

In 1570 and 1571 the viceroy of Peru, Francisco de Toledo, adopted a series of measures which revolutionized the Huancavelica system and profoundly affected the whole viceroyalty. He expropriated the Huancavelica mine on behalf of the Spanish crown and provided it with a domestic outlet for its product by personally supervising experiments which led to the adoption of the amalgamation process at Potosí, thus bringing about what, according to an early chronicler, he called "the most important marriage in the world, that between Potosí and Huancavelica." He also established the *mita* system of forced Indian labor for the benefit of both of these mining centers, and drew up ordinances for their government which remained in effect with relatively little alteration for the next two centuries.

These measures not only gave a great impulse to the growth of Huancavelica and increased the royal revenue from its mines from 10,000 to 400,000 pesos a year, but also brought unprecedented prosperity to Potosí and the whole of Peru. The key to this prosperity was the mercury mine of Huancavelica. . . .

In view of the great importance of mercury in general and particularly of the Huancavelica mine, it is not surprising that under Toledo's ordinances private exploitation was subordinated to government control to a much greater extent in the case of mercury mining than in the case of silver and gold mining. . . .

Instead of operating the mine on government account, however, Toledo leased it to the miners' guild, or *gremio de mineros,* of Huancavelica. This plan was adhered to for more than two centuries, throughout which the *gremio,* although loosely organized, inefficient, and unruly, was nevertheless a power to be reckoned with. It was originally composed of the six discoverers of the mine, and in the eighteenth century, when its membership had grown to about thirty, descendants of the discoverers were given preference over other applicants for admission to it. This hereditary element gave the *gremio* the strength of continuity; while custom, based upon its monopoly of experience in mercury mining, gave it a vested interest which the court could not refuse to recognize. With it the viceroys negotiated at irregular intervals the *asientos* or contracts under which the mine was operated. When, as often happened, the miners were not satisfied with the terms of the *asiento* or the court's conduct under it, they retaliated by bootlegging mercury and otherwise flouting the obligations of their contract and the law of the land. For long periods they were able to pursue these practices with impunity, for they often succeeded in bribing or intimidating the officials set over them, and their influence extended to the viceregal capital itself. The mine was also the principal support of the numerous churches of Huancavelica, and the *gremio* directly contributed a substantial part of their revenues.

Until the latter part of the seventeenth century the contracts between crown and *gremio* were frequently revised; but in 1683 one was negotiated by the viceroy, the Duque de la Palata, which remained in force until 1744. According to its terms the crown was to provide the miners with 620 Indian *mitayos,* advance them 125,000 pesos a year on the mercury to be produced, and pay 74 pesos and 2 reales a quintal for the mercury, a sum which, after the deduction of certain taxes, netted the miners 58 pesos a quintal. The *mitayos* were to be supplied by certain designated *provincias mitantes,* which included Angareas (in which Huancavelica was located) and several neighboring provinces; and each *corregidor* was assigned an annual quota of *mitayos* whom he was required to deliver at the mine. The miners on their part undertook to produce a minimum of eleven quintals of mercury per annum for each *mitayo,* or a total of 6820 quintals. This gave a margin of about 15 per cent over the normal consumption of mercury by the Peruvian mines, which was about 6000 quintals. . . .

In the course of the seventeenth century many serious defects and flagrant abuses developed in the Huancavelica system and these were well known to the authorities at Madrid as well as Lima. Yet it is hardly surprising that they took no effective steps to correct the situation, for the worst sufferers were mere Indian *mitayos* and, despite wide and sometimes violent fluctuations in the rate of production, the mine was on the whole successful in performing its main function, which was to provide the silver mines of Peru with an adequate supply of mercury. So long as this was the case, conservatism counseled and inertia agreed that it would be imprudent to disturb a system that was so important a factor in the economic and fiscal régime in Peru.

Another deterrent to change in the existing system was the realization that while the *gremio* certainly had its faults, it was by no means solely responsible for the faulty operation of the mine. This was most clearly brought out in a report prepared in 1689 by the Duque de la Palata, the viceroy who had recently negotiated the contract that was to govern the operation of the mine until 1744. In his opinion, the welfare of the mine depended upon two essential conditions, neither of which had it been in his power to fulfil completely and neither of which was under the control of the *gremio*. The first of these and the most difficult of all was the delivery of the 620 Indian *mitayos*, which had been rendered impossible by the destructive earthquakes of 1687 in Angaraes and other *provincias mitantes*. The other essential condition was the prompt payment of the government's annual advance of 125,000 pesos to the miners. Realizing the importance of this aid, the viceroy had charged it against what seemed at the time the most dependable source of revenue in Peru, which was the receipts from customs duties; but since 1684 the coast of Peru had been infested by pirates who had reduced its commerce so greatly that he had never been able to pay the *gremio* the whole amount of the advance.

The government's remissness in this respect continued for many years to come and stimulated the growth of a practice that was regarded by the authorities themselves as undesirable. The improvident miners apparently seldom accumulated capital reserves, and when the government failed them they generally had to borrow from the *aviadores* or merchants of Huancavelica who, in return for staking the miners for a season, received an option on all the mercury that they produced at a price which was about 25 per cent below the government's buying price for mercury under the *asiento*. For example, at one time the *aviadores* were buying mercury from their dependent miners at 43 pesos a quintal and selling it to the government for 58 pesos. Thus to a considerable extent the profits and financial control of the mine were passing into the hands of a group of finance capitalists who had no standing in the contract under which the mine was supposed to be operated.

It was not until the eighteenth century, however, that the situation at Huancavelica developed to the point where it seemed to call for corrective action on the part of the court. Even the Duque de la Palata's confessed inability to fulfil the two essential conditions of the mine's prosperity did not necessarily discredit the system, for he ascribed it to causes which were external to that system and were, indeed, external to any human system, since they were acts of God — that is, earthquakes and piracy. And so it was that the Huancavelica system rocked along virtually unchanged to the close of the seventeenth century.

The first two decades of the eighteenth century witnessed developments which altered both the terms of the Huancavelica problem and also the court's attitude towards it. An important factor in the change was the War of the Spanish Succession (1701–1713). On the one hand, this war imposed a great strain upon the whole Spanish Empire, aggravating old evils and adding new ones, in Peru as in other dominions. On the other hand, the war resulted in the establishment of the Bourbon dynasty on the throne of Spain. The new dynasty brought with it a new zeal for reform and renovation; and while these were primarily designed to increase efficiency, revenue, and authority, they also bore a strong imprint of humanitarianism.

In this spirit the court confronted the problem of Huancavelica at the end of the war, considering it in its two familiar aspects: first, as a unique problem involving the only mercury mine in America; and second, as an integral part of the whole problem of Peru. For the moment, the latter aspect seemed the more important of the two. Once the richest and most flourishing dominion of the crown, Peru now presented an alarming picture of decay, in which the most striking features were administrative demoralization and a decline both in the Indian population and also in mineral production.

Huancavelica was not only an outstanding example of both aspects of this decay but was also regarded as a cause of it. The production of mercury had always fluctuated widely from year to year; but since the closing years of the seventeenth century these fluctuations had shown a constant and pronounced downward trend such as had never occurred before. The average annual production was about 5200 quintals from 1660 to 1679. Dropping to 4110 in the decade 1679–1689, it was brought back up to 4544 in the years 1689–1701; but from 1701 to 1709 it fell to the alarmingly low level of 3059 and remained at about the same point during the next two decades.

This decline was all the more alarming because of its adverse effect upon silver production throughout the viceroyalty. What was the reason for it? Some attributed it to corruption and inefficiency on the part of the miners and the colonial officials; others, to the fact that the richest deposits had been exhausted. An important sector of opinion, however, pinned the blame on the *mita,* and for a variety of reasons the problem was first attacked at this point.

That the *mita* was a grievous burden to the Indians of Peru had long been notorious. Now it began to be regarded as harmful to Spanish interests as well; and the history of the Huancavelica mine vividly illustrated the evils of the *mita* at its worst. In the first half of the seventeenth century, when working conditions in the mine were most atrocious, there were four main occupational hazards. The first was mercury poisoning, which was contracted through handling the ore either in the mine or at the furnaces and resulted in a lingering and horrible death. The second was a gas, apparently carbon monoxide, which formed in deep and unventilated recesses of the mine and snuffed out life suddenly and without warning. The third was pneumonia, which was common because the laborers were constantly coming and going between the mine, where even a Spanish official admitted that the heat was infernal, and the outside air, which, at this high altitude, was usually frigid. The fourth consisted in the frequent cave-ins and other accidents of the mine.

That labor in the Huancavelica mine was a thing of horror at this time is established by the testimony of many responsible colonial authorities. Juan de Solórzano Pereira, who was governor and superintendent there from 1616 to 1619, subsequently wrote in his classic *Política Indiana* that sooner or later even the strongest *mitayos* succumbed to mercury poisoning, which entered into the very marrow of their bones and made them tremble in every limb, and that he had never known one who had survived it more than four years. His testimony was borne out by the viceroy of Peru at that time; and under another governor a generation later the mortality rate among the Indians was so high that the mine had to be shut down until a ventilation shaft, begun thirty-four years earlier, was completed (1644). It was reported that this brought about a great improvement in working conditions, especially by reducing the danger from pneumonia and carbon monoxide gas. Yet it was necessary to open a second ventilation shaft in 1734 and a third in 1760; mercury poisoning seems to have continued to be frequent until well on into the eighteenth century; and the cave-ins never ceased, the worst of them all occurring near the close of the eighteenth century.

The death of many *mitayos* in the mine and the flight of many more to escape the dread service in it led to a sharp decline in the population of all the provinces subject to the Huancavelica *mita.*

This depopulation in turn reacted unfavorably upon the mine, for after the early part of the seventeenth century the full quota of *mitayos* was never supplied and by the close of the century the number actually delivered at the mine was seldom more than about half the quota.

Thus by the time the new Bourbon dynasty was well established in Spain it seemed clear that self-interest as well as humanity required the abolition of the *mita;* but here reforming zeal ran into a stone wall: the authorities in Peru had always maintained that the *mita* was indispensable to the prosperity of Huancavelica and probably even to its very existence.

Out of this dilemma, the Marqués de Santo Buono, who was viceroy of Peru from 1716 to 1719, wrought a heroic solution: since the mine could not live without the *mita* and the *mita* had become intolerable, the mine must be abandoned. As for the silver miners of Potosí, they could import their mercury from the Spanish mine of Almadén. This was the most drastic remedy ever proposed in the whole history of the problem. Indeed, it was entirely too drastic, for while it doubtless represented a generous reaction of the spirit of the renovation against gross inefficiency and crying injustice, it failed to take into account either the strength of vested interests and the force of custom or the exigencies of imperial policy. A mine that had been regarded as the keystone of Peruvian economy for nearly a century and a half was not to be destroyed by a stroke of the pen. And it was by no means certain either that Almadén could supply Peru as well as Mexico and Spain or that, at a time when Spain had sunk to the rank of a third-rate sea-power, the silver mines of Peru and Mexico ought to be made wholly dependent upon a mercury mine on the other side of the Atlantic Ocean.

The court did take the viceroy's proposal seriously enough to submit it to Dionisio de Alcedo y Herrera, who had held an important post in Peru for a number of years and was now one of the court's chief consultants on South American affairs; but Alcedo condemned it as both impractical and unnecessary and it was rejected. Instead, it was decided to approach the larger problem of Peru from another angle, and in 1720 the king issued a cedula prohibiting the *mita* throughout the viceroyalty. The enforcement of the measure was, however, suspended in view of strong representations from colonial authorities as well as miners, and the *mita* continued in operation until the end of the colonial period, modified only by the increas-

ingly common practice of commuting the personal service by a
money payment. . . .

The case of Huancavelica raises doubts about the accuracy of
the familiar picture of an enlightened Spanish court constantly baffled by its selfish, corrupt, and short-sighted officials and other subjects in America. In this case, the court itself had much to answer
for. To be sure, much may be said in explanation, and even in ex-
tenuation, of its errors. For one thing, from the economic point of
view, the very importance of Huancavelica discouraged experimen-
tation that might upset the existing order; and from the political
point of view, the unrest which was rife in Peru in the eighteenth
century made it unwise to alienate the powerful Huancavelica interest, whose influence extended to the viceregal capital itself. It
must also be recognized that, as the subsequent history of the mine
shows, the problem was one of extraordinary difficulty; and for
Spain its difficulty was increased because it had to be considered in
the intricate context of imperial interests.

And yet, when all allowances have been made, the fact remains
that the court showed a persistent lack of energy, firmness, and
good judgment in dealing with the situation, which might at least
have been ameliorated even if it could not have been saved. Ignoring good advice repeatedly given, the court failed to come to grips
with the problems of the *mita* and the *gremio,* which were left to
solve themselves at an unnecessarily heavy cost to Peru and to Spain
itself. The court also failed to support the new governors of Huancavelica, who were both competent and thoroughly honest, and
failed to apply to the problem of the mine the considerable body of
scientific talent developed in eighteenth-century Spain. At the elev-
enth hour, it did despatch the Nordenflicht mission to Peru; but
this not only came late but would probably have been a poor substitute at any time, since Nordenflicht and all his companions were
foreigners. Their failure was due in part to this simple fact, and
one wonders why the court lacked the foresight to send an Elhuyar
to Peru as it did to Mexico. At any rate, by these omissions and
otherwise it made itself in large measure responsible for the long
agony of Huancavelica. . . .

Although they are too few and faint to permit confident generalization, the story of the Huancavelica mine also throws some tan-
talizing sidelights on the social and cultural development of Peru.
For instance, one is struck by the fact that, if the Spanish court was

slow to offer the Peruvians instruction in modern mining methods, they were still slower to accept it — witness the fact that as late as 1816 the silver miners had not learned either the smelting process learned in Mexico or the newer Born amalgamation process, though nearly thirty years had elapsed since the court had sent a dozen mining experts to teach the latter process to them for their own good.

Similarly, by the beginning of the eighteenth century, the mercury miners of Huancavelica seem to have lost the capacity for adaptation. At an earlier period they had clearly possessed it and had made a technological contribution of their own — the Bustamante or *aludel* furnace — which had been copied by the Spanish mine of Almadén; but when in 1734 the superintendent of the Almadén mine studied the methods then in use at Huancavelica he found them absurdly antiquated, and substantially the same judgment was passed upon them by other competent judges down to the end of the colonial period. This deterioration can hardly be explained by the remoteness of the town, for though remote, it was not culturally isolated from Spain, as was shown by the character of its celebration of the accession of Charles III in 1760. Perhaps the explanation lies in the *gremio's* monopoly, which, so long as it was secure, bred indifference to improvement, and, when it was threatened, developed a defense mechanism that tended to condemn indiscriminately all efforts of whatever kind to change the existing order. One notes also an apparent increase of racial antagonism, which, on the part of the whites, became more marked when, towards the end of the colonial period, the hitherto submerged Indians began to challenge their economic supremacy.

Finally, the history of Huancavelica in the eighteenth century seems to illustrate the widespread contemporary trend towards the liberation of land, labor, and enterprise — a movement which was beginning to sweep over both Europe and America and was to continue on through the next century. While the *mita* was not formally abolished until the close of the colonial period, in actual practice voluntary wage labor had largely supplanted forced labor at Huancavelica by the middle of the eighteenth century. A generation later the ancient monopoly of the miners' guild (*gremio de mineros*) was destroyed, and shortly thereafter most of the mine was thrown open to free enterprise (*pallaqueo*). In these respects the movement of liberation, which brought unexampled prosperity to a large part of the world in these two centuries, had made important progress at Huancavelica while Peru was still under the yoke of Spain.

At Huancavelica, however, the progress of liberation coincided not with the growth but the disappearance of prosperity and with the ultimate ruin of the mine. Thus its experience in the last century of the colonial period failed to bear out the assumption, widely accepted in both Spanish and English America in that period, that increasing liberty would beget economic expansion and prosperity. . . .

On the whole, the unhappy results of the progress of liberation in the case of Huancavelica seem to have been due in considerable measure to the social heritage of three centuries of Spanish domination. This had developed a ruling class which, so long as it retained power, was either indifferent or hostile to change, even when change meant improvement, and a submerged mass which, when it was freed, possessed neither the moral qualities nor the mental and technical training necessary for effective leadership. Thus for Huancavelica the earlier stages of liberation resulted not in recovery but in continued decline under new auspices; and, in the next stage, the establishment of Peruvian independence put the final seal on the ruin already accomplished.

C. A Modern Interpretation

5. The Fall of the Spanish American Empire

R. A. HUMPHREYS

At the time of the Napoleonic invasions of the Spanish peninsula in 1807–8, the Spanish empire in America stretched in unbroken line from California to Cape Horn. From Stockholm to Cape Town is less distant, and within the area ruled by Spain all western Europe from Madrid to Moscow might lie and be lost.

R. A. Humphreys, "The Fall of the Spanish American Empire," *History* (October, 1952), pp. 213–227, *passim*. Reprinted by permission.

A hundred years earlier, at the beginning of the eighteenth century, Spain had been a major battlefield of Europe. That experience was now to be repeated, and this time foreign invasion spelt imperial destruction. The French Revolution in its Napoleonic aspect was the occasion, if not the cause, of the emancipation of Spanish America. But in the years between the war of the Spanish Succession and the wars of Napoleon, Spain herself had risen with remarkable resilience from the decrepitude into which she had fallen in the seventeenth century. Her economic decline had been first arrested and then reversed, and under Charles III and during the early years of Charles IV she enjoyed what seems in retrospect to have been an Indian summer of prosperity.

What was true of Spain was true also of her empire. Of the empire during the long years of Spain's weakness and decay we know all too little. But of its material and intellectual advance during the so-called century of enlightenment there is abundant evidence. And Spain, like Britain, undertook in the eighteenth century the task of imperial reorganization and reform. At home and in the empire the administrative system was overhauled. New viceroyalties and captaincies-general were created. The establishment, in the very year of the North American Declaration of Independence, of the viceroyalty of the Río de la Plata, covering the whole, indeed more than the whole, of what is now Argentina, marked a period in the history of Spanish America. And the attempt to systematize and centralize colonial government by the division of the colonies into intendancies — "to unify the government of the great empires which God has intrusted to me," as Charles III expressed it in the Great Ordinance of Intendants for New Spain — was scarcely less important.

The reforms in the imperial economic system were equally radical. The Spanish system of colonial and commercial monopoly differed not in kind from the colonial policy of other powers, but in the extraordinary rigour with which it was applied. There were special reasons for the severity and minuteness of these economic regulations, and special reasons for the quite disastrous consequences that followed. But though the policy of colonial monopoly was never abandoned, it was, in the eighteenth century, liberalized. Slowly and cautiously the natural trade routes of the Indies were opened up. Where once Cádiz and Seville had enjoyed a monopoly within a monopoly, and the fleets and galleons had divided between them the commerce and treasure of Mexico and Perú, step by step the ports of America and the ports of Spain were opened, the age-old restrictions on inter-colonial commerce were lightened, and the tariffs and duties hampering trade revised. The so-called Decree of Free Trade of 1778, by which all the more important ports of Spain and of Central and South America were allowed to trade, if not freely at least directly, with one another, was as much a landmark in the economic history of the later empire as was the establishment of the viceroyalty of the Río de la Plata in its political history.

The reasons for these striking innovations were, in the broadest sense of the word, strategic. Efficiency in administration, the rehabilitation of colonial trade, were not so much ends in themselves as means to an end; and the end was imperial defense, the protection of the empire against foreign aggression, particularly English aggression, the elimination of foreign economic competition, and the restoration of Spanish maritime and military power in Europe. And as in British colonial policy after 1763, so in Spanish, the financial problem was paramount. Defence demanded revenue, "it being necessary," as Charles III instructed his visitor-general to New Spain,

> on account of the large sums needed in attending to the obligations of my royal crown, to exhaust all means which may appear conducive to increasing as much as possible the income from the revenues.

This was a dominant consideration both in administrative and in economic reform. And what Britain in part proposed to effect by tightening up the acts of trade, Spain in part proposed to effect by their relaxation.

The results, or the apparent results, were remarkable. The volume of imperial trade notably increased. At Buenos Aires, now the capital of the viceroyalty of Río de la Plata and no longer a dependency of Lima, the economic life of the colony was transformed. Its customs receipts, its exports, its shipping, its population, all alike rapidly increased. At Havana, Cuba, where six vessels had sufficed for the trade of Spain in 1760, two hundred were insufficient in 1778, and more than a thousand, Spanish and foreign, entered in 1801. New Spain, or Mexico, repeats the same story — a larger volume of shipping, swelling revenues, greater exports. In Perú, when the legislation of 1778 first came into effect, "speculations were multiplied to so extraordinary a degree" in the first fervour of novelty that the merchants resorted to the now familiar device of destroying their goods in order to maintain the price level. And even remote Chile experienced a new and vigorous impulse of economic change.

Whatever truth, therefore, there may be in the legend of the stagnation and decay of Spain and of the Spanish American empire in the seventeenth century, it does not hold for the eighteenth. Within Spain's transatlantic dominions the signs of an expanding economy and of a growing prosperity were everywhere, or almost everywhere, writ large. "It is just . . . to observe," wrote a competent British observer, that Perú, during the late eighteenth century

> was not only in a flourishing state both in respect to her mines and to her commerce, but also as referable to the capitals possessed by individuals, to the comparative extent of her manufactures, and to her navigation. Between the years 1790 and 1800 there existed in Lima a *commercial* capital of above 15 millions of dollars; whereas in the present year [1826] it is under one million.

Humboldt, in Venezuela, noted that "everything seemed to announce the increase of population and industry." In New Spain the public revenues increased more than sixfold in the eighteenth century, and so also did the produce of the mines. And though more than half of the world output of the precious metals still flowed from Spanish America, and though there is a lively superstition that the Spanish American colonies were made of gold and silver and nothing else, agriculture as well as mining, as the great Gálvez tells us, were the basis of their prosperity. The value of the gold and silver of the Mexican mines, says Humboldt, was less "by almost a fourth" than that of the agricultural produce. Of Venezuela and Cuba he observes that agriculture "founded more considerable fortunes" than had been accumulated by the working of the mines in Perú, and in southern South America, where the mines were few, but where Buenos Aires and even Montevideo were rapidly rising in importance, the pastoral and agricultural industries, then as now, were the economic staples.

It is reasonable to conclude, with Professor Haring, that as the eighteenth century closed the peoples of Spanish America were probably more prosperous than at any time in their history. True, in a colonial and developing area, there was no considerable growth of manufactures. Nor was there in the English colonies. But domes-

tic manufacturing was in fact more widespread than is commonly
supposed. True, also, the whole population of Spanish America was
certainly not greater than that of the British Isles in 1811. But its
increase in the eighteenth century was remarkable. In 1800 Mexico
City was the leading city of the western hemisphere, larger than
any city of Great Britain and Ireland except London and Dublin. Its
rival, Lima, compared with Bristol and was itself outstripped by
Havana. Even long-neglected Buenos Aires was as large as New
York or Philadelphia in 1790. And the growth and embellishment
of the cities (not merely the capital cities) illustrates the same ex-
pansionist trend. Here, at least, in public buildings and public display, were the marks of opulence; and it is no accident that here
also, at the end of the century, there was an efflorescence of intellectual activity, in the universities and academies, in the growth of
a periodical press, in literary societies and in clubs. In Santa Fé, Perú
and Mexico, observed an English merchant in 1804, there was not
only a greater degree of knowledge and a greater degree of progress
in civilization than was commonly supposed in Europe, but, he
added, though perhaps with prejudice, "much more than exists in
Old Spain."

The disruption of this society by a violent cataclysm which
would, within a few years, destroy much of its wealth, would seem,
at first sight, an improbable event. The Conde de Aranda, one of
the more far-sighted of Spanish statesmen, indeed foresaw it. "We
must imagine" he wrote in 1782 "that sooner or later in [Spanish]
America there will occur revolutions like those of the English colonies." And Canning's retrospective judgment, on the effect of the
American Revolution, that "the operation of that example" was
"sooner or later inevitable," is well known. The influences of eighteenth-century rationalism and of the French Revolution were
equally powerful dissolvents. The continent, despite the censorship
of the Inquisition, was not closed to ideas. Forbidden literature is
always the most enticing of literature. A cultivated minority was
certainly acquainted with the writings of the *philosophes,* of Rousseau, of Locke, even of Adam Smith. These were to be echoed,
along with the Declarations of Independence and the Rights of
Man, in the pronouncements and charters of revolutionary leaders
and revolutionary governments. Yet despite the activities of an ad-
venturer like Francisco de Miranda, who knew the "brace of
Adamses" and had seen the French Revolution at first hand, de-

spite occasional conspiracies and even outright rebellion, there was little specifically revolutionary activity in Spanish America before Spain herself fell a prey to Napoleon. The revolution, when it came, rose like a sudden tide from still, or comparatively still, waters.

Yet Spain's colonies were lost before the revolution began. The Bourbon reforms came too late, they did not go far enough, they were given insufficient time, to save the empire. And politically at least they contained no concession to the newer movement of ideas.

> "Instead of considering its colonies as a place of refuge for the idle, the profligate, and the disaffected, where they might learn to amend their lives, and, if possible, forget their errors," wrote the *Edinburgh Review* in 1806, "the Spanish Crown has watched over its foreign settlements with the solicitude of a duenna, and regulated their government as if they were to be inhabited by Carthusians."

The quotation, perhaps, is mainly interesting for the light it throws on the value placed on colonies in early nineteenth-century Britain. But it contains a solid grain of truth. The empire, from first to last, was built on paternalist and absolutist lines. It could not, in point of fact, be quite so centralized as theory might imply. The royal will was always limited by circumstance. But the price of paternalism was procrastination and inefficiency, a tradition of legalism and a disrespect for law, a class system which almost, but not quite, became a caste system, and a mounting jealousy between Spaniards born in Spain and Spaniards born in America, between, that is, the governors and the governed. "The most miserable European" wrote Humboldt "without education, and without intellectual cultivation, thinks himself superior to the whites born in the new continent." The creoles, excluded generally from the higher administrative posts, found almost their sole representation in municipal institutions. "Even in the most despotic states" says Robertson in his famous *History* "this feeble spark of liberty is not extinguished." But even here it was the local, not the representative, character of the *cabildos,* or town councils, too often closed corporations, petty oligarchies, which caused them to play so prominent a part in the events of 1808 to 1810.

There was no relaxation of this paternalistic system in the eighteenth century. On the contrary, enlightened despotism sought to rationalize and simplify the machinery of imperial administration both in Spain and in America in the interests of order, uniformity, centralization, efficiency. And though, for a time, a new life was breathed into the imperial system, the political aspirations of the creoles were forgotten, or ignored. In so far as the newly appointed intendants, invariably Spaniards, superseded minor, but creole, officials, and trespassed, moreover, on the functions of the *cabildos*, the Spanish American creoles were, in fact, still further removed from the work of government. "We were left" Bolívar was to say "in a state of permanent childhood."

And, paradoxically enough, the measures designed to secure a still closer integration between Spain and her colonies had precisely the opposite effect. In Spanish America, as in Spain, local and regional loyalties were always strong. Customs, conditions, varied enormously. Cities and squares, law and administration, might be drawn to a pattern, but the life of the colonies flowed in its own individual channels; and at a time when the Bourbon economic reforms gave to the several regions of Spanish America a new economic autonomy, the creation of new viceroyalties and captaincies-general promoted and consolidated a growing sense of regional nationalism. Colonial self-consciousness was directly stimulated. It can be no accident that the revolution, when it came, gained its first successes in those areas whose economic and political status had thus been raised. The origins of the new Spanish American nations must properly be sought in the developing life of the eighteenth century.

Apart from a small minority, an intellectual *élite*, it is possible that the rising creole middle class of lawyers, merchants, landowners and soldiers might have reconciled themselves for some time longer to their political inferiority, however much they resented their social inferiority, to the Spaniards. The loyalists, or royalists, were always far more numerous during the Spanish American revolutions than they were during the revolution for North American independence. But whatever the prosperity of Spanish America, whatever the rehabilitation of Spain, in the second half of the eighteenth century, the economic foundations of the empire had been irretrievably undermined. The recovery of Spain had failed to keep pace with the expanding economy of her colonies, and the imperial economic reforms of Charles III were no more than palliatives of a condition imperfectly understood. The trade of the empire was still a closed monopoly of Spain, but the monopoly was imposed by a country which could still not successfully apply it, a country out-stripped in financial and technical resources, in facilities and skills, by its greatest colonial rival, Britain. The empire, Professor Whitaker has observed, "fell not so much because of decay within as because of pressure from without"; and from this point of view its fall was no more than a corollary of the commercial expansion of Europe and particularly of England.

What really stimulated the economic expansion of Spanish America in the eighteenth century, perhaps, were not so much the imperial economic reforms as the European search for Latin American markets and the European demand for Latin American products. And for the continued growth of European interest in Spanish America there were, apart from considerations of strategy and politics, three main reasons. First, Spanish America provided dollars, the gold and silver coin and specie which was the lubricant of international trade. The bullion supply was as interesting to the continental as it was to the British and North American merchant. Secondly, Spanish America supplied a number of raw materials, such as drugs and dyewoods, hides and skins, increasingly important for industrial and commercial purposes. Thirdly, it afforded a market for manufactured goods, particularly textiles and hardware. The market, perhaps, was not infinitely extensible as was sometimes imagined, but its potentialities were great, some English and some continental merchants knew it far better than might be supposed, and it was undoubtedly profitable.

There were, also, two ways of tapping the resources and trade of Spanish America. The first was to do so indirectly by way of Cádiz and, still more indirectly, by way of Lisbon and Rio de Janeiro. The second was the direct or contraband trade. Both had long been practiced. At the end of the seventeenth century everybody knew that the fleets and galleons at Cádiz were stocked with foreign, principally French and English, not Spanish goods, that the Spanish merchants were little more than agents or shippers, and that the returns which flowed to Spain immediately flowed out again.

"We owe to Divine Providence," Philip V complained, "the special blessing of vast dominions in America, the centre of abundant precious metals; [yet] the Crown has always seen that . . . this is the kingdom which retains the least."

Or, in Pufendorff's phrase, which Mr. Christelow has recently quoted, "Spain kept the cow and the rest of Europe drank the milk."

Spain, in short, could not supply her colonies herself. But she maintained the pretense of so doing. What was more, she insisted that colonial products should flow only to Spain. Since the tonnage of the galleons fell by three-quarters in the seventeenth century, it is obvious that the volume of imperial trade had seriously contracted. Not only this, high duties and restrictive freights combined with the monopolistic interests of the merchant houses in Seville and Cádiz to raise the price level in America to fantastic heights. An increase of two to three hundred per cent above the prices in Spain was not uncommon. And if Spain could not herself supply her colonies with enough or cheap enough goods, neither could Europe obtain from Spain all that she wanted of colonial products. The result was an enormous contraband trade. This was the second method employed by the French, the English and the Dutch, the direct or contraband trade; and the more debilitated Spain became, the greater grew the contraband, the more the contraband, the greater Spain's debility, and the weaker her empire. . . .

The effect on Spain can partly be measured in the continuing decline in the tonnage of the fleets and galleons and in the irregularity of their sailings. When the galleons sailed for the last time in 1737 they were unable to dispose of their goods because the markets were already overstocked. Royal decree after royal decree complained of the presence of foreigners and foreign goods in the Indies. Foreigners must be expelled. Officials who connived at contraband trade should be punished with death. Even their immortal souls would be imperilled, for in 1776 the Church was recommended to teach that contraband was a mortal sin. Finally, of course, the great series of economic and commercial reforms which began in 1740 with the permission given to register ships to sail round Cape Horn and culminated in the legislation of Charles III, reflected the acute anxieties of the crown.

The reforms could alleviate, but they failed to remedy the situation. It is true that they did much to rehabilitate Spanish commerce. Though the old monopolists protested, new and more enterprising Spaniards and Spanish Americans entered trade. Shipping and revenue increased. But the contraband continued. To tap the trade of the Gulf of Mexico and the Spanish Main, the British, in 1766, established free ports in Dominica and Jamaica, extending the system, after 1787, to other strategic points in the West Indies. And there is no doubt that, despite temporary vicissitudes, the free port trade, encouraged in time of peace and specially licensed in time of war, was, as the board of trade found it, when reviewing the Free Port Acts themselves, highly "beneficial." The Spaniards might properly complain. But it was no part of British policy to enforce the Laws of the Indies. And whatever may have been the prospects that the imperial reforms of Charles III could have arrested foreign economic pressure upon the walls of the empire and that Spain herself could have been brought successfully to compete in the swelling volume of international trade, the doom of Spanish hopes was sealed by two events. The first was the death of Charles himself in 1788 and the accession of the incompetent Charles IV. The second was the entry of Spain into the French revolutionary wars.

The war of 1779 to 1783, when Spain had actively promoted the independence of England's colonies, had been costly enough. For the first time in Spanish history the crown was forced to issue paper money, soon to be inflated. The brief war with France, from 1793 to 1795, was a further blow. But when, in 1796, Spain again went to war with England, and, with a brief interval of only two and a half years, remained at war for twelve years more, the result was disaster. This was the crisis of the empire. Spain and her colonies were severed. The Spanish economy was seriously deranged. The Spanish navy was almost destroyed. And the colonies were thrown upon their own and foreign resources.

There had been occasions, in earlier years, when Spain had been compelled to tolerate the trade of friends or neutrals in Spanish America. In 1782, for example, Louisiana had been allowed to trade with France. Cuba, in 1793, was permitted to trade with the United States. In the years after 1789, moreover, the slave trade had been thrown open and foreigners allowed to engage in it. But when, on November 18, 1797, the crown opened the ports of Spanish America to neutral shipping, the measure was one of desperation. The order was indeed revoked in 1799 because it had "redounded entirely," as the decree of revocation complained, to the injury of the state and of the interests of its subjects. But what the law forbade, local regulation continued to tolerate and the crown itself to license; and though the old system was restored at the peace in

1802, with the renewal of the war once again the ports were opened.

The result, or partial result, was the rapid growth of North American shipping and North American trade, from Cuba to Buenos Aires and Buenos Aires to Chile. And more than one American, perhaps, like the young Richard Cleveland of Massachusetts, carried in his cargo a copy of the Federal Constitution and of the Declaration of Independence, conveniently translated into Spanish. But it was not only American trade, legitimate and illegitimate, that grew. So also did British trade. The contraband flourished at the free ports in the West Indies. It flourished at Trinidad, which alone was said to supply the Spanish colonies with goods to the value of one million pounds a year. It flourished at Vera Cruz, as Viceroy Marquina bitterly complained. It flourished at Buenos Aires. And, even on the Pacific coast, where the South Sea whalers were actively engaged in it, it extended and strengthened its hold.

There was still to be fought out in Spanish America the battle between monopoly and free enterprise, between the beneficiaries of an old order and the partisans of a new. But the issue was already resolved. It was impossible to re-enact the Laws of the Indies. The economic emancipation of Spanish America was determined before its political emancipation began.

And so far as political emancipation was concerned, the years from 1796 to 1808 were equally decisive. As Britain had formerly wavered between plundering the Spanish American colonies and trading with them, so now she hesitated between their conquest and their emancipation. In 1797 the governor of Trinidad was specifically instructed to encourage revolution on the Mainland. The invasion of Buenos Aires was prepared, and cancelled, in the same year. And there were other plans, in the mind of the British government as well as in that of Francisco de Miranda, so long plotting in England and America the emancipation of Venezuela. But fundamentally Britain was more interested in trade than territory. Her designs were commercial and strategic rather than imperial, and when, in 1806, Sir Home Popham captured Buenos Aires, it was at his own responsibility. *The Times,* indeed, rejoiced. It knew not, it said, how to express itself in terms adequate to the national advantage obtained. But the government vacillated. It did too little and that little too late. Buenos Aires was recaptured and Montevideo lost. The whole affair, said *The Times,* was "a dirty, sordid enterprise, conceived and executed in a spirit of avarice and plunder," and the chief source of the calamity was the unauthorised beginning of it.

But for Spanish America its end was all important. The viceroy of Río de la Plata had fled. It was the creoles who defeated the British, deposed the incompetent viceroy and appointed a new one. Spanish America had seen the deposition and imprisonment of the legal representative of the king. It had seen a creole militia defeat a European army. It had seen a colonial port crowded with British ships and flooded with British goods. It was not a revolution that took place at Buenos Aires as a result of the British invasions. But it was a political and economic transformation that contained the seeds of revolution.

Suddenly, however, the situation changed. Napoleon invaded Spain. The crown fell into captivity. A usurper sat upon the throne. From an enemy Britain became, overnight, the ally of Spain, and the army which Wellesley was preparing in Ireland for the liberation of Spanish America sailed, not to emancipate Spanish America from Spain, but to liberate Spain from France.

The news of the fall of the monarchy, and of the invasion of the mother country, stirred the loyalty and moved the indignation of the colonies, and, superficially, the resistance movement in Spain was almost exactly imitated in Spanish America. As juntas sprang up in Spain in the name of Ferdinand VII, so in Spanish America juntas and *cabildos* assumed the powers of viceroys, presidents and captains-general, the agents, now, of an authority which had ceased to exist. Extraordinary circumstances called for extraordinary measures. The colonists took thought for their own protection and their own future. Power reverted to the people, though by "the people" nothing more can be meant than a small but active creole minority: the revolutions in Spanish America were the work of the few, not of the many.

But that a movement which began as an assertion of independence from France should have ended as an assertion of independence from Spain was due quite as much to Spain herself as to the creole minority in her colonies whose thwarted aspirations in government and trade were thus fulfilled. For though the monarchy had collapsed, though the Peninsula was overrun, the Spaniards still clung to the principles of imperial monopoly and colonial subordination. Crown, Regency, Cortes, showed themselves equally blind, equally determined. The colonies, declared the Junta Central, in

1809, were an integral part of the Spanish monarchy, and the deduction soon followed that they owed obedience to the extraordinary authorities erected in Spain. That was not the Spanish American view. Nor had it been the Habsburg view. "Estos y esos reinos," "these and those kingdoms," was the famous phrase used to define the royal possessions in Spain and the Indies. The Indies had never belonged to Spain. They were the property of the crown of Castile, united to the kingdoms of Spain merely by a dynastic tie. The Bourbons forgot, or ignored, this Habsburg view; and so did the Spaniards. But the creoles remembered it. Just as the English colonies, in the eighteenth century, refused to accept subordination to the sovereignty of parliament, so the Spanish Americans refused to accept subordination to the people of the Peninsula. And in both cases what reason failed to arrange, force was left to decide.

BIBLIOGRAPHIC SUGGESTIONS

1. Bobb, Bernard E. *The Viceregency of Antonio María Bucareli in New Spain, 1771–1779* (Austin: University of Texas Press, 1962).

1a. Boxer, Charles R. *The Golden Age of Brazil, 1695–1750* (Berkeley: University of California Press, 1962).

2. Burns, E. Bradford. "The Enlightenment in Two Colonial Brazilian Libraries," *Journal of the History of Ideas,* XXV (1964), pp. 430–438.

3. Cardozo, Manuel. "The Brazilian Gold Rush," *The Americas,* III (1946), pp. 137–160.

4. Fisher, Lillian Estelle. *The Last Inca Revolt, 1780–1783* (Norman: University of Oklahoma Press, 1966).

4a. Humphreys, R. A. and John Lynch, eds. *The Origins of the Latin American Revolutions, 1808–1826* (New York: Alfred A. Knopf, Inc., 1965).

5. Hussey, Roland D. *The Caracas Company, 1728–1784* (Cambridge, Mass.: Harvard University Press, 1934).

6. Lanning, John Tate. *The Eighteenth Century Enlightenment in the University of San Carlos de Guatemala* (Ithaca, N.Y.: Cornell University Press, 1956).

7. Lynch, John. *Spanish Colonial Administration, 1782–1810* (London: The Athlone Press, 1958).

8. Means, Philip A. "The Rebellion of Tupac Amaru II, 1780–1781,"

Hispanic American Historical Review, II (1919), pp. 1–25.

9. Merino, Luis. *Estudio crítico sobre las "Noticias Secretas de América" y el clero colonial (1720–1765)* (Madrid: Instituto Santo Toribio de Mogrovejo, 1956).

9a. Mörner, Magnus. *The Expulsion of the Jesuits from Latin America* (New York: Alfred A. Knopf, Inc., 1965).

10. Shafer, Robert J. *The Economic Societies in the Spanish World (1763–1821)* (Syracuse: N.Y.: Syracuse University Press, 1958).

11. Whitaker, Arthur P., ed. *Latin America and the Enlightenment* (Ithaca, N.Y.: Cornell University Press, 1958, 2nd ed., 1961).

12. ———. "Antonio de Ulloa," *Hispanic American Historical Review,* XV (1935), pp. 155–194.

13. ———. "The Elhuyar Mining Missions and the Enlightenment," *Hispanic American Historical Review,* XXXI (1951), pp. 557–585.

14. Valcárcel, Daniel. "Estado de la investigación histórica sobre la rebelión del cacique Tupac Amaru, 1780–1783," *Mar del Sur,* III, No. 7, (Sept.-Oct., 1949), pp. 42–53. Summarizes and examines critically, and chronologically from Humboldt's essay until 1949, the publications on this rebellion. Analyzes the problems involved, and suggests what still needs to be done.

Section X

Historians and Historical Controversies

The readings in this section have been selected to show that "history" is not precisely the past, and must always be regarded as the product of men's researches and thinking about earlier times which only partially recover the real past, which is irrecoverable. What is history? What we call history has been written and will be written in the future by men deeply concerned to recover as much as possible of what happened before their time. They have used and will continue to use the sources they can discover and, bringing their own powers and attributes to the task, strive to record and interpret what they believe they have learned. So history is never written once and for all time. It is a continuing enterprise undertaken by many individuals in every generation. A historian cannot be, after all, more than a man both of his own time and his own cultural background.

The special problems involved in writing the history of Latin America have been obvious since the sixteenth century. Iberian writers and those native to the New World were bound to clash, and have done so resoundingly through the centuries, in presenting both the facts and their significance, and historians elsewhere have brought their various points of view to bear. One of the most penetrating approaches was that of a German scientist, Karl F. P. von Martius (1794–1868), in his essay on how the history of Brazil should be written (Reading X.1). Martius learned about Brazil when he accompanied Archduchess Leopoldina to Rio de Janeiro, where she became the wife of dashing young Prince Pedro. During the years von Martius lived there, he traveled extensively in his search for botanical specimens. When the Brazilian Geographical and Historical Institute was established in 1838, one of its principal objectives was to encourage the writing of a national history. But how should it be written? The Institute sponsored a contest, and von Martius as a Corresponding Member submitted the proposal that was judged the best. His basic thoughts on how important was the amalgamation of races and on how significant were unity and diversity in the development of Brazil might well be applied to the history of all of Latin America.

Selecting what to write about has sometimes perplexed historians. Prescott frankly confided in his diary how he made his decision and how he proposed to do his work (Reading X.2). Another American historian, Hubert Howe Bancroft, who started out as a businessman in California, ended up producing, in the latter part of the nineteenth century, some forty stout volumes of history. By applying business methods to the collection of materials and the composition of history, he alienated some of his contemporaries. He decided therefore to explain his methods and did so in a wonderfully interesting volume appropriately entitled *Literary Industries* (Reading X.3).

The nature and extent of the sources available to historians greatly influence the way in which they write their works. Spaniards had a keen sense of history and collected historical materials on a monumental scale (Reading X.4). Portuguese interest in learning about Brazil developed late, and no body of comparable material was collected.

No matter what sources a historian discovers, his use of them, his own imaginative power, and his writing style determine the kind of history he writes. The Scottish historian William Robertson never saw the New World, but he wrote one of the two classic histories in English of the Spanish conquest of America. Professor R. A. Humphreys of the University of London, who has written an excellent brief biography of William H. Prescott as well as one of Robertson, considers the latter's *History of America* (1777) ". . . the most moving account of the discovery of América in the English language" (Reading X.5). Predispositions and prejudices also influence a historian's work, as Professor Charles C. Griffin of Vassar College demonstrates of the Chilean historian Francisco Encina (Reading X.6).

Controversy has often characterized the writing of history. Whether chickens existed in America before Columbus is not a world-shaking matter, but the amusing story Professor Carl O. Sauer, eminent geographer at the University of California, Berkeley, tells about New World chickens, indicates how firmly an idea can remain fixed in a scholar's mind (Reading X.7).

A. Ideas and Methods

1. How the History of Brazil Should Be Written

KARL F. P. VON MARTIUS

General Ideas About the History of Brazil — Anyone who undertakes to write the history of Brazil, a country which promises so much, should never lose sight of the elements which contributed to the development of man there. These diverse elements come from the three races, namely: the copper-colored, or American; the white, or Caucasian; and the black, or Ethiopian. Because of the reciprocal and changing relations of the three races, the present population consists of a novel mixture, whose history therefore has a very particular stamp. . . .

Each physical and moral peculiarity characterizing the different races offers a special force in this development of a new people. The more energy, number, and dignity that characterize the race, the more will be its influence on the common development. Thus it necessarily follows that the Portuguese, as discoverers, conquerors, and masters greatly influenced this development; and because the Portuguese created the conditions and the physical and moral guar-

Karl F. P. von Martius, "How the History of Brazil Should Be Written," *Perspectives on Brazilian History*, E. Bradford Burns, ed. (New York: Columbia University Press, 1967), pp. 23–41, *passim*. Reprinted by permission.

antees for an independent kingdom, they emerge as the most powerful and vital force. However, it certainly would be a great error for the principles of a pragmatic historiography if we disregarded the force of the natives and the imported Negroes, who likewise contributed to the physical, moral, and civic development of the whole population. The natives as well as the Negroes resisted the dominant race.

I know very well that there will be whites who will charge that such a linking of these races disparages their ancestry. But, I am also certain they will not be found among those seeking to write a philosophic history of Brazil. On the contrary, the most enlightened people will discover from this investigation that the Indian and Ethiopian races have been and still are involved in the historic development of the Brazilian people. This investigation will be a new stimulus for the profound and humane historian.

The history of peoples, as much as that of individuals, shows us that the genius of world history, which leads mankind in directions whose wisdom we should always recognize, frequently resorts to mixing the races to obtain the world order's most sublime ends. Who can deny that the English nation owes its energy, resoluteness, and perseverance to the mixture of the Celtic, Danish, Roman, Anglo-Saxon, and Norman peoples?

Perhaps even more important, the genius of history proposes the blending of peoples of the same race with races so entirely different in their individualities, moral character, and physique in order to form a new and marvelously organized nation.

We will never be permitted to doubt that providential will predestined this mixture for Brazil. The powerful river of Portuguese blood ought to absorb the small tributaries of the Indian and Ethiopian races. This mixture has taken place in the lower classes. As in all countries, the upper class is developed from elements of the lower class, vitalized and strengthened by them. Thus the highest class of the Brazilian population is made from this mixture. For centuries this mixture has had a powerful influence on the elevated classes and transmitted to them that historical activity for which the Brazilian Empire is noted.

I believe that the philosophic writer, comprehending the doctrines of true humanity and enlightened Christianity, will find nothing in this opinion that could offend the Brazilians' sensitivities. The current *conditio sine qua non* for the true historian is to appre-

ciate man according to his true value, as the Creator's most sublime
work, and to disassociate this from his color and background. This
transcendent humanitarianism, which appreciates man in any situation in which he discovers him, as an instrument to work for and to
serve — knows the infinity of the world's order and is the animating
spirit of the true historian. Thus I consider the Brazilians' personal
relations, which allow the Negro and the Indian to influence the
development of the Brazilian nationality, to be a benefit for the destiny of the country. I can contrast this with attitudes in other areas
of the New World, where these two inferior races are excluded
from the general development as unworthy by birth or because
their small number in comparison to whites makes them of little
importance.

The reflective historian's essential task should be to show that
the conditions were established during Brazil's development for
the improving of the three races, which are placed next to each
other in a manner previously unknown in history, and that they
should help each other in every way.

This reciprocity in the history of the development of the Brazilian people offers a picture of an organic life. The task of a truly
human legislation will be the proper appreciation of this. The historian can judge the future from what has been done for the Negroes' and the Indians' moral and civic education so far. From this
history, he can become a sibyl prophesying the future, and he can
offer some useful projects, etc. The stronger his defense of the interests of these unprotected peoples, the greater will be the merit
of his work. It will have the stamp of noble humanitarianism that
our century requires of the historian. The historian who doubts the
perfectibility of mankind allows the reader to suspect that he does
not know how to rise above odious and partial opinions.

The Indians and Their History as a Part of the History of Brazil
— If the above-mentioned general ideas deserve the approval of
the Brazilian historian, he ought to undertake the meticulous investigation of the American aborigines' life and the history of their
development. He should extend his investigation beyond the time
of the conquest, and scrutinize the history of the primitive inhabitants of Brazil. Their history presently is not divided into distinct
periods, nor does it highlight important events. It is still wrapped
in obscurity. For this very reason, it excites our curiosity.   . . .

Until recently, the generally accepted opinion was that the American Indians issued forth directly from the Creator's hand. The Brazilian aborigines were considered as an example of the development possible in man deprived of any divine revelation, and directed only by his innate reason to follow the path of his needs and physical inclinations. As seen by this mistaken philosophy, this was man's primitive state, from which he tried to derive the most extraordinary organs of public law, religion, and history. The more profound investigations have proved for the unbiased person that he was not dealing with man's primitive state. On the contrary, the sad picture offered by the present-day Brazilian Indian is that he is a remnant of a very ancient, though lost, history.

As soon as we have understood this concept, the difficult but interesting task remains to use it to illuminate the obscure past of the American race. The path that the historian should follow is, first, to consider the physical being of the Brazilian and to compare it with that of neighboring peoples of the same race. The next step will lead us to their soul and intelligence. This is connected with the investigation of their spiritual activity and how this is manifested in historical documents.

The Indian languages should be the most general and significant document. One cannot overemphasize the need for research in this rarely studied field. The American languages are found to be fusing increasingly, and some of them are becoming extinct. There is much to say on this subject, but I suppose few Brazilian historians will interest themselves with linguistic studies. I take this occasion to express my desire that the Brazilian Historical and Geographical Institute select some linguists to edit grammars and dictionaries for these languages. These scholars should be in contact with the native speakers. I would especially recommend the investigation of the roots of the Tupi language and its dialects, from the Guaraní on the banks of the Rio da Prata to those of the Amazon. The vocabulary that the Empress Catherine ordered made for the Asiatic languages would be a good model for such a Brazilian dictionary. The most important vocabulary to collect should refer to natural objects, legal definitions, and social relations.

The principal language of the past spoken throughout the vast extent of Brazil was Tupi, or the *lingua geral* [universal language]. It is significant that a great number of Brazilian tribes understand this language. As in Peru with Quechua and Aymará, Tupi extended over the vast Brazilian territory. There is no doubt that all the tribes that used it belong to a unique and great people which possessed its own history and its own civilization, which declined to the present state of degradation and dissolution, the same as occurred in western South America among the Incas. It should not pass unnoticed that the Caribs in the Guianas and the Antilles spoke a language related in syntax and vocabulary to Tupi. This fact is made more interesting when one realizes that the Caribs were pirates who extended themselves from Florida and Bermuda to South America. In this way studies of the language of the Brazilian aborigines assume a wider importance, taking on ethnographical considerations and spreading out to a large part of the New World.

Language ought to be linked to studies of the mythology, theogony, and geogony of the Brazilian races. A philosophical observer will not fail to discover still extant in the remnants of the myths and in the poetic gibberish some very significant vestiges of a lost natural philosophy and of a still enigmatic religion. A superficial look at the contemporary religion of the Brazilian Indians tempts one to consider it as a fetishism or witchcraft; but such an explanation will not satisfy a philosophical historian, who sees in the present examples of religious ideas and ceremonies purer antecedents and forms of an ancient religion, of which the human sacrifice of prisoners, cannibalism, and numerous customs and domestic habits can be considered a brutal degeneration and only in this way explicable. Such researches will lead us necessarily to those phenomena related to superstition, to the curative powers of Indian magic, witch doctors, and mystics, and from these we will continue on to investigations concerning the wisdom of the Indians in relation to natural phenomena and the position of the priest class among them and the relations of the *Pagé* [priest], witch doctor, and chief toward the social community.

The Portuguese and Their Part in the History of Brazil — When the Portuguese discovered and settled Brazil, they found only a few primitive Indians. Thus the Portuguese colonies developed and expanded almost without caring about these Indians. Only when the Portuguese colonists were forced by threat of hostile attacks did they create a defensive institution, the system of militias.

The militias were an important influence for two reasons: First, they encouraged and maintained the spirit of adventure, the voyages of discovery, and the extension of the Portuguese domain; secondly, they furthered the development of self-governing municipal institutions and helped to nurture a bold citizenry that took up arms to oppose the governing authorities and the powerful religious orders. We also find that this was the reason for the success of Portuguese arms against the invasions of the French in Maranhão and Rio de Janeiro, and of the Dutch along a great part of the northeastern coast.

Establishing himself in Brazil, the Portuguese abandoned some of the rights he possessed in Portugal from the monarch, because in place of a king he here had an overlord. For this reason as well, the colonists were constantly armed and always ready to fight. Ever armed they continuously moved inland from specific focal points on the coast, where European civilization was first established. In the interior no one recognized any superior, and they either forcefully overcame the Indians and made slaves of them or deceitfully induced them to serve the invader.

The Portuguese colonist's warlike relationship with the Indians greatly contributed to the rapid exploration of the interior as well as the expansion of the Portuguese domain. Still Brazil's particular nature, especially the abundance of gold, was of no small moment. First came the plundering raids to enslave the Indians, and then the journeys to discover mineral wealth.

We should not judge the Portuguese immigration to sixteenth-century Brazil, which laid the foundation for the present empire, by the principles which regulate today's colonization. Today's colonization, with few exceptions, is a private undertaking made by the poor who want to improve their conditions. These immigrants consist of farmers and artisans, almost never the nobles and the rich. Such was not the case in the beginning of the colonization of Brazil. It was a continuation of the bold undertaking directed toward India and carried out by princes, nobles, and their followers. The Portuguese nation became very famous and rich from these enterprises. The desire to immigrate was not born out of religious crises as in England. It was a consequence of the great Portuguese discoveries and commercial undertakings along the west coast of Africa, the Cape, Mozambique, and India. The same powerful reasons that gave such a driving movement to Europe's smallest nation, causing it by itself to create a monumental epic within the flow of universal history, influenced the immigration to Brazil.

This period of the discovery and early colonization of Brazil can be understood only in relation to the Portuguese maritime, commercial, and military achievements. This period never can be considered as an isolated event in the history of the active Portuguese people. Brazil's importance to and relations with Europe are the same as those of the Portuguese expansion. As the Portuguese expansion had an important influence on European politics and commerce, so did it also affect Brazil.

These observations might seem to belittle the historiography of Brazil. But it should never be forgotten that the history of world commerce of the time formed a part of the history of the colonization of Brazil and its civil and legislative developments. Although the East Indies did not have the same commercial products as Brazil, still it would not be difficult to compare the commercial history of India and Brazil if we wanted to understand the European's motivation for immigrating to India or the New World. In the study of the history of Brazil, the historian must point out and deal with the different commercial routes — the use of the Red Sea or the rounding of the Cape of Good Hope — and the effect of these sea and land routes on the price of the commercial products.   . . .

The Portuguese, who immigrated to Brazil in the beginning of the sixteenth century, brought the time's characteristic spirit and courage with them. Although exempt from the immediate effects of the Lutheran schism, the Portuguese colonist represented the period's peculiar temperament. Because of the numerous conflicts with Spain and the greater part of Europe, he was more accessible then, than later, to the great intellectual movement of that century. If the Brazilian historian intends to describe these men who came from across the ocean to found a new Portugal, he cannot avoid drawing his picture from the customs of the fifteenth century.

The historian should follow closely Portuguese legislative history and the Portuguese social conditions in order to be able to show the gradual development of the very liberal municipal institutions, their transplantation to Brazil, and what were the causes for their perfection in Brazil. A very interesting task for a historian, who sees this legislation as a mirror of the times, would be to show how immune the old Portuguese legislation of Dom Diniz was from the influence of the Roman law propagated in Portugal by the Spanish kings.

At this point the historian should discuss the relations between the Crown and the Church. It is important to do so because the ecclesiastical orders often found themselves opposing the municipalities or the inhabitants and favoring the Indians, as they did also in Spanish America. According to my understanding of the ecclesiastical establishment in Brazil, its actions did not proceed solely from Brazilian decisions but were owed to decisions made in the metropolis or in Rome.

Of all the religious orders in Brazil, the Jesuits played the most important role. Their buildings are the only monuments left from that remote time. Their institutions have not entirely disappeared nor lost their influence. Because of their missionary activities, the Jesuits obtained the most varied and important information on the Indian languages, civil and domestic life, etc. Many of these accounts still remain unused and lie buried in the various archives of the order or in the libraries which obtained them after the suppression of the order. . . .

Other religious orders, such as the Franciscans, Capuchins, Augustinians, Carmelites, and Paulists, also had missions in Brazil. Their reports might disclose some important material on Indian ethnography as well as the history of the customs of the European settlers. The activity of these orders was not generally unfavorable for Brazil. Often they were the only carriers of civilization and education to a restless and turbulent people. At other times, they protected the oppressed from the powerful. Because of this, their numerous disputes with the city councils (illustrated in repeated references in Bernardo Pereira de Berredo's *Chronica do Maranhâo*) cannot be understood without reference to the clergy — mainly the orders — the foundation of their convents, asylums, missions in the interior of the country, and the mercantile speculations that they undertook. The colonists' opposition to these generally philanthropic orders resulted from their apparent conflict of interests.

The Portuguese government was vigilant toward the religious orders' influence on the population and suspiciously guarded the crown's prerogatives. The prohibition on founding convents in the province of Minas arose from this distrust of the orders. The history of the expulsion of the Jesuits was clearly related in Portugal to the

Jesuits' political position in Pará; and in Spain, to the Jesuits' power in Paraguay. This kind of event, so important in the annals of universal history, is deeply rooted in the history of Brazil.

An interesting task for the practical historian would be to study the establishment and development of the arts and sciences in Brazil as a reflection of European life. The historian should bring us into the colonists' homes, show us how they lived in the city and the country in various periods and developed their relationships with their neighbors, servants, slaves, and customers. He should depict church, school, and government for us and take us into the fields, the plantations, and the sugar mills. We should learn something of the rural economy, the agriculture, and the colonial commerce of Brazil. It would be interesting to learn how and where the colonists gradually introduced European plants and trees to Brazil. How did the present system develop? What part was played by the Portuguese knowledge of naval construction, navigation, and the sea?

The historian who studies the Brazilian schools, their teaching methods, and the quality of the instruction must investigate the Portuguese educational system. Thus the Brazilian historian should analyze the progress of poetry, rhetoric, and the other sciences in Portugal; compare them with the rest of Europe; and show their influence on the scientific, moral, and social life of the Brazilians.

To complete this aspect of the Brazilian historical picture, many questions should be asked about the influence of Portuguese military life. What were the methods employed in military recruitment, education, command, and duty? Were the strategic concepts based on Brazilian experience, which is so much different from European conditions? There is no lack of data on the wars with the Dutch. The few written documents buried in various archives in Brazilian cities and towns should be sought out in order to describe little-known expeditions of discovery of the Paulista *mamelucos* into the Brazilian interior and their wars with the Spanish and the missionaries in Paraguay.

Most Brazilian chronicles relate the monotonous and routine events of the community, which have minimal significance. Therefore, the historian will be drawn to the variety of the narrations of the many expeditions and forays into the hinterland from the coast. These *entradas* were undertaken to procure gold and precious stones or to capture Indians and make slaves of them. The participants in the *entradas* had the energy, ingenuity, perseverance, and courage of a Cortés, a Balboa, or a Pizarro, and their adventures are worthy of posterity's admiration. One can seriously hope that rigorous research in municipal archives will furnish us with more documents similar to those that referred to the romantic adventures of Bueno da Silva, who discovered Goiás on September 19, 1740. His adventures were worthy enough to inspire an epic poet, as well as the more tranquil muse of the historian. . . .

A deeper investigation of these expeditions will acquaint the historian with the numerous fascinating legends about Brazil's subterranean wealth. These romantic legends gave the Brazilians a substitute for the many European tales of ghosts or chivalry which were such an inexhaustible source of European popular poetry. In evaluating the popular Brazilian superstitions found in these tales, the historian should not forget to consider the Negro's contribution. The Negro's love of talking, his African way of thinking, and his fetishism supplied him with different poetic thoughts about the supernatural, and miraculous events. The special orientation of the inhabitants of Minas, São Paulo and Goiás can be discerned in the development of their complete set of fables about Pluto.

There are no vestiges of this in the Amazon region with its majority of Indians. The Amazonian fables revel in the fantastic monsters of the Indian's imagination, which is saddened by the jungle's dismal solitude and the terrors of menacing Nature. Everywhere one encounters the horrible monsters, satyrs, and mythical animals of which the European first learned from the extravagant accounts of Sir Walter Raleigh and his companions.

The historian who is familiar with these popular myths certainly will not disregard them. He will give them the particular importance they merit as a key to understanding the daily life of the inhabitants, as well as the extent of their intellectual achievements in general. The diversity of the origins of these tales offers the historian a chance for many observations, both historic and ethnographic.

The African Race and Its Relation to the History of Brazil — There is no doubt that Brazil would have developed differently without the Negro slaves. The historian will resolve the problem of whether it was for the better or the worse after considering the influence the African slaves exerted on the civil, moral, and political development of the contemporary Brazilian population.

If we want to show the Negro's influence on Brazil, it is important to investigate the Negro's background, customs, civil attitudes, natural discernment, preconceptions, superstitions, and his race's particular defects and virtues. As the Portuguese had visited Africa before the discovery of Brazil and had extracted great commercial advantages from that continent, Africa doubtless had already influenced the customs and political development of Portugal. We should analyze the conditions in the Portuguese African colonies, which all sent slaves to Brazil. This analysis should indicate the slave trade's influence on the industry, agriculture, and commerce of both the African colonies and Brazil.

The primitive Portuguese trading posts on the coast and in the interior of Africa, and the organization of the slave trade, make fascinating subjects and are almost unknown in Europe. Some recently published English material presents one side without adequately clarifying the management and conduct of the slave trade in the interior of Africa. On the other hand, the Portuguese literature tells us little about the history of the world slave trade.   . . .

The Brazilian historian must never forget that his task is larger than simply to describe the development of one people; Brazil's crises and experiences are a part of the larger scope of world history. Furthermore, Brazil is still in the process of change and development. He must not consider Brazil's unique fusion of different elements as unfavorable, but rather see them as a fortunate and important union. The history of Brazil will always be primarily a history of a branch of the Portuguese. However, if Brazilian history is to be complete and to deserve the name history, it can never exclude the roles played by the Ethiopian and Indian races.

Some Observation on the Form of a History of Brazil — The works published up until now on the separate provinces are of inestimable value. They abound with important facts and minutely examine many events. Nevertheless, they do not satisfy the requirements of a real historiography, which demands more than mere chronicles. These historical works monotonously repeat many insignificant facts and certain information of slight historical importance. All this lessens the work's interest and bewilders the reader

about the point of the work. What is gained by repeating each provincial governor's acts and omissions, or by relating unimportant
facts about the administration of cities, or bishoprics, etc., or by a
scrupulous list of citations and records of dubious historical authenticity? My opinion is that all this should be excluded.

The vast extent of Brazilian territory presents the historian with
a difficult problem, for he is surrounded by an immensely varied
natural setting, and by a population composed of very different elements with different customs and practices. As Pará has an entirely
different climate from Rio Grande do Sul, different soil, natural
products, agriculture, industry, customs and necessities, the same
is true for Bahia, Pernambuco, and Minas. In one province the white
descendants of the Portuguese predominate; in another an Indian
mixture has the majority; in a third, the African race manifests its
importance; and each of these exerts a special influence on the state
of civilization in general. The author who does not see this broad
interplay of forces risks the chance of writing, not a history of Brazil, but only a series of special histories of each province. Another
historian who does not give these peculiarities the necessary attention runs the risk of not discovering the special local temperament
that is indispensable when he is trying to rouse the reader's interest,
to give vitality to his description, and to impress the reader with
the ardor that we so much admire in the great historians.

In order to avoid these difficulties, it seems necessary to begin by
describing the general state of the whole country in well-chosen
epochs, including relevant relations with the mother country and
the rest of the world. Passing on to those parts of Brazil that are basically different, only those provinces that have a real historical significance should be emphasized. By proceeding in this manner, it
will not be necessary to start from the beginning in each province,
and all the repetitious material can be omitted. Those parts of Brazil
that are similar in physical conditions and belong with each other
can be treated together. Thus, the history of São Paulo, Minas,
Goiás, and Mato Grosso converge into one; Maranhão and Pará
can be treated as one; Ceará, Rio Grande do Norte, and Paraíba form
a natural group influenced by Pernambuco; and finally, the history
of Sergipe, Alagoas, and Pôrto Seguro will be the same as Bahia's.

For such a work, it seems indispensable for the historian to visit
these provincial areas and to penetrate the peculiarities of nature

and population with his own eyes. Only in this manner will he be able to evaluate properly all the historical events that have taken place in whatever part of the empire, explain them by the particularities pertaining only to inhabitants of the place where it occurred, and connect them with other events in the area. How different is Pará from Minas! They possess divergent natural conditions, different men, different needs and passions, and consequently are influenced by different historical forces.

This diversity is not sufficiently recognized in Brazil. Because few Brazilians have visited all of the country, many erroneous ideas have been developed about local conditions. Without any doubt, this fact contributed to the length of time it took to extinguish the political turmoils in some provinces. Since the officials in Rio de Janeiro could not recognize the true causes of these vexing situations in the distant provinces, they did not administer the appropriate remedies. If the historian thoroughly acquaints himself with these local peculiarities, and presents them exactly, the administration will often ask him for his useful counsel.

If the reader is not acquainted with the details of the local natural setting, he will neither be interested in nor be able to develop an intimate knowledge of Brazil. Following the system of Herodotus, the father of history, the historian will find many opportunities to include enchanting pictures of Nature. He will make his work attractive to the inhabitants of Brazil's different regions, for the reader will be able to recognize his own home in these descriptions and identify himself with the greater Brazilian scene. The European reader will be especially interested in such a rich and varied book.

In conclusion, I ought to add an observation about the position of a Brazilian historian toward his country. History is the master of the present and the future. It can spread noble patriotic sentiments among contemporaries. A history of Brazil ought to stimulate the love of country, courage, constancy, industry, fidelity, prudence — in a word, all the civic virtues — in its Brazilian readers. Brazil suffers from a politically immature population. There we see republicans of all complexions and of all types of ideologies. It is precisely among them that many people will be discovered with an interest in the history of their homeland. A book should be written just for them, to correctly convince them of the impracticability of their utopian plans, of the impropriety of licentious discussions about public business, of the undesirability of an unrestrained press, and of the necessity of a monarchy in a country where there is a large number of slaves.

Brazil has just begun to feel that it is united. Many provincial prejudices still prevail; they ought to be removed by judicious education. Each part of the empire should turn its face toward the others. They ought to attempt to prove that such a vast, rich country as Brazil with so many varied sources of good fortune and prosperity will attain its most favorable development when its inhabitants firmly support the monarchy and establish a wise organization of reciprocal relations among all the provinces. Often foreigners have tried to sow discord among the different parts of Brazil, and by the principle of "divide and rule" obtain an important influence in the State's affairs. The patriotic historian ought to take advantage of every occasion to show that the provinces belong together by organic law and that their progress can be guaranteed only by a closer union among them.

Brazil's greatness and power are based on its very vastness, the variety of its products, and also on its inhabitants who are sons of the same land with the same historical background and same future aspirations. In order to render his fatherland a real service, the historian should write as a constitutional monarchist, a real unitarian in the purest sense of the word. His work should not exceed one sizable volume, written in a popular though noble style. It should satisfy the intelligence as well as the heart, not be written in a pompous language, nor be overburdened with a heap of sterile citations. It should avoid taking on the character of a mere chronicle or a dry, purely erudite historical investigation. As any history that deserves the name of history, it will be an epic! A really popular epic is written only when the people still believe in progressive development.

As Brazil is a country entering a phase that demands dynamic progress, it surely is a worthy subject for a popular history. Its author will find in the favorable development of the land a propitious stimulus to present in his work all his patriotic zeal and love, that poetic fire appropriate for youth, to which at the same time he can apply the depth of judgment and firmness of character belonging to a mature and virile age.

2. The Historical Methods of William H. Prescott

Prescott Chooses His Life Work

Dec. 25, 1825 . . . I have been hesitating between two topics for historical investigation: Spanish hist[or]y fr[om] the invasion of the Arabs to the consolidation of the Monarchy under Charles V. — or — a Hist[or]y of the revolution of Ancient Rome which converted the republic into the Empire. — A third subject which invites me is a biographical sketch of eminent geniuses, with criticisms on their productions & on the character of their ages. — I shall probably select the first, as less difficult of execution than the second, & as more novel and entertaining than the last. —

I must discipline my idle fancy, or my meditations will be little better than dreams. —

I have devoted more than 4 h[our]s per diem to thinking or dreaming on these subjects. — . . .

January 8, 1826 . . . I have decided to abandon the Roman subject. A work on the Revolutions of Italian Literature has invited my consideration this week. A work which without giving a chronological and minute analysis of authors, should exhibit in masses the most important periods, revolutions, and characters in the history of Italian letters. The subject would admit of expansion or contraction *ad libitum* & I should be spared what I detest, hunting up latent barren antiquities. The subject would require a mass of knowledge, & a critical knowledge of the Italian in particular. It would not be new after the production of Sismondi, — and the abundant notices in modern reviews. Lit[erar]y hist[or]y is not so amusing as civil. — Cannot I contrive to embrace the gist of the Spanish subject without involving myself in the unwieldy barbarous records of a thousand years? * (* This was the first germ of my conception of "Ferd [inand] & Isabel" May 1847) What new & interesting topics may be admitted, not forced, into the reigns of Ferdinand & Isabella?

From *The Literary Memoranda of William Hickling Prescott,* edited and with an introduction by C. Harvey Gardiner. (Norman: University of Oklahoma Press, 1961), Vol. I, pp. 65–90, Vol. II, pp. 29–33, *passim.* Copyright 1961 by the University of Oklahoma Press.

Can I not indulge in a retrospective picture of the constitutions of Castile & Aragon; of the Moorish dynasty — the causes of its decay & dissolution? Then I have the Inquisition, with its bloody persecutions, — the conquest of Granada a brilliant passage, — the exploits of the "Great Capt[ain]" in Italy, a proper character for romance as well as hist[or]y, — the discovery of a new world, my own country — the new policy of the monarch tow[ar]ds the overgrown aristocracy &c. &c. — A biography will make me responsible for a limited space, only, — will require much less reading, a great consideration with me, — will offer the deeper interest which always attaches to minute developm[en]t of character, & a continuous closely connected narrative. — The subject brings me to the point whence English hist[or]y has started, is untried ground, & in my opinion a rich one. The age of Ferdinand is most important as cont[ainin]g the germs of the modern system of European politics, & the three sovereigns Henry VII, Louis XI, & Ferdinand were important engines in overturning the old system. It is in every aspect an interesting and momentous period of hist[or]y. The materials authentic, ample. — I will chew upon this matter. — & *decide this wk.* . . .

July 3, 1828 . . . Finally for the hundredth time, after a full & accurate reflection on the whole matter, I confirm my preference & choice of the Spanish subject. I am convinced that a history written on this matter, which shall exhibit general views on all occasions, showing the influence & importance, both as regards Spain & Europe of the policy pursued by Ferdinand & Isabella, — in their domestic & foreign relations; which shall give copious illustrations, &c. of the Arabian, Spanish, & criticisms on the Italian literature; which shall select only interesting details to be narrated, & narrate them circumstantially; & which, finally, shall aim at wide rather than deep views, at a popular rather than erudite compilation, avoiding intricate research, particularly in antiquities, & particularly too on topics relating to constitutions of government, or economy, —will be easy eno', & perfectly safe for me to write, & may be made novel, elegant, useful, & very entertaining. — What more can I desire? . . .

The Conception of Prescott's *History of Mexico*

July 14, 1839 . . . Mem[o]: Describe the features of those parts of the country which are the scene of operations, as existing at that time, and at the present. Give life to the picture by the exhibition of the various natural products peculiar to those regions. In short, be minute in the localities, and everything relating to them, topographical, physical, & historical — transporting the reader to the country, and to the age.

Omit no trait which can display the character of Cortés, the *hero of the piece,* round whom the interest is to concentrate. The narrative is a beautiful epic. It has all the interest which daring, chivalrous enterprise, stupendous achievements, worthy of an age of knighterrantry, a magical country, the splendors of a rich barbaric court, and extraordinary personal qualities in the hero — can give.

There is not a diversity of very conspicuous characters — the interest being nearly absorbed in that of Cortés — who is, in truth, not merely the soul, but the body, of the enterprise, present everywhere in person,* (*This is in this History as published.) In the thick of the fight, or in the building of the works, with his sword or his musket, sometimes leading his soldiers, and sometimes directing his little navy. The negotiations, intrigues, correspondence, are all conducted by him; and, like Caesar, he wrote his own Commentaries, in the heat of the stirring scenes which form the subject of them. His character is marked with the most opposite traits, embracing qualities apparently the most incompatible in its composition. He was avaricious, yet liberal; bold to desperation, yet cautious and calculating in his plans; magnanimous, yet very cunning; courteous and amiable in his deportment, yet inexorably stern; lax in his notions of morality, yet (not uncommon) a sad bigot. The great feature in his character was constancy of purpose; a constancy not to be daunted by danger, nor baffled by disappointment, nor wearied out by impediments and delays. His address secured the cooperation of men who set out with being his enemies, and effectually combined into one harmonious whole, the motley mixture of Indians of different tribes, and Spaniards of hostile parties. He was inexhaustible in resources, and when all outward means were withdrawn, seemed to find sufficient to sustain him, in his own bosom. Witness his extremity after the flight from Mexico; his enemies victorious, his allies doubtful, his own troops discontented, his cause in his own country deserted and betrayed. From all this he rose triumphant, and finally succeeded, with a handful of men, in overturning the most powerful of the barbarian empires of the New World. He was the only man alive, probably, who, with such means, could have effected such results. The Conquest of Mexico was the greatest miracle in an age of miracles.

As to the other, subordinate characters, they are not without interest. There is Sandoval, a frank and generous soldier; Alvarado, fierce and daring; Marina, the Indian captive, full of intelligence and amiable qualities, and, from her knowledge of languages, capable of rendering the most important services to the Spaniards; the worthy Father Olmedo, a rare pattern of Christian toleration in an age of intolerance; Bishop Fonseca, efficient, artful, and vindictive; Narváez, weak and presumptuous; the unfortunate Montezuma, the victim of destiny, whose fate seemed to be announced before the arrival of the white men, and who yielded to it with an unresisting weakness that forms an affecting contrast with his naturally bold and somewhat cruel character; Velazquez, mean, selfish, and vacillating; the young Tlascalan chief Xicotencatl, rash, restless, a barbarian Hotspur; and Guatimozin, the last of the Aztec line, and closing the series of warlike princes with a brave, heroic devotion, worthy of a better fate.

For important battles, we have those of Tabasco, Tlascala, the Noche Triste, Otumba, and the final siege of Mexico. For particular incidents of interest, there are the storming of the great temple, and the narrow escapes of Cortés then, and twice on the causeways, the gallant capture of the standard of Otumba by him, the seizure, imprisonment, and death of Montezuma, the torture of Guatimozin, the valiant night assault on Narváez, the suppression of various conspiracies and mutinies of the troops, the execution of the Mexican general Quauhpopoca, the reception of Cortés by Charles V., &c. &c.

The principal address in managing the narrative will be to vary the tissue of blood and battle, which is to form the staple of the story, with other circumstances of milder complexion, so distributed as to relieve the reader's mind, without impairing the interest. The parts thus interspersed should come in natural pauses, and be not too long. They should be suggested by, and serve to illustrate, the narrative — not in the form of disquisitions. Such materials may be found in the characters of the great actors; the state of the mother country, and its politics, somewhat; the progress of maritime discovery, previous and contemporary; the conduct of Velazquez, when first engaging with Cortés; *his suit subsequently prosecuted in Spain,* together with that of Cortés, before the Regent, and the Emperor; (this is an affair of much interest, and may be introduced at various times, *or perhaps best* at *the close of the narrative of the Conquest*) the description of the grand and picturesque scenery through which the Spaniards march; faithful discussions of the various architectural remains, of the vegetable products, the mountains, the towns, &c., contrasted, moreover, with their present condition, affording an agreeable and instructive variety, and giving life and coloring to the picture; the description of Montezuma's palace, court ceremonies, way of life, his gardens, collections of natural history, &c.; the city of Mexico, its buildings, market, manners of the people, &c., such as fell under the personal observation of the Spaniards; (the national institutions will be discussed in the Introduction) the various intrigues and negotiations of Cortés with his Mexican enemies, with the soldiers of Narváez, and his own mutineers; the rebuilding of the capital; the personal history of Cortés, both before and after the Conquest, &c. &c. Care must be taken to avoid enumeration of lifeless details, in the progressive subjugation of the Indian tribes, both during and after the Conquest; the leading events may be brought distinctly before the eye, but the subordinate ones thrown into the shade, or omitted wholly.

In short, the true way of conceiving the subject is, not as a philosophical theme, but as an *epic in prose,* a romance of chivalry; as romantic and as chivalrous as any which Boiardo or Ariosto ever fabled, — and almost as marvellous; and which, while it combines all the picturesque features of the romantic school, is borne onward on a tide of destiny, like that which broods over the fictions of the Grecian poets; — for surely there is nothing in the compass of Grecian epic or tragic fable, in which the resistless march of *destiny* is more discernible, than in the sad fortunes of the dynasty of Montezuma. — It is, without doubt, the most poetic subject ever offered to the pen of the historian. Is it, for that reason, the best? At all events, being the most poetic, it must be regarded from this point of view, to be treated with full effect. — The Introduction, embracing comprehensive views of general causes and their results, and the Conclusion, taken up with the personal history of Cortés, are of a different cast from the narrative of the Conquest: the Introduction being a *philosophical* subject, and the latter *biographical.* They may seem, at first sight, to match badly with the main story. But it seems to me, if well managed, the general views of the first will prepare the reader for the particulars of the Conquest; and the great public events narrated in this, will, without violence, open the way to the remaining personal history of the hero, who was the soul of it.

3. The Historical Methods of Hubert Howe Bancroft

My system of historical work requires a few words of explanation, since not a little of the criticism, both favorable and unfavorable, has been founded on an erroneous conception of its nature.

In order to comprehend clearly the error alluded to, it is well to note that the composition of an historical work involves labor of a twofold nature, the dividing line being very clearly marked. Material in the nature of evidence has first to be accumulated and classified; subsequently from the evidence judgments have to be formed and expressed. . . .

My system, then, applies only to the accumulation and arrangement of evidence upon the topics of which I write, and consists in the application of business methods and the division of labor to those ends. By its aid I have attempted to accomplish in one year what would require ten years by ordinary methods or on a complicated and extensive subject to collect practically all the evidence, when by ordinary methods a lifetime of toil would yield only a part.

To illustrate: Let us suppose an industrious author, determined to write the history of California, at the start wholly ignorant of his subject. He easily learns of a few works on California, and having purchased them studies their contents, making notes to aid his memory. His reading directs him to other titles, and he seeks the corresponding books in the libraries, public and private, of the city where he resides. His search of the shelves and catalogues of the various libraries reveals many volumes of whose existence he had not dreamed at first; but yet he continues his reading and his notes. . . .

Now the reader will permit me to trace my own course through a similar routine of investigation, pursued, however, by different methods. Like my imaginary friend, I was determined to write the

Hubert Howe Bancroft, *Literary Industries* (New York: Harper and Brothers, 1891), pp. 330–338, *passim*.

history of California, and had almost as vague an idea as he of the task assumed. He purchased some books as tools with which to work, selecting such as were known to bear on his subject; I began ten years before I was ready to write, and bought through agents in all parts of the world every book that could be had concerning the Pacific States, thus obtaining twenty thousand volumes, sure to include, as I thought, all existing material about California. To search among my twenty thousand for two thousand on California was a less formidable undertaking than for him to search the shelves of different libraries and catalogues for his five hundred volumes; but it was too slow for my purposes, and from ten to fifteen men were employed to index the whole and furnish me a list of California material with reference to volume and page. My imaginary author plods industriously through each work as he finds it, making careful notes of such matter as he deems of value, while I put ten men at work, each as capable for this kind of labor as he or I, to extract everything under its proper heading. Like him, I am more and more astonished at the apparently never ending mass of material encountered, but I can see my way through it if only the treasury department sustains me. So I tunnel the mountain of court records and legal briefs, bridge the marsh of United States government documents, and stationing myself at a safe distance in the rear, hurl my forces against the solid columns of two hundred files of California newspapers.

Like him, I see about me many living witnesses, and from several hundreds of them obtain, by aid of stenographers, as well as reporters, detailed statements respecting early times. I more than suspect the existence of important papers scattered in private hands, and proceed to buy, borrow, and beg, until the product fills a hundred volumes. The six hundred bulky tomes of public and mission archives rise up before me, but there is no such thing as retreat at this point of procedure; I have no fifteen years to spend in plodding through this pathless waste, but fifteen searchers reduce the time to one year, and the archives are transferred to my library. Meanwhile my note-takers continue their labors; each volume, pamphlet, manuscript, and newspaper is made to give up its evidence, little or much, on one point or many and nothing is omitted or slighted.

At last the preparatory work is ended, and the evidence on each specific point is laid before me, as my friend had his before him, but with this difference: I have practically all where he had only part — he hardly realized, perhaps, how small a part. He had two or three witnesses whose testimony he had selected as essential on a certain topic: I have a hundred whose evidence is more or less relevant. From this point our progress lies practically in the same path, and the race is well-nigh run. Had he the same data as I, his results would be superior to mine if he were my superior as a thinker and as a writer. Our respective methods and systems have little or no influence in the matter, save perhaps that in my experience with my assistants I have been able to select a few to whom I can intrust the preparation of systematized notes on special topics, and thus still further to shorten my labors.

My work at last completed, I have been able to accomplish thoroughly in fifteen years what my friend, quite as zealous, industrious, and able as myself, has done superficially in twenty-five years, and what he could not have done as thoroughly as myself in half a dozen lifetimes. And yet our respective methods differ after all in degree rather than in kind. I have done scarcely anything that he has not attempted. He has purchased books, studied books, handled newspapers, deciphered manuscripts, and questioned pioneers; I have simply done twenty times as much as he in each of these directions, much more easily and in much less time. . . .

The primary endeavor in all my historical writings has been to exhaust the subject, but presenting it always in as condensed a form as possible. In the text is given the information complete, the full narrative in the fewest words.

It was ever my aim to tell the story clearly and concisely, taking a common-sense practical view of things, and arranging them in natural sequence, giving an episode as much as possible in one place, even though in its relation to other episodes it overlapped a little. Analysis of character, as applied to leading personages, I endeavored to make a feature, giving, with physical description, bent of mind and natural and acquired abilities. In cases where characteristics were not directly specified they might be arrived at from the acts of the individual. A little colloquy was deemed not ineffective when short, terse, and in language appropriate to the persons and the time. A short story, pointedly given, is effective to enliven the text, but it must not be carelessly done. The notes were for reference to authorities, for proof, elucidation, discussion, illustration, balancing of evidence, and for second-class information. To this end quotations from authorities were deemed in order, not as repetitions, but as presenting the subject in its several shades and opposite positions. Though not illustrated, maps and plans were inserted in both text and notes wherever needed. In regard to bibliography, it was my aim to give every important book and manuscript formal notice in the most suitable place; the title to be given in full and in italic characters. The contents of the work were then briefly epitomized, after which a criticism and a biographical notice of the author were given. The biographies of leading historical characters were of course presented in the text, these of themselves constituting history; though for want of space some may have been crowded into notes, where also were given those of the pioneers.

B. Sources

4. The Other Treasure from the Indies

LEWIS HANKE

Historians must ever be grateful for the keen sense of history and the almost unconscious and certainly widespread recognition by the early Spaniards that their actions in the New World would one day be carefully scrutinized by posterity. Columbus started the practice of writing about America, and many followed his example. The conquest so excited the imagination of Spaniards that they came to look upon it as the greatest event since the coming of Christ. Even as the conquistadores roamed over vast areas of land and sea and missionaries attempted to christianize millions of Indians, they collected historical materials and composed histories on a monumental scale. Eventually this concern that the record of their deeds be known and the nature of the overseas lands be described led the Council of the Indies to establish . . . the office of a Cosmographer and Cronista Mayor, whose obligation it was to devote him-

Lewis Hanke, "The Other Treasure from the Indies," *Karl V. Der Kaiser und Seine Zeit* (Cologne: Böhlau-Verlag, 1960), pp. 94–103, *passim*. Reprinted by permission of Böhlau-Verlag, Cologne.

self to writing the history of the Indies on a year-round basis.   . . .

In the days of Charles V the writing of history in and about America was not so much an officially approved activity as it was a manifestation of the Spaniard's conviction of his high destiny in the New World and of his Renaissance zest for life. The ever-present ecclesiastics shared this feeling, too, for scarcely a decade after the Franciscans reached New Spain they appointed one of their number to compose a history of their accomplishments to date. There was a derring-do spirit, moreover, in Spanish actions in America. The youthful conquistador Diego de Ordaz yearned to find out what lay beneath the outpouring smoke of a Mexican volcano and finally wrung a reluctant approval for the ascent of the crater from his chief Cortés, who authorized the dangerous enterprise only "in order that the Indians might see that nothing is impossible for a Spaniard."

It is true that the Crown stimulated its representatives to report carefully and in a detailed way on the new dominion; the conquistadores were even "charged with prying out the secrets of those new lands to see if there were mosques and Moslem priests." At times, too, such a chronicler as Gonzalo Fernández Oviedo y Valdés seemed to be indulging in exaggerated accounts of the New World for the benefit of the folks at home. He wrote, for example, that he had heard of a Peruvian monkey that "was no less extraordinary than the griffins," for it had a long tail, with the upper half of its body covered with many-hued feathers and the lower half with smooth, reddish fur. It could sing, "when it felt like it," in the same dulcet tones as a nightingale or a lark. Oviedo also noticed that roosters crowed less frequently and less raucously than in Spain, and even the tom-cats of the Caribbean made so little noise at night that his studies were not interrupted as they often had been when he was at the University of Salamanca. On the whole, however, one gets the impression from reading the numerous early chronicles that Spaniards were deeply and seriously conscious of the historic importance of the mighty events in which they were participating, and that there was indeed "nothing that a Spaniard could not do," or at least would not try to do.   . . .

The broad interests of these early chroniclers, which today would be dignified by some such resounding phrase as "interdisciplinary coordination," must be recognized too. They viewed the conquest in the round, and discoursed on disease and death, art and cooking, linguistic matters, child-raising, and a galaxy of other topics which interested them in the New World. Even Las Casas, best known for his staggering statistics of Indians killed during the conquest and for his polemical writings, also revealed a concern for education, a competence in psychology, and an interest in nature that even now are not fully appreciated.

All these and other similar chronicles have long been known and used; indeed, one may say that they have been exploited by historians in the same way that the early miners at Potosí drew off the richest deposits of silver lying easily accessible at hand. In both cases, however, much valuable material was left untouched for future generations to use. Even such a standard and obvious source as the official reports drawn up for their successors by the hundred or more viceroys in Peru and Mexico have not been adequately or fully published, though active consideration is being given now to remedying this deficiency. And the "encomienda" — that basic economic, social, and religious institution — has yet to find a historian who has made full use of the pertinent though scattered and somewhat refractory manuscripts. . . .

The letters of friars also reveal a pungent and noteworthy quality of observation. Vast quantities of manuscripts exist in European and American archives on the Indians. . . .

The voluminous private correspondence of Spaniards in America, who exercised a most unusual freedom of speech at least during the epoch of Charles V; the truly impressive number of "legajos" of judicial and notarial records in which are embedded valuable historical data; and the biographical statements drawn up by conquistadores seeking a pension or preferment from the Crown all will undoubtedly produce some day a rich yield if systematically worked over. The "residencia" manuscript records alone constitute a largely unexploited collection of considerable value for reaching a more realistic picture of life in America than the rosy views which official documents sometimes produce. The most weighty proof of the almost inexhaustible detail on certain aspects of the achievement of Spain in America is to be found in the many-volumed opus of Huguette and Pierre Chaunu, *Séville et l'Atlantique, 1504–1650,* which surely marks a significant advance in this field. When these official data are joined with the economic information of a "local" character — such as the early account books of the "haciendas" of that same Diego de Ordaz who was so eager to peer down into the smoking volcanoes — we are confronting an almost frightening quantity of economic data.

The number of stimulating historical problems to be found in this copious documentation is as impressive as its sheer bulk. Even in such a relatively well-worked field as that of legislation on the Indies, Richard Konetzke has demonstrated that the mass of laws that Spain produced in such bewildering variety has not yet been fully exploited by historians. The analysis of the origins of the Spaniards who went to the New World has just begun to receive the attention it deserves. And what more curious commentary on Spaniards and on the shock of a conquest that brought together peoples of such different development can be found than item 24 in the 1512 Laws of Burgos, the first code drawn up to regulate Indians, which provides: "That no one may beat or whip or call an Indian dog [perro] or any other name unless it be his given name."

Perhaps we need not agree with the dictum that "History to be interesting and valuable should be recorded by persons of talent and prejudice or by chambermaids who listen at keyholes," but has the time not come for a much greater emphasis on the social and economic history of Spain in America? Once this truth has been recognized, the historical data recorded concerning the America of Charles V will prove to be a treasure trove which will give historians cause for delight as well as for professional profit. . . .

As a conclusion, one generalization may be hazarded concerning both treasures from America. In one respect at least the prospecting for mineral wealth and its primitive extraction in the Emperor's New World domains was markedly similar to the task historians face today in the location and utilization of that "other treasure." In both cases there can be seen plenty of work for all available hands. The Crown insisted that Indians as well as Spaniards — indeed, everyone — be encouraged to participate in the feverish hunt for silver and gold so urgently needed in Europe. And despite the opposition of Spaniards, the natives did discover mines. Thus began an economic and social movement in America, marked by considerable social mobility — a movement that is still going on.

So today, the sheer size of the mass of documentation yet to be located and studied is so enormous that historians will doubtless work over these sources for many years, just as Spaniards extracted mineral wealth from the New World for almost three centuries. Moreover, a variety of specialists must be drawn into the labor —

anthropologists, economists, geographers, and sociologists, to suggest but the most obvious of the disciplines whose members will find rich data for their studies. In fact, none of the representatives of the social sciences and few of the humanities will go away empty-handed. Let us therefore invite all interested scholars to the common task — and I appeal especially to my colleagues in Germany and other European countries.

If this attack is carried on along a broad front, can anyone doubt that this "other treasure from the Indies" will help us to achieve the objective set up by the late Carl Becker of Cornell University: "The attempt to reconstruct, and by imaginative insight and aesthetic understanding, make live again that pattern of events occurring in distant places and times past," which we call history? Even if we do not wholly achieve this objective, will not the rich and copious historical documentation produced in and about the New World during the epoch of the Emperor Charles V be a powerful aid in deepening and perhaps transforming our knowledge of America, and of Europe, in those decisive decades of the sixteenth century?

C. Interpretations

5. William Robertson and His *History of America*

R. A. HUMPHREYS

There are two classic histories of the Spanish conquest of America in the English language. The one is the splendid narrative of Prescott, written more than a century ago, but still unrivalled. The other, equally celebrated in its day, but now almost forgotten, is William Robertson's *History of America*, published at London in two volumes on May 28, 1777.

R. A. Humphreys, *William Robertson and His History of America* (London: The Hispanic and Luso-Brazilian Councils, 1954), pp. 5–7, 14–25. Reprinted by permission of the author.

Robertson died three years before Prescott was born. In 1759, when, as a thirty-seven-year-old Scottish Presbyterian clergyman, he was as yet barely known outside his beloved Edinburgh, he had enchanted the literary world of England with a *History of Scotland during the Reigns of Queen Mary and of King James VI*, which is properly to be regarded as a major contribution to the new historiography of the eighteenth century. Ten years later — he was now Historiographer Royal in Scotland and Principal of the University of Edinburgh — he had capped this success with a yet more resounding triumph, a *History of the Reign of the Emperor Charles V*, which was read all the way from Paris to St. Petersburg and brought him European fame. His third great history, the *History of America*, was his most distinguished achievement. It arose, naturally and inevitably, from his European subject. And, in origin at least, it was no more than a by-product of his work on Charles V.

Prescott, sixty years later, trod a similar path. Prescott made his name with a *History of the Reign of Ferdinand and Isabella*, and Spain was his first and his last love. But as *Charles V* had led Robertson, so *Ferdinand and Isabella* led Prescott from Europe to America; and Prescott was to tell in detail the story which Robertson told in outline. "The most poetic subject ever offered to the pen of the historian," he calls it. "A perfect epic," he says a little later, "and as full of incident as any tale of chivalry." And, again, when his *Conquest of Mexico* was nearly finished: "The story," he writes, "is so full of marvels, perilous adventures, curious manners, scenery, etc., that it is more like a romance than a history, and yet every page is substantiated by abundance of original testimony."

But Prescott, with far richer resources at his disposal than Robertson could command, never forgot what Robertson had done before him. In his two great American histories and elsewhere he is generous with his praise of the "illustrious historian of America" — such is his phrase. "It is very absurd," he says in one of his letters, "to consider the pennyweight of commendation that might be conceded to my efforts as any deduction from the solid worth of Robertson." And hidden in his private journals there lies a warning note. "Beware of Robertson," he writes. "Never glance at him till after subject moulded in my mind and thrown into language." So, across the years, one great historian of the New World saluted another.

Prescott was a product of the nineteenth-century "flowering of New England," Robertson of the eighteenth-century "awakening of

Scotland." He was born in 1721, two years before Adam Smith. A studious and rather awkward lad, brought up, as his friend Dr. Alexander Carlyle says, never to dance, to attend the theatre, or to play cards, he entered the University of Edinburgh at the mature age of twelve, was licensed to preach before he was twenty-two, and soon afterwards was presented to the small living of Gladsmuir, no great distance from the capital. Here he remained for fourteen years, active in the affairs of his parish; riding into Edinburgh to consult the shelves of the Advocates' Library or to attend the sessions of the General Assembly of the Scottish Church; looking after six sisters and one younger brother — the sisters, as Brougham, his great-nephew, noted many years later, always addressed their brother as "Sir"; marrying his cousin; and in, about, 1753, beginning his first great history. . . .

The *History of America,* as Robertson gave it to the world, was a history of Spanish America. More particularly, it was a history of Spanish America in the great age of discovery and conquest, "the most splendid portion," as he calls it, "of the American story." As a prelude to discovery, however, he traced the course of European exploration from ancient times to the fifteenth century, when, as he says, "the glory of leading the way . . . was reserved for Portugal." And, as a conclusion to the story of the conquest, he appended a remarkable chapter, Book VIII, in which he analysed the nature and effects of Spanish colonization in the New World and discussed also contemporary imperial reforms. He was at pains, moreover, to examine, so far as he could, the indigenous cultures of Mexico and Peru, and in what he called a "View of America when first discovered, and of the manners and policy of its most uncivilized inhabitants," he showed, as Professor Black has pointed out, a quite unusual awareness of the relation between geography and history, and no sympathy at all with the legend of the "noble savage." Whatever Rousseau's opinions might be, Robertson was under no illusion that "the most perfect state of man" was, as he dryly observed, "the least civilized."

In all this Robertson broke fresh ground. Englishmen, when his book appeared, knew even less about Spanish America than they do now — if that is possible. The man of letters might have dipped into one or another translation of early Spanish chronicles and histories and into one or another collection of voyages. The merchant was familiar with the transatlantic commerce of Cádiz and Lisbon, and with the profits and hazards of the contraband trade, and he long retained memories of the famous *Asiento,* or contract to supply slaves to Spanish America, of the South Sea Company, and of the South Sea Bubble. Grub Street provided some indifferent manuals, of which the most informative — despite its author's capacity, if Boswell is to be believed, for drinking thirteen bottles of port at a sitting — was *A Concise History of the Spanish America,* published by Dr. John Campbell in 1741. And one work of real merit, *An Account of the European Settlements in America,* which Robertson himself praises, and which is attributed to Edmund Burke, appeared in 1757. Travellers' accounts, moreover, such as the celebrated *Voyage to South America* of the two young Spanish naval officers, Juan and Ulloa, were eagerly read. And when the Abbé Raynal's *Histoire philosophique et politique des établissements et du commerce des européens dans les deux Indes* came out in English dress in 1776, it proved so popular that fourteen editions were called for by the end of the century.

But Raynal's famous "philosophic history" — dreary enough reading now — contained as much fiction as fact. The literature of travel was all too meagre. And, as Robertson himself observed, Spain, "with an excess of caution," had "uniformly thrown a veil over her transactions in America." The wealth of the Indies was legendary; and from the days of Elizabeth to those of George III successive British governments had attempted to take a bite at the Spanish American cherry. But of the history or institutions of Spain's empire in America little was known; and to an Englishman, nourished in Elizabethan and Cromwellian traditions, what was known was usually thought to be discreditable to Spain.

Robertson lifted the veil. "The longer I reflect on the nature of historical composition," he wrote, "the more I am convinced that . . . scrupulous accuracy is necessary." It is impressive to notice his close scrutiny of his sources and the judgements which he passes on the early Spanish chroniclers and historians: on Garcilaso de la Vega, for example, who, he remarks, is unable to distinguish between "what is fabulous, what is probable, and what is true"; on Herrera and Solís; on Cieza de León; and on Bernal Díaz del Castillo, whose account, he says, "bears all the marks of authenticity, and is accompanied with such a pleasant *naïveté,* with such interesting details, with such amusing vanity, and yet so pardonable in an old soldier who had been (as he boasts) in a hundred and nineteen battles, as renders his book one of the most singular that is to be found in any language."

Impressive also was his eagerness to seek out first-hand evidence. "Emboldened," he says, "by a hint" from Gibbon, he printed a catalogue, or bibliography, of the Spanish books and manuscripts which he had consulted and collected — a notable departure from eighteenth-century practice. It contained most of what was of importance to his subject then in print, and the Advocates' Library in Edinburgh, which refused to buy his Spanish collection for £100 odd in 1781, must often have repented of its folly. In Spain the archives of Simancas were closed to him. The great Arabic scholar, Gayangos, was one of the first persons to be allowed to use them, on Prescott's behalf, nearly seventy years later, and his description of what he found makes amusing reading. But Robertson was able to procure copies of other Spanish manuscripts through the good offices of the Rev. Robert Waddilove, then the chaplain to the British Embassy in Madrid and later Dean of Ripon. He instituted a search in the Imperial Library at Vienna for the first letter sent by Cortés to Charles V from New Spain — it is still lost — and discovered instead a copy of the famous letter written by the town-council of Vera Cruz and a copy also of Cortés's account of his expedition to Honduras. To support his theory that the American Indians were probably descended from the "rude" tribes of Tartary, and to prove how easily man might have passed from the old world to the new, he secured from St. Petersburg a translation of the manuscript journal of the expedition which had been sent in 1768 to continue the progress of Russian exploration off the north-eastern shores of Asia; and this helped to confirm Robertson in an opinion, soon shown to be correct, that Asia and America were only separated by a narrow strait. He prepared a questionnaire, which was sent to a number of Spaniards who had lived in the New World, asking for information on various colonial institutions and practices, on the population of Spanish America, the royal revenues, and the like; and he addressed a further set of queries both to Spaniards and to non-Spaniards, dealing with the customs and habits of the American Indians. Finally, he consulted, among others, the surviving members of the French scientific expedition which had been sent to measure an arc of the meridian at Quito in 1735.

The result was the first modern history of Spanish America. Contemporaries, Gibbon and Burke, for example, were fascinated by

Robertson's account of the Indian aboriginals. But, not surprisingly, this is the part of his work which has worn the least well. So far as the preconquest cultures of Mexico and Peru are concerned, it is only necessary to compare Robertson's pages with those of Prescott to see the bareness of his ground; and in some respects at least, though certainly not in all, the gulf between Prescott and the modern ethnologist and archaeologist is not less wide than the gulf between Robertson and Prescott. Not, indeed, till 1839 did John Lloyd Stephens and Frederick Catherwood begin their explorations of the ruined cities of Central America which were to result in the discovery of the civilization of the Mayas. Compelled to rely almost wholly on literary sources alone, and these inadequate, Robertson, as Prescott wrote to Stephens, "underestimated everything in the New World. It was little understood then," adds Prescott, "and distrust which had a knowing air at least was the safer side for the historian."

Yet Robertson's discussion of the American Indian was far more considered and careful than was common among his contemporaries. The *philosophes* had discovered the American Indian. Rousseau, though he had not created the legend of the "noble savage," had greatly strengthened it by his glowing descriptions of the virtuous simplicity of primitive life. Rousseau, it is true, knew nothing of the American Indian, and indeed barely mentioned him. But Buffon had surveyed the world from China to Peru, and Buffon had found him. The animals of South America, he had noted, were different from, and smaller than, those of the Old World. There were no elephants and rhinoceroses, for example, no lions and tigers, and no giraffes. The domestic creatures transported from Europe had diminished in size. The men had no beards; their constitutions were feeble. And, putting these matters together, Buffon had arrived at the conclusion that the greater part of the New World was a young continent where nature had not yet "had time to establish all her plans," and where man himself was only an animal of the first rank. Finally, de Pauw, the notorious de Pauw, rejecting this theory of the youthfulness or immaturity of the New World, had maintained that America was not young but degenerate, and had included in one ferocious condemnation its climate, its fauna, and its native inhabitants. Where Rousseau had seen the "noble savage," de Pauw found the "ignoble savage."

But the *philosophes,* as Robertson complained, "too impatient to inquire," hastened to decide, and "began to erect systems, when they should have been searching for facts"; and it was facts that Robertson wanted. There is, it is true, much of Buffon in his pages, though nothing at all of Rousseau. But he was careful to test the opinions and information which he had collected and collated by the experience of scientists, missionaries, and administrators who had had first-hand knowledge of various parts of the Americas. Were the bodily constitutions of the Indians, he inquired, as vigorous and robust as those of the inhabitants of similar climates in the ancient continent? Was the absence of a beard natural to the Indian? Was he defective in animal passions, the passion of love for example? What was his attitude in regard to parental affection or filial duty? What ideas did he have of property? And what conception did he entertain of a future life? What was the genius and what the structure of the Indian languages? Moreover, did European animals which propagated in America improve or degenerate? Were animals which were common to both continents greater or smaller in size? And other questions of a like kind.

"If, in advanced years," Adam Ferguson had written, "we would form a just notion of our progress from the cradle, we must have recourse to the nursery." Robertson went to the nursery. "That state of primaeval simplicity, which was known in our continent only by the fanciful description of poets," he remarked, "really existed in the other." And whatever its errors and inconsistencies, his analysis of primitive Indian life must be regarded as one of the earliest critical inquiries into the subject. Though Buffon, morever, had realized the significance of Russian discoveries in the sea of Kamchatka, it was left for Robertson to demonstrate the probability that man first reached the New World by way of the Bering Strait. His conclusion failed, alas, to check that "extravagance of conjecture," as he called it, which found the origin of the American Indian in the hills of Wales or the lost ten tribes of Israel. But informed opinion had long supported it.

If time has done much to destroy the value of Robertson's chapters both on the aboriginal Indians and on the higher cultures of Mexico and Peru, it has also done much to vindicate an attitude of mind which shocked and distressed some of his contemporary critics namely, his refusal to accept what has come to be called the "black legend." And here again Robertson differed widely from the fashionable doctrines of Raynal, de Pauw, and others of the *philosophes*.

"I am satisfied," he wrote, "that upon a more minute scrutiny" into the "early operations" of the Spaniards in the New World, "however reprehensible the actions of individuals may appear, the conduct of the nation will be placed in a more favourable light." He did not disguise the acts of cruelty and perfidy, the licentiousness, the tyranny, and the rapacity, which stain the annals of the conquest. He noted the terrible toll of human life taken in Hispaniola and Puerto Rico by the sword, by barbarity, by famine, and by disease. Of Mexico he remarked that "in almost every district of the Mexican empire, the progress of the Spanish arms" was "marked with blood, and with deeds so atrocious, as disgrace the enterprising valour that conducted them to success." The agreement made between Pizarro and his associates, which was to result in the conquest of Peru, moved him to the biting comment that "in name of the Prince of Peace" they "ratified a contract of which plunder and bloodshed were the objects." And the execution of the Inca, Atahualpa, he characterized as an action "the most criminal and atrocious that stains the Spanish name, amidst all the deeds of violence committed in carrying on the conquest of the New World."

On the other hand, Robertson declined to take at their face value the sweeping charges made against the sixteenth-century Spaniards by one of the greatest of them all — Las Casas. He perceived the strange mixture of motives mingling in their breasts: "religious enthusiasm," he says, united with the spirit of adventure, and both with avarice. He was lost in admiration at their "fortitude and perseverance." Of the march which Cortés made to Honduras, he remarks that what Cortés suffered "from famine, from the hostility of the natives, from the climate, and from hardships of every species, has nothing in history parallel to it, but what occurs in the adventures of the other discoverers and conquerors of the New World." Above all, though his description of the "bustling, indefatigable activity" of Las Casas was certainly unhappy, Robertson insisted on the devoted labours of the missionary orders, on the humanity of the Crown, and on the royal concern for the welfare of the native Indians. And he rightly remarked that "in no code of laws is greater solicitude displayed, or precautions multiplied with more prudent concern for the preservation, the security, and the happiness of the subject, than we discover in the collection of the Spanish laws for the Indies."

Robertson's narrative ends with the civil wars in Peru. It begins with Columbus and ends, as Prescott was to end his own fine history, with the conciliatory mission of that great ecclesiastical statesman, Pedro de La Gasca. It deals only briefly with events outside the major theatres of Spanish operations, and it touches only lightly on such matters as the territorial organization of the colonies and the beginnings of royal government. Discovery and conquest, not colonization, are its main themes.

But Robertson was not content with this alone. The Spanish Crown, he observed, "having acquired a species of dominion formerly unknown," formed "a plan for exercising it, to which nothing similar occurs in the history of human affairs." The successors of Ferdinand and Isabella were "the universal proprietors" of the territories which their subjects had conquered. "It is true," he continued, "that when towns were built, and formed into bodies corporate, the citizens were permitted to elect their own magistrates, who governed them by laws which the community enacted. Even in the most despotic states, this feeble spark of liberty is not extinguished. But in the cities of Spanish America, this jurisdiction is merely municipal. . . . No political power originates from the people. All centers in the crown, and in the officers of its nomination."

His narrative ended, Robertson appended, therefore, in Book VIII, a review of Spanish colonial policy and administration from the sixteenth century to the Bourbon reforms of his own time, and surveyed also the internal development of the colonies during this period and their economic impact upon Spain and Europe. Here he examined the effects of the flow of American treasure upon Spanish commerce and industry, pointed out the disproportion between Spain's economic capacities and her colonies' economic needs, discussed the rise of the contraband trade, and concluded with an account of contemporary imperial reorganization. The chapter, as Burke remarked, threw "quite a new light" on the state of Spanish America; as an example of Robertson's analytical powers it deserves to be compared with his famous introduction to the *History of the Reign of the Emperor Charles V;* and for the modern historian it retains its value after the lapse of nearly a hundred and eighty years.

Inevitably, of course, Robertson sometimes fell into errors of fact, though these, like the obvious *lacunae* in his work, were more often a reflection of deficiencies in the sources of his information than of carelessness in himself. Prescott, after all, was able to draw on a far greater corpus of materials, both printed and unprinted. Sometimes, also, Robertson's critical sense in the use of his authorities failed him. But the outstanding impression created by the *History of America* is one of general truthfulness and fairmindedness. It was a pioneer history, and destined to be superseded as the archives were opened and new documents brought to light. But, as a pioneer history, it was good history, and, what is more, it is extremely good reading. . . .

6. Francisco Encina Interprets Colonial Chile

Charles C. Griffin

The writing of full-length, multivolumed national histories which was so conspicuous a feature of the nineteenth century has practically disappeared in our time. The professionalizing of the writing of history has discouraged would-be literary historians in the grand manner; cooperative enterprises by groups of scholars have supplied the demand for large general works of reference for students and teachers; the changing and expanding reading public has sought a literary diet far removed from that of the nineteenth-century educated gentlemen on whose library shelves the works of Macaulay, Guizot, George Bancroft, or Diego Barros Arana reposed in massive dignity. It is therefore an event of no small importance that at mid-century a twenty-volume national history of Chile should have been published, and an even more astonishing fact that this voluminous work should have become an outstanding *éxito de librería*.

The interest aroused by Francisco Encina's history is surely not due to its extraordinary length. It is doubtful whether it will be followed by competitors on the same scale, and it has even been felt desirable to publish a three-volume condensation in order to overcome, in part, the extraordinary effort demanded of the reader of the original work. To what, then, can we ascribe the popularity of this history? There appears to exist in Chile a large public interest in a fresh interpretation of the national past. Compilations based on earlier syntheses no longer speak meaningfully to those who face

Charles C. Griffin, "Francisco Encina and Revisionism in Chilean History," *Hispanic American Historical Review*, XXXVII (February, 1957), pp. 1–27, *passim*. Reprinted by permission of the Duke University Press.

the multiple problems of the Chile of today. The last volume of the only comparable work, the classic *Historia jeneral de Chile* by Diego Barros Arana was published almost half a century before the first of Encina's came from the press. Though the former was unquestionably the most masterly achievement of Spanish and American historiography in the nineteenth century and will remain indispensable to all investigators of the Chilean past, it selected and interpreted its materials from the point of view of a scholarly nineteenth-century liberal for whom national independence, the growth of individual liberty, and the evolution of representative constitutional government were the main themes. Since Barros Arana wrote, though Chilean historians have been very active, they have not devoted themselves to a new general synthesis and the time was ripe for an attempt to be made.

Francisco Encina has presented a unique and highly personal view of Chilean history as his contribution toward meeting the need for a new look. It outrages scholars because of the cavalier way in which it disregards all the rules of the professional historian's craft; it outrages present-day liberals because of its attack on Barros Arana and on the whole liberal tradition in Chilean historiography; it shocks the filio-pietistic sentiments of many by ruthlessly cutting down to size the figures in a whole gallery of *patri patriae* and magnifying the historical role of other heroes; it titillates the Hispanist sentiments of one sector of the Chilean intellectual world while it infuriates *indigenistas* and Americanists. Above all, the book appeals to those who share the author's robust and deepseated faith in the national destiny, and it does this not by flattering and magnifying Chilean national accomplishments, but by attacking all who have sought either larger or smaller aims: ideological or international on the one hand, or local and partisan on the other. Closely coupled with this is Encina's constant demand that the economic problems and policies of Chile be regarded realistically and be dealt with in such a way as to maximize productive labor and economical use of natural resources, and his severe criticism of what he considers to have been either romantic, or dogmatic, or casual and shortsighted economic ideas and policies.

What sort of man is the author of this provocative, ambitious, and controversial work? What are the dominant ideas, prejudices, and other influences which have shaped him? What are his views about the nature and function of history? It would be ridiculous for one who has not had the advantage of personal acquaintance to attempt a character sketch, but there is so strong a personal imprint on the pages of the *Historia de Chile* that a few comments are justified.

First of all, he is a Chilean *hasta la médula de los huesos*. No one can doubt that. Throughout the long reaches of the centuries Encina suffers with every catastrophe, swells with pride in every heroic deed, feels shame over every betrayal. Pedro de Valdivia is the father of Chile. He does not glorify the conquistador so much for his manifold talents and virtues of bravery, constancy, endurance, and statesmanship, as for the urge to create a nation which he ascribes to the founder of Santiago. The standard of criticism throughout the work is national. In the numerous conflicts which fill the pages of Chilean history Encina always assumes the position of judge as well as that of chronicler and his verdict on individuals is not based, primarily, on his admiration or disapproval of personal traits or ideals, but on the consequences of their acts, as he sees them, for the growth of the Chilean nation.

The aristocratic viewpoint of the author is also evident. It is of the provinces, somewhat aloof from that of the capital. Born in the province of Talca and educated in his early years in the little city of that name, a scion of a landed family long established in that region, Encina exhibits in his writing many characteristics of rural Chilean aristocracy: its respect for courage, will, responsibility, its paternalistic sense of kinship with the *huaso,* its love of the vineyards, the wheatfields, and the blooded horses, and a kind of contempt for the bureaucrat, the *tinterillo,* the members of the half-educated white-collar class.

Another obvious trait is arrogant self-confidence. Encina never finds it difficult to come to a conclusion about a person or a problem. Whether he takes a middle ground or an extreme one, his view is always right and every other possible opinion is wrong. This assurance is most frequently apparent in the hundreds of biographical sketches which appear in his volumes. One man is labeled the greatest mind of his time; another, granted private virtues, is completely lacking in political sense, or in *don de mando;* still another is a *tarado* [*sic*] *mental,* or is a hysteric living in a permanent *estado delirante;* yet another is a *desconformado cerebral.* Encina sees men in sharp chiaroscuro. He is interested in character, but tends to give oversimplified judgments, often based on family or group traits presumed to be dominant.

Our author was an omnivorous and voracious reader in his youth, widely acquainted with the classical works of European literature, philosophy, and history from Plutarch and Don Quijote to Gibbon, Macaulay, and Comte. Though he completed the course in law at the University of Chile, served as a deputy, and held for a time certain administrative positions in the government, Encina's active career has been primarily that of a landowner deeply concerned with the economic problems of the nation. A generation ago he published in book form a series of articles on that subject. From economics his interest moved on to history in general and in middle age he devoted himself to wading through the increasingly voluminous collected printed materials of Chilean history, dipped deeply into the Medina transcripts of colonial documents and spiced his interest still further by a study of his own and other family records. When all this long-continued reading finally led him to write he began with a biography of Diego Portales. Many years later, in 1935, he published a book which might be considered an advance prospectus of his *magnum opus. La literatura histórica chilena y el concepto actual de la historia* gives evidence of the crystalization of a personal philosophy of history and the amalgamation of a number of interpretative concepts with regard to Chilean history in the light of which he condemned his predecessors and set up a conceptual framework for the history to which he was to devote himself for over a decade. Though a reader of the history will find in the earlier work some illumination of the intellectual origins of the *Historia de Chile* and a more connected exposition of the author's theory of history than is provided here and there through its twenty volumes, there is no evidence that Encina's opinions changed significantly in the interval between the publication of the two books. However, theories are more clearly manifest in conjunction with their application, and the ensuing comments on them, therefore, are mainly based on the *Historia*, which contains a large number of disgressions on historiography.

In the first place, Encina makes a sharp distinction between the historian and the historical scholar (*investigador erudito*). In his opinion the two functions cannot well be combined. The task of archival research is too laborious and time-consuming to permit its devotees to get beyond the publication of documents or their detailed study in monographs. Even more important, the kind of mind which can concentrate on minutiae is not capable of the synthetic thought — the broad outlook — required of the historian. The latter must have read widely in history, literature, philosophy, and social science, and he must also have the knowledge of men and affairs which is not easily acquired by the burrowing scholar. The object lessons here are José Toribio Medina and Diego Barros Arana. The talent, almost approaching genius, of the former as a biographer and a collector of historical materials is fully recognized; the latter is praised as an investigator also, and both are considered to lack qualifications for writing history. Professional historians (*los profesores*) are looked down upon and their contributions are largely disregarded or waved aside.

If Encina means that no general history can any longer be written completely and directly from the sources, he is on sure ground. It is also true that many scholars who have distinguished themselves in the production of monographs have not equally excelled in the task of synthesis. However, if he means to draw a sharp dividing line between the two functions he is in more dubious territory. It would not be hard to cite numerous examples of success in both fields and it would be equally hard to justify the idea that the critical discipline demanded by research is not also valuable to the general historian. As a matter of fact, this notion is not even exemplified in Encina's own work. Though he has leaned heavily on the work of others, both editorial and monographic, there is plenty of evidence of detailed work with documents throughout the *Historia.* Some of the digging may have been done by research assistants, but there can be no question about the broad familiarity of the author with the sources of Chilean history.   . . .

Encina envisages history as more than a series of events. His work is definitely an attempt at a history of civilization in Chile. More broadly than any previous writer, he has tried to deal with the evolution of the diverse aspects of society in Chile during four centuries. When it comes to a general theory of cultural dynamics he awards the primacy to race and inheritance. Next, in his view, comes the personal influence of great men, who serve as catalytic agents in critical situations. He also recognizes the modifying effect of geographic environment and the importance of collective attitudes of mind such as those of the Counter-Reformation, the Enlightenment, and Romanticism. The idea of race predominates, however. The reception of other influences is determined by attitudes presumed to derive from blood inheritance.

Encina's racism is extreme and dogmatic. It is in conflict with contemporary anthropological theory which tends to deny the possibility of isolating any pure racial groups in Europe or the attribution of particular traits of character or temperament to a racial strain. Encina quotes with approval an earlier Chilean work which takes a view similar to his own, but his attitude seems to derive ultimately from Gobineau and his successors and to ignore recent anthropological theory.

One example will suffice to illustrate Encina's racism. As he sees it, the population of Spain at the time of the discovery of America consisted of a Germanic (Gothic) element mixed with a larger nondescript strain. The Gothic Spaniards were physically distinguished by fair hair and a rugged physique and were by nature leaders, men of action, fighters, endowed with great energy and courage. The opportunities offered by the New World acted selectively to draw from the peninsula the representatives of this type who continued to appear as distinct racial elements in sixteenth-century Spain. Encina makes much of the supposed high incidence of fair hair among the conquistadores. Encina also considers the qualities of vigor and tenacity which marked the Indians of Chile resident south of the Bio Bio, the Mapuche, to be the result of peculiar racial differences from the other Indian inhabitants of the country.

At times Encina seems to manipulate his racial theories with a certain flexibility, as when he recognizes that children of Spaniards and Indian women living in or near Santiago, the center of Spanish culture, tended to be more European, and that children of Mapuche warriors and captive Spanish women living among the unconquered Indians tended to approximate Indian characteristics. At other times, however, as when he denies the possibility of any real Christianization and civilization of the Indian population, except through a secular process of admixture of European blood, he thinks of race as a fixed and determining force. The Mapuche had a cerebral organization with fixed limits which no amount of cultural contact could affect in the slightest degree. He was bound by his blood inheritance to his tribal culture — the *admapu* of his ancestors.   . . .

It is to be noted that for the colonial period Encina's history follows Barros Arana in basic organization, varying from it in greater volume accorded to some subjects in the topical sections and, of course, in its very different interpretation. This points up a matter of considerable importance. Encina takes the solid ground-work of Barros Arana as a point of departure and leans heavily on him for material, while at the same time he makes much of the deficiencies of his great precedessor. Encina recognizes the preeminence of Barros Arana among nineteenth-century historians of Chile, but he is so strongly opposed to the anti-Hispanism and liberalism of the earlier work that he is less than generous in admitting the extent to which he is indebted to it. The same holds true for the attitude of Encina toward more recent Chilean historians. Though there are very occasional references in the text, and more often in bibliographical listings at the heads of certain chapters, to the contributions of other historians, in general their work is unmentioned, even when it is obvious that he has profited from it.   . . .

When he deals with the remote prehistory of Chile Encina, quite properly, recognizes the impossibility of providing a connected or clear story. However, he has few doubts about the Indians whom the Spaniards found in Chile and their culture. Following Latcham, he is able to present a good picture of the ways in which influences from the north (Atacameño, Diaguita, and finally Inca) found their way into Chile, but he tends to present a very simple view of what is a highly complex archeological record. Recent anthropological literature does not support conclusively Encina's view of a racially distinct Mapuche invasion from the east and tends to think of the three main groups of Araucanians (Picunche, Mapuche, and Huilluche) as regional variants of a common culture with unknown racial antecedents. Encina may be right, but his view represents plausible speculation rather than established fact.

There is little new in Encina's account of the discovery and conquest of Chile. He tends to soft-pedal the accounts of Spanish cruelty and brutality to the Indians as many recent authors tend to do in reaction against the exaggerations of the *leyenda negra*. Original with him appears to be the view that the conquistadores "en su inmensa mayoría eran hombres sanos de alma, empujados como Valdivia, por la sangre, a la creación de un nuevo pueblo." Elsewhere, Encina somewhat modifies this generalization, recognizing that most of the conquistadores were impelled by "móviles egoístas y pequeños."   . . .

However sympathetic Encina may be toward supposedly trans-

cendental motivation of the conquistadores, he has no patience with
the "mysticism" of the missionary churchmen who clashed with the
former in their eagerness to civilize and convert the Indians. Only
"cerebros desconformados por las ansias místicas" could have
dreamed of the conversion of the Indians except through the long
process of miscegenation. The whole company of clerics from Montesinos and Las Casas to Fray Luis de Valdivia, who could not
realize the impossibility of putting their hopes and ideals into effect, were victims of "fantasía, lindante en la iluminación." Their
Christian sentiments provoked in them "el estado delirante en todo
lo concerniente a las relaciones entre españoles e indígenas." The
civilization of the Indians was "una imposibilidad que emanaba de
la distancia excesiva en el grado de evolución mental y de la índole
demasiado diferente de sus estructuras cerebrales." The identification of cultural and biological differences can hardly go further than
this.

As the reader may suspect from the above, Encina believes in
the necessity of forced Indian labor and defends the practices of
the encomenderos. He sees more merit in the Tasa de Santillán,
which attempted to regulate Indian labor, but he has nothing but
condemnation for the Tasa de Gamboa, which attempted to put
into effect royal orders to end *servicio personal* altogether. . . .
Taking issue with Barros Arana, who doubted the extent of prosperity at the end of the sixteenth century, Encina tries to prove
that there was economic progress at the same time that revenues
declined owing to the lack of labor in the mines, and that encomenderos were ruined by the requisitions of men, horses, arms, and
provisions for the war on the southern frontier. It is hardly possible
to hold all these positions. If the war caused distress it was not
due to the Tasa de Gamboa. If there was a growth of agriculture
and stockraising until the coming of the military disaster in 1597 it
can hardly be true that Indians and Spaniards alike lived in misery
after 1580.

Apart from these arguments which grow out of Encina's passionate war against the philanthropic policies of the churchmen and
the Crown, the material on the economic, social, and cultural life
of the early colony is most abundant and interesting.

Much of Encina's attention from 1600 on is devoted to an elaborate critique of the defensive policy on the frontier, together with
the efforts at pacification under the leadership of Luis de Valdivia.

His attacks on Fray Luis know no bounds. Barros Arana, who notes the failure of the Jesuit policy, does not give it the tragic significance that Encina ascribes to it. Granting the possible theoretical soundness of Encina's opinion from the point of view of military strategy, it is hard to see how he expected Chile and Spain in the seventeenth century to provide the enormous economic and military effort that would have been required in order to carry on a steadfast war of attrition against the Mapuche for which they lacked resources. It is difficult to accept, therefore, the author's condemnation of the peace policy, though he is undoubtedly right in condemning the sporadic raids which only irritated the enemy, and also right in condemning the policy of trying to hold isolated forts in Indian country.

Looking at the seventeenth century as a whole, Encina sees it as the epoch in which, despite earthquake, floods, Indian forays, and excesses of popular religious mysticism, Chile managed to survive, thanks to the Peruvian *situado* and the permanent standing army of the frontier. More than that, it was the period in which the "Chilean race" was formed and the character of the people established.

Topics which occupy major attention in Encina's view of the eighteenth century are: the influx of the Basques and their influence on the Chilean aristocracy, the impact on Chile of the Enlightenment and of the Bourbon reforms, and activities of the Jesuits and the significance of their banishment.

Encina attributes vast importance to the coming of the Basque merchant immigrants in the early eighteenth century. There can be no doubt about the fact of this immigration or that the newcomers were more hardworking and business-minded than the earlier creole aristocrats. They soon intermarried with the wealthier old families of the kingdom, most of which, according to our author, were of northern Spanish descent. The *elemento meridional*, he believes, tended to go down hill economically and socially and to be elbowed out of place by the new aristocracy which Encina refers to as *castellano-vasca*. . . .

Encina goes on to ascribe to this group: industry, foresight, economy, common sense, lack of imagination and of the spirit of adventure. He believes that these characteristics remained stable and colored not only the independence movement in Chile but also the political evolution of the country in the nineteenth century.

The aristocracy of Santiago in the eighteenth century undoubtedly possessed many of these traits, though it is dubious whether there existed as complete a homogeneity of attitudes as that suggested, but it is hard to believe that such traits need to be explained entirely in terms of the Basque race. Not all Basques share in the spirit of business enterprise. In other parts of America new Spanish immigrants from many different Spanish provinces played a role similar to that of the Basques who went to Chile. Much of the differences between the newcomers and their predecessors can be explained by the different environment in Spain and America of the later colonial centuries. We have here one more example of Encina's racism.   . . .

Unlike many recent historians who have tended to place a high value on the accomplishments of the Bourbon dynasty in Spanish America, Encina tends to minimize the Enlightenment. He respects the laborious and patriotic efforts of kings, viceroys, ministers, and governors, but he is critical of what he considers to be artificial and unrealistic reformism from the top down, based on rationalist notions which did not sufficiently take into account the necessity of linking reforms and progress to the character and capacity of the people. He quite enjoys pointing out some of the failures of the economic plans of Ambrosio O'Higgins and the impracticality of some of the notions and schemes of Manuel de Salas. The Enlightenment in Chile, despite Salas, Rojas, and others, was not as brilliant as it was in some other portions of the Spanish empire and this may be one reason for Encina's relatively caustic view.

A major theme in the later colonial era, of course, is the role of the Jesuit order. Encina believes that its earlier missionary zeal had largely evaporated or had become embalmed in the pious historical works produced by the order. In the eighteenth century the Jesuits concentrated their efforts on the education of youth and the development of economic resources. Our author has nothing but admiration for the patient and intelligent industry of the order and its achievements in agriculture, industry, and the arts and crafts. Practically everything new or progressive in the era is ascribed to the Jesuits, but Encina feels that their efforts were sterile. When they were expelled by the Bourbon monarch they left all they had in the colony, but this wealth evaporated and disappeared because they had done nothing to spread their practical knowledge and skills beyond their own circle, imposing a completely literary and nonpractical education on the youth of the upper class almost exclusively trained in their schools and colleges. Expulsion, consequently, led to a depression in Chile which had not come to an end when the movement for independence began. Encina treats many Jesuits, however, with great respect, especially Molina, whose scientific work he feels has been undervalued in the past. On the other hand, he does not feel that the exiled Jesuits had much of anything to do with the development of conflict between Chile and the mother country and he is very convincing in his discussion of this point. . . .

It is hard to give a general judgment on this paradoxical, brilliant, and uneven series of volumes. Most readers will be repelled by Encina's racism and will remain unconvinced that Chilean history can be explained so largely in such terms. Yet, part of Encina's racism is a matter of vocabulary. Though he would be the first to deny it, much of what he interprets racially can be translated into cultural terms by the reader. Individual and group temperaments and attitudes which Encina explains in terms of blood inheritance are no less present even if they can be better explained in other ways. Readers must recognize in this history a remarkable sensitivity to group attitudes. In this, as in other aspects of the book, readers will be repelled by the dogmatism and arrogance which accompany the vigor and the imagination also present. They will sometimes find themselves undervaluing insight into phenomena because they reject the manner and form in which that insight is clothed.

The contribution Encina has made will be variously estimated. To Chilean historians who are specialists in national history the positive value of the book will not appear as great as it may to non-experts. The experts will tend to weigh defects more heavily and to profit less than others from the bringing together of so vast an amount of historical material. However, they will find in it a number of stimulating hypotheses and theories, particularly in the latter portion of the work, which they must take into account. To readers in Peru, Bolivia, and Argentina, Encina will at many points be distasteful because of his assumption of Chilean superiority and his prejudiced and derogatory judgments on the character of the people and of leaders in neighboring republics. This holds true in spite of Encina's attempt to give credit where credit is due, as to Santa Cruz, Pardo, Mitre, and others. By those who look at the Chilean scene from a distance the work will be most highly appreciated because of its lively and full treatment of aspects of Chilean history neglected in other general histories and because, for all its dogmatism and other faults, it has a clear interpretative scheme which gives meaning to material which has often been presented in a confusing manner. If such readers are at all sophisticated they will be able to separate from the rest that which is most dubious.

Serious students of history will regret the unwillingness of the author to use the accepted methods of professional historians with regard to documentation which greatly hampers any attempt to subject Encina's views to critical verification. Fundamentally, however, the book should be judged on broader grounds than its eccentricities of style, its unorthodox method, its often tiring repetition, and its many careless errors of detail. The basic question is: Does Encina's panoramic vision of the birth, growth, and development of the Chilean nation make a contribution to the understanding of Chilean history? The present writer believes that it does. There is something inspiring in the very vastness of the effort, and the extensive study of the relationship of political, social, economic, and cultural history within a single conceptual scheme is stimulating. The book is a monument, as well, to a remarkable personality. It is essentially a *tour de force* by a vigorous and opinionated mind interested not so much in gaining the accolade of professional historians as in making the average literate Chilean change his view of his own national past.

D. Controversy

7. Chickens in America Before Columbus?

CARL O. SAUER

In 1922 Erland Nordenskiöld published a memoir on the spread of certain culture elements through South America. One of the ele-

Carl O. Sauer, *Agricultural Origins and Dispersals* (New York: American Geographical Society, 1952), pp. 57–60. Reprinted by permission of the American Geographical Society.

ments that he discussed was the domestic fowl. The known historical record begins with Magellan's party which secured supplies of fowls in 1519 from Indians on the coast of southern Brazil. Hence, so Nordenskiöld thinks, they were introduced by Cabral in the discovery of Brazil in 1500 or by someone else shortly thereafter. No document mentions anything of the sort, though the journals of Cabral's voyage are quite detailed. The Cabral landing took place a thousand miles to the north of the Magellan incident. In 1526 Cabot's men not only got hundreds of fowls in the coastal villages of South Brazil but sent for additional supplies to a distance of forty leagues inland. Later explorers of the interior from Paraguay to the Orinoco commonly found chickens being kept in Indian villages never before visited by whites. "Domestic fowls were evidently taken inland by Indian traders to far-off places long before these were explored by whites." Nordenskiöld elaborates this statement by lengthy and careful documentation. The name of the Inca Atahualpa is accepted by him as the Quechua word for domestic fowl; he traces the distribution of this name and other native names from the Araucanians to Amazonian tribes. "Not a single tribe living in an area bordering on the old territory of the Inca Empire calls the fowl *gallina* or *gallo* or uses any name traceable to Spanish." Doggedly Nordenskiöld worked out an enormous distribution of the fowl through remotest agricultural South America before Spanish contact, documenting it with the distribution of native names, ceremonial uses of the fowl, and selection for white plumage, as a remarkable example of explosive rapidity of diffusion. He did not concern himself with the question as to how chickens could have multiplied so rapidly as to have been spread over hundreds of thousands of square miles in a very few years, nor about the probable rate of acceptance of a strange new animal, including ceremonial acceptance, into a wide range of native societies. That the chicken could have been brought only by white men was a premise that it never occurred to him to question.

Ten years ago I went on a field trip in Chile with a Chilean zoologist. We were served boiled blue and olive green eggs at an inn. I was surprised at seeing them and he was surprised that we had no eggs of such colors. I then learned that the Indians, that is, Araucanians, like to raise a breed of chickens that lays such eggs and that white folks do not care for such fowl or their eggs. We saw them in Araucanian village after village, obviously cross-bred with ordinary races. My education in the blue- or green-egg fowl continued at the hands of Don Ricardo Latcham in Santiago who, I found, knew a lot about the question and had written in the same year as Nordenskiöld another study on the chicken in the New World. Using much the same documentation, he had come up with the opposite conclusion, that the Indian chicken was of a quite different breed from any European ones, that it had been introduced long before European contacts, and that it survived as the Araucanian fowl. Don Ricardo seemed to me to have the best of the argument. Few people seem to know this study of his, nor has this fine scholar and gentleman ever had full recognition outside of his adopted country for the range and depth of his insight into native cultures. To him belongs the credit for discovering the pre-Columbian chicken of the New World.

On returning home, I found that the blue-egg chicken was a *cause célèbre* in poultry genetics. Professor Punnett of the animal genetics laboratory at Cambridge had established this color factor as a dominant gene. It is unknown in the Old World. Such dominant mutations arise very rarely under domestication, being ordinarily primitive genes of remote origin. The Cambridge experiments were made from Chilean stock. An Englishman resident in Costa Rica supplied Punnett with a further note of "original" chickens laying green eggs; this was among mountain Indians of Costa Rica, a small outlier of Chibchan culture surviving in mountain fastnesses. Thus, from the southernmost extremity of the New World vegetative planters to their northern limit there existed and in part still exists a greatly aberrant form of chicken, the like of which is unknown elsewhere. The Europeans could not have brought it, for they did not have it. Its economic qualities are inferior to European breeds and it survives vestigially as a marker of vanishing Indian cultures. Hybrid origin (which Latcham surmised) appears impossible for the New World has no nearly related fowl other than the turkey. A miraculous post-Spanish mutation can be ruled out; this is an Indian fowl, Indian cultures were in retreat and breaking down by Spanish conquest, and Chilean and Costa Rican Indians were not in contact with each other.

To the mystery of the chicken in the New World Dr. J. P. Harrison of our National Archives adds a further item from the journal of T. A. Dornin, *U.S.S. Brandywine*, May 30, 1828, Paita, Peru: "The poultry here have black combs and black feathers, have also black meat, except a small white streak on their breasts — the bones are black, which is unfavorable in appearance only, for they are the sweetest and tenderest here. Prejudice is powerful, some of our mess would not eat them." This internal blackness has been noted for Asia and Africa as a quality of a ceremonial breed preserved in the ornamental Silkies. The source is apparently from Southeast Asia; an introduction by way of Europe is unlikely.

BIBLIOGRAPHIC SUGGESTIONS

A. *Historians*

Few biographies have been written of historians concerned with Latin American colonial history, but there is a valuable bibliography on what has been done:

1. Esteve Barba, Francisco. *Historiografía indiana* (Madrid: Editorial Gredos, 1964).

1a. Hanke, Lewis. "Gilberto Freyre: Social Historian," *Quarterly Journal of Inter-American Relations*, I, No. 3 (July, 1939), pp. 24–44.

1b. ————. *Bartolomé de Las Casas: Historian* (Gainesville: University of Florida Press, 1952).

1c. Humphreys, R. A. "William Hickling Prescott: The Man and the Historian," *Hispanic American Historical Review*, XXXIX (1959), pp. 1–19.

1d. Simpson, Lesley B., trans. and ed., *Cortés, The Life of the Conqueror by His Secretary*, by Francisco Lopez de Gomara (Berkeley: University of California Press, 1964).

1e. Phelan, John L. *The Millennial Kingdom of the Franciscans in the New World: A Study of the Writings of Gerónimo de Mendieta* (Berkeley: University of California Press, 1956).

2. Manchester, Alan K. "Some Brazilian Colonial Historians," *Bulletin of the Pan American Union* (Sept., Oct., 1934), pp. 634–647, 698–707.

2a. Von Hagen, Victor W., ed. *The Incas of Pedro de Cieza de León*. (Norman, Oklahoma: The University of Oklahoma Press, 1959).

B. *Collecting Sources*

Historians must have adequate sources if they are to write sound and interesting works, and they depend upon libraries. The story of how the great collections on Latin American history have been built up is absorbing, as the following items will show.

3. Bancroft, Hubert Howe. *Literary Industries* (New York: The Bancroft Co., 1891). A perfect mine of information on how Bancroft built up his library, how he selected his colleagues, and his views on history.
4. Butler, Ruth Lapham. "Edward E. Ayer's Quest for Hispanamericana," *Inter-American Bibliographical Review*, I, No. 2 (1942), pp. 81–90. Ayer laid the basis for the Newberry Library's excellent collection. For a description of the way in which William B. Greenlee developed Newberry's extensive collection of Portuguese history and literature, see Charles R. Boxer's account in the *Newberry Library Bulletin* (May, 1951).

C. *Ideas*

5. Cardozo, Manuel. "The Idea of History in the Portuguese Chroniclers of the Age of Discovery," *The Catholic Historical Review*, XLIX (1963), pp. 1–19.
6. León-Portilla, Miguel, ed. *Broken Spears* (Boston: Beacon Press, 1962). History is usually written by the conquerors. Here is a collection of Indian reactions to and accounts of the Spanish conquest of Mexico.
7. Morse, Richard M. "Some Themes of Brazilian History," *South Atlantic Quarterly*, LXI (1962), pp. 159–182.
8. Zavala, Silvio. "La colonización del Nuevo Mundo por los europeos," *Memoria de El Colegio Nacional*, IV, No. 3 (1960) pp. 21–59.
8a. Bernstein, Harry and Bailey W. Diffie, "Sir Clements R. Markham as a Translator," *Hispanic American Historical Review*, XVII (1937), pp. 546–557.

D. *Controversies*

9. Nowell, Charles E. "The Discovery of Brazil — Accidental or Intentional?" *Hispanic American Historical Review*, XVI (1936), pp. 311–338.
10. Rau, Virginia and Bailey W. Diffie, "Alleged Fifteenth-Century Joint-Stock Companies and the Articles of Dr. Fitzler," *Bulletin of the Institute of Historical Research*, XXVI (London, 1953), pp. 181–199.

General Bibliographic Suggestions

Bibliography is not necessarily a dismal science cultivated by pale-faced librarians but should be an important part of the intellectual equipment of every student. Knowledge of where to look for material is particularly important for Latin American history, because its publications appear in many countries, and without guidance one may spend much time without visible result. Moreover, great strides have been made in this field during the last decade or so; the quantity and quality of historical publications have sharply increased, which makes the problem of finding pertinent items more serious than ever before. Great improvement may be expected a few years hence when Charles C. Griffin completes the *Guide to the Historical Literature on Latin America* he is preparing, with the assistance of a number of specialists, under the sponsorship of the Conference on Latin American History of the American Historical Association. Another basic volume now in preparation is the third edition of the standard C. K. Jones, *A Bibliography of Latin American Bibliographies.*

Everyone eventually discovers for himself his own bibliographic and reference tools based on his experience and his needs. Some basic works exist, however, and the following list, as well as the "Bibliographic Suggestions" at the end of each section, is intended to save the time of students by indicating a few of the most useful works.

I. GENERAL

1. *Handbook of Latin American Studies.* Harvard University Press published this annual bibliography from 1936 through 1939, and since 1940 the University of Florida Press has issued it. Prepared by the Hispanic Foundation of the Library of Congress, the *Handbook* has become an

indispensable reference work. An index to the first 25 volumes is now in preparation.

2. *Hispanic American Historical Review.* A quarterly, published by Duke University Press, whose volume 50 will appear in 1970. Two useful guides have been prepared: Ruth Lapham Butler, ed., *Guide to the Hispanic American Historical Review, 1918–1945* (Durham: Duke University Press, 1950); and Charles Gibson and E. V. Niemeyer, *Guide to the Hispanic American Historical Review, 1946–1955* (Durham: Duke University Press, 1958).

3. Humphreys, R. A., *Latin American History: A Guide to the Literature in English* (London: Oxford University Press, 1958). This little volume brings together in an organized way reliable information on the large amount of material available in English on Latin America.

II. PORTUGAL AND BRAZIL

4. Burns, E. Bradford, "A Working Bibliography for the Study of Brazilian History," *The Americas,* XXII (1965), 54–88. The most useful list for general purposes.

5. Cobb, Gwendolyn B., "Bancroft Library Microfilm: Portugal and Her Empire," *Hispanic American Historical Review,* XXXIV (1954), 114–125.

6. Greenlee, William B., "A Descriptive Bibliography of the History of Portugal," *Hispanic American Historical Review,* XX (1940), 491–516. "A summary of the chief sources for the history of Portugal, both in Europe and the Orient, as a background for the needs of the student of Brazilian history."

7. Welsh, Doris, *A Catalog of the William B. Greenlee Collection of Portuguese History and Literature and the Portuguese Materials in the Newberry Library* (Chicago: The Newberry Library, 1953). A fundamental work based upon the rich collection in the Newberry Library.

III. SPAIN AND SPANISH AMERICA

8. *Índice Histórico Español.* Editorial Teide, Barcelona. Established in 1953 by the late Jaime Vicens Vives, the distinguished Catalan scholar, this annotated bibliography immediately became the best source of information on current publications relating to all periods of Spanish and Spanish American history. Despite the death of the founder in 1960, the *Índice* continues to appear.

9. Sánchez Alonso, Benito, *Fuentes de la historia española e hispanoamericana,* third ed., 3 vols. (Madrid: Consejo Superior de Investigaciones Científicas, 1952).